By Hazard Adams

NONFICTION

The Academic Tribes

FICTION

The Horses of Instruction
The Truth About Dragons: An Anti-Romance

CRITICISM

Blake and Yeats: The Contrary Vision
William Blake: A Reading of the Shorter Poems
The Contexts of Poetry
The Interests of Criticism
Lady Gregory
Philosophy of the Literary Symbolic
Joyce Cary's Trilogies
(in press)

EDITED BY HAZARD ADAMS

Poems by Robert Simeon Adams
Poetry: An Introductory Anthology
Fiction as Process (WITH CARL HARTMAN)
William Blake: Jerusalem, Selected Poetry and Prose
Critical Theory Since Plato

Philosophy
of the
Literary Symbolic

PHILOSOPHY
OF THE
LITERARY SYMBOLIC

Hazard Adams

A Florida State University Book
UNIVERSITY PRESSES OF FLORIDA
Tallahassee

Quotations from *Collected Poems* of William Butler Yeats are reprinted
with permission of Macmillan Publishing Company (copyright 1919, 1928,
1933 by Macmillan Publishing Company, renewed 1947, 1956, 1961 by
Bertha Georgie Yeats; copyright 1940 by Georgie Yeats, renewed 1968
by Bertha Georgie Yeats, Michael Butler Yeats, and Anne Yeats) and of
Michael and Anne Yeats and Macmillan London Limited.

Library of Congress Cataloging in Publication Data

Adams, Hazard, 1926–
  Philosophy of the literary symbolic.

  "A Florida State University book."
  Bibliography: p.
  Includes index.
  1. Symbolism in literature.   I. Title.
PN56.S9A3   1983   809'.915   82–24785
ISBN 0–8130–0743–7 (cloth)
ISBN 0–8130–0771–2 (paper)

University Presses of Florida is the central agency for scholarly publishing of the
State of Florida's university system. Its offices are located at 15 NW 15th Street,
Gainesville, Fl 32603. Works published by University Presses of Florida are evalu-
ated and selected for publication by a faculty committee of any one of Florida's nine
public universities: Florida A&M University (Tallahassee), Florida Atlantic University (Boca Raton), Florida International University (Miami), Florida State University
(Tallahassee), University of Central Florida (Orlando), University of Florida (Gainesville), University of North Florida (Jacksonville), University of South Florida (Tampa),
University of West Florida (Pensacola).

© 1983 by the Board of Regents of the State of Florida
All rights reserved

Printed in the U.S.A. on acid-free paper.

Dianae

. . . one portion of being is the Prolific,
the other the Devouring: to the Devourer it
seems as if the producer was in his chains;
but it is not so, he only takes portions of
existence & fancies that the whole.

—Blake

Contents

Tables and Figures

Acknowledgments

In this book I have attempted to work out a problem that I struggled with in my work on Blake and Yeats many years ago and that has concerned me ever since, in part because of the terminological confusions it has engendered—"a large terminal moraine of confusion," Northrop Frye has aptly called it; and more recently because of the growth of interest in allegory in contemporary critical theory and the debates connected with it. I am in the debt of several journals whose editors have published essays by me on the subject of the symbolic or literary theory generally. In a few places in chapters 4, 11, and 12 I have used in greatly revised form remarks made in those journals: *Centennial Review*, *Journal of Aesthetics and Art Criticism*, *Criticism*, *New Literary History*, *Contemporary Literature*, and *Blake Studies*.

My principal debts are to the Guggenheim Foundation for a fellowship which, combined with sabbatical leave from the University of California, Irvine, gave me the academic year 1974–75 for research and writing, the National Endowment for the Humanities for a summer research grant in 1974, the British Library, the Warburg

Institute, and the libraries of the University of California and the University of Washington. The School of Humanities at Irvine supported preparation of the manuscript, which has been typed and edited by Mary Gazlay, to whom I owe many thanks. Among the many colleagues whose remarks have stimulated me through the years of work on this book, I wish to single out Murray Krieger for his most generous interest. I also want to thank particularly Charles O. Hartman and Leroy Searle for helpful advice at a late stage of revision and Otto Goldschmid for his help with the German translations. Finally, I wish to express my appreciation to members of my graduate seminars at Irvine, who engaged themselves in the study of the theory of the symbolic. I am especially grateful to students in my seminar at the School of Criticism and Theory there during the summers of 1976 and 1979. They were subjected to ideas expressed in this book, and surely their criticisms have crept into the final text.

Hazard Adams

Newport Beach, California
1977
Seattle, Washington
1981

Philosophy
of the
Literary Symbolic

I

Introduction

This book sets forth a ground for literary theory in the "philosophy" of literary symbolism, or the symbolic (which I prefer to call it since I am uncertain that there really is such a thing as a literary symbol in the sense in which the term is used to signify a type of trope). The book is an effort to see whether the terms "symbolic" and "allegory" can be rescued for theory from the "terminal moraine" in which Northrop Frye alleges that "symbol" and "allegory" are embedded as the result of the common late eighteenth- and early nineteenth-century distinction between the two.[1] In short, I hope to show that the moraine is not necessarily terminal, but in part terminological. Rather than opposing the terms to each other at the expense of "allegory," as in Goethe and much subsequent romantic theory, and rather than valorizing "allegory" at the expense of "symbol," as in the recently influential work of Walter Benjamin and some who have followed him like Paul de Man, I would like to rehabilitate "symbolic" as a term that contains and does not negate "allegory" as a perfectly legitimate poetic device.[2] Both Frye and Angus Fletcher take this position, but their work is to my mind schematic and practical, whereas mine seeks a ground for theory.

My procedure is partly historical, but for the most part analytical.[3] To read certain recent critics, one would conclude that the history of thought about the literary symbol is entirely one of folly and self-mystification. Such was the view of Walter Benjamin. Perhaps there is some folly in any line of thought, but under benighted conditions an important searching (and even an advance) can take place. I have chosen to go back to Kant's "aesthetical idea" and the Goethean and romantic distinction between symbolism and allegory in order to determine what possibilities were opened up by them, what problems the terms used generated, and what value may be gleaned from acquaintance with certain "moments" in the theoretical events that followed. After discussion of Kant and the romantic distinction as it variously appears, I turn to William Blake's use of "allegory" and "vision" as a basis for a notion I shall develop as the book proceeds. Then I examine some of those "moments" that I regard as either typical developments in thinking about literary symbolism or especially important to my effort to rehabilitate the term "symbolic" without negating the allegoric. I must admit that often, perhaps most often, the "moments" I discuss yield mostly negative value for the theory of the symbolic with which I conclude, but I treat these "moments" nevertheless because as parts of the history of my subject they both illuminate it and maintain the power to rise up and perpetuate old confusions. This process proceeds through an examination of nineteenth-century *symbolisme*, theories of the dream, the concept of fictions, symbolic forms, sentimental archaism, the work of Frye, and Yeats's idea of conflict, to a presentation in the light of several recent trends of what I call a "secular" form of symbolic.

The notion of the symbolic that I wish to rehabilitate becomes larger than a literary notion, or—to put it another way—the literary notion expands beyond the conventionally literary. In this matter, I side with Ernst Cassirer's broad usage of the "symbolic" against Paul Ricoeur's deliberate narrowing of the term's range.[4] In examining the symbolic I am interested penultimately in a theory of the liberal arts and sciences and ultimately in that theory's implications for structures of academic organization, both intellectual and bureaucratic. My last chapter approaches these issues, leaving much for a later "practical" work.

In the remarks above I alluded briefly to the dangers of negation in the romantic symbol/allegory distinction. The term "negation" I employ in its Blakean, not its Hegelian, sense.[5] My own theorizing is much in the debt of William Blake's scattered remarks on naming, creation, and contrariety, and some related ideas of the earlier anti-Cartesian thinker Giovanni Battista Vico. Since I employ these things frequently in this book, it is best to make some of them familiar at once, though the Blakean notions will be more fully examined in chapter 4.

1. Some Blakean and Vichean views

IN THE chapter that is devoted wholly to Blake's views, I shall make a distinction between "myth" and "antimyth" that will carry over to the book's conclusion. Please make no assumptions yet about what these words mean, for the meanings rise out of the later discussion of Blake. I now offer four fundamental Blakean notions, and overlap them with three fundamental notions found in the writings of Vico. Though Blake, to my knowledge, had never heard of Vico, he might as well have.

1. Blake wrote in *The Marriage of Heaven and Hell*:

The ancient Poets animated all sensible objects with Gods or Geniuses, calling them by the names and adorning them with the properties of woods, rivers, mountains, lakes, cities, nations, and whatever their enlarged and numerous senses could perceive.

And particularly they studied the genius of each city and country, placing it under its mental deity.

Till a system was formed, which some took advantage of, and enslaved the vulgar by attempting to realize or abstract the mental deities from their objects: Thus began priesthood.

Choosing forms of worship from poetic tales.[6]

This is a complicated passage, which I shall examine again in chapter 4. Here I want to note Blake's idea that the poetic capacity, which he identifies with primordial naming, is the source of language and culture. This means that the true model of language is trope and not the abstract ideal form of symbolic logic. This is not a unique view. It had been enunciated by Vico; it was picked up by Herder; and it became a popular notion in romanticism. But with respect to the culture at large it has always been, I think, what Blake would call a "reprobate" view. Blake drew his notion of the "reprobate" from the biblical image of the visionary crying in the wilderness; it is an ironic reversal of the Calvinist meaning. For Blake, greater and greater forms of linguistic abstraction arise from poetic sources and in turn generate need for interpreters, or what Blake calls "priesthood," which would include those we now call critics. He goes on to remark that in this historical process something is lost:

> And at length they [the priests] pronounced that the gods had ordained such things. Thus men forgot that all deities reside in the human breast.[7]

Blake implies that his "primitive and original ways"[8] are designed to restore a golden age before the fall into separation of words from their contained objects, of man from his gods.

2. Blake also wrote in the *Marriage* a sentence that I have chosen as the epigraph for this book:

> . . . one portion of being is the Prolific, the other the Devouring: to the Devourer it seems as if the producer was in his chains; but it is not so, he only takes portions of existence and fancies that the whole.[9]

Here the "prolific," with which Blake connects the naming power of the "ancient poets," is made a constant social force, from which emanates cultural food, so to speak. The food is *devoured* by an abstracting, interpreting, using, hungering society. It is easy enough for the devourers to become deluded into thinking that the prolific are merely their captives. The history of the arts in the nineteenth century suggests that many prolifics came to feel that this was their fate. But Blake says it is never really so, which is at worst a defiant remark, at best a truth.

3. Blake offers in his longer poems a notion involving his own special use of the terms "center" and "circumference."[10] If you are at a center or are a center, everything is outside you in the form of nature or matter. When you study yourself analytically you put yourself outside yourself in this material field. If you are at a circumference your experiences are inside you and a part of yourself. You contain the world in the form your imagination, including your power of language, gives it. You become an ancient poet. On the other hand, at a center you are a priest or alien interpreter of an outer world.

4. Finally, Blake made in *Milton* and *Jerusalem* an important distinction between "contraries" and "negations," which is the basis for his un-Hegelian dialectic.[11] A negation is a situation in which, in an opposition like soul/body or good/evil, one side is privileged over the

other, that is, one side negates the reality or authority of the other, attempting to suppress it. This is, in Blake, definitely a historical notion. Blake's example in the *Marriage*, where the term "contrary" is first introduced, is the opposition soul/body: In the history of religion the soul has negated the body, connecting it with evil. This is a process that developed from original visionary acts toward priesthood, which bureaucratizes the interpretation of the act into law. In the Christian "church," a term indicating an era for Blake, the law is that of "chastity" or sexual repression. The process turns soul/body into good/evil. A "contrary" would be an opposition in which the distinction itself (or the reasoning that creates it) is on one side, and on the other is the denial of the distinction in favor of the identity of the two things in the term "energy," with neither side negated.

"Identity" is a tricky word applied to Blake. More will be said about it. Here let me state that "identity" is not indifference, but instead the contrary of the distinction difference/indifference.[12] This is the first of three negations, the contraries of which I shall seek. The second, subject/object, concerned Blake himself pretty directly, though he did not employ the terms. The third is symbol/allegory and is deeply involved with the first two. To consider this and romantic and postromantic efforts to find a contrary to the negation to which Goethe and others gave the name is my historical theme. I have not, however, tried to write a history as such, either of the distinction between symbol and allegory or of the symbolic. In his book, *Allegory*, Angus Fletcher wisely declined to write a history of his subject. It would have been impossible, because as he treats his subject he discovers that there is really no end to it.[13] I am in the same situation and have therefore chosen moments of exemplary importance to my theoretical theme, which is centered on the pursuit of contraries to the three negations I have mentioned above.

I come now to the three overlapping notions in Vico. He has been much written about in recent years by both theoreticians of history and semioticians, and his views have been digested and clearly presented along with those of J. G. Herder by Isaiah Berlin.[14] The first two notions involve two distinctions Vico makes. The first distinction is between "poetic logic" and conceptual logic, and the second is between "imaginative universals" and abstract universals. Both "poetic logic" and "imaginative universals" he connects with primitive people.

1. "Poetic Logic": The keys to Vico's new science of man are his claims that in the childhood of the world men were by necessity "sub-

lime poets" and that the first science to be mastered before more can be known about man is that of mythology.[15] The first wisdom of the gentile world was what Vico calls "poetic wisdom" operating by "poetic logic"—"a metaphysics not rational and abstract like that of learned men now, but felt and imagined as that of the first men must have been, who, without power of ratiocination, were all robust sense and vigorous imagination."[16] The fundamental difference here between Vico and others who held similar views[17] is that Vico does not consistently denigrate as hopeless because they are irrational the qualities he mentions above; in some moods he even celebrates them. Nor does he try to rationalize examples of "poetic logic" by claiming that myths hide rational statements by allegory. The term "poetic" in Vico refers to a mode of thought that does not work toward abstract concepts, but in Blake's terms toward the expansion of centers. "Poetic logic" gave rise first to history, not poetry (in the sense of imitation and feigning, at least); and the first history was created by poets, for "all gentile histories have their beginnings in fables."[18] Mythologies are really "civil histories of the first peoples, who were everywhere naturally poets."[19] This view of Vico's differs from most allegorical euhemerism in that it does not claim myths to be early impressions of historical fact corrupted into fable over time, but events formulated originally in the mode of "poetic logic." In him there is no notion of an original enlightened condition of Deistic reasonableness before a Fall into debased religion. Jove by the "poetic logic" of metaphor is the sky *and* the first of the gods. One does not *stand for* the other. This all follows from the nature of primitive thought, which for Vico is never far divorced from primitive language, which is animistic, incapable of abstraction, and fundamentally tropological. Indeed, language is the form of thought. Ideas and words are of a twin birth.[20] Vico goes so far as to say, anticipating modern structuralist thought, that minds are formed by the nature of language, not vice versa.[21]

Fundamental to Vico's notion of the origins of language in the concrete and poetic are three of the four major tropes: metaphor, metonymy, and synecdoche. (Irony appears somewhat later.) These tropes, which are treated by classical thought simply as devices of rhetoric spread upon a fabric of conceptual logic, Vico treats as the fundamental "corollaries" of "poetic logic," the "necessary modes of expression,"[22] thereby implicitly joining thought to language. He expresses his important reversal of the classical view of tropes as follows:

By means of these three divinities [Jove, Cybele, and Nep-
tune] . . . they [primitive men] explained everything appertaining to the sky, the earth, and the sea. And similarly by
means of the other divinities they signified the other kinds of
things appertaining to each, denoting all flowers, for instance,
by Flora, and all fruits by Pomona. We nowadays reverse this
practice in respect of spiritual things, such as the faculties of
the human mind, the passions, the virtues, vices, sciences, and
arts; for the most part the ideas we form of them are so many
feminine personifications, to which we refer all the causes,
properties and effects that severally appertain to them. For
when we wish to give utterance to our understanding of spiritual things, we must seek aid from our imagination to explain them and, like painters, form human images of them.
But these theological poets, unable to make use of the understanding, did the opposite and more sublime thing: they attributed senses and passions, as we saw not long since, to
bodies, and to bodies as vast as sky, sea, and earth. Later, as
these vast imaginations shrank and the power of abstraction
grew, the personifications were reduced to diminutive signs.[23]

There appears here the idea of a primordial "sympathetic nature," as
well as that of shrinkage to a Blakean center. Modern man's mind is
"so detached from the senses, even in the vulgar, by abstractions corresponding to all the abstract terms our language abounds in" that
we cannot form any image of such a nature, at least not without an
immense effort.[24] The tropes are "corollaries" of a "poetic logic"
identical to that exercised by Blake's "ancient poets."

2. "Imaginative Universals": According to Vico, the earliest people did not possess "intelligible class concepts of things," but they
nevertheless had to move in thought and expression from particulars
to some sort of universals, "to which, as to certain models or ideal
portraits" they could "reduce all the particular species which re-
sembled them."[25] A Vichean "imaginative universal," the special
product of "poetic logic," remains animate in its universality by
retaining all the qualities of any particular referred to it. "It is an
eternal property of the fables always to enlarge the ideas of particulars,"[26] and, I might add, to insist on the "identity" with the particular of that enlargement.

We are not surprised, therefore, to find that metaphor is the
"most necessary and frequent" corollary of "poetic logic" by which

the first poets "attributed to bodies the being of animate substances, with capacities measured by their own, namely sense and passion, and in this way made fables of them."[27] Vico notes how many inanimate things are verbally formed by metaphors from the human body, its parts, senses, or passions, and concludes that "as rational metaphysics teaches that man becomes all things by understanding them (*homo intelligendo fit omnia*), this imaginative metaphysics [poetic logic] shows that man becomes all things by *not* understanding them (*homo non intelligendo fit omnia*); and perhaps the latter proposition is truer than the former, for when man understands he extends his mind and takes in things; but when he does not understand he makes the things out of himself and becomes them by transforming himself into them."[28] Like metaphor, each metonymy and synecdoche creates a fable in miniature. Vico classes the gods and some traditional heroes as "imaginative universals"—Hercules, Homer, Aesop, Horatio, and Orlando, for example. Homer, the heroic character of Grecian men "insofar as they told their histories in song," is an "imaginative universal." All the inconsistencies that surround Homer as a singular individual during a particular period are made consistent by this view, which Vico develops to some length, anticipating Blake's remark in the annotations to Reynolds's *Discourses*, "Every class is individual."

3. The third Vichean notion is that of "fictions": If myth and poetry developed in the way Vico describes, so originally did jurisprudence. The most ancient laws of the gentiles arose out of single instances and were only later given general application. They were not conceived before the acts occurred that made them necessary. Vico introduces the idea of "fictions" into his account of Roman law, which he calls as a whole a "serious poem." By this he means a historical development out of the practice of "poetic logic." His treatment of law as fictions in which "what had happened was taken as not having happened, and what had not happened as having happened" anticipates Hans Vaihinger's theory of "as if" (which I shall discuss in chapter 7) by two centuries, even down to the type of illustration used, and it emphasizes not the untruth of a fiction but the notion of a fiction as a making, implicit in the Blakean idea of the "prolific" activity of the "ancient poets."

There is in Vico, however, a latent positivism, with which a theory of symbolic cannot go along. He seems to regard "poetic logic" as principally and perhaps only a necessary precursor to philosophy. He writes that in fables, as in embryos or matrices, we have discovered the outlines of all esoteric wisdom. And it may be said that in the fables the nations have in a rough way and in the language of the human senses described the beginnings of this world of sciences, which the specialized studies of scholars have since clarified for us by reasoning and generalization.[29]

For Vico, the early poets were the "sense" and the philosophers the "intellect" of human wisdom. The latter, working upon the crude and confused accomplishments of the former, made humanity "complete."[30] It would seem that each metaphor or "fable in brief" provides the materials for abstract thought, but once abstract thought assimilates metaphor, the metaphor's formative power is lost and there is decay into a "false" figure of speech, useful for illustrative purposes perhaps, but dangerous when extended beyond its now diminished realm. At the same time, Vico remarks that it was the very "deficiency of human reasoning power" that gave rise to the great sublime poetry of the heroic age and that "the philosophies which came afterward, the arts of poetry and of criticism, have produced none equal or better, and have even prevented its production."[31] This sounds nostalgic, like Blake's story of the "ancient poets" and the subsequent "priesthood." As an antidote to that nostalgia Vico offers not a theory of the persistence of "poetic logic" in art but only the *recorso*, the theory of the growth, maturity, and decline of a civilization, whose apotheosis seems to occur as the "abstract" mind gains complete ascendancy over the "poetic." The growth of the "abstract" marks the decadence of the "poetic," but the supreme dominance of the abstract marks also the decadence of the culture.

Vico offers a theory based on a keen appreciation of the facts of flux, and this enables him to search back into origins, to find the dynamic character of myth and language. But his sensitivity to change leads him to an inner conflict. On the one hand, he demonstrates sympathy for "poetic logic" as a mode of thought. It seems to provide a Blakean contrary to that excess of abstraction which leads man away from his own life in the world. On the other hand, he seems to regard "poetic logic" as a stage in human development to be passed through. His third great age—the Age of Man—liberates man from myth. Vico offers to a philosophy of the literary symbolic a view of language that makes "poetic logic" more fundamental than abstract conceptualization and thereby tends, as Croce said of him, to "suppress the dualism between poetry and language" that has long dogged our civilization.[32] Further, his attempt to distinguish "imaginative universals" from abstract ones shows him grounding the poetic in a process that is clearly not the mode of romantic allegory as I shall soon describe it. But Vico does not take the crucial step to a view of language as fully creative and symbolic. He cannot free himself entirely from certain assumptions about human progress that make him at times seem to denigrate the poetic almost as much as did the Cartesianism he sought to revise. This failure allows us to read him as a supreme historical ironist, with civilization buffeted between the poles of poetry and abstract thought in an endless cyclical movement. What he needs is a Blakean notion of "prolific" contrariety to oppose to the cyclicity which negates now "poetic logic," now "conceptual logic." The contrary must also oppose the idea of straight-line progress from "poetic logic" to a culture of the pure concept.

2. TYPES OF ROMANTIC ALLEGORY

NEXT I want to set forth a relatively simple schema of the romantic distinction between symbol and allegory. In chapter 3, I will look closely at specific ways in which that distinction appears in certain romantic writers. This is merely a preliminary map.

The distinction between symbolism and allegory uttered by so many theorists of the romantic age was not fundamentally one between types of poetic tropes, or between a metaphysical and a rhetorical term, but between what was regarded as the poetic and the non-poetic.[33] It may, therefore, be regarded as a negation of allegory, and it arose in response to a previously implied negation of the poetic (as the romantics understood poetry) by neoclassical criticism and the dominating epistemologies of that age. This difference was not clearly seen, however, by many theorists, and the terms tended to slip back to designating tropes, quite frequently muddying discourse as they did so. It must be understood, therefore, that romantic use of the term "allegory" was varied and inconsistent. At the outset one should consider it a term independent of "allegory" as it has been used in traditional rhetoric and practical criticism. The problem for contemporary criticism is to rescue both "allegory" and "symbolism" from a historical negation which cyclically privileges one term over the other in a Vichean round where, as Blake remarks, both sides adopt the same story—just different sides of it.

The distinction was very often expressed in connection with the concepts of particularity and universality. For the romantic writers on this subject, in "allegory" the so-called universal is declared to be of primary importance, while in the "symbol" the particular is privileged. "Allegory" becomes a term of reprobation, "symbolism" a term of approbation. The outcome of this view seems to be a division of the allegoric into three fundamental types, which I shall take the liberty of calling the "Platonic," the "religious," and the "empirical," respectively.[34] No romantic theorist so systematically divides the allegoric, but many tend to single out one or two of the three types for concentration when they discuss allegory. In all three cases, allegory is treated in the way that romantic poets and theorists characteristically deal with poetry—as an expressive form or human activity.[35] In each of the three types, the poet appropriates a particular experience or object and proceeds to signify with it a "reality" beyond it which is superior to and separate from it.

In the first or "Platonic" type, the poet regards himself as making an appearance or copy to signify an "idea" or universal form for which the copy stands. Let me say here at once, however, that by "Platonic" I mean a view *derivable from* Plato, not Plato's own. The Plotinian form of the "Platonic," for example, tends to rescue the mere "allegorical" appearance from the severity of Plato's critique and makes it an emanation of the "idea" or what I shall shortly call the "miraculous" form of the romantic symbol.

In the second or "religious" type, the poet begins with a phenomenal, particular world, which is regarded as a veil that tantalizingly intimates the existence of a hidden realm of ultimate truth, of silence, of nothingness, or noumena, or of God. Because the signifiers are arbitrary, occult means must be learned in order to "read" the veil and gain intimations of the reality beyond. Two modes appear under this type: the mode of intellectual intuition or theology and the mode of mystical negative vision. The difference, which I overstate at this point for the purpose of getting the argument started, is that between a process of religious vision that is willing to employ the rational intellect and one that insists on radical abandonment of the reason and even language itself at an early stage. I say mystical "negative" vision because in this mode words or things only *signify* a hidden reality. Their connection to it is not "emanative" and is by way of a secret code, and thus vision is not vision in any sensuous sense at all.

In the third or "empirical" type, one makes the particular into a sense datum or instance and abstracts from it toward a general principle or universal natural law, which is given a status in being greater than that of the instance itself. The process, in contrast to the deduc-

Table 1.1. Romantic Allegory
The Particular

	(1)	(2)	(3)	(4)
Appearance:	false copy	veil	instance, phenomenon, secondary qualities of experience	trope
Location of reality or the universal:	Platonic form or idea	truth, silence, nothing, noumena, God	general principle, natural law	behind the text behind the trope
Name:	The Platonic	The Religious (1) Intellectual Intuition (2) Mystical Vision	The Empirical	The Substitutive (1) codal (2) mythic (3) oneiric
Form:	philosophy	theology	science	rhetoric
Guardian angel:	Socrates	(1) St. Thomas Aquinas (2) Hermes Trismegistus	Bacon, Newton, Locke	(1) Quintilian et al. (2) Euhemerus (3) Freud

tive "Platonic," is inductive. One notes this form, mixed with the "Platonic," in the theorizing of Sir Joshua Reynolds.[36] The "empirical" type of allegory develops out of the subject-object distinction, or, in Locke's terms, the distinction between "primary" and "secondary" qualities of experience. Reality in this system is located in a world devoid of all that is not measurable, a world that can be regarded as "out there" in the form of A. N. Whitehead's "soundless, scentless, colourless" universe: "merely the hurrying of matter, endlessly, meaninglessly."[37] Such a world, however, under the pressure of philosophical critique—that set in motion by Berkeley—can be further reduced to a "creation" of the human understanding. It becomes a purely abstract world of natural law that phenomena obey, a world that turns into mathematic form. It is not surprising that Blake should have recognized an affinity between this abstract, "empirically" derived law and the hidden god of the "religious" type of allegory, who in Blake's view is a human "creation" revealing himself to man (or rather hiding himself) only in another kind of law, the arbitrary moral code. By the same token, it is not surprising that John Crowe Ransom in our own century should have identified the abstract world of natural law with the "Platonic," using the latter term to lump type 1 and type 3 together.[38]

In each of the three types reality is located not in the particular but in the universal, so called—a universal that can be known only by a process which abandons the sensuous—though in the third type, "general" is a more appropriate term than "universal." And in each case the relation of word to referent is a relation of sign to something hidden. In the "Platonic" the relation is hopefully mimetic; in the "religious" and "empirical" it is admittedly arbitrary. To each of the three types I assign a guardian angel, or, as Blake would call it, a "covering cherub." For the "Platonic" there is Socrates. For the "religious" there is St. Thomas Aquinas (for the first mode) and the fabulous Hermes Trismegistus (for the second). For the "empirical" Blake's triple form of Bacon, Newton, and Locke will serve. It is possible, with some oversimplification, to consider that the three types arose in Western civilization in the order in which I have presented them. It is also possible to see that each has generated its own war with poetry: Socrates himself refers to the ancient war between philosophy and poetry. In Boethius's *Consolation of Philosophy* the struggle between philosophy and poetry is reaffirmed, but here philosophy has really become theology, so that it can be seen that the second type generates a war between religion and poetry. The third type produces a war between science and poetry, which was the romantic theorists' own particular concern—indeed their obsession. The pressure of this third struggle, added to that of the older ones, was enough to generate the terminology of symbol/allegory among literary theorists as a bulwark against a threefold enemy, though there were various efforts at this time to seek treaties with the "Platonic" and the "religious" in the concept of the symbol itself.

In the romantic view there is a fourth type of allegory which subsumes the three I have mentioned yet frequently appears in forms independent of them. This is the "substitutive," which has a history as old as literature and is theoretically contained in the tradition of classical rhetoric, where it is treated as an extended metaphor. One treatment of metaphor in this tradition is as a verbal substitute for another word: There is a tropological text which hides another text. It is convenient to think of three modes of this type. The first is a deliberate secret code. The second is a text that is regarded as having become a code through historical accident, as myths are regarded in the tradition of euhemerism. The third is an oneiric text, or dream, the modern mode of allegorical interpretation here being that of psychoanalysis. The guardian angels are Quintilian et al., Euhemerus, and Freud, respectively. Clearly the three types of romantic—"Platonic," "religious," and "empirical"—can be regarded as "substitutive," though they do not produce exact substitutions. In fact, in all three types the substitution can be regarded as a kind of failure (sometimes involving a Fall), since none reaches reality or truth. The *purely* "substitutive," on the other hand, being only substitutive, gives nothing new; it merely reveals a text behind a text, which then must be interpreted in one of the other three ways. One has, therefore, failure after all, and possibly an infinite regress. It goes without saying that this view of allegory does not always square with a reader's literary experience. Angus Fletcher, for one, points out that allegory can add something of its own, that is, that the literal level itself may offer something to the reader. Romantic use of the term "allegory" usually doesn't allow for this. If it did, of course, that would be all the more reason to insist on the discontinuity of levels and the literal level's swerving away from the truth.

Romantic efforts to provide a poetic opposition to philosophy, religion, and science all at once began as all efforts to formulate a revolt begin, in the coils of a terminology established by the principal enemy. This was a terminology of subject and object, primary and secondary qualities—the language of the empirical tradition or the age's dominant mode of what I shall call "antimyth." To fly either to subjectivity (as in some phases of *symbolisme*) or to the object (as in naturalism) was to remain trapped to some extent inside the mode. Many brave nineteenth-century forays turned out to be retreats to the extremity of one or the other pole of that mode's negation. The immense concentration of romantic thought on this issue, under which became subsumed the wars of poetry with philosophy and religion along the lines I have suggested in Blake and Ransom, led to a revision of the old distinction enunciated by Aristotle between poetry and history. Aristotle wrote:

> The true difference is that one relates what has happened, the other what may happen. Poetry, therefore, is a more philosophical and a higher thing than history; for poetry tends to express the universal, history the particular.[39]

But for romantic thought, nothing is more particular than poetry, which has become personal and biographical; while history, as historians came to imagine it, becomes a form of the "empirical," moving in its major nineteenth-century utterances toward the establishment of historical law.

To privilege poetry in opposition to the romantic types of allegory required a new word. But men do not coin words from nothing. They make words anew from the verbal material at hand. The source in this case was religious ritual. The term "symbol" had been adopted from its early Greek form and connected in Christianity with the sacraments.[40] In the Eucharist, Christ's body and blood are not simply *represented* by the bread and wine but are declared to be miraculously present in and as the bread and wine. Romantic criticism begins the process of appropriating this miraculous occurrence, secularizing it, and applying it to poetry under the name of "symbolism," a word which in itself seems to have come from a secular term meaning simply the use of one thing to stand for another. It was adopted and put into its new role by the church fathers to indicate not a rhetorical trope but a mystery, in which a word or object embodies or actually contains in its very nature the being of the thing it stands for. The displacement of this concept continues to exist in most romantic parlance. Whereas in allegory as the romantics saw it the thing stood for is forever separate from the word or object—like the hidden God of the Gnostics—the symbol bears at least a trace of the Christian notion of actual appearance or coming into being.

Yet except in forms of ritual like the Eucharist the symbol is not quite a radically complete presence. Rather, it is the sign of a metaphysical connection between two levels of being—a connection that is not arbitrary, as in allegory, but one in which the symbol partakes of the thing it stands for. It is in an indestructible relation to it. It is in itself sensuous, and this sensuousness is part of its connection with what it stands for, not something that misleads us about the stood for or veils it, but actually embodies a spiritual aspect of the stood for. Still, this stood for is treated as beyond or mysterious and not sensuous at all. So it must be said that the symbol in this sense is not identical with its stood for but a sort of fallen form of it, which may yet provide mediation with the truth beyond.

What I have just described I shall call the romantic symbol of the first type. Its connection to romantic allegory of the second or "religious" type is clear enough, and the difference is perhaps only a matter of degree. In the "religious" the connection of allegory to a stood for is purely conventional, dogmatically accepted, and arbitrary. In the romantic symbol of the first type the connection is "miraculous." In both cases there *is* a distance, though in the symbol the gap is partial in that the symbol contains something of the stood for but in a lower or sensuous degree. The relation is not arbitrary but one of what is called in, say, Swedenborg, "correspondence." Such correspondence is *given* and not arbitrary, though some, like Blake, would argue that it is *arbitrarily given*. The alternative to this would be a mimetic relation of some sort, as in the "Platonic."

There is a second type of romantic symbol, and it is the emergence of this second type that is my primary concern. It is only an emergent type in romanticism because a ground is never quite fully articulated for it. I intend to observe certain moments of its partial and fleeting appearances, which occur usually in conjunction with the "miraculous" first type. It already seems clear enough that because the "miraculous" symbol is "fallen," it tends to slip back to become a form of "religious" allegory; and its advocates are particularly subject to charges of self-mystification.

The first thing to say about the second type of symbol is that in romanticism it is only emergent, if that. Perhaps, for this reason, it should not be called romantic at all. The second thing is that in the form in which I hope eventually to see it developed here, it is not a negation of allegory but a contrary to the negation allegory/"miraculous" symbol. The third thing is that it is "secular." It presses for separation from miraculism and the idea that it either incarnates or stands in a fallen state for a spiritual mystery. It arises out of epistemological issues presented to us by the tradition of empiricism. Its language is appropriated from and struggles with that tradition. In the "secular" symbol, as I shall call it, there is recognition of particularity as real. From Goethe onward, with some backsliding, it is the particular that is declared by literary theorists to *contain* the universal, not *point to it* or provide a transparency for it. One must add to these notions the idea that the particular does not negate the universal, recalling Vico's "imaginative universals."

But for the particular to contain the universal seems as miraculous as the power of the symbol to embody God. In the "secular" symbol, however, the universal becomes not something previously there to be contained but something *generated by* the particular as the seed generates the plant or the poem such interpretations as we make of it. This is the sense in which the particular *contains*. Two Blakean notions previously mentioned are relevant here. The first—center and circumference—applies because to be at a center is to be in a condition where one points outward *toward* everything, as allegory is always pointing us *to* something. To be at a circumference is to contain, as mathematical form contains physical reality or the poem its so-called meaning. The second notion is that of "prolific" and "devourer." Under "prolific" comes the symbol, which points to nothing beyond it (neither Platonic idea, mystical nothingness, nor natural law) but instead generates from itself food for "devouring"— interpretation. Nothing is interposed between us and a hidden being on the other side of the symbol, for the other side is not another world at all. It is only a potentiality to be shaped by the creative power of the symbol itself, and in that sense it is in the symbol, not elsewhere. The concept of circumference as container is, however, finally not quite right, since it implies form as a receptacle for a content. The Blakean idea of prolific is preferable to circumference, since prolific doesn't contain. It generates. The idea of form is thus an idea of a shaping action rather than a mold, and the governing idea is one of temporal process rather than spatial location. These notions are, of course, usually treated under the rubric of romantic "expressivism." Indeed, in the tradition of the expressive I wish to think not of symbols but of *symbolic activity*, substituting the notion of the symbolic eventually for that of the symbol *as such* as an object or trope in the poem. The term "symbolic" always has for me this notion of activity about it, rather than the stasis or silence that, say, Walter Benjamin attributes to the romantic symbol.[41]

Of course, we may erect an interpretation between ourselves and the symbolic expression. The symbolic is there to be devoured or to be built upon by our thought. It is principally a source, not, as Saussure and others would have it, principally a signifier. Goethe declares it to be "inscrutable," a sort of immanence of itself, and Blake declares it to be hidden to the "corporeal" (by which he means "empirical") understanding. There is a sense in which it is partly hidden *by* such understanding, because, as I have said, the interpretation erects a veil and often treats the symbolic as a mystery in the manner that the allegorist of type 2 treats whatever is behind the veil of phenomena.

In the beginning, romantic thought did not distinguish the two types of symbolism I discover—the "miraculous" and the "secular." Through recourse to the miraculism of the symbol's sacramental sources in the church fathers when the romantics begin to formulate the "secular" notion, their language tends to slip back into the "miraculous," thence to "religious" allegory. The "miraculous" form of the symbol has ineradicable allegoric elements insisted on by the religious notion of the Fall of man into the alien realm of matter, sense, and appearance, with the result that the "miraculous" symbol always has to have a fallen and corrupting element separating it from its ultimate source even as that separation is vehemently denied in the form of religious ritual and belief. It is on this point that I want to distinguish the literary symbolic from religious forms of expression.[42]

In the beginning also, the romantic distinction between symbolism and allegory was not stated as a distinction between kinds, usages, or ways of considering language, but ways of perceiving or experiencing without particular concern for the mediation of language. This tendency in itself illustrates the extent to which even critics of empiricism were captured by the terms and oppositions in which the empirical tradition worked, the empirical approach being by way of a critique of perception and the establishment of the duality of subject and object. Indeed, in the discourses of Goethe, Kant, Schelling, and others, it is not clear whether the writers think of words as symbols or only things as symbols or whether the question of words and their possible hand in conception or creation has arisen for them.[43] But for twentieth-century theorists this makes all the difference, and the question becomes to what extent language in itself is principally creative or principally significatory. A philosophy of literary symbolism building on the "secular" concept of the symbolic would seem to require a theory of the radically creative power of language; otherwise it relaxes into a theory of universal allegory or signification, in other words a theory of rhetoric only.

One of the reasons that Coleridge's *Statesmen's Manual* is so interesting is that there Coleridge faces the question of the word, albeit the biblical word. Is it a creative *container of* or *pointer* backward *to* events? As readers of his discourse, we soon discover ourselves reading Coleridge's remarks about the Bible as if he were discoursing about poetry generally. We feel he has invited us to do so. We believe him to be on the way to asking questions about how much and what kind of reality actually inheres in or is constructed by our language. We wonder whether in some sense the romantic impulse to valorize symbolism was not an insight still in the process of formation in the direction of a theory of symbolic expression, part of a struggle to make the claim for language as fundamentally poetic and poetry as the source of our capacity to create such cultural reality as we are capable of producing.

A concept that was deliberately made to lie outside the romantic distinction between symbolism and allegory should be mentioned here, for I shall study it as a special mode in chapter 3. This is what Hegel called in his *Philosophy of Fine Art* (1835) "romantic art." In that work Hegel named three types of art: the "symbolic," the "classic," and the "romantic"; and he saw them as phases through which art passes in man's quest for the absolute. Hegel's "symbolic" art is clearly romantic "religious" allegory. His "classic" art, more difficult to place in my scheme, has some relation to the romantic symbolic. His "romantic" art is in some respects a return to the mode of romantic allegory but on what he conceived of as an entirely different and higher spiritual level. Because of Hegel's unique premises—principally his refusal to admit the kind of beyond posited in the three types of allegory I have mentioned—I do not identify his romantic art with romantic allegory, at least not until I study it further toward the end of chapter 3. It must suffice to say here that romantic art for Hegel marks the beginning of art's disintegration or encompassment and man's passage to a higher form of religious consciousness, which in turn disappears into philosophy. The Hegelian path, which for many reasons has proved attractive to recent theorists, is not the one that the theory of the symbolic which emerges here takes. Rather, from my point of view the Hegelian path is a circling back in the direction of allegory—with a difference, a devouring of art in religion and then in philosophy. I shall call it specially the "Hegelian." It plays a role in this study of the symbolic, for its influence appears on both

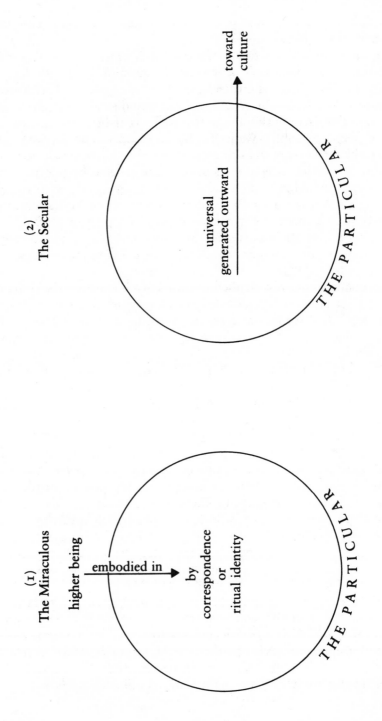

Figure 1.1. Romantic Symbolism

sides of the romantic distinction right up to the present, and it influences theorists as opposed as Walter Benjamin and Paul Ricoeur.

It is to be noticed that neither of my charts, except where the "substitutive" is mentioned, indicates the presence of language. If, for example, we were to add the realm of language to the "Platonic" type we should have to regard language as a copy of the "false copy" listed under "appearance" or an arbitrary signifier of a false copy, in either case declaring the linguistic term an allegory twice removed. In my chart of romantic symbolism, either we should have to place language outside the circumference of each circle, pointing toward it, in which case we would have something pointing outward toward an inwardness ("substitutive" allegory again), or we should have to develop a theory of language as itself a containing circumference or a "prolific." It is the latter choice, of course, that I wish to make. A philosophy of the literary symbolic requires a theory of language as the "prolific." This is a concept quite different—at least in its emphasis on the act any linguistic expression contains—from the concept implicit in classical rhetoric, the normative concept of "ordinary" language, the ideal mathematical model of positivistic tradition, or the significatory model of modern semiotics.

3. THE PROGRAM

THE DISTINCTION between allegory and symbolism began as a defensive strategy against Cartesian rationalism and British empiricism in their most intolerant antipoetic forms. But the distinction itself ran the continual danger of capture in the enemy's enclosure. Even to this day it generates a cyclical valorization of one term, then the other. This cyclicity, of which the falling away from the "miraculous" symbol into some form of the romantic allegoric is the most common example, is the cause of much confusion in thought about the symbolic. My aim in this book is to argue once again for the *importance* of the poetic. I am concerned with the tradition of theorists of the symbolic since Kant, Goethe, and the romantic critics who used the symbol/allegory distinction; and my effort is to rehabilitate the symbolic by insisting on a notion of it as the creator, through intellectual contrariety, of culture. My strategy as I proceed is one, I hope, of careful elimination of theoretical stances that are irreducibly problematic or, in some cases, just plain trouble-making (moraine depositing), while at the same time I try to push ahead, gathering what is of value as I go. Thus the deliberate combination of historical treatment and polemic.

Every literary theory has a central term, often analogous to other central terms in other theories. This raises the question of why one chooses the term one does, particularly when one's term does not dominate all the discourses one is obliged to discuss. In part, of course, my term "symbolic" is a matter of choice. But more important, it is, I think, the word most abused yet most prolific for theoretical use. It is the maker of important reverberations, far beyond the realm of what we usually call literature, into questions involving all of the liberal arts and sciences, the organization of learning and of universities. This and its astonishing modern persistence and ubiquity alone call for clarification.

The cyclical movement to which I refer characterizes the work of most theorists I consider and accounts for the need to find so many of them wanting even as one learns from them. One sees in Kant, for example, a slipping back from the possibility of a "secular" symbolic to a conventional form of allegoric. One sees in Goethe a struggle with the terms of the romantic distinction, and in several romantic theorists an attempt to make the "miraculous" sustain itself against tremendous pressure. Though Blake never uses the word "symbol" it is from him and what Vico had in common with him that I set out toward a notion of the "secular" symbolic, connecting it as I go with the important modernist terms "myth" and "fiction." Along the way are many valorous partial achievements. The French *symboliste* movement, with its brilliant theoreticians, could not break the cycle, in spite of the powerful wrenching of terms that this movement achieved. The psychoanalytical movement became a battleground of allegorists against "miraculous" symbolists. The sentimental archaists, as I call Mircea Eliade, Philip Wheelwright, and others, attempted to rehabilitate the "miraculous" symbol after the ravages of Freud, but they submerged art in the "religious" again. In this history the line of thought most congenial to me runs from Blake through theorists of fictions and myth, Cassirer, Frye, and the notion of conflict in Yeats. But even here are pitfalls, as in Cassirer, who proceeds from a treatment of myth to discussion of language and art, distinguishing between the two while at the same time using the linguistic art of poetry among his examples of art. The opposition he offers between language and art is contradicted by his examples. A submerged positivistic eschatology wars with his respect for what he calls "mythical thought," much as it does in Vico, estranges language from poetic art, and forces the very struggle that he wants to avoid.

There is perhaps an excuse for this. Every literary theorist occupies an "ironic" position, that is, a position requiring him to separate his work on the one hand from poetry and on the other from science, but at the same time identifying it with both. That position is the only place from which he can do his job, which requires a kind of empathy and, at the same time, distance. It involves being apart and yet seeing the thing from its own point of view, a notion wrapped up in the image of the Blakean vortex. Both Vico and Cassirer speak of the difficulty and yet the necessity of such a vantage. In *The New Science*, Vico remarks on the difficulty of coming to understand the way human thinking arose in "poetic logic." He tells us that he expended twenty years in the effort to understand that development from inside itself; "We had to descend from these human and refined natures of ours to those quite wild and savage natures, which we cannot at all imagine and can comprehend only with great effort." [44] Cassirer, who is much in his debt, observes, "We cannot reduce myth to certain fixed static elements; we must strive to grasp it in its inner life, in its mobility and diversity, in its dynamic principle." [45] The problem with respect to the treatment of poetry is the same as that with respect to myth. Even the most careful of discursive approaches betrays at some point an alien perspective. Cassirer and Vico, as I have indicated, are examples. The old classical attitude toward tropes as deviant recurs also in the language of contemporary structuralism, even sometimes when certain tropes are *declared* to be fundamental to language. The problem of self-contradiction in Vico and Cassirer, the allegoric element in structuralism, and the return to rhetoric in current mixtures of poststructuralism and Anglo-American linguistic criticism come from positivistic assumptions negating the poetic in spite of the interests and values sometimes directly expressed in these discourses.

The danger in structuralism, as far as poetry is concerned, is that it is captured by a positivism that would turn all criticism into an "allegoric" social science, the term "human science" to the contrary notwithstanding. [46] My position has some appearance of affinity with modern phenomenological criticism, but I seek to develop a theory of contrary "fictions" rather than moving from the rhetoric of "unconcealment" in Heidegger to phenomenological hermeneutics. These matters I shall deal with in my last chapter. It is well to say here at the outset that I accept from the tradition of J. G. Herder and Wilhelm von Humboldt the idea that language is constitutive of thought, that thought takes form in language, form being more than frame, appearance, or order, and not a term opposed to "content." Rather, form is a mode of activity that shapes and projects. Humboldt says, "languages are not really means for representing already known truths but are rather instruments for discovering previously unrecognized ones."[47] But language is not merely an instrument to look through; it is radically creative, and "no object is possible without it for the psyche."[48] One could go so far as to say that concepts inhere *in* and *as* language, and they are not properly regarded as separate from language once they have been created *by*, *in*, and *as* language. However, even though concepts are creations *inside* and *as* the very form of language, language hypostatizes or projects concepts and fictionalizes an apartness for them. This is what I shall later call the creation of "antimyth"—the fictive projection to an "outside" of something language really retains in itself (thus the creation of the fiction of difference) followed by the fiction that the outside preceded its container. It seems to me that Humboldt was working toward some such idea when he wrote:

> The least advantageous influence on any sort of interesting treatment of linguistic studies is exerted by the narrow notion that language originated as a convention and that words are nothing but signs for things or concepts which are independent of them. This view up to a point is certainly correct but beyond this point it is deadly because as soon as it begins to predominate it kills all mental activity and exiles all life.[49]

Humboldt builds on Herder and Kant to arrive at a theory of language which can pave the way for a philosophy of the literary symbolic—a "secular" symbolism—rather than a return to allegory.[50] Yet Humboldt recognizes the enclosure of language:

> Man thinks, feels, and lives within language alone. . . . But he senses and knows that language is only a means for him; that there is an invisible realm outside it in which he seeks to feel at home and that it is for this reason that he needs the aid of language. The most commonplace observation and the profoundest thought, both lament the inadequacy of language, both look upon that other realm as a distant country toward which only language leads—and *it* never really. All higher forms of speech are a wrestling with this thought, in which sometimes our power, sometimes our longing, is more keenly felt.[51]

He observed that human beings are sometimes actually hostile to language because it is regarded, in these moods, as too confining to the psyche and distorting to its pure utterance,[52] but he recognizes that thinking is dependent on language, even to some degree upon specific languages.[53] When all this is said, however, Humboldt is more celebrative of human power through language than he is concerned about human limitation because of it. He holds that language "reorders the *merely* [my italics] perceptive psychic capacities."[54] Language makes the past and thereby makes culture. True, for those who seek a beyond, language fails. It cannot present or represent things-in-themselves, and there is always this romantic metaphysical regret. But for Humboldt it is not an unquenchable thirst. Poetry has apparently enough to do without solving ultimate theological questions. He finds language involved in making nature, which is a nature beyond all nature[55]—not beyond it toward a "Platonic" or "religious" transcendent realm but beyond it inasmuch as nature alone is mere phenomena and unordered potentiality. Language makes a true nature of nature. This power of the word Humboldt compares to that of a work of art: "a word reveals itself as an individual with a nature of its own which bears resemblance to an object of art."[56] For Humboldt also, objectivity is something that is made by man, emerging as it does from the energy of subjective individuality.[57] It is what I call, following Vico, a "fiction." Thought here seems to expand outward from a verbal, poetic center. Though Humboldt runs afoul of the traditional dualism of poetry and language that carries even into Cassirer (he says art "by no means acts through language"), the whole drift of his argument leads to claims that there is indeed a "prolific" literary art and that language provides a methodology for endless self-renewal.

Generally, discussion of poetry has had to struggle with the deeply ingrained notion that words allegorically stand for a previous meaning or the negation of this—the notion that what meaning we can find is the product of a verbal interpretation of a previous verbal structure which always defers its meaning. Humboldt was apparently trying to get at this point, but ever so tentatively, when he attempted to distinguish poetry from prose:

> The characteristic difference between poetry and prose . . . is that prose declares by its form that it wishes to accompany and serve. Poetry cannot do without at least appearing to control thought or actually bringing it forth.[58]

His language verges on that of Heidegger in the idea of bringing forth and hints at the duplicity that deconstructionists like to find in all verbal structures. I choose to see another side—secular creative expression—and claim that from poetry's point of view the poem makes a language, which creates and contains its signified and allows it to emanate into the world to be devoured; though I shall recognize that from the opposite point of view, which I shall call "antimyth," it copies or signifies only and cannot contain or radically form. And I shall hold that both views are necessary fictions—Blakean contraries from which a desirable culture can, but admittedly may not, emerge. This book is an attempt to build a language that expresses this situation of contraries as fundamental and necessary.

My study begins with Kant, where modern theorizing about human symbolic creativity began. A philosophy of the literary symbolic is involved with the concept of a human constitutive power. Though Kant limited constitutive power to what he called the understanding and did not explicitly connect it with language, his thought leads toward the concept of a linguistic imagination. This is not to say that the history of this subject begins here. It goes back, of course, through Herder and Vico to Plato's *Cratylus* and perhaps beyond. But one must begin somewhere, and in any case my *ultimate* concern is not history but the most instructive "moments" of my problem.

2

The Kantian Symbolic

To characterize the fundamental difference between modern and earlier concepts of literary symbolism is to acknowledge the emergence of a modern concept giving the symbol a status absent in earlier definitions. To characterize this status, one faces the question of whether "symbol" can be regarded as "constitutive," thereby acknowledging the profound influence of Kant, who uses both terms but never joins them. Indeed, Kant's use of "symbol" and "symbolical" is not the fundamental source of interest in him with respect to this question, though it is important to know how he uses the terms. In *The Critique of Judgment*, Kant's use of them is limited to a few pages at the end of the "Dialectic of the Aesthetical Judgment."

1. SCHEMA AND SYMBOL

In Section 59, Kant divides all *hypotyposes*, by which he means presentations or sensible illustrations, into the *schematical* and the *symbolical*. In the *schematical*, "to a concept comprehended by the understanding, the corresponding intuition is given."[1] Schemata are direct demonstrative presentations of a concept. In terms of generals and particulars, this means that a particular represents an empirically derived general. In the *symbolical*, "to a concept only thinkable by the reason, to which no sensible intuition can be adequate, an intuition is supplied with which accords a procedure of the judgment analogous to what it observes in schematism, i.e. merely analogous to the rule of this procedure, not to the intuition itself, consequently to the form of reflection merely and not to its content."[2] Both hypotyposes are distinguished from "designations of concepts by accompanying sensible signs which contain nothing belonging to the intuition of the object,"[3] i.e., symbols in the sense in which the term is used in symbolic logic or (in Kantian terms) arbitrary *characterization*.

The difference between *schemata* and *symbols* for Kant has to do with the connection between *schemata* and the understanding on the one hand and *symbols* and the reason on the other. The symbol offers a situation in which there is an attempt to present an intuition adequate to an idea of the reason, which for Kant is impossible. Thus the presentation is indirect and analogous only, as compared to *schemata*, where the concepts of the understanding are given a direct presentation by recourse to intuition, upon which the understanding directly built. Kant goes on to say:

> Thus a monarchical state is represented by a living body if it is governed by national laws, and by a mere machine (like a hand mill) if governed by an individual absolute will; but in both cases only symbolically. For between a despotic state and a hand mill there is, to be sure, no similarity; but there is a similarity in the rules according to which we reflect upon these two things and their causality.[4]

What has happened here is that the judgment applies the concept to an object of sense and then applies the rule of the reflection on the intuition to a different object, one becoming the symbol of the other. This is a conventional enough analysis and might not detain us if Kant himself did not consider it insufficient and did not at once remark, "it deserves a deeper investigation, but this is not the place to linger over it."[5] He then limits his observations to two: (1) The German language is full of indirect, symbolical presentations "in which the expression does not contain the proper schema for the concept, but merely a symbol for reflection."[6] The result is an analogy "by the transference of reflection upon an object of intuition to a quite different concept to which perhaps an intuition can never directly correspond";[7] and (2) the beautiful is the symbol of the morally good, but only in that both "give pleasure with a claim for the agreement of everyone else."[8] I shall return to these points.

Kant's failure to linger here is unfortunate. It is part of a general absence of any direct confrontation with problems of language in the critiques and particularly language as exhibited in literary art. It is only in Section 49 of the *Critique of Judgment*, preceding the remarks alluded to above, that Kant refers to poems in connection with his notion of the "aesthetical idea." This notion is related to the symbol, but it is introduced in a cryptic and vexing way, to which I also shall return. Kant never does expand the term "symbol" to make it a constitutive form. For Kant, we think in a mental form that is constitutive—the understanding; but to what extent that form is linguistic is not broached. This is true even though Kant proceeds to all of his philosophy from a consideration of the verbal structure known as the syllogism. The Kantian notion of the constitutive does, however, influence literary theory indirectly. It does so via a distortion, for some later critics have carried the notion of the constitutive over into literary art even though Kant claims that only the concepts of the understanding can be regarded as constitutive. In order eventually to see how this extension of the constitutive occurred, it is necessary briefly to recall the idea as Kant presented it in *The Critique of Pure Reason*.

2. Aesthetical Judgment of the Beautiful

Kant begins with the so-called things-in-themselves. Though they exist, they can never be known. What can be known is the product of our thought, which is generated from appearances. Appearances are intuited and ordered temporally and spatially by the sensibility, whereupon the understanding synthesizes and produces thought. (In Kant, intuition is always of appearances or phenomena and never of noumena or the supersensible.) The understanding performs its synthesis via a priori categories and is constitutive, making and ordering our experience in concepts. The mediating power between the sensibility and the understanding is the imagination, joining image to concept. The reason performs what Kant regards as a quite natural human act: Man desires completion and full explanation, and the reason strives to produce from the constitutive concepts of the understanding thought that would discover, so to speak, the final unifying idea, were it possible to do so. But the reason can produce only regulative ideas, not constitutive ones, that is, ideas that can never be verified, ideas of objects that can never be known. If reason attempts to prove the existence of such objects, it falls into logical contradictions or antinomies. Thus reason comes back in a circle to a confrontation with the unknowability of things-in-themselves, or noumena.

Kant, however, recognizes a gap between the reason and the understanding. This he fills with the judgment, which he divides into two types, the aesthetical and the teleological. Kant's clearest exposition of the role of the aesthetic judgment occurs in Section 58 of the *Critique of Judgment*. There he imagines and rejects a situation in which there is no judgment but only understanding and reason:

> To begin with, we can either place the principle of taste in the fact that it always judges in accordance with grounds which are empirical, and therefore are only given *a posteriori* by sense, or concede that it judges on *a priori* grounds. The former would be the empiricism of the critique of taste, the latter its rationalism. According to the former, the object of our satisfaction would not differ from the *pleasant*; according to the latter, if the judgment rests on definite concepts, it would not differ from the *good*. Thus all beauty would be banished from the world, and only a particular name, expressing perhaps a certain mingling of the two above-named kinds of satisfaction, would remain in its place. But we have shown that there are also *a priori* grounds of satisfaction which can subsist along with the principle of rationalism, although they cannot be comprehended in *definite concepts.*[9]

Kant thus rejects the possibility of an empiricism of taste, which would refer judgments of the beautiful to the understanding, and a rationalism of taste, which would refer them to the reason. The judgment fills this gap and prescribes to itself a "law," which though it seems to be experiential is a transcendental principle. It represents "the peculiar way in which we must proceed in reflection upon the objects of nature in reference to a thoroughly connected experience."[10] It is not a constitutive but a regulative principle. This principle is the purposiveness of nature. Aesthetically, purposiveness involves our judging things assuming that nature is in harmony with our faculties; teleologically, it means that we assume that things fit into a plan or design. Kant says, "The attainment of that design is bound up with the feeling of pleasure."[11] Both sorts of judgments are based on the transcendental principle of purposiveness, though when

Kant comes to his discussion of the sublime the purposiveness there is not nature's but human nature's. The principle of purposiveness is to be distinguished from natural laws, which are given by the understanding and are mechanically conceived and constitutive, whereas purposiveness is organically conceived and regulative only. The teleological judgment furnishes the conditions under which something is seen as belonging to a purposiveness attributed to nature. The aesthetical judgment decides by taste the harmony of an object with our cognitive faculties insofar as this decision rests not on any agreement with concepts but on feeling.

Aesthetical judgments divide themselves into judgments of the beautiful and the sublime both in nature and in art. Kant's discussion begins with the beautiful in nature; only a very small part is devoted to art, but much of the commentary on the beautiful and sublime in nature has been taken over into the theory of art by later theorists without much attention to Kant's distinction between art and nature, partly because Kant's discussion doesn't deal adequately with the presence of the artistic medium. His discussion is principally concerned with how the judgment determines beauty, but he also concerns himself with what is required to produce the beautiful in art, namely genius and taste, and, after discussion of the sublime, with "aesthetical ideas," which are converse parallels to the ideas of reason. The latter are ideas to which no intuition or representation of the imagination is adequate. The former are ideas which occasion much thought but to which no concept is adequate.[12]

We must be content, for the moment, with these remarks about the two critiques and proceed to those elements in Kant that affect subsequent ideas of literary symbolism. The purpose of the summary I have made is to remind us that Kant's discussion of art exists in the context of a total philosophical system that creates special meanings for his "aesthetical idea" and "symbol."

The Critique of Pure Reason provides the seed of probably the single most important idea of modern theories of literary symbolism collected around the notion of "symbolic form," which I shall discuss later on in this book. This seed, as I have indicated, is the idea of the constitutive. Without a constitutive understanding, with its ordering and creative powers, experience is for Kant an undifferentiated manifold of sensation. As a result of the irredeemable gap between our knowledge and things-in-themselves, what we do know we know only from the processes of the understanding. Kant, then, never says that art constitutively produces knowledge, a term which always has a special, limited meaning for him that is connected to products of the understanding. What the artist can produce are aesthetical ideas, which are regulative only and not constitutive, and seem to be like Kant's "symbols."

One may remark here that certain later stages of thinking about art as constitutive could not occur until the whole question of the languages of art and other symbolic structures surfaced and the concentration of Kant on how the mind works turned into a concentration on how language works or how the mind works with or in language. This is the very point at which Kant's discussion of symbols stops short. The question became to what extent not the mind's thoughts but symbolic systems themselves (whether of art or science) are constitutive. This development changed meanings normally attached to the term "symbol" and allowed for the development of what I call the "secular" form of the symbolic. While the concept of the constitutive, displaced as it later was, is probably Kant's main contribution to an idea of the "secular" symbolic, the *Critique of Judgment* contains ideas that influenced almost every theorizing about literary symbolism. To exhibit these will require a brief account of a fundamental principle and four points made in the *Critique*.

Kant says that the judgment legislates for feeling, mediating between understanding and reason. The judgment, he says, is determinant or reflective. In a determinant judgment, the universal is given, and the task is to subsume particulars under it. In a reflective judgment, only the particular is given, and the universal must be found.[13] In order to accomplish the latter, the reflective judgment "requires . . . a principle that it cannot borrow from experience":

> This principle can be no other than the following: As universal laws of nature have their ground in our understanding, which prescribes them to nature . . . , so particular empirical laws, in respect of what is in them left undetermined by these universal laws, must be considered in accordance with such a unity as they would have if an understanding (although not our understanding) had furnished them to our cognitive faculties, so as to make possible a system of experience according to particular laws of nature.[14]

Such laws must not be thought to belong to nature but to the faculty of judgment itself: "The judgment . . . prescribes not to nature (autonomy) but to itself (heautonomy) a law for its reflection upon nature."[15] The principle Kant enunciates as such a universal is, as I have already indicated, the "purposiveness of nature in its variety."[16] This principle has its origin solely in the reflective judgment; it is a priori, but Kant insists it is "neither a natural concept [of the understanding] nor a concept of freedom [of the reason], because it ascribes nothing to the object (of nature), but only represents the peculiar way in which we must proceed in reflection upon the objects of nature in reference to a thoroughly connected experience, and is consequently a subjective principle (maxim) of the judgment."[17]

Now "the subjective element in a representation, *which cannot be an ingredient of cognition*, is the *pleasure or pain* [the feeling] which is bound up with it."[18] The purposiveness of a thing belongs not really to the thing but is a subjective a priori principle of the judgment and has nothing to do with cognition as governed solely by the understanding. Hence, "the object is only called purposive when its representation is immediately combined with the feeling of plea-sure, and this very representation is an aesthetical representation of purposiveness."[19] Under the circumstances of what Kant calls "inter-nal purposiveness" the object is called beautiful, and though the judgment is subjective, to call something beautiful, as against calling something merely pleasant, is to claim universality for the judgment. The faculty of such judgment Kant calls taste.

With respect to the aesthetical judgment, Kant makes four points which are analogous to the four modes of the categories of the under-standing as they were presented in *The Critique of Pure Reason*:

1. (Quality). "*Taste* is the faculty of judging of an object or a method of representing it by an *entirely disinterested* satisfaction or dissatisfaction. The object of such satisfaction is called *beautiful*."[20]

2. (Quantity). "The *beautiful* is that which pleases universally without requiring a concept."[21]

3. (Relation). "*Beauty* is the form of the purposiveness of an ob-ject, so far as this is perceived in it *without any representation of a purpose*."[22]

4. (Modality). "The *beautiful* is that which without any concept is cognized as the object of a *necessary* satisfaction."[23]

It must first be remarked that objects to which Kant is referring here are objects of nature, not art. (The discussion of a method of representation in conclusion number 1 above does not refer to a work of art as a representation but to the act of taste in representing an object to oneself.) Kant's point here is to describe the judgment of taste as not logical, as subjective, but at the same time separated from self-interest. In asking of the faculty of taste whether something is beautiful or not, *all* we are asking is whether or not the object is accompanied in us with satisfaction, and with a satisfaction which we declare would exist for anyone else. If self-interest is involved, the judgment becomes personal and is referred to some desire or end and can no longer be claimed to be universal. In other words, the viewer's subjective purpose has been introduced into the judgments: "Everyone must admit that a judgment about beauty, in which the least interest mingles, is very partial and is not a pure judgment of taste."[24] The oft-stated platitude that the work of art *must* be useless, as for example uttered by the character Vivian in Oscar Wilde's "The Decay of Lying," is a corruption in the direction of *reductio ad absurdum* of this position. In the first place, Kant is not talking here about works of art, though the idea does apply to them. In the second, he is not saying the object must be useless but only that in a judgment of taste the use of the object must not enter as part of the consideration, that a selection of sorts takes place; otherwise, self-interest and an external standard are introduced and the judgment as a pure judgment of taste is destroyed. Further, a judgment in which self-interest is a factor is always either purely conceptual, referable to categories of the understanding, or purely sensuous and referable directly to personal pleasure or pain and not universal. In neither case is it any longer a judgment of taste. There can therefore be no *concept* of beauty to which a judgment of taste is referred, because by definition judgments of taste proceed beyond concepts, which are of the understanding. As a result, judgments of taste must always be singular judgments. We can judge a particular rose to be beautiful, but to say roses are beautiful is to make a concept generalizing from a number of singular judgments of taste. In this case the understanding has been brought into play in the judgment, and the conclusion is not aesthetic.

Judgments of taste Kant nevertheless defines as universal. He distinguishes these sharply from cases in which an individual feels pleasure but is not prepared to claim everyone else would feel it. It would be better if Kant began by distinguishing clearly between these cases, but he first uses "pleasure" (*Lust*) and the "pleasant" (*Angenehm*) for both, proceeds to identify them with "gratification" (*Vergnügen*), a term connected with judgments not deemed universal, and adopts "satisfaction" (*Wohlgefallen*) in connection with judgments of taste. Coleridge, who took over Kant's argument in *The Principles of Ge-*

nial Criticism, distinguished in the same way between an apprehension of the beautiful and the merely agreeable. In any case, Kant regards the beautiful as a disinterested satisfaction, and, because it is disinterested, the viewer can claim universality for it, although it is still, of course, subjective.

We have already struggled with the question of purposiveness. In the third point above, Kant presents us with an apparent paradox. He has already stated that the judgment of the beautiful works from a sort of fictive principle of nature's purposiveness, and this idea, when we see our empirical concepts of the understanding conform to it (or when we make them conform to it), gives us pleasure. Now he says that in an aesthetic judgment of taste one connects the object judged to such a principle, but without judging it according to its use in proving or establishing nature's purposiveness *as a mechanical law*, which can never be *proved* anyway, since it is only a regulative principle. To try to prove it would be to refer the whole question to the understanding and to remove it from the domain of judgment. Further, though the aesthetic judgment acknowledges the purposiveness of the object as part of nature and in conformity to the regulative teleological principle, at the same time it cannot claim to be acting according to how well the object fulfills any external purpose, since that again would refer the whole matter to the understanding. Thus, paradoxically, though the object has purpose in the eyes of the aesthetic judgment in one sense, that purpose cannot be analyzed, and the object, viewed as aesthetic, cannot be said to have purpose in another sense.[25] Further still, but this I have already discussed, the use or purpose to which the viewer may happen to put or have put the object may not enter into a judgment of taste (though this does not prevent the object from being useful) since the viewer would no longer be disinterested and, of course, the judgment would then no longer be universal. So we are talking not about the object in all of its possible manifestations, but only the object as it comes under the reflective aesthetic judgment of taste.

The fourth point also presents a paradox in that Kant refers to an object of which there is no concept, which is nevertheless cognized. By this he means that no concept of the understanding is adequate to the object as beautiful. Thus the beauty of the object cannot be cognized by the understanding, though Kant then allows the term of "cognition" to be applied to the object in a quite different sense as the activity of the faculty of taste. These conclusions, Kant's theory of art, and his concept of the production of aesthetic ideas (the latter two still to be discussed) have far-reaching consequences for a theory of the literary symbolic.

It has already been remarked that when Kant uses the term "symbol," he treats symbols as standing for or representing something other than themselves by analogy. But there has also developed out of Kant, partly as a result of Kant's doctrine of the constitutive understanding and unknowable thing-in-itself, the un-Kantian idea of the symbol not as analogical hypotyposis but as constructing in itself and its relation to other symbols such reality as we can know. A symbol of this sort, strictly speaking, would have no referent as such but would instead be a bringing into verbal or plastic form of a previously undifferentiated manifold. For the present I merely wish to suggest that this would involve the Kantian conception of aesthetic judgment under the principle of the purposiveness of nature being shifted over from regulative to constitutive. Art would then be declared to make knowledge even though referable with respect to purposiveness to nothing beyond itself.

The Kantian object, considered as an object of the judgment of taste, and thus as having no concept adequate to it, leads by analogy to a view of the work of art as being in the ultimate sense uninterpretable, because to interpret it fully would be to bring it under a concept of the understanding, which act is self-contradictory. This has certain results in modern literary theory of the symbol. One is the well-known "heresy of paraphrase," enunciated by Cleanth Brooks, and another is the popular distinction between symbol and allegory, invented during the romantic period, the subject of the next chapter, in which true art is defined as symbolism, and allegory is defined as conceptual statement disguised as art. I am not claiming that Kant is responsible for the distinction, only that it could be deduced from one line of argument in *The Critique of Judgment*. The principle is the Kantian one that the beauty or the artistic nature of an object cannot be brought under a concept.

This idea forces a critic, who nevertheless wishes to discuss an object as a work of art, to acknowledge that as such it does not have meaning in the usual sense but that it does have being. From there the critic must go on to construct a mode of analysis of the object's artistic being in defiance of Kantian strictures. (I say "artistic being" here because there is good reason to think that the notion of a work of art in the sense derived from Kant as fully determinant of any object is too fixed and narrow, many objects being more than works of art and yet possessing art.) There are usually two procedures here. First, a method of describing the object's internal structure of relations is developed. This is a form of hermeneutic which attempts always to stay within the work considered as a context. Strict formalisms are of this type, but they prove sterile unless they begin to allegorize, though allegorizing too can produce sterility. Therefore, a second procedure is usually mixed with the first: The critic strenuously proceeds to conceptualize the work only to admit failure with every conceptualization, thereby indicating the work's inexhaustibility in the form of the paradoxes of his own allegorizing commentary. This inexhaustibility becomes a "proof" of beauty or art. But at this point Kant is left behind, for Kant declares that a judgment of the beautiful is not subject to demonstration. Also, the beautiful has been brought under a concept, which is self-contradictory. The concept of inexhaustibility is, of course, called in much modern criticism the concept of complexity, but it could just as well be called the concept of simplicity or invulnerability, since the complexity discovered is the complexity of the interpretation's relation to the object. In these remarks I have used the term "interpretation" not in the sense that has developed in phenomenological hermeneutics, but roughly in the sense of "analysis," as that term was used in the wake of the New Critics. Analysis in this case tries to have its Kantian cake and eat it too, in that the analysis is designed to demonstrate the impossibility of its own completion. For the interpreter to succeed is to fail, or vice versa. This establishes the work as "symbolical" rather than "allegorical," in one of the senses in which these terms have been popularly contrasted since the time of Goethe, but it also reintroduces allegorization as a critical rather than artistic activity. In turn, this critical activity begins to look at least artful, if not artistic, because its own complexity is expressed through tropes such as irony and paradox. As a result, though a difference between art and criticism is maintained, it is a difference which is perhaps encompassed by a similarity or a relation.

3. THE AESTHETICAL IDEA AND THE SUBLIME

EVERYTHING that we have observed thus far in Kant has to do with objects of nature, however, not necessarily objects of art. Kant says of art that we regard it as if it could only prove purposive as play, as an occupation that is pleasant in itself; yet he acknowledges that there is something not free but compulsory in it. This is the technical aspect of the artist's labor, the handling of the medium.[26] "Beautiful" art is a mode of representation, "purposive for itself and which, although devoid of definite purpose, yet furthers the culture of the mental powers in reference to social communication."[27] This comment is unfortunately not much developed, and the social role of art remains unprobed in Kant. Instead, concern with technical problems turns him away from his characteristic approach via the viewer to dwell, as the romantics who follow him tend to do, on the situation of the producer of art, who must possess for success both genius and taste. Genius is the "innate mental disposition (*ingenium*) *through which* nature gives the rule to art."[28] It is a talent for producing that for which, however, no definite rules as such can be given. Genius is opposed in this way to imitation (of predecessors), even though there are for Kant works of previous artists that are inspiriting. While Kant recognizes the element of technical training and of tradition, he cannot allow either very much leeway without seeming to establish concepts of the beautiful to which individual works would have to be referred. Thus nature's laws in this matter are again not really laws or at least cannot adequately be uttered. They are regulative ideas that the theorist uses to construct an idea of artistic creation. We can say then that Kant's remarks about the artistic activity are not empirical. They are efforts to round out a system. What Kant notes about genius is *fictively* located in the object, just as the beautiful is. Genius is

> the faculty of expressing *aesthetical ideas*. And by an aesthetical idea I understand that representation of the imagination which occasions much thought, without however any definite thought, i.e. any *concept*, being capable of being adequate to it; it consequently cannot be completely compassed and made intelligible by language.[29]

The aesthetical idea as fundamental to art severs the imitative, referential relationship of art to nature, since an aesthetical idea really cannot be a representation of a natural object, the aesthetical idea going beyond nature. This is not to say that aesthetical ideas do not employ representations of nature or use nature as material, but such representations are not present for the external *purpose* of imitation. Clearly "purpose" here is not definable as what the maker of the object may or may not have intended, since that is an empirical question. This is purpose seen under the judgment of taste and is always internal and reflectively posited. Free of imitation in this sense, aesthetical ideas rise above and free of nature. But not really free of the reason.

Kant has connected "aesthetical ideas" with symbolical hypotyposes, to be introduced in Section 59, by indicating that they "re-mold experience, always indeed in accordance with analogical laws."[30] With some reluctance, perhaps, he allows them the status of *ideas*:

> Such representations of the imagination we may call *ideas*, partly because they at least strive after something which lies beyond the bounds of experience and so seek to approximate to a presentation of concepts of reason (intellectual ideas), thus giving to the latter the appearance of objective reality, but especially because no concept can be fully adequate to them as internal intuitions. The poet ventures to realize to sense, rational ideas of invisible beings, the kingdom of the blessed, hell, eternity, creation, etc.; or even if he deals with things of which there are examples in experience—e.g. death, envy, and all vices, also love, fame, and the like—he tries, by means of imagination, which emulates the play of reason in its quest after a maximum, to go beyond the limits of experience and to present them to sense with a completeness of which there is no example in nature.[31]

There is a problem with the word "concept" at this point, since Kant employs the term above with respect to both the understanding and the reason. In his discussion of poetry, the word refers to the reason.

> Of all the arts poetry (which owes its origin almost entirely to genius and will least be guided by precept or example) maintains the first rank. It expands the mind by setting the imagination at liberty and by offering, within the limits of a given concept, amid the unbounded variety of possible forms accordant therewith, that which unites the presentment of this concept with a wealth of thought to which no verbal expression is completely adequate, and so rising aesthetically to ideas.[32]

"Concept" elsewhere refers to the understanding. Further, there are determinable concepts and undeterminable ones. The concepts of poetry are of the latter type.

> [Poetry] strengthens the mind by making it feel its faculty—free, spontaneous, and independent of natural determina-

tion—of considering and judging nature as a phenomenon in accordance with aspects which it does not present in experience either for sense or understanding . . .[33]

So, though the "aesthetical idea" is beyond understanding, it is not beyond reason. It is

> a sort of schema for, the supersensible. It plays with illusion, which it produces at pleasure, but without deceiving by it; for it declares its exercise to be mere play, which, however, can be purposively used by the understanding.[34]

"A sort of schema" is really Kant's "symbol," not a schema as defined in Section 59, with which we began this chapter, but to which Kant has not yet come. Such symbolical hypotyposes would be "epistemologically unreliable," as Paul de Man has remarked, since they would give to ideas of the reason only the "appearance of objective reality."[35] We already know that ideas of the reason have no intuitions or representations of the imagination adequate to them. We are now told that no concept is adequate to an aesthetical idea as an internal intuition. But "concept" here means a concept of the understanding.

However, past this, Kant seems to make further, conflicting claims for the aesthetic idea. It presents attributes of an object (not a natural object) that its rational idea cannot present. This seems almost to mean that the aesthetical idea is ungraspable by the reason. It takes the place of the logical presentation of an object with the result that the mind is enlivened by the prospect of an "illimitable field of kindred representations," which allows it to think more than could be comprehended in a concept and therefore in a "definite form of words." But this goes on in an "undeveloped way."[36] It is almost as if Kant saw in the aesthetical idea something beyond or apart from reason. But there is finally overwhelming evidence that he does not or that his system cannot.

At this point it is important to consider that the discussion of aesthetical ideas follows on Kant's treatment of the sublime. Kant's analysis of the sublime parallels that of the beautiful in that he treats it according to quantity as universally valid, according to quality as devoid of interest, according to relation as subjectively purposive, and according to modality as necessary.[37] The notion of the sublime is, however, contrasted at every step with the beautiful. Both are indefinite in comparison to the definiteness of the understanding and the reason, but the beautiful parallels as an indefinite form the concepts of the understanding and the sublime the ideas of the reason. The beautiful is identified with rest, the sublime with movement. The beautiful is identified with positive pleasure, the sublime with negative.

The notion of negative pleasure is arrived at as follows: Natural objects are not in themselves sublime. Rather, sublimity inhabits the mind, for the notion of sublimity surpasses all sense, and with the sublime feeling comes a curious mixture of pain with pleasure. The pain arises from "the want of accordance between the aesthetical estimation of magnitude formed by the imagination and the estimation of the same formed by the reason."[38] The imagination founders, so to speak. The pleasure comes from the same want of accordance, because it involves our realization in the sublime experience of the mind's transcendence of nature in the reason:

> in the immensity of nature and in the insufficiency of our faculties to take in a standard proportionate to the aesthetical estimation of the magnitude of its *realm*, we find our own limitation, although at the same time in our rational faculty we find a different, nonsensuous standard, which has that infinity itself under it as a unity, in comparison with which everything in nature is small, and thus in our mind we find a superiority to nature even in its immensity.[39]

It is therefore the mind that is sublime, not the objects of nature: "The sublime is that, the mere ability to think which shows a faculty of the mind, surpassing every standard of sense."[40] Instead, the sublime's disinterest lies in that it pleases in opposition to the interest of sense.[41]

Clearly the aesthetical idea arises out of the connection between the sublime and the reason, of which the sublime is an indefinite form. The aesthetic idea may have qualities of indefiniteness that "gives life to [the poets'] concepts,"[42] but it is inconceivable that Kant would have allowed an aesthetic breakthrough to the noumenal world any more than he would countenance the notion of an intellectual intuition. That would have meant the embodiment of noumena in images of sense, as implied by the notion of the "miraculous" romantic symbol. There lurks in Kant the possibility of a constitutive aesthetic form, but it is continually suppressed and is perhaps more potential in the notion of the beautiful than in the "aesthetical idea" as that was generated out of the idea of the sublime. Aesthetical ideas are finally only illustrations to sense of ideas of the reason; and, though they have something in sense that is their own, they remain always symbolical hypotyposes or allegorical images subject to rational completion, even though Kant on occasion seems to be granting them more than this.[43]

Still, after all this, Kant's notions of indefinite concept, aesthetical idea, and the beautiful tantalize with the possibility of a constitutive "secular" symbolic form. Kant's language never quite seems to hem in these notions, which maintain their "unbounded variety" and "wealth of thought." The dominance of the reason over these subversively indefinite forms is maintained under great stress. The aesthetical idea is resistant. Kant's poet is important because he does not bring his play under the categories of the understanding, but presents it as material like nature that inspires and quickens thought. But in Kant, after all, thought always surpasses this play and must leave the poet's play a husk, exhausted by a devouring reason. What I am trying to reach here is a distinction between Kant's aesthetical idea, which is exhausted by reason (though not by the understanding) and a "secular" symbolic form that is "prolific," not exhaustible by the reason but not "miraculous" either.[44]

Kant's aesthetical idea is torn between earth and spirit. He observes that for the imagination the transcendent is like an abyss in which it fears to lose itself.[45] Art may be interpreted as a longing to go beyond which fails, that is, a form of romantic "religious" or "Platonic" allegory, which constantly tells the same story. Art is here subsumed under religion or philosophy. The alternative is to recognize in art—even in the so-called sublime—a deliberate pulling back (sometimes in spite of the author) from the abyss. The "fear," as Kant calls it, is really a desire to create a human culture in this world. Involved here is the attempt to build a "contrary" to the notions of division implied in religion and science—body/soul, subject/object, with their consequent asceticism and abstraction. Even allegory (as it is actually practiced in art) is, as Angus Fletcher has amply shown, a sensuous form.[46] It can certainly be regarded as a "contrary" effort to pull the reason back to sense, a balance against an excess of noumenal desire that leads man to the disillusioned negation of his culture.[47]

At this point, we leave Kant, but take along a remembrance of the struggle his reason has with the idea of a poem. At the end of the "Dialectic of Aesthetical Judgment," Section 59, as I have pointed out, Kant for the first time in *The Critique of Judgment* uses the term "symbol," and declares that beauty is the symbol of morality. This analogical relationship (for that is all the term signifies in Kant), he explains, accounts for the fact that the beautiful gives "pleasure [satisfaction] with a claim for the agreement of everyone else."[48] He then offers four points of analogy and goes on to remark that we habitually make a symbolic relation between beauty and morality in the common terms we employ to describe beautiful objects. But for Kant beauty is not the *good*, it is beneath it or on the way to it, or supplementary (in its indefiniteness) to it. This analogical relationship, like that of the relation of aesthetical ideas to ideas of the reason, suggests to us what romantic theory classifies as an allegorical relationship. Kant reminds us in *The Critique of Judgment* that "beauty and sublimity are aesthetical modes of representation which would not be found in us at all if we were pure intelligences." This appears to be, for Kant, a matter for regret.[49] Kant is more fundamentally a moralist than an aesthetician. He does not build his ethic on a base of aesthetics, but fits his aesthetics into a gap—a very large gap, which it fills— in his philosophy. Nevertheless, his establishment of the analogy of beautiful and good has much to do with a tendency of later theorists to base ethics on aesthetics (Schiller's theory of play, for example), in which an embryonic form of the "secular" begins to take shape and in which disinterest becomes an ethically higher form of purpose.[50] Kant's critiques served as grounds upon which later theorists constituted their own positions, sometimes deviating radically from his spirit, as in the tendency of some romantics to seek transcendence to a quite un-Kantian form of the supersensible in the symbol and thus turning the possibility of a "secular" symbol back into a "miraculous" form or even into a form of "religious" allegory.

3

Romantic Distinctions between Symbol and Allegory

The practice of distinguishing between symbol and allegory that began late in the eighteenth century and continues to this day is a historically crucial source of confusion.[1] Certain influential versions of the distinction and their grounds illustrate problems that frequently arise in thinking about the symbolic. The cases differ. Goethe, whom I shall consider first, seems to present a distinction seeking a ground. One observes Goethe struggling for a language that will explain his sense of what poetic activity is. Schelling, on the other hand, seems to generate his version from an epistemological ground and thus to come *to* his idea of the artist as the supreme maker of knowledge. Coleridge works eclectically both ways. What is a rudimentary "secular" notion in Goethe tends toward the "miraculous" as we pass through Schelling to Coleridge, who wrote in 1800: "I would endeavor to destroy the old antithesis of *Words* and *Things* elevating, as it were words to Things, and living things too."[2] Through most romantic distinctions runs the notion of the symbol as having its own being, which embodies something of its referent, unified with its tendency toward transparency; while allegory is merely arbitrary, and in this sense disposable—in other words, "substitutive." In the idea of transparency, the terminology employed to describe the symbol carries over something of the preceding terminology of imitation and traditional rhetoric, and therefore their epistemologies, as well as the miraculism of ritual. The symbol's partial transparency calls in question the purity and value of its being or purely internal referentiality and introduces the notion of a Fall, from which the symbol's "miraculism" can be only a partial recovery. What was needed was not merely to make words into things considered as alien objects (were one to maintain a subject/object distinction), but to replace in some way the concept of the sheer material thing with the culturally creative word. After treating the distinctions made by Goethe, Schelling, and Coleridge as significant moments on a quest toward a concept of a "secular" symbolic, I turn to Carlyle's *Sartor Resartus* considered as a quest for a concept of fictions, a necessary step toward establishing the idea of a *cultural* reality that symbols generate rather than merely transparently stand for. The poet's role in this ought to be important, as Shelley tried to argue when he claimed that the poet was the constant remaker of language and that every language was originally "in itself the chaos of a cyclic poem."[3] The chapter concludes with a brief attempt to clarify Hegel's special use of the term "symbol" in his *Philosophy of Fine Art* and to characterize a special form of romantic allegory—the "Hegelian."

I. GOETHE'S SYMBOLIC

IN RENÉ Wellek's *History of Modern Criticism*, we are told that it is "to Goethe that we apparently owe the distinction between allegory and symbol, which was then elaborated by Schelling and August Wilhelm Schlegel and from there taken over by Coleridge."[4] Goethe formulates the distinction several times over a long career. The uses of the terms that Goethe received from his age give no compelling reason to distinguish the two.[5] "Symbol" tends to mean "allegory" in the common usage of that term. Goethe seems to have been impelled to make his distinction as a result of discussions with Heinrich Meyer, who in an essay of 1798 takes a rather traditional view of these terms.[6] I am interested in Goethe's essay, "Über die Gegenstände der bildenden Künst" ("On the Subjects of the Plastic Arts") because it reveals Goethe trying to make an accepted terminology say something new.

In this essay (a translation of which appears as an appendix to this book),[7] Goethe at first tries to distinguish two principal kinds of artistic "subjects."[8] The first are natural and realistic, representing "well known common things as they are, although raised to the level of an artistic unity" by what he calls "mechanical treatment."[9] In contrast, the second are what he calls "idealistic" subjects that are not merely the thing "as it appears in nature."[10] Rather, in this second kind, the thing meets the treatment of the artist as an "already completely formed subject."[11] Goethe remarks, "Nature produces the former, the human spirit in most intimate association with nature the latter."[12] The artist raises the former through "mechanical treatment" to a certain level of merit, whereas the "mechanical treatment" is really not the critical issue with respect to the latter.[13] Indeed, Goethe seems to be saying that the latter sort of subject makes "mechanical treatment" unnecessary or superfluously decorative or so completely and naturally in harmony with the subject that there is no sense of such treatment having occurred.

At first, then, it appears that Goethe considers certain subjects in themselves to possess particular authority, and these subjects tend to unify themselves with the poet's spirit and shine forth absorbing intuition and expression (to use Croce's terms) in a single act which is loosely identified with "spirit" and made antithetical to the "mechanical." "Mechanical treatment" is apparently a sort of passivity, while spirit is an active principle. Idealistic art, he says, involves capturing the thing on a level where it is divested of all common and individual traits and becomes universal. Though here Goethe does not specifically state (as he does elsewhere) that the artist begins with the particular, we may assume it, the spirit of the artist being for Goethe the faculty that merges particular and universal. Goethe comes finally in his essay to warn against the very worst kind of art—worse by far than the realistic. In this third type of art the attempt is to "embody the highest abstractions in sensible representations," in other words, allegory.

It appears that the idealistic work of art represents not nature (as in the first, realistic kind Goethe mentions) but the artist's mental act, which he seems, oddly enough, to have described as a process of generalization from sense data toward abstractions. But this must surely be the result of Goethe's struggle with an intransigent critical vocabulary; it is surely not what Goethe intended us to understand; that would be an "empirical" form of allegory, and he warns us against allegory. But it does illustrate the difficulty that he has in emancipating himself from deeply ingrained "allegorical" assumptions. He struggles out of this problem as the essay proceeds: In making idealistic art, the artist produces a representation of a mental act, which, because it is an act of spirit "in the most intimate association with nature," produces something that is "idealistic," but *not* general. It remains particular and sensuous.

Such remarks lead us on to Schelling. It is also possible to see past Goethe's statement to a distinction later enunciated by Coleridge between fancy and imagination; works of fancy are equivalent to the allegorical, works of imagination to idealistic art. Coleridge's distinction brings over into the theory of art a contrast between two theories of mind, the first of which is based on both the Lockean concept of the mind as a passive receptor of sense data and the Hartleyan concept of the association of ideas, the mind arriving at knowledge by combining and recombining the units of perception into various structures. The second attributes creativity to a mind that, acting upon nature, brings its own formative or transformative powers to bear upon intuition. To find these concepts opposed is to distinguish between a mind that is fundamentally a *tabula rasa* and one that is constitutive, but whose constitutive powers are not limited to those of the Kantian understanding.

At the same time, to have made such a distinction is to have said nothing about artistic *productions* as such. Coleridge tried to apply his distinction to works of art—to discover in texts themselves evidence of fancy and imagination—with limited success (but still with greater success than almost anyone else has had) because of an insufficient establishment of the connection between the acts of the mental powers he names and the labor of expressing and externalizing (to use Croce's terms) those acts. The same problem exists here for Goethe.

Since Goethe does not inherit an adequate critical vocabulary and seems so contemptuous of "mechanical treatment," one is not surprised that he declares certain subjects to be in themselves more artistic than others. The artistic element, after all, has to be either in the subject or the treatment. Still, when he does this he tempers his remark by involving the human spirit in the making of the artistic product in some vague way after all. He has put the subjects of highest art *out there* in nature ready to cooperate with nature, but he is not satisfied with this because the artist is not doing enough. After denigrating "mechanical treatment," he now has to create some other activity for the artist and another name for the artist's role, or abandon the idea of the artist's creativity.

The next step in Goethe's essay is to recapture the subject from externality and to regard it as really coming into existence in the individual mental act of the artist. Each subject under these conditions must be unique, particular, and individual. Goethe comes around to saying that the work of highest art is "self-explanatory at first sight as a whole as well as in its parts."[14] Nothing else can possibly explain it, since it refers to an act of which it is, itself, the only evidence. To arrive at this concept takes some doing: "treatment" is released from the adjective "mechanical"; the term "symbol" is introduced.

> Although in all works of art the subject can never be considered by itself [as it appears Goethe has attempted to do], except as it is treated, it must be said of the three kinds so far described that they have been considered chiefly with reference to the object. In the following we shall consider more the treatment and the spirit of the treater; and thus then are subjects determined: through deep feeling, which if it is pure and natural will coincide with the best and highest subjects and possibly make them into symbols. Subjects represented in this way only seem to stand naked by themselves but are freshly and deeply significant on account of the ideal, which always carries universality with it.[15]

This does not explain to us how "deep feeling" will necessarily coincide with the "best and highest subjects" unless the artist *makes* the subjects himself instead of drawing them as objects from nature. It begs the question or is tautological. It introduces the term "ideal" without accompanying clarity. Nevertheless, Goethe does fairly clearly warn against certain disasters that can befall the ambitious who seek after the "best and highest subjects." There is, for example, the sort of deep feeling that is corrupted by fanaticism. There is also hollow sentimentality. But these dangers are pale in comparison to those posed by the allegorical. Though allegory can contain many attractions, such works

> destroy the interest in the representation itself and drive the spirit back into itself, so to speak, and remove from its eyes what is actually represented. The allegorical distinguishes itself from the symbolic in that the former signifies directly, the latter indirectly.[16]

This passage and the conclusion of the essay do not banish allegory entirely from the realm of art, but they certainly indicate that it is its lowest form.

The semantic slough—not quite yet a terminal moraine—through which I have been trying to navigate is created by Goethe's concern as a poet over the bifurcation of subject and object and his struggle with a language that seems to insist on the bifurcation at every turn. Thus the uncertainty in the language of Goethe's essay as to the location, so to speak, of the artist's "subject"; and thus, too, the inadequate reflection upon what happens in the conversion of an object of nature into a subject, if indeed there is an object and that is what does happen. Goethe referred once to this tendency in himself as "stiff-necked realism."[17] This sort of struggle with the subject/object distinction, however difficult its expression, illustrates an effort to assert a radical artistic creativity that goes on for well over a century in literary thought. Goethe's is one of the earliest attacks on all so-called generality and abstraction in art, commonplace in the tradition with which we are concerned.

Nevertheless, Goethe was one of the few poets of his or any later age to insist that there was no conflict between the two roles of poet and scientist, that they could blend rather than foment the furious opposition his own attack on abstract thought sets in motion. Cassirer says of Goethe,

> Wherever he could no longer look and see, he could no longer comprehend and understand. It was this which always kept him away from mathematics—especially the modern form of analysis discovered by Leibniz and Newton.[18]

It was this too that finally limited his achievement in science. His desire is to maintain the sense of concrete experience at all costs. Thus, first, his emphasis on process, which is not limited to or derived from a theory of purely literary creation but is developed in his scientific studies—for example, his genetic view of plant development as against the previous generic method of classification in Linnaeus. Thus, second, his suspicion of anything smacking of Platonic idealism, as in the conversation he reports with Schiller:

> I vigorously expounded the metamorphosis of plants, and with many suggestive strokes of the pen let a symbolic plant arise before his eyes. He listened to and looked at everything with great interest, with decided power of comprehension; but when I ended he shook his head and said: "That is not empirical, that is ideal" ["*Das ist keine Erfahrung, das ist eine*

Idee"]. I was taken aback and somewhat vexed; for he had emphatically stated the point that divided us. . . . But I collected myself and replied: "I am very glad that I have ideals without knowing it and even see them with my eyes."

Schiller had been using the term "ideal" in the Kantian, not the Platonic sense.[19]

Even so, Goethe's remarks on the subject of abstract ideas, whether Platonic or general (i.e., "empirical"), are virtually made from the point of view of the practicing poet and might even be construed to imply wholesale criticism of German philosophy. In the following passage from the conversations with Eckermann, the question of poetry seems to be superseded by a question of ethics, with the theory of art as the basis for an ethic:

> The Germans are, certainly, strange people. By their deep thoughts and ideas, which they seek in everything, and fix upon everything, they make life much more burdensome than is necessary. Only have the courage to give yourself up to your impressions: allow yourself to be delighted, moved, elevated; nay, instructed and inspired for something great: but do not imagine all is vanity if it is not abstract thought and idea.[20]

He is careful to say of *Faust* that it was not conceived as an abstract idea. That would have been to write allegory:

> It was in short not in my line, as a poet, to strive to embody anything *abstract*. I received in my mind impressions, and those of a sensuous, animated, charming, varied, hundredfold kind—just as a lively imagination presented them; and I had, as a poet, nothing more to do than to round off and elaborate artistically such views and impressions, and by means of a lively representation so to bring them forward that others might receive the same impression in hearing or reading any representation of them.[21]

In his desire to eliminate any hint of the abstract and allegorical Goethe seems in the two passages above to have classified his own *Faust* as a product of the first type of art that he mentioned in the 1797 essay, where the artist is passive in relation to his subject. It seems in this particular instance that Goethe has to retreat to a passive concept of the artist if he is to eliminate abstraction from the artist's thought. I mention this here not as characteristic of Goethe but as representative of a problem that we have already seen in his essay and that keeps coming up in critical theory. I shall return to it.

Meanwhile it is important to know that Goethe himself admits to having presented abstract ideas in shorter poems and even in *Wahlverwandtschaften*, which he calls an exception among his longer works. He will not, he says, claim to have made it better by having made it available to the understanding. He goes as far as to say, "I am rather of the opinion, that the more incommensurable, and the more incomprehensible to the understanding, a poetic production is, so much the better it is."[22] Still Goethe remarks of *Faust*, as if he is tantalized by the idea of accomplishing a complex work that expresses a single coherent abstract idea, "It would have been a fine thing indeed if I had strung so rich, varied, and highly diversified a life as I have brought to view in *Faust* upon the slender string of one pervading idea."[23]

Certainly Goethe did not intend to classify *Faust* among either naturalistic or allegoric works. He seems in his remark (with its reference to reception of his impressions and his assertion that all he did was to round off and elaborate) to be describing the first type of work and to be advocating a sort of wisely unconscious, passive receptivity. But this is probably accounted for by his obvious desire in the passage to avoid use of images of activity that the listener might associate with the making of the work into an abstract idea. If this is the case, Goethe is on the horns of a dilemma by no means unique to him, for it keeps reappearing in various forms throughout the nineteenth century. If in order to preserve the particularity of experience he characterizes the artist's actions as passive reception, he is in danger of giving such acts no creative power. If he emphasizes the artist's activity as constitutive he begins to make the artist's activity sound like that of a Kantian understanding, which produces abstract ideas, thereby losing the particularity of art and creating something like romantic allegory. Goethe lacks here an adequate terminology for a creative act that does not move toward higher and higher levels of generality. As a result he retreats to hint at the old Platonic concept of the artist as a vessel of receptivity. Yet even this gives him trouble, because he draws a line between the artist's receptivity, which seems passive, and the merely technical rounding off that the artist does, leaving no place between for the creative spirit.

In the 1797 essay, then, Goethe toils to make a statement that

evades characterizing the higher kind of art as involving passive reception of sense data; but he wants also to hold on to the idea of
nature and the artist working together actively to effect what appears
to be an imitation, though not a passive one to be judged by canons
of accuracy. The language which is frustrating him and which he
needs to overthrow is the traditional language of imitation and the
epistemology of subject and object.

In the conversations with Eckermann many years later, Goethe
evades any hint that nature as the objective is being imitated and
turns to the image of the artist as a vessel of inspiration. But here
again—perhaps especially here—the act is made to seem more passive than was his intent, because again all of the artist's conscious
activity is classified with the rounding off and elaboration, and a split
between intuition and mechanical treatment is acknowledged. He attempts to rescue himself from this by referring to the mind as having
received impressions "just as a lively imagination presented them."[24]
But this imagination is difficult to locate. Is it his own, or is it divine,
or is it nature working through him? In his retreat from the allegorizing understanding Goethe struggles to evade attribution of the poem
to Plato's divine, passive madness.

I want now to place before us Goethe's best-known and later remark distinguishing allegory from symbolism. It is well first to remember Goethe's apparently tautological assertion in the conversations with Eckermann that all poems must be occasioned by a poet.
Reality provides material, but a "particular event becomes universal
and poetic by the very circumstance that it is treated by a poet."[25] As
in many writers of the nineteenth century, poetic mental activity is
regarded as going on here without necessarily resulting in poems, because the term "poet" is defined by mental acts, not production of
poems, or at least, if we are again to use Croce's language, not the
externalization of them. Here Goethe emphasizes the active nature of
the poet in contrast to his emphasis on receptivity in his remark on
Faust. However, we must remember that in the 1797 essay Goethe
identifies poetic "treatment" with a somewhat passive mechanical
technique.

The well-known statement in the *Maximen* of 1822 follows:

There is a great difference whether the poet seeks the particular for the universal [*Allgemeine*] or sees the universal in the
particular. Out of the first method arises allegory, where the
particular serves only as an example of the universal; the latter

procedure, however, is really the nature of poetry: it speaks
forth a particular, without thinking of the universal or pointing to it.[26]

Goethe still does not say that an allegory is never a poem, for he is
not really talking about poems as discrete existences but about a
power of the poet that defines his mental acts. Also, to equate the
poem as a whole with the poetic or with poetry is not characteristic
of the thought of the time. Just as "poet" does not seem to be defined
exclusively as someone who produces poems, so a poem is not necessarily entirely poetic, as Coleridge remarked; for poetry is regarded
as a sort of quality or condition of the imagination that poems in
various measures possess. The symbol has become more than a trope
but less than the poem as a whole. For Goethe, symbolism does not
define a poem in its entirety, but it is the quality that a poem must
possess in some degree.

Further, Goethe does not here treat the question of the poem as a
produced object. He is talking about the poetic process, and he does
not provide in his distinction any advice to critics as to how to distinguish symbolism from allegory when faced only with a text. But
Goethe would probably have little patience with such criticisms as
this one, since for him a true poem expresses the author's spirit, reveals its own process, and only an insensitive reader would not be
able to intuit the presence of the symbolic. Still, the distinction
Goethe makes refers only to the process of the author's thought, and
the relation of the finished work to the process remains theoretically
problematical.

There has been a difficulty in reading Goethe's statement distinguishing symbolism from allegory. In his translation of the passage,
René Wellek renders "*Allgemeine*" as "general," not "universal," and
thereby introduces a much more strictly neoclassical bias into Goethe
than the passage seems to warrant.[27] "General" implies to the English
reader that Goethe is thinking strictly about generalizations from
sense data. We naturally, then, associate the remark with those of
critics like Samuel Johnson and Joshua Reynolds, both of whom are
influenced by the empirical language of the Lockean tradition. "Universal" seems to me the better translation; it should not, however, be
taken to refer to Platonic ideas or to an ultimate archetype, but instead to something more like the immanent spirit of nature: "True
symbolism is where the particular represents the more universal, not
as a dream and shadow, but as a living momentary revelation of the

inscrutable."[28] Goethe does not regard the inscrutable as the unapproachable that lies beyond appearances of phenomena—the "Platonic" or the "religious." Instead he regards it as approachable by the process of art that he advocates, which process he equates with the symbolic. The "inscrutable" is only that which is unapproachable by the understanding in its Kantian sense. "Scrutability" is a word referring to the powers of the understanding.

Angelo Bertocci has quite correctly distinguished Goethe's view from the Neoplatonic:

> For him, too, as for Plotinus, art is the mediator of the inexpressible. But he rejected in Plotinus what left him cold in Plato, that eventual separation of the world of the Idea from the world of sense. For man there cannot be any knowledge, even on the highest level, severed from sense.[29]

As Karl Viëtor has remarked, the phenomenon in Goethe is not less than "the idea of which it is the realization."[30] An idea for Goethe can only be grasped "in the midst of a Becoming,"[31] and does not exist apart from becoming. There is for Goethe no theoretical absolute, "no special essence or spiritual principle apart from the phenomenon and capable of being abstracted from it."[32] Goethe's "idea" is not an indefinite product of the reason. It appears to be "secular." Cassirer has pointed out, "Goethe recognized no sharp boundary between intuition and theory; for such a boundary would have contradicted his own experience as scientific investigator."[33] Thus his poetic attitudes remain on this point one with his views as a scientist. Unfortunately, Goethe had no term to distinguish his sense of immanent universality from abstract generalization. He lacked Vico's notion of the "imaginative universal."

The difference from Plotinus has very important consequences for a theory of the symbolic, throwing emphasis on the temporal, the phenomenal, and the mental acts of the poet themselves—the living human process—and relegating much of what had been previously thought of as symbolism to the romantic allegoric, whether of the "empirical" or the "Platonic" type. In *Maximen* 1112 and 1113, Goethe elaborates his distinction:

> Allegory changes a phenomenon into a concept, a concept into an image, but in such a way that the concept is still limited and completely kept and held in the image and expressed by it.

The symbolic changes the phenomenon into the idea, the idea into the image, in such a way that the idea remains always infinitely active and unapproachable in the image, and will remain inexpressible even though expressed in all languages.[34]

The poet who proceeds by allegory, we now note, does not begin with a concept at all, but is moved at the outset by phenomena. Then, perhaps as a result of the German habit to which Goethe refers in his conversations, the artist is compelled to conceptualize, to abstract from experience immediately toward a concept, and to locate truth in the concept. Allegory does not seem here to be the "Platonic" type but rather "empirical" generalization. Goethe's objection to this is finally ethical, since the precious individuality of things is drained out in the process.

Goethe does not wish, any more than T. E. Hulme, the self-styled modernist adversary of romanticism, to fly off into the "circumambient gas."[35] His "idea" is not "Platonic," "religious," or "empirical." Nevertheless, there slips back into Goethe's treatment of it as symbolic some of the elusiveness that he is so intent on expunging from art. What he needs is a clear statement that the symbolic "idea" is "unapproachable" by rational processes, not "unapproachable in the image," but *created* in the image and fully there. For this, the term "idea" carries a burden of otherness which tends to imply the "miraculous" after all.

Something of what Goethe was striving for seems to have been accomplished by someone often regarded only as a disciple of his. Karl Philipp Moritz distinguishes mythological poetry from hieroglyphics and from allegory in exactly the same way that Goethe separates symbolism from allegory. Jupiter, for example, signifies himself and all that the imagination has ever included in him (as in Vico's "imaginative universal," a term which, however, Moritz does not use). This total inclusiveness obviates the need for the symbol to look outside itself.[36] The poem as a whole is a symbol having the same characteristic of self-containment. Meaning lies within the poem even though it mirrors life. And the gods are not signs of abstract powers but the powers themselves: "because the imagination flees all generalizing concepts, and seeks to make its creations as individual as possible, it transfers the concept of a higher prevailing power to beings which it now represents as actual. . . ."[37] These passages go beyond Vico in their linking art with myth and their consideration of mythological poetry as a primal source, rather than a signifier. But there is a problem in Moritz's attempt to blend poetic art and religious consciousness. In him the religious impulse does not result in "religious" allegorization but in a problem of belief and a confusion about the precise location of creative power. His introduction of the idea of play ("Its [the imagination's] nature is to form and shape; to this end it creates for itself a broad realm of play") might suggest an idea of purely random behavior. Indeed, as we have seen, Goethe, in his zeal to emancipate the poet from allegorizing, does occasionally give the impression of the poet as a "free" consciousness who simply responds to stimuli. But such a consciousness would not be free. It would be determined by external power. Moritz does not think of play in this sense; instead he imagines it as developing its own rules— play become game. The game is a game of radical creation. The "rules" of such play can be expressed only in the act itself. At least they can be expressed *positively* only in the act. The difficulty is that Moritz's pagan religious zeal wins out over his aesthetic, and art becomes the ultimate form of this religiosity. The "miraculous" concept takes over at a crucial point where art becomes the vehicle of religious understanding.

2. SCHELLING—ART AND NATURE

BEFORE proceeding to Schelling's version of the distinction between symbol and allegory, I want to take note of his famous oration *Über das Verhältnis der bildenden Künste zu der Natur"* ["On the Relation of the Plastic Arts to Nature"] (1807), principally because it connects the epistemology of the Schelling of this period to the distinction between symbol and allegory. Schelling's views changed over the years, and I am not concerned with tracing nor competent to trace that growth, which has been done in any case quite fully elsewhere.[38]

Schelling begins by attributing to the ancients and endorsing the idea that art stands as a "uniting link between the soul and nature."[39] At the same time he attacks all commonly held ideas of imitation, denying that they provide a satisfactory explanation of the linkage of nature and soul. His argument is that most critics who hold to a theory of imitation also treat nature as if it were a dead object or a congeries of the Lockean primary qualities of perception. It is almost as if Schelling would accept the idea of imitation, were it not corrupted by what he regards as false definitions of the so-called object of imitation, nature, so that it is rendered unreal at the outset. His own conception of the relation of art to nature is based on an epistemology in which art plays the supreme role. With Schelling the so-called Absolute or Idea lies in the intercourse of subject and object, man and nature, though man is really part of nature. Nature without man is unconscious, mere potentiality, but is also the means of bringing about consciousness in man, for without nature there would be nothing to be conscious of. By the same token, without man nature could not rise to consciousness of itself. Schelling does not view this situation from man's point of view only, as does Fichte, who sees nature generated as object by the subject. Rather, man is part of nature and is that necessary subject through which nature as object knows itself.

A succinct summary of Schelling's position is attempted by Copleston. It is misleading in an interesting way, and a moment's attention to it may be instructive. He pictures "the Absolute as eternal essence or Idea objectifying itself in Nature, returning to itself as subjectivity in the world of representation and then knowing itself, in and through philosophical reflection, as the identity of the real and the ideal, of Nature and Spirit."[40] There are two problems here, if we apply Copleston's summary to the Schelling of 1807. First, the statement implies that the absolute in Schelling is somehow Platonically previous to nature, where it would be better to state that the absolute is generated as idea in the act that makes nature conscious. This is a fundamental difference between Schelling and Plotinus, for Schelling emphasizes always, though not with consistent language, the living *process* as the source of reality. The tendency to connect Schelling too resolutely to his Neoplatonic forebears needs to be resisted. Still, I must admit that there are occasions on which Schelling is not clear enough for me to claim that Copleston's Plotinian Schelling does not lurk somewhere in spectral form.

Second, in his summary Copleston does not give to the artistic act the status that Schelling does, or at least did in 1807. It is in such acts, for Schelling, that nature comes supremely to know itself, even to a greater extent than through "philosophical reflection," for art actually *performs* the unification of subject and object, of particular and universal. As early as *The System of Transcendental Idealism*, Schelling, playing with the notion of genius offered by Kant, asserted, ". . . it is art alone which can succeed in objectifying with universal validity what the philosopher is able to present in a merely subjective fashion."[41] Also, it might be added to Copleston's remark that for Schelling the term "nature" plays two roles. One is nature strictly as mute object apart from and other than man—not the real, completed, conscious nature. This is the initially posited nature that Schelling passes through to get to the real one, which is nature as genera-

tor *with or by means of man* of the absolute, in which the initial
notion of the otherness of nature is transcended. The former and inadequate nature we tend to think of abstractly and spatially; indeed,
at a stage in the process we must posit it as object. The latter nature
we then come to think of dynamically as the mental act of unification
itself—the idea—in which the former is seen to be partial if not false,
or at least rudimentary—a lesser form of reality, or only a potential
form. As one reads Schelling it becomes clear that he frequently en-
gages in struggles with an initially inadequate terminology of this
sort, and that his writings are themselves *processes* in the creation of
a philosophical language rather than *analyses* of objectively posited
things. Indeed, the process is designed to move beyond the positing
of objects as objects. It is a kind of *bildung*. Insofar as language tries
to keep to a spatial, static world, or to construct an abstract world of
primary qualities of experience, Schelling struggles to overcome language. This turns him ever toward the arts and myth, where struggles
with a fixed language become triumphs *in* a dynamic one. It also accounts in part for Schelling's emphasis on the importance of language, without which there would be no consciousness. In any case,
Schelling frequently establishes terms in his discourse and then transcends them. For example, he talks about imitation and then introduces in the process of philosophizing a higher form called "genial
imitation," and he proceeds from the "actual" to the "genuinely actual." This process is consistent with his view of the philosopher's
role, which is to engage in the process of creation that his philosophy
comes to declare is reality. Schelling philosophizes from the point of
view of poetry as if poetry were the beginning and end of philosophy.
Indeed, so he stated in 1800:

> Philosophy was born and nourished by poetry in the infancy
> of knowledge, and with it all those sciences it has guided to-
> ward perfection; we may thus expect them, on completion, to
> flow back like so many individual streams into the universal
> ocean of poetry from which they took their source.[42]

After his attack on the idea of imitation offered by those who
equate nature with dead matter, Schelling criticizes the traditional
idea of art as an improvement on nature or a "surpassing of the actual"[43] and the idea of imitating not nature but the artistic works of
antiquity. In the former idea, it is still possible to detect a view of

nature as a dead otherness, and not the unconscious potential force of creation Schelling posits. In the latter, there can result merely a cold formalism. In all of these efforts, "the miracle by which the limited should be raised to the unlimited, the human become divine, is wanting."[44] The rigid form of nature regarded merely as *out there* must be melted so that the "pure energy of things may flow together with the force of our own spirit."[45] In order for this to occur, "we must transcend form, in order to gain it again as intelligible, living, and truly felt."[46] The term "form" here is slippery. At this point, it seems to mean abstract qualities of extension, spatial relations, and the like. Against "form" is placed "essence" or the idea or absolute, for these are by definition filled with the creative force of the subject. But form, in another sense, becomes the vital shape taken by essence: "Determinateness of form is in nature never a negation, but ever an affirmation. Commonly, indeed, the shape of a body seems a confinement; but could we behold the creative energy, it would reveal itself as the measure this energy imposes upon itself. . . ."[47] Schelling does not identify the body with matter but with spirit itself in determinate form.[48] Insistence on the determinateness of objects as less a limitation than an enabling quality reminds us of Blake's concept of "human form divine" and his emphasis on the bounding line, and leads us to Schelling's own concentration on the particular and individual. Rather than regarding the particular as partial, as one might imagine him doing, considering that he regards man as a part of nature, Schelling instead allows the particular to embody the "vital idea" that in objective nature alone is unconscious:

> Certainly we desire to see not merely the individual, but, more than this, its vital idea. But if the artist has seized the inward creative spirit and essence of the idea, and sets this forth, he makes the individual a world in itself, a class, an eternal prototype.[49]

Implicit here is a collapse of measurable space, the idea of the world contained microcosmically by the particular. Schelling rejects the conventional measurable space implied by an already rejected, dead, primary nature. He then locates reality in the constructive act of the mind, which he calls idea, absolute, or essence: "How comes it that, to every tolerably cultivated taste, imitations of the so-called actual [Goethe's first type of art], even though carried to deception, appear in the degree untrue—nay, produce the impression of specters; whilst a work in which the idea is predominant strikes us with the full force of truth, conveying us then only to the genuinely actual world?"[50] Here Schelling characteristically transcends the merely "actual" to the "genuinely actual" in order to abolish the specter of objective nature as the ultimate reality. He substitutes an act that joins subject and object, creating or revealing the idea: "Whence comes it, if not from the more or less obscure feeling which tells us that the idea alone is the living principle in things, but all else unessential and vain shadow?"[51] Creating or revealing? Does Schelling see the imaginative act as itself the reality, the absolute—the world, perhaps, in every particular instant—since nature when alone is dead and man without consciousness of nature would not himself be conscious? Is the world born anew in each instant, or does Schelling regard the act of consciousness as a penetration to an absolute that is archetype of all reality, a something previously hidden? Is eternality a process (or act) preserved by art, or is the eternal some other timeless world made to seem immanent by the imaginative act? For the development of a theory of the symbolic a dynamic rather than a Platonic or Plotinian Schelling is the important one. The dynamic Schelling finds in the intercourse of subject and object, rather than a window into a Platonic sort of archetype, the actual construction in each instant of a particular reality *behind* which there is nothing. The act of consciousness is a making. Dead nature is denied. Nature only slumbers like Blake's Albion, and this sleep is a metaphor for the presence of a pure potentiality to be awakened in the act of perception. All is act; there is no separate object, there is no separate subject. Man is, then, his acts, or more accurately nature acting, since nature too is the act itself.

As an act, the production of the work of art is a combination of unconsciousness and consciousness or the bringing of the unconscious to consciousness. Rather than the artist being purely a vessel *through* whom nature acts, the artist is the act himself.

We have noticed already that "nature" does multiple duty in Schelling: it is first posited as the objective, but in its higher sense it is the force that conspires with man. In still a third sense, it is what is self-made out of man's intercourse with itself (in the first sense), or it is the process of that intercourse. The term does duty finally for the absolute. As a result of all of this, we see more than one way of considering the work of art or of locating it: (1) *As an act*, that is, as the temporal activity of the artist, the *work* of art in its literal dynamic sense; (2) *as the object produced*, the work being preparatory for the result. At this point it would be necessary to introduce a new usage of the term "object," since Schelling's whole aim has been to collapse what he calls "object" and "subject" into unity. Thus the art object must be a different sort of object, a sort of ultimate realization of the act. But would it not, after all, be only a copy or residue? As a copy it would be an attempt to approximate verbally the act. Is the original act a verbal act? If it is, then the act must be fully capturable as words. We would have preserved as the sign of the act virtually the act itself. But if the act is not linguistic by nature, what is the relation of the resultant verbal structure to it? Does a miraculous transformation take place, and if so, of what sort? It is here that we desire a more explicit theory of the creative power of language than Schelling gives us at this point. The connection between poetry, myth, and language needs more complete exploration in a theory of the poet as mythmaker or constant restorer of reality *in* language, and this Schelling attempts elsewhere, where he emphasizes the importance of myth and declares that without language consciousness itself would be impossible.[52] If we do not have that, the reality fades behind the language in which it merely "appears" or is occultly allegorized, and interpretation becomes a sort of archeology, a tendency characteristic of postromantic criticism in the form of literary biography, restoration of the act taking precedence over the residual object, which is, in Shelley's words, a feeble shadow in any case.[53]

Schelling began his oration with an attack on ideas of imitation mainly because he rejected their implicit concepts of nature. But the idea of imitation appears even in Schelling, once he creates a new meaning for "nature." Perhaps the best-known passage from the oration is:

> . . . in all things in nature, the living idea shows itself only blindly active; were it so also in the artist, he would be in nothing distinct from nature. But, should he attempt consciously to subordinate himself altogether to the actual, and render with servile fidelity the already existing, he would produce larvae, but no works of art. He must therefore withdraw himself from the product, from the creature, but only in order to raise himself to the creative energy, spiritually seizing the same. Thus he ascends into the realm of pure ideas; he forsakes the creature, to regain it with thousandfold interest, and

in this sense certainly to return to nature. This spirit of nature working at the core of things, and speaking through form and shape as by symbols only, the artist must certainly follow with emulation; and only so far as he seizes this with genial imitation has he produced anything genuine.[54]

Brief consideration of Goethe's essay should have helped us with this passage. Still, it is difficult. As I understand it, the artist withdraws himself from any effort to make a copy of nature (thought of as separate, primary, and fundamentally only measurable). By ascent into the realm of pure ideas Schelling means the mental act that transforms and obliterates subject and object, creating something else. The terms "ascent" and "pure ideas" are misleading. Here they do not signify a purgation of particular mundane experience or a flying upward into the realm of Platonic ideas. Instead, their use is meant to affirm the fullness of the imaginative act.

Because nature works through man in this act and because nature is universal, the imaginative act of consciousness is always a joining of nature's universality with the artist's particularity. In this sense it is possible to say that for Schelling each imaginative act symbolizes, indeed is, nature as a whole, not nature as extended in space, however, but nature as the moving spirit constituted as an act. "No particular exists by means of its limitation, but through the indwelling force with which it maintains itself as a particular whole, in distinction from the universe."[55] A symbol is not merely a trope; it is the defining quality of a work of art; the term does not refer to what the work contains but to what it is, and it is an act. Also symbolization is what Schelling really means by a "genial imitation": it is not a copy of nature as matter or extension but an assertion of the act of consciousness that awakens nature in the particular moment.

But we have moved with Schelling too easily between the mental act creating spirit and the verbal or other sort of structure which is the artistic formulation or object. In the passage I have quoted, Schelling mentions nature working through man to produce art, which speaks through its "form and shape as by symbols only." Form and shape are the principal delineators and particularizers of the artistic object, the object itself being a particular which as a whole symbolizes nature, understood in its dynamic Schellingian sense. The restricting form of the object is paradoxically the means by which the particular embodies the qualities of unity and dynamic form that are implicit in nature. It is an achieved object embodying the achievement itself. "Object," with its suggestion of primary abstraction, is really not, for Schelling's idea here, the right word. Something like "spiritual body" might be the right word.

There is another symbolization of universal by particular in art implied by Schelling; and it carries on the metamorphosis of aesthetics into ethics:

> The spirit of nature is only in appearance opposed to the soul: essentially, it is the instrument of its revelation: it brings about indeed the antagonism that exists in all things, but only that the one essence may come forth, as the utmost benignity, and the reconciliation of all the forces.
>
> All other creatures are driven by the mere force of nature, and through it maintain their individuality: in man alone, as the central point, arises the soul, without which the world would be like the natural universe without the sun.
>
> The soul in man, therefore, is not the principle of individuality, but that whereby he raises himself above all egoism, whereby he becomes capable of self-sacrifice, of disinterested love, and (which is the highest) of the contemplation and knowledge of the essence of things, and thus of art.[56]

Here Schelling has worked toward the idea of conjoined universality and particularity by concluding that the work of art is the result of a process carrying man out of his own ego at the same time that he remains firmly attached to particular acts and experiences. The work of art in its universality symbolizes man's soul, conceived of as that which rises above self-interest. There is a hint here of the artist disappearing into his work, so to speak. Schelling in his own way has taken into his philosophy Kant's idea of purposiveness without purpose and Schiller's idea of art as disinterested play. Kant saw the beautiful as the symbol, but only (in his limiting terms) the analogy, of the good. Schiller saw what he called play as the supreme act of man because in its purposiveness without purpose there is a purgation of self-interest. Schelling takes the same tack and constructs an ethic on Kantian aesthetic grounds.

Schelling's distinction between symbol and allegory is made in the *Philosophie der Kunst*, written in 1802 but published many years later. It distinguishes among three things:

That representation (*Darstellung*) in which the universal signifies the particular or in which the particular is shown forth
through the universal is *Schematism.*

That representation, however, in which the particular signifies the universal, or in which the universal is shown forth
through the particular is allegoric.

The synthesis of these two, where neither the universal
signifies the particular, nor the particular the universal, but
where both are absolutely one, is the symbolic.[57]

As Todorov has observed, following Sørensen, Schelling's addition of a third element to the Goethean opposition is an appropria-
tion from Kant.[58] But it is different from Kant in that it gives a kind of
independent power to the symbol. Schelling's distinction implies that
in the synthesis the symbol does not merely signify but is what it signifies, and he connects this idea in the *Philosophie der Kunst* with the
idea of myth as tautegorical, a term picked up later by Coleridge.

But Schelling and his contemporary Friedrich Schlegel pass
through a period of theorizing during which immense claims are
made for myth, and myth, symbolism, and poetry seem to have been
made identical. Poetry is for both at this time a faculty of the mind
like the reason and understanding. Their concept of myth as a mode
of thought is similar to that of Moritz, with emphasis on the immanence of the deity in nature, the importance of sympathy, the indwelling of the universal in particulars, and the fundamentally metaphorical nature of such thought. Schlegel extends his interests into Indian
language and myth and notes that Sanskrit embodies the characteristics of myth in its highly metaphorical nature.[59] The early Schlegel is
concerned with the problem of the alienation of the poet in his subjectivity, and advocates what comes to be famously called romantic
irony as an answer to this alienation; but such irony, though it expresses awareness of the problem, hardly provides a contrary to sub-
ject/object. It does, however, allow the poet to express the difference
of his condition from that of the ancient myth-making poet, which is
to be regarded as the desirable and truly ideal state. In this state, now
lost,

. . . mythology and poetry are one and inseparable. All poems
of antiquity join one to the other, till from ever increasing
masses and members the whole is formed. Everything inter-
penetrates everything else, and everywhere there is one and

the same spirit, only expressed differently. And thus it is truly no empty image to say: Ancient poetry is a single, indivisible, and perfect poem.[60]

But the modern poet, facing the alienation of object from subject bequested by the Lockean and Cartesian traditions, finds himself bereft of that sense of the solidarity of life implied by ancient myth, which had not learned of the modern bifurcations of reality. For the earlier Schlegel, Goethe was the unusual modern poet who managed to overcome such oppositions, but modern conditions make the effort nearly superhuman. The old mythological structure has declined into philosophical pantheism and allegory. The modern poet is left to create from inside himself, and though many have done so brilliantly, each one begins anew from nothing; because modern poetry "lacks a focal point, such as mythology provided for the ancients."[61] Schlegel sees the possibility of such a myth or recognizes that we must work to create one. However, conditions being different, "it will come to us by an entirely opposite way from that of previous ages, which was everywhere the first flower of youthful imagination, directly joining and imitating what was most immediate and vital in the sensuous world."[62] It will come via idealism, which is the true realism, not its opposite, as is so often thought. For Schlegel, idealism incorporates realism because it does not throw up the barrier of scientific abstraction between man and his experience. While rationalism abstracts *from* the real, idealism gathers the real into its forms. It would appear that myth and poetry, as a mode of thought, deliver particularity unscathed to man. Rationalism is a distancing force, but the poetic mode in its very essence begins to "cancel the progression and laws of rationally thinking reason, and to transplant us once again into the beautiful confusion of imagination, into the original chaos of human nature, for which I know as yet no more beautiful symbol than the motley throng of the ancient gods."[63] The gods maintain that particularity admired by Vico; the historical movement to subjectivity begun with Descartes, which culminates in Fichte's ego, turns inside out, so to speak, and becomes the true realism. It reconstitutes nature, not as abstract, primary, and isolated from the subject, but as particular, experiential, and uniquely objectified through the forms of human thought, one of which is the mythico-poetic.

In their introduction to Schlegel's *Dialogue on Poetry*, Ernst Behler and Roman Struc describe the new mythology as consisting of "transformation and transfiguration of the objective world surrounding us."[64] Though it is accurate in its way, the phrase can mislead, because Schlegel is not thinking of "transforming" an objective world. The whole point of the new mythology is to obliterate the subject/object distinction. It also might be better to say that the new mythology is not to "transfigure" but to constitute reality in its own terms. These are perhaps fine distinctions, but they are necessary, I think, to get at the principal point of Schlegel's analysis, which requires a sweeping away of the assumptions of "rationally thinking reason." This is not to say that Schlegel himself does not on occasion fall into the terminology of "transfiguration," but the occasions on which he does so are lapses from his fundamental effort.

Schelling is in some ways more rigorous than Schlegel. This can be seen in their respective treatments of Spinoza. For Schlegel, Spinoza's pantheism is an image of that unifying force that obliterates false reasoned bifurcations and breathes as spirit through everything. But Schelling criticizes Spinoza for his reduction of everything to abstract objects ("things") and his consequent determinism, which amounts to the denial of all that one identifies with the mythic and poetic mode of thought:

> The error of [Spinoza's] system is by no means due to the fact that he posits all *things in God*, but to the fact that they are *things*—to the abstract conception of the world and its creatures, indeed to external Substance itself, which is also a thing for him. Thus his arguments against freedom are altogether deterministic, and in no wise pantheistic. He treats the will, too, as a thing, and then proves very naturally, that in every case of its operation it must be determined by another, and so forth, endlessly. Hence the lifelessness of his system, the harshness of its form, the bareness of its concepts and expressions, the relentless austerity of its definitions, so admirably in accord with the abstract outlook.[65]

Schelling's movement from a concept of an immanent natural god like that of myth, identified with process and flux, to an absolute which *is* and from which all flows, marks a turning away from myth similar to Schlegel's later turning. The Schelling whom we have just studied is the Schelling who identifies symbolism and what he calls "tautegorical" myth and thinks of art as the only true revelation, the only organon of philosophy. Schelling's notion of the "tautegorical" in myth makes myth a constitutive form, and it is a major step in

what Paul Ricoeur calls "the dissolution of the myth as explanation
. . . the necessary way to the restoration of the myth as symbol . . . a
criticism that is no longer reductive but restorative."[66] In advocating
myth, Schelling sees the same problem for the modern poet as does
Schlegel, but imagines art to be capable of healing the cultural bifurcations Schlegel deplores. Schelling has much in common with Moritz in his sense of the concrete universality of myth and laments the
disappearance of this quality—the symbolic—in modern poetry,
which has turned allegoric. For Schelling, language itself is a sort of
deadened mythology, and he seems to be suggesting that only mythological thought of the Vichean sort can revive a language that is perpetually deadening to thought itself.[67] In the modern world, God is
sought, but modern thought cannot achieve the goal of finding God
immanent in the world. In the middle of Schelling's career this failure
seems to him redeemable by rediscovering the true nature of symbolism and art in myth. The artist will create "lasting forms out of the
fickle formlessness of the age."[68] But the later Schelling thinks of the
artistic synthesis, so important in his system, as only a "moment" in
man's progress toward a higher realm, in which the spirit moves back
to God, up the scale of ideality, transcending all form. Form must finally be obliterated in the idea of God that defies representation.
Even though this development in Schelling seems to undercut his emphasis on the dynamic and changing as the core of reality and relaxes
back into Neoplatonism, his sense of the dynamic reasserts itself in
his version of romantic irony: Art remains to claim its moment in a
progressive act, an Odyssey of the spirit toward pure freedom.

Schlegel too lost interest in the power of art to heal a bifurcated
culture. For him, the isolation of man came to be not merely a characteristic of the age but a metaphysical condition to be transcended.
Converted to Catholicism, Schlegel redrew the line between infinite
and finite; art no longer leaps it. The relation of finite to infinite, real
to ideal, becomes again allegoric, and romantic irony reveals itself as
the highest expression of the poet's striving for the unattainable infinite, even as he recognizes that it is unattainable. Myth is relegated
to the past or achieves the status of a sort of ideal unfallen or pre-fall
condition in which the world was unified and God immanent, but
now unattainable except by the annihilation of the very same spirit
that strives. The historical interpretation of myth wins out over the
aesthetical. Myth characterizes a particular historical epoch, and its
disappearance is nostalgically lamented. The modern poet will pro-
fess mythic values but will never quite achieve a condition that makes

them possible. Poetry may be defined ideally as myth, but it is really an expression of the self's search for an always receding, elusive mythic state. From this, there follow those typically romantic efforts to set up past "natural" conditions as nostalgically desirable, to find the true nature of poetry in folk literature, in myths themselves, but always with a sense of distance, desire, and loss. And, of course, finally in this we see the source of recent turnings in criticism back to the valorization of allegory (in its "religious" form) and the demystification of the "miraculous" symbolic.

3. COLERIDGE—NATURE AND BOOK

COLERIDGE's statement contrasting symbolism and allegory occurs in *The Statesman's Manual* in connection with an argument advocating the Bible as a practical textbook for statesmen, and I shall examine it in that context, for that provides its peculiar interest. The quality of the Bible mentioned by Coleridge which gives rise to the distinction is its alleged "freedom from the hollowness of abstractions" in contrast to the "histories of highest note in the present age." Coleridge praises the "applicability" of passages from the Bible to such subjects as the change and fortunes of empire. From virtually any passage, he argues, "some guiding light" may be struck. The Bible is symbolical, not allegorical. It is, in fact, the example par excellence of the symbolical because it can be regarded as historical and thus unquestionably particular: "While the later [histories of highest note in the present age] present a shadow-fight of Things and Quantities, the former [the Bible] gives us the history of Man, and balances the important influence of individual Minds with the previous state of the national morals and manners, in which, as constituting a specific susceptibility, it presents to us the true course of both the influence itself, and of the Weal or Woe that were its Consequents." [69]

Coleridge attributes the abstractness of contemporary historical writing to a "general contagion" of "mechanic philosophy," the product of an "unenlivened generalizing Understanding": and he goes on to attribute the power of the Bible to the imagination, which is "that reconciling and mediatory power, which incorporating the Reason in Images of the Sense, and organizing (as it were) the flux of the Senses by the permanence and self-circling energies of the Reason, gives birth to a system of symbols, harmonious in themselves, and consubstantial with the truths, of which they are the *conductors*." [70]

I shall return to this. It is important first to observe that Coleridge discourses on symbolism and allegory with respect to the Bible and history rather than to art. We recall that in Goethe's distinction one problem not dealt with was how to determine from a text whether indeed symbolism or allegory were present, because Goethe treats the question in terms of the author's motive and provides no criterion of judgment where we are faced with the text itself. In presenting to us a work declared to be both historically and spiritually truthful, Coleridge would offer an unambiguous example. There is no way to argue, without attacking Coleridge's premises, that the particulars of the Bible are merely shadows arbitrarily invented to stand for universals or general ideas. The particulars of the Bible, he says, are "consubstantial with the truths of which they are the conductors." These particulars, or events, carry their meanings inside themselves.

Also, Coleridge thinks of the Bible as a system of symbols and implies that one of the qualities of such a system is a sort of internal harmony. All of this leads him to his distinction between allegory and symbolism. About allegory he says:

> It is among the miseries of the present age that it recognizes no medium between the *Literal* and *Metaphorical*. Faith is either to be buried in the dead letter, or its name and honors usurped by a counterfeit product of the mechanical understanding, which in the blindness of self-complacency confounds SYMBOLS with ALLEGORIES. Now an Allegory is but a translation of abstract notions into a picture-language which is itself nothing but an abstraction from objects of the senses; the principal being more worthless even than its phantom proxy, both alike unsubstantial and the former shapeless to boot.[71]

Coleridge appears to shift the definition given us by the Germans from a focus on the poet and his activity to the language of the work itself. The terms "literal" and "metaphorical" appear to direct us more to the verbal structure than do the terms of either Goethe or Schelling. Indeed, Coleridge seems to be loosening the terms "symbol" and "allegory" from their designating tropes in a discourse to designating the discourse as a whole. However, this is not by any means a clean break. Elsewhere Coleridge clearly uses "allegory" in its tropological sense: "We may . . . safely define allegorical writing as the employment of one set of agents and images with actions and accompaniments correspondent, so as to convey, while in disguise, either moral qualities or conceptions of the mind that are not in themselves objects of the senses, or other images, agents, actions, fortunes, and circumstances, so that the difference is everywhere presented to the eye or imagination while the likeness is suggested to the mind." [72] Also, Coleridge seems to have formulated his distinction defensively, as is so often the case in such matters, in order to provide a contrary to certain notions in the British empirical tradition. The assumption he attacks is the location of truth in generality only and the assumption that language apes a thought that moves from particulars to higher and higher levels of generality and "law." A particular under these conditions becomes significant only as an instance of general law, the only model of thought being the inductive method. Coleridge rejects this notion because the notion erects an unsurmountable barrier between what Goethe called the phenomenon and the universal. Coleridge's use of the term "metaphorical" is important because it seems to declare that he is introducing a notion of metaphor that removes it from the list of classical tropes, expands its range of meaning, and gives it special status as fundamental to both thought and expression. If he were to develop this notion, promulgated first in modern times by Vico, he might further close the gap between language and thought that we imagine him already beginning to close by focusing on the verbal structure or text rather than the author's mental act. He does indicate that the particular or "literal" thing, or word denoting such a thing (he is not clear about whether he is discussing language or phenomena), can also be more than its literality, as the events or words of the Bible are more than their historical specificity:

> . . . its contents present to us the stream of time continuous as Life and a symbol of Eternity, inasmuch as the Past and the Future are virtually contained in the Present. According therefore to our relative position on its banks the Sacred History becomes prophetic, the Sacred Prophecies historical, while the power and substance of both inhere in its Laws, its Promises, and its Comminations. In the Scriptures therefore both Facts and Persons must of necessity have a two-fold significance, a past and a future, a temporary and a perpetual, a particular and a universal application. [73]

In Coleridge's theory the theological bent of his mind asserts itself, the tradition of typological interpretation standing behind his remarks. It is uncertain, yet, whether Coleridge finds in literary art (other than the Bible itself, which may have unique status for him in this regard) the collapse of linear time into eternity, of literal into metaphorical, to occur in language or to be a hidden realm of reality that language seeks a way to represent. This collapse is for Coleridge characteristic of the Bible, which is both act (even history) and word, the acts not being separate from the words that express them, but being *the word*. The acts to which the Bible appears to refer Coleridge does not regard as being *interpreted* by the authors of the Bible but as being set forth, presented, preserved, and eternalized, containing their own meaning, which then comes directly, that is, *presently*, to us in our reading. The idea of the symbol is, for Coleridge, to be derived from this model: the question remaining, I must repeat, is how far this concept of the symbol can be extended to less privileged literary works. It appears that a concept of symbolism, similar to that applied by Coleridge to the Bible, could not very well have been applied to literary works during a period in which the Bible had unquestioned, supreme, and unique status as *the word*; for no other verbal structure could, under these conditions, be raised to its eminence. Coleridge's remarks in *The Statesman's Manual* are now frequently treated as applicable to other works, the growth of the modern concept of literary symbolism being concurrent with and perhaps impossible without the decline of the Bible into literariness.

Following his attack on allegory, Coleridge defines the symbol:

> a Symbol (ὁ ἔστιν ἀεὶ ταυτηγόρικον) is characterized by a translucence of the Special in the Individual or of the General in the Especial or of the Universal in the General. Above all by the translucence of the Eternal through and in the Temporal. It always partakes of the Reality which it renders intelligible; and while it enunciates the whole, abides itself as a living part in that Unity, of which it is the representative.[74]

This passage is more elaborate than Goethe's, and in some ways more careful. Coleridge seems determined to include in his definition all terms that have plagued previous discussions. These he arranges in a hierarchy having its sources in his studies of Kant and Schelling. He sees the universal or absolute, familiar to us from Schelling, shining through the general and the special to the individual itself. The special is meant in its literal sense of the species that the individual embodies. The species he seems to consider not something established by man through generalization from sense data (though one assumes that the concept of species is arrived at in such a way); rather, the species has a status in being that a generalization does not have, similar to Goethe's prototype of plant or animal or what Blake called an individual class. It is perhaps connected with the Schellingian vital idea in nature. The general exists at a greater level of abstraction, disembodied—a product of the understanding, not of nature itself. The universal transcends the purely humanly constituted general. Between these last two, Kant drew a firm line that Coleridge blurs: The understanding, which produces generalizations, works by its own categories and is "constitutive." But beyond such general principles the mind can produce through the reason only "regulative" ideas, into which class Kant would put Coleridge's universals. Coleridge rebelled against the Kantian refusal to allow reason the power to produce constitutive ideas, to make things-in-themselves knowable, and redefined the reason. Wellek observes that in Coleridge's thought Kant's "doctrines on the limits of our knowing power become a sort of back-door through which the whole of traditional theology is admitted."[75] This is not quite correct. The *whole* of theology does not reemerge, but enough does to make it possible to restore the notion of "intellectual intuition," which Kant claimed to be an impossible contradiction. It becomes the vehicle by which man rises to an apprehension not merely of things-in-themselves but of the ultimate thing-in-itself. Coleridge transforms the reason into "an organ bearing the same relation to spiritual objects, the Universal, the Eternal, and the Necessary, as the eye bears to material and contingent phenomena."[76] And the sensuous image or symbol becomes a medium of expression of the reason's intuition of noumena. That the unknowableness of things-in-themselves did not torment Kant seems to have tormented Coleridge, who doubtless saw in the word "to know" a valuable symbol that could not be lost to acts of faith and requiring what Kenneth Burke calls a "stealing."[77] This tendency in Coleridge leads him in the end to emphasize the "miraculous" rather than the "secular" form of the symbol. Though Wellek says this is a return to traditional theology, it is at least trying to be something more because Coleridge is flirting with the idea that his reason is linguistically constitutive and that reason can express itself as a *poetic* logos.

For Coleridge, then, the symbol moves up a hierarchy, mediating among the levels he delineates. He explicitly includes the possibility of allegory as trope *in* symbolism, while at the same time insisting on an essential difference between them. The symbol can contain allegorical levels, but ultimately the symbol encompasses all levels in a circumferential form that defies an abstract interpretation. This view moves toward making "symbol" a term *for* a work of art rather than a device *in* a work. The allegorical is identified with the working of the understanding and the fancy. The symbol, at its ultimate, is identified with the imagination. At the same time, the distinction is hard and fast since it contrasts two different processes by which the mind comes to knowledge. Allegory is the result of an empirical process by which man reaches generalizations. It provides an image representing such generalizations. Symbolism offers an image that is unique and contains its own significance. Reason builds upon understanding toward antinomies in Kant; reason is embodied ultimately in the poetic word in Coleridge, or at least he would like it to be. And such a word would be the ultimate metaphor, connecting all discrete words in one relation of identity that encompasses differences yet maintains particulars.

It appears that for Coleridge allegory is a man-made thing—a verbal or representational image. Literary or other artistic symbols, on the other hand, seem to be direct representatives of specific instances of the intercourse of mind with phenomena. In an appendix note to *The Statesman's Manual*, Coleridge affirms this:

> I seem to myself to behold in the quiet objects, on which I am gazing, more than an arbitrary illustration, more than a mere *simile*, the work of my own Fancy. I feel an awe, as if there were before my eyes the same Power, as that of the REASON —the same power in a lower dignity, and therefore a symbol established in the truth of things. I feel it alike, whether I contemplate a single tree or flower, or meditate on vegetation throughout the world, as one of the great organs of the life of nature.[78]

Whether the phrase "more than an arbitrary illustration" (allegory) indicates that such acts of the mind really may be that *and more* or whether Coleridge is distinguishing *in kind* is not clear. The term "simile" is to be identified with allegory because it avows only a partial relationship, not the identity claimed by metaphor. Clearly Coleridge is investing in "objects" (regarded as the creation of the intercourse of subject and object) a symbolic power capable of evoking the highest religious intuition. Reason, not regulative as in Kant (not "merely speculative or purely practical" and not "abstract reason, not the mere organ of science") is for Coleridge the science of the universal, the "science of All as the whole," and is in effect the instrument of religion. Coleridge defines religion not as the moral law but as the practice of intellectual intuition. He sees religious ends as the motivating force for the arts, which are "symbolic" and operate by the same mental powers as religion:

> The Reason first manifests itself in man by the *tendency* to the comprehension of all as one.
>
> To this tendency, therefore, RELIGION, as the consideration of the Particular and Individual (in which respect it takes up and identifies with itself the excellence of the *Understanding*) but of the Individual, as it exists and has its being in the Universal (in which respect it is one with the pure Reason)—to this tendency, I say, RELIGION assigns the due limits, and is the echo of the 'voice of the *Lord God* walking in the garden.' Hence in all the ages and countries of civilization Religion has been the parent and fosterer of the Fine Arts, as of Poetry, Music, Painting, &c. the common essence of which consists in a similar union of the Universal and the Individual.[79]

Observing this near identity of religion and poetry, one wonders on what grounds a difference might be established. Since "poetry" is a mental activity and is not interchangeable with, but only occasionally produces, poems, there really seems to be no difference at all. It follows that a poem is a product of the striving to express the intellectual intuition that goes by the name of religious experience, or poetry. There are dangers of a collapse here back into a form of the "religious" or "Platonic" allegoric, as in "The Destiny of Nations":

> For all that meets the bodily sense I deem
> Symbolical, one mighty alphabet
> For infant minds; and we in this low world
> Placed with our backs to bright Reality,
> That we may learn with young unwounded ken
> The substance from its shadow.[80]

Coleridge does not doubt that the word of God came into the Bible, though it is an "immediate derivation from God," through the verbal acts of men. Coleridge's departure from Kant in his attribution of intellectual intuition to man opens up the possibility that individual men can create symbolic works like the Bible. The Bible's status is no longer unique; it is now prototypical. It is the model poem, a complete success except where it has been corrupted by editors.[81]

There is another book immediately derived from God, and that is the "great book of his servant Nature":

> That in its obvious sense and literal interpretation it declares the being and attributes of the Almighty Father, none but the *fool in heart* has ever dared gainsay. But it has been the music of gentle and pious minds in all ages, it is the *poetry* of all human nature, to read it likewise in a figurative sense, and to find therein correspondencies and symbols of the spiritual world.[82]

Poems would seem to be the product of man's effort to create a verbal nature with the status of the Bible itself. In this sense, poems are not imitations of natural objects. They are the product of man's imitation of God's act in creating nature and of God's creation of a verbal nature, the Bible. The power of creation in God has no name and is symbolized by its products. The act of imitating that power is the act of imagination defined briefly by Coleridge in the famous chapter thirteen of the *Biographia Literaria*. Imagination in its primary sense is unconscious. In its secondary sense it is a sort of imitation ("echo") of the former, and it "struggles to idealize and to unify." [83] As Virgil learned that Homer and nature are one, so Coleridge avers that the Bible and nature are one.

Yet this for Coleridge does not mean that one copies biblical stories or records phenomena. The relationship or echo of which he speaks is a formal one of process. When Coleridge gazes on natural objects, each one of them

> upholding the ceaseless plastic motion of the parts in the profoundest rest of the whole . . . becomes the visible organismus of the whole *silent* or *elementary* life of nature and, therefore, in incorporating the one extreme becomes the symbol of the other; the natural symbol of that higher life of reason. . . . Thus finally, the vegetable creation, in the simplicity and uniformity of its *internal* structure symbolizing the unity of nature, while it represents the omniformity of her delegated functions in its *external* variety and manifoldness, becomes the record and chronicle of her ministerial acts, and inchases

the vast unfolded volume of the earth with the hieroglyphics
of her history.[84]

With nature and book formally identical, the organic metaphors to
describe the former are carried over to the latter in the literary criticism of Coleridge best known to us.

Before I examine that criticism with respect to our subject, some
questions are in order. To a skeptical age is it enough to assert that
because the Bible closes the gap between word and reality, the poet
too can achieve such closure in his poem? This would seem to be a
miraculous, even holy, power, and if it were to become the standard
of poetic achievement might well drive any poet to the statements of
"Dejection: An Ode" or the conclusion of "Kubla Khan." In our own
time, of course, the Bible's historical adequacy and its status as infal-
libly God's word are in doubt, and it can be regarded for our purposes as no more (which is quite a lot) than an encyclopaedic literary
work of unparalleled cultural influence.

But it can be said of Coleridge finally that, though the Bible is a
model for his definitions of the symbolic, he does not consider it to be
the model only because it is declared to be God's word and immediately equivalent to nature. He claims in *The Statesman's Manual*
that the Bible has symbolic authority and thus value to modern life.
On this ground the Bible has to be defended as a verbal structure like
any other rather than as the report of a structure of events full of
significance if only put down faithfully. The meaning would have to
inhere in the verbal structure rather than the events as such. One
would have to develop a way of demonstrating this strictly from a
text. But is this possible? What demonstration there is in *The Statesman's Manual* is disappointing and tends to turn the Bible into what
Coleridge has already called an allegory: it is said there, for example,
that the prophet Isaiah can be read as a commentary on the French
Revolution.[85] It is rather in Coleridge's so-called practical criticism
that we find the stirrings of the analogy between nature as book or
word and poem as nature. It is with respect to the formal identity of
these things that Coleridge makes his claim for the authority of the
poet's word.

Nature is already regarded as a unity, its parts microcosmically
reflecting the internal structure of the whole. It needs only to be read.
The poem also strives for this same unity, and this Coleridge attempts
to demonstrate in his practical criticism as inhering in the language
of the poem itself. This is a fundamental issue in the *Biographia Lite-*

raria from the beginning, where Coleridge disparages his own early work and "the faults of my language, though indeed partly owing to the wrong choice of subjects, and the desire of giving a poetic colouring to abstract and metaphysical truths,"[86] in other words, his own tendencies toward allegory. He objects to "translations of prose thoughts into poetic language" and to "language mechanized into a barrel-organ."[87]

These few remarks early in the *Biographia Literaria* suggest some sort of distinction not merely between symbolism and allegory as processes of thought but between actual *kinds* of language, there being "poetic language" (symbolism) and simply "language." Presumably such a difference should be demonstrable. The commentary on Wordsworth at least demonstrates that "poetic language" is not the language of "low and rustic life," but it does not provide us with a general theory of poetic language, nor does the discussion of meter appended to it. There are numerous remarks in the *Biographia Literaria* that contribute to a theory of poetry, but the term "poetry" in Coleridge never clearly means poetic language nor the poem as language. This is not to say that he does not offer tantalizing hints of some profound identity between words and things. The letter to Godwin of 1800, to which I alluded at the beginning of this chapter, teases with questions: "Is *thinking* impossible without arbitrary signs? &—how far is the word 'arbitrary' a misnomer? Are not words &c. parts & germinations of the Plant? And what is the Law of their Growth? In something of this order I would endeavor to destroy the old antithesis of *Words* and *Things*, elevating, as it were, words to Things, & living Things too."[88] Fourteen years later he writes: ". . . do not let me forget that Language is the medium of all Thoughts to *ourselves*, of all Feelings to others, & partly to ourselves—now a . . . thing cannot be a medium in the living continuity of nature but by essentially partaking of the nature of the two things mediated."[89] There is something only hopeful in these and other remarks, such as when he talks in the *Biographia* about thinking *in* a language.[90] He takes another position at times: that language follows upon acts of the mind and that the "language of words" is only the vehicle of the "language of spirits." The untranslatableness of a poem seems not to be the result of the thought being thought or created *in* language. Instead it is because the language is "framed to convey not the object alone, but likewise the character, mood and intentions of the person who is representing it."[91] This is an inadequate way of presenting the idea of the mind's creative role, if we examine it in the light of what we know from the letter to Godwin to have been Coleridge's desire. It too nearly suggests that poetic language is somehow facts absorbed in subjectivity or emotion.

Nor does Coleridge affirm that images are the essence of the poetic: "They become proofs of original genius only as far as they are modified by a predominant passion: or by associated thoughts or images awakened by that passion: or when they have the effect of reducing multitude to unity or succession to an instant: or lastly, when a human and intellectual life is transferred to them from the poet's own spirit."[92] This passage begins by exhibiting the same problems as the one previously commented upon, but it goes farther toward relating poetic imagery to the creative and transforming acts of the mind that Coleridge attributes to the imagination, which ought after all to have something to do with the making of images. Yet while Coleridge seems so often to be talking about poetic language or to be verging on a definition, he seldom does more than describe the poet's mental activity, which seems separate from language. The critical passage of this sort, where the connection between nature as book and poem as nature is nearly found, is in the essay on Shakespeare's genius. Mechanic form, that old Goethean monster, which produces allegory, is contrasted to organic form, the symbolic:

> The form is mechanic, when on any given material we impress a predetermined form, not necessarily arising out of the properties of the material: as when to a mass of wet clay we give whatever shape we wish it to retain when hardened. The organic form, on the other hand, is innate; it shapes, as it develops, itself from within, and the fullness of its development, is one and the same with the perfection of its outward form. Such as the life is, such is the form.[93]

Yet here again we are not able to conclude that the material for poetry is language. It appears more likely that the material is the poet's intuitions likened to the forms created by nature, indeed, identical to the form of nature if we assume that Coleridge, employing an idea of Schlegel, is thinking along Schellingian lines: "Nature, the prime genial artist, inexhaustible in diverse powers, is equally inexhaustible in forms, each exterior in the physiognomy of the being within its true image reflected and thrown out from the concave mirror: and even such is the appropriate excellence of her chosen poet, of our own Shakespeare, himself a nature humanized, a genial understanding, directing self-consciously powers and an implicit wisdom deeper even than our consciousness."[94] Even here the plays and poems of Shakespeare are not mentioned, unless the term "Shakespeare" is to be taken to represent his works. This we cannot do, however, since clearly it is the *process* of Shakespeare's imagination to which Coleridge refers. Coleridge is merely repeating his oft-stated metaphor identifying the poet with the spirit of nature in its creative performance. This process does not seem *fundamentally* to be the process of linguistic creation. It is, in fact, "deeper than our consciousness," and seems to be the mental act of the secondary imagination.[95] There is finally no completed theory of poetic language as thought to bridge the gap between poem and poetry in Coleridge. Going beyond Goethe, Coleridge still does not quite fill the gap between mental act and pure poetic technique, such as meter and rhyme. But he tantalizes us constantly with possibility.

Coleridge identifies the organic with the symbolic, but neither finally with language, except by the analogy he establishes between nature and art. *The Principles of Genial Criticism* attempts to connect the organic and symbolic, derived from Schelling and Schlegel, with the Kantian beautiful. Coleridge is not nearly as careful with Kant's distinctions as Kant was, and the essays do not contribute anything original to our particular subject. It is important, however, to remark that in the *Principles* the beautiful, which Kant so circumscribes and allows only an analogical and (in his terms) symbolic relation to the good, Coleridge distinguishes from the good. According to the *Principles* the good is always "discursive," the beautiful always "intuitive."[96] But this does not square with the remarks he makes in *The Statesman's Manual*, where distinctions of this sort are made ultimately meaningless by his identification of poetry with religion. The terms "discursive" and "intuitive" draw a hard and fast distinction. The former means that the good can be linguistically expressed in precepts, but the latter means that the beautiful cannot. But since poems can express the beautiful and are linguistic structures, Coleridge seems to imply, without demonstrating it, that language is of two different sorts, not perhaps in substance, but in form. What is needed in Coleridge is an expansion of hints we find here and there in the *Biographia Literaria* about the nature of metaphor. Meanwhile, in addition to those hints we have the description of the beautiful in the *Principles*: "The sense of beauty subsists in simultaneous intuition of the relation of parts, each to each, and of all to a whole: exciting an immediate and absolute complacency, without intervention, therefore, of any interest, sensual or intellectual."[97] The beautiful here seems identical to the symbolic in that the symbolic identifies particulars with the universal as beauty identifies multeity with unity. Yet no claim is made for beauty's relation to the good, while in *The Statesman's Manual* the symbolic is the very basis of all religious experience and of art.

At the same time in the *Principles* Coleridge seems to arrive at a concept of the beautiful that is an ironic negation of the possibility of its definition. The beautiful is "frequently produced by the mere removal of association," and

> When I reflect on the manner in which smoothness, richness of sound, &c., enter into the formation of the beautiful, I am induced to suspect that they act negatively rather than positively. Something there must be to realize the form, something in and by which the *forma informans* reveals itself, and these, less than any that could be substituted, and in the least possible degree, distract the attention, in the least possible degree obscure the idea, of which they (composed into outline and surface) are the symbol.[98]

From the point of view of expression, then, the "idea" is very nearly an absence, a silence; and poetic technique is the means of producing a special sort of transparency in language, an absence of language in language. The Faustian distrust of language is balanced against a faith that poetic language can destroy discursiveness and reveal the "idea." Criticism still struggles with a normative concept of language which tends to exclude the poem or to think it deviant. The struggle of the symbolist critics must be against the separation of poetry from language as well as the separation of language from thought. In the end, too, there must be a distinction between a "miraculous" and a "secular" form of symbolic. Coleridge's attempt to make the symbolic "idea" constitutive rather than merely regulative, as in Kant, is derived from a theological interest and is directed at establishing a religious intellectual intuition which would give hope of the "miraculous" immanence in language of the noumenal, though this would be inevitably in a fallen form.

4. CARLYLE—BOOK AND CLOTHING

THOMAS CARLYLE's *Sartor Resartus* (1831) is not a work of pure speculation; it is not principally the presentation of a discursive argument. Instead it is a sort of anatomy in Frye's sense, which plays with an intellectual theme, while at the same time it takes advantage of and castigates a tendency among us to relegate the playful to the trivial or unserious.[99] It stands in the early nineteenth century to preceding theories of the symbol much as Yeats's *A Vision*, which I shall examine in chapter 11, stands to thought about fictions in the early twentieth. Indeed, it is about fictions, and the "clothes" of Carlyle are related to the "masks" of Yeats. Further, the two books share a fictive device, discovery of a lost or obscure text which is then interpreted by an "editor," the extent of whose competence to understand or sympathize with his text is never quite certain but of whose good will we are convinced. The curious relation of text to editor and other ambivalent situations in *Sartor Resartus* tend to reflect in themselves the nature of the symbolic that is the ostensible subject of discussion. As we have come to expect from theories of the symbolic, expressed from the point of view of the norm of discourse, the symbol is regarded as indirect, inscrutable, and mysterious.

The obscure text in this case is that of a German professor named Diogenes Teufelsdröckh (Devilsdung), of unknown parentage and apparently now disappeared, having left behind, in addition to the published tome, a number of bags, each marked with a zodiacal sign, containing miscellaneous notes and autobiographical fragments. His book is entitled *Die Kleider, ihr Werden und Wirkin* (*Clothes, Their Origin and Influence*), in which there is presented a "philosophy of clothes"—in fact, a well togged out theory of symbols. The editor, after introducing the author and his general theory, indulges in an archeological investigation that seems to be demanded by the romantic conception of poetry—the recreation of the author's life. This particular recreation is *truly* archeological, for, as Teufelsdröckh has commented with respect to most of man's past, his own life is left to us entirely in symbolic remains, contained in the paper bags that the editor ransacks for information. Having completed his archeology as best he can, the editor himself begins to question the archeological method, even to think that he has been made a fool for having imagined all he has worked with to be literally authentic:

It is a suspicion grounded perhaps on trifles, yet confirmed almost into certainty by the more and more discernible humoristico-satirical tendency of Teufelsdröckh, in whom underground humors and intricate sardonic rogueries, wheel within wheel, defy all reckoning: a suspicion, in one word, that these Autobiographical Documents are partly a mystification! What if many a so-called Fact were little better than a Fiction: if here we had no direct Camera-obscura Picture of the Professor's History; but only some more or less fantastic Adumbration, symbolically, perhaps significantly enough, shadowing-forth the same![100]

While at the same time the subject of the book is clothes as symbols or symbols as clothes, the fictive structure of the book and the materials upon which it is based declare their own problematic nature. They are part of an elaborate clothing for Carlyle himself, though the question remains, as we shall see, as to whether Carlyle is not coexistent with his clothing, even in the last analysis is not *only* his clothing.

One chapter of *Sartor Resartus* and of Teufelsdröckh's book is entitled "Symbols," the former being an excerpt of the latter by the editor. In it Teufelsdröckh praises the virtues of concealment, of secrecy, of silence. The commentary on these virtues exemplifies the ironic habit of Teufelsdröckh that so perplexes the editor. There is a design in it, however, since the curious praise of silence eventuates in a definition of the symbol: "In a Symbol there is concealment and yet revelation: here therefore, by Silence and by Speech acting together, comes a double significance."[101] Silence turns out to be a metaphor for the Goethean inscrutable that, it is said, cannot be spoken directly, but only indirectly. The symbol would seem to be a special use of language that is characterized not by one side of a set of negations, not by establishing a contrary to the set, but by a "miraculous" embodiment of one in the other. The negations are familiar: silence/speech, infinite/finite, poetry/prose: "For it is here [in the joining of them in the symbol] that Fantasy with her mystic wonderland plays into the small prose domain of Sense, and becomes incorporated therewith."[102] In this and a few other passages it seems to be implied that the lower level of reality—sense—loses its status as reality when separated from the higher, though this idea is not pressed very hard and is more or less played with, as are all ideas, in Teufelsdröckh's characteristically perplexing fashion.

The symbol, not just a literary symbol, begins to take on the status of a "miraculous" reality itself: "In the symbol proper, what we can call a Symbol, there is ever, more or less distinctly and directly, some embodiment and revelation of the Infinite: the Infinite is made to blend itself with the Finite, to stand visible, as it were, attainable there."[103] Symbols are subsumed under the general name "clothes." Since they are given such status, Teufelsdröckh, who is a strong advo-

cate of personal freedom, rather annoys the editor by claiming bene-
fit of clergy and right of trial by jury for scarecrows. Though he does
not explain this, it is clear enough that a creature purely of clothes,
like Carlyle's metamorphosed into his book, merits in Carlyle's eyes
this consideration. It is no wonder that the editor at this point loses
his aplomb and imagines that his elaborate archeological investigation of Teufelsdröckh's life may have been a mistake, the true life
of Teufelsdröckh being his book and Teufelsdröckh now apparently
vanished off the face of the earth. If we disregard the editor's coy
speculation that Teufelsdröckh is secluded in England, we can conclude that his only existence is in or as the text, that his presence
there is not a "miraculous" emanation from another world where he
persists as purely unfallen spirit. This eliminates the *throughness* of
the symbolic and maintains the *in-ness*. But Carlyle does not eliminate throughness, and the editor's coy speculation is an oblique insistence on it.

Words, of course, are regarded by Teufelsdröckh as symbols, but
he complains like Faust about words. When he does this, however, he
is speaking of that "small prose domain of Sense" in which words are
employed to make "axioms, and categories, and systems, and aphorisms."[104] The symbol is the opposite of words in this sense, but this
sense is the dominant sense of what language normatively is. Like
others in the symbolist tradition, Carlyle tends to treat symbols as
opposed to language rather than as a kind of language or even fundamental to the nature of language, while ironically meaning the very
opposite. This phenomenon lingers through the history of our subject even in a writer like Cassirer, whose aim is actually to combat it.
Part of the reason for its persistence is that both the rationalist and
empiricist traditions identify the essence of language with representation, signification, or copying of the phenomenal, material, or external worlds (or realities) as posited by these traditions. Fleeing from
these assumptions about the location of reality, opposing theorists
left the term "language" to the opposition, it being attached to the
"finite," and the "other"; then they adopted "silence" and the like to
stand for the inscrutable, which became identified with the "infinite."
Because "language" becomes in this usage representative of but one
dimension of reality—the "empirical"—(being caught on one side of
a negation), the term "symbol" (though clearly there are linguistic
symbols) comes to be the term opposing "language" and then eventually is made to transcend this opposition, gathering both sides into
itself.

Teufelsdröckh's struggle to get at this matter requires the sloughing off of established terms, their redefinitions, and the establishment of an irony confusing to his editor. Thus while he deplores words, he glorifies them when they are symbols. In one of his moods he treats man as a fundamentally naked creature and scandalizes his editor by confessing that he has imagined people in dignified ceremonies as without clothes, implying that he is seeing them in their reality and knows "not whether to laugh or weep." In this mood he sees man as "without vestments, till he beg or steal such, and by forethought sew and button them." He sees something great in the moment "when a man first strips himself of adventitious wrappings; and sees indeed that he is naked. . . ."[105] But this is not by any means the whole Teufelsdröckh, for he also imagines man virtually created by symbols, as in the playful remark about the scarecrow and the following, which the editor regards as frivolous:

> By symbols, accordingly, is man guided and commanded, made happy, made wretched. He everywhere finds himself encompassed with Symbols, recognized as such or not recognized.[106]

And: "It is in and through *Symbols* that man, consciously or unconsciously, lives, works, and has his being."[107] Teufelsdröckh even claims that those ages that prize symbolic worth are the greatest ages, and he obviously equates the drive to symbolize—to clothe—with cultural growth. It is no surprise that the literal-minded editor is confused about the substantiality of clothes.

"In and through": Symbols are clearly of different sorts. To live through symbols (not in the sense in which I previously used the term) would seem to be to use them and perhaps to manipulate them coldly and abstractly. To live *in* symbols would be to have created a coherent structure of culture. This is perhaps connected to the distinction Teufelsdröckh makes between extrinsic and intrinsic symbols, which appears parallel to the familiar romantic one between allegory and symbolism. Extrinsic symbols are arbitrary ones—heraldic coats-of-arms, banners, sectarian costumes, and the like: "They have no intrinsic, necessary divineness, or even worth,"[108] they acquire abstract authority. They are what the general semanticists called symbols, warning against confusing the symbol with the thing itself. This sort of symbol is at the very bottom of Teufelsdröckh's hierarchy. At the top is that sort of symbol in which "the Godlike is manifested to sense," in which "Eternity look[s] , more or less visibly, through the Time-Figure (*Zeitbild*)." These highest symbols are not tropes in discourses but prophetic works of art, to which extrinsic values often add themselves over time. Such symbols correspond to what I have called the "miraculous" and involve throughness in the earlier sense.

In spite of this throughness Teufelsdröckh contributes two particularly interesting things to the notion of a "secular" symbolic. First, he expands the concept of symbolism to suggest that human culture is a symbolic world:

> Society sails through the Infinitude on Cloth, as on a Faust's mantle, or rather like the Sheet of clean and unclean beasts in the Apostle's Dream; and without such Sheet or Mantle, would sink to endless depths, or mount to inane limboes, and in either case be no more.[109]

We live in a "reality" of our own construction. For Teufelsdröckh, culture is itself symbolic. He seems finally to see man unclothed as incomplete, uncreated, only a potentiality. His reality is in the making. Thus reality always includes a humanly made future, which must be purely symbolic, and toward which everything is always directed.

Second, Teufelsdröckh points out that symbols "wax old" and die. Part of this process is the tendency of intrinsic symbols to become extrinsic, or romantic "allegory." They have lives like that of terrestrial garments. In many textbooks of composition today there are sections warning against the use of clichés, which are usually described as metaphors worn out from overuse. This description does not explain how it is that some symbols entirely avoid this fate or achieve rebirth. Teufelsdröckh is aware of the need to make explanation, but may not fully succeed:

> Homer's *Epos* has not ceased to be true; yet it is no longer our Epos, but shines in the distance, if clearer and clearer, yet also smaller and smaller, like a receding Star. It needs a scientific telescope, it needs to be reinterpreted and artificially brought near us, before we can so much as know it *was* a Sun.[110]

By and large, symbolist theory has not quite wanted to face the issue raised here. Perhaps this accounts for the persistence of a mystical element that makes theorists uneasy with a purely "secular" concept of the symbol and turns them to the "miraculous" at the cost of imposing a sort of Platonic stasis on the symbol. Teufelsdröckh does not want to relegate Homer to oblivion, but he has trouble maintaining the dynamism of his theory of symbolic culture and the constant or eternal value of Homer at the same time. His solution is to require the classics to be reinterpreted for modern life, but he seems to mean by this that they should be reinterpreted as documents in the history of symbolic culture, not as living symbols. Yet they are not extrinsic symbols, because they are reinterpreted. This sort of argument is a rationale for the German tradition of *Geistesgeschichte*. At the least, Teufelsdröckh's theory will require an explanation of why it is important to reinterpret, what works deserve reinterpretation and how we are to tell, and why a culture requires a symbolic past.

Up to the establishment of these questions and only a little beyond does Teufelsdröckh take us: "Of this thing, however, be certain: wouldst thou plant for Eternity, then plant into the deep infinite faculties of man, his Fantasy and Heart; wouldst thou plant for Year and Day, then plant into his shallow superficial faculties, his Self-love and Arithmetical Understanding, what will grow there." [111] Here the answer is that at the top of the hierarchical ladder of symbols are the truly lasting works. They have something that maintains the highest level of symbolicity. They apparently are immortal and mean more to succeeding generations than evidence that they *were* suns. But we are proceeding in a tautological circle. Further, either Homer's works are not among these or Teufelsdröckh has contradicted himself. Certainly, while Teufelsdröckh wants to maintain the idea of the true work of art as eternally valuable, he does not really allow for this in his dynamic theory of the birth and aging of symbols. As for providing some criterion by which we can recognize the highest art, to be able to do that would be self-contradictory. To assert that something is a symbol of the highest sort is to declare its inscrutability and singularity. And so we are reduced to tautology and to irony, which pervades the structure of *Sartor Resartus* from the outset. The struggle that goes on between Teufelsdröckh's editor and the text, the questioning of the documents and their meaning, the perplexity of the editor over the elusiveness of Teufelsdröckh's thought: all are an embodiment and symbolization of a curious paradoxical situation in which while we think of clothes as covering us we must also imagine ourselves as our clothes.

For Teufelsdröckh, language seems to be *fundamentally* metaphorical, and as such it partakes of the same paradox mentioned above: it is not merely the clothing of thought but also its body. Carlyle provides in Teufelsdröckh's general remarks the embryo of a theory of language that seems to be lacking in his predecessors. But it is far broader than a theory of language alone, since as a "philosophy of clothes" it encompasses a vast area of symbolism. One can, of course, steal the term "language" and declare that there are other sorts of language than the linguistic, or one can stick with the terminology of Carlyle and declare that there are other systems of symbols than words. In Carlyle the theory of literary symbolism is connected, however loosely, to a general theory of culture, but this theory requires further sophistication before it can return to a literary theory within and consistent with it.

We have noticed a hierarchy in which body is regarded as clothing of spirit and language is the garment of thought:

> . . . however, it should rather be, Language is the Flesh-Garment, the Body of Thought. I said that Imagination wove this Flesh-Garment; and does not she? Metaphors are her stuff: examine Language; what, if you except some few primitive elements (of natural sound); what is it all but Metaphors recognized as such, or no longer recognized? [112]

Like Vico a century before him, Teufelsdröckh concludes that the metaphoric is not a special tropological device or use of language, but the "muscles and tissues and living integuments" of language itself.[113] The *indirectness* of language when symbolic (in Goethe's sense) is paradoxically its metaphorical *directness*. We are able now to note that there was something curious in Goethe's treatment of the symbolic as indirect and the allegorical as direct. One would think that, from the point of view of Goethe and the whole tradition, allegory with its arbitrary relation of sign to object would be considered indirect, while the symbolic, which in Coleridge's words always partakes of what it symbolizes, would be regarded as direct. But the virtues implicit in the word "direct" had long been captive of the rationalists and empiricists, and so "indirect" became the term to oppose the indirect directness of the enemy.

5. The "Hegelian"

The romantic distinction between symbolism and allegory threatens to annihilate itself in a return via the fallen "miraculous" to a form of "religious" allegory or something bordering on it. The form which this circling back takes in Hegel is particularly important because Hegel systematizes so many elements of thought on the subject and stands at a point of culmination. It must first be said that Hegel is well aware of the problems that a mystical or religious *beyond* creates for the artist. The basis of his philosophy, like that of Schelling, is a rejection of the Kantian thing-in-itself as an unknowable *beyond*. For Hegel, Kant is a sort of "Platonic" allegorist with the difference that he refuses to allegorize about the beyond that he posits. The whole noumenal world Hegel seeks to recapture for mind or spirit (as the term "*Geist*" is variously translated). On the other hand, the "external, sensuous, and transitory" world of naïve realism Hegel also obliterates in the activity of spirit. At the beginning of *The Philosophy of Fine Art*, Hegel puts it as follows:

> The world, into the profundity of which thought penetrates, is a supersensuous one, a world which to start with is posited as a Beyond in contrast to the immediacy of ordinary conscious life and present sensation. It is the freedom of reflecting consciousness which disengages itself from this immersion in the "*this side*," or immediacy, in other words sensuous reality and finitude. But the mind is able, too, to heal the *fracture* which is thus created in its progression. From the wealth of its own resources it brings into being the works of fine art as the primary bond of mediation between that which is exclusively external, sensuous and transitory, and medium of pure thought, between Nature and its finite reality, and the infinite freedom of a reason which comprehends.[114]

This statement seems to attack the principle on which romantic allegory is based—a dualism of spirit and matter, noumena and phenomena, idea and appearance. For Hegel there can be no such thing as truth unless it appears. But this act of penetration, as it is called above, is the product of a process that Hegel imagines both historically and dialectically. In history the process is endless, that is, always emergent. Dialectically the process is imagined as a movement from art to religion and finally to philosophy. However, the movement or odyssey of spirit is never seen in terms of some result. Rather, the result is meant to include the process of arriving at it:[115] "The length of the journey has to be borne with, for every moment is necessary."[116] Thus nothing past or passed is obliterated. And the whole or absolute idea "is merely the essential nature reaching its completeness through the process of its own development."[117] Man is fully man only in the form of this movement and progress, "cultivated reason, which has made itself to be what it is implicitly."[118]

There are two common views of whether Hegel has or has not accomplished the annihilation of the dualisms I have mentioned. Stace thinks not: ". . . in spite of his frequent reiteration of the doctrine that thought is all reality, he nevertheless allowed himself to be seduced by a lingering trace of the idea which he had himself explicitly repudiated, that there is some mysterious entity in or behind things in addition to the universals which compose all we know of them."[119] But others take the view of Copleston: ". . . for Hegel the Absolute is not an impenetrable reality existing, as it were, above and behind its determinate manifestations: It *is* its self-manifestation."[120] From this point of view reality is, by paradox, the very process of its own "penetration" (a word I take from the quotation from Hegel above). Both views may be correct, though seeming to disagree. Stace's criticism really suggests that Hegel's language betrays him. Copleston tries to move through the language to Hegel's intention. If we consider the Hegelian movement from symbolic to classic to romantic art, thence to religion and finally to philosophy dialectically rather than historically, the problem Stace mentions is eased. Yet Hegel tempts us to do both, and if we do, the dialectical becomes "Platonized" as a sort of *beyond*. We begin by thinking of art as a mediation between the *beyond* and ordinary consciousness, an opposition to be gradually obliterated as we pass up the dialectic toward the idea and "the infinite freedom of a reason which comprehends." Ordinary consciousness is of a low order, merely the beginning on the path, and the most rudimentary kind of art is a first step. On the other hand, "fine art is not art in the true sense of the term" until it establishes itself in "a sphere which it shares with religion and philosophy."[121] It is, however, only on the edge of the sphere. It is midway, so to speak, between the sensuous and the external on the one hand and the ideality of pure thought on the other; but in art the sensuous is "show" rather than matter:

> . . . though the sensuous *materia* is unquestionably present in a work of art, it is only as surface or *show* of the sensuous that it is under any necessity to appear. In the sensuous appearance of the work of art it is neither the concrete material stuff, the empirically perceived completeness and extension of

the internal organism which is the object of desire, nor is it the universal thought of pure ideality, which in either case the mind seeks for.[122]

Here Hegel's language differs from Goethe's in that there is an identification in Hegel of the concrete and particular with matter, and he sees art as a step toward purging sensuousness of its corporeal grossness while maintaining particularity. The sensuous presence (note the somewhat condescending language below),

> albeit suffered to persist in its sensuousness, is equally entitled to be delivered from the framework of its purely material substance [not abstract matter but matter in something like the Plotinian sense]. Consequently, as compared with the immediately envisaged and incorporated object of Nature, the sensuous presence in the work of art is transmuted to mere semblance or *show*, and the work of art occupies a midway ground, with the directly perceived objective world on one side and the ideality of pure thought on the other. It is not as yet pure thought.[123]

There is something ambiguous about this because it appears that Hegel has made a distinction in kind between materiality and sensuousness as "show," but as we read on we recognize that it is only one of degree. Sensuousness as "show" is still somewhat clogged with matter. Therefore, so, in Hegel's view, must be particularity. It is not surprising that Hegel comes to a declaration of the death of art.

Hegel's desire to spiritualize art to a midway point leads him to declare that true art's sensuosity is limited to the two "theoretical" senses of sight and hearing. This idea is in an adaptation from Schelling's previous distinction between "real" and "ideal" arts. The other senses—smell, taste, and touch—"come into contact with matter simply as such."[124] This distinction among senses has its source in the Kantian treatment of the beautiful as distinct from the agreeable. In Hegel's version, smell, taste, and touch can be agreeable or disagreeable; but there is nothing of spirit or the beautiful in them. Sound and sight are senses separated from matter yet sensuous as well. There is something right about the distinction: Critics have always been wary of treating as artistic or beautiful things whose appeal is to smell, taste, and touch. But there is something unconvincing about Hegel's explanation of the distinction, for sight and sound can be reduced to materiality as easily as the other senses. The true difference lies in the idea that words allow for the presence of purely symbolic mediation, while the other senses do not. It is the element of mediation, in fact, that turns Hegel toward his own form of allegoric.

Hegel is just as interested in indicating the limit of art as he is in its spiritual powers. Art is a means to a higher end than itself (though Hegel also insists that the means is contained by and therefore present in the end). That end is, of course, the idea. Though the whole aim of life is to "render the universality of the notion wholly intelligible," this cannot be done "through the medium of sense."[125] Art achieves a spiritual unity between sense and idea, but this unity is not a perfection or an end, only a bridge for spirit to traverse from matter to idea.

All three of Hegel's types of art are defined in terms of the relation between a sign and a signified. This is the reason that Benedetto Croce, rightly, I think, claims that Hegel begins his thought about art with art already behind him.[126] The first Hegelian type of art is the "symbolic," which is really a form of the "religious" romantic allegory, as I have described it in chapter 1. Hegel says three fundamental things about symbols: (1) "There is no necessary connection between the thing signified and its modus of expression whatever,"[127] when we consider the symbol merely as sign; (2) in an expanded and artistic sense symbols can denote objects that have something of the quality of the signified in them, as for example the fox signifying cunning; (3) however, "though the content which is significant, and the form which is used to typify it in respect to a *single* quality, unite in agreement, none the less the symbolical form must possess at the same time still *other* qualities."[128] Where a lion is made to equal strength or courage one can see that a similarity is located within a difference. There is no complete coalescence of the two terms. One might observe about this that the analogous trope is simile, not metaphor. In such a situation the idea is shown to be fundamentally alien to natural phenomena or matter, and symbolic art performs a mediation in which a forcing of relationships occurs.

Classic art, which marks a step upward, seems to be like the "secular" symbolic, but in the end Hegel's conception of the classical prevents our finally identifying the two. In Hegelian classic art there is the greatest possible appropriateness of sensuous shape to the idea. For Hegel this appropriateness exists only in the human body, "the natural shape appropriate to mind [spirit]."[129] But the "defective excrescences which adhere to it in its purely physical aspect" have to be purged.[130] This sounds rather like the classicism of a Joshua Reynolds, but Hegel does not have in mind Reynolds's "general nature" —itself a combination of "Platonic" and "empirical" concepts. He is interested in concrete spirituality. In classic form art attains the highest excellence of which sensuous embodiment is capable, but it is not the highest excellence of which spirit is capable. The representation of the body, in the words of Byron's First Destiny in *Manfred*, "clogs the ethereal essence."[131] So from this point onward art is striving to escape the limits of art.

At the same time the escape from art is art's apotheosis. Romantic art causes a sundering of the image and that signified by it, but at a new and exalted level far above that of symbolic art, where the signified was mysterious. Classic art was but a moment:

> In the classical type [art] sets up the perfected coalescence of spiritual and sensuous existence as adequate conformation of both. As a matter of fact, however, in this fusion mind itself is not represented agreeably to its *true notional concept*. Mind [spirit] is the infinite subjectivity of the Idea, which as absolute inwardness, is not capable of freely expanding in its entire independence, so long as it remains within the mould of the bodily shape. . . .[132]

But so is art, taken as a whole, only a moment; and romantic art represents a culmination in which art transcends itself and ceases to be art. The human form that Blake calls divine is not so divine after all. Therefore romantic art cancels the completed union of the idea and the body—a union that has therefore been tenuous;[133] and "the new content secured thereby is consequently not indefeasibly bound up with the sensuous presentation, but is rather delivered from this immediate existence, which has to be hypostatized as a negative factor, overcome and reflected back into the spiritual unity."[134]

This is not a return to symbolic art. In symbolic art the spiritual is regarded as an enigma and the perspective toward it is that of matter, which provides the sign of spirit. In classic art the spirit is embodied in the external form most appropriate to it. In romantic art the perspective is that of spirit in the act of overcoming "sensuous externality of form," which is thus represented as "unessential and transient." But it is still represented, for art requires such an "external vehicle of expression."[135] The vehicle most free of externality or matter is sound, the word. Music and poetry are, therefore, the romantic arts, and poetry is the romantic art par excellence because of the greater spirituality of the word:

> For sound, the only remaining external material retained by poetry, is in it no longer the feeling of the sonorous itself [as in music] but is a mere sign without independent significance. And it is, moreover, a sign of idea which has become essentially concrete, and not merely of indefinite feeling and its subtle modes and gradations.[136]

The word always goes out and infuses nature with its spirituality. For Hegel, Adam began this process when he named the beasts, nullifying them as mere beings and turning them into ideal things. Poetry he sees as the "*original* imaginative grasp of truth," but it "fails as yet" to free spirit from matter.[137] It remains attached to the Image. Thus poetry is a threshold art. The poetry of Adam was unintentionally idealizing. Poetry as romantic art is self-conscious and exists in a world where unidealizing prosaic expression already exists to be reckoned with. Poetry is, therefore, now "fully conscious of the sphere from which its task is to detach itself."[138]

Yet for Hegel there is something inadequate about sound itself. It is a materiality which nears ideal purity. Hegel says poetry uses sound *merely* as sign, but this is a straining toward an ideality that poetry cannot reach. The threshold state of poetry as romantic art marks the "disintegration of art itself." Only by turning into religion can art continue the odyssey of spirit toward a knowing which, as Werner Marx has put it, is "not, as in Kant, a giving of form to what was previously formless, but a becoming manifest to itself of the movement of the concept, which, as Logos, rules in everything."[139] In *The Phenomenology of Spirit*, Hegel had remarked:

> ... man's mind [spirit] and interest are so deeply rooted in the earthly that we require a like power to have them raised above that level. His spirit shows such poverty of nature that it seems to long for the mere pitiful feeling of the divine in the abstract, and to get refreshment from that, like a wanderer in the desert craving for the merest mouthful of water.[140]

One would think that a "like power" would be a balancing, contrary power; but Hegel sees the whole movement of humankind, from Adam's naming of the animals, as a process that raises spirit permanently above the earthly. The "like power" becomes the supreme power. Art becomes "a sign-post . . . to that which stands beyond her border."[141] The process is irreversible and upward.

Art fails to satisfy man's highest desires and is therefore part of a hierarchy in which all human activities are placed. When works of art are no longer regarded as divine signs for something greater, man makes ready the disintegration of art itself; this time is upon us:

> We are beyond the stage of reverence for works of art as divine and objects deserving our worship [the surrogate signs of symbolic art]. . . . Art is no longer able to discover that satisfaction of spiritual wants, which previous epochs and nations have sought for in it and exclusively found in it. . . .[142]

Thus art is not to be treated in terms of an end which its own nature defines but in terms of a single ultimate human spiritual desire. It is a moment in an odyssey that ends in the apotheosis of philosophy itself—pure self-thinking thought, absolute spirit.

In this system, it seems to me, Hegel invents a new and special form of romantic "allegory." I have said that Croce argues that Hegel begins his meditation on the phases of spirit at a point where art is already behind him, though he does not recognize this.[143] What Croce is driving at can be seen clearly in Hegel's treatment of language. Hegel believes that language produces "signs," which are arbitrary in their relation to matter and phenomena and thus in his view purely intellectual and universal; Croce writes of Hegel:

> Owing to this logical form, language tries to express the individual, but cannot do so: "you wish to say *this* piece of paper, upon which I am writing, or rather have written—precisely *this*, but you do not say it. What you say is a universal, the *this*."[144]

Thus language cannot embody particulars and always moves to the universal and ultimately to the pure idea. Croce's point about this is that Hegel always abstracts every language act from its context, which is always particular. Though Hegel does on occasion deplore the alienation that this causes, for the most part he sees it as a spiritualization that lifts language by its very nature above art to the realm of the idea. Language is by nature ascetic, since for Hegel sensuousness and spirit are at odds, or rather the sensuous is a low form in the process of spirit. For Croce, language is in essence poetry and the development of artificial prose has not changed this fact. Hegel begins with the "allegoric" idea of the abstracting, idealizing sign, while Croce begins with the concrete particularizing symbol and thus claims to begin with language as poetry.

Hegel's aesthetics marks an escape by art into the ideality of language, but Hegelian ideality robs art of its particularity and thus art is eventually annihilated in its own striving. Hegel's ideality has no place *in the end* for the particular. It is present only as part of the process. But before we place Hegel among the "Platonic" or "religious" allegorists of art, we must remember that for Hegel every moment of the journey is necessary and that the process of the unfolding of the absolute is part of the absolute itself. Thus Hegel seeks to redeem art as a part of the whole, while at the same time moving beyond it. There is nothing like this paradox in either the "Platonic" or the "religious" modes of romantic allegory as I have proposed them.

But Hegel's process is analogous to the process of reading that Coleridge describes in the *Biographia Literaria*, where the journey toward the end of a true poem is *as important as*, indeed, *is* the end of reading. In this matter Hegel adopts the romantic emphasis on process and rejects all dualisms, even as he includes "Platonic" and "religious" outlooks. The "Hegelian" is not romantically allegorical, for the idea is not merely "represented." It is not an other. It is merely not here yet. It is in the making. It is not translatable. But the "Hegelian" is not "miraculous" symbol either, because it does not embody an other. It is not "secular" because it is on the way to completion in the idea. It is a stage in the disclosure of meaning, which is rational and must be regarded as exhausting art, if we could ever get to that point. If we were there, thought would be the beyond achieved, and we would gaze *back* to a totally different sort of beyond—a beyond which *is* where we were and in that sense is a within, a part of where we would be. It would include art. Hegel begins at a center of matter and tries to expand it until matter is totally enclosed first by art, then religion, and ultimately at the circumference philosophy, which can look back into and contain in the idea the form of its own expansiveness. His system, nevertheless, overcomes art with reason and challenges Schelling's conception of art as the actual vehicle of the absolute. Charles Taylor is right in remarking that Hegel "sees conceptual clarity as an achievement, won through the forging of a more and more adequate descriptive language, and the transposition into the clarity of representative thought of insights originally expressed in non-representative consciousness." [145] In this sense, his views and Schelling's negate each other, and we require a contrary.

4

The Blakean Symbolic

I seek the necessary contrary in William Blake's potentially "secular" notion of "vision." "Symbol" or "symbolism" and "myth" are words that never appear in Blake's extant writings, yet Blake has long been regarded as a symbolist and myth-maker—even as the first symbolist—as such appellations have been vaguely and indiscriminately used in modern criticism. I shall make no attempt here to chart the history of the application of these terms to Blake. Instead, I seek to acknowledge the significance of Blake's own statements about "allegory" and "vision" and to discover Blake's contribution to the idea of poetry as a "secular" form of symbolic.

1. ALLEGORY AND VISION

BLAKE'S version of the symbolism-allegory distinction of his time differs semantically from that of all other writers familiar to me. Although its terminology varies through his career, with the term "allegory" being used in different senses, it is static in its fundamental idea. Blake employed the term "allegory" in his writing in four different senses, one honorific, two derogatory, and one neutral. In its single honorific sense, "allegory" is identified with the "sublime" and the "intellectual powers" in the well-known letter to Thomas Butts of 6 July 1803. In that same letter, however, Blake indicates that the value of allegory is lost if it is addressed to the "corporeal understanding": "Allegory address'd to the Intellectual powers, while it is altogether hidden from the Corporeal Understanding, is My Definition of the Most Sublime Poetry."[1] The honorific use of the term is reinforced six years later in the *Descriptive Catalogue*, where, influenced by the syncretic mythographers, Blake refers to the Druidical age as that which turned "allegoric and mental signification into corporeal command."[2] However, Blake's earliest use of the term, in *Europe* (1794), connects allegory derogatorily with abstract generalizing thought. The "allegorical abode where existence hath never come"[3] mentioned in *Europe* is echoed in the distinction Blake later makes in *A Vision of the Last Judgment* (1810) between "Spiritual Mystery," that which is hidden to the corporeal understanding (and is identical to "vision" in his vocabulary) and "Allegoric Fable," which he identifies with the debasement of original vision into the "Druidical" use of poetic figures to stand for abstract ideas: "Let it here be Noted that the Greek Fables originated in Spiritual Mystery & Real Visions, which are lost & clouded in Fable & Allegory, while the Hebrew Bible & the Greek Gospel are Genuine. Preserv'd by the Saviour's Mercy."[4] This attitude is one shared with Vico even down to the exemption of the Bible from the ravages of history. In *Jerusalem* allegory is also identified with the drift toward the privileging of abstract ideas and subsequent Druidic degeneration, which in the inverted vocabulary Blake applies to fallen man is "allegoric generation."[5]

Very late in his life Blake refers ironically to the god of Dr. Thornton's translation of the Lord's Prayer as "only an Allegory of Kings & nothing Else," and he there clearly reasserts a relationship he has often made between allegory and the moral law, which he regards as a product of abstract ideas.[6] This use of "allegory" is the second sense in which its employment is derogatory, but it is really a subclass of the first sense. Both *The Four Zoas* and *Jerusalem* contain such usages. In those poems, "allegory" is coupled with "moral virtue," which in *The Four Zoas* VIIb:24 creates secret lust and in VIII:169 is identified with the tree of the knowledge of good and evil that caused the false idea of sexual morality to develop.[7] In *Jerusalem* allegory is identified with moral restraint (30:18; 85:1; 88:31; 89:5;

89:45) under the domination of the negative, abstractive female will.[8] Blake's fourth usage of the term occurs in *The Everlasting Gospel* and is without any implication of approbation or derogation.[9]

Though Blake contrasts two kinds of allegory in the letter to Butts, he usually opposes allegory to the highly valued "vision," a term he consistently identifies with "imagination" and which maintains a fundamental meaning from as early as 1788, when he uses it in an annotation to Lavater's *Aphorisms*.[10] The first full indication of its importance occurs in Blake's rather angry reply to Dr. Trusler, author of *The Way to Be Rich and Respectable, Hogarth Moralized*, and other works whose titles might well have seemed to Blake affronts to all he stood for. Trusler had been disappointed in a design he had commissioned from Blake and wrote to him, "*Your fancy*, from what I have seen of it, & I have seen variety at Mr. Cumberland's, seems to be in the other world, or the World of Spirits, which accords not with my Intentions, which, whilst living in This World, Wish to follow *the Nature* of it."[11] Nothing could have irritated Blake more than Trusler's dualistic assumption that Blake's fancy took him out of this world, indeed that the world of spirit negated the body. Blake held as a fundamental tenet of his whole existence and activity that there might be levels of vision, but there was only one reality. The visionary knows that reality in its fullness, the "eternal now," as he calls the object of vision in his annotation to Lavater, by looking with his mind through the senses:

I feel that a Man may be happy in This World. And I know that This World Is a World of imagination & Vision. I see Every thing I paint In This World, but Every body does not see alike. To the Eyes of a Miser a Guinea is more beautiful than the Sun, & a bag worn with the use of money has more beautiful proportions than a Vine filled with Grapes. The tree which moves some to tears of joy is in the Eyes of others only a Green thing that stands in the way. Some See Nature all Ridicule & Deformity & by these I shall not regulate my proportions; Some scarce see Nature at all. But to the Eyes of the Man of Imagination, Nature is Imagination itself. As a man is, So he Sees. As the Eye is formed, such are its Powers. You certainly Mistake, when you say that the Visions of Fancy are not to be found in The World. To Me This World is all One continued Vision of Fancy or Imagination.[12]

In Blake's vocabulary there is not the Coleridgean distinction between imagination and fancy, but the latter term in Coleridge is very
like Blake's "allegory" in its derogatory sense.

Blake makes clear that to claim *this* world to be a world of vision
is to create an art that will be difficult for the abstractionist to grasp:

> You say that I want somebody to Elucidate my Ideas. But you
> ought to know that What is Grand is necessarily obscure to
> Weak men. That which can be made Explicit to the Idiot is
> not worth my care. The wisest of the Ancients consider'd
> what is not too Explicit as the fittest for Instruction, because
> it rouzes the faculties to act.[13]

Edward B. Hungerford claims Blake to have been in sympathy with
those he calls the "symbolists among the mythographers," i.e., allegorists, but in fact Blake does not accept the dualistic and/or mystic
premises of those interpreters of myth.[14] He goes along with them as
far as to say that the Greek fables as we now know them originated
in but are now corruptions of "spiritual mystery," but he does
not mean by this that "spiritual mystery" originally veiled abstract
ideas.[15] For Blake, Greek and Roman myths have become allegorical,
but they were not debasements of original abstract philosophy or
corruptions of history. They were debasements of original "vision."
It is true that Blake usually identifies "mystery" derogatorily with
"moral virtue" and allegoric abstraction, but here it is clear enough
that "spiritual mystery" is meant to be that which is hidden to "corporeal understanding." He is defending a vision that is expressed in
what he calls elsewhere his "primitive & original ways of Execution."[16] It is not even that the world of spirit is immanent in nature.
Blake does not employ the word "nature" in a sense interchangeable
with "spirit" or "vision." "Nature" he usually identifies with the material world of the Lockean primary qualities of experience. Blake
tries to establish a contrary to the Lockean distinction between primary and secondary qualities. "Nature" in this sense is an abstract,
dead, unreal, "allegoric" concept of the "corporeal understanding."[17]
Thus "corporeal" has the ironic upside-down meaning of abstract
bodiless nothingness, rather than the particularity characteristic of
the objects of vision. Such particularity is the truly infinite, because
not objectively measurable. Blake speaks in an early, happier letter to
Trusler of "Infinite Particulars," a paradox from the point of view of

the "corporeal understanding."[18] Infinitude, like God, is always particular and present. The imagination does not dwell in vagueness or effluvium, but instead has a "clear idea, and a determinate vision of things."[19] The "corporeal understanding," which is immersed in the concept of abstract primary matter, exists in what Blake's Los calls

> No Human Form but only a Fibrous Vegetation,
> A Polypus of soft affections without Thought or Vision.[20]

Against this is put "every Space larger than a red Globule of Man's blood," which is "visionary."[21] Visions are not "cloudy vapour" but "organized and minutely articulated." The prophets of the Bible saw what they saw distinctly and in this world.[22] The poetic logic of metaphor, being the earliest speech, is the visionary way of expressing directly (indirectly only to the corporeal understanding) one's vision.

Blake's emphasis on bounding line, minute particularity, the definite and the determinate in his annotations to Sir Joshua Reynolds's *Discourses* does not, therefore, have to do only with artistic technique, which he refuses to think of in isolation, but with vision and expression as a single act of the mind: "Invention depends Altogether upon Execution."[23] Art is not a matter of generalizing from a previous experience and then expressing that generalization in an artistic medium:

> I have heard many People say, "Give me the Ideas. It is no matter what Words you put them into," & others say, "Give me the Design, it is no matter for the Execution." These people know enough of Artifice, but Nothing of Art. Ideas cannot be Given but in their Minutely Appropriate Words, nor can a design be made without its minutely Appropriate Execution.[24]

When Reynolds questions whether we should understand literally certain "metaphors or ideas expressed in poetical language," Blake is quick to pounce upon his language, identifying vision and imagination with the literality of metaphor, by which he means that there is a language of art, which is the true human language, and that such language does not require interpretation in the direction of abstract generality in order that it may be grasped (not "understood").[25] This "primitive and original way" of thought is the way of the "imaginative universal," rather than the abstract universal, into which Blake thinks Reynolds wants to turn all painting. Reynolds has written, ". . . it is from a reiterated experience, and a close comparison of the objects in nature, that an artist becomes possessed of the idea of that central form, if I may so express it, from which every deviation is deformity" and ". . . in each of these classes there is one common idea and central form, which is the abstract of the various individual forms belonging to that class."[26] For Reynolds this is what the artist searches out, reducing "the variety of nature to the abstract idea."[27]

"What Folly," remarks Blake in response to this last remark,[28] and to the first he says,

> One Central Form composed of all other Forms being Granted, it does not therefore follow that all other forms are Deformity. All Forms are Perfect in the Poet's Mind, but these are not Abstracted nor Compounded from Nature, but are from Imagination.[29]

For Blake to speak of a class is to speak of an imaginative, not an abstract, universal: "every class is individual."[30] Blake, therefore, treats Chaucer's Canterbury pilgrims not as romantic allegorical abstractions but as individual poetic class concepts.[31] By the same token, when Berkeley writes in *Siris*, "Plato and Aristotle considered God as abstracted or distinct from the natural world. But the Aegyptians considered God and nature as making one whole, or all things together as making one universe," Blake remarks, "They also considered God as abstracted or distinct from the Imaginative World, but Jesus, as also Abraham & David, consider'd God as a Man in the Spiritual or Imaginative Vision."[32] Blake's difference from Hegel with respect to the notion of particulars should be noted here, because it is a diametrical opposition. For Hegel, as Charles Taylor puts it, ". . . the particular and its affirmation is the essence of evil, for it is that which cuts men off from the universal."[33]

Blake does not relegate the logic of vision to a bygone age but insists on its presence as the fundamental way to know in any age. Though he also utters a myth of the decline of visionary power under the domination of abstract thought, he uses that myth to declare that through the practice of art the Golden Age, by which he means the habit of vision in a people, can be created.[34] By the same token he does not locate the Fall in an alien past or the Last Judgment in the future. Both are potential in any moment and present to a reading of the Bible.

2. MYTH AND ANTIMYTH

WE SAW in the first chapter a passage from *The Marriage of Heaven and Hell* where Blake offers a fictive history of how poetic vision became reduced to abstract moral code and, as a result, ". . . man forgot that All deities reside in the human breast."[35] That phrase offers a picture of the prelapsarian condition, for the version of dissociation of sensibility he offers in *The Marriage* and the Fall are identical. Human consciousness was, or properly is, to use Blake's characteristic terms, the "circumference" of experience or reality rather than its "center." One human breast properly contains the Gods, who always should be, according to Blake, the servants of Man. The senses existed originally in an "enlarged" state and contained the world. This gathering in of experience was not contradicted by the first poets when they named and composed. Indeed, their activity, which we take to have been the creation of language, was the means by which "vision," as we now understand it, was established. Given Blake's emphasis on creativity, the statement about this at the beginning of the passage is put rather curiously, however: "The ancient Poets animated all sensible objects with Gods or Geniuses. . . ." Were the "sensible objects" existent previous to their animation by the poets? Only, I think, as potential possibilities of vision. Blake did not intend us to imagine men, at that critical moment of the invention of language, originally confronting real inanimate sensible objects. Rather, he intended the poets by the constitutive power of language—namely metaphor—to have *created* those objects in the way a circumferential power gives life—by anthropomorphizing them. It is in words that the "calling" and the "adorning" mentioned in the passage from *The Marriage* must continually take place. The enlargement of the senses and their increased number are sustained by these acts of "calling" and "adorning." The additional senses, lost in the fallen state, can be described collectively as constitutive power, or what I shall call "myth," as against a notion of passive reception of subsequently named sense data, or what I shall call "antimyth."

As the poets built language, regarded as fundamentally metaphoric, the world became realizable in words: "Till a system was formed, which some took advantage of." That brought the dissociation, for, as Blake says, "some took advantage" of what the "system" formed from myth provided. To take advantage of something is to externalize it (to make it an "it,"), or in Blake's terms, to retreat to what he calls the "selfish center" from an imaginative circumference that holds everything together. This thrusts everything outside and turns the outside into inanimate or "sensible" objects, abstracted from their "mental deities," which are relegated at this point to subjective illusions and arbitrary signs by the dominating epistemology of subject/object. The object is *before* the word, the world *before* language, both temporally and epistemologically. Object negates subject. To put it another way, the poetic verbal universe is destroyed by a competing idea of language that claims for language only the power to point outward toward *things* beyond which lies nothing; or only the power to point outward toward *things* which stand "Platonically" or "religiously" for an order of ideas or mysterious beings disembodied behind the veil of those things. With language no longer containing reality in mythic form but only *pointing toward* an alien reality, a mediating or interpreting force is required, namely what Blake calls a "priesthood," to rationalize the mysteries of this "allegoric" separateness. Now what we have here are two fundamentally opposed views of language. In that of Blake's "ancient poets," metaphor is absolutely fundamental, not merely a collection of tropes or devices added on to an assertion that points outward from itself. Trope as device is all that is left of the synthetic and myth-making powers of language after it has been redefined by priestly practice.

The difference is that between what Blake once called "allegory addressed to the intellectual powers," but usually "vision," and allegory which is available to the "corporeal understanding." Both are forms of language, the former that of the poets, the latter that of the priesthood, the former mythical, the latter antimythical. But it is important to notice that the priesthood came after the poets and chose "forms of worship from poetic tales." The original mode of language was poetic, and the whole process of externalizing language was built outward from that original mode. Poetry and myth, regarded as a way of knowing, preceded religion, if one thinks of religion as a system of rational interpretation leading to a system of beliefs, to which are attached codes of behavior. Inasmuch as Blake's archetypal priest Urizen is also his archetypal scientist, it would appear that for Blake myth precedes science in the same way. But the main implication is that we are talking about language. To what extent is the world that Blake talks about a linguistic world or "secularly" symbolic?

Before proceeding to that question I return to a previous one answered arbitrarily and only provisionally for the sake of launching the inquiry: Were the sensible objects Blake mentions in the passage existent previous to their animation by the poets? Or is Blake for the sake of rhetoric simply acceding to our deeply ingrained antimythical habits of externalization or *pointing to* in order to get *his* argument going? This is like asking what the original Edenic condition was in Blake's mythology. But that mythology does not allow us to locate Eden by pointing outward and back to it, locating it at the beginning of a linear stretch of external time. Blake's mythology is mythical, and we should not choose forms of externality from poetic tales. If we stick as closely as possible to Blake's terms, we can avoid externalizing. There is some help here in the story of the shapeless, bodiless form of Urizen—the nonentity that Los must in some way constitute; there is the sleeping body of the world-giant Albion, whose unorganized dreaming state is, as an alien history, the substance that must be transformed into the living vision. Both of these figures seem to imply the possibility of a living, human, unified world, adornable with the "properties of woods, rivers, mountains, lakes, cities, nations"—in other words, subject to, indeed requiring, the process of poetic naming. These horrific sleepers in Blake are the *potentiality* of imaginative creation. As potentiality they are not in time and history; neither are they matter that is *there* for the poets to confront as such. They are sheer possibilities of the imagination. Existence can be said to have its beginning in their mythical apprehension.[36] Another part of *The Marriage of Heaven and Hell* throws some light on this and suggests how language acts as a creative force and dynamic container of reality. In one of his "Memorable Fancies" Blake describes a printing house in Hell where "lions of flaming fire" melt metals into living fluid, passing the fluid to "unnamed forms" who cast the metals into the expanse, there to be received by men in the shape of books arranged in libraries.[37] This, according to Blake, is how knowledge is transmitted from generation to generation. The body of earth—the mass of potential reality—is turned to flux, and then, in naming, it is formed linguistically. As a result, history becomes not simply an outward objective linear arrangement of events to which words arbitrarily refer but is embodied as the presentness of words. The past comes into the present—belongs to it—because the only place that we can find it is in its construction in words, present to our reading. This may clear up the apparent oddity of Blake's method of drawing the "visionary" heads of historical personages, for he declared that they were actually present to him as he drew them. Without resort to theories of ghosts or madness, one can argue that Blake believed he was bringing these people to presentness in his paintings—by painting them as he *sees* (*in* his mind and *through* his eyes)[38] them according to their presentness in the words of history books.

The Marriage suggests an idea of culture as embodied in words and, perhaps, an idea of history as more real when located *in* or *as* a verbal structure than externalized, distanced, and objectified as a past. Indeed, the latter is quite impossible without making a verbal structure indulging the perfectly acceptable antimythical fiction of pastness, which in turn becomes itself a presence. Blake's idea of verbal presence, the only real existence of the past, he no doubt took from his reading of the Bible. Blake interprets Jesus' second coming as His continual presence in the presence of the book itself. Blake has nothing good to say about the historical or so-called past Jesus, who is the supreme form of Antichrist. He is "outward Ceremony,"[39] meaningless ritualized behavior that mindlessly copies or points out and backward to an historically lost and forgotten or only vaguely remembered event, memory always being identified with corruption of the truth. The opposite of this would be a shaped imaginative form, living in the immediate present, like the Bible and what it contains.

But of course it would have to have been shaped. When it is shaped we do it the honor of referring to its events in the present tense. We can say that Jesus *comes*. To treat the matter otherwise is to externalize the events from the words and tacitly admit that the words don't contain and shape but only point to—in this case point *back to*—a lost past. So we may argue that when we talk of a verbal universe made by the ancient poets there is no point in referring to a *before* external to it that they transformed into a present. Blake, facing what he will later call the "stubborn structure of the language," was merely acceding to our manner of speaking. The passage from *Jerusalem* in which he uses the phrase "stubborn structure" shows that we can apply our concept of *potentiality* to language itself, which the poet faces and must shape and, in the sense that the poet works in history, must reshape constantly, since it tends to harden and die into "allegory." The phrase I have mentioned appears in Plate 40 [36] of *Jerusalem* as a parenthetical statement by the author himself and suggests what Los's supreme task is:

(I call them by their English names: English, the rough basement.
Los built the stubborn structure of language acting against
Albion's melancholy, who must else have been a Dumb despair.)[40]

By "them" Blake refers to the cities of England, who have become in the poem part of an elaborate parallel-identity with the tribes of Isreal. Blake has already told us in *Milton* that he will not let his sword sleep in his hand until Jerusalem has been built in England, and his poem *Jerusalem* is a plan for that building—the establishment of an identity in the time and space of "poetic logic" between holy Jerusalem and resurrected London. At this point in the poem he calls his cities by their English names; he shapes the biblical vision into the English tongue. Language is the fundamental form of constituting reality mythically, and the mythic form is fundamental to the antimythical, which grows from it. It stands like Los at the base of culture. Los is described here as the archetype of the ancient poets. It is he who actually makes and remakes language as a receptacle for culture. This act constantly provides the sleeping giant Albion with the power of speech, of awakening, of shaping his nightmare world of flux and disorder into a reality. No longer will he be surrounded like a dumb beast by a buzzing confusion, which he has allowed to grow up "around" him by his inarticulateness, his tropological poverty, his delusion that his language only points to things, his succumbing to the powers of the cultural antimyth of subject and object and which Blake identifies with the "allegoric" mind. Antimyth I derive as a term from the parallel concept of Antichrist as Blake would see it. Antichrist, as I have already remarked, is the historicized or objectified and distanced Jesus.

The linguistic structure or creation of the ancient poet Los is "stubborn," and the word is harsh enough to make us query it. Freed as we now should be from the need to address ourselves to the problems of beginnings, we can see that in the myth, where to query beginnings is pointless, Los's activity is really continuous, ever-present, or eternal in the moment. The stubbornness of the structure is twofold: From the "allegoric" point of view, language has the capacity to resist the stasis reason desires and stubbornly frustrates those who—like Urizen, Satan, and the "priesthood"—would choose to abstract a single form of worship from it (try to reduce it to a system pointing outward only to that one form—the clock world of deism or the ideal world of Platonism). This capacity to resist is its mythical, Los-like structure. On the other hand, language resists stasis only as a result of the struggle that Los has with its equally dangerous (from the poet's point of view) but necessary antimythical susceptibility to externalization and hardening. Its stubbornness, then, can point either way.

What Blake calls in the prophetic books Golgonooza is, in one of its aspects and perhaps in its primary aspect, the city of verbal form, the "stubborn structure" itself. As it is built by Los, so does it also fall by dint of those who abstract forms of worship from it, continually exhausting its possibilities in externalization and use. As a result, Los has to be at work continually.

> Here, on the banks of the Thames, Los builded Golgonooza,
> Outside of the Gates of the Human Heart beneath Beulah
> In the midst of the rocks of the Altars of Albion. In fears
> He builded it, in rage & in fury. It is the Spiritual Fourfold
> London, continually building & continually decaying desolate.[41]

The work is always accomplished in the midst of the ruins that are continually made of it. In my own "allegoric" or priestly reading of the passage above, the rocks are matter or Lockean substance that is made from language by forms of verbal externalization. The altars are the forms of worship abstracted from mythical thinking or "poetic logic" by a priesthood. The process is eternal—timeless because internalized and thus lifted from linear, measurable time, endless when seen in time because of the constant need to refurbish the mythico-linguistic structure as it is plundered by those who use it to their selfish purposes. The structure must remain dynamic. It is, as Blake tells us, a "terrible eternal labor."[42]

The labor is the eternal recreation of the act that Blake attributes in *The Marriage* originally to the "ancient poets." Since *The Marriage* is present to us, however, it is more appropriate to say that the act is not a *recreation of* but is *identical to* the act of the poets. Seen cyclically, Los's work as the builder of language is a "striving with Systems to deliver Individuals from those Systems."[43] As the system that was formed from language (a mythology) is taken advantage of and corrupted into externality, or, in other Blakean terms, becomes the spectre of its original self, Los's eternal act of building the "stubborn structure of the language" can be seen as a struggle with a spectral or "allegoric" system grown like a "polypus" upon his original system (original not in the historical sense but in the sense that his system represents the fundamental nature of language—its mythical nature). Thus, Los is engaged in a struggle with his spectre—language converted to "allegory" or antimyth. Confronted by the deterioration or purposive plundering of his system into an opposing system, he

. . . stands in London building Golgonooza,
Compelling his Spectre to labours mighty; trembling in fear
The Spectre weeps, but Los unmov'd by tears or threats remains.
"I must Create a System or be enslav'd by another Man's,
I will not Reason & Compare; my business is to Create."[44]

Like those in *The Marriage* who work with molten metal to make books, Los, who is a blacksmith, uses ladles of ore, shaping potentiality into the spiritual sword.

I have argued against the idea that the "ancient poets" confronted an originally spectral situation. Los, when viewed in history, however, seems to be in a more embattled position. Thus, in spite of my argument from one point of view—the mythic—that the action of Los is not recreation in time but original creation, I must from another point of view—that of externality or "fall" and, ironically enough, of critical interpretation—claim that Los, as the creative spirit of time, the container and maker of significant time, does have to rebuild a stubborn structure that is always turning by deterioration into its spectral negation and threatening to surround him in the form of determining history. The spectral negative stubbornness of language is for Los and for Blake the tendency of language toward generalization, abstraction, and dead trope:

. . . it is the Reasoning Power,
An Abstract objecting power that Negatives every thing.
This is the Spectre of man. . . .[45]

One of Los's duties is to try to turn a negative relationship into a true contrariety. What we have regarded as cyclical and yet without external temporal beginning we shall consider provisionally as a dialectical contrariety between opposed linguistic tendencies. One is the purely prolific tendency of the free myth-making imagination and the other the devouring tendency of the externalizing, purposive, object-making and thus also subject-making, "allegoric," "antimythical" rationality: I have already mentioned Blake's notion of "prolific" and "devourer." The devourer attempts to ingest the myth-making power of language. But, in the process, that power can only turn into its opposite, because the devourer is a machine for externalizing. For the devourer to take something inside is really for him to externalize it at once in the form of the "antimyth" of subject and object. The devourer can never be at the circumference of his thought, but only at the center, no matter how much he devours, for devouring is using and to use is to externalize. Ultimately, however, the devourer is at the circumference of a kind of myth of his own, but actually what I shall call an antimythical fiction that insists paradoxically on placing him at the center of experience and surrounding him with infinite space and time. If he does not appreciate the powerful irony of this situation and bring in the contrary, he is in trouble. Thus the curious difficulties Urizen has in finding a place to stand in *The Four Zoas* and his inability to attain to a circumference. He does not grasp that his antimyth is a created fictive form. He makes it surround and determine him as a fixed "reality."

I pause now in the argument to expand a point made in passing. In measurable or externalized time, Los would seem to be condemned to a Sisyphus-like existence, building language as myth only to see it deteriorate, and then building it again. This surely sounds as if it were Hell, and it would be Hell if Los lived only in the externalized time that is antimyth to his myth. Instead, he lives in prolific work, where every moment is imaginatively created. To put it more accurately, time and the unfallen counterpart of Hell are *in him*— the area of human energy out of which come Blake's famous proverbs. It is not too much to say that this energy is artistic shaping in a language, whether of words or lines or musical forms, that this unfallen Hell at the bottom of the world (the strong legs and feet of unfallen man) is an unremitting source of the symbolic. The work done here—in the mines and at the forge—is not easy, for it is accomplished against the pressure of antimyth. From the mythic point of view, antimyth obfuscates particular reality with generality and primary, abstract nothingness. The following passage declares the radical creativity of the imagination:

> Some Sons of Los surround the Passions with porches of iron & silver,
> Creating form & beauty around the dark regions of sorrow,
> Giving to airy nothing a name and a habitation
> Delightful, with bounds to the Infinite putting off the Indefinite
> Into most holy forms of Thought; such is the power of inspiration
> They labour incessant with many tears & afflictions,
> Creating the beautiful House for the piteous sufferer.[46]

The porches are the forms taken by the metals of the "memorable fancy" I have already examined, mythico-linguistic shapings from crude potentiality. The "regions of sorrow" or fallen Hell—unshaped because symbolically uncontained and therefore rampant spectral anxieties—are made part of, enter into, a larger containing form. The House of Albion is a house of cultural myth that shapes his acts:

> Others Cabinets richly fabricate of gold & ivory
> For Doubts & fears unform'd and wretched & melancholy.[47]

The passage I have quoted from *Milton* ends with a description of the artist:

> Antamon takes them [the spectres] into his beautiful flexible
>   hands:
> As the Sower takes the seed or as the Artist his clay
> Or fine wax, to mould artful a model for golden ornaments.[48]

Blake is very critical of antimyth: his own age has come to be so dominated by it that people tend to think only in its terms, which are for Blake the terms of Bacon, Newton, and Locke. It has tended, in its cultural domination, to render myth trivial or material for psychoanalysis by accusing it of subjectivity while reserving objectivity for itself. When antimyth negates myth in this way Blake is prone to call it simply "error," the completion of the Fall in opacity and contraction—Newton's trumpet blast.[49] Everything is reduced thereby to Lockean material substance or the nothingness of the abstract. The antimyth comes to be regarded as the source of the single vision of truth and reality, but Blake always insists that this vision (or from Blake's point of view "allegory") is a human construction like myth; indeed, it is built like an antitype or fallen analogy on (or, to be consistent, underneath) the very same mythic structures that it relegates to subjectivity—poetry and the other arts. It is unimaginable without the work of those original ancient poets who established the world of vision.

Therefore, both myth and antimyth are, as I apply the terms to Blake, modes of imaginative construction that result in what may be called fictions. The antimyth creates the fiction of the subject-object split and proceeds to divide everything by analysis into smaller and smaller units, thus draining substance of life, freedom, and will. Blake opposes the dominance of antimyth in his time by giving myth the fictive historical primacy we noted in *The Marriage of Heaven and Hell*. He also gives it a formal primacy by considering it to be the fundamental mode of imaginative construction. It puts together or provides, and antimyth takes apart or devours. Because both are modes of activity and not themselves copies of anything, the question of which has truth or correspondence to reality is not a possible question; indeed, the question is merely a reflection of a category, to borrow Kant's term, of the antimythic mode, and is meaningful only within its terms.

Blake's insistence on the historical and formal primacy of myth suggests that without myth, antimyth starves. In this sense, myth potentially contains antimyth (as the seed does the plant): antimyth can never contain myth, though it is engaged in a constant effort to devour it. Its own tendency to externalize everything prevents its self-completion and its victory.

Art, the creator of the fiction of myth and the prolific to the antimyth's devourer, the seed of thought, becomes for Blake the contrary of everything that operates by abstraction toward law—not just science but religion and, to some extent history, when history rises up the scale of abstraction to form a deterministic outlook. But art, as the fundamental activity of making languages, is also the source upon which all of these modes feed, distorting the source and requiring its rebirth in the process.

3. *JERUSALEM*, PLATE 98

IN THE 98th plate of *Jerusalem* the four Zoas, who comprise Albion, are revealed in what we must take to be the ultimate act of prolific work, the making of reality in the languages of man:

> And they conversed together in Visionary forms dramatic which
>   bright
> Redounded from their Tongues in thunderous majesty, in Visions
> In new Expanses, creating exemplars of Memory and of Intellect,
> Creating Space, Creating Time, according to the wonders Divine
> Of Human Imagination throughout all the Three Regions immense
> Of Childhood, Manhood & Old Age; & the all tremendous
>   unfathomable Non Ens
> Of Death was seen in regenerations terrific or complacent, varying
> According to the subject of discourse; & every Word & Every
>   Character
> was Human. . . .[50]

We realize here that apocalypse is not the *completion* of work in any temporal sense but the *doing* of work under the right conditions, and that it is a "secular" event always potentially present. These conditions are those of true contrariety—the "war and hunting" of heaven—in which real work is the constant building of languages, contrary to language's own tendency to decay. Languages contain in themselves space, time, history, science, and art. Languages are the human forms or circumferences of reality.

One of the aspects of the Fall was that words became separated from their humanity, and the covenants of Jehovah became abstract, tyrannical moral codes: "allegory" replaced humane vision. In the 98th plate this is rectified, for Blake there sees:

> the Words of the Mutual Covenant Divine
> On Chariots of gold & jewels, with Living Creatures, starry &
>   flaming,
> With every Colour, Lion, Tiger, Horse, Elephant, Eagle, Dove, Fly,
>   Worm
> And the all wondrous Serpent clothed in gems & rich array,
>   Humanize
> In the Forgiveness of Sins.[51]

Forgiveness of sins, the true Christianity, is the effective abolition of abstract, external moral law in which the word has become arbitrary and detached from humanity.

As the poem ends Blake discovers the name of the Emanation of all human forms—the name of all that Man loves and desires, the *completion* in vision of all that man with language can do—the imaginable world named Jerusalem. Named, it becomes a possibility.

In a sense then, though Blake's poem ends, it contains not an end but keeps reasserting its beginning, and the poem as a whole is work being done. It shows us the "reprobate" contrary quality of language, seeking to constitute at every moment the system that according to *The Marriage of Heaven and Hell* "some took advantage of." Blake's poem is the prolific that provides food for the twentieth-century literary theorist to devour—but to devour gently and always with a measure of regret—in order to externalize the critical doctrine of the "secular" symbolic, by which that theorist then interprets Blake.

Blake's "secular" view suggests that we create symbolic worlds, and that these are for all practical purposes the only worlds we have. What we have made them makes us what we are. We can only make a world with a language, indeed *in* a language. Practically speaking, there is nothing imaginable independent of a medium to imagine *in*.

Our languages constantly die into use and must be reborn. Further, each language has its own limits and requires its opposite. Blake's vision of all language was that myth precedes science and reason, that the latter feeds on the former. But he also believed that in his time the devourer's language had so dominated reality in the form of "Single vision & Newton's sleep"[52] that civilization itself was in danger unless the contrary mythic language of poetry and art rose to the challenge of spiritual warfare. Fully antimythical language—always only an ideal of symbolic logic—is the contrary that must be reshaped back into its opposite, but only in order that the devourer may consume that opposite once again in prolific use. This is the "fitness and order" Blake sought; the vision of it leads to his remark: "What is the Life of Man but Art & Science?"[53]

5

Symbolist Symbolism

The notion of the literary symbolic is, of course, popularly associated with the French *symboliste* movement, which is frequently regarded as a culmination in synthesis of previous romantic thought about the symbol. At the center of the movement are the struggles of Charles Baudelaire and Stéphane Mallarmé to establish their symbolist theories in the face of a hostile positivism.[1] At the side are the many lesser theorists, who return to notions of allegory or subjective obscurity.[2] This chapter studies the theoretical efforts of Baudelaire and Mallarmé, concluding with a glance at the symbolist ideas of the early Yeats and Oscar Wilde.[3] The chapter is one of a series on which I now embark to ascertain how far toward and how far short of a workable notion of secular symbolic certain groups of influential theorists have managed to come. I am interested in positive achievements but also in ascertaining and pointing out blind alleys that these theorists may have taken, for contemporary theorists wearing bright new terminologies still tend to be lured down them. Thus at the end of each of the next several chapters

I shall seem to have located an impasse as well, perhaps, as a road onward.

1. Baudelaire, Mallarmé, and the book

THE OLD idea of nature as book and of the Bible as word and reality rolled into one—as a sort of supreme nature—we found to be taken up by Coleridge in *The Statesman's Manual*. An idea with some connection to it is expressed by Baudelaire and developed further with subtlety, but also toward extremity, by Mallarmé. Baudelaire took his cue as early as 1846 from a remark by the painter Delacroix, who called nature a "vast dictionary."[4] Delacroix's idea struck Baudelaire strongly enough that he mentioned it again in "The Salon of 1859" in a discourse on the nature of the imagination: "'Nature is but a dictionary,' he [Delacroix] kept on repeating."[5] Baudelaire proceeded to list the usages to which a dictionary can be put—the discovery of meanings, genealogy, and etymology. However, although a dictionary is a book,

> no one has ever thought of his dictionary as a composition, in the poetic sense of the word. Painters who are obedient to the imagination seek in their dictionary for the elements which suit with their conception; in adjusting those elements, however, with more or less of art, they confer upon them a totally new physiognomy. But those who have no imagination just copy the dictionary.[6]

Baudelaire accuses such painters of banality and of failure to feel and to think.

This idea of the painter as creating a composition from the disordered or arbitrarily ordered dictionary of nature raises some interesting issues if the metaphor is pushed a bit further. It gives great authority to the artist as the shaper of life, but it also raises the question of from what the dictionary was compiled, since a dictionary does not come into being out of nothing. After all, a dictionary is based upon an existent language. It is an arbitrary, mechanical, alphabetical ordering of that language. Baudelaire does not explicitly say this, but in his notes for an article on realism he does jot down the phrase: "This world, a dictionary of hieroglyphics."[7] He implies here the existence of *another* world and makes our own world a dictionary derived from it. The other world would seem to be a completely unified and harmonious text (a term I shall query shortly), like what we think of as the perfect work of art; nature, or this world, would be abstracted from it and disordered into the arbitrary, mechanical "order" of a dictionary, whose terms point allegorically to their referents in the other world. The metaphor leads us to Baudelaire's theory of "correspondences," which I shall examine shortly, and eventually returns us to his use of the term "imagination." It is worthwhile noting, however, that although Baudelaire is fond of the image of the dictionary, he elaborates his idea with other images, perhaps recognizing its limitation after all:

> The whole visible universe is but a storehouse of images and signs to which the imagination will give a relative place and value; it is a sort of pasture which the imagination must digest and transform. All the faculties of the human soul must be subordinated to the imagination, which puts them in requisition all at once.[8]

I shall return to Baudelaire on the imagination. Here it is worthwhile to note that even in the metaphor of the storehouse the phrase "images and signs" presumably refers to an invisible other universe, and the imagination's need is to turn via an appropriate ordering of those signs to an apprehension of the invisible referent. The image of the pasture does not have this implication, but it is proffered more tentatively than that of the book or storehouse and is left undeveloped except as an illustration of how the material of the imagination is thoroughly reworked. Unfortunately, the image cannot be carried very far without the whole matter of digestion and defecation hopelessly complicating it and threatening to reduce it to absurdity.

It appears that Baudelaire's image of the dictionary of nature implies that the imagination of the artist reorders something that has been disordered by the arbitrary alphabetizing of its parts. Baudelaire is, of course, discussing painters, not poets, in his "Salons," so he is not implying that nature is literally composed of words from A to Z, or that the other, "real" world is a world of words. He is not here speaking of verbal texts. He seems to be implying the existence of nature as some sort of manifold of sensation, but since the "dictionary," disordered in one sense, is ordered in another, perhaps it might be possible to say that it is the world as mechanically ordered (as a dictionary is), the world created by eighteenth-century empiricism and nineteenth-century positivism. Nor does he deal at all with the relation of the artist's medium to the dictionary. He seems to be thinking about the artist's mental activity as separate from the medium in which he works, the mind as ordering the materials of the dictionary and then expressing that order in a medium. One could look further at the whole question of poem-nature-hidden referent and consider the possibility that for Baudelaire everything is a "text" to be "read" but not all texts are verbal—and the ultimate text never is. Coleridge sought to emphasize the *word* as ultimate source. In Baudelaire the ultimate text seems to be a nonverbal mystical source—a true silence, except that for Baudelaire silent things other than words do speak. This view of Baudelaire's thought must not be overstated, because he frequently plays on the edge of the idea of a verbal source, one that the poet creates rather than one to which he refers. But in the end the balance seems to be tipped toward a theory of "religious" allegory: Nature is a dictionary of a nonverbal text. This text the poet has to reconstruct with verbal signifiers.

Mallarmé goes further. He invents a famous phrase, which one imagines must have been influenced by Baudelaire, and he repeats it in various contexts. It is reported tantalizingly but not developed by Jules Huret in an 1891 interview now treated as part of the Mallarmé canon: "In the end, you see, the world is made to end in a beautiful book."[9] The statement comes at the very end of the interview, and we search back through the preceding paragraphs to find the key to it, only to discover that Huret has apparently not recorded the preceding utterance. However, in another essay, "The Book: A Spiritual Instrument," Mallarmé elaborates on his statement, and reveals that he is talking neither about Baudelaire's dictionary nor, strictly speaking, about language. He means "book" literally. The book has come to represent for him not only itself but all the possibilities of language arranged in print and enfolded in the white blankness of its pages, the whole book in its physical existence, including those spaces, becoming a language.[10] Mallarmé does not linger here; throughout his life he imagines creating the ultimate book, the "great work," which would include everything and indeed bring an end to things.

But Mallarmé's "great work" was never written.[11] Observation of his aesthetic has prompted A. G. Lehmann to remark that it never could have been, for Mallarmé was driven to "doctrines frankly beyond the sanction of common sense." One can hardly escape the conclusion, Lehmann observes, that a "fanatic mysticism at bottom [drove] him to an extreme of fastidiousness and to unheard-of demands upon his talents."[12] However, elsewhere, either predicting his own failure to produce *the* book, or recognizing it only as an ideal (or both), Mallarmé does relegate *the* book to another realm than the paper and binding of a single volume or even a single author. If the book is to be made, it will extend beyond the volume itself and be the work of many who will inscribe "on spiritual space, the amplified signature of genius, anonymous and perfect like a being of art."[13] This ultimate book, though the work of many, he goes on to view as already existent in an ideal realm: "more or less, all books contain the fusion of a few repeated accounts; likewise there is only one bible—the world, its law." Individual works are merely interpretations of the one "veracious text."[14] This bible is not, of course, Coleridge's Holy Bible, but instead the text to be found or made. Of pertinence at this point is the clash within Mallarmé's essay between an idea of the poet as creating and that of his discovering by divination the single great text. This latter idea reveals a mystical Mallarmé who does not trouble himself with the unruly shapeless "dictionary" nature of Baudelaire, but is seeking to pass a threshold by means of a heroic act of creative search.

However, there is another and more essential Mallarmé, apart from this one, who seems to have bypassed the question of nature as shaped or shapeless and concerned himself fundamentally with the condition in which the poet finds language itself. This concentration on language sets Mallarmé off from other theorists of his time and makes him of particular interest to us.

Language is characterized by what Mallarmé calls "le Hazard," the "brute unpoetical quality of unorganized language," as Lehmann puts it.[15] Thus Mallarmé sees creation as a linguistic act, but we have not found in him any single utterance that enables us to know exactly what or how much is being created when language is poetically shaped. Thus, though Mallarmé raises the problem of poetry to the level of language, which Baudelaire does not, it threatens continually to slip away back to where Baudelaire left it, or language seems to become detached from everything else in an absolute idealism.

But not without a struggle. To understand the ground on which the struggle takes place, we must return to the generally acknowledged source of French symbolist theory—the famous doctrine of correspondences. Writers on the French symbolist movement and its English offshoots are generally agreed that the doctrine of correspondences came to Baudelaire via Swedenborg[16] and that in the movement there is a strong occultist element.[17] Swedenborg's theory is an elaboration of the old Hermetic concept "as above, so below," everything in nature having its heavenly analogy. The idea of correspondence suggests the Baudelairean "dictionary." It is interesting to ob-serve that in 1810 a dictionary of Swedenborgian correspondences was actually published, extracting its materials from Swedenborg's writings.[18] Baudelaire's correspondences are an elaboration of and variation upon Swedenborg's fundamentally mystical and theologi-cal concept. Baudelaire sees correspondence as a universal repository of all metaphor, and though he accepts the occultist "vertical" corre-spondence of "as above, so below," which is fundamental to Sweden-borg's theory, he also develops a theory of "horizontal" correspon-dences, which gives his concept a "secular" twist and leads to his emphasis on synaesthesia. Critics have often emphasized the mystical and occult—what I would call the "religious"—in the symbolist movement as it rises out of the "vertical" concept. This was the em-phasis of Arthur Symons in one of the earliest books on the subject[19] and continued to be that of Maurice Bowra, who asserted that the symbolists were poets who "attempted to convey a supernatural ex-perience in the language of visible things and therefore almost every word is a symbol and is used not for its common purpose but for the association which it evokes of a reality beyond the senses,"[20] "be-yond" in this case meaning "above." The "vertical" concept is di-vided into two parts by L. J. Austin. The first is called "symbolique," the concept nearest to the Swedenborgian, where the ideal other world is figured forth. The second is "symbolisme," which performs a reversal and signifies the use of images to express human inner ideas and feelings.[21] This distinction Austin makes less semantically confusing by substituting the terms "transcendental" and "human" for the former and latter respectively. Charles Chadwick adopts these terms in a little book on symbolism: Transcendental symbols are those of a "vast and general ideal world of which the real world is merely an imperfect representation." Human symbolism is the "art of expressing ideas and emotions" by suggestion, the inner life made outer.[22] Austin had seen Baudelaire moving from "transcendental" to "human" symbolism.[23] Chadwick views Mallarmé as having moved in the same direction in the late 1880s. Verlaine is said to exhibit lit-tle of the "transcendental" but much of the "human."[24] And Valéry displays neither, Chadwick placing him among the symbolists only stylistically.[25] What Chadwick never gets clearly stated is that the symbolists sought to resolve the two types, since there is a clear effort to equate "above" with "inner," an idea not new with the symbolists but worked out by Blake.[26] That the truth above was also inner truth for the symbolists, or at least ideally so, is rather arcanely recognized by Joseph Chiari in a remark that takes us a bit further than we are prepared to go at the moment: "For the symbolist writer, form was all, and form was only the veil of the unseizable reality whose core was not the will-centered 'ego' of the romantics but the uncommunicable self or the 'thing-in-itself' of Kant."[27] Both the self and the ideal are driven back to the same source in this theory. Both require a revelation by an adept.

But neither are these vertical correspondences ultimately separate from the horizontal ones. It is from the inner self of dream that Baudelaire draws his idea of the synaesthetic harmony of things, which indicates the potential order that the poet's imagination can give to the disordered or mechanically ordered dictionary of nature. In the "Salon of 1846," he offers on this matter the quotation from Ernst Hoffman that seems to have meant so much to him:

> It is not only in dreams, or in that mild delirium which precedes sleep, but it is even awakened when I hear music—that perception of an analogy and an intimate connexion between colours, sounds and perfumes. It seems to me that all these things were created by one and the same ray of light, and that their combination must result in a wonderful concert of harmony. The smell of red and brown marigolds above all produces a magical effect on my being. It makes me fall into a deep reverie, in which I seem to hear the solemn, deep tones of the oboe in the distance.[28]

Baudelaire himself indicates that the intensification of perception takes one into an infinite realm that is characterized by the harmony of the senses themselves. The vertical and horizontal movements become one:

> Edgar Poe has it somewhere that the effect of opium upon the senses is to invest the whole of nature with a supernatural intensity of interest, which gives to every object a deeper, a more willful, a more despotic meaning. Without having recourse to opium, who has not known those miraculous moments—veritable feast-days of the brain—when the senses are keener and sensation more ringing, when the firmament of a more transparent blue plunges headlong into an abyss more infinite, when sounds chime like music, when colours speak, and scents tell of whole worlds of ideas?[29]

The major exhibit of this idea in Baudelaire has always been for critics the sonnet "Correspondances." Anna Balakian has claimed that the poem is a "contradiction in terms," that it really contains two poems.[30] The octave she sees as expressing a Swedenborgian vertical symbolism, while in the sestet the symbolism is synaesthetic or horizontal. She sees this synaesthesia as strictly earthly and the conclusion as without spirituality, the English translators usually confusing the issue by translating "esprit" as "spirit" instead of something, I presume, like "mind":

> La Nature est un temple où de vivants piliers
> Laissent parfois sortir de confuses paroles;
> L'homme y passe à travers des forêts de symboles
> Qui l'observent avec des regards familiers.
>
> Comme de longs échos qui de loin se confondent
> Dans une ténébreuse et profonde unité,
> Vaste comme la nuit et comme la clarté,
> Les parfums, les couleurs et les sons se répondent.
>
> Il est des parfums frais comme des chairs d'enfants,
> Doux comme les hautbois, verts comme les prairies,
> —Et d'autres, corrompus, riches et triomphants,
> Ayant l'expansion des choses infinies,
>
> Comme l'ambre, le musc, le benjoin et l'encens,
> Qui chantent les transports de l'esprit et des sens.

The question is whether Baudelaire is thinking along the lines of his remarks about the dictionary. True, nature is here a temple and a forest, both images offering the possibility of hidden meaning, the former suggesting the rites of imagination to be performed by the poet-priest, the latter the possibility of strange hidden creatures lurking just beyond perception. There is a link to the dictionary image in a "nature" that emits a confusion of words. The words clearly require ordering, but it is not merely words that make up the ultimate order. Words here seem only themselves a metaphor for messages of all sorts via all the senses, and the ultimate message is the harmonious order represented by the poem's synaesthesias. Synaesthesia is, in one sense, a mass of horizontal symbolism; but, more than that, it represents the harmony lacking in the dictionary or in the temple before the rite of imagination is performed, or it represents the harmony lacking in nature when it is still dark and terrifying. This harmony is a sign of the harmony above, and is sometimes declared to be an actual recreation of it. Vertical and horizontal symbolism end in the same place, being two aspects of the symbolization of another world. Balakian seems to me mistaken in the strict separation she declares. Baudelaire remarks of correspondence, ". . . what would be really surprising would be that sound *could not* suggest color, that colors could not convey a melody, and that sound and color were unsuited to translating ideas, things always having been expressed by a reciprocal analogy since the day when God created the world as a complex and indivisible whole."[31] It is the order of harmony in the other world that the unity of the senses in this world suggests.

There have been traditionally two theories of knowledge that have vied with one another throughout the history of modern philosophy. The first, a correspondence theory, sees our symbols as referring directly to things in the outer world; the second, a coherence theory, judges our symbols on the basis of their capacity to form organized wholes.[32] Baudelaire combined correspondence and coherence by claiming that the coherence or harmony of the senses is a sign of or correspondence with the coherence and harmony of the ideal world. To apprehend the harmony is to apprehend the formal nature of that other world.

I have treated Baudelaire as a dualist, but the line in his thinking between dualism and a concept of immanence is very thin. From time to time in him there is a strong indication, not lacking in "Correspondances," of an achievement of total experience in the harmony of the senses, the other world immanent in this one, actually evoked by the poem. Critics of Baudelaire usually emphasize one or the other of these stances. The apprehension of universal analogy seems on the one hand to be the ultimate experience of the "voyant." He discovers the relations that imply finally the "overriding order and unity of all created things,"[33] but the concept of "all created things" leaves God separate: "I shall never believe that the spirit of God inhabits plants,"[34] so that in Baudelaire, even as we are tantalized by the world itself as the ultimate unity and harmony, we are drawn away from it to another world it copies, where the complete synaesthesia is achieved and maintained.[35] This returns us to the idea of the natural world as mere dictionary, with the human imagination "creating" the horizontal correspondences, or rather "recreating" them from the disorder of nature. This "recreation" is also a "discovery" of the ideal conditions of the other world. The dictionary world, which is also the mechanical world of science, is reordered by the artist's mind on the principle of harmony.[36] I say "mind" because there is no indication in Baudelaire that language itself is involved in the creativity or recreativity of which he speaks. Lehmann is quite correct to remark: ". . . putting his experiences into words is in his perspective a secondary side of the poet's activity, which is first and foremost mystical, a-linguistic,"[37] even as he points out that Baudelaire does claim that poems are the result of formal constructiveness. This maintenance of the duality of thought and language accounts, I think, for Angelo Bertocci's conclusion that Baudelaire would have had no sympathy for the "secularization of the symbol"[38] that occurs in later theorists, a phenomenon with which his work ironically had a good deal to do. Symbols for Baudelaire are finally not in language but in nature itself. Until the whole question of symbolism is raised to the level of language, the connection of *symbolisme* with the occult remains, and the "symbolic" natural world is itself a system of signs, an allegory to be read, though not linguistic.[39]

But the possibility from the time of Kant that the question might be raised to the level of language seems—except with Blake and, in some of their moods, Schelling, Coleridge, and Humboldt—to have been effectively frustrated by the prevailing positivistic idea of language as fundamentally consistent with a correspondence theory of knowledge. On this side is the positivistic concept inherited from the Cartesian-Lockean tradition of the separation of subject and object. The opposite view is one that is contextual, creative, consistent with a coherence theory, and looking backward to the sources of language in a Vichean "poetic logic" rather than forward to a perfected language of logical analysis. It opposes the subject/object antimyth. The dominance of the positivistic view, which the *symboliste* tradition itself never fully escaped (having fought it on its own terrain), led usually not to this true contrariety but to establishment of a number of strategies within its despotic terms. These had to do with the equation of art and mystery, with the concept of "suggestion," and with the connection of poetry to dream and music. Except in certain ways with Mallarmé, the question is not made one of language but of mediumless thought or experience previous to language. As a result, poets and literary theorists frequently retreated to a strict subjectivity, the ultimate statement of the position being Walter Pater's famous conclusion to *The Renaissance* (1873):

Experience, already reduced to a group of impressions, is ringed round for each one of us by that thick wall of personality through which no real voice has ever pierced on its way to us, or from us to that which we can only conjecture to be without. Every one of those impressions is the impression of the individual in his isolation, each mind keeping as a solitary prisoner its own dream of a world.[40]

Subjectivity was staked out as a realm of art, but subjectivity is itself based on the subject/object distinction, which was an invention of the same profoundly antiartistic attitude that the retreat to subjectivity was supposed to resist. The distinction trapped the theory of art in a small corner of the enemy's terrain. It would be extremely difficult under these circumstances to claim any sort of universality for art, relegated as it was to alien territory. One recognizes a futile attempt to stake out a claim in this territory by Edgar Allan Poe, who accepts the banishment of thought (the objective) from his poem and claims for poetry the domain of feeling (the subjective, further reduced to emotion), yet Poe's theory of poetry, as set forth in two well-known essays, is radically exclusivist, even to the extent of banishing the long poem from art as a "contradiction in terms" because it cannot sustain a *feeling* in the reader over a period of about half an hour.[41] Poe's theory is the precursor of Aldous Huxley's ironic "feelies," a reduction of art to feeling and feeling to pure sensation. His division of everything into the truthful and the poetical leaves poetry in an alien corner of a hostile world and reduces the theory of poetry to a theory of rhetoric advocating strategies for eliciting subjective *response*. The symbolist movement carries along some of this theoretical baggage, which frequently frustrates its potentially successful theoretical statements.

The popular terminology of the symbolist movement tends, as I have suggested, to illustrate Croce's "duality of poetry and language." The trend is seen early in Carlyle's play with the word "silence," an antilinguistic term meant to express ironically the qualities of language that go against the grain of positivist definition, but the play is into the enemy's hands. "Mystery," "suggestion," "dream," and "music" end the symbolists in the same place.

Baudelaire makes "suggestion" into a term of general approbation. *Madame Bovary* is declared to be "essentially suggestive,"[42] and suggestion is identified with magic and strangeness which in turn is equated with beauty: "The beautiful is always strange,"[43] the familiar world obviously being the world of positivism, and being given real status. Baudelaire on occasion struggles out of the trap of the subjective to declare that this strangeness is actually the result of the *joining* of subject and object.

> What is the modern conception of pure art? It is the creation of a suggestive magic containing both the object and the subject, the world outside the artist and the artist himself.[44]

Baudelaire's attempt to set up the imagination as the creative power to achieve synthesis is evident in his "Salon of 1859," as we shall see. But one always senses in him the pressure of positivistic terms on his thought.

So too with Mallarmé whose concentration in this matter is, as I have suggested, more on language. Mallarmé obviously equated the direct presentation of objects in language with a positivistic idea of language as referential. Thus all terms alluding to such a process are rejected:

> To *name* an object, that is to suppress three quarters of the enjoyment of the poem, which comes from divining little by little: to *suggest*, that is the dream. It is the perfect use of this mystery which constitutes the symbol.[45]

The unconscious irony here should be particularly evident to one who has just come from Vico or from Blake's *Marriage of Heaven and Hell*, where the role of the poet is precisely *to* name things, to create them in their words. Mallarmé's squeezing of the significance out of an object by suggestion expresses a capitulation to the assumptions of the positivistic critique of language, which regards metaphor as false or at least *indirect* signification and language as a process of generalization. The terms of Vico and Blake are reversed, and Mallarmé has only the irrational procedures of the magical left to him. Under the domination of an alien epistemology he drives himself into the alien corner already mentioned.

Yet there is a sense in which Mallarmé, Vico, and Blake are in agreement, though their languages are opposed: "They [the Parnassians] present things directly; I think that, on the contrary, there should be only allusion," Mallarmé remarks.[46] An argument could be made that in Mallarmé's ironic inverted language his "directness" is what Blake would call art addressed to the "corporeal understanding," while his allusiveness is the metaphorical speech of Blake's "vision." Still in their opposed use of terms there is a very considerable difference of gesture which is nearly as important as the agreement. The difference, though never clearly enunciated, lies in Mallarmé's retreat toward the idea of the poet as priest or hierophant presiding over a mystery—a real mystery, a mystery which must be protected from the mob of potential intruders. This is the expression of a profound disillusion that French thought has tried to make a virtue ever since Descartes. It is a disillusion that we see tempting Blake in his fierce reply to Dr. Trusler. Trusler is typical of the "intruders" of whom Mallarmé speaks. What is needed, Mallarmé says, is "an immaculate language—hieratic formulas the study of which would blind the profane and goad the inevitably patient."[47] Unlike Mallarmé, Blake desired Trusler's approbation, always hoping that Trusler's faulty vision might be "redeemed." Trusler, of course, failed him, as did many others including his patron Hayley; but it was never Blake's intent to ward off or blind the mob, only to bring their imaginative powers to action. Mallarmé above seems to have reached conclusions that imply the hopelessness of such a task. Yet there is another side to this complex man, for he feels that art must be challenging and, to use Blake's phrase, "rouse the faculties to act."[48] Allusion, suggestion, and the rest play that role: "The Parnassians, they take the thing entirely and show it: in so doing, they forfeit mystery; they fail to provide the spirit that delicious joy of thinking that it creates."[49] Even here, however, there is skepticism or perhaps disillusion. Mallarmé does not say that the spirit *is* creating something, only that we are put into the state of mind of *believing* it does.

Blake's idea is of the poet as a man who speaks his mind in metaphor (which he regards as the direct mode of speech) and whose voice is imaginatively graspable by children. Beneath this is an idea of the fundamentally metaphorical nature of language and of such creativity as naturally communicative. The concept of poetic mystery and a priesthood to interpret it is one actually developed from the point of view of a positivistic concept of language, no matter what protests Mallarmé might raise.

This situation sends Mallarmé in now one direction, now another. It leads back to a pure subjectivity in which he claims that we should not describe the object but the effect it produces on us,[50] this effect being reproduced in the reader. We find a similar attitude in Baudelaire, poetry being, in other words, an intersubjective medium or simply the effect of rhetoric on the feelings, as in Poe. Or it leads to a form of mysticism in which the soul is evoked as an ideal from another world: ". . . to evoke an object little by little to show a state of soul; or inversely, to choose an object and from it to rescue a state of soul by a series of decipherings."[51] Poetic language becomes a coy, hieroglyphic, enigmatic mode of expression. (It is perhaps not surprising, given Mallarmé's remark, that Blake should have thought of a priesthood as the protector of the "female" religion of chastity.) Reverie and contemplation become terms for a mental activity of both poet and reader, opposed to analytic objectifying thought: "The contemplation of objects, the image taking wing from the reveries aroused by them."[52] The fear of analytical activity is pronounced. Mallarmé believes that poetry taught in school inevitably is reduced "to the level of science,"[53] all discussion designed toward understanding being translation of the poem into discourse, or what the romantics called allegory. But one is not sure whether Mallarmé dislikes this because meaning is not discoverable or because he fears the mystery *will* be explained.

The symbolist reaction against everything that seemed even an analogue of positivistic science turned the principle of *ut pictura poesis*, its connections being with imitation, signification, and space, into *ut musica poesis*. Pater's statement that all art aspires to the condition of music was preceded by Poe's idea that music is the perfection of the soul of poetry, and Baudelaire's remarks in praise of Wagner that music should "express the undefined part of feeling that words, which are too specific, cannot render."[54] Here Baudelaire follows Poe in arguing that poetry should strive for an indefiniteness of effect. The term "indefiniteness," as I have already suggested, signifies a retreat from the rigors of a positivist referentiality in language, but is unfortunate in some of its nevertheless positivistic implications. It treats poetry from positivism's point of view. A struggle over the term "definite" rages all through the nineteenth century. Blake insists on holding it in the arsenal of art, and considers the language of science *in*definite because of its abstractness and its insistence on claiming abstract objectivity as the true reality. He bequeaths this attitude to the later, but not the earlier, Yeats. Blake calls objectivity "indefinite" in a reversal of the common usage; and he asks, "What is General Nature? is there Such a Thing? What is General Knowledge? is there such a Thing?"[55]

The habit of Poe and to some extent Baudelaire in this matter leads to T. E. Hulme's charge that the romantic poets ascended into the "circumambient gas" and that their expression of feeling was indefinite indeed.[56] On the same side is T. S. Eliot with his desire for an "objective correlative" that will make feeling definite.[57] The problem is perhaps resolvable by a declaration that there are different sorts of definiteness and precision, definable only in terms of the mode of thought or expression being employed. To adopt such a stance is to recognize, I think, that Hulme's antiromanticism is directed curiously against the same romantic antipositivism that he himself espouses in different terms. No doubt he would have considered romantic "indefiniteness" an example of sentimental retreat, but his own championing of a precise but sterile imagism merely goes to the opposite extreme of response.

Baudelaire does finally, however, give to poetry and music a definite object of reference. It is through them that "the soul glimpses the splendors beyond the tomb."[58] These glimpses are not in their own terms thought vague by Baudelaire. Rather than tilting directly with the question of definiteness or indefiniteness, Mallarmé makes an opposition between music on the one hand and allegory and abstraction on the other. "Scenic art is now strictly allegorical, empty, and abstract, impersonal; in order to move with verisimilitude, it needs to employ the vivifying effluvium that music pours forth."[59] Though music is offered to us as breath or liquid, there is nothing vague about it. Mallarmé introduces in connection with music his idea that it expresses, like literature, the Idea: "The alternative aspect releases toward the obscure—scintillant there with the assurance of a single phenomenon—the Idea, as I shall call it."[60]

This concept leads us to consider the Baudelairean and the Mallarméan ideas of imagination: whether, according to them, the imagination discovers or creates, or in some special way accomplishes both in a single act; and finally whether or not it acts in language. Margaret Gilman has observed that from the outset of his criticism Baudelaire searched for a word that would embody his whole thought. "Correspondances" is one of those he used, but "imagination" is the ultimate "quintessential and all-embracing" term of his criticism.[61] It is the imagination which alone comprehends universal analogy or "*la correspondance*." As in other things, Baudelaire is in the debt of Delacroix and Poe for his concept of the imagination. Usually opposed to imitation, it is now a creative, now a combining power. It is regarded as a sign of man's divinity. It perceives "immediately and without philosophical methods the inner and secret relations of things, the correspondences and the analogies."[62] Unlike Vico's primitive "poetic logic," which is an open and direct mode of imagination, Baudelaire's imagination emphasizes the occult and secretive. It appears that for Baudelaire this was not historically always the case, the truths which it can know being secret and veiled only apparently in modern culture, to which Baudelaire's intellectual antipathy is profound. In a sense, the imagination is an exiled ruler or a prophet in the wilderness. Sometimes Baudelaire seems to say that the imagination gives us insight into *another* world; sometimes he says that it actually makes *this* world; and sometimes he suggests that it makes a new world better than any we can know. Baudelaire's introduction of the element of secrecy is still another expression of profound disillusion with the culture and assertion that a "dissociation of sensibility" has occurred:

> It is the imagination that first taught man the moral meaning
> of colour, of contour, of sound and of scent. In the beginning
> of the world it created analogy and metaphor. It decomposes
> all creation, and with the raw materials accumulated and dis-
> posed in accordance with rules whose origins one cannot find
> save in the furthest depths of the soul, it creates a new world,
> it produces the sensation of newness. As it has created the
> world (so much can be said, I think, even in a religious sense),
> it is proper that it should govern it.[63]

Baudelaire picks up support for his conception of the imagination in part from Mrs. Crowe's garbled version of Coleridgean and Germanic definitions: it is constructive, it is constituted partly by the memory, it perceives the other world, it *makes* the other world, it makes *this* world, it combines, it transforms, it discovers, it decodes.[64] But there is no single statement of Baudelaire on the subject that gathers together and then either blends all the terms or eliminates those that do not fit. So, finally it seems to be the expression of the negative side of prevailing positivistic currents. The credo he attacks is the one that says, "I believe in Nature and I believe only in Nature. . . . I believe that Art is, and cannot be other than, the exact reproduction of Nature."[65] The world is divided by him into two camps: The realists (positivists) who claim: "I want to represent things as they are, or rather as they would be, supposing that I did not exist." And the imaginatives who say, "I want to illuminate things with my mind, and to project their reflection upon other minds."[66] This opposition is stated in other ways, but one must note that there is frequently the tacit assumption that the positivists are right in claiming their reality to be *out there* as such, and the poet is reduced to distorting or decorating it, or following it through his subjectivity to no clear purpose. This—in spite of so much talk about the imagination as creative. Baudelaire thus vacillates between a never quite stated concept of a truly creative imagination and a rebellious perverse desire to create the monstrous and deviant. He is so under the domination of the detested positivistic concept of copying and imitation that he seeks to steal the term "imitation," albeit with much irony, for an imitative theory of his own by a deliberate misinterpretation. The tendency is revealed fully in his most complete utterance on the subject in "The Queen of the Faculties":

> In recent years we have heard it said in a thousand different ways, 'Copy nature; only copy nature. There is no greater delight, no finer triumph than an excellent copy of nature.' And this doctrine (the enemy of art) was alleged to apply not only to painting but to all the arts, even to the novel and to poetry. To these doctrinaires, who were so completely satisfied by Nature, a man of imagination would certainly have had the right to reply: 'I consider it useless and tedious to represent what *exists*, because nothing that *exists* satisfies me. Nature is ugly, and I prefer the monsters of my fantasy to what is positively trivial.' And yet it would have been more philosophical to ask the doctrinaires in question first of all whether they were quite certain of the existence of external nature. . . .[67]

He goes on to hedge against his own boldness:

> So far as I have been able to understand its singular and humiliating incoherences, the doctrine meant—at least I do it the honour of believing that it meant: The artist, the true artist, the true poet, should only paint in accordance with what he sees and with what he feels. He must be *really* faithful to his own nature. He must avoid like the plague borrowing the eyes and the feelings of another man, however great that man may be; for then his productions would be lies in relation to himself, and not *realities*.[68]

Baudelaire is coming around to the argument that true realism, a term he also seeks to steal, always involves the poet *and* nature:

"Every good poet was always realistic."[69] But elsewhere he abandons "truth," and thus the realistic, to the enemy: "Poetry cannot, under penalty of death or failure, be assimilated to science or morality: it does not have truth as its object, it has only Itself."[70] There are occasions when Baudelaire identifies "truth" with the breakdown and annihilation of the subject-object split, clearly an act of imagination, but his argument is not pressed to a conclusion, and his Kantian idea of the end of art as itself is not explicitly connected to an epistemology that makes such an end truth.

There presses into Baudelaire's thought at this point a competing concept of "le rêve," the world of imaginative activity seen as a wakeful dreaming where, as Lehmann points out, "the criteria of truth and falsehood are abolished."[71] The imagination, then, is either not concerned at all with knowledge, is concerned with the knowledge produced by an identity of subject and object in perception, or is concerned with the creations of *le rêve*, which in turn may or may not be symbolic or, in my terms, allegoric of another higher world or consciousness. One finds here most of the choices but no resting place. I think finally that Lehmann is right to insist that Baudelaire's theory of symbols left "no room for the part played by language in art."[72] By this I take it that Lehmann is trying to say that Baudelaire lacks an idea of language which makes it not hieroglyphic like his dictionary nature but creative and formative of nature, implying that thought is bound up with language and does not precede it.

Anna Balakian has used a phrase to describe the symbolists that illustrates what prevents them from achieving the end that Lehmann desires for them. She refers to their "unsuppressible metaphysical thirst."[73] One recognizes this thirst in both Baudelaire and Mallarmé and, in much simplified form, in followers such as Jean Moréas, who tend to reduce to allegorism the formulations so laboriously worked out by their predecessors. In Mallarmé, however, if we see this thirst never fully assuaged, there is a far greater recognition of the role of language in poetic thought. Mallarmé's strategy varies, but for the most part it seems to be based on an attempt to bypass the whole question of perception as the basis of a theory of knowledge, presumably because that route has been taken by the positivists and their apes, the realists:

The childishness of literature up to now has been to think, for example, that to choose a certain number of precious stones and put the names on paper, is to *make* precious stones. Not at all! Poetry consists of *creation*: it must take up in the human soul states, glimmers of a purity so absolute, well sung, and well placed and illuminated as in effect to constitute the jewels of man: there, there is symbol, there is creation, and the word "poetry" has its meaning.[74]

Mallarmé simply admits, in one of his moods at least, that nature exists and we cannot change her. What we do by being true to an inner vision is "at will to extend, simplify the world."[75] We tend to decompose the world, or ignore it, only to rebuild it from an absolute nothingness deep inside the mind. This idea of the nothingness out of which the poet creates is central to Mallarmé, and I shall return to it, but first it is important to summarize, having come this far, the role that the ideal or the idea plays in Baudelaire and Mallarmé. This brings us back to the terms "allegory" and "symbolism," only for us to learn that Baudelaire, as we may have suspected, does not distinguish between them. He calls allegory "one of the noblest branches of the art" in the "Salon of 1845"[76] and continues to use the term interchangeably with symbolism: "Rabelais . . . is directly symbolic. His comedy nearly always possesses the transparence of an allegory (apologue)."[77] And Wagner's melodies are "in a sense, *personifications of ideas*."[78] Allegory for Baudelaire, as Guy Michaud has pointed out, is one of the primitive and most natural forms of poetry.[79] Symbolism and allegory are avenues to an ideal realm.

But the ideal is then often pulled into the realm of experience by being made a characteristic of, therefore present in, beauty, which is always earthly. On the other hand, beauty is also an earthly harmony that by its order corresponds to the ideal or suggests it. The first view is Kantian: "Absolute and eternal beauty does not exist, or rather it is only an abstraction creamed from the general surface of different beauties."[80] The second ties beauty to earth. At the best it is something intermediate—a mode of suggestion: "All forms of beauty, like all possible phenomena, contain an element of the eternal and an element of the transitory."[81] He also quotes Stendhal as holding that "ideal beauty" occurs in poetry "derived from a temperament."[82]

There is, however, another statement from this time in his career (1846) that relegates the ideal itself to an abstract fiction and sees beauty as *created*:

> . . . the absolute ideal is a piece of nonsense. . . . poets, artists, and the whole human race would be miserable indeed if the

ideal—that absurdity, that impossibility—were ever discovered. If that happened, what would everyone do with his poor *ego*, with his crooked line?[83]

The last sentence undercuts the previous one with an irony that calls the whole statement into question. Profound skepticism and disillusion enter the discourse, and we are suddenly cut loose from any commitment to location of an ideal either made *here* or copied from *there*. It is no surprise, in the light of all this, that commentators have constructed more than one Baudelaire. Such a remark as the one above leads Bertocci, for example, to opt for a Baudelaire whose symbolism is neither subjective nor idealistic and transcendent.[84] And there are grounds for such an interpretation, but there are grounds for others, too. Baudelaire will sometimes adopt a sort of Kantianism grafted onto ideas of Poe and contradict his own doctrine of correspondences by releasing poetry entirely from reference and truth of any sort. A poem will in this mood have "no other goal than itself."[85]

In Baudelaire, therefore, we see various ideas of the symbol. It is sometimes an arcane expression of a nonexistent abstraction. It is sometimes an expression of a hidden reality above, through correspondence or through the corresponding harmony of the whole poem to which it belongs. Yet this harmony, or beauty, is not the ideal, but distanced from it while yet, one supposes, suggesting it. Symbols are not linguistic but are natural objects themselves, and such symbols are really signs. Thus, the return of romantic allegory. Sometimes the work of art is cut off from both of these referents and is only itself. This last view is not bolstered systematically with a statement about its function or an elaboration of its nature or a theory based on its being a linguistic structure.

In Mallarmé, there is a persistent struggle to define the ideal in a way that will escape the uncertainty of its Baudelairean location. Mallarmé's ideal often sounds like the "Platonic" realm of the above that is somehow brought into apprehension through art, which is identified with "dream" and "fiction," terms I shall query in later chapters: Grasping of the ideal is pleasure, which is always generated from beyond. Yet a key idea in Mallarmé competes with and overthrows this simple "Platonism." The key idea is Mallarmé's "nothingness," a term full of irony and obviously constructed to *épater le materialisme*, but also one through which Mallarmé sought his way out of the sort of imitative theory of art practiced by naïve realists, who think one can build "with brick and mortar" inside a book.[86] In the concept of nothingness Mallarmé attempts to clear an absolutely pure, empty space for the imaginative word or symbol to fill. According to Michaud and others, Hegel is the origin of Mallarmé's idea of nothingness and the idea that nothingness is "not an end but a point of departure."[87] But Mallarmé deviates from Hegel to identify nothingness with beauty and absolute purity. It is that pure blank space out of which comes the symbol, which therefore copies, signifies, decodes, or interprets nothing.[88] Yet it is the necessary something to that nothing—its perfect complement and Hegelian negation. Insofar as the poem comes from the artist, the artist becomes that void, as in Hegel concepts negate objects. As Michaud points out, the poet seeks self-negation and impersonality so that he can become a source of revelation of "the mystery immanent in the universe."[89]

But although Mallarmé may succeed in this way in freeing the symbol from representing an idea in another world and thus from all traces of allegory and reference in this sense, the problem of freeing the symbol from the representation of phenomenal nature *as the positivists see it* is trickier. Mallarmé's recourse to the idea of nothingness is also a strategy for dealing specifically with the false (but domineering) objective world of positivism. In trying to annihilate that world Mallarmé seems driven to annihilate every other world as well, leaving us with either solipsism or the pretense of an allegoric mystery.

Or Mallarmé risks a fall back into imitation because he does not present a systematic theory of perception to rescue his concept of creation; yet he needs such a theory because if he cannot present us with a creative theory of perception it would appear that he must assume that the poet grasps objects from the outer world, puts them into the void of himself and somehow refines them out of such existence into generalized abstractions. I believe that Mallarmé does not want to say quite what he says:

> Why the miracle of transposing a thing of nature into its vibratory near-disappearance by the play of the word, if not to draw out from the constraint of the near or concrete, recalling the pure notion?
>
> I say: A flower! and from the oblivion to which my voice banishes every form, something different—the sweet idea itself—from the usual calices musically arises that which is absent from all bouquets.[90]

This is the presentation of language as the Hegelian means of annihilating the world in the concept—a radical idealism. But it differs

from Hegel in that it is a bodily kind of concept, maintaining the
thingness of the flower even as it annihilates the materiality of the
flower. It is a pure image rather than a concept. It is a form of radical
creation that must destroy the world to create its own dream. It does
not in the end use the world as potentiality; it thoroughly annihilates
a world that it despises. One might wish it possible to claim that Mallarmé refers in all this to the poet's power to counter the antimyth of
the natural object generated by the theory of primary qualities of experience. But Mallarmé's aestheticism sometimes seems as ascetic as
Hegel's idealism in its annihilation of the world.

In Mallarmé's effort we recognize a shift over to a concern with
language. His distinction between the newspaper and the book is in-
dicative of such a movement. He identifies the newspaper with description and rhetorical design upon the reader, therefore purposiveness, and thus "speech." The book is identified with allusion,
suggestion, and "silence," the annihilation of externality. The newspaper assumes the role of reporter of *external* events. The book generates from its interior a being. It draws forth something from
nothing—a purely ideal being. Mallarmé speaks from the heart
when he amusingly says he will contemplate all the intricacies of the
idea of the book if he can be free of his "domineering newspaper."[91] In
the image of the newspaper is gathered all Mallarmé's contempt for
the world created by positivism, which he equates (unfortunately, I
believe) with the outer world of nature in any form whatever and
which he therefore feels he is compelled to annihilate. However, Mallarmé's own irony reveals that it cannot be exorcised. So it is really
flight. When he flees, he does so not just from the world that positivism insists on, but from any world at all, all phenomenal reality being
eschewed, so great is the symbolist's sense of entrapment. The French
tradition does not have a Coleridge to work out the problem of imagination as it faces the world of phenomenal experience. Instead, it
continues to struggle with the thorough bifurcation established by
Descartes, a spirit that broods over all subsequent French theory.
Mallarmé's linguistic creativity is cut off from the world. His choice
is that of a temperament and an experience different from Blake's
and under greater cultural stress. While Blake will invade the world
he sees and compel it to become material for his poem, Mallarmé will
withdraw from that world by invoking the magicality of annihilation
into a poem which is a self-mirroring object.[92] "Silence" becomes a
word to describe not only the annihilation but also the whole formal
structure of the work as well as the nothingness displaced by the
work. "Everything is suspended, disposition of fragments with alter-

nation and relation contributing to the total rhythm, which will be the poem itself, to the point of blankness, translated only—in its own style—by each pendentive."[93] This is the nature of the total, "new word" which poetry fashions, as against the simplistic abstract language of the newspaper.[94]

But it is not all that simple. In the same essay in which he talks about silence, he also says, "I think—by a doubtless ineradicable prejudice of the writer—that nothing will endure without being spoken,"[95] recognizing the need to generate that very same noise that the image of silence and self-mirroring denies to him. He knows also that the poet must use the language of the marketplace, borrow it, so to speak, and though he complains about this, he also recognizes the needs of it: Art seems to have to be "like an orchestra, wings spread, but with its talons rooted in your earth."[96] Mallarmé's self-reflexive language in its silent space is not, in most of his moods at least, a vehicle by which to copy a realm of ideas or archetypes either above or within. The poem, examined from this point of view, is purely creative of and out of "nothingness." But the problem of referentiality still dogs Mallarmé's critical language. If "silence" is meaningful as a term, there must be noise somewhere. There is simply no solution to this problem as long as his vocabulary is either rooted (albeit by negation) in the epistemological assumptions of positivism, which do not allow for a theory of the mind as creative in its facing "outward" to the manifold of sensation, or is so negative as to force the disappearance of the world.

We have arrived at a position similar to that of Lehmann, who laments, ". . . the insistence observed throughout all the cases we have explored up to this point, to make the central feature of a literary symbol, and the source of its special aesthetic value, reside in the fact of its making a reference to something else—some transcendental order of experiences or not, as the case may be."[97] I would add that the problem is even more complex than Lehmann has allowed. If Mallarmé is to cut off his poem from the referentiality he never quite avoids, he must in some way demonstrate a new form of relation to a world that is in some sense still there as a possibility. If Mallarmé could rid himself of what Lehmann calls the "obsession"[98] of positivist premises, he would also rid himself of the solipsism that threatens him, and he would reconstitute the whole relation of mind and of poem to world. Lehmann's provocative book fixes upon the problem but provides finally no solution to this dilemma except to state that the solution lies in the realm of language.

2. THE EARLY YEATS

THE FALL of a theory of the symbol into romantic allegory, often of an occult "religious" variety, is common enough at the end of the nineteenth century. It is exemplifed by the early Yeats. The usual assumption, or at least an assumption that is dying very slowly, is that the theories of French *symbolisme* were introduced into England by Arthur Symons and worked an influence on Yeats through Symons's best-known book, *The Symbolist Movement in Literature* (first version 1899). The situation is far more complicated than that. Ruth Z. Temple was able to write a book on the introduction of *symbolisme* to England that pays little attention to Yeats, focusing on those English critics who actually wrote on French writers—Arnold, Swinburne, Symons, Gosse, and Moore.[99] Edward Engelberg has rightly criticized people who argue that Yeats was not a *symboliste* because "he got his doctrines secondhand from Arthur Symons and could read French only slowly and with great difficulty."[100] The truth is that Yeats did not need Symons's book or even Symons to move along his own symbolist road. The influence of Swedenborg and his occult studies, leaving alone Blake, would have sufficed him. Richard Ellmann argues convincingly that Yeats was the dominant force in the friendship with Symons, that Yeats had already developed symbolist ideas in his work on Blake with Edwin J. Ellis, and that Symons followed Yeats to Blake and to mysticism.[101] The last point is crucial, for Symons was apparently not by nature attracted to the so-called transcendental aspects of mysticism, even though his emphasis throughout his book is on those very aspects as fundamental to the whole symbolist movement. In his dedication to Yeats, he acknowledges as much:

> I speak often in this book of Mysticism, and that I, of all people, should venture to speak, not quite as an outsider, of such things, will probably be a surprise to many. It will be no surprise to you, for you have seen me gradually finding my way, uncertainly but inevitably, in that direction, which has always been to you your natural direction.[102]

We may conclude that Symons's interpretation of the French *symbolistes* is, in fact, influenced by Yeats, traveling his own road.

Ruth Temple is right, I think, in claiming that Symons erred in failing to distinguish the "artist's delight in the visible world" from materialism.[103] This failure, which perpetuates a difficulty that we have already observed in *symboliste* theory, was also the early Yeats's and is analogous to perpetuating the distinction Blake attacked between body and soul. All dwelling upon mundane existence, upon any idea of an external world, Symons and the early Yeats connect, as Mallarmé tends to do, with the hated materialist science. Symons establishes this early in his book as its principal theme: ". . . after the world has starved its soul long enough in the contemplation and rearrangement of material things, comes the turn of the soul."[104] Such contemplation is apparently for Symons the exercise of Coleridge's "fancy" or Blake's "memory," the mere rearrangement of fixed blocks of matter according to the Hartleyan process known as the association of ideas. The problem in Symons, and in Yeats, and among the symbolists generally, was that the revolt against fancy became a revolt against all that was not of another, supersensible world. Symons writes: "Here, then, in this revolt against exteriority, against rhetoric, against materialistic tradition; in this endeavor to disengage the ultimate essence, the soul, of whatever exists and can be realized by the consciousness; in this dutiful waiting upon every symbol by which the soul of things can be made visible; literature, bowed down by many burdens, may at last attain liberty, and its authentic speech."[105] The emphasis is on all but appearance. It seems that Symons has banished seeing, touching, and hearing, and has left only disembodied contemplation. Literature is described as liberated, but it could just as well be described as having abandoned a huge range of experience.

Yeats expresses a similar view and criticizes any literature written on materialist premises: "The scientific movement brought with it a literature which was always tending to lose itself in externalities of all kinds, in opinion, in declamation, in picturesque writing, in word-painting, or in what Mr. Symons has called an attempt 'to build in brick and mortar inside the covers of a book';[106] and now writers have begun to dwell upon the element of evocation, of suggestion, upon what we call the symbolism of great writers."[107] Symons had said that symbolism is a characteristic of all great writing, making it virtually the defining term of literature in the manner of Goethe and the romantics.[108] But in fact, it becomes with both Symons and Yeats an exclusivist term as well, referring now to the essence of art, now to a specific literary movement determined to redefine what is art by excluding from it every remotely scientific attitude. According to Yeats, the age has been one of scientific and political thought, unfriendly to art.[109] Symbolism is not merely antimaterialistic and antiscientistic. It is also antimoralistic, antirhetorical (antipurposive), and antirealistic.[110]

It would not be necessary to take Yeats into account if this were all he had to say. It would merely be Mallarmé trivialized. Mallarmé's aim was to discover nothingness, to generate an essence that would annihilate all else, thus escaping the copying of or even the acknowledging of the existence of externality. In the quotation above from Symons, one sees what may be an effort to express this idea, but one is uncertain whether or not Symons quite understands it. Yeats may not understand it either, but Yeats is important because he attempts to generate his own rationale for the symbol, and because he maintains, under the surface of his earliest thought, a skepticism about the separation of spirit and matter, even as he seems to build his arguments on that very negation. I shall return to this. He is important also because as his work developed in the twentieth century he turned away from such negations, as we shall see in chapter 11. Yet the early Yeats did not overcome the failure that Ruth Temple notes in Symons to distinguish materialism from the imaginative treatment of nature. In every case Yeats and Symons found themselves, in contrast to Blake, positing the symbol as a sign of something unexperienceable through the eyes, a sign often generated by trance.[111] Symons defines symbolism as "a form of expression, at best but approximate, essentially but arbitrary, until it has obtained the force of a convention, for an unseen reality apprehended by the consciousness."[112] This marks a retreat from the boldness of Mallarmé's effort to create all spirit or essence in words, an act clearly a parallel on the spiritual side or in the world of spirit to the materialist's building in brick and mortar inside the covers of a book. It is a retreat in spite of the qualification Symons makes: "It is sometimes permitted to us to hope that our convention is indeed the reflection rather than merely the sign of that unseen reality."[113] It is a retreat to romantic allegory under the banner of the "miraculous" symbol.

The matter of poetic convention is emphasized in one guise or another throughout Yeats's early theorizing on the symbol, Yeats putting great stock in the idea of a tradition of poetic utterance suppressed in modern positivism. Sometimes he sees the tradition as having undergone a gradual deterioration from a primitive way of thought, which he regards as fundamentally occult (thus allegoric), similar to that attributed by some of the eighteenth-century mythographers to the ancient Egyptians or the Druids. Sometimes he considers the tradition to have been maintained in Celtic folklore. And sometimes he regards the two sources as the same, a sort of Vichean "poetic logic" mixed with occultism. In an important essay of 1898 he wrote: "Each of these writers [authors of the Kalevala, Homer, Virgil, Dante, Shakespeare] had come further down the stairway than those who had lived before him, but it was only with the modern poets, with Goethe and Wordsworth and Browning, that poetry gave up the right to consider all things in the world as a dictionary of types and symbols and began to call itself a critic of life and an interpreter of things as they are."[114] A Baudelairean dictionary with its implication of a hidden supersensible reality becomes the guiding principle of true poetry. But this idea Yeats took directly from Swedenborg.

It is through Swedenborg and other occultists that Edwin J. Ellis and the young Yeats interpreted Blake in their huge edition of 1893. Perhaps the most interesting part of the three volumes is a brief essay written by Yeats, but clearly influenced by Ellis, called "The Necessity of Symbolism."[115] This essay, never reprinted, is earlier than any essay published in Yeats's earliest collection, *Ideas of Good and Evil* (1896–1903), and more important to an understanding of his early conception of poetry than anything he had published previously. With this said, it must also be admitted that it throws considerable confusion into the study of Blake. The reason fundamentally is that Yeats tries to force Blake into Swedenborg's language instead of generating his understanding out of Blake's own ample terminology. The key Swedenborgian terms are "correspondence" and "degree," which Blake seldom uses and, except where he is annotating Swedenborg, never uses in Swedenborg's sense.

The definition Yeats offers of "correspondence" raises a problem at once: ". . . 'correspondence,' as Swedenborg called the symbolic relation of outer to inner, is itself no product of nature or natural reason, beginning as it does with a perception of a something different from natural things with which they are to be compared."[116] The statement might be brought into line with Blake's view if we were to conclude that Yeats means by "natural things" objects *created* by the abstraction and separation out from perception of the so-called primary qualities of experience—creations of what Blake calls Urizen.[117] But it is not at all clear that Yeats has this in mind. Instead, it is fair to say, he is expressing a purely dualistic and occultist mysticism quite opposite to Blake's emphasis on the visionary here and now of his own self-styled "primitive and original ways."[118] This opinion is enforced by Yeats's own account of his occult studies in the *Autobiogra-*

phy and the *Memoirs*. For example, in his study with the Theosophists in the eighties, he was taught that "every organ of the body had its correspondence in the heavens, and the seven principles which made the human soul and body corresponded to the seven colours and the planets and the notes of the musical scale."[119] The statement indicates a belief in both vertical and horizontal correspondence.

The system that Yeats attempts to apply to Blake, so convinced does he seem to be that a poet merely passes on a received wisdom, distinguishes in a Swedenborgian manner between "continuous" and "discrete" degrees of correspondence. Discrete degrees are specific stages marking the spaces between this and the other world. Continuous degrees, like the appearance of light, are indistinguishable from one another. Continuous degrees are horizontal and as such merely "symbols of the 'discrete degrees'," which are vertical. "Symbol" means here a sign of the relationship of things below to things above. Curiously enough, Yeats identifies continuous degrees with the thought of the scientist, because the scientist reduces all spiritual things to material explanation or single degree. Discrete degrees are the vehicles of mystical thought, which distinguishes and, perhaps we can say, protects spirit from matter.[120]

The problem with the distinction is that Yeats is dealing with Blake and there is no place for Blake in it. Yeats wants to put Blake with the dualistic mystics, but Blake rejects both positions Yeats sets up, attacking not the existence of the body but only the identification of the body with Lockean matter, and attacking the concept of upper and lower worlds as implied by discrete degrees. Yeats says that Blake goes *beyond* Swedenborg: "Blake goes further and asserts that 'the poetic genius,' as he calls the emotional life, 'is the true man, and that the body or outward form of man is derived from the poetic genius.'"[121] But Blake does not think of a separated "emotional life." To do so, for Blake, is an error. And it is not that Blake goes *beyond* Swedenborg; it is that he rejects him. Yeats's difficulty is that he does not really understand Blake's two different uses of the term "body." In one sense the body is that abstraction created by "Bacon, Newton, Locke" (and, let us add, Descartes). But in another more common Blakean sense it is a spiritual body, an indivisible entity, the form of the soul, though the soul is not its content.[122] (Indeed, the term "soul" is better not introduced, since its common usage performs all over again the bifurcation Blake opposes.)[123]

Perhaps the central theme in the early Yeats's theory of symbolism, as we piece it together from a number of essays, is "mood." As

Table 5.1

(1) *Yeats*	(2) *Christianity*	(3) *Swedenborg*	(4) *Cabala*
Bodiless mind	Father	Celestial	Neschamah
Surging thought	Son	Spiritual	Ruach
Thing	Holy Spirit	Natural	Nesphesch

(5) *Theosophy*	(6) *General*
unmanifest eternal	universal
manifest eternal	particular
manifest temporal	concrete

far as I know, the term is first used by Yeats in the edition of Blake and finds further expression in a short essay published in 1895.[124] All nature seems to be regarded as the lowest degree of moods or emotions. Everything is an emanation downward or outward of a "central mood" or the "poetic genius" to some Swedenborgian "degree." "Mood" in its lowest degree becomes matter and takes precedence over it. Yeats thinks his concept has an analogue in all the religious or mystical systems of man. He schematizes in table 5.1. There is finally a "mood that goes through all moods,"[125] which is what Yeats thinks Blake meant by the "poetic genius"; but Yeats can find no triad by means of which he can include Blake in his scheme, Blake having treated all triads as the products of error. Although the early Yeats gives lip service to a sort of human creative power, he returns always to those same separations that Blake's idea of creative imagination working in poetic language denies. Yeats believes in the separations he posits as having an objective existence in the same externality he so desperately desires to avoid. Blake believes the separations are created by our discursive way of thinking and expressing. It is not a question of different actual worlds but of different ways the mind and its forms construct the worlds of culture.

As a result of Yeats's unsteadiness on this point one senses a sort of schizophrenia in his discourses on Blake. The interpretation he makes of Blake threatens to turn any distinction he draws between allegory and symbolism into a distinction without a difference or to render his various statements inconsistent. But the distinction runs through much of his early prose, and we must face it. Yeats claims Blake as the founder of symbolism in modern times, by which he means that Blake reestablished an ancient tradition. It is Yeats who is the first to declare Blake's distinction between allegory and vision to be really the same distinction as that between allegory and symbolism.[126] But Blake's "vision," though it may be Goethe's "symbolism," is not Yeats's. Yeats writes: "A symbol is indeed the only possible expression of some invisible essence, a transparent lamp about a spiritual flame; while allegory is one of many possible representations of an embodied thing, or familiar principle, and belongs to fancy and not to imagination: the one is revelation, the other amusement."[127] The introduction of invisibility and essence causes the distortion. The distinction is really one between a "religious" form of allegory and an "empirical" one, with the additional claim that in one case the sign is arbitrary and in the other it is not. He criticizes Johnson's dictionary for not distinguishing between allegory and symbolism: ". . . it calls a symbol 'that which comprehends in its figure a representation of something else'; and an allegory 'a figurative discourse, in which something other is intended than is contained in the words literally taken'."[128] But he accepts, albeit with some reservation, a modern dictionary's definition "that calls a symbol 'the sign or representation of any moral thing by the images and properties of natural things,' which, though an imperfect definition, is not unlike 'The things below are as things above' of the Emerald Tablet of Hermes."[129] He does not seem to realize that he has accepted here a definition of symbolism that makes it a subclass of Johnson's definition. The subclass is an allegory in which the something else intended is a thing above and apparently a moral abstraction to boot. The connecting link is occult correspondence.

Yet if this is what symbolism is, how can Blake be a symbolist when Yeats himself says that Blake was a "symbolist who had to invent his symbols"?[130] To invent one's own symbols would be, according to Yeats's idea of an occult source of symbols and of the lack of arbitrariness in them, a contradiction in terms. What Yeats would have to agree to (or abandon the dictionary definition) is that Blake didn't invent but had to rediscover a lost system of correspondences which reflect *truth* in a sort of preordained signifier. In order, perhaps, to deal with this problem, Yeats introduces here and there the ideas of lost tradition or lost book and sacred book to be written. For him, Blake was a dispossessed poet in a culture which thrust him on his own. Blake's difficulty was that "he was a man crying out for a mythology and trying to make one because he could not find one to his hand." Yeats imagines that a medieval Blake would have used Catholic myth, a modernist Blake Norse myth as did Wagner, or if he were Irish (which Yeats tried to make Blake by ancestry) he would have gone to the peasant folklore. But he "spoke confusedly and obscurely because he spoke of things for whose speaking he could find no models in the world about him."[131] This view of Blake is echoed by Eliot some years later.[132]

There is another well-known statement of Yeats about Blake. On the surface, it strikes one as apt: Blake is "a too literal realist of the imagination." But Yeats adds, "as others are of nature," and goes on to argue, ". . . he believed that the figures seen by the mind's eye when exalted by inspiration, were 'eternal existences,' symbols of divine essences. . . ."[133] The literality of Blake's approach is not in doubt, but Yeats's concept of the objects of Blake's imagination is misleading, for there are no essences approximated by signs in Blake. What Blake sees is what he claims there is, no more and no less.

From Blake's point of view, Yeats's symbolism is allegory. This situation explains the inconclusive use in Yeats of these terms in the early essays. In his essay on Spenser, Yeats begins by hardly distinguishing between them, calling them both "natural" languages by which communion between worlds is accomplished. Both, he says, can "speak of things which cannot be spoken in any other language, but one will always, I think, feel some sense of unreality when they are used to describe things which can be described as well in ordinary words."[134] But he does not here say that the latter is allegory. Here the Mallarméan creative power of the symbol seems to have disappeared completely, both allegory and symbol being "descriptive." Later in the essay he does come to distinguish the two, symbolism being "the only fitting speech for some mystery of disembodied life." Allegory is now reduced to the sort of description that can be done as well in other terms, though how one description can be equated to another is not clarified. Yeats merely calls allegory for the most part boring and identifies it as the activity of what Blake called the "daughters of memory."[135] There is no indication that Yeats knows that Blake meant by memory the process of Hartleyan association of ideas or the fancy in Coleridge's sense. Yeats further confuses us by declaring that allegory worked for Dante because it was natural to him but didn't for Spenser because Spenser was a sensuous poet. This begins to make Dantean allegory look like the symbolism of the previous definitions and allowable if the poet is intent on a certain purpose, even though Yeats elsewhere thinks it for the most part boring. Ultimately the distinction collapses for Yeats. He ends by calling the parts of Spenser he likes "mythological and symbolical, but not allegorical" and leaves the matter.[136]

An essay of four years earlier (1898) evades some of these problems and protects Yeats from too specific commitment by defining symbolism through the voice of a German painter doing his portrait: "The German insisted with many determined gestures that symbolism said things which could not be said so perfectly in any other way, and needed but a right instinct for its understanding; while allegory said things which could be said as well, or better, in another way."[137] To have left the matter simply at this would have freed the symbolic from being always necessarily a mystical sign of another world and would have left the possibility of its being a mode of language that creates all kinds of experience in its own forms. But the early Yeats is too heavily burdened by the pressure of materialist science and must at once restrict the German's statement, calling the symbol the giving of a body to a bodiless thing. In order to abandon the processes of analytical description, Yeats thinks he must abandon also the senses.

Nevertheless, Yeats's interest in Dante, Spenser, Blake, and Shelley indicates that he is drawn strongly to poets who build a language that captures the world in its structure, a "system of ordered images," as he calls it with respect to Dante's achievement.[138] Eventually Yeats will come no longer to insist that this sort of "myth" is principally a sign of an essence or mood. Until the end of his career he will, however, speak of the "great memory," which is a term that gathers much together for him in the way that "imagination" did for Baudelaire. The "great memory," which in one place is called "the memory of Nature,"[139] is far different from the "nothingness" of Mallarmé or from the "memory" of Blake. It is eternal, it is disembodied, and it is a "dwelling-house of symbols, of images that are living souls."[140] Yeats's whole idea of tradition and convention is tied to this concept, which he associated with Blake's "bright sculptures of Los's halls," and with the experience of magical evocation: "Anyone who has any experience of any mystical state of the soul knows how there float up in the mind profound symbols, whose meanings, if indeed they do not delude one into the dream that they are meaningless, one does not perhaps understand for years."[141] But they do have meaning to be discovered. This great memory, because it is itself composed of symbols or is the storehouse of them, does not seem to be the ultimate reality, only the language pointing to essence or the single mood from which all moods or gods emanate, descending by degrees into our minds. These last are messengers from the deep truth which apparently Shelley's Demogorgon rightly characterized as imageless.

On the other hand, Yeats occasionally indicates that the great memory is actually stocked by man himself: "Whatever the passions of man have gathered about, becomes a symbol in the Great Memory."[142] The issue of who or what makes or made the great memory or its contents (depending on whether the great memory is a storehouse or a collection) is not resolved. The symbols that are in some way related to it are characterized in two conflicting ways. They are regarded as the product of long associations, developing their power through repeated human use; but they are also regarded as possessing "preordained energies."[143] The resolution of these two ideas is not easy without some concept of the creative imagination, and the early Yeats does not provide it, or, if he does, it is so elusively presented in a prose frightened by discursiveness that we miss it. The distinctions Yeats attempts between "inherent" and "arbitrary" symbols[144] or "emotional" and "intellectual" ones [145] break down as soon as he creates them. The types, he admits, are mixed and blend in dreams, trance, madness, and meditation.

Though the symbol takes us to the great memory, to the moods, to essence, withdrawing from material, from all nature, from body, and though the early Yeats invests much in the symbol as a harbinger of a new supernaturalism,[146] there is another early Yeats. It is one who wishes to hang on to the particular and concrete. When he was a Theosophic student in 1890 he was actually asked to resign from the Esoteric Section because he said to the teacher, "By teaching an abstract system without experiment or evidence you are making your pupils dogmatic and you are taking them out of life."[147] In the *Autobiography*, he says with reference to the same period, "I generalized a great deal and was ashamed of it. . . . I began to pray that my imagination might somehow be rescued from abstraction."[148] This ambition fought with his tendency to be interested only in "intellectual essences."[149] By 1906 he could write: "Art bids us touch and taste and hear and see the world, and shrinks from what Blake called mathematic form, from every abstract thing, from all that is of the brain only, from all that is not a fountain jetting from the entire hopes, memories, and sensations of the body."[150] From at least this point, Yeats tends to distinguish the poet's role from that of the more abstract mystic.[151] By 1924, when he is preparing his early essays for a new edition, he adds a note to the essay on Blake's Dante illustrations. It says in part:

> Now, in reading these essays, I am ashamed when I come upon such words as "corporeal reason," "corporeal law," and think how I must have wasted the keenness of my youthful senses. I would like to believe that there was no help for it, that we were compelled to protect ourselves by such means against people and things we should never have heard of.[152]

"Corporeal" Yeats had appropriated erroneously from Blake. He seems not to have understood that Blake used the term quite precisely to refer to the abstraction that a Lockean epistemology makes of the body rather than his own idea of the spiritual body. At any rate Yeats recants, recognizing that he had been driven into a defensive and negative posture. By 1906 he had begun development of a distinction between poet and "saint" around which he builds for the rest of his career a drama of the poetic imagination, intimately bound up with body and earth. The worrying of the issue of symbolism as such is abandoned. Yet in another sense, which we are to study in chapter 11, Yeats becomes a more profound theorist of symbolic forms.

3. WILDE—ART AND NATURE

AMONG ENGLISH critics of the end of the nineteenth century, it was not the early Yeats who came closest to seeing his way out of a language all the rules of which positivism had imposed, but Oscar Wilde. Wilde has seldom been treated with the seriousness he deserves, and the reasons are obvious. First, the tragic end of his career and the flamboyance of the public personality he created made him appear a subject for the Mallarméan newspaper, not a creator of the book. Second, his epigrammatic style with its flippant play of ideas does not invite one to examine with any particular solemnity such underlying ideas as may or may not be expected to exist. Third, Wilde seems often merely to mouth fashionable decadent ideas. For example, one of the characters in the dialogue "The Critic as Artist" seems to be repeating a common antipositivistic cliché or to be extending an idea to absurdity for the sake of a joke: "Nowadays, we have so few mysteries left to us that we cannot afford to part with one of them."[153] However, much as Wilde plays with the attack on externality that leads to the glorification of mystery in the symbol, his fundamental effort is to restore art's relation to that externality. In spite of the usual view that Wilde separates art from life in an aesthetic world, the fact is that he often moves toward a redefinition of life and toward a theory of art as a cultural and social force. In this process he detaches art from all of those terms that he imagines positivism to have captured and deadened, including "morality." And he turns "imitation" on its head.

Ultimately Wilde's view is that art is creative of the forms into which we cast our perceptions of nature. Nature, of course, can have several meanings. It can be "simple instinct as opposed to self-conscious culture," but Wilde holds that work produced by those who hold this view is always old-fashioned and dull. On the other hand, we can think of nature as the "collection of phenomena external to man," and in this case man discovers in nature only what he himself brings.[154] But Wilde's is by no means a pure and relativistic subjectivism. For Wilde, nature exists in an unformed state. The question is whether man is going to copy it (a fruitless effort) or transform it. The former route is purely subjective and results in slavery to fashion; the latter is civilized and creative of culture. In "The Decay of Lying," Vivian remarks:

> What Art really reveals to us is Nature's lack of design, her curious crudities, her extraordinary monotony, her absolutely unfinished condition. Nature has good intentions, of course, but, as Aristotle once said, she cannot carry them out.[155]

Wilde's theory is thoroughly biased toward the creative: Men are not created by their times; it is men who create those times.[156] Nature is something to be subdued. Houses are preferable to the open air because they are our creations and thus subordinate nature. Fogs in London did not *really* exist until they were given artistic form so that we could see them.

> At present, people see fogs, not because there are fogs, but because poets and painters have taught them the mysterious

loveliness of such effects. There may have been fogs for centuries in London. I dare say there were. But no one saw them.
They did not exist till Art had invented them.[157]

Wilde then laments that fogs are now carried to excess. Sunsets too
have become old-fashioned, principally through the immense influence of Turner. Asked to a window by a pretty young woman to see a
glorious sky, Vivian reluctantly goes, and reports: "It was simply a
very second-rate Turner, a Turner of a bad period, with all the painter's worst faults exaggerated. . . ."[158] The upshot of all of this is that
nature copies art, or to put it another way, nature conforms to the
forms of human artistic creation. The language of art is the container
or maker of the reality that nature copies or becomes. A corollary of
this is that words are more real than action and harder to handle
than nature:

> It is very much more difficult to talk about a thing than to do
> it. In the sphere of actual life that is, of course, obvious. Any-
> body can make history. Only a great man can write it. There is
> no mode of action, no form of emotion, that we do not share
> with the lower animals. It is only by language that we rise
> above them, or above each other—by language, which is the
> parent, not the child of thought.[159]

The novelty of this is that art is the language *in which* the creation of
forms takes place.

It is in this sense that Wilde claims art only to express itself.[160]
This statement is usually taken to mean that art separates itself off
from life and culture. But Wilde really means that art shapes and contains culture, giving it meaning and true existence. Wilde's comic,
flippant tone has misled readers. Many with good reason dislike the
idea of culture implicit in his work. Also, throughout his writing
there is a desire to perplex. The result is the clichés that have developed about decadent escapism and the like. The cultural concerns of
the following deliberately exaggerated statement are discounted:

> I am certain that as civilisation progresses and we become
> more highly organised, the elect spirits of each age, the criti-
> cal and cultured spirits, will grow less and less interested in
> actual life, and *will seek to gain their impressions almost en-
> tirely from what Art has touched.* For Life is terribly deficient

in form. Its catastrophes happen in the wrong way and to the wrong people. There is a grotesque horror about its comedies, and its tragedies seem to culminate in farce.[161]

Readers assume that "art" here means something isolated from life; that is, they apply positivistic assumptions to a discourse that by the time this paragraph occurs has much enlarged "art's" meaning and destroyed positivism's hold on key terms. There is even in this passage the appearance of a moral premise. Artistic form defines the tragic and provides a standard of judgment which is aesthetic but moral as well.

Art for Wilde replaces the Kantian understanding as the preferred way to order nature. Wilde obliterates the subject-object distinction by playing the terms to death:[162] He claims the most objective-appearing artistic productions to be the most profoundly subjective and *vice versa*. There can be no creation of any kind that does not emerge from a creator. Shakespeare never speaks to us directly, but is always present: "Man is least himself when he talks in his own person. Give him a mask, and he will tell you the truth."[163] The conclusion is that Shakespeare's disappearance is *into a creation*, thus an appearance, while direct speech is rhetorical and purposive, implying a desire to manipulate an external nature that already exists as a formidable otherness, rather than to create. This destroys the self because the self is isolated from nature, which becomes an object. Wilde thus presents us with the image of man as a creator of symbolic forms of reality in the languages of art. Wilde's extremism is not in this but in his particular notion of high culture and his admonition that a work of art should have no use. This takes a Kantian idea to extremity. Kant never declared that a work of art must not be useful, only that viewed aesthetically an object is not externally purposive. But even here Wilde is often misunderstood because by this time Wilde has so identified "use" with a limited, shortsighted utilitarianism that we can take his concept of uselessness to mean appropriate cultural creation. As the tyranny of materialism seems to have driven Mallarmé from all externality, so apparently did the tyranny of positivism force Wilde into declaring for the uselessness of art, even as he claims paradoxically that art in its cultural role is the most useful—but not purposive—of all things.

6

The Modern Dream

I come now to consideration of the first of two terms—"dream" and "fiction"—that play special roles in connection with the poetic. Though "dream" has long been a metaphor for art, the modern treatments of dreams do not at the theoretical level shift over to poetry as easily as is often supposed. This does not imply that modern literature does not contain psychoanalytical allegories. It does imply that modern psychoanalysis, though it speaks much of the symbol, in the end does not treat poetry as a "secular" symbolic but rather as a form of allegory only.

The first lines in Yeats's *Collected Poems* lament the replacement of dreaming in modern life by the "grey truth" of modern science. The poem goes on to advise a return to dreaming as a defense against scientific modernism, which is identified with materialism and mechanization. I have already mentioned the symbolist use of the words "dream" (*rêve*) and "reverie" to express antipositivistic sentiments and to construct an alternative to positivism's capture of "thought."[1] The recourse to "dream" is not, of course, invented by the symbolists. Since antiquity, dreams have been considered conveyors of special knowledge, and dreams and visions had already been a subject for, if not the alleged form of, poetry. Yet one detects increased activity with respect to the word "dream" in the early nineteenth century, where "dream" comes to be expressive of internal spiritual states and identified with the freedom of the spirit rather than a conveyor of messages from some *beyond*. Keats's nightingale teases him out of "thought" into a state of mind that *may* be identifiable with "dream." Novalis finds that dreams free the imagination and reunite the adult with his childhood. For Nerval, dreams are a preferable second life. Baudelaire quotes Ernst Hoffman on the visionary synaesthesia of dreams.[2] Mallarmé's attempt to establish a radical creativity out of the nothingness of the self suggests connections to dreams not lost on his followers. One symbolist magazine was called *Le Rêve et L'Idée*, which was to glorify the import of the dream as the container of truth. This attitude is not restricted to poets but appears in theorists of the dream. In 1814, G. H. von Schubert's *Die Symbolik des Traumes* argued that dreams emancipate man from the natural world and raise him to a higher level of experience. K. A. Schermer in 1861 held that dreams possess a "productive" power.[3]

The word "dream" among the symbolists represents a radical subjectivity that often calls in question the status of the external world while at the same time staking out the internal world as the domain of poetry. The famous passage from Pater that we have already noticed keeps the "dream" a subjective enclosure: "Every one of these impressions is the impression of the individual in his isolation, each mind keeping as a solitary prisoner its own dream of a world."[4] Here the term signifies an attempt to recapture for the imagination, and in its terms, the whole realm of perception, but at the risk of solipsism. Of all nineteenth-century writers, Pater seems most succinctly to have expressed the curious situation of the romantic imagination faced with the narrowing of its domain and surrounded by an externality it never made and cannot know.

1. FREUDIAN ALLEGORY

BUT SUCH defensive maneuvers as those grouped around the identification of "dream" with poetic vision barely survived the end of the century. The connection of dream with poetic vision suffered a severe blow when Sigmund Freud captured still more of the intellectual terrain for positivism by making the dream subject to analysis, thereby objectifying and externalizing it. Up to the time of Freud, the scientific study of dreams had not influenced the poets' use of the term to any great extent. The prevailing medical opinion that dreams were the result of external physical stimuli during sleep was easy to ignore because it explained so little by explaining so much. Freud seemed to be in revolt against the prevailing currents of scientific opinion, but he illustrates the simple logical principle that for two people to be against something does not necessarily unite them. His view is clearly positivistic: Supernaturalist interpretations of dreams must give way as science moves ahead: "We may leave on one side pietistic and mystical writers, who, indeed, are perfectly justified in remaining in occupation of what is left of the once wide domain of the supernatural so long as that field is not conquered by scientific explanation."[5] His own recapitulation of the history of the theory of dreams[6] seemed to align him to some extent with a long tradition of dream interpretation even as he declared his break with all that had gone before. He quotes Schiller on the dangers of the domination of reason over the creative activity, favoring Schiller's view that one must be free of the analytic and the critical in order to create.[7] However, he applauds Schiller's remark not because he believes *higher* truths will emerge from relaxation of the critical faculty but because it is a statement that out of Schiller's context can be taken to illustrate a state of mind in which a patient undergoing psychoanalysis is most able to release valuable information through free association. There is nothing "creative" in Schiller's sense about this. There is no pretense in Freud that Schiller's heights and these newly discovered depths are connected. For Freud, the views of Schubert, the younger Fichte, and Schermer are "scarcely intelligible" and are now "repeated only by mystics and pietists."[8] Yet these views were hardly supernaturalistic in the occultist sense. Rather, they were metaphysical.

Very soon after Freud, and because of him, the challenge to critics was as much to distinguish poetry from dreams as to identify poetry with them.[9] There had already been mechanistic theories of dreams and even the reduction of art to sexuality and repressed or unconscious desires,[10] but never one, like Freud's, so apparently capable of making powerful explanations. The situation was muddled, however, by Freud's own remarks about art, some of which seemed to glorify the artist almost as much as any symbolist might wish, others of which tended to reduce art to infantile play.[11] As a result of this, two aspects of Freudian theory must be kept separate in considering his thought about symbolism. The first is the analogy to be drawn from his work between dream and poem, and, by extension, between analysis and literary criticism. The second is his occasional tendency to treat the analogy as an identity. I shall consider each, but shall make no attempt to resolve them with each other, for they cannot be.

Freud pays some attention to two past methods of dream-interpretation, the so-called "symbolic" and the "decoding." The former "considers content of the dream as a whole and seeks to replace it by another content which is intelligible and in certain respects analogous to the original one."[12] His objection to the "symbolic" method is that it breaks down in the face of so many confused, unintelligible dreams. The decoding method "treats dreams as a kind of cryptography in which each sign can be translated into another sign having a known meaning, in accordance with a fixed key."[13] Freud believes the dream as a whole cannot be taken as the unit initially to be interpreted. Instead, the "separate portions of its content" must be read. Freud claims to be nearer to the "decoding" method than to the "symbolic," for dreams are of a "composite" character.[14] At the same time, Freud does not necessarily acknowledge the existence of those fixed meanings for dream "symbols" popular among the decoders before his own work appeared. Indeed, it is only with reservations that he acknowledges the existence of any fixed dream "symbols," and he warns against leaping to conclusions about the manifest symbols of dreams.

Freud's concept of the dream is simple and schematic. There are the "latent dream thoughts," which, through what he calls the "dream work," are displaced, condensed, and represented by a "manifest dream content." This content is, in fact, a scrambled and coded version of a hidden, or repressed, original. The analysis or interpretation of the dream has as its task restoration of the original "latent dream thoughts." This circle from latent dream thought back to dream thought via interpretation is, in Freud's view, traversable without loss, at least theoretically. There is nothing to the manifest dream that is not either simply the mechanism of displacement, condensation, and representation or the masked original thoughts. The "dream work," in other words, adds nothing of its own to the content of the dream, and form is of no account. The latent dream thought is regarded as fully expressible in discursive form. It appears that to Freud the dream thought *is* fundamentally a discursive linguistic form, but Freud does not raise explicitly the crucial question of the authority of this language, and it has only been with structuralism that attention has been turned to what Freud had to have meant, if one grants the structuralist premise of a linguistic chain that contains both signifier and signified.[15] Here the latent dream is a linguistic structure. If one does not accept this structuralist assumption, one looks for discussion of the relation of the linguistic structure of the latent dream to the unconscious, but Freud does not pretend to know anything about the mysterious unknown that the latent dream thought represents, if the dream thought is not the fundamental creation, beneath which is nothing. Freud has no theory of creativity at either manifest or latent level. The Freudian unconscious, then, seems to be an unknowable sort of interior thing-in-itself. But unlike Kant, in his confrontation of the unknowable external thing-in-itself, Freud does not indicate that any active creative power makes the latent dream thought from an internal manifold. What he in one place calls "dream composition"[16] he regards not as the construction of the original thought but only the "dream work" of displacement, condensation, and representation, which adds no meaning. "Composition" is not productive at all but is, in fact, a kind of destruction of the logic of the original thought.

One part of the condensation is a turning of a discursive thought into images that express it.[17] Different dreams express different relations between latent and manifest content. There are those whose manifest contents have a clear sense on the surface and at the same time fit clearly into our mental life. There are those that have a clear sense but do not seem to fit into our life. And there are those—the majority—that are confused, disconnected, and apparently meaningless. In all of these cases psychoanalysis seeks the "essential [latent] dream thought"[18] by restoring all the logical connections which the dream work has destroyed in condensation. It then can interpret the symbols that are the result of displacement and representation. The hypothesis in every case is that the connections are there to be found and that the "latent dream thought" is a thought expressible in discursive form, that indeed such is its true form, language fully expressing the unconscious, perhaps (though Freud does not broach the issue) being indeed the form or very nature of the content of the unconscious.

There is an analogy, but only an analogy, possibly to be drawn between the triad of latent dream thought—manifest dream—analysis (which is the latent dream again in its appropriate discursive, explanatory form) and the Baudelairean triad of correspondence: Upper world—dictionary nature—work of art. In both cases, the triad's middle term is a sort of chaos that the creator of the third term has to reorder in its original form (or, in Baudelaire's case, something like its original form). The difference is critical, however; Baudelaire's upper world is not a discursive idea but instead has all the qualities of a formal aesthetic unity, while Freud's "latent dream thought" appears to be an abstract idea. It is further to be noted that in Freud's triad it is the manifest dream that is analogous to the work of art, while in Baudelaire the work of art is the end product of the triad, not the analysis of it.

Jack J. Spector is quite right, at least with respect to the fundamental Freudian analogy, to point out that Stanley Edgar Hyman errs in his claim that Freud believed all artists to be analysts.[19] Freud's analogy, of course, requires that the analyst be the critic, not the artist. Indeed, for Freud the dreamer would seem unconsciously to act like, say, a political poet speaking by an obscure allegory in order to protect himself against charges of heresy or treason. But this is not finally an adequate analogy, because the manifest dream is usually quite confused and more like a coded message or a message passed into a scrambler than a poem. The dream is hieroglyphical, but not as a whole: ". . . one can never tell whether any particular element in the content of a dream is to be interpreted symbolically or in its proper sense, and one can be certain that the *whole* content of a dream is not to be interpreted symbolically."[20] By "symbolically" here Freud means an interpretation which takes the manifest dream as a unity like a poem which can be given a single unified reading. But his concern in making this remark is only with the *process* of interpretation; he claims that one cannot begin work with the manifest dream considered as a unified whole, but must examine each part with respect to everything else one can learn from the patient. The manifest dream will seek to frustrate any simple reading of its content. Of course, it could be argued that at another level the manifest dream is a *unity of evasiveness* (my term) and that as a whole it has a purpose to which all of its parts can be referred. No doubt, Freud would agree with this, for in his system the dream in theory can finally be explained. But Freud would not be able to argue that such a unity is more than the expression of the logic of the mechanisms of condensation, displacement, and representation. It is not a unity working *toward* a meaning, but away from it.[21] It is not an aesthetic unity, which works toward its own forms of clarity rather than obfuscation. Perhaps this is why Freud speaks of the manifest dream as a "dream *content*" [my italics] and does not treat the manifest dream as having a form. Nor is the latent dream content an aesthetic unity. It is, however, apparently a discursive unity, a unity of what Kant might have called external purposiveness.

The term "symbol" in Freud does multiple duty, for it refers to more than the so-called "symbolical" mode of dream interpretation. It also refers to the parts of the manifest dream as they are isolated for analysis: ". . . unlike other forms of indirect representation, that which is employed in dreams must not be immediately intelligible. The modes of representation which fulfill these conditions are usually described as 'symbols' of the things which they represent."[22] The processes to which the latent dream thought is submitted generate an apparently arbitrary relation between "latent dream thought" and the manifested "symbol" that stands for it.

The abstract, discursive nature of the "latent dream thought" that the "symbol" stands for makes the Freudian dream "symbol" analogous not to romantic symbolism but to romantic allegory. The apparently arbitrary relation between thought and symbol is not, of course, arbitrary in another sense. Freud's evidence suggests that with experience the analyst is able to understand the meaning of the separate elements of the manifest content of a dream, in some cases even whole dreams, without having to ask the dreamer for his associations.[23] This is because dreamers who speak the same language, and even some who don't, often seem to employ similar symbols in dreams.[24] Thus, if the relation of symbol to "latent dream thought" is being obfuscated, there seems to be a common mental mechanism that produces the same symbols in different people. This idea verges on the same concept of fixed meanings for manifest symbols, the too easy acceptance of which Freud elsewhere cautions against.

We have already noticed that Freud himself sometimes allows the analogy of dream and art to become an identity. When he distinguishes between them it is usually on the ground that most dreams from the point of view of analysis resemble "a disordered heap of disconnected fragments," and such dreams are just as valuable as those that have been "beautifully polished and provided with a surface."[25] But despite this phrase, the "dream work" is in no way creative, that is, "it develops no fantasies of its own, . . . it makes no judgments and draws no conclusions; it has no functions whatever other than condensation and displacement of the material and its modification into pictorial form, to which must be added as a variable factor the final bit of interpretative revision."[26] Absolutely nothing here suggests even the naïve idea of a fundamental material being worked into something new by poetic shaping. All shaping is the result of the mechanism of evasion and *absolutely nothing more*. The activity of the "dream work" is not really, then, the activity of the artist, as the basic analogy demands, even a so-called "allegoristic" artist. Freud, in any case, sees the so-called formal or aesthetic aspects of art as quite separate from art's content, and he often admits to little interest in the former.[27]

Nevertheless, he occasionally persists in speaking as if there were a complete identity of art and dream. When he does so it appears that all the separated, so-called formal and aesthetic elements come to be regarded as part, not of an evasion perhaps, but at least of a device of bribery to a reader to continue to show interest in the author's egotistical expression. Having made the connection between the creative writer and day-dreaming in a well-known essay, he remarks: "The writer softens the egotistical character of the day-dream by changes and disguises, and he bribes us by the offer of a purely formal, that is, aesthetic pleasure in the presentation of his phantasies."[28] The aesthetic element here is detachable from the work's meaning and is defined purely in terms of an external purposiveness. By his own admission Freud paid scant attention to this so-called aesthetic element and always treated it as separable: ". . . the subject-matter of works of art has a stronger attraction for me than their formal and technical qualities."[29] Curiously, he goes on to state that these qualities are nevertheless foremost to the author; having said this, if he had been pressed on this point he would have had to indicate that in his opinion they were foremost to the author because of their power of bribery.[30] As Spector reminds us, Freud avoided making any claim to a "comprehensive theory of aesthetics."[31] This is not surprising considering the narrowness of meaning he gives to the term "aesthetics."

The analogue of poem and day-dream connects the poet with the child at play. The adult no longer plays as the child does, but constitutes "phantasy" for play with real objects.[32] In the Freudian system, of course, unfulfilled wishes are the "driving power" behind fantasies.[33] All imaginative productions can be traced back to the original "naïve day-dream" by an uninterrupted series of transitions. Of course, adult fantasy is more closely in touch with reality, a term Freud uses loosely and thus makes problematic itself, than the play of children. The model of latent dream thought—manifest dream—analysis still prevails, with the work of art playing the middle term and "aesthetic" form being the result of the destructive "dream work." It is involved in the attempt to mask the egocentricity of the day-dream.

The analogy of the dream extends in Freud to myths, fairy tales, and even jokes. Indeed, it is a formula that threatens to encompass all so-called fictive creations. In addition, Freud argues that we generally underestimate the role of the unconscious in nonartistic activity as well as artistic. Although he believes this to be true and although he dwells on the relation of myth to dream, he feels compelled to draw a distinction "between poets who, like the bygone creators of epics and tragedies, take over their material ready-made, and those who seem to create their material spontaneously."[34] In "The Relation of the Poet to Day-Dreaming" he recommends that we examine only the latter and, of these, less highly esteemed writers. He curiously assumes that romances, novels, and stories of this less esteemed sort will be more susceptible to his approach; though it ought to have been obvious enough to him that such works are usually doggedly and obviously conventional and often written to the external formula not of "his majesty" the author's ego, but, if anything, the publishing world's idea of the *reader's* wishes. The distinction Freud uses is also used by F. C. Prescott in his *Poetry and Dreams* (1912).[35] It is as troublesome to him as it was to his master and to the apostate Carl Jung, who produces his own version of it.[36] Freud does not work out a concept of literary convention, perhaps because the line he draws between form and content leaves him no place for a clear perception of it.

There is another aspect of the analogy between dreams and literature in Freud that is exploited by later critics and writers who find potential illumination in it. In his study of dreams, Freud discusses the absence in the manifest dream of the normal relational concepts of discursive thought—"because," "either-or," "no," "if," and the like. Discursive incompatibles are present together in the manifest dream.[37] Before Vico and even back to Plato it had been often thought that poetry employs a sort of ordering or logic different from or even antithetical to that of what Kant called the categories of the understanding, and Freud's analysis of dreams opens up the possibility of further exploration of this. But, of course, Freud does not give to this antilogic any status as a true mode of constructive thought, because, as always in his view, there is a key to the confusion that will reveal it as a systematic allegorical destruction of a quite logical structure in the "latent dream thought" itself. There is finally no concept of the symbolic, creative imagination in Freud.

With respect to the connections of myth to art through the concept of the dream, Freud remarks outright that myths are probably "distorted vestiges of the wish-fantasies of whole nations—the agelong dreams of young humanity."[38] The series of analogies which emerges from Freud's writings fails to provide us with any discussion of language that might clarify the relationships the analogies suggest. Though he never states this outright and might well have some serious reservations about it if he did, at the source of the dream thought there appears to be a verbal structure. Its first appearance to the analyst is "unusual." Such thoughts "are not clothed in the prosaic language usually employed by our thoughts, but are on the contrary represented symbolically [in my terms, allegorically] by means of similes and metaphors, in images resembling those of poetic speech."[39] But this is a "constraint imposed upon the form in which dream thoughts are repressed." It is anything but an advance on the original it distorts. Freud expresses the typical positivistic view of language as fundamentally discursive and of tropes and figures as deviations from the norm of language and thought. Freud shows much interest in language with respect to jokes and verbal play, but he never really probes the linguistic implications of his own conception of the dream thought. The role that language plays in a structure that is either the ultimate reality of the unconscious or an emergence from an unknowable depth is left for discussion by followers like Lacan. Freud's theory of the dream and of the poem is allegoristic in the simple sense of the substitutive. All meaning is reducible to that expressible in the language of the understanding and all else is without meaning. Poetry can finally be nothing more than such meaning either imagistically condensed or cunningly displaced in order either to bribe the reader with some sort of pleasure added on or to hide from some readers what is really being said.

2. JUNGIAN ALLEGORY

THE GREAT apostate of the psychoanalytical movement is, of course, Carl Jung. If Freud is a preromantic allegorist, Jung at first glance seems more like a symbolist, though it will be necessary to determine just what Jung meant by the term. "The contrast between Freud and myself," Jung remarks, "goes back to essential differences in our basic assumptions. Assumptions are unavoidable, and this being so, it is wrong to pretend that we have made no assumptions."[40] It is this challenge to Freud's basic but unstated assumptions that makes Jung of particular importance. It has been argued by René Wellek that all of the traditional theology that Kant had dispensed with flows back into Coleridge's philosophy. It has been said of Jung that the "mystical and pietistic" attitudes that Freud lays to rest reappear in Jung's recourse to metaphysical issues. There is ground for thinking this to be true in both cases, though no overwhelming reason to assume that either Coleridge or Jung can be dismissed as wrong because of it.

In dealing with Jung the dream-poem analogy is again our principal concern, and we shall soon come to it. However, it is important first to affirm that Jung attempts to enlarge the realm of possible meanings of dreams. For him all dreams cannot be reduced to wish-fulfillments: "Dreams may give expression to ineluctable truths, to philosophical pronouncements, illusions, wild fantasies, memories, plans, anticipations, irrational experiences, even telepathic visions, and heaven knows what besides."[41] Thus he implies that no single reduction of dreams is possible. Further he complains that Freud's reduction of dreams to a sexual source involves an unwarranted expansion of the concept of sexuality, which becomes "so vague that it can be made to include almost anything."[42] The reduction that occurs in Freud ends in classifying everything from the activity of the glands to that of the "highest reaches of the spirit" under the single term. Jung rejects any Freudian effort so to reduce the work of art, which is "something in its own right, and may not be conjured away."[43] What any psychologist has to say can only apply to the "process of artistic creation" rather than to its "innermost essence."[44] In certain ways, Jung makes the dream-poem analogy seem to be a closer one than Freud did. First, he considers the dream on the analogy of a text: "We say that the dream has a false front only because we fail to see into it. We would do better to say that we are dealing with something like a text that is unintelligible, not because it has a facade, but simply because we cannot read it."[45] Second, he defines the dream-symbol much as the literary symbol came to be defined in the nineteenth century, distinguishing his usage of the term from Freud's:

> . . . it is the indefinite content that marks the symbol as against the mere sign or symptom. It is well known that the Freudian school operates with hard and fast sexual "symbols"; but these are just what I should call signs, for they are made to stand for sexuality, and this is supposed to be something definite.[46]

Jung never tires of making the point that what Freud calls symbols are not true symbols but "signs" or "symptoms."[47] But Jung is not totally consistent in his own treatment of symbols. He says that he prefers to regard the symbol, even what he calls "relatively fixed symbols,"[48] as "the announcement of something unknown, hard to recognize and not to be fully determined."[49] He speaks of images that are "true symbols because they are the best possible expressions for something unknown—bridges thrown out towards an unseen shore."[50] However, he also makes remarks, in the same essays, implying that what is unknown may yet become known: "It is far wiser in practice not to regard the dream-symbols as signs or symptoms of a fixed character. We should rather take them as true symbols—that is to say, as expressions of something not *yet* consciously recognized or conceptually formulated [my italics—H. A.]."[51] This positivistic influx cannot be regarded quite as a careless oversight, even though it conflicts with the previous statements, for the same assertion appears twice in another essay: "The true symbol . . . should be understood as an expression of an intuitive idea that cannot yet be formulated in any other or better way,"[52] and "true symbols are . . . attempts to express something for which no verbal concept yet exists."[53] And a little farther on, "meaning" seems to be equated with "verbal concept": ". . . a symbol is the intimation of a meaning beyond the level of our present powers of comprehension."[54] There is no resolution of this contradiction between a symbol that can by its very nature never have a verbal concept equivalent to it and one that does not *yet* have an equivalent verbal concept but may eventually.

In the light of this, we are torn two ways when we learn that Jung calls *Faust* Part Two a symbol and differentiates it from allegory, which "points to something all too familiar." *Faust* is "an expression that stands for something not clearly known and yet profoundly alive."[55] Does the statement imply that this thing "not clearly known" may in time become better known and conceptualized in other terms, whereupon we may abandon *Faust*?

It is possible, indeed probable, that Jung does not quite mean to say what he has said and has lost a battle with the "stubborn structure" of language recognized by Blake. For Jung does not, I think, ever offer us the example of a symbol that has been successfully fully conceptualized. He seems really to be saying that the symbol proceeds from unconscious sources and is in its very nature not conceptual. Yet it can be meditated upon, in much the way that Yeats speaks of in his essay on magic,[56] to achieve nondiscursive intuitions. Symbols are thus not merely personal but universal. The example Jung most often employs of such a symbol is the mandala, which takes myriad forms in dreams and art and which he describes as a symbol that "stands for a psychic happening," covering an experience of the inner world. The mandala symbol is a sign after all, but a sign of

something that cannot be known—"no doubt as lifelike a representation as the famous rhinoceros with the tickbirds on its back."[57]

Jung applies this principle to both poems and dreams, and connects the work of the individual poet to mythology: "I am assuming
that the work of art we propose to analyze, as well as being symbolic,
has its source not in the *personal unconscious* of the poet, but in a
sphere of unconscious mythology whose primordial images are the
common heritage of mankind. I have called this sphere the collective
unconscious."[58] These primordial images or "archetypes" appear
"wherever creative fantasy is freely expressed."[59] The difference from
Freud appears in the insistence on creativity and freedom.

Jung is similar to Freud in his need to divide literature into two
types. He adopts an analogy to Schiller's distinction between naïve
and sentimental poetry, calling them extroverted and introverted respectively and concluding that the extroverted sort is submissive to
the "demands of the object" (by which he vaguely means the poet's
materials or external nature), while the introverted asserts an author's conscious intentions against the demands of the object. Part
Two of *Faust* is evinced as extroverted, where the consciousness of
the poet is "not identical with the creative process."[60] Another distinction in another essay is related to this via the example of *Faust*.
There poetry is divided into the psychological and the visionary. The
psychological mode is represented by *Faust* Part One. It

> deals with materials drawn from the realm of human con-
> sciousness. . . . This material is psychically assimilated by the
> poet, raised from the commonplace to the level of poetic ex-
> perience, and given an expression which forces the reader to
> greater clarity and depth of human insight by bringing fully
> into his consciousness what he ordinarily evades and over-
> looks or senses only with a feeling of dull discomfort.[61]

The visionary mode involves, by contrast, the expression of "primordial experience which surpasses man's understanding, and to which
he is therefore in danger of succumbing,"[62] an example being *Faust*
Part Two. Both Freud and Jung seem to have divided literature because of their sense that what they have to say about it applies more
convincingly to some of it than equally to all of it. Indeed, it appears
that Jung's distinction makes the term "symbol" apply only to the
visionary mode and is not a term interchangeable with literature as it
seems to have been with some romantic theorists. Visionary litera-

ture is "true symbolic expression—that is, the expression of something existent in its own right, but imperfectly known."[63] Jung believes man suppresses this "something" because of our modern fear of superstition and metaphysics. This fear is the result of modern life's tendency toward conceptual or "directed" thinking to the exclusion of all other possible modes.[64] The problem is to get behind language so conceived to determine what lurks there yet to find expression. This implies the familiar dualism of poetry and language that Croce noted.[65] Visionary literature apparently does this through the symbol. But Jung creates even a further dualism differentiating the symbolic from the aesthetic, stating that the truly symbolic breaks up the aesthetic unity of a work:

> A symbol remains a perpetual challenge to our thoughts and feelings. That probably explains why a symbolic work is so stimulating, why it grips us so intensely, but also why it seldom affords us a purely aesthetic enjoyment. A work that is manifestly not symbolic appeals much more to our aesthetic sensibilities because it is complete in itself and fulfills its purpose.[66]

In fact, Jung comes to identify the creative process itself with the "activation of an archetypal image," and "the elaborating and shaping of this image into the finished work."[67] But this leaves the psychological mode of art, and the aesthetic as well, outside art entirely, if art is to be identified with creativity. But is it, or can it be in this system? As we shall see, it cannot.

With all aesthetics pretty well disposed of, what is the function or purpose of art? It is to shape the archetype:

> . . . the artist translates it [the archetype] into the language of the present and so makes it possible for us to find our way back to the deepest springs of life. Therein lies the social significance of art [but apparently only visionary art]: it is constantly at work educating the spirit of the age, conjuring up the forms in which the age is most lacking.[68]

Visionary art is a compensation for the "one-sidedness of the present."[69]

What Jung is giving us is a psychologistic version of symbolist symbolism, with an identical concern about the mechanistic direction of culture and a quarrel with language, which is normatively conceived of only as discursive. Jung's language seems tacitly to assume that anything brought fully into the consciousness, as "psychological" literature brings things, is conceptualized. Conceptualization and consciousness are treated as identical. Any full expression of something is apparently a conceptualization of it. Therefore, symbols are not really full expressions of what they signify but only intimations of something sometimes considered permanently unknown, sometimes considered only for the present unknown. A work of the "psychological" mode begins to look like either a purely discursive statement or an allegory in the romantic sense, which merely masks a purely discursive statement.

Literature, therefore, for Jung becomes two very different things. Though both types use words, Jung does not have a theory of language that clearly includes both. The "visionary" mode is really an unlinguistic literature where words, if any attention is paid to them at all, are regarded only as signs or symbols of unknown things. The less attention paid here to language, which is always "directed" in modern life and a symptom of modern life's one-sidedness, the better. "Directed language" is what we think in: "language directed outwards to the outside world."[70] Such thinking, like Herder's thinking, is in verbal form the content of which is inseparable from that form.[71] Jung sees language as developing from emotive and imitative sounds into a complex system of conceptualization, the end of which would seem to be scientific abstraction. This thinking seems to be equivalent to what Kant called the activity of the understanding. Between this and what William James called "associative thinking" (Jung calls it "thinking in images" or "dreaming or fantasy-thinking"), there seems to be for Jung no middle ground.[72] This leaves the verbal art of literature in neither camp unless one either ignores its verbal character and pretends that it is merely the play of signs of true symbols, which are pure images, or calls it allegory in the romantic sense and considers it a covert form of "directed thinking." Jung seems to do both: psychological literature is the latter; visionary literature the former, the problem of words being ignored. Visionary literature is identified with dreams and mythic images. Apparently the formal elements of a work, separated from content, are identified with the verbalization and contribute little or nothing to the power of visionary literature. As we have already observed, Jung creates a dualism of the visionary and the aesthetic. We see now that the visionary must be, for him, profoundly antiverbal. The language of visionary literature must come to be identified only with rhetoric and decoration, very near to the Freudian "bribery."

Jung's civilized form of language is "directed" to the external world. It is part of man's striving to dominate nature by the discovery of a system of natural causes.[73] The result of this harnessing of the natural world in language is, however, a splitting of the human experience into an externalizing on the one hand and on the other an internalizing apparently impervious to linguistic action or conceptualization. Archaic man did not suffer this split,[74] and at the "deeper levels" of every modern man's psyche there is an archaic man.[75] The archaic man, unencumbered by a conceptual language, is "unpsychological," that is, "psychic happenings take place outside him in an objective way,"[76] which is apparently Jung's way of saying that archaic man does not distinguish inside from outside, that it is modern man who invented the inside and outside. Jung seems to imply that archaic man's condition is the condition of true creativity, because the primordial images are not suppressed within by the domination of the discursive intellect, but flow forth as they did in the forms of myth in ancient life. Jung begins to sound here like Yeats, who recommended that poets "copy the pure inspiration of ancient times."[77] "Thinking in primordial symbols," a sort of depth thinking beneath language, is for Jung the source of art and apparently of health. But primitive man for Jung is not prelogical, as Lévy-Bruhl argued. He merely has different presuppositions. But Jung does not show what sort of logic sustains these presuppositions. He declares that artistic creation is characterized by a return to a state of what Lévy-Bruhl called "*participation mystique*," where individuality is buried in communion.[78] Yet in another essay Jung quarrels with the application of the term "mystical" to this state,[79] since from the primitive point of view there is nothing mystical in the attitude. Before there can be mysticism there must be a bifurcation between the interior and exterior of the self. All bifurcating terms—"matter," "mind," etc.—are merely "symbols" for Jung,[80] but he cannot mean they are symbols in the sense in which he has used the term to mean representations of the primordial unknown. They must rather be *mere symbols* considered as the creations of a mind thinking *in* language and creating a structure of an outside and inside.

The irony finally perceptible in the Jungian system is that, as much as Jung claims for the work of art "something in its own right," implying something *created* in its construction, the only real creativity we can be sure of when we view his system as a whole, is that involved in "directed" thinking in language. The farther we get toward what Jung obviously regards as the greatest literature, the "visionary" and "extroverted," the closer we come to a version of the old Platonic divine madness and a "Platonic" form of allegory verging upon the "religious," though it must be said that Jung's mandalas and archetypal symbols are sometimes treated as "miraculous" symbols.

This connection of "visionary" and "extroverted" may still appear curious, and it is probably useful to recapitulate how it comes about. I have established in Jung the following equations:

Schiller's naïve = extroverted = visionary = *Faust* Part II
Schiller's sentimental = introverted = psychological = *Faust* Part I

In the introverted-psychological the "material is mastered by the conscious intentions of the poet."[81] In the extroverted-visionary the material is distinguished by its "refractoriness."[82] We recall that Jung says that archaic man is not "psychological" and that he has no "inside," so to speak. In Jung, the bifurcation of external-internal is transcended by the term "external" in contrast to, say, Berkeley, where the transcendence is in roughly the opposite direction. Thus for Jung the "visionary" is identified with archaic man's unpsychological extroversion. Curiously enough, this makes the introverted-psychological work more "creative," because the artist asserts his aims against the demands of the object while the extroverted-visionary submits to an external force. Thus the literature Jung is most interested in and admires the most is in our terms the least creative.

The visionary poet discovers or experiences symbols and expresses signs for them, but finally he makes nothing. It is man creating language, moving ever apparently toward higher and higher levels of abstraction, who is creative. But he is creative only finally of those bifurcations that threaten his own health. Jung, therefore, continues to assert the old dualism of poetry and language and adds to it his own dualism of vision and aesthetic as well as that of the highest poetry and creativity. His bifurcations raise problems as perplexing as the bifurcation of nature into outer and inner that he deplores.

These problems, though never analyzed by Jung, seem to stand at the threshold of his own consciousness, for he attempts to draw the line between a psychologist's approach to art and an approach staying "within the sphere of art,"[83] thereby obliterating, at least for art, the bifurcations he has created. From its own point of view, he declares, art has no "meaning," at least as we understand "meaning":

Perhaps it is like nature, which simply *is* and "means" nothing beyond that. Is "meaning" necessarily more than mere interpretation—an interpretation secreted into something by an intellect hungry for meaning?[84]

But outside the sphere of art it is "impossible for us not to speculate."[85]

One senses Jung's dissatisfaction in a situation for which Jung himself has no cure within the mode of interpretation he follows. It is a dissatisfaction which leads to an abandonment of the analogy between art and dream in much modern criticism and among poets, or at least to an insistence on strict limitation of the analogy along the lines enunciated by Charles Lamb a century before: "The poet dreams being awake. He is not possessed by his subject but has dominion over it."[86] If a term served to replace "dream" to characterize poetry in the modern period, it was "form," and Jung, as the great dissenter from Freud, was quite in line with modernist critical thought to the extent that he questioned the application of the term "meaning" to poetry and worried about the unsatisfactoriness of a situation in which interpretation has to "meet the demands of science."[87]

3. BACHELARDIAN REVERIE

BECAUSE in chapter 12 I shall be contrasting my own position to that of certain phenomenological critics, it is important to consider, in connection with the dream as a literary concept, the anti-Freudian phenomenological critical theory of Gaston Bachelard. Is Bachelard's anti-Freudianism useful to a philosophy of the literary symbolic?[88] Bachelard, who began his career as a philosopher of science and then astounded his colleagues by writing meditations on the primordial elements, such as *The Psychoanalysis of Fire* (1938),[89] held that in order to deal with such things as reverie and poetry, the philosopher had to break with his past habits of research.[90] It is the same, he thought, for the psychoanalyst. The psychoanalyst "thinks too much" and "does not dream enough."[91] Yet Bachelard means "dream" in a quite special way here, and eventually his need to give obeisance to Lamb's idea requires him to distinguish "dream" from "reverie," only the latter providing a connection with poetry. The former is referred to as the "night dream." The distinction is expressed in terms of consciousness:

The night dreamer cannot articulate a *cogito*. The night dream is a dream without a dreamer. On the contrary, the dreamer of reverie remains conscious enough to say: it is I who dream the reverie, it is I who am content to dream my reverie, happy with this leisure in which I no longer have the task of thinking.[92]

There is apparently a creative element in reverie, but not in the "night dream." Bachelard distinguishes this creativity from "thinking," which is apparently always discursive. We shall see that Bachelard identifies the state of reverie with freedom. Not so, the night dream, in which the subject loses his "being."[93] The night dream, according to Bachelard, must be left to the psychoanalyst and the anthropologist, who will compare it to myths. But these comparisons will have little or nothing to do with reverie, for they reveal only the "immobile, anonymous man" or the "man without a subject."[94]

By contrast to the night dreamer, the dreamer of reverie, "if he is a bit philosophical, can formulate a *cogito* at the center of his dreaming self." There is always a "glimmer of consciousness" in reverie,[95] even though this *cogito* is less lively than that of the thinker, less sure than that of the philosopher. It is not quite clear how this lessened activity and sureness contribute to a greater freedom, since they seem to draw the subject closer to the nonbeing of the *cogito* of the night dreamer. Nevertheless, Bachelard identifies reverie with freedom by comparison to "thought" because he imagines the dreamer of reverie escaping that old horror, the subject-object problem. In reverie the dreamer's *cogito* is not "divided into the dialectic of subject and object."[96] In an important statement Bachelard claims that "objects privileged by reverie become the direct complements of the dreamer's *cogito*."[97] Active life is rooted in the subject-object problem and thrusts us on to a position outside or opposite to things and to the world,[98] and this position is not for Bachelard truly free, caught as it is in the toils of our modern bifurcation. But in reverie nothing is opposite to the dreamer. The dreamer is "in an *inside* which has no *outside*."[99] Whether this is a radical subjectivity or a denial of the whole subject-object opposition is not quite clear. I suspect it is the former.

Clearly reverie, as a psychic condition not to be confused with dream,[100] is for Bachelard the source of poetry, which produces pleasure for others. This source Bachelard calls the "image," and often the "poetic image," which is an image of reverie before it is an image *in a poem*. Such images, Freud to the contrary notwithstanding, "can only be studied through the image. It is nonsense to claim to study imagination objectively, since one really receives the image only if he admires it." "Admiration" here is obviously meant to be a word free of "thought." In connection with this idea and consistent with his phenomenological stance, Bachelard cuts the poetic image off from all antecedents, all causality. In contrast to the Freudian symbol, which is always pursued to a source, it is radically unique, a "pure sublimation."[101] The issue with Freud is put at the outset of *The Poetics of Reverie*:

> The poetic image, appearing as a new being of language, is in no way comparable, as with the mode of the common metaphor, to a valve which would open up to release pent-up instincts. The poetic image sheds light on consciousness in such a way that it is pointless to look for subconscious antecedents of the image. Phenomenology, at least, is set up to consider the poetic image in its own being, distinct and independent from any antecedent being, as a positive conquest of the word. If one were to listen to the psychoanalyst, he would come to define poetry as a majestic Lapsus of the Word.[102]

The phrase "conquest of the word" is ambiguous in translation and means "conquest by the word," but as yet Bachelard has not really indicated that words are involved in the poetic images of reverie, that reverie is a linguistic act. Does Bachelard posit a radical linguistic creativity *in* reverie? Clearly he claims, as I have claimed, that in Freud we get a search *back* to an alleged true source for dream, daydream, and even art. In Bachelard is the movement always *forward to* completion, not return? I believe that Bachelard seeks to establish such creativity in the poem, but fails because he falls into the ancient chasm between form and content. How this happens we shall see.

Since there is no antecedent to the image produced by reverie, it would appear that Bachelard has turned the nothingness of Mallarmé into a psychological field from which the poetic image emerges. The poetic image emerges into consciousness as a "direct product of the heart, soul and being of man, apprehended in his actuality."[103] Indeed, it appears that this nothingness is so named because it is the opposite of the somethingness we identify with the objective. Bachelard's approach to the image of reverie, which he calls the "poetic image," is by avoiding its objectification: "the 'objective' critical attitude stifles the 'reverberation' and rejects on principle the depth at which the original poetic phenomenon starts."[104] Bachelard seems actually to echo his antagonist Freud in this passage, the Freudian dreamer also being asked to relax his critical attitude when he indulges in free association. But Bachelard goes beyond Freud here and insists that the "reader" (analyst) also relax his critical or analytical stance. A reverie, according to Bachelard, cannot be "recounted." It must, in fact, be written down, "written with emotion and taste." At this point, we have to question how the reverie can be transferred to language from whatever form it is generated in, if the reverie is not linguistic in its very nature. In *The Poetics of Reverie*, Bachelard believes that the reverie is "being relived all the more strongly" by the fact of its being written.[105] But in *The Poetics of Space*, he says that "one would not be able to meditate in a zone that preceded language,"[106] and meditation seems to be identical to reverie. At the same time, in *The Poetics of Reverie*, he says that the psychologist will have to study "life in speech (*la vie en parole*), life which takes on meaning in speaking."[107] Yet the poem is finally for Bachelard not quite the reverie itself. I find it difficult to trust his language on this point, however:

> The poet retains the consciousness of dreaming distinctly enough to manage the task of writing his reverie. What a promotion of being it is to make a work out of a reverie, to be an author in reverie itself![108]

He speaks of poems as "direct complements for our dreamer's *cogito*."[109] They are not the *cogito* itself. And he says that when he considers the "poetic image at its origin" he leaves aside the "problem of the *composition* of the poem as a grouping together of numerous images."[110] Reveries he sometimes regards as beneath poems, and he admits that one can never be sure that the reverie beneath is the "poet's reverie," by which I presume he means the content of the poem itself. At this point Bachelard talks about affect and sees the poem as channeling the dreams of the reader.[111] But he does not specifically link these with the poet's reveries, if the poet's reverie can be known. We do not know what the "promotion" of a reverie to the level of a poem means, but it appears to be the formalizing of a previous content, in which form and content are thus regarded as separate, one a container—but an elegant container—for the other.

In spite of this problem, Bachelard goes on to offer his own version of the distinction between symbolism and allegory. The idea of radical creativity in reverie, with which he flirts and which he imagines as the expression of a radical freedom, much like what emerges from Mallarmé's nothingness, he calls "a state of open symbolism." The contrast is to "immobile heraldry," which retains "antiquated aesthetic values," presumably because they are filled up with meaning or thought and are not really the products of reverie.[112] They are like what Freud claims to find in dreams—allegorical images in the preromantic sense.

Finally, however, Bachelard's equation of reverie and the poetic seems to include language as well. The poetic image, which, it must be repeated, is not necessarily the image in the poem, but the image of reverie, is nevertheless regarded as an "emergence from language" and always "a little above the language of signification."[113] And Bachelard speaks of the idea of "language-as-reality."[114] But *even if this is so*, the poem is a "promotion" from such linguistic reverie no matter how shaped that reverie may have been. The art of writing a poem follows:

> . . . the Poetics of Reverie . . . is in no way a Poetics of Poetry. The documentation of the awakened oneirism with which reverie provides us must be worked on—often worked on at length—by the poet in order to take on the dignity of poems. But in the end, those documents formed by reverie are the most propitious matter to fashion in poems.[115]

About this "dignity of poems" Bachelard is silent. And yet must not this activity be either a prolongation of reverie into the very act of writing or the imposition of the object as object upon the subject and a revivification of the subject-object dialectic that the act of reverie was to obliterate in the first place? Has the poem become a "phenomenon of freedom" after all?[116]

It may be objected that I have unfairly mixed together statements from two works of Bachelard to produce these problems, that each work is a meditation that must be taken on its own terms. But I think it is fair to state that Bachelard only tantalizes us with an idea of linguistic creativity and that the activity of "open symbolism" that is radical creativity is not located clearly enough to suit us, any more than it is in Jung, whom Bachelard quotes in his own support.[117]

The phenomenological method claims to "attempt communication with the creating consciousness of the poet."[118] "Reverie" is a term for a state open to intersubjective communication. But there is admitted a distance of some kind between the reverie and the poem. Once the existence of that space is allowed, we seem to have to fill it with (1) an act of imitation of the reverie, (2) a "promotion" of the reverie by decorative form (thus splitting content and form), or (3) the objectification of the work and the artist's progressive struggle with his own emerging creation. None of these choices satisfies the aim of Bachelard at a pure intersubjectivity—to keep the line between reverie and reader completely undrawn by the dreaded objectification. To deny the object in favor of a radical subjective creativity is not finally to obliterate the objective but, like Pater and others, merely to assert its brooding presence and to denigrate the power of imagination really to affect a reality still located *there*. In that sense, Bachelard's works mark a return to the anxieties of nineteenth-century writers.

7

Symbol, Fiction, Figment

The notions of myth and antimyth offered early in this book lead to the identification of both as "fictions," that is, in my terms, humanly created forms of symbolic. I am interested, therefore, in the development of the idea of the fictive and its connection with human creative power. One place where the idea of symbolic and the idea of fiction converge is in the work of Benedetto Croce.[1] I now proceed to it, and then to Hans Vaihinger's expansion of the term "fiction" to include practically all areas of human thought.[2] Then I consider the relation of "symbol" and "fiction" to "myth" in recent critical discourse influenced by Vaihinger.

1. CROCE'S INTUITION, EXPRESSION, AND EXTERNALIZATION

No TWO positions would seem to be more opposed than Croce's idealism and Vaihinger's "critical positivism," though both arose out of Kant. In Croce, however, there is finally a more fundamental influence—in addition to the influence of Hegel. It is that of Vico—lacking in Vaihinger—and it makes a huge difference. Croce argues that the importance of Vico's theory of poetry has hitherto never been adequately appreciated.[3] In his *Aesthetic*, he remarks that for Vico language and poetry are substantially the same thing[4] and then proceeds to base his whole aesthetic on this Vichean idea. From here, he declares the identity of aesthetics and linguistics.[5] Croce is influenced by Vico to hold that language was born as poetry and in the course of history was turned (dare we say corrupted?) into signs,[6] the impression Croce leaves being that the sign is not—as much as we may think it is—language's natural state or fundamental nature or even its real present condition. On this point, Croce consciously "corrects" and "completes" the thought of Vico, who tended to consider poetic language characteristic of a bygone stage of culture.[7] In fact, Croce would seem to wish to turn philosophy itself back toward the mode of apprehension that Vico called "poetic logic." For Croce, philosophy is properly a sort of science of the concrete. This idea is perhaps best seen in his discussion of rhetorical tropes, where it becomes clear that he believes not only thought but also intuition to be linguistic in form, in much the same way that Blake identified his artist Los with the legs of primordial Albion, the foundations of culture and mental life.

We have noted that the usual definitions regard tropes as deviations from normal expression. Like Vico, Croce sees them as absolutely fundamental to expression. The usual definitions, he says,

> either grasp the void or fall into the absurd. A typical example of this is the very common definition of metaphor as of *another word used in place of the proper word*. Now why give oneself this trouble? Why substitute the improper for the proper word? Why take the worse and longer road when you know the shorter and better road? Perhaps, as is commonly said, because the proper word is in certain cases not so *expressive* as the so-called improper word or metaphor? But if this be so the metaphor is exactly the proper word in that case, and the so-called "proper" word, if it were used, would be *inexpressive* and therefore most improper.[8]

From their own point of view, so to speak, tropes are nothing but pure expression, pure creation, and are referable to no norm or to anything beyond themselves. They are, in fact, not subject to definition. The discussion of metaphor above implies that expression is intuition, and that actuality or reality is not some objective "other" such as is hypothesized by science and surely not some static "thing," but, as A. Wildon Carr has remarked in connection with Croce, "the living change itself in its concrete activity."[9] Croce's idealism locates this activity in mind and more precisely in language.

It is not surprising that, after Vico, Croce is drawn to Herder's thought, where language is regarded "no longer as purely mechanical or as something derived from arbitrary choice and invention, but as a creative activity and a primary affirmation of the activity of the human mind."[10] For Croce, language is so radically creative that words have no "logical sense" and true sense is "conferred upon [them] on each occasion by the person forming a concept."[11] Gian N. G. Orsini has put it well when he remarks, "For Croce, language is not a sign or system of signs, a sign being something which has only referential value, obtained from the external objects that it supposedly refers to; language has its object within itself, the representation of thought which is identical with its expression."[12] Croce's view requires a sense of flux as absolute and the idea that each use of a word is a radical creation. Dictionaries are therefore for him mausoleums of dead language.

Further, language has no real existence in any abstract sense at all: "Languages have no reality beyond the propositions and complexes of propositions really written and pronounced by given peoples at definite periods; that is to say, they have no existence outside the works of art (whether little or great, oral or written, soon forgotten or long remembered, does not matter) in which they exist concretely."[13] Orsini points out that Croce is at variance with Hegel when he denies that words are general terms,[14] but the point really is that Croce regards each general term as a uniquely particular creation. Each term is made anew as part of a unique intuition every time it is uttered. It is therefore always concrete. But Croce means by language not merely words; there are other languages in which intuition works. The term *intuizione* Croce employs in the Kantian sense of *Anschauung* and has nothing to do with any sort of sixth sense. It also does not imply the opposition of subject and object that characterizes the terms "perception" and "sensation" in the history of modern philosophy: "In our intuitions we do not oppose ourselves as empirical beings to external reality, but we simply objectify our impressions, whatever they may be."[15] Croce reconstitutes the meaning of "objectify" here, making the objective the product of free mental creation and paving the way for Cassirer's treatment of art as leading to an "objective" view of life. No longer does "objective" refer to a previous, given externality which intuition is alleged to represent or copy. The so-called external or primary world of science is objective not because it is *out there* but only because it is linguistically constructed. But in creative acts pure intuition does not submit to Kantian categories or to any other categories. It lacks "reflective consciousness" such as that of the historian or critic.[16] Each of its acts and products is unique.[17]

The identification of intuition and expression requires examination before we can understand Croce's remarks about symbolism. According to Croce, "every true intuition or representation is also *expression*. That which does not objectify itself in expression is not intuition or representation, but sensation and mere natural fact."[18] As he does in his book on Vico, Croce in the *Aesthetic* notes the resistance even among the greatest thinkers to the "identification of language and poetry." He attributes this to the persistence of definitions of art in extra-artistic terms, the treatment of the languages of art as merely means of conveying preexisting concepts:

> Yet, now that we have established the concept of art as intuition and of intuition as expression and, therefore, by implication, the identity of the latter with language, the above identification appears to us as unavoidable as obvious, provided, of course, that language is taken in its whole extension (that is, without arbitrarily limiting it to so-called articulate language, or without arbitrarily excluding its tonal, imitative, or graphic forms) and in its whole intension. . . .[19]

The identity of intuition and expression means that there is a continuum "from the qualities of the content [of an intuition-expression] to those of the form."[20] In one sense, Croce claims that content and form are one and the same. In another sense, he admits a distinction only to dissolve it when he argues that content cannot be known independently of the form given it by intuition.[21] (The analogy seems to be between content and the Kantian thing-in-itself.) But in intuition the content is dissolved in the all-inclusive term "form," the latter term standing for the perpetration of a radical creativity. For Croce, "imitation" is a useful word only when it is regarded as "representation or intuition of nature, a form of knowledge," but not when it is regarded as reproduction or duplication in the Platonic sense. All errors such as the split of content and form and the confusion of imitation with duplication arise from the unwarranted assumption that only intellectual cognition is knowledge, that content is always concept.[22]

The matter of the crucial distinction that Croce introduces between intuition-expression and externalization I shall examine shortly. First, it is important to note that for Croce conceptual thought follows upon expression:[23] ". . . to reason well is in fact to express oneself well, because the expression is the intuitive possession of one's own logical thought."[24] Yet at this point Croce indicates that "considered abstractly" a concept is "inexpressible," even though in equating thought with expression he has come to the brink of declaring that the inexpressibility of the concept (the idea of the concept as merely *signified* by language rather than embodied in it) is a sort of fiction:

> The concept, the universal, considered abstractly in itself is *inexpressible*. No word is proper to it. So true is this, that the logical concept remains always the same, notwithstanding the variant of verbal forms. In respect to the concept, expression is a simple *sign* or *indication*.[25]

This is apparently a turnabout. It has often been said that art seeks expression of the inexpressible. The whole point of Croce's *Aesthetic*, however, is that things can't be considered in their concrete reality and at the same time abstractly. Therefore, reality must be located in the concrete. Thus Croce must declare the uniqueness of each expression of a concept. It seems to me, however, that the idea of the inexpressibility of the concept is an antimythical fiction. The fiction is that the expression is distinct from the concept. This hypostatizes the concept as a separate substance that each expression strives to signify.

It is actually this fictive relation that Croce is tempted to call "symbolic"; this would of course turn the term completely away from any relation to intuition-expression and art. But he recognizes the semantic violence he is perpetrating (given the history of the word back to Goethe) in separating the term off from its history of relations with art. His problem is that if he is to call art symbolic, what can a work of art in a theory of radical creativity possibly symbolize (in the sense of "signify")? Faced with the romantic tradition of thinking about art, Croce is rather in the same position as Aristotle trying to rescue "imitation" from Plato. "Certainly," says Croce in the *Guide to Aesthetics*, "art is symbol, all symbol, that is, all significant. But symbol of what?"[26] Not the concept; not the thing-in-itself, for Croce believes art is not conceptual and not in a significatory relationship to the mysterious. It is sheer creative form. In Croce's system art can only, in a supreme tautology, signify itself. It cannot even signify the act of intuition because it is identical with intuition.

In the earlier *Aesthetic* Croce wrote,

> . . . symbol has sometimes been given as the essence of art. Now, if the symbol be conceived as inseparable from artistic intuition, it is a synonym for the intuition itself, which always has an ideal character.[27]

If we allow for the least distance, the least gap between symbol (in the sense of signifier) and thing symbolized (signified), we have allegory, and consequently we do not have art: ". . . we fall back again into the intellectualist error: the so-called symbol is the exposition of an abstract concept, an allegory: it is *science*, or art aping science."[28] The distinction is the venerable romantic one, radically purified on the symbolic side by a positive declaration of the absolute impossibility in art of any kind of significatory relationship—whether labeled imitative, symbolic, allegorical, or whatever. Croce simply leaves the symbol with nothing to signify and nothing to imitate, paving the way for the reconstitution of the word "symbol" in Cassirer's phrase "symbolic form," where a form creates rather than copies a reality. The attack on "imitation" by a follower of Cassirer, Eliseo Vivas, follows from this.

Allegory remains to take up the whole task of signification, which appears to be a fictive task:

> Allegory is the extrinsic union, or the conventional and arbitrary juxtaposition of two spiritual facts—a concept of thought and an image—whereby it is posited that *this* image must represent *that* concept. Moreover, not only does recourse to allegory fail to explain the integral character of the artistic image, but, what is more, it deliberately sets up a duality. . . . thought remains thought and image remains image.[29]

Still, Croce is not entirely consistent in limiting the term "symbol" to art and sometimes employs it to mean sign. Fundamentally, however, he swallows the term up in "intuition-expression." One suspects he is willing to accept it in this way only because of its long nineteenth-century history. At the same time, Croce notes that in the nineteenth century the terms "symbolic" and "realistic" came merely to mean either "artistic" or "inartistic," depending on the predispositions of the user. It is clear finally that he regards "symbol" as a troublesome term just as well dispensed with.

The *Aesthetic* retains the term "allegory" for the act of interpretation. It is interpreters who create allegory. Interpretation is intellectualization, or it is "an expression externally added to another expression": "A little page of prose is added to the *Gerusalemme*, expressing another thought of the poet; a verse or strophe is added to the *Adone*, expressing what the poet would like to make a part of his public believe; to the statue nothing but the single word: *Clemency* or *Goodness*."[30] These examples are additions—expressions and/or interpretations—attached by the artist, but the principle applies to all interpretation, which is either really intuition-expression and therefore art itself or intellectualization and therefore allegory.

What about figures who are created parts of intuition-expressions? Are they symbols? Clearly only so far as they tautegorically signify themselves. Are they types in the usual sense of abstract concept? Only if they are "allegorical," but then they are, by Croce's definition, not part of the intuition-expression. In a discussion of whether Don Quixote is a type or not, Croce's approach is derived from Vico. It is an effort to declare the Vichean poetic universal distinct from abstract concept and still fundamental to modern human action:

> Don Quixote is a type, but of what is he a type, save of all Don Quixotes? A type, so to speak, of himself. Certainly he is not a type of abstract concepts, such as the loss of the sense of reality, or of the love of glory. An infinite number of personages can be thought under these concepts, who are not Don Quixotes.[31]

Usually, then, "type," as above, is misleading, for we really mean by it something "aesthetic." Croce has tried to release Vico's "poetic logic" from its place in a bygone primitive age and make it a perpetual mode of human creativity.

Yet when Croce speaks of the aesthetic, now identical to the symbolic, he is using the term specially in his own linguistic creation. It is at the same time narrower and broader than most common usage. It is broader because it includes the act of intuition in its entirety. It is narrower because it excludes what Croce calls "externalization." This introduction of externalization, late in his book almost as an afterthought, cannot be ignored. It is a separate unaesthetic, unsymbolic element, and it raises unresolvable problems, even though Croce be-

lieves the distinction between expression and externalization to eliminate many traditional dilemmas in aesthetics.[32] Croce says, "We cannot will or not will our aesthetic vision: we can however will or not
will to externalize it, or rather, to preserve and communicate to others, or not, the externalization produced."[33] The distinction raises
problems on two levels. First, since Croce considers thought identical
with language and language identical with expression, there may not
be too serious a problem in separating the external act of writing or
actual speaking from the expression (since the expression is already
linguistic); but one wonders whether the physical act of drawing or
sculpting can be classified as external to expression quite so easily.
The act of expression seems deeply involved in artistic materials just
as the act of literary expression is admittedly deeply involved with
language. One asks in what the so-called languages of these other
arts consists if it is not, in some part, these materials. Are these languages composed of imagined sounds and imagined plastic forms?
Can one visually imagine a three-dimensional statue in a single intuition? Can one "see" a picture and copy it with materials? More to
the point, is this what really happens? There is the related problem of
technical training, but Croce claims that every act of technical training is itself intuition and expression, though most artists would certainly insist on a difference in kind somewhere here.[34]

Second, unless Croce intends to insist on a kind of atomization of
the creative act, even with linguistic art he must deal with the fact
that the poet composes through a constant revision, deletion, and addition. And surely Croce doesn't imagine that a poet's intuition is already, before externalization, formed as, say, a sonnet. This revision
is a sort of conversation between himself and the expression, which
gains more and more externality as he proceeds, unless one is to
imagine that the artist's memory is grotesquely prodigious. In order
to escape this conclusion, Croce must claim that every minute mental
act of composition, every minute act of revision and deletion, creates
a new poem. In any case, Croce acts as if writing always occurs after
expression, whereas the act is often the generator of intuition; though
he also says that the artist may make an externalizing stroke of the
pencil or brush without intuition "as a kind of experiment and in order to have a point of departure."[35] But if such an act and the external evidence for it is only a point of departure and not part of the act
of intuition-expression, does it not mean (if it remains unexpunged
in the completed externalization) that the externalization contains
something extraneous and is therefore a distortion? Or if it is judged

by the artist to be part of the work as a whole, then must it not be admitted that this act of will has somehow invaded the intuition as the intuitive process has proceeded? Of course, it may be answered that the moment of invasion was really an intuitive act in the artist's mind that accommodated the wayward beginning brushstroke or word or whatever, but this returns us to atomizing to preserve the distinction between expression and externalization.

Of course, in Croce's theory, all performance is relegated to externalization, unless one wishes to claim that performance is an intuition of an intuition. But how can an intuition be of a previous expression when intuition is supposed to be radically creative? Here there has to be a gap between sign and signified, such as Croce claims only for allegory. And how can we ever really know a play in performance if we must suffer the indignity of an externalization cluttering our reproductive intuition of it?

The difficulty is marked by the terrible problem one has in stating Croce's position at all. Carr, for example, says, "In Croce's view art is purely and only mental, and there is no such thing as an external work of art. What is external in the work of art, the physical thing in which we see, or to which we give, beautiful form, is itself quite extrinsic to the art or to the aesthetic quality."[36] But even to state that the externalization is external to the "aesthetic quality" makes the externalization the container for as much aesthetic content as the artist is able to transfer from his mind to the material of his art, and we have returned on another level to the form-content duality that Croce's whole separation of expression and externalization was designed to protect against. Of course, it can be said that at least these problems are the viewer's and not the artist's, who seems oddly released from responsibility in these matters, except in the realm of practicality.

The issues I raise here, which need to be followed further than I have taken them, have to do with determination of the idea of symbolism, or as Croce prefers to call it, the aesthetic. The traditional concepts of imitation and allegory require us to put our emphasis on some external object or idea to be reproduced in a medium. This requires not merely an external but also a prior object. The thrust is backward in time. In contrast to this view, Croce insists on expunging the external, prior object, or at the least claims it to be unknowable. Content does not exist prior to form. His concentration is on the present, the act itself, as free creativity. His way of doing this, however, atomizes the process into a series of discrete acts, which seem infinitesimally divisible. Croce has protected the realm of art from allegory, and the symbol stands freer than ever before. But possibly too free.

There is another possible perspective. What if the activity of the artist can be regarded as *radically directed to the future*, toward formulating an intuition never really brought into being until fixed in the so-called externality of paint, stone, or page, and requiring that exercise before intuition-expression is really achieved?

In an able defense of Croce, Orsini invokes for us no alternative to Croce except either defeat by or victory over language, considered as external and alien.[37] But it is not necessary to hold that language as writing is a villain to be subdued if one can claim that the process of creative intuition actually involves externalization. Further, it is possible to claim that the act of intuition is freely directed toward a future, without a past (except a symbolic past), and makes its presentness in preserved words. While Croce may preserve the unity of art from one point of view, he violates the experience of creation, and he leaves the viewer without art, only with the dead external signs of intuition. Such signs require interpretation, which for Croce is allegorization, from which art is forever separated.

The argument over externalization continues to rage, and later definitions of "symbol" can easily become entangled in it. Even Croce seems to have doubts about it. On the matter of "myth" Croce is of far less interest, despite his connections with Vico. He notes in his *Guide to Aesthetics* that there is a difference between art and myth and that it is tied up with the problem of belief. To the believer, myth is revelation and knowledge of reality, but to the nonbeliever myth can become art or "metaphor."[38] I shall not pause to query Croce's use of the term "metaphor" here in the light of his attack on tropes. Nor shall I ask what he means by "belief," which is a rather misleading term with respect to primitive thought in most of its commonly recognized senses. Instead I shall note that the statement implies that myths, when not believed, have aesthetic value as what they must be—fictions.

Interestingly enough, the term "fiction" appears in the *Guide to Aesthetics* in connection with science:

> that character of ideality, which the natural and mathematical sciences appear to assume as against the world of philosophy, religion, and history, and which seems to bring them closer to art (and owing to which the scientists and mathematicians of

our day are so eager to brag about being creators of worlds, of *fictiones*—a term similar, even as far as language is concerned, to the one designating the tales or inventions of the poets), is gained at the expense of a surrender of concrete thinking, at the expense of a generalization and an abstraction—which are arbitrary actions, decisions of the will, practical acts, and, as such, alien and hostile to the world of art.[39]

Croce consistently opposes aesthetic to science: "art displays much more antagonism toward the positive and mathematical sciences than toward philosophy, religion, and history."[40]

But where oppositions may be conceived there are also similarities. And to examine them may make possible some movement from what threatens in Croce to be the dead center of the theory of symbolism. The term "fiction" and its possible relation to "myth" may be a means by which a new light is thrown on literature and art generally and the connections between them and other cultural forms, some of which may in parallel or opposition help to fix art's meaning for us.

2. VAIHINGER'S "AS IF"

THE TERM "fiction" has, of course, long been a word connected with literature. But it has been employed by philosophers with respect to science and the usages have affected literary theory in the post-Kantian era. Our primary exhibit of the use of "fiction" in the philosophy of science is Hans Vaihinger's *Philosophy of "As If."* The work, which has recently enjoyed something of a vogue among literary theorists, proposes a broad concept of fictions, which Vaihinger derives from Kant, but in a positivistic, rather than idealistic, direction. It is true that Vaihinger calls his philosophy at one time "positivist idealism" or "idealistic positivism"; but his idealism is a far cry from Croce's, and he is probably more accurate when he describes his position as "critical positivism." His principal focus is upon science and the usefulness to science of what he calls fictions. In the process of his account of fictions, he must take notice of mythological, religious, and aesthetic fictions, but he tends for the most part to set them aside as not quite belonging to his subject, and there is good reason for this. Fundamentally he has little interest in them.

Vaihinger tells us that his awareness of fictions began with his introduction to Plato and his reading of Herder, but these were to him only early intimations of his theme. The fundamental influence is

Kant, particularly Kant's concept of the ideality of space and time and "Kant's discovery of the contradictions with which human thought is faced when it ventures into the realm of metaphysics."[41] Vaihinger regarded Kant's special importance to be his having shown that most "ideational constructs" are subjective.[42] But Kant did not take the next logical step, which was to conclude that they are "fictions," which are means that the mind constructs for attaining certain purposes. For Vaihinger, Kant's thing-in-itself and the ego are fictions; Kant's categories are fictions; and both subject and object are fictions:

> From the standpoint of Critical Positivism . . . there is no Absolute, no Thing-in-itself, no Subject, no Object. All that remains is sensations, which exist, and are given, and out of which the whole subjective world is constructed with its division into physical and psychical complexes. Critical Positivism asserts that any other, any further claim is fictional, subjective, and unsubstantiated.[43]

Yet Vaihinger does not mean that fictions are of no value. On the contrary, they are of immense importance, because it is through them that man makes his conceptual world. Human thought converts sensation into its own terms and as it does so "becomes increasingly entangled in its own forms."[44] Indeed, thought asserts its own autonomy. Setting out in one direction, often it takes another: "an original means working towards a definite end has the tendency to acquire independence and to become an end in itself."[45] This process Vaihinger calls the Law of the Preponderance of the Means over the End. When it operates, however, thought

> sets itself problems to which it is not equal because it has not developed for this purpose; and finally the emancipated thought sets itself problems which in themselves are senseless, for instance, questions as to the origin of the world, the formation of what we call matter, the beginning of motion, the meaning of the world and the purpose of life.[46]

This passage, turning Kant's antinomies into "fictions," and placing them on a level with understanding as the immediate result of intuition, illustrates Vaihinger's positivism, his total dedication to the concept of practical value; but out of context it also tends to mislead one into thinking he may denigrate fictions. In fact, the tendency to create fictions has its good side, because many fictions, in spite of their senselessness, are useful, and use is Vaihinger's criterion of value. Furthermore, the fictional world, as a "nail to which the sensations are attached as attributes," is all that stands between us and the manifold confusion of sensation:

> The "as if" world, which is formed in this manner, the world of the "unreal" is just as important as the world of the so-called real or actual (in the ordinary sense of the word); indeed it is far more important for ethics and aesthetics. This aesthetic and ethical world of "as if," the world of the unreal, becomes finally for us a world of values which, particularly, in the form of religion, must be sharply distinguished in our mind from the world of becoming.[47]

In spite of this loftiness, Vaihinger fails to penetrate the worlds either of aesthetics or of religion. He seems capable of compartmentalizing them and, in his emphasis on the practical nature of "truth," relegating them to inferior status. The value of Vaihinger's concept of fictions to literary theory is not in his concept of aesthetic fictions at all, which remains completely undeveloped, but in any analogies that others may find between his scientific or conceptual fictions and literature. Vaihinger's emancipation of thought from "reality" may be the basis for such analogical thinking. He sees conceptual thought as beginning with slight deviations from reality and ending with constructs that are not mere deviations but actual contradictions of reality. He goes so far as to state that without such deviations thought cannot attain its purposes. This is quite natural because thought by its very nature must manipulate and elaborate the given. There can, therefore, be no identity of thought and reality, because the "world" is merely "an instrument of thought," something made and used to another purpose: "behaviour, and ultimately *ethical behaviour*."[48]

Vaihinger attempts to distinguish scientific fictions from hypotheses, an effort which gives him considerable difficulty but which he regards as crucial to his whole argument. Fictions are first of all thoughts that are *arbitrary* deviations from reality. Since "reality" is *only* sensation, it is a little difficult to see just how a fiction can *deviate from* a sensation, since it has already been asserted that thought and reality have not met in the first place. What he means is that fictions posit statements that have all the appearance of violating our concept of the factual or logical. For a fiction to be a fiction, there must be awareness that the fiction is such a deviation, and the fiction must be a means to a definite end. Fictions contain, in other words, an element of deliberate error. If they are regarded apart from their purposes, they are mere "husk[s] without content such as $\sqrt{-1}$."[49] Vaihinger remarks of the Greeks that their fear of contradiction in mathematics prevented their making discoveries that modern mathematicians have made via the construction of fictions.[50] Yet one feels that in these remarks Vaihinger puts a false emphasis on the purposeful and deliberate and forgets his own Law of the Preponderance of the Means over the End, which introduced a broad idea of conceptual play and purposelessness leading to discovery—practical attainment still, but by means of thought that one has allowed deliberately to take over to its own ends. It is possible that Vaihinger here is so much under the influence of Kant's distinction between the purposiveness of conceptual thought and the purposiveness without purpose which Kant limits to the aesthetic that he does not see that he has found this latter element of free play in conceptual thought as well. What he has seemed to find is a notion of purposelessness with a purpose—play which must be fictively regarded as play but with a sly unknown end.

The distinction between fictions and hypotheses is begun as follows: While fictions are consciously false, hypotheses are probable assumptions, the truth of which may be proved by further experience.[51] Both are employed because of their utility, but only the latter because of their possible truth. However, there is some question about this distinction because it appears that truth has been identified all along in Vaihinger as that which proves its utility. For Vaihinger, many things usually regarded as hypotheses are in fact fictions. Certain systems of classification—that of Linnaeus, for example—are fictions and were so regarded by their creators. Adam Smith's concept of self-interest was a conscious fiction. Goethe's animal or plant archetype was a fiction: "we are invited to proceed *as if such an animal could have existed.*"[52]

> As long as such fictions are treated as hypotheses without a realization of their nature, they are *false hypotheses*. They derive real value only if it is realized that they have been deliberately constructed as provisional representations.[53]

The distinction is also made on the basis of the theoretical object of a hypothesis and the practical object of the fiction. Hypotheses are supposed to fill the gaps in knowledge, but fictions are not in themselves creative of any knowledge.[54] The hypothesis attempts to eradicate contradictions, but the fiction actually calls contradictions into existence.

The distinctions leave us in difficulty as to whether at any given time we can tell the difference with infallibility. The question of the self-conscious awareness of the perpetrator of a fiction is more vexed than Vaihinger admits. True, he tries to distinguish between a false hypothesis and a fiction, but what about a false hypothesis that turns out to be useful? Is such a phenomenon retroactively dubbed fiction in spite of the perpetrator's attitude toward it? One sees looming here an analogy to the long argument about "belief" that dominated literary criticism during the ascendancy of the New Criticism. Vaihinger expresses a half-awareness of this problem when he produces his Law of Ideational Shifts and for a moment at least regards fictions, hypotheses, and dogmas as states through which ideas may pass, either from fiction through hypotheses to dogma, or in the opposite direction. In Vaihinger's eyes it was the great merit of Schleiermacher to have transformed religious dogma to fictions. In any case, hypotheses are judged by probability and must be verified. Fictions are judged by usefulness and must be justified. Fiction making should be placed on an equal footing with induction and deduction.[55]

It is not surprising to discover that the area of the fictive is huge indeed. Vaihinger finds the fictive method to some extent in all science. There are fictions of artificial classification (Linnaeus); abstractive fictions which deliberately neglect certain elements of reality (Adam Smith); schematic, paradigmatic, utopian, and tropic fictions (Goethe's animal types); symbolic or analogical fictions (Kant's categories); juristic fictions; personificatory fictions; summational fictions (general ideas); poetical (ethical) fictions; mathematical fictions, and so on. In fact, practically every human intellectual and aesthetic construct becomes a fiction. In every case, the conceptual worlds that thought creates are not "a *picture* of the actual world but an *instrument* for grasping and subjectively understanding that world,"[56] though in another place Vaihinger asserts that the world can't be *understood*, only known, by which he really means "used."[57] It appears that despite the emphasis on hypothesis and dogma as well as fictions, the term "fiction" becomes for Vaihinger the whole conceptual structure by which man constructs a cultural world. For Vaihinger this construct is never really an end in itself, despite his own Law of the Preponderance of Means over the End. The true end of fictions is to render action possible. Scientific fictions do this by determining actual sequences and coexistences and by giving "ideas with which we invest reality a more concise, more adequate, more useful and more harmless form."[58]

There remains the question of aesthetic and religious fictions, since all that has preceded refers to the fictive nature of science. Vaihinger finds the original fictive parent of all the present fictive forms in myth, which was "the first expression in free constructive activity of the inventive faculty, of imagination and of phantasy."[59] But he wishes to distinguish scientific fictions from all others by giving the others the name of "figments":

> For instance, Pegasus is a figment, atom, a fiction. This [use of the word] would certainly facilitate distinctions. The opponents of the fiction misrepresent it in so far as they regard it as a mere figment. "Fictio," in legal terminology, has already acquired the secondary meaning of practical utility.[60]

This statement is made in a footnote, and the program is not carried out in the rest of the book. But the implications are crucially revealing. Though Vaihinger declares that the purpose of the distinction is a practical one only, it is important to remember that for Vaihinger only practical actions are of value, and a hierarchy of value is surely implied in his effort to perform a Burkean theft of the term "fiction" for science and to deny it to art and religion by substituting a less honorific term. Indeed, by the Law of Ideational Shifts the movement from dogma to hypothesis to fiction would always really be a movement to figment, as in the case of Greek mythology, where the Greeks preserved originally religious dogmas as "fictions,"[61] though precisely why Vaihinger is unable to tell us.

Aesthetic fictions or figments for Vaihinger are closely related to mythological and religious fictions, sometimes are former religious dogmas. They include all similes, metaphors, and such. They include those ideational forms that deal even more freely with reality. This is an interesting point because Vaihinger generally regards fictions as arbitrary and violent:

> Violence must be done not only to reality but (in real fictions) also to thought itself. The arbitrary way in which thought operates corresponds to the violence to which it subjects reality and the logical Law of Contradiction.[62]

Vaihinger sees the same psychical processes occurring in the creation of aesthetic fictions that occur in scientific ones. But Vaihinger's commitment to positivism and its practical ends makes it impossible for him to be precise or convincing about the value of aesthetic fictions:

> Aesthetic fictions serve the purpose of awakening within us certain uplifting or otherwise important feelings. Like the scientific, they are not an end in themselves but a means for the attainment of higher ends.[63]

Vaihinger notes that both scientific and aesthetic fictions have given rise to bitter controversies of a roughly similar sort, the question being how far the imagination may deviate from nature:

> As in science, so in poetry . . . fictions have been greatly abused, and this has frequently led to reactions, based on exactly the same grounds as those resulting from the misuse of scientific fictions. The real criterion as to how far such fictions are to be admitted into either field, and one which has always been adopted by good taste and logical tact alike, is simply the practical value of such fictions.[64]

But until Vaihinger can provide us a more precise idea of the end— the practical end of aesthetic fictions—or of life itself, we have very little chance of making judgments based upon his too general assertion. On the one hand, it appears that he wishes to distinguish between art and the production of the understanding in a Kantian way that refuses purposefulness, precisely delimited, to art; yet in order to allow art a place at all in his positivistic system he must find a practical and thus purposive role for its play to play. Vaihinger never resolves this dilemma, and his attempts flounder in failure to establish meaning and purpose in the fictive activity generally.

Vaihinger's philosophy places human creative thought in a symbolic relation, not to things-in-themselves but to the manifold of sensation, but he has nothing to say about the actual internal structure of human creations and thus is finally unable satisfactorily to distinguish one from another except on the ground of the intention of the creator. In fact, he is rarely able to determine what an intention is. In spite of Vaihinger's protestations we are uncertain finally of the way to distinguish hypothesis from fiction without personally asking the perpetrator what he himself thought he was making—a hypothesis or a fiction. And with respect to a wide range of durable constructs, we see at once that there was a time when Vaihinger's distinction was unknown to the perpetrators, that some scientific fictions no longer "useful" have become merely "aesthetic fictions," whose "use" is, in his system, unclear, yet whose durability requires explanation. One sees that the concepts of purpose and practical end are virtually useless to distinguish types of fictions from each other and fictions from hypotheses, unless the internal structure of each is the defining element rather than the final cause.

In fact, Vaihinger reduces aesthetic purpose to ethical ends, though *The Philosophy of "As If"* does not quest very far into the area of ethics as such. One senses that Vaihinger would graft the *Critique of Practical Reason* onto his positivistic philosophy, but the *Critique of Judgment* is beyond the pale. "All the nobler aspects of our life are based upon fictions," and "a pure ethic can only be established by the recognition of its fictional base."[65]

One of the balances that Vaihinger's position tries to strike is that between nominalism and realism. Nominalism, of course, considered all generalizations to be what he calls fictions, but it never gave to these fictions the positive meaning that they have for him. Conceptual realism goes to the other extreme, objectifying the subjective and hypostatizing the purely logical. For Vaihinger "the individual phenomena, the successive and coexisting phenomena are the only real things."[66] But he believes that though the nominalists were right in one way, they were wrong in another, for pure sensation is not of any *use* until ordered by the imagination and made the *material* of symbols.

With remarks of this sort, Vaihinger helps shift the problem of knowledge from wherever it was to the linguistic level, to which Croce also shifts it. Vaihinger does not discuss the question of which is prior, thought or language; but this "fiction" certainly can be regarded as a linguistic construct, though he does not subject language to analysis.

3. Fictions after Vaihinger

ONLY RECENTLY—particularly in books by Frank Kermode and Harold Toliver—has Vaihinger's work received much attention from literary critics.[67] The first explicit use of it known to me occurred in a work on Yeats and is particularly relevant to our study, since Yeats has helped me to the conclusions I reach. The work is Donald Stauffer's *The Golden Nightingale*, published in 1949.[68] From the beginning, Stauffer's concern is the problem of belief—not so much the reader's problem in appreciating the statements of a poet whose views seem outdated or absurd, but the relation of the poet to his own work. The issue naturally centers upon Yeats's *A Vision*, and Stauffer seeks help in Vaihinger's concept of fictions in order to confront Yeats's so-called system and the more general question of "what the poet knows, or more precisely . . . what is the nature of *poetic* knowledge."[69] Sir Philip Sidney's remark that the poet "never affirmeth" is invoked, and then the name of Vaihinger, who is described as bringing out the "hypothetical nature of the poet's statement."[70] Of course, strictly speaking, Vaihinger's poet does no such thing, since Vaihinger distinguishes between hypothesis and fiction and then separates poetry off even from fiction with his term "figment." Stauffer is aware of this, but he deliberately shies away from the term "fiction" because of the "emotional contempt which the word 'fiction' might stir up in our age of scientific 'truth'."[71] What strikes Stauffer about fictions is their expedience and our apparent need for them, as demonstrated by their persistence. Yet the fictions he is concerned with—what we popularly call myths—are not really those that interest Vaihinger, whose positivism always turns toward science. While praising Vaihinger's book too lavishly as one which tells poets what they are doing, Stauffer inveighs, with Yeats, against the "scientific, pragmatic, and sociological" impulses of our age. He doesn't seem to realize that in Vaihinger we have a supremely pragmatic philosopher of science, who has no inclination even to discuss poetic "figments," let alone consider their use.

In his discussion of Yeats, Stauffer notes that Yeats himself recognized his own fantastic beliefs as fictions: "In his system Yeats has given us a brilliant series of fictions, innumerable bold sallies into the region of 'As if,' that confident jugglery with hypotheses which shows his complete awareness of the way in which the artist lives with knowledge."[72] It is interesting to see that while Croce implies that scientists have stolen the word "fiction" from literary artists, Stauffer steals the word "hypothesis" from scientific procedures. It is as if both camps sense that there is something lacking in their arsenal and seek the solace of the opposite. Here it is important to observe Stauffer trying to formulate the artist's role with the use of Vaihinger. But finally Yeats's work is more helpful to Stauffer than anything Vaihinger has to say. Stauffer claims that Yeats's road is the road of images, *mimesis*, and *mythos*, proceeding by a "constant throwing out of alternatives and hypotheses that keep us alive to the possibilities of choosing."[73] This does not differentiate Yeats's fictions from those of science; one can imagine Vaihinger attributing this cultural function to things other than art.

What is the difference? The key for Stauffer is apparently the process. *Mythos* means the particular, not the abstract path of science; and the fictions of the artist are not figments but conveyors of what Stauffer calls "presentational" knowledge. The term is no doubt adopted from Susanne K. Langer's *Philosophy in a New Key*, first published in 1942. Langer's work, which I shall discuss in the next chapter, was heavily influenced by Ernst Cassirer's theory of "symbolic forms." Stauffer roughly distinguishes "argumentative" knowledge from the "presentational," which "lives in pictures, not abstractions; . . . is tied to particulars as inextricably as experience itself."[74] Stauffer makes no explicit effort in his treatment of fictions as presentation to imagine them embodied in language. He seems to have revived in modern disguise the venerable opposition of symbol and allegory, concrete and abstract. His book moves from the concept of the fictive in its first chapter to the mature Yeats's concept of the symbol in the second. I shall return to this topic in chapter 11. Here it must suffice to recognize that in Stauffer's confrontation with Yeats's work he seems quite consciously to have apprehended the close relation of symbol to fiction, in a sense derived but also liberated from Vaihinger and applied to art. He goes to some length to describe the symbol as Yeats used and talked about it, and he is fascinated with the problem of the relation of *A Vision* to truth—the "presentational" truth he had opposed to the "argumentative." It is clear that for him *A Vision* is fictive, by which he also means symbolic in the paradoxical sense that we have seen developed through Croce: The symbol does not symbolize (signify). It does, for Stauffer, however, *mean*, though its meaning is untranslatable. Stauffer doesn't explicitly state that meaning under this condition must be totally internalized within a system of symbols to which the symbol belongs, but he claims that Yeats agrees with Croce that intuition is identical with expression. His treatment of *A Vision* declares that a fiction or *mythos* is a cluster of symbolic interrelations. Stauffer's discourse is cluttered with terms that have very nearly caused a Fryean "large terminal moraine of confusion" in modern criticism equal to that perpetrated by the distinction between symbolism and allegory. The terms are the triad of "meaning," "truth," and "knowledge," all three valuable objects frequently stolen and recreated in the discourses of the New Criticism.

In *The Sense of an Ending*, Frank Kermode offers a theory of fictions that would solve the problem Vaihinger creates when, dismissing aesthetic fictions as figments, he finds no use for them unless they are moral allegories. Kermode nowhere explicitly recognizes that Vaihinger has dismissed such fictions as figments; his aim is to establish a parallel Vaihinger would have rejected between scientific fictions and literary ones and to establish for them a use. His true mentor is the poet Wallace Stevens, whose own theme of fictions he traces to Vaihinger, Nietzsche, and the American pragmatists. For Kermode's book, there are numerous possible epigraphs in Stevens, some of which he employs, as for example the following:

> . . . the nicer knowledge of Belief,
> that what it believes in is not true.[75]

But the text Kermode might best be imagined to have written on is from Stevens's *Adagia*:

> The final belief is to believe in a fiction, which you know to be a fiction, there being nothing else. The exquisite truth is to know that it is a fiction and that you believe it willingly.[76]

This is hardly belief in any popular sense of the word. Kermode dismisses the notion of belief entirely from fictions, but he maintains its connection to myths. Belief is what is wrong with myths, for belief is exceedingly dangerous. The important, liberating thing about fictions is their conscious falsity, their difference from the real; when they come to be believed, they degenerate into myths. Kermode does not directly face the idea that to have consciously created a fiction as a falsity is to have defined it as false with respect to some accepted truth—a reality of *some* sort. But all such "realities" for Kermode are myths as soon as they elicit belief. The terms of his discourse require that he deconstruct the reality tacitly assumed by his conscious fiction-making.

Myths try to rearrange the world in their terms, and such world-rearrangement is dangerous. Kermode calls to witness the myth of the Third Reich, describing myths as "agents of stability," within which term he includes totalitarian oppression. Fictions, on the other hand, are for "finding things out." They are "agents of change" and ways of making sense of the present.[77] This accounts, in Kermode's view, for the happy fact that fictions, being free of proof or disconfirmation, simply fall into neglect when they have lost "operational effectiveness."[78] For Kermode, like Vaihinger, fictions differ from hypotheses in that hypotheses are subject to proof or falsification and discardable therefore on a different principle.

Now all of this is not Vaihinger's positivism, much as it has been influenced by it, but instead is strictly pragmatic. Fictions are clearly for a use which includes comfort. The matter of comfort falls under the pragmatic and hedonistic, clearly an influence of Kermode's mentor Stevens. The hedonistic proceeds to existentialism and beyond in Kermode's embrace of the Sartrean absurd. It is not very far from Kermode's idea of the fiction to Jacques Derrida's recent deconstruction of texts. Deconstruction can be seen as grounded in a theory of fictions *all* of which are shown to be not false but "undecidable" by virtue of the notion that referentiality is always totally internalized in the linguistic chain and meaning infinitely deferred. Croce rejected the sign as the defining feature of language. Derrida achieves his idea of infinite enclosure in the linguistic chain by recourse to the Saussurean sign. He ends where he does by beginning with the idea of the sign as referential and then deconstructing the notion of reference, but the notion of reference, as I know he would admit, always remains as a trace in his discourse. When a myth becomes fixed in an interpretation, according to Kermode, it stultifies culture. But, on the other hand, the infinite regress that the Derridean notion of "differance" and the undecidable leaves us in is also potentially a stultification with no escape into hope that a fiction can have any sort of purpose whatever, except as pure play. But this is not Schiller's play with its origin in Kant's purposiveness without purpose, nor is it Vaihinger's purposelessness with purpose.

Kermode's sense of myth is different from mine in the distinction I make between myth and antimyth. Kermode always thinks of *myths*, specific decadent fictions, while my notion of myth is one pole of a continuum of prolific and devouring *ways* of thinking and expressing. When Kermode calls something a myth it is already, in his eyes, a fixed structure eliciting belief and it already has wrought intellectual havoc.

My notion of myth is in the tradition of certain nineteenth-century theories of myth, but it departs from them wherever the tendency to allegorize toward fixity intrudes, as it does in so many theorists of the age. It accepts the idea of fictive creativity and emphasizes possibilities for culture rather than dwelling on the folly of referentiality as the preserve of the signified, as in recent deconstruction. It is now time for us to reexamine that more productive line of thought in the philosophy of symbolic forms, steeling ourselves provisionally against deconstructive skepticism and accepting the possibility of the cultural value of the literary fictive, which is to say the symbolic.

8

The Philosophy of Symbolic Forms

Ernst Cassirer's work charts a direction in its seeking for a general theory of symbolic culture in which literary symbolism can find its place. The first volume of Cassirer's *Philosophie der symbolischen Formen* was not translated into English until 1953. It was followed by the second in 1955 and the third in 1957.[1] In a review of the translation of volume one, written in 1954, Northrop Frye was quite right to observe that the translation came after Cassirer's ideas had been rather fully assimilated by English and American critics.[2] The fundamental source of this influence was the book Cassirer had written in English and published in 1944 entitled *An Essay on Man*.[3] *The Philosophy of Symbolic Forms* may now be regarded as a prelude to *An Essay on Man*, which, though Neo-Kantian, emancipates itself from rigidly Kantian organization and procedure, is more sophisticated with respect to linguistics, and introduces into the argument considerable new material on symbolic processes in animals and man. Further, it contains a full chapter on art as a symbolic form, whereas the earlier work, though it mentions art here and there, and seems to be leading up to a discussion of art at the end of volume two, never quite develops the implications for art that the work as a whole contains. But Cassirer's commentary on art, even in the *Essay*, cannot stand apart from his total philosophy, and his commentary on language and myth in that book has had more influence on literary theory than has his commentary on art as such.

Cassirer's early interests were principally in epistemology and the philosophy of science. This is particularly important, because it explains a tendency in him to privilege scientific discourse even as another side of him tends to establish an equal role for art in culture. But it also prevents him from neglecting science and rescues him from recourse to the "miraculous" or to the denigrations of scientific knowledge characteristic of some phenomenological critics.

I shall begin with a brief account of *The Philosophy of Symbolic Forms* and proceed to an examination of the theory of symbolic forms expressed in the *Essay* and its implications for a philosophy of the literary symbolic. Then I shall examine developments from his theory in the work of Susanne Langer and Eliseo Vivas.

1. LANGUAGE AND MYTHICAL THOUGHT

IN *The Philosophy of Symbolic Forms*, Cassirer seeks to broaden epistemology beyond what he regards as the relatively narrow boundaries of scientific cognition, to which it had been confined when Descartes, with the term "cogitatio," relegated consciousness to "pure thought." The modern philosophy of science, Cassirer's specific starting point, discredits the "naïve copy" theory of knowledge: "The fundamental concepts of each science, the instruments with which it propounds its questions and formulates its solutions, are regarded no longer as passive images of something given but as *symbols* created by the intellect itself."[4] Moving from this beginning, Cassirer finds a similar activity of creation in other modes of human behavior:

> Every authentic function of the human spirit has this decisive characteristic in common with cognition: it does not merely copy but rather embodies an original, formative power. It does not express passively the mere fact that something is present but contains an independent energy of the human spirit through which the simple presence of the phenomenon assumes a definite "meaning," a particular ideational content. This is as true of art as it is of cognition; it is as true of myth as of religion. All live in particular image-worlds, which do not merely reflect the empirically given, but which rather pro-

duce it in accordance with an independent principle. Each of these functions creates its own symbolic forms which, if not similar to the intellectual symbols, enjoy equal rank as products of the human spirit. None of these forms can simply be reduced to, or derived from, the others; each of them designates a particular approach, in which and through which it constitutes its own aspect of "reality." They are not different modes in which an independent reality manifests itself to the human spirit but roads by which the spirit proceeds toward its own objectivization, i.e., its self-revelation.[5]

How Cassirer determines what functions of the human spirit are "authentic" and that symbolic forms are of equal status *The Philosophy of Symbolic Forms* never quite comes to explain. Further, since some forms are historically prior to others and later ones build upon former ones, there is confusion about whether equality means independence. *An Essay on Man* makes a firmer attempt to face these issues, but inconsistently, and the characteristic of "authenticity" may be unprovable by virtue of the relegation of the process of proof to one symbolic form only. Also, just how a symbolic form "constitutes" a "reality" both *in* and *through* itself requires development or amplification, since it is clearly paradoxical. The term "reality," in quotation marks in the passage above, requires redefinition, as does "spirit," lest we apply Schelling's or Hegel's sense in too rigid a manner. Finally it is worth noting now that Cassirer has stolen the term "objectivization" from the purely positivistic theories of knowledge that he wishes to correct and has applied it to the activities of art, language, religion, and myth, as well as science.

The authority upon whom he first calls for support is Heinrich Hertz, who in his *Die Prinzipien der Mechanik* (1894) argued that the object of knowledge is defined only "through the medium of a particular logical and conceptual structure."[6] In this system there is no simple object to be regarded as a "transcendent prototype to the empirical copies."[7] According to Cassirer, Hertz's concept of the symbol is that of a free "fiction." The physical concepts of space, time, mass, force, and the like are examples of such fictions, created, according to Cassirer, "in order to dominate the world of sensory experience and survey it as a world ordered by law, but nothing in the sensory data themselves immediately corresponds to them, yet although there is no such correspondence—and perhaps precisely *be-*

cause there is none—the conceptual world of physics is entirely self-contained."[8]

But far previous to Hertz's theory of fictions are the influences of Kant and Schelling. Cassirer claims Kant to have seen that limiting objectivity to scientific cognition was insufficient. Cassirer's view is that Kant proceeded to correct the trend of the *Critique of Pure Reason* in his ethics and aesthetics, but in fact Kant never regards acts of the aesthetic judgment as processes of objectivization. They can claim only subjective universality. It was Schelling who made the greater claim of objectivity for art with his theory of absolute spirit and his denial of the unknowability of the *Ding an sich*.

There is influence of Schelling in Cassirer, but it is thoroughly transformed, for if Cassirer will not respect the limits that Kant puts upon cognition, he also does not posit the act of spirit in quite the same way that Schelling does. What Cassirer calls "reality" in quotation marks is not merely the object of cognitive knowledge produced by Kant's understanding, nor is it the Schellingian self-reflexive *act* of consciousness in which nature and mind meet in absolute spirit. "Reality" is not a world of "things," a world of images of things, or a world of acts only. True, the human spirit knows itself through the "reality" it creates, but this reality is a cultural reality in which man expresses himself to himself, not in which nature expresses itself through intercourse with man. The human spirit produces fixed centers of form and meaning in which consciousness articulates itself. The highest objective truth that man can reveal to himself is the form of his own activity. Cassirer acknowledges that the question of what constitutes absolute reality apart from the functions of the spirit remains ever unanswerable, as it does in Kant. Yet Cassirer argues that as we think more and more on the matter the question of things-in-themselves dissolves into an "intellectual phantasm" for "the true concept of reality cannot be squeezed into the form of mere abstract being."[9] Thus Cassirer seems to attempt a mediation between Kant and Schelling, enlarging Kantian objectivity and differentiating modes of knowledge that Schelling tends to blend together in a single spiritual act.

What Cassirer presents is a general concept of culture, not of the so-called world. Since culture "makes" the world, the question of cultural forms must for Cassirer always precede, encompass, and to some extent obliterate the question of the world. In this sense Cassirer's Neo-Kantianism is both idealistic and humanistic.

Appropriating the Schellingian organicism that is so familiar a mark of romantic theory, Cassirer emphasizes the importance of context for meaning, the indissolubility of content and form, the idea that any concept—that of the aesthetic object, for example—belongs to a whole that it signifies, for "every notion of a part already encompasses the notion of the whole, not as to content but as to general structure and form." Theoretically any single concept, image, or myth of a culture implies the form of the rest, like Blake's "world in a grain of sand." Thus, the concept of the aesthetic object would seem to depend for its very existence on the total structure to which it belongs, while at the same time it empties the form of that structure.

The first volume of *The Philosophy of Symbolic Forms* is on the subject of language. As he finds the limitation of the term "objective" to the results of scientific cognition too narrowing, so does Cassirer reject the traditional view of language that is dominant in both the empirical and rationalist traditions. Both rationalists and empiricists, though opposed in many of their views of language, agree in regarding language exclusively as an "instrument of cognition," and both regard it principally with respect to its "theoretical content."[10] Whether one begins with Descartes and sees language as a mode of logical analysis on the model of mathematics or with Hobbes and Locke and sees language in its psychological function,

> whether it is interpreted as the immediate work and indispensable organ of reason, or as a mere veil which conceals the basic contents of knowledge, the true and "original" perceptions of the spirit: in either case the goal of language, by which its positive or negative value is determined, is seen as theoretical cognition and its expression.[11]

But this view misses much, perhaps most, of the substance of language—particularly the element of feeling and spontaneity which seems to have played the major role in language's formation. The thinkers to whom Cassirer turns for resources in his own theory are mainly Vico, Herder, and Humboldt, all of whom in his view sought to enlarge the scope of language. Vico, who is admired by Cassirer because he was the thinker who "first attempted a comprehensive, systematic outline of the cultural sciences," developed a concept of "poetic metaphysics,"[12] in which he saw poetic tropes and metaphors as absolutely fundamental to the nature of language, not artificial devices of rhetoric and art, or, worse, diseases of language, as in the theories of Max Müller. Herder attempted to mediate between Vico's view, as transmitted to him by Hamann, and the Leibnizian rationalism in which he had been trained. Cassirer is interested in Herder because for Herder, language fuses the analytical element with feeling. It is both the "product of immediate sensation and at the same time entirely . . . a product of reflection: because reflection is not something external that is merely added to the content of feeling; it enters into feeling as a constitutive factor."[13] Language is dynamic and has its own inner principle of development, a factor in the Kantian "synthetic structure of consciousness" itself.[14]

Humboldt, according to Cassirer, is the first to apply a Kantian critique to the philosophy of language and thus may be regarded as the founder of the tradition Cassirer continues. For Humboldt,

> the metaphysical opposition between subjectivity and objectivity is replaced by their transcendental correlation. In Kant the object, as "object in experience," is not something outside of and apart from cognition; on the contrary, it is only "made possible," determined and constituted by the categories of cognition. Similarly, the subjectivity of language no longer appears as a barrier that prevents us from apprehending objective being but rather as a means of forming, of "objectifying" sensory impressions. Like cognition, language does not merely "copy" a given object; it rather embodies a spiritual attitude which is always a crucial factor in our perception of the objective. Since the naïve-realistic approach lives and moves among objects, it takes too little account of this subjectivity; it does not readily conceive of a subjectivity which transforms the objective world, not accidentally or arbitrarily but in accordance with inner laws, so that the apparent object itself becomes only a subjective concept, yet a concept with a fully justified claim to universal validity.[15]

And, to quote Humboldt directly, "Because of the mutual dependency of thought and word, it is evident that the languages are not really means of representing the truth that has already been ascertained, but far more, means of discovering a truth not previously known."[16] Humboldt's Kantianism follows the master in reserving the term "objectivity" (that valuable coin of the realm) for the understanding, subjective universality rather than objectivity being in Kant characteristic of the aesthetic judgment. The way Cassirer gets from the traditionally Kantian discrimination between the objective and subjective universality to his own claim for the objectivity of all symbolic forms is, nevertheless, via Humboldt:

> for Humboldt each single language is such an individual view of the world, and only the totality of these views constitutes the objectivity attainable by man. Accordingly, language is subjective in relation to the knowable, and objective in relation to man as an empirical-psychological subject. For each language is a note in the harmony of man's universal nature: "once again the subjectivity of *all* mankind becomes intrinsically objective."[17]

In this view, language takes on a characteristic similar to that of space and time as pure forms. Kant describes these as subjective in that they are the spectacles we wear, but objective in that we cannot remove them.

Objectivity is no longer imagined as a *given* requiring merely description. Instead it is an end to be achieved by a "process of spiritual formation," namely expression. Also fundamental to Cassirer is Humboldt's idea that inquiry into language must proceed generically (but not with respect to its purely temporal development) in that we must recognize "the finished structure of language as something derived and mediated."[18] To this generic principle Cassirer is doggedly faithful, for both *The Philosophy of Symbolic Forms* and *An Essay on Man* proceed chapter by chapter through an analysis of the development of the subjects at hand. Finally, Cassirer takes from Humboldt the concept of language as a synthetic force: Linguistic meaning is not to be found in the particular word but in the structure of the sentence. Language is an activity of formalization. For the purposes of *The Philosophy of Symbolic Forms*, Vico, Herder, and Humboldt provided enough linguistic theory to buttress Cassirer's own analysis.

In his attack on the copy theory of language Cassirer argued that the meaning of the form of language cannot be found in what it expresses but in its manner and modality and its own inner laws of expression. Space and time being the Kantian pure forms of thought, Cassirer analyzes language in their terms. He notes that language renders intellectual concepts by spatial metaphor, logical and ideal relations becoming available to consciousness only when "projected into space and there analogically 'reproduced'." In setting forth things, in fixing boundaries in spatial terms, language brings the object into symbolic being. Language begins apparently in the quite concrete realm of the situation of the speaker and spreads out in ever wider circles from that point. In fact, the body becomes a model according to which man constructs his world as a whole. Even where language has become extremely abstract, the metaphors of space and body linger. Thus language does not merely reproduce an objective presence but constructs relations, beginning with the "I" and proceeding outward.

Time is a more complex problem because unlike two points in space, two moments of time are not given simultaneously to consciousness. As a result, the "whole fact of the representation of time is never contained in immediate intuition."[19] Language characteristically spatializes time. What begins as a simple distinguishing of separate points in time becomes transformed into the concept of a "mutual dynamic dependence."[20] At the furthest removal from the simplest spatializations of time lies the realm of numerical words, leading finally to mathematical construction of temporal order.

> In three diverse but closely related phases, language develops the three basic intuitions of space, time and number and so creates the indispensable condition for all intellectual mastery of phenomena and for every synthesis of these phenomena into the unity of a "world concept."[21]

The paradox in the idea of symbolic forms is that the control of "reality," indeed the creation of it, comes as language develops its own freedom and abandons its role as a copier of an assumed pre-existing objectivity.

Cassirer regards number as a particularly sophisticated kind of or development from language. There is a tension, in fact, between linguistic and what he calls the "purely intellectual symbols"[22] of mathematics. He distinguishes numerical concepts from language as such by arguing that language can never escape from intuition and the intuitive representation of things. Language clings, and must cling, to concrete objects and processes. Yet paradoxically, Cassirer says, this very clinging to the sensuous is itself a liberation, for without this base the system of number could not have come into being. Here Cassirer seems to imply that somehow the failures of language are redeemed by its having engendered mathematics, but although he exhibits this tendency from time to time, he suppresses it as he builds his system and claims authority for various symbolic forms.[23] Number also starts from the human body and its members and works outward to the distinction between "I" and "thou." Only gradually in its primitive stages does number emancipate itself from the designation of things and attributes, various occult systems of number being persistent examples of this.

The relation of "I" and the world is fundamental to the formation of all language. Cassirer sees language, after Humboldt, as a vehicle of the process in which the "I" comes to grips with the world, in which the limits of the two are clearly defined. Language is a process of differentiation growing out of a relatively undifferentiating state.

I have suggested that the critical technique that Kant applied to the mind Cassirer turned toward language and man's other expressive forms. Though Kant began *The Critique of Pure Reason* with the analysis of various kinds of statements, he never really treated the problem of thought as a problem of language. Cassirer claims that all logical analysis of concepts leads to the study of words. It is only "in and through" speech that the opposition between true and false arises. The question of the origin of the concept takes us back to the origin of the word. To language Cassirer gives the power of the primary formation of characteristics and classes.

> . . . we do not simply seize on and name certain distinctions that are somewhat present in feeling or intuition; on the contrary, on our own initiative we draw certain dividing lines, effect certain separations and connections, by virtue of which distinct individual configurations emerge from the uniform flux of consciousness. In the usual logical view, the concept is born only when the signification of the word is sharply delineated and unambiguously fixed through certain intellectual operations, particularly through "definition" according to *genus proximum* and *Differentia specifia*. But to penetrate to the ultimate source of the concept, our thinking must go back to a deeper stratum, must seek those factors of synthesis and analysis which are at work in the process of word formation itself, and which are decisive for the ordering of all our representations according to specific linguistic classifications.[24]

Language implies objectification, not the attribution of an independent reality to its content but a fixing of the content symbolically "for knowledge."[25] This is an important statement because it reveals what Cassirer means by the "objective," which he has turned away from its common usage. Humboldt thought each language had a "specific inner form" and differed in its perspective of the world. Accepting this view, Cassirer nevertheless claims overall perspective for language itself. This perspective has points of contact with other forms—scientific cognition, art, and myth. There is always in Cassirer's theory of forms the attitude that the whole precedes the parts, language as a formative power (not a content) preceding languages, the sentence preceding the word.

In that curious region between the extreme concreteness of some primitive languages and the pure abstraction of mathematics, language as we usually think of it performs its task. Its connections with mythical thought Cassirer goes on to explore in the second volume of *The Philosophy of Symbolic Forms*. It is in this investigation of the form of myth and its relation to language that Cassirer's main importance for literary theory becomes most apparent, though this significance is not systematically worked out by Cassirer himself.

It must first be understood that when Cassirer speaks of myth he is not referring to what we commonly think of as myths. Myths in the usual sense are the content of "myth," or the expression in language of "mythical thought," which is always to be understood in a formal sense and is really a term for a category of human symbolic activity. Cassirer begins his account of myth characteristically with a short history of thought about the subject. He makes a number of interesting observations here, a few of which are worth comment. First, he sees the classical tradition of interpreting myths allegorically as an attempt to justify the primitive stories as expressions of a preparatory stage for the new and more sophisticated world of *logos*. Second, for him Plato regarded myth as "the conceptual language in which alone the world of becoming can be expressed,"[26] as against the more real world of being; therefore, Plato found a place, albeit a secondary one, for myth. But, third, he observes that the Stoics and Neoplatonists unfortunately returned to the "old speculative-allegorical interpretation,"[27] which was then handed down to the Middle Ages and the Renaissance and has tended to cloud our understanding of mythical thought.

Vico and Schelling are Cassirer's two most important predecessors for the theory of myth. Vico saw myth as an "independent configuration of man's *consciousness*."[28] Schelling "replaces the allegorical interpretation of the world of myths by a tautegorical interpretation, i.e., he looks upon mythical figures as autonomous configurations of the human spirit, which one must understand from within by knowing the way in which they take on meaning and form."[29] But Schelling's idealism runs the danger of absorbing everything into one and not differentiating myth from other symbolic forms.

Beginning with these thinkers, Cassirer posits the objectivity of myth: "It is objective insofar as it is recognized as one of the determining factors by which consciousness frees itself from passive captivity in sensory impression and creates a world of its own in accordance with a spiritual principle."[30] It appears that myth has its genesis in the sense of "a magical force inherent in things,"[31] exemplified by the concept of *mana* and the division of things into the sacred and the profane. It is a form of concretion, characteristically repelling all merely abstract factors. It is defined principally by the following formal characteristics.

In myth there is an "indifference" of the various levels of objectification that are characteristically distinguished by empirical thinking.[32] Science submits change to abstract law; but in myth metamorphosis knows no such law. It is individual and unique.[33]

Where empirical thought sees merely representation myth sees the real identity of image and thing. Word and name do not merely describe or portray but contain the object and its power. This principle extends to that of *pars pro toto*, where, rather than the whole consisting of parts and resulting from them, the part and the whole become identified.

Myth lacks the category of the ideal. In order to apprehend true signification, myth has to transpose it into a concretion. The characteristic drive of myth toward the animation of everything is not a "spiritualization," but an example of concretion. Myth clings to bodies. The principle of sympathy in myth and magic passes over spatial and temporal differences and submerges similarity in indifference.

Using his characteristically Kantian vocabulary, Cassirer claims that it is not the quality of its categories of thought that differentiates myth from empirical-scientific thinking but the modality of those categories. Both involve unity, multiplicity, coexistence, contiguity, and succession. But in myth there are no "ideal, relational forms which constitute the objective world." Instead there are only "concrete unifying images."[34] While science combines elements only by distinguishing among them, myth "seems to roll up everything it touches into unity without distinction."[35] In scientific cognition relation comes "between" elements as an ideal signification, but in myth there is simply a "*concrescence or coincidence of the members of a relation.*"[36] The ideal space is not present.

As he does with language, Cassirer examines mythical space, time, and number. In a sense there is no mythical space but only spaces, and a space is regarded as part of the thing that occupies it. Space, in other words, is not abstract but concrete. Further, there is an indifference or blending of inward and outward, "I" and nature: ". . . each, rather, is reflected in the other, and only in this reciprocal reflection does each disclose its own meaning."[37] In a sense, the "whole mythical life form" is characterized by this relation.

Mythical time develops, as we have seen with language, through spatial relations. The past is an absolute past:

> All the sanctity of mythical being goes back ultimately to the sanctity of the origin. It does not adhere immediately to the content of the given but to its coming into being, not to its qualities and properties but to its genesis in the past. By being thrust back into temporal distance, by being situated in the depths of the past, a particular content is not only established as sacred, as mythically and religiously significant, but also justified as such.[38]

The principle of *pars pro toto* applies in mythical time, and differentiations in time are blurred or never existed. Even as in the development from the most primitive concepts of time certain differentiations begin to occur, the fundamental principle of the unity and "single dynamic and rhythm" of life persists.[39]

Cassirer sees religion, as he sees art, grow out of mythical thought. Indeed, religion is never entirely removed from this source. But although their contents are interwoven, the forms of religion and myth differ:

> Religion takes the decisive step that is essentially alien to myth: in its use of sensuous images and signs it recognizes them as such—a means of expression which, though they reveal a determinate meaning, must necessarily remain inadequate to it, which "point" to this meaning but never wholly exhaust it.[40]

Mysticism, in Cassirer's view, moves beyond this attitude and strives actually to negate the realm of the actual, rejecting both mythical image language and "historical elements of faith."[41] For the mystic both the concrete and abstract expressions of religion are inadequate. Yet the attempt to move beyond image and the attachment to the world Cassirer sees as the characteristic quality of the religious consciousness. The world of things is, in this constant opposition, transformed into a world of signs. Things and events signify something transcendent. The comparison with language is obvious. In their own ways both religion and language cling to the sensuous and yet strive to surpass it. Religion's typical way of doing this recalls for us romantic and idealistic concepts of literary allegory, and Cassirer notes the relation:

> In religion the sensuous and the spiritual by no means coincide, but nevertheless they point continuously to one another. They stand to one another in a relationship of analogy, by which both are interrelated and separate. In religious thinking this relation occurs wherever a sharp line divides the world of the sensuous and the suprasensory, the spiritual and the corporeal—but where on the other hand the two worlds undergo their concrete religious formation by reflecting each other. Hence "analogy" always bears the typical features of "allegory": for no religious understanding of reality flows from itself; in it the reality must be related to something else, through which its meaning becomes known. This progressive process of allegoresis is illustrated above all in medieval thought.[42]

Indeed, for Cassirer to say that "the reality must be related to something else" tends to misplace reality, which from the religious point of view must then *be* that something else. Yet Cassirer's point is that the process of allegoresis allows religion to remain in the "particular and the given" without being confined strictly to it, since the world becomes a book to be read, as it were, but a book which "copies" or "reads" a hidden reality. Religious consciousness turns mythical thought in the direction of "tropological thinking," physical reality to "mere trope." The medieval religious mind invented an elaborate art of hermeneutics to organize the tropological conventions.[43] Cassirer claims that religion depends on a tension between a hidden meaning or reality and a sensuous image of it. Resolution of that stress cannot occur in religion.

On the last page of the volume on mythical thought, Cassirer brings us to art:

> The striving for such an equilibrium points . . . to another sphere. Only when we turn from the mythical image world

and the world of religious meaning to the sphere of art and artistic expression does the opposition which dominates the development of the religious consciousness appear to be in a sense appeased, if not negated. For it is characteristic of the aesthetic trend that here the image is recognized purely *as such*, that to fulfill its function it need give up nothing of itself and its content.[44]

It would appear, then, that we have in science, or what I call the realm of the "empirical" form of allegory, a symbolic form the structure of which asserts the separation of subject and object and identification of the "real" with the objective realm. In religion, or what I have called "religious" allegory, we have a structure asserting the separation of sensory and suprasensory realms in which the suprasensory is identified with the "real." In mythical thought we have an indifference of subject and object and an immanence of the supernatural rather than a hidden supernature. At the end of the volume on mythical thought it would appear that Cassirer regards art as filling a gap in a system of cultural forms. Myth as a primitive form of thought gives way historically to science on the one hand and to religion on the other. In the latter the supernatural is replaced by the supranatural. Yet in each of these more sophisticated forms the solidarity of life is bifurcated. He hints at art as a third force evolved from myth that in itself binds meaning to image. Yet a discussion of art is lacking at this point, and we must turn to *An Essay on Man* to find it, for the third volume of *The Philosophy of Symbolic Forms*, entitled "The Phenomenology of Science," takes us in another direction.

2. *An Essay on Man*

IN ADDITION to providing chapters on art and history, *An Essay on Man* approaches its subject through new material. Animal and human behavior are contrasted, and man is defined as the *animal symbolicum*. Symbolic processes in man are described with reference to the linguistic development of Helen Keller and Laura Bridgman, to cases of aphasia, and by comparison to the behavior of apes. In the chapter on language, there is reference to linguists unknown to Cassirer twenty years before, particularly Saussure and Bloomfield. The chapter on art reveals also a considerable study of the history of literary theory.

Before I examine the discussion of art, it is well to review briefly Cassirer's short chapter on the symbol. The term, of course, is in no way limited to the literary symbol, and in some respects it has little apparent relation to common literary usage of the term. Nevertheless, it is important to the concern of this book, because it goes beneath common usage to locate a broad base—too broad a base, in Paul Ricoeur's opinion.[45] Carrying out his contrast between animal and human behavior, Cassirer claims that between the "receptor system" and the "effector system," which are found in all animals, the *animal symbolicum* possesses the "symbolic system." A *human* response is not an "organic reaction." There intervenes between stimulus and response a "slow and complicated process of thought."[46] This process can be regarded as of questionable value from one perspective, but from Cassirer's it is an obvious advance and is the process that allows us to refer to such things as the human "spirit," a term to which Cassirer gives no metaphysical or mystical grandeur but which characterizes the *animal symbolicum*. In any case, Cassirer claims no more anxiety about this "reversal of the natural order" than does Kant about the unknowability of things-in-themselves:

> Man cannot escape from his own achievement. He cannot but adopt the conditions of his own life. No longer in a merely physical universe, man lives in a symbolic universe. Language, myth, art, and religion are parts of this universe. They are the varied threads which weave the symbolic net, the tangled web of human experience. All human progress in thought and experience refines upon and strengthens this net. No longer can man confront reality immediately; he cannot see it, as it were, face to face. Physical reality seems to recede in proportion as man's symbolic activity advances. Instead of dealing with the things themselves man is in a sense constantly conversing with himself. He has so enveloped himself in linguistic forms, in artistic images, in mythical symbols or religious rites that he cannot see or know anything except by the interposition of this artificial medium.[47]

This passage is liable to misinterpretation out of context and is even slightly misleading in context. For a moment, it would seem that Cassirer is implying a preprimitive golden age before Faustian man surrounded himself with the encumbrances of culture. But Cassirer posits no such age. The choice for Cassirer is between human culture and the condition of the beast that can never create one: even that is no longer a choice, if it ever was. The "physical reality" to which he refers above is not the "reality" of physical science or of religion. It is only the Kantian manifold of sensation. The "realities" of the physical sciences (indeed their "objectivities") and of religion are symbolic constructions, composed according to their own categories.

The symbol, for Cassirer, does not really exist as an isolated entity. What Cassirer sees is a range of related symbolic constructs or wholes that have expressive and "constitutive" power. The purest, most radical example of such a system, which is not a system of objects or entities, but a system of forms or relations, is mathematics. Mathematics does not copy the world, though in its primitive stages it was thought to do so; instead the world is cast into the form of mathematics. Plato was wrong, therefore, when he claimed in the *Republic* that "the spangled heavens should be used as a pattern and with a view to that higher knowledge."[48] Mathematics does not copy nature; the "spangled heavens" are "constituted" in mathematical form. Such a form, for Cassirer, is not, however, their only form.

Nor is Cassirer sentimental about mythical thought, though on occasion he seems to admire it. At the same time, he has difficulty expressing his concept of its cultural role. In *The Philosophy of Symbolic Forms* he goes to great trouble to argue that myth has to be understood on its own terms, from inside itself, at which point its own logic becomes clear. And he makes this claim for every symbolic form. At the same time he regards mythical thought as a stage in human culture that is there to be surpassed or to be built upon, and he refers to it early in *An Essay on Man* as "a false and erroneous form of symbolic thought that first paved the way to a new and true symbolism, the symbolism of modern science."[49] But if this is so, what criterion has been employed to judge a symbolic form erroneous and untrue? Cassirer has already warned us against judging myth by some external criterion. It appears that all such judgments in Cassirer ought to be based upon purely internal considerations to which such terms as "organic unity" and "coherence" have popularly been applied. And if one such symbolic form is to be declared erroneous by principles external to it, what is to prevent all such forms coming under the same sort of attack?

The fact is that for Cassirer all symbolic forms that he discusses are not to be lined up and treated equally. Some are germinative, so to speak, others presumably more final, though not fixed in the way that Aristotle regarded the forms of tragedy to be, Aristotle's forms being substantial and Cassirer's not. Cassirer always allows for development; but science, art, religion, and history emerge from the primitive forms of language and myth, which are inextricably related in their genesis. This is not to denigrate myth but to assert that it gives shape to more sophisticated forms, and the fundamental quality of these new forms is their self-consciousness *as forms*, which completely changes the nature of human belief in what they constitute. Religion, art, and science are all viewed as forms which sophisticate myth in some special direction.

Cassirer remarks that we are constantly struck by the "close kinship" of myth with poetry, but just as we recognize only a primitive chemistry in alchemy, so do we see a fundamental difference. Cassirer approaches this difference by recourse to Kant's remarks on aesthetic contemplation and distinguishes art from myth on the basis of the absence of belief in the aesthetic contemplation of the former. The actual *connections* between myth and poetry are not enumerated, though it is obvious that the characteristics of myth enumerated in *The Philosophy of Symbolic Forms* have analogues in literature.

Meanwhile Cassirer's discussion of language and art creates a terminological quagmire for those who wish to employ his insights for literary criticism. Though literature is a *linguistic* art, Cassirer tends to draw contrasts *between* language and art, even as he treats literature as an art. This confusing procedure has its roots in a scientific positivism that lingers on in his vocabulary, even though he has been moving away from it in his philosophy. In his chapter on language, Cassirer tends to assume that language's progressive development is strictly toward conceptual abstraction. Everything he mentions tends to demonstrate language's emancipation from myth in the direction of science. Then in the chapter on art, art is contrasted to language and science by being shown to perform another function. Cassirer seems momentarily to forget that there is, in his own view, a linguistic art that emerges from myth to develop its own symbolic form. Cassirer's contrast is expressed in this way:

> Like all other symbolic forms art is not the reproduction of a ready-made, given reality. It is one of the ways leading to an objective view of things and of human life. It is not an imitation but a discovery of reality. We do not, however, discover nature through art in the same sense in which the scientist uses the term "nature." Language and science are the two main processes by which we ascertain and determine our concepts of the external world. We must classify our sense per-

ceptions and bring them under general notions and general rules in order to give them an objective meaning. Such classification is the result of a persistent effort toward simplification. The work of art in like manner implies such an act of condensation and concentration.[50]

But for Cassirer, language and science are "abbreviations of reality," while art is an "intensification of reality."[51]

There are semantic difficulties here. First, to say that language and science are the two main processes "by which we ascertain and determine our concepts of the external world" is ambiguous. It *can* imply the very same "ready-made, given reality" that Cassirer has already rejected. The "external world" ought to be regarded by Cassirer here as itself built up conceptually, not as a thing. Second, to refer to language and science as "abbreviations of reality" raises the same problem, for it prejudges the location of a reality which these forms are supposed to make. Cassirer seems to be making a judgment of the symbolic forms of language and science from a point external to those forms, a procedure he has already warned against. The terms he uses seem to imply judgment rather than description alone.

Yet, if we clear away this problem we come to a more satisfactory contrast:

> Language and science depend upon one and the same process of abstraction; art may be described as a continuous process of concretion. . . . what science is searching for is some central feature of a given object from which all its particular qualities may be derived. . . . But art does not admit of this sort of conceptual simplification and deductive generalization. It does not inquire into the qualities or causes of things; it gives us the intuition of the form of things.[52]

Like all theorists Cassirer has found it easier to talk about what science does than about art. The contrast is difficult to make because of the problem of discussing art in what Cassirer has declared to be a separate symbolic form—in conceptual language. It is also a problem that the contrast between abstract and concrete is really inadequate, for it is possible to say, as Susanne Langer comes to say, that there is a process of abstraction from the manifold of sensation in *all* symbolic forms. The difference between science and art in this case would seem to be a process of abstraction toward the general in science and abstraction toward the concrete in art. This is the same distinction that Vico offered between abstract and poetic universals.

However, there is something to be said against the term "abstraction," or at least a clarification is necessary. There must be something to abstract *from*, and Cassirer's position is that symbolic forms are constitutive, not mimetic. Thus the term "abstract" must be taken to mean the constitutive process, if it is to be used at all, and must contain no implication of copy or imitation.

It is only with these semantic reservations and substitutions that we can follow Cassirer consistently through a remark such as the following:

> Science means abstraction, and abstraction is always an impoverishment of reality. The forms of things as they are described in scientific concepts tend more and more to become mere formulae. . . . It would seem as though reality were not only accessible to our scientific abstractions but exhaustible by them. But as soon as we approach the field of art this proves to be an illusion. For the aspects of things are innumerable.[53]

Here he teeters on the edge of a copy theory, and in his zeal to establish a place for art employs the derogatory term "impoverishment" to describe scientific abstraction. No symbolic form can "impoverish" in Cassirer's system unless it is isolated from all other forms and becomes the sole vehicle of cultural life. And in that case, it seems to me, every form would impoverish. Cassirer's rhetoric leads to a plea for a recognition of the necessity of a culture of interlocking forms, but his language threatens to give away the gains he has made and to revert to a theory of naïve representation.

He has, of course, gone to great lengths to combat just such a theory. Indeed, his criticism of nineteenth-century romantics and realists turns on this very point. The romantics under the influence of Schlegel thought erroneously of art as a "symbolic representation of the infinite" and considered the finite world of things only a veil. The realists denied the "pure forms" of the idealists and insisted on the "material aspect of things."[54] Unfortunately in their theories the realists fell back on the doctrine of imitation and failed to discover the "symbolic character of art" out of fear of dropping back into the net of romantic theory. The two schools were each half right: "Art is, indeed, symbolism [as the romantics say], but the symbolism of art must be understood in an immanent, not in a transcendent sense."[55] Cassirer considers, then, that the romantics posited art as allegorical in their sense after all. This leads him to regard romantic theory as an attempt to blur the distinction between art and religion, since he has identified religion in *The Philosophy of Symbolic Forms* as also an allegorical symbolic form. For Cassirer the very nature of symbolism in art is that it keeps to the concrete and does not move beyond it. But it is not accurate any longer to say symbolism *in* art; we must say symbolism *as* art or art *in* symbolism, for symbolism now has a much broader range; moreover, symbolism when applied to art is not any longer a trope but the form of art. Indeed, the old romantic opposition between allegory and symbolism seems to be replaced by an image of allegory contained in symbolism, like the center in the Blakean circumference. Though Cassirer is not explicit about this, we are now required to treat allegory as a form *within* art, while symbolism is to be treated as the form *of* art.

In spite of his own problems of expression, Cassirer regards symbolic forms as being one with their respective media, so to speak. He is attracted to Croce's idea that intuition and expression are identical but rejects the distinction Croce makes between expression and externalization. Cassirer tends to emphasize the creation of a work of art as a process by which intuitions are achieved and fixed, and he declares that the medium of an art is not mere technical apparatus. In fact the medium is not a medium but a form, and poetic creation is a process in which the intuition is discovered, not transferred into words, rhythms, or colors. Context and form are one. He quotes Mallarmé to the effect that poetry is not written with ideas but words. Yet he then goes on to say it is written with "images, sounds, and rhythms," when it would have been better to mention these not as other basic stuff of poetry but properties of language.

His distinction between language and art still dogs him in these remarks. One of the reasons for his having made the distinction in addition to its incipient positivism is that he is carrying on a quarrel with Croce:

> Croce insists that there is not only a close relation but a complete identity between language and art. To his way of thinking it is quite arbitrary to distinguish between the two activities. Whoever studies general linguistics, according to Croce, studies aesthetic problems—and vice versa. There is, however, an unmistakable difference between the symbols of art

and the linguistic terms of ordinary speech or writing. These two activities agree neither in character nor purpose; they do not employ the same means, nor do they tend toward the same ends. Neither language nor art gives us mere imitation of things or actions; both are representations. But a representation in the medium of sensuous forms differs widely from a verbal or conceptual representation.[56]

As we have already observed, the distinction between language and art in Cassirer leaves poetry in the void unless Cassirer is prepared to offer a theory of poetic language and explain how it differs from language as he has for the most part used the term. Otherwise, the use of Cassirer for a theory of the literary symbolic threatens to collapse, since as language, literature would then have to adhere to his description of language as constantly moving toward generalization, and as a result we would have left only a purely allegorical theory (in the romantic sense) of literary statement. To claim that literature is not made of language but of the things that are properties of language would return us to some variation of the old Horatian *ut pictura poesis* principle and lands us in a purely imitative or copy theory. Either way would destroy the elaborate constitutive power that Cassirer gives to literature as a symbolic form and with it his claim that such a form is a structure creative of his brand of objectivization.

When at the end of his chapter on art Cassirer claims that "conceptual depth" is discovered by science and "purely visual depth" by art,[57] we are certain that he suffers from that traditional lack of an appropriate terminology for art that so many critics have bemoaned. "Visual" is hardly an adequate word for all art. Perhaps "appearance" is somewhat better—a term he shifts to—but it, too, is inadequate. In any case, he claims for art not only the term "objective" but also the term "knowledge." This "knowledge" is the result of the "multiformity and diversity of intuitions," not the "uniformity of laws," and rather than "theoretical description" art consists in "sympathetic vision."[58] With this word "sympathy" the relation of art to myth again appears, and we sense that the characteristics of myth enunciated in *The Philosophy of Symbolic Forms* are analogous to the characteristics of that poetic language which needs to be described in order to complete Cassirer's theory as a theory of *literary* symbolic. Indeed, as I have suggested, it is in this undeveloped analogy that Cassirer's main contribution to literary theory lies.

There is yet another point to be made. The analogy between literary art and myth begins with their common indifference of subject and object. But art differs from myth in its self-consciousness. It knows it "makes" something; the artist and reader are therefore both inside and outside it at the same time, while primitive thinking is forever inside. Art is said by Cassirer to join subject and object. But to say they are *joined* by art implies that they are somehow separate in some reality independent of all symbolic form. But *where* they exist or *if* they exist as things in themselves is forever unknown. Meanwhile Cassirer hints that the variety of symbolic forms is not a wild discord but a Heraclitan contrariety, a crucial idea that cries out for development.

3. Langer's "new key"

The most ambitious effort to develop a theory of the arts out of Cassirer's concept of symbolic forms has been made in a series of books by Susanne K. Langer. I say "theory of the arts," because Langer attempted in her *Feeling and Form* to distinguish among the arts while establishing a general theory.[59] We have noted that Cassirer didn't entirely eradicate the old opposition between poetry and language complained of by Croce. Indeed, in his chapter specifically on art in *An Essay on Man* he did not proceed very much beyond Croce and might have been as well off free of Croce's influence. Langer pays more attention than Cassirer to specific arts, though whether she succeeds in moving beyond him remains to be seen.

Cassirer was not the only influence on Langer. Clearly her concept of art as "presentational form" emerges from Cassirer's concept of "mythical thought," but it is possible to say that temperamentally Langer's affinities are with the tradition of empiricism and with logical positivism, as her allusions to the early Wittgenstein show. Her *Philosophy in a New Key* is dedicated to Whitehead; and her stance is not that of critical idealism.[60] Instead she seems deliberately to seek enlargement of the boundaries of logical positivism to include a workable theory of the *logic* of art. The concept of the symbolic plays the central role in this effort.

Langer employs a distinction between signal and symbol similar to that of Cassirer between sign and symbol. In her treatment, the symbol is not necessarily located in language but in what she calls the "image": "No human impression is only a signal from the outer world, it is always *also* an image in which possible impressions are formulated, that is, a symbol for the conception of *such* experiences."[61] The exact nature of the image is not clear. Does it exist as a

sense datum or as a Crocean internally expressed form or as an externalized form? The term seems to function as the first part of an in-
tegrated process resulting in the end in what Croce called externalization. Langer says that the image exists at a "very low level of
symbolization,"[62] though sometimes "image" seems to equal the
completed symbol. In any case, the signal calls our attention to an
objective situation, whereas a symbol "is understood when we conceive the idea it presents,"[63] the term "presentation" apparently emphasizing creation of something rather than mediation. Apparently
also, the signal indicates a passive mental condition, while the symbol indicates an active one. But signals regarded as objects rather
than pure acts can also be symbols.

The symbolic activity Langer calls "abstraction": ". . . we
promptly and unconsciously abstract a form from each sensory experience, and use this form to *conceive* the experience as a whole, as a
'thing'."[64] Abstraction (or symbolization) is broadened from its positivistic connection with generalization based upon sense data (Cassirer's "impoverishment of reality") to include artistic activity. Langer notes that because of the common positivistic usage she seems to
have created a paradox in assigning the term "abstraction" to "a
mode supposed to be characterized by concreteness."[65] But for her,
the terms "abstract" and "concrete" are not opposites, concretion
being the specific mode of abstraction resulting in art. She claims that
our various senses create their own kinds of abstraction and "consequently dictate their own peculiar forms of conception."[66] This view,
which simplistically assigns each art to a sense, she tends, however, to
abandon in her later *Feeling and Form*, though not without occasional continued flirtation. The term "conception" is also among
those she expands. It includes concrete art symbols as well as those
general ideas with which we have connected the term to this point.
Concepts, for Langer, can be fantasies which are built up from many
impressions but remain concrete and contain an element of the "image."[67] The notion is reminiscent of Vico's "poetic universals," but in
spite of Cassirer's use of Vico, Langer nowhere mentions him.

In its expanded form, abstraction includes all symbolic formulation and representation. In taking this step, Langer criticizes some
previous thinkers who, she acknowledges, have been on her track. In
penetrating remarks on Henri Bergson, she argues that Bergson saw
one issue clearly: all conceptual formulations (in the common positivistic sense) designed to represent time abstract toward an impoverishing general concept of our experience of it. But Bergson errone-

ously concluded that *all* symbolization thwarts our true experience of time (and of everything else). He held, therefore, that we must have recourse to pure intuition, which he regarded as unmediated experience. Langer argues that it is not a prison house of conceptual symbolism that makes us think we fail to grasp "lived" time, but our too narrow positivistic sense of the conceptual and symbolic, which limits it to what she calls "discursive forms." It is necessary, then, to see art as a mode of symbolic formulation which has a logic of its own. Bergson's unmediated intuitive knowledge is really mediated by a nondiscursive symbolism not to be identified with "systematic, explicit reasoning."[68] Langer seeks the "logical structure of a type of symbol that logicians do not use."[69] In this she is strictly a follower of Cassirer.

Croce she thinks fails ultimately on the same point as Bergson does: ". . . by contemplating intuitions as direct experiences, not mediated, not correlated to anything public, one cannot record or systematize them, let alone construct a 'science' of intuitive knowledge."[70] Her complaint against Croce is that the identification of intuition and expression, which regards the work of art as "something in the artist's mind" makes the depiction of that something "in material terms" (Croce's "externalization") simply incidental to art.[71] She wants to argue that the externalization is "part and parcel of the creative drive."[72] Rather than splitting this drive as Croce does (she really desires to imagine it as a unified process), she threatens to split it, at least with respect to the literary work, all over again between the unified expression-externalization and the previous, though very rudimentary "image." She also complains that for Croce there are no different kinds of intuition, but only the various mechanical externalizations of one fundamental kind of intuition, whereas she assigns intuitions of different things to different arts. Croce's "science" of aesthetics is thus for her a contradiction in terms. In her view Croce's follower R. G. Collingwood reaches the same impasse,[73] and a similar problem is implicit in Freud, who turns all art into natural self-expression instead of "hard won intellectual advance"[74] from image to art object via the process of symbolic abstraction.

Langer's theory begins with a distinction between "two symbolic modes rather than restricting intelligence to discursive forms and relegating all other conception to some irrational realm of feeling and instinct. . . ."[75] The two modes are discursive and presentational (nondiscursive) forms. Both forms are said to proceed from "the basic human act of symbolic transformation."[76] This distinction gives her considerable trouble with respect to literary art, because of the fixed positivistic view of language as pure discourse with which she begins. Langer's presentational forms are described as "matters which require to be conceived through some symbolic schema other than discursive language,"[77] language being by no means our only "articulate" human product. The problem, as she sees it, for a positivistic approach is that nondiscursive symbols "cannot be defined in terms of others, as discursive symbols can."[78] A piece of discourse is always part of a symbolism; a work of art is a "prime symbol" or a system of its own.[79] In this sense, art objects could in fact be called "presented forms," a term that as far as I can tell, Langer uses only once and perhaps without conscious intent.[80] Once having made her distinction, Langer gradually in *Philosophy in a New Key* comes to declare that it does not rigorously correspond to another distinction she employs between "literal" and "artistic." She comes to state that some presentational symbols are in fact merely proxy for discourse, while true artistic symbols have a sense which is untranslatable, being "bound to the particular form which it has taken."[81] But here there is a contradiction because, as we have seen above, she does not regard works of art as *containing* symbols but *being symbolic* as wholes, and this tendency to be tempted to think of symbols as parts of works of art muddles her discourse. Unartistic presentational symbols would be maps, diagrams, and flags, which have a "purely literal significance."[82] It does not seem possible to make this claim, since such symbols would seem to be referential objects that can be considered parts of a symbolic system larger than themselves. She only declares that "in a general way literal meaning belongs to words and artistic meaning to images invoked by words and to presentational symbols."[83] It would appear by this that words never in themselves are presentational symbols, nor can they combine to create one; only the images invoked (called on, summoned up?) by words are. Yet a discursive statement she declares to be symbolic on the face of it, creating in itself a conceptual structure of a certain sort which has apparently transformed *into language* the way things objectively are. Here the symbolic element lies in the language, unless we are to assume that the symbolic structure is only in the concepts created or signified and *pointed to* by language, these concepts having a being apart from language. But for a linguistic art, she seems to declare, the symbolic element lies not in the language at all, which is by her definition always discursive in nature, but in the images summoned up by the discourse. Thus the language of literature would seem to be a set of signals to a reader to recall these images, and the images themselves would constitute the symbolic system of the literary art object. This argument is further complicated by her double use of the term "image," which sometimes means a very rudimentary beginning of the symbolic process and sometimes the completed artistic object. We are not certain whether her concept of the image allows for a real symbolic transformation or is merely a sense datum that is signaled by language. Fundamentally her problem here is that her lurking positivistic concept of language insists on pure abstraction as the linguistic model and cannot firmly regard language as in any way *creating* or *containing* the image.

In the end she would bifurcate the poetic process, in spite of her argument in the following remark: "Croce and many other serious aestheticians to the contrary notwithstanding, the final process of figuring forth an idea in sensuous appearance is *not* a mechanical affair, but is part and parcel of the creative drive."[84] One even detects another implicit bifurcation because here the original thing "figured forth" is an idea (an abstract idea?) that is to be *put into* sensuous terms.

Another way to look at this problem is to note a certain unsteadiness in Langer's treatment of the term "symbol" itself. Langer seems to use it in more than one sense with respect to art. In the first sense, which contradicts the one I have already mentioned, it is an element of a work of art which seems to have some status independent of its context. In a second sense, it is the work of art itself as a total form. There is even a third sense lurking in Langer's theory as a whole which tells us that "symbol" refers to no object but to the *activity* of abstraction, or various activities of abstraction, including both presentational and discursive forms. Langer's theory as a whole must abandon the first usage above, since her argument declares that no part of an artistic work can formulate artistic meaning except as part of the total artistic context, which is the symbol in sense two. The term "symbol" simply cannot in her system be used to refer to parts of artistic works if it is to be used to refer to the special presentational mode of abstraction which denies that inside its own activity there is anything but self-ordering.

The connected problem of the relation or disrelation of image to word generated in Langer's theory arises perhaps out of her use of music as a sort of paradigm of art. This use is not unfamiliar to us, since we have seen flirtations with it in the nineteenth-century remarks of Baudelaire, Mallarmé, Wagner, and, of course, Pater, who was only one of the thinkers of the time to claim that all art aspires to the condition of music. The remark itself should give us pause, since "aspiration" implies a significant difference that cannot be rationalized away by making the teleologically conceived ideal into a norm. Perhaps if we examine Langer on music we can determine why she must make literary symbols prelinguistic "images."

A "purely connotational semantic," music is, she says, "peculiarly adapted to the explication of 'unspeakable' things."[85] It is not strictly a language because for Langer language implies discourse. At least it can only "inexactly" be called a language.[86] It does not produce meaning in the sense that language does. On the other hand, it is not spontaneous utterance. In essence, it is neither the cause nor cure of feelings, but their logical (in her expanded sense) expression. The logic is that of presentational musical form. In *Philosophy in a New Key*, Langer calls music an "unconsummated symbol,"[87] presumably because it does not generate meaning in the way discourse does. Language is a symbolism in which equivalent terms may be interchanged, but a musical work is a symbol in itself. The term "unconsummated," however, may have made Langer uneasy, and in *Feeling and Form* she does not use it. She well might have been uneasy because it is positivistic in perspective. From that point of view, the term can only mean that music always falls short of delivering true meaning, that is, it only *aspires to the condition of language*. For Langer's theory it would, in fact, be better to say that music is a "consummate" symbol.

To this point, a musical work seems to be a pure, radical formulation only of itself, but to say this seems to cut it off from life and leaves us and criticism with only the statement that any work of music is what it is or means itself. Langer is not satisfied with that, but she seems to have no recourse except to seek something that a work of music expresses or represents after all. She studiously avoids terms like "copy" or "imitation," but here her language becomes unsteady again. She says that representation is really formation, and she tries to make the term "articulation" imply a radical creativity. Such creativity seems to be a search into musical forms to discover something. Yet there is still present a hint that music is not discovering but copying something. It articulates *feelings* or, sometimes, in order to emphasize the abstractive, symbolic role, it articulates the *idea* of feeling. Indeed, the latter is a far preferable way for her to put it because the feelings which are the *materials* of the symbolic transformation must be transformed into something else. "Concept" would perhaps be a more consistent term, since her whole argument is that artistic form, or abstraction in the direction of the concrete, is another way of making concepts, which should not be limited to scientific cognition, as in logical positivism. The feelings are made presentable to intellect via presentational forms. One sees that articulation is another term for abstraction or symbolic transformation, though sometimes it looks as if articulation is imitation.

Yet literature is made from language or with language, which in Langer's positivistic usage has not been associated at all with the articulation of feeling but only with the articulation of logical concepts. Some of Langer's early treatments of language in *Philosophy in a New Key* are narrow indeed. Language is described as "a very poor medium for expressing our emotional nature": "It merely names certain vaguely and crudely conceived states, but fails miserably in any attempt to convey the ever-moving patterns, the ambivalences and intricacies of inner experience, the interplay of feelings with thoughts and impressions, memories and echoes of memories, transient fantasies, or its mere runic traces, all turned into nameless, emotional stuff."[88] Language is "essentially discursive."[89] Wordless symbolism is untranslatable, impossible of definition within its own system and cannot directly convey generalization. Later, Langer hedges and calls language as defined above "language in its literal capacity," and she speaks of language in that sense as "stiff" and unable to express new ideas, which "usually have to break in upon the mind through some great and bewildering metaphor."[90] This remark makes metaphor seem to be an unlinguistic or at least prelinguistic phenomenon, as if it were fundamentally "image" rather than "word." I shall return to Langer on the metaphor. Here we detect her trying to find a role for nondiscursive forms in the development of culture and giving a powerful creative role to metaphor. It is a role prior to language as positivistically defined: ". . . it is only where experience is already presented—through some other formative medium, some vehicle of apprehension and memory—that the canons of literal thought have any application."[91] Since she has identified "literal" thought with language, it seems that she is placing all nondiscursive forms historically prior to language. At the same time, she goes so far as to assert that our "primary world of reality is a verbal one."[92] Language allows us to remember in ways that other animals cannot. Language is fundamentally "the formulation and expression of conceptions rather than the communication of natural wants." Its motive is the transformation of experience into concepts, and its source is not pragmatic but "purposeless lalling-instincts, primitive aesthetic reactions, and dreamlike associations of ideas. . . ."[93] In the declaration that both discursive *and* presentational forms are indeed formative there is the possibility that distinction between them might break down. In the statement below, Langer's positivistic use of the term "language" is no longer quite workable:

> Just as verbal symbolism has a natural evolution from the mere suggestive word or "word-sentence" of babyhood to the grammatical edifice we call a language, so presentational symbolism has its own characteristic development. It grows from the momentary, single static image presenting a simple concept, to greater and greater units of successive images having reference to each other; changing scenes, even visions of things in motion, by which we conceive the passage of events. That is to say, the first thing we *do* with images is to envisage a story; just as the first thing we do with words is to tell something, to make a statement.[94]

There are several problems here. One is a confusion of terminology that results from a mixing of generic and teleological (in the guise of normative) definitions of language. Langer adopts a generic approach to her discussion of language only by fits and starts, in contrast to Cassirer, whose approach is basically and more consistently generic. Another problem is the statement that stories are presented in images, not words. Langer has fallen back on the idea of images because her latent positivistic definition of language cannot admit that language itself is or can be presentational. Thus she is tempted to press stories back into so-called prelinguistic images which language then can signify or signal in a way acceptable to a positivistic view. This insistence on the image as the medium of literary art makes language merely a code or set of signals for presentation. A purely linguistic art, then, becomes for her a contradiction in terms even as she insists on its existence.

Sometimes Langer *starts out* to treat all language as fundamentally poetic:

> . . . the poetic use of language is essentially formulative. Poetry is not a beautified discourse, a particularly effective way of telling things, although poetic structures may occur in discourse with truly artistic effect. Poetry as such is not discourse

at all, it is the creation of a perceptible human experience, which, from the standpoint of science and practical life, is illusory.[95]

But she is always dragged back to the same problem: Either language is not always language, or language is not always discourse, or poetry does not inhere in language but in something language points to. But if poetry does inhere in language, positivistically defined, how can it be the creation of a *perceptible* human experience? Poetry on a written page is not a sensuous medium like music to the ear, and poetry spoken is only a set of signals. Is Langer saying again that poetic language refers to mental images? If so, she retains her positivistic view of language but at the cost of stealing from poetry what would appear to be its substance—words. If we follow along in this line, poetry becomes the only art that does not *present in* its apparent medium. It only signals a presentation of images, which the reader must evoke or call up. We have found a split in Langer as difficult as the one Langer finds in Croce between expression and externalization. An example of the result is the curious phrase in *Philosophy in a New Key*, "a metaphor of wordless cognition,"[96] where the term metaphor is wrenched from its connection with language as rudely as it was forced by classical rhetoricians to become merely a device of discourse. Yet in another breath metaphor is declared to be the means by which language, poverty-stricken almost by definition, is to restore itself, and metaphor is also the fundamental "power whereby language, even with a small vocabulary, manages to embrace a multimillion things."[97]

In *Feeling and Form*, Langer points out that an artist would probably insist that his metaphor is literal truth, but in so insisting would have recourse to myth, which is a "stronger symbolic mode than metaphor."[98] Langer calls myth both a "nondiscursive symbolism" and "the primitive phase of metaphysical thought."[99] Myth can only abstract toward presentation. When in a culture the literal truth of myth begins to be questioned, its power is exhausted,[100] and it has become fully rationalized by discourse, or it gives rise to aesthetic forms. Of these, she declares the epic to be one of the first: "It is not merely a receptacle of old symbols, namely those of myth, but is itself a new symbolic form, great with possibilities, ready to take meanings and express ideas that have had no vehicle before."[101] The connection with myth is not rigorously explored. It is declared that myth is ex-

haustible; so are artistic forms.[102] It is declared that in our time the
current myth (in the sense of a total cultural structure of "mythology") is reaching total exhaustion:

> There must be a rationalistic period from this point onward.
> Some day when the vision is totally rationalized, the ideas ex-
> ploited and exhausted, there will be another vision, a new
> mythology.[103]

A dialectic of myth and reason is here turned into a cyclical historical
movement reminiscent of Vico's *ricorso*, Blake's circular fallen world,
and Yeats's wheel. Langer adds little at this point to Cassirer's analogy between myth and art.

In addition to difficulties surrounding the terms "language," "image," and "myth," a crucial problem in Langer is the question of just
how symbolic activity should be described. Does it transform, create,
express, or do all of these things in some way that our discourse has
not been able to get into a single word? In *Philosophy in a New Key*,
she employs the term "transformation" in such a way as to make us
wonder whether or not she has introduced the wolf of imitation in
sheep's clothing. When she comes to discuss what is formed in the
transformation, we are not sure whether she is referring to an original stuff remade or something radically produced; it is, she says, "the
verbally ineffable, yet not inexpressible law of vital experience, the
pattern of affective and sentient being."[104] Is the "law" and "pattern"
the *result* of the abstractive process she calls artistic symbolization?
Do we really read *law* and *pattern* in art? Are these terms adequate
to describe the product of an abstractive process that is supposed to
result in concretion? In *Feeling and Form*, a symbol is said to articulate "ideas of something we wish to think about, and until we
have a fairly adequate symbolism we cannot think about it."[105] Here
what we wish to think about seems to be present previous to the creation of the symbol, and the symbol seems to be only a mnemonic device after all. Art is elsewhere the "creation of forms symbolic of
human feeling,"[106] where again the symbolic seems to have lost its
radical power to create those feelings and only "allegorically" recalls
them. Music is "symbolic expression of the forms of sentience."[107]
We are still uncertain whether "expression" means the statement of
something already present in some other state ("image"?) or symbolic *creation* of an idea of feeling. A piece of music is "a highly articulated sensuous object, which by virtue of its dynamic structure can

express the forms of vital experience which language is peculiarly un-fit to convey."[108] Setting aside here the old bugaboo of "language," we are overwhelmed by the welter of portentous words. Langer's strategy may be deliberate, as she comes up against the walls of her own discourse, which seems always to be demanding a return to some version of imitation. Her recourse to Roger Fry's now venerable term "significant form" represents both her defiance of imitation and her retreat from the vanguard. With respect to the term "significant form," an oxymoron which certainly needs discussion, she says "the factor of significance is not logically discriminated but felt as a quality rather than recognized as a function."[109] Recognition is "without conscious comparison and judgment" but direct, and it is recognition of the "forms of human feeling: emotions, moods, even sensations in their characteristic passage."[110] But how can we say that such recog-nition is direct when we have already, in our criticism of Bergson and in our concept of symbolization, claimed that intuition is not direct but mediated?

Langer's ultimate effort to escape from imitation lies in the argu-ment in *Feeling and Form* that art presents a pure "illusion" and a "semblance," both terms being collected in the concept of the "vir-tual," which is balanced against the "actual." Language she identifies with the actual. But poetic language she must now declare to be only the *materials* of poetry,[111] presumably like the painter's paint. In this way, she tries to relieve poetry of the necessity of statement in the mode of actuality, poetry not being "genuine discourse" at all but an "illusory" 'experience,' or a piece of virtual history, by means of dis-cursive language."[112] In what sense it can be said that true discourse, since it also is a symbolic mode of abstraction, is not also "virtual" is not developed. That is, Langer does not proceed to the theory of fic-tions or "as ifs" that her analysis seems always to be about to drive her. She does not capitalize on Cassirer's use of Hertz's conception of free fictions.

But of course for her the discursive language of the poem is merely material and not true discourse. One wonders why man would go to such great lengths to express the idea of feeling in such recalcitrant and contrary materials if one already has truly non-discursive arts like music to do the job. Langer's distinguishing of modes of feeling expressed by the different arts does not go very far toward convincing us of the need for a nondiscursive verbal art. Mu-sic as virtual time, plastic art as virtual space, dance as virtual ges-ture, literature as virtual memory—these concepts threaten to draw us back to imitation, seem to define the arts wholly in terms of the representational relationship.

Langer's flurry of terms illustrates the lengths to which a theorist who attempts to proceed from a positivistic concept of language must go to establish a theory of the symbolic. That Langer never really shakes free is finally illustrated by her remarks on ambivalence and irony. We have already noted that in describing music as an "unconsummated symbol," Langer has treated music from a point of view that assumes consummation to occur only in discourse. From the same point of view, she attributes irony and ambivalence to artistic forms.[113] Her argument is that literal discourse (or "discourse") can only declare the separateness of emotions like joy or grief, while art can synthesize them in a "dynamic structure."[114] However, a synthesis is surely not an ambivalence but an assertion that the literal opposition is merely a creation of discourse. The irony and ambivalence ought then to be located not in the synthesis, but in the condition of discourse—its inability to achieve the synthesis that art declares to be, in its own terms, actual (a condition Langer does not ascribe to art). In this sense, perhaps it can be said that criticism is ironic, not art. Irony is thrust upon art as a projection of the bifurcations established by discourse. Langer goes so far as to project a "pervasive ambivalence" back behind art to "human feeling" itself,[115] which is an area in her system that we ought not really to be able to talk about but only to build symbolically from. It might be noted here that it is very doubtful that artistic forms exhaust themselves, though Langer says that, like myth, they do. What seems to be true is that a critical discourse about them is exhaustible as discourse, and artistic works endlessly generate the need to renew discourse.

Langer has attempted to build on Cassirer's theory of the radically creative symbolic form, and she has extended that theory into a complex of the forms of art, but she struggles with many of the problems that beset Cassirer and with the irony that must be present in any discourse about art. In the end, though she criticizes Croce for his bifurcation of the artistic process, her own discourse threatens to split the literary artistic process into image and word and to divorce the poet from his true materials. In her system the poet can work with language, but not in it.

4. VIVAS'S "CONSTITUTIVE SYMBOL"

THE TERMINOLOGIES of Cassirer and Langer have been frequently employed by literary critics in loose ways without much attention to their philosophical underpinnings.[116] Both the extension into criticism and critique of them as such has been powerfully made by only one man, Eliseo Vivas, whose work has been in both philosophy, especially ethics and aesthetics, and literary criticism, practical and theoretical. He is one of the few thinkers who has insisted on and put into practice in his own work the idea that "to be responsible, criticism must be based on an aesthetic which in turn must be based on a complete philosophy, including an epistemology."[117] Much of the impulse for his early work must have been his sense that the so-called New Criticism lacked a philosopher and an adequate philosophical underpinning. He attempted to provide both with a development of the philosophy of symbolic forms.

Vivas's view of Kant is that Kant's categories are too narrow and do not really allow for art.[118] Cassirer improved on Kant in that he introduced a concept of the evolution of categories and made room at the same time for more than the narrowly cognitive mode of conceptualization. But Cassirer tended erroneously to put all the activities of the mind on a single plane. For Vivas, the aesthetic or artistic mode is more basic than the others.[119] In taking this view, Vivas is similar to Blake, who assigns to Urthona, the artist, a place at the base of archetypal man. Langer, Vivas argues, falls back into imitation in the end by making each art form a different mode of imitating feeling, though she denies this and, in fact, employs the term "expression" instead of "imitation."[120] Vivas is very hard on the term "imitation," since in all its common usages he regards it as taking away creative power from the artist. He recognizes, of course, the efforts that have been made to escape the term, even Langer's, but notes that substitute terms like "immanent meaning," "reflexive meaning," "presentational symbol," and "aesthetic icon" all leave something to be desired.[121] Vivas himself, however, resorts to some of these terms at critical points.

Vivas divides human cultural activity into four modes—the aesthetic (including the artistic), the moral, the cognitive, and the religious. Beneath these is what he calls the "basic symbolic activity," which he associates closely with the aesthetic, which by virtue of this is more "basic" than the other three.[122] Vivas views basic symbolizing as Cassirer and Langer do. There is a difference between a sign or signal and a symbolization, the latter being the product of a radically creative process.[123] Vivas does not dwell at length, however, on the role language plays generally, or on its involvement in the basic symbolic activity. In some remarks he seems to hold that it is so involved:

"Give the animal the ability to constitute the world by means of language and release him for a minute only from the urgency of animal needs that demand peremptory satisfaction, and he discovers the world an object worthy of intransitive attention."[124] "Intransitive attention" is Vivas's term for the aesthetic experience. In any act of symbolic transformation or constitution there is a fundamental aesthetic element, that is, a creation of an object for free contemplation rather than purposive use. He remarks that the "basic symbolic capacity is operative in what is usually called the aesthetic response—the beholding of objects for their own sakes."[125] At the same time, such activity can be "employed for utilitarian ends" and becomes "stereotyped" and "makes up what we consider our common-sense perception of our world."[126] In any case, the act of symbolization in its most basic sense is an "organization of the primary subject matter of experience."[127] Further, it proceeds by concretion and a dramatic sense of its subject matter and does not at once refine that matter to abstract "data." In other words, to employ Vico's terms, the imaginative universal logically precedes the abstract universal. Cognition builds on top of aesthetic. Like Langer, Vivas has recourse to the idea of the "image." It is the capacity to create the image that makes us "able temporarily to frustrate the tendency to respond behaviorally to the stimulus."[128] The image is "constitutive," and the "proto-image . . . antedates phylogenetically the birth of language."[129]

Vivas obviously must believe in some sort of close relationship between the image and language, for in his mind both are constitutive. At least, he says that the image is constitutive—that is, symbolically creative—because we have no grounds to think it merely a mental copy of physical stimuli. But Vivas does not satisfactorily develop his concept of the image, and when he comes to language he is unable to state language's precise connection to the image. Language is constitutive, but it does not seem to be constitutive of images, which, as in Langer, seem to precede it:

> I assume that when man first invented language he did not first invent separate words, which he attached to proto-images. What he did was invent signs that from the beginning were interrelated to one another systematically.[130]

To say this is to avoid the dreaded "imitation" theory, but it sets language completely free in its own universe, and doubly removed from brute reality, since the image seems to stand *between* it and that domain. Perhaps we can expand on and complete Vivas here and claim that in his view of the image there is only a very rudimentary constitutive element and that it must be given true form in a symbolic mode. Language as system provides the form, but in the formalization something happens to the image.

This line of thought must stop here, however, for Vivas himself provides us with an entirely different terminology to describe the act of symbolic formulation. Two sets of terms are proffered: creation and discovery, and the triad of subsistence, insistence, and existence. The terms "creation" and "discovery" harbor a paradox:

> From the standpoint of culture, the mind creates new values, for these were not there before for the creative mind or for the culture. But the mind discovers them by bringing them up from the realm of subsistence, into the poem, from where they get carried away by its readers and put into circulation, so to speak, in the market place.[131]

We have a model of inchoate subsistent values floating in the culture but unformed and therefore ungraspable, like Kant's manifold of sensation operating at the level of intellect rather than at the level of pure perception. It takes a symbolic formalization which is a radically *creative* act to *discover* them. The poet "makes the effort to extricate the import and order of his experience and body it forth in language."[132] Vivas admits that he speaks of these subsistent values prior to their creation-discovery in the poem "as if they were identical with themselves after the poet has caught them in the constitutive means of his language,"[133] but they are not. Exactly what they are in the condition of subsistence is a problem for philosophers that he agrees to bypass. A Kantian, we assume, would declare them unknowable, and a pure idealist would say they were nonexistent. For Vivas, who claims to be a "value realist,"[134] the values are *there* but present in such a way as to be undisposable until given symbolic form. Thus there is throughout Vivas's work an immense tension between the terms "discovery" and "creation" since for all that he claims to be creating values, he does not give up his claim to their objectivity—their ontological subsistence—beyond the confines of a given cultural situation. But values that merely subsist do not somehow in themselves have any value.

The distinction between subsistence and insistence is, therefore, of the greatest importance. It is the difference between chaos and or-

der, mere substance and "informed substance" or symbolic form. Insistence is the condition of the work of art. It is what makes the work
"self-sufficient." This does not mean that the poet can employ a language he creates from nothing.[135] Instead, a poem is self-sufficient
when it is "able to capture attention *intransitively* upon itself and is
thus able to prevent the mind from seeking comparisons between it
and the actual world."[136] This involves controlling the reader's response, so that the reader is in a state of "rapt, intransitive attention
in its full presentational immediacy."[137] There is no reference through
the object to consequences.[138] The object is, if we translate into Kantian terms, purposive without purpose. Of course, intransitive attention is a normative concept. In this state the reader apprehends the
work's "immanent meanings and values."[139] Insistence maintains,
therefore, the reader's and the object's freedom in what Vivas calls
the "artistic transaction."

Vivas would maintain the word "meaning" for poetry, while
abandoning the word "reference." The poem will *create* immanent
meaning, but refer to nothing: "What the poem says or means—or,
in other words, the object of the poem—is, genetically speaking, the
full-bodied, value-freighted, ordered, self-sufficient world it presents
to us for the first time."[140] But the poem is not quite opaque after all:

> What does the poem mean or say? What it means is not a
> world it reflects or imitates or represents in illusion, in the
> sense of a world as envisaged by the mind prior to the poetic
> activity in the manner in which it is envisaged in poetry. What
> the poem says or means is the world it reveals or discloses *in*
> and *through* itself, a new world, whose features, prior to the
> act of poetic revelation, were concealed from us and whose
> radiance and even identity will again be concealed from us the
> moment our intransitive attention lapses.[141]

"In" and "through" in this combination echo Cassirer. This sort of
meaning, free of reference, available only in the moment of "rapt, intransitive attention," it is difficult for us to understand as shining
"through" the poem, if at the same time Vivas claims that nothing
the poem says can be compared with an independent reality. In one
place, at least, Vivas nearly says that the "in" part of his formula refers to the musical and rhythmic (or "intrinsic") powers of language,
in which there is "no less power of revelation than in the language's
function merely to denote,"[142] but this merely raises an image of the

old form and content opposition that he surely means to avoid at all costs. It is the *throughness* that raises problems for us, particularly since Vivas seems to have treated language as a system of relations rather than denotations. It does not appear that "meaning" is merely that which is projected from the in-ness of the poem, that is, made by it or generated in it.

The problem Vivas had lies in his own value realism's terminology. It forces him to claim that a poem has an *object* that is in some sense not the poem and in which the poem's meaning lies. He must then distinguish this sort of object crucially from the sorts of objects to which "ostensive," not poetic language, refers. The latter objects may be real, ideal, or fictive, but "whatever they are, they are external to the language by which I point to them, and in a sense can be exhibited independently of it." The poem's object has no "discoverable *existential* status independent of the language that reveals it."[143] If we accept this, why must we then distinguish, as Vivas says we must, "the language of the poem from the object it reveals"?[144] Why is the familiar terminology of referentiality—"object" and "meaning"—being forced on the poem in spite of the poem's obvious recalcitrance? Vivas's answer here, for what it is worth, is to continue to play the paradox. The object of the poem is the "values and meanings" which are "embodied" in it. Presumably these values and meanings have been floating unembodied in the realm of subsistence—like all Platonic subsistents. They do not have bodied or objective status until they "insist" in the poem's language.[145] Yet previous to the poem they are called "values" and "meanings." Perhaps "things" might be imagined in a Platonic sense to "subsist," but it is difficult to grasp how "meanings" can themselves be subsistent. One would imagine that if the poem as act of symbolization were anything in this sort of system it would be an act which *confers* meaning and does not take meanings and merely give them a form. Yet Vivas claims that the meanings and values "subsist by themselves and are actually, to some extent at least, operative in the culture prior to their discovery by the poet."

The terms "object" and "meaning," it seems to me, finally betray Vivas's argument. They force a distinction between form and content upon him and display a realism, with which the theory of symbolic forms is incompatible. The closer we look at Vivas's use of "meaning," the more difficult it is to understand it.

The question of the subsistence of "values" is perhaps different from that of the subsistence of "meanings." Plato attempted to establish the idea of the ontological status of values, and Vivas's value realism seems to follow from that attempt. But if meanings are conferred rather than subsistent, can we consider values to pre-exist meanings? Can values be other than the product of the act of creating meaning? In any case, it is time to turn to Vivas's concept of the literary symbol as it grows out of his theory. In an appendix to his study of D. H. Lawrence, Vivas offers us three senses of the symbol or "constitutive symbol" (all symbols for Vivas are constitutive) germane to literary art. The first sense, and the broadest, is that of "symbolic form" in Cassirer's usage. In describing this symbolization, incidentally, Vivas gives to it the power of *creating* meaning:

> A constitutive symbol, in the first meaning, is a symbolic form by means of which the world is apprehended. But in this sense, the symbol is a basic and elementary form. By virtue of its relations to other forms, the world is apprehended as orderly—or, more exactly, as containing such order as the interrelationships among the forms used to apprehend it allow. The apprehension gives the world *meaning*.[146]

In the second sense, the symbol is the work of art as a unit in itself. This Vivas calls "an organized complex of dramatic and moral categories."[147] "Dramatic" seems to mean "concrete" and "experiential," that is, holding on to the image rather than abstracting toward the "general," or toward Vico's "abstract universals." Thus Vivas can identify it with our grasp of the world at the "basic level of ordinary practical living."[148] But at this point Vivas's trouble with the *throughness* of the symbol raises its head again and he speaks of an "interanimation between [the symbol] and the thing or process it symbolizes," where this thing or process is clearly not what is created but what is there prior to the act.[149] In his book on Lawrence this prior existence is called "substance," and the act of symbolization is called an "informing" of substance, the terms being much like Aristotle's, as much as Vivas dislikes Aristotle's recourse to imitation to describe a similar process.

There is for Vivas a third sense of constitutive symbol. And it is here that the old romantic trope *in* the poem, which had fallen out of my discussion of symbolism in Cassirer and Langer, reappears in rather more sophisticated dress than we have yet seen it. The symbol here is a component of a work of art, and Vivas appears to give to it potentially all the powers that the work as a whole might have. This symbol functions much as does Joyce's "epiphany." It is: "a complex situation or scene, . . . which gathers the significance of events preceding it and illumines the scenes or situations that follow."[150] A number of observations can be made about this idea:

1. The statement implies that the symbol in sense 3 in a work is a creator of meaning inside the work in much the same way that a constitutive symbol in sense 2 gathers up the potentiality of a preceding subsistent manifold of events and gives that "substance" form. With respect to narrative fiction, which Vivas is discussing here, one assumes that the materials the symbol gathers together and informs are the preceding narrative, not anything from outside the work (outside the symbol in sense 2). Perhaps what Vivas has done here is to speak to the old problem of whether a poem can be all poetry (as Coleridge put it). By making the symbol in sense 3 a component of the symbol in sense 2, he makes the symbol in sense 3 depend for its existence on the context and at the same time inform the context with significance. The symbol in sense 3 cannot therefore stand alone as significant, because its power is created radically by its context. Thus poetry is not identified with the symbol in sense 3 and thus a poem can be *all poetry* after all.

2. However, there is another way of looking at the matter. If the analogy between the symbol in sense 3 and the creative act of symbolization of sense 1 is to be pressed, this reduces the preceding parts of the narrative to a sort of subsistence which is brought to insistence only in the component symbol, thus calling in question the value of the context of the preceding narrative after all, since it seems to be unformed in the sense at least in which the component symbol is an *in*formation of the context's mere subsistence. But since it has already been claimed that the poem as a whole (symbol in sense 2) is constitutive, there would seem to be a contradiction between two different constitutive forms in this line of reasoning, unless we have a hierarchy of symbolisms in which at each level the previous constitutive form becomes merely subsistence in relation to a following constitutive act. This would give to the component symbol in sense 3 a supreme authority which would threaten to explode the very context on which, for its very existence, it apparently depended, unless it were constantly reasserted that the symbol (in sense 3) must constantly be referred back to the context, from which it *cannot* ever be separated. This contradicts the idea that the component symbol brings what only subsists in the context to insistence.

3. If we go back to the relation of insistence to subsistence that we

find in the relation of poem to what the poem works upon, and if we apply the idea of context to this relationship, we find that, of course, the poem has no pre-existent context because a context must be formed and subsistence is formless, though Vivas insists on applying the terms "meaning" and "values" to this unformed chaotic domain.

4. There is a moment when we think that Vivas is tempted to give to component symbols a being independent of the context to which he limits them. He does not do this in his own discussion of Lawrence's component symbols—the doll, the fox, the rocking horse. Where he does do it is in a not adequately developed discussion of the difference between Cassirer's concept of the symbol and Jung's. Here he begins to speak of symbols, in the case of Jung at least, as not contextually formed but, of course, primordial and ultimately of an unfathomable or hidden meaning of the sort we noted in chapter 6. Such a symbol operating in a literary work (symbol, sense 2) would not necessarily gather up the significance of the preceding narrative but bring into this a previously established primordial insistence. The symbol would an interpreter rather than a maker, not a romantic symbol but an allegorical image.

If Vivas is to maintain his component symbol as creative in the spirit in which he offers it, he must absolve it of any hint of previous meaning—primordially mysterious or otherwise. Jung's symbols, for Vivas's work of art, can only be subsistent and awaiting meaning.

We have seen that in romantic theory there is a tendency for the idea of symbol as trope in a work to be replaced by the idea of the work as symbolic. With Vivas there is an attempt to allow the component symbol to flow back into the work, but only now that the work itself is seen as a symbolic form or constitutive symbol. The component symbol is no longer the kind of trope it was, nor is it presumed that all language is simply referential or propositional. What seems to have developed is, within the concept of symbolic form, a concept of a dialectical relationship of the poem's parts to its whole. The component constitutive symbol draws its substance from a subsistence in the culture, but it is created new from that material. The concept of symbolic form, in other words, becomes the means by which the component symbol is held to its context and is made to be readable (to insist) only in that context and not in terms of some presupposed table of correspondences or other independent doctrine.

Where is criticism in Vivas's system? Here must be introduced Vivas's idea of *ex*istence. It is culture that uses art and does so by extracting ideas or images from it by a conceptual process. The condition of "intransitive attention" in which the real human connection with the art object is made evanesces into a condition in which purposiveness, or Blake's "devourer" intrudes. When this occurs, the object of the poem or its created "meanings" and "values" enter our world of practical intercouse in an impure condition because they are submitted to the alien forms of the discursive. Here they are passed about as ideas, but in a thinned condition until they become clichés or habitual concepts.

One glimpses a cyclic situation here which culture, as Blake argued, must make into a constant dialectic of intellectual "war" and "hunting"—terms similar in Blake to Vivas's "creation" and "discovery." For as the ideas projected out of the poetic context use themselves up, so to speak, and fall back into sheer subsistence, there must be renewal by the human power to symbolize, and now those dead cultural clichés are added back in to the world of subsistence that art works upon, creating from these materials a new insistent vision. I take it that this is what Vivas was coming to when he argued that "art plays a constitutive role in the rest of life, and the rest of life offers itself to art as matter to be transubstanced into the substance of art."[151] The rest of life is always reducing itself to the mute and inglorious subsistence that the artist brings to awakening as Los works upon the shapeless abstract body of Albion.

Vivas attempts to turn the philosophy of symbolic forms directly to the problems of literary criticism, and his work is particularly to be valued for this reason. Further, he strenuously seeks a way to establish literature's cultural function. He establishes along the lines of Cassirer and Langer the concept of the poem as symbol—an idea that, as we have seen, is developed only in a confused way in the nineteenth century. He has his own problems with the old tradition of imitation and struggles heroically with it. His own brand of realism gives him difficulty, as does his inadequate discussion of the relation of the "image" (as a rudimentary symbolic form) to language. Assuredly the image-making power antedates language, but surely those images that antedate language are images in a very crude form, and are exceedingly unstable and evanescent. With language and other symbolic forms developed, surely the image is rarely pure but is now an indistinguishable part of a complex of symbolic constitution in language or some other form. Is it not possible to lodge full creativity in that complex and not before it, language in fact becoming an image *making* power, once man has evolved it? The problem for the poet is to maintain the power of the image as a linguistic thing that has no formal antecedent and creates a symbolic reality that is other and, in terms of value, *more than* the so-called real world of science. Vivas remarks that "scientific activity gives us *the real world*, in a partial and highly eulogistic sense of the word 'real'—the structure of the physical world." He calls that world "the necessary but not sufficient ground of culture."[152] This is a nice statement, but it is somewhat misleading in the light of his own position and his own claim that Cassirer errs in putting all symbolic forms on the same plane. The necessary ground of culture is, in Vivas's argument as a whole, actually art, because it is more fundamental, more closely related to the basic symbolic activity, the source from which other symbolic forms sprang historically, and the source of cultural renewal. Yet there is a sense in which scientific forms seem today to have usurped this role. Cassirer's own latent positivism—in his treatment of language as progressive to higher and higher levels of abstraction, purifying itself of the image—certainly illustrates this point. Which symbolic form is regarded in our culture as fundamental, but not necessarily privileged, must have consequences for the value we put upon human life.

9

Sentimental Archaism

Alongside modern theorizing about myth and symbol such as we have examined in the previous chapter, there seems frequently to exist the tendency to look to the primitive past and to admire some aspect of the mind of archaic man that is allegedly now lost or repressed. Blake himself begins his thought with this fiction. The idea of a golden age, often antediluvian, is evoked in various forms: The ancients are revered at the expense of the moderns; a "dissociation of sensibility,"[1] to use Eliot's famous phrase, is located somewhere in the past; a holy book is lost; the book of nature is declared to be closed, or the hermeneutical key forgotten. Frank Kermode has found the myth of dissociation to be the product of the doctrine of the "image,"[2] as he calls it, in modernist literature, but the myth is not one invented by literary people alone. It flows through theology, psychology, and anthropology and then returns to literary theory. I propose now to examine work of three writers who illustrate different moments of modern sentiment about myth. Their views span a range from "religious" allegory to "miraculous" symbolism. None reaches a concept of a secular symbolic, but each raises the problem of the relation of poetry to religion.

1. CAMPBELL'S "MONOMYTH"

IN THE heyday of the New Criticism and in the period before Northrop Frye's attempt to order aspects of so-called myth criticism into a coherent literary theory, a book concentrating on comparative mythology and psychoanalysis and typifying the modernist anxiety appeared. Written by a student of Joyce's *Finnegans Wake* and evoking Freud and Jung, the book made its new kind of syncretic mythography felt in literary circles, though it did not pretend to be a work of literary criticism or theory in any specific sense. This book was Joseph Campbell's *The Hero with a Thousand Faces* (1949).[3] It evoked the alleged wisdom of archaic man, or rather it advised restoration of the mode of thought that opens the door to that widsom.

Campbell's thesis was not really that the holy book is lost. The book is forgotten, which in Campbell's terms is to say that it is repressed. The gods are not dead but sleeping like old Finn and will return upon call. We must rediscover the language in which to call. That language is myth, for myth is "the secret opening through which the inexhaustible energies of the cosmos pour into human cultural manifestation."[4]

What has been the cause of the repression of ancient wisdom? Fundamentally, according to Campbell, a combination of things: "The democratic ideal of the self-determining individual, the invention of the power-driven machine, and the development of the scientific method of research." These events have alienated man from the "long-inherited timeless universe of symbols."[5] But this universe has merely become a shadowy underworld, where each of us still possesses a "private, unrecognized, rudimentary, yet secretly potent pantheon of dream."[6] The fundamental modern problem is that this venerable, indeed eternal, pantheon is dispossessed: "The lines of communication between the conscious and the unconscious zones of the human psyche have all been cut; and we have been split in two." Group meaning has been suppressed by the "self-expressive individual."[7]

For Campbell the great opportunity to heal this split has been provided by psychoanalytical research, which demonstrates the correspondence of myth and dream. As a result "the long discredited chimeras of archaic man have returned dramatically to the foreground of modern consciousness."[8] Campbell claims in his enthusiasm that mythology *is* psychology and criticizes all those who read it as history, biography, cosmology, and so forth. As he sought to provide a "skeleton key" to *Finnegans Wake*,[9] so he attempts like so many before him to provide the key to universal mythology, which is a door or perhaps a clouded window to ancient and eternal truth. The key is the same key, really, that was supposed to have unlocked Joyce's great work. This key helps to turn unconsciousness back into primordial superconsciousness and destroys the hold on us exercised by the phenomenal world, which is identified with the categories of a Kantian understanding.

But Campbell admits that myth is not exactly dream. Both arise from the same source—"the unconscious wells of fantasy"—and they have the same grammar. Myths are not dreams because they are not spontaneous products. They are a communal "powerful picture language for the communication of traditional wisdom."[10] Curiously, Campbell's myth, as much as he regards it as a means to unlock repression, is quite determined. The symbols of myth are not "manufactured," nor are they "invented," nor can they be "permanently suppressed."[11] The myth-maker is apparently only a vessel into which is poured and shaped some imageless truth. But the shape itself is apparently a distortion like the Freudian manifest dream. The organs of human apprehension and the categories of thought confine the mind so as to frustrate true knowledge. Thus mythological symbolism has to be read in a certain way in order for it to become translucent and to reveal that which is beyond. Indeed, "the full system of correspondences" which "represents" the repressed unknown actually does no more than awaken the mind, calling it past itself and pointing the way.[12] Symbols are only "vehicles," not "tenors":

> No matter how attractive or impressive they may seem, they remain but convenient means, accommodated to the understanding. . . . The problem of the theologian is to keep his symbol translucent, so that it may not block out the very light it is supposed to convey.[13]

We must note briefly here that this translucence lends considerable abstractness to the symbol: To construct it as a translucence is to devalue its concreteness and earthiness. The attitude suggests a fall. It is that of "religious" allegory and connects efforts toward concretion with materialism. At the same time, it seems to invest the symbol with a "miraculous" quality. But myth and symbol are only "penultimate." The ultimate Campbell describes as "openness," "void," "being beyond the categories," or "silence."[14] He describes myth as on that borderland where it is "manifest" yet permeated by the "silence."[15] It appears that the language of myth is still within the "categories"[16] (in the limiting Kantian sense), while at the same time it points toward a condition of freedom from the categories. This curious halfwayness Campbell never actually describes. Indeed, his focus is not on language. But he does on occasion think of the language of myth as moving toward cosmic paradoxes, which are at the "brink of a transcendent illumination, the final step to which must be taken by each in his own silent experience."[17] To these paradoxes he gives a mediating authority not present in Kant's antinomies of the merely regulative reason.

For Campbell, the phenomenal world is the world of shrunken consciousness, and the unconscious world becomes the metaphysical world,[18] which is the single source of energy. The whole aim of man must be to dissolve the phenomenal world back into the world of superconsciousness, which was the prelapsarian condition and is now the "timeless dark,"[19] approachable through myth and dream. Personal achievement of this quest renders up the problem of communicating the experience, which defies speech. The nearest language can approach to this silence is myth itself, which must be read in its own terms. But its own terms are not the "tautegorical" terms of Schelling or the internalized terms of Cassirer. Campbell identifies myth with psychology, which becomes the supreme human science, presiding over all the others. No other science has the right to reduce myth to its own terms, yet myth is declared to be "amenable as life itself to the obsessions and requirements of the individual, the race, the age."[20]

If, indeed, there is a supreme human science, then Campbell subsumes all else under it. Everything must speak its language. But if there is not, then clearly Campbell has reduced myth to psychology in just the same way that he has accused biographers, historians, and the others of reduction. In any case, Campbell's emphasis is not on making but on interpreting, a myth being a kind of arcane psychoanalytical interpretation. Further, it is a mode of interpretation that is psychoanalytically syncretic. It draws no distinctions between schools of psychoanalysis, but instead picks what it wishes where it finds it.

All this, curiously enough, after so much reservation about the repressive tendencies of scientific processes! In fact, Campbell applies a very old scientific procedure in a heavy-handed way to his interpretation of myth: reductive generalization. He finds in all myths "the one shape-shifting yet marvelously constant story." It is his "monomyth" of the "composite hero."[21] While he performs this reduction it occurs to us that the translucence he claims for any myth is really only the abstractable qualities it has in common with all other myths known to him. In another voice, however, he claims that there is "no final system for the interpretation of myths, and there never will be any such thing."[22] Then, in a piece of acrobatics that seems to anticipate Lévi-Strauss, he asserts that myth accepts all of its interpretations.[23] This presumably means that its translucence cannot be fully expressed in any language other than its own. But his own induction draws from every myth the one "composite" meaning which he must regard as privileged. In fact, he goes so far as to claim, once he has abstracted his monomyth into existence, that if some part of the monomyth is absent in any single instance, the absence itself has meaning. Further, although Campbell usually thinks of a myth as a translucence mediating between silence and the language of the understanding, he does say at one point that it is uncertain whether philosophical statement precedes myth or myth precedes philosophy.

The result of all this is recourse to a sort of universal occult doctrine built upon the monomyth of the quest of the hero (microcosm) and the cosmogonic cycle (macrocosm). This doctrine is declared to be, however, a dim copy of the true silence or darkness. It is nevertheless a statement of timeless principles involving "ubiquitous power"[24] in the universe.

Though Campbell obviously regards myth as a positive force, there lingers in his discourse a sentimental version of the archaic condition, in which man is declared to have been superconscious in his supersilence. But not quite, or never fully, because if archaic man thought in myth, which involved language, that translucent linguistic veil was present and he was thus condemned from the beginning to repression. The reason for this dominant regressive nostalgia in Campbell is his very restrictive sense of language. He ties it to the categories of the understanding and then connects the categories to our grasp of the phenomenal world. We have no other way in his system to express our grasp of that world, which is as fully fallen as is the understanding itself. This double condemnation leads Campbell to seek a better, extraterrestrial condition. Here the concept of myth has returned under modernist psychologistic guise, as it so often does, to a venerable tradition of religious mysticism that requires arcane interpretation of a hidden truth that is displaced in language by a fall. There is neither immanence of the holy in nature nor such experience radically created in and by language itself.

Campbell's book is significant to us because in its establishment of a theory of archetypes based on the generalized "monomyth," it expresses most fully at a critical moment the dominant regressive elements that seem constantly to threaten the symbolic as ground for a literary theory: the recourse to reductiveness (including the triumph of the "general" over the "particular"), the turn to mysticism, the acceptance of a positivistic norm for language, the resultant obliteration of any sense of differences in the way language may be employed. In this theory we find an unconsious return to romantic "religious" allegory even as the rhetoric of the presentation denigrates allegory in favor of the "miraculous" symbol.

2. ELIADE'S "ARCHAIC MAN"

SENTIMENTAL ARCHAISM is also well illustrated, though in a more sophisticated form, in the anthropological theory of Mircea Eliade. Eliade, who is an unashamed apologist for the relevance of Christianity to modern life, declares outright that he detects "a certain nostalgia in modern man for the 'primordially mythical'."[25] His own views are by no means free of it, particularly with respect to archaic man's treatment of time. Eliade claims, somewhat more lightly than Campbell, the same connection between dream and myth and notes the same difference of "ontological significance":[26] the dream lacks the constitutive dimensions of myth—those of the exemplary and universal. The dream is only personal and subjective. There is an indication here, as in Campbell, of displeasure at the triumph of individualism, the domination in modern life of a "personal thinking,"[27] which is declared to be relatively absent in traditional societies. In short, there is little religious community in modern life, presumably because of the relative absence of mythical thought. As we shall see, however, Eliade detects its presence in secular forms and declares that it persists in modern Christianity.

Eliade, who generally draws sharper distinctions than Campbell, delineates the nature of myth more clearly and in a narrower way. Myth is "ontophany," which implies "theophany" or "hierophany," revealing a structure of reality that involves "an irruption of the sacred into the world."[28] The principal form of the myth is that of the sacred history of creation. This moment of creation is in fact an extratemporal event that contains all reality. Paradoxically, sacred history is therefore an abolition of time. Archaic man, according to Eliade, recognized the need to regenerate himself through the periodic "annulment of time,"[29] or at least the annulment of time's irreversibility. This annulment is achieved by a ritual return to origins. To erase temporal differences is to identify contemporary acts with the primordial act of creation. In archaic or traditional life, no act is significant or real unless it is identified with the primordial archetype: "Reality is acquired solely through *repetition* or *participation.*"[30] Eliade claims, then, that for archaic man objects or acts achieve value only when they are perceived to participate in a reality that "transcends" them. Such objects and acts have no autonomous intrinsic value. This view of mythical thinking has some things in common with Cassirer's, but it differs crucially in that it implies the existence of a transcendent realm in archaic thought, while in Cassirer the mythical thinker thinks only in terms of immanence. From Cassirer's point of view, therefore, Eliade's recourse to transcendence, and ultimately to a theory of ritual imitation, condemns him to the very same nostalgia or sentimental archaism that he notes in modern life. Similarly, the idea of repetition in Eliade merges with the idea of copying. It is not surprising that Eliade connects "archaic" or "primitive ontology" with Platonic structure, suggesting that Plato could be regarded as "the thinker who succeeded in giving philosophical currency and validity to the modes of life and behavior of archaic humanity," the Platonic doctrine of ideas being the "final version of the archetype concept."[31]

Yet to establish this relationship is to ignore the fundamental difference between mythical thinking and rational modes that lies at the bottom of Eliade's many books. The Platonic form or idea is achieved in Plato by a rational process, and the form is always declared to be different from and vastly superior to the copy. The mythic qualities of immanence and indwelling energy for which anthropologists have appropriated the Polynesian term "mana" are not present. With the Platonic come the concepts of imitation, distance, and transcendence, and finally the nostalgia that Eliade detects in modern life. Though Eliade's language declares there to be a distance between the archaic and the Platonic structure of thought that he sees emerge from it, he does not characterize that distance in terms of language or of modes of creation or creative power. The result is a tendency to blend again the Platonic and the mythic and to force us to call in question his distinction between archaic and modern thought.[32] Eliade tends to vacillate between a concept of "archaic thought" and one of "primitive thought," sometimes declaring archaic man not to be primitive at all and sometimes using the terms interchangeably.[33]

In Eliade's view, cyclical theories of history are nostalgic and express the pull toward archaic thought. In cyclical theories the historical event has no significance unless assimilated to the archetype of primordial creation. Cyclical theories are thus attempts to find "trans-historical justification for historical events";[34] they represent yearnings for sacred meaning. Messianic history, which seems to be eschatological and linear, is also declared to be cyclic because involved in a time between two identical atemporalities.

As Eliade identifies cyclical and messianic historical thinking with archaic man so does he connect literature with return to origins:

> From a certain point of view, we may say that every great poet is *remaking* the world, for he is trying to see it as if there were no Time, no History. In this his attitude is strangely like that of the "primitive," of the man in traditional society.[35]

Or, to put it in a brief phrase, literature contains "some residues of 'mythological behavior'."[36] The similarity here to Blake's remarks in *The Marriage of Heaven and Hell* is apparent enough.[37] There is recourse to a myth of beginnings, and there is the struggle against time. But the struggle against time in Blake is a struggle against time *as it is constructed only by the categories of measurement*; and Blake's struggle is one in which there is no effort to obliterate this construction but only to provide it with a contrary. Though Blake says that he wishes to restore the golden age, he does not sentimentalize that age back to a realm of irrational childish innocence. Instead it is a realm where reason and imagination discover their appropriate roles, a "present" that is outside of the single tyranny of measured time and a constantly renewed product of the imaginative act, which is always new and unique like a Kantian apprehension of the beautiful. Blake tries to turn Eliade's primordial moment of creation into a continuous, supremely historical and temporal event, generated out of the opposition of reason and energy working in the languages of man. For Blake, human life *falls* into cyclic patterns when the creative opposition fails and we cannot grasp each moment, which presents us always with a radically new possibility.

Eliade calls the poet's attitude *recreation*, perhaps because his view of all "primordial" activity in modern life is that it nostalgically and vainly copies:

> . . . poetic creation, like linguistic creation, implies the aboli-
> tion of time—of the history concentrated in language—and
> tends toward the recovery of the paradisiac, primordial situa-
> tion; of the days when one could *create spontaneously*, when
> the *past* did not exist because there was no consciousness of
> time, no memory of temporal duration. It is said, moreover, in
> our own days, that for a great poet the past does not exist: the
> poet discovers the world as though he were present at the cos-
> mogonic moment, contemporaneous with the first day of the
> Creation.[38]

In the end, this cannot be creation but recapitulation and imitation, a backward seeking. This drift toward transcendence and return is coupled in Eliade with a tendency to think of art as radically private utterance. The situation of the alienated *symboliste* poet is regarded as the universal condition: "All poetry is an effort to *re-create* the language; in other words, to abolish current language, that of every day, and to invent a new, private and personal speech, in the last anal-ysis *secret*."[39] This attitude, heavily influenced by the *symbolistes*, runs counter to Blake's claim that the poet is appropriately an orator, as does Eliade's account of the modern reader, who reads to escape from the constrictions of time into a timeless realm, where there is apparently the soothing "illusion of a *mastery of Time*."[40] The ar-cane difficulty of works of art makes reading a sort of initiation into the mysteries rather than an open rousing of the faculties to act.[41] Reading is the "supreme 'distraction'."[42] We are here nearer, I think, than Eliade wants to be to the narcotic theory of Freud. Modern man, for Eliade, has reversed the order of things as it obtained in archaic society, where every "responsible" occupation was an escape from time and from the self. All acts not immersed in ritual were then trivial and unreal.

But Eliade does not claim in the end that myth has completely disappeared in the modern world, nor does he claim that it is present only in unconscious, repressed form, as does Campbell. True, mod-ern life is impoverished with respect to myth, except in "the dreams, the fantasies, and the longings of the modern man,"[43] who seeks over and over in the rituals of the year, the birth of a child, or the building of a house to reactualize the mysteries. Further, modern secularized myths exist. Marxian communism and national socialism are mythic in structure. But finally it is Christianity which can still be a living expression of mythic transcendence "prolonging a 'mythical' conduct of life into the modern world."[44]

It appears that for Eliade, where literature is not trivial escape, its values are religious, in contrast to Cassirer's view, where religious and artistic values are distinguished by being produced from different symbolic forms. His symbols are unlinguistic objects signified by words. The holy book is a nature full of correspondences in the manner of a Baudelaire: "In the last analysis, *the World reveals itself as language*."[45] This means that the world is a language, not that language constitutes a world. The archetypes exist beyond our language, and our language is signification and imitation of the true language, which is the world itself. That world is a "miraculous" symbolism, full of "man," partaking of what it silently signifies, which is immanent in it. Eliade's own myth is that of a titanic archetypal figure who reads nature silently without the mediation of language and who is properly called archaic but not "primitive." This titan was not one of Blake's "ancient poets." For Eliade, when the poets began to name things, the fall had already begun, whereas for Blake the opportunity to create had occurred and time had become the "mercy of eternity."[46]

3. WHEELWRIGHT'S "DEPTH LANGUAGE"

SOME OF THE religious concerns of Eliade lie behind Philip Wheelwright's study of symbolism, *The Burning Fountain*,[47] but its emphasis on the role of language makes his approach seem at the outset more fruitful for a philosophy of the literary symbolic than either Campbell's "religious" allegory or Eliade's "miraculous" symbolism of the world. His effort to examine literary language as such absolves him to some degree at least from the charge of sentimental archaism. In the end, however, his approach blurs the distinction between religion and art in the way that any theory of the "miraculous" must. The problems that this creates for him become apparent in his discussion of archetypes. Like Vivas, Wheelwright had connections with the New Criticism and was interested in providing a philosophical foundation for critical practice. Both were influenced by Cassirer, and both were critical of the psychologistic aesthetics of I. A. Richards, whose practical criticism had such a strong influence in the New Criticism, even though his behaviorism was anathema. Wheelwright attempts to develop an anti-positivistic semantic to which he can attach a theory of myth and archetype.

Study of Wheelwright's work is complicated by the fact that *The Burning Fountain*, his major statement, was first published in 1954 but reissued in a revised version in 1968. The revised version employs more phenomenological terminology than the earlier. In 1954, he writes that the aim of his book is to show that "religious, poetic, and mythic utterances at their best really mean something, make a kind of objective reference, although neither the objectivity nor the method of referring is of the same kind as in the language of science."[48] In 1968 the word "trans-subjective" replaces "objective" in the sentence above, and from that point the sentence reads: ". . . make a kind of trans-subjective reference, although their methods of referring and the nature of what is referred to need to be understood and judged on their own merits, not by standards of meaning imported from outside."[49] This signifies an abandonment of Cassirer's strategy, which was to claim a special kind of objectivity for art. Wheelwright now seeks instead to enlarge the boundaries of the subjective, under the influence no doubt of Kant's subjective universality, but in the terminology of phenomenological criticism. A further terminological addition in 1968 is the concept of the "phenomenological object," the "what is referred to" of the revised sentence above.[50] I shall consider it shortly. Finally, Wheelwright departs from Cassirer in throwing together religion, poetry, and myth—a blending that will cause him some difficulty.

In what follows I shall concentrate on the 1968 version of *The Burning Fountain*, where certain shifts of emphasis do count for something. In 1954 Wheelwright began his book with a chapter on what he called "man's threshold existence," in which he is concerned with the human existential condition: "To be conscious is not just to be; it is to mean, to intend, to point beyond oneself, to testify that some kind of beyond exists, and to be ever on the verge of entering into it."[51] In 1968 he added to this sentence the following: ". . . although never in the state of having fully entered." And a new sentence followed: "The existential structure of human life is radically, irreducibly *liminal*."[52] These additions suggest the greater consciousness of phenomenological approaches. But more important, in 1968 this chapter became chapter two, and what had been chapter two, "Symbol, Language, Meaning" became chapter one, emphasizing the book's concern with language and expressive symbolism. The "liminal ontology" of the new chapter two is to provide the "philosophical background, or underground," of the entire book.[53] "Expressive language," it is declared, will be shown to be "[superior] to steno-language, principally in its ability to suggest, largely by its overtones and paradoxical indirections, something of that ineluctably liminal character of human experience."[54] The 1968 version, therefore, begins with a discussion of the symbol, which encloses consideration of the thresholds of experience, presumably in the light of an analysis of language. This change strikes one, however, as more cosmetic than substantial, for Wheelwright never really sees threshold experience in terms of language. More of that later.

Wheelwright describes the symbol in a number of ways. In phenomenological terms it is more in "intention" than in "existence." In other words, it has "meaning," or in an earlier vocabulary it is "ideally self-transcendent."[55] It is also "contemplative" rather than "directive" or "pragmatic."[56] It is not a natural sign. Here Wheelwright invokes I. A. Richards's terminology of "vehicle" and "tenor" and describes the symbol as having a relation between vehicle and tenor that is not determined by "natural causation" but by "human choice."[57] The symbol as such has a sort of "stability." It can endure in time in the way that a sign or signal cannot. There are types of symbols. Common symbols are habitually employed and are no more than linguistic reflexes. Presumably even these had a poetic or expressive source and have grown old and lost their tension. Stipulative symbols are agreed-upon forms, abstractly applied, symbols of measurement being of this sort. It is to be noted here that for Wheelwright symbols are not all "poetic" but are characteristic of the whole range of human thought. Finally there are "organic," "expressive," or "depth" symbols.[58] The terms "organic" and "expressive" carry overtones of creativity. The term "depth" carries overtones of search into the liminal. In depth symbols, temporal stability is not accidental, because these symbols are searches into an ever present liminality. Presumably such symbols, though changing perhaps in vehicle, have a stable tenor. The stability is "developed and modulated by the creative and discriminating activity of man, in his human capacity as the being who can apprehend and express meanings through language."[59] Creativity and search are both implied in this remark.

All symbolism, of course, is not linguistic, nor is all language symbolic. Nevertheless, Wheelwright regards linguistic symbols as the most flexible and powerful of symbolic forms. Wheelwright divides the function of symbols into two types. There are "steno" symbols (or "steno-language"). Such symbols designate clearly for purposes of communication.[60] Their standard is one of designatory purity. There are "expressive" or "depth" symbols, which aim to "express" with "humanly significant fullness." No single standard of purity can be applied here.[61] Wheelwright states emphatically that the distinction between steno and depth symbols has nothing to do with the subject-object or the appearance-reality distinction, in spite of the fact that he uses the term "trans-subjective" to describe "depth" statements. Nor is the distinction an outright dualism. In everyday behavior, for example, there is a mixture of the two types, further blended with phatic utterance. In 1968 Wheelwright declares steno-language to be "the negative limit of expressive language, its absolute limit"[62] in seven ways, which he proceeds to enunciate. The principal traits of expressive language, which he now takes to be the real characteristics of language, are "referential congruity," "contextual variation," "plurisignation," "soft focus," "paralogical dimensionality," "assertorial lightness," and "paradox."[63] In all cases the negative limit of language (the steno) is a place where the freedom implicit in these seven traits is purged and an artificial ideal form of language created. Steno language must be "stipulative," (or, in 1954, it must possess semantic discreteness);[64] it must be "univocal," not equivocal; the symbol must have only one legitimate reference; its focus must be "hard" and clear, without a "connotative fringe"; it must keep separate the concrete instance and the general rule; it insists on truth-falsehood value; and it must contain no internal contradiction.[65] The negative of expressive language is a pure form of abstraction. At one point Wheelwright calls this "analogous to . . . silence,"[66] reversing the ironic identification that Carlyle and Mallarmé made between the poetic and silence. Expressive language he refers to as "full human song."[67]

The effort to deal with expressive language as such comes at the end of a long struggle by philosophers to transfer the epistemological issue established by Kant to the arena of language. One senses an analogy between Kant's categories and Wheelwright's traits of language. But Wheelwright's point is that true categorization, such as Kant attempted for the understanding, can occur only with respect to language at the negative limit of language—at the limit of abstract silence. The reason is that language at the expressive end is an open form, so to speak, capable of violating any categorical rule.[68]

In the 1968 version of *The Burning Fountain* the concept of the threshold or liminal is introduced after the steno-expressive distinction has been established. This is followed by an analysis of the "four ways of imagination." These are critical chapters for those of us who would discover whether or not threshold experience and imagination are in truth closely tied to language, and, if so, language in what condition. There are three thresholds—those of time, otherness and upwardness. Wheelwright's discussion of the threshold of time declares that the conceptualizing of time for purposes of utility is narrowing and that a whole other insight into time is possible. The argument is reminiscent of Bergson and does not go beyond Bergson's warning against the spatialization of time in our language as it proceeds toward the steno pole. Wheelwright does not really discuss time in terms of language until he makes a statement about paradox at the very end of his commentary, though he claims his inquiry to be "ontological and semantic."[69] The question remains whether at the expressive pole language *creates* time according to its more open forms or is a transparency behind which existential time appears somehow merely less spatial. It is not made clear how this is possible, except through paradox; and it is at paradox that Wheelwright's study of this threshold comes to rest.[70] Unlike Kant's ideas of the reason, which are only regulative and to which no single intuition or representation of the imagination is adequate, Wheelwright's paradoxical intimation of existential time expresses a threshold situation, an intellectual intuition of something not completely present in language.

The same thing is the case with the other two thresholds. The liminal always appears paradoxical when it is verbally expressed. It is the task of the poet, faced with liminal otherness, to "bring us back, by evocative cadence or the jolt of a fresh metaphor, to the bright ambiguity of our primal situation."[71] We should note that Wheelwright says "primal" here, not "primitive," and does not make extravagant claims for primitive mentality. Neither does he lament the passing of a golden age. At the same time he regards the "primal situation" as in itself ambiguous. This raises the question of whether or not the primal situation is a linguistic situation or independent of language, or in some strange way both.

Nevertheless, Wheelwright's argument, if it is not sentimental about the primitive condition, tends to associate the primal with origins if only because the steno seems the result of a progression away from an original source. The poet is regarded as returning us to the center of language, the condition of expressiveness itself. The inertia of culture is outward toward the negative limit. As language proceeds outward it takes us farther and farther away from intimations of the liminal mystery and constructs a purely abstract "reality" or system. In this situation, we might observe, the steno has curiously become the result of human creativity, while the expressive has become the transparency by which we intuit a beyond or an above. Yet Wheelwright claims that the poet operates by the "creative magic of the word."[72] What is it that he creates? It can only be, in these terms, the situation in language by which transparency is possible. It cannot be a radical creativity such as occurs at the steno pole in, for example, mathematics.

The poet's activity, in any case, is declared to be a softening or extending of the borders of the subjective, or what is called the subjective, "the ordinarily narrow areas of shared mentality." This is to be accomplished by "sly linguistic maneuvers," a phrase somewhat reminiscent of Mallarméan withdrawal.[73] This area of shared mentality is the trans-subjective," substituted in 1968 for the Cassirerian poetic objectivity. Wheelwright calls the liminal otherness that is sought the "presential" or "sheer experienced otherness."[74] But how can this be sheerly experienced if it is always other and the poet is always searching, as in the following?

> The bard and his hearers may perhaps move a little forward (who can ever say how far?) along the unsure threshold. The radically presential, the pristine *such*ness of it, is not hopelessly and totally incommunicable; it offers an ever shifting challenge to communicative ingenuity and taste.[75]

The problem here is that if the presential is available, why must the poet tamper with it except to point out its presence, which should be easy enough in a form less confusing than that of expressive language? "Presential" appears to be a term derived from Langer's "presentational," applied not to language or symbolic form (as in Langer) but to the liminal otherness itself, which lurks *there* as a tempting challenge, coyly unavailable.

The threshold of "upwardness" introduces the question of the relation of poetry to religious utterance. For Wheelwright, steno language's only response to religion is either positivism or supernaturalism. It is clear that Wheelwright regards the question of religion as in part a semantic one. Language seems to be a means either of experiencing or of putting a prior experience into some form. The question, with respect to the latter alternative, would be whether or not language sullies the purity of the experience. Wheelwright does not ever really come to grips with this problem and leaves us vacillating between an idea of the shaped, "expressed" experience, which is in language, and the intimation and mystery that is merely sensed, but which in its mere being sensed may be more real than the linguistic form, even though it is mute. Wheelwright claims that the implicit paradox of upward liminal experience needs to be "expressed and presented," but just how this is possible or to what end is not made clear unless it is to remind those of us who do not have the experience that others do have it, or, that such experiences are available to be had.

It is here apparently that for Wheelwright poetic and religious utterances converge and to some extent overlap. All religious utterance would seem to be poetry; some poetry, and obviously that of the higher sort, would be religious. Any religious utterance would be of a higher sort than unreligious poetry. What a nonpoetic religious utterance could possibly be is not clear. This issue is not mentioned at all by Wheelwright, but it seems critical to his whole theory, and I shall return to it.

There follows on the discussion of thresholds an exposition of the "four ways of imagination." We may ask at once in what sense, if at all, imagination is itself linguistic. Wheelwright says that poetic language is immediately "presentative,"[76] which must mean that it is the vehicle of the "presential." The four ways of imagination are "confrontative imagining," "imaginative distancing," "compositive imagining," and "archetypal imagining." These are terms for familiar concepts.

Confrontative imagining involves particularization and intensification. Wheelwright claims for it a "bracketing off" from the "reputedly 'real' world with its demanding network of causal and definitional associations"—making possible contemplation of the "phenomenological object."[77] The concept of the phenomenological object, as I have said, is absent in the 1954 version of *The Burning Fountain*. In 1968 it becomes the paradoxical place in between, where the presential and the presentational somehow join, an "object" looking both ways. This mode of imagining frees itself of the steno context and employs the more elastic mode of depth—or expressive language. But this too is a linguistic context, and the so-called phenomenological object must be created to some extent by it. This would seem to separate such an object from the truly *phenomenal* object to be confronted. Wheelwright sees this situation as inevitable and paradoxical:

There is unavoidable circularity here, and unavoidable paradox. For on the one hand the poetic consciousness largely
makes and articulates its own phenomenological object—and
makes it, too, through the articulating of it—while on the
other hand the phenomenological object confronts the poetic
consciousness with relevant properties of tenderness and aus-
terity, offering certain possibilities, indefinitely limited, of one
sort or another for poetic response.[78]

This inevitable indwelling paradoxicality in the phenomenological
object persists in most of what Wheelwright has to say about the
confrontative, but in one place at least he seems to abandon the paradox and opts for a simpler idea of the phenomenological object as a
sort of imitation of phenomenal experience. He has remarked that
Hobbes's ideal of a sort of steno language is inadequate for dealing
with "the living flow of experience which is not yet formalized into
definite concepts."[79] (We might well ask here, as we did with Jung,
whether indeed he means "yet" or "not susceptible to being.") The
concept of the phenomenological object is necessary for the following reason: ". . . the semantic character of the language employed
must have more flexibility in order to be relatively close to the fluc-
tuating character of the experience in question."[80] There are "referentially intimate meanings." This idea of intimacy suggests a "miraculous" element.

But referentially intimate meanings are still referential.[81] Wheelwright's language reopens—or, better, destroys the bridge over—the
gap he tries to close or mediate by his concept of the phenomenological object—the gap between experience and expression, sign and referent. The liminal threatens to be cut off once again. The poem is
split from primal consciousness, if such consciousness exists.

Curiously enough, Wheelwright's strenuous effort to find a way
to establish our consciousness of the liminal via the poetic ends with
a concept of poetic creativity that is far more problematic than the
creativity he has made evident in the workings of steno language.
Steno language creates a whole abstract system—what I have called
antimyth. Steno language can live serenely with the gap between sign
and signified, subject and object, for it has made these gaps a part of
its structure, which radically creates *conceptual* objects. In the end, it
appears that Wheelwright's phenomenological object may be a conceptual object after all, but a surrogate for an unknown. Such an object may be a "religious" allegorical or "miraculous" symbolical

creation of religious thought, but is it a poetic object? Can there be a poetic object?

All this is to say that Wheelwright has not only the problem caused by his departure from Cassirer's language but also the difficulty of distinguishing between religious and poetic utterance. When the gap between signifier and signified is accepted by poetry (as seems to be the case in Wheelwright's idea of the phenomenological object) the gap between religion and poetry disappears. The value of the phenomenological object comes to reside in its intimations of the upward liminal world, not in its power to form a vision from a potentiality. The mode of poetry is no longer what I have called "myth" but a "religious" form of antimyth.

Although Wheelwright has tried to give credence to the creative activity of the poet, it is not a radical creativity but a paradoxical situation in which creativity is subordinated to search. Search is never quite a discovery but an endless moving-toward.

Nothing in Wheelwright's treatment of the other three ways of imagination will move us to revise this estimate. "Imaginative distancing" is Wheelwright's version of Kant's "internal purposiveness," Cassirer's artistic "objectivization," and Edward Bullough's "psychical distance."[82] Since the previous way of imagination was supposed to put us in close relation with otherness, this "way" represents the other side of a paradox. Distancing is paradoxically distancing of the phenomenological object from our tendency to make of the same material a conceptual object. It is thus fundamentally a freeing of the object from the demands of utility into our free play with it. In this sense imaginative distancing is also paradoxically identical with Keatsian empathy. Here again the emphasis is on search for the identification with the object on the part of the poet rather than on making in language.

"Compositive imagining" is Wheelwright's version of the Coleridgean "esemplastic power." It has connections with Kant's unifying act of the mind, thrown into the symbolic "new key" of Langer. Wheelwright himself mentions José Vasconcelos's Neo-Kantian concept of the "unification of the heterogeneous,"[83] which like Langer's "new key" is an analogy in the realm of artistic creation to Kant's concept of the understanding as creative. It is a synthesis without the use of abstract universal class concepts.

Finally, Wheelwright develops the theory of "archetypal imagining." Here we return to the problem of the upward threshold. His recourse is to the Goethean concept of the concrete universal and the distinction between allegory and symbolism. Such universals, Wheelwright reminds us, "cannot be separated from the given context, cannot be logically explicated, without suffering distortion."[84] Archetypes for Wheelwright are not necessarily Jungian. What he has to say about them is independent of whether or not they express a "collective unconscious" or are "transmitted by inheritance."[85] Archetypes are here clearly associated with depth meaning and religious experience. It is declared that in poetry the depth meaning, now clearly identified with the upward threshold, is not all that matters (though what in the end *can* matter in the face of the huge import of the upward threshold is not really made clear). In religious utterance, however, "the depth meaning is *all* that matters."[86] A curious statement appears a few pages later: "*Poetic discourse* is a species of expressive discourse, in which the main part of the meaning is controlled by the poet's art rather than by developing social customs as in the case of shared archetypal symbols."[87] The last phrase is syntactically ambiguous as well as vague in itself. It is not clear whether an archetype's meaning is or is not independent of a poetic context. Certainly symbols are not archetypal unless they are in some way shared, but how they are both shared and controlled by the poet's art is not sufficiently explained. Perhaps Wheelwright is moving toward some theory of subsistence and insistence, such as is presented by Vivas. If so, he tries to apply it to his threshold of upwardness, whereas Vivas applies his concept to a threshold of otherness and without recourse to a theory of archetypes at all. In the end, for Wheelwright poetry is concerned with all three thresholds and religion only with the upward. This seems to divide poetry into a greater and lesser type, the religious and the secular.

Wheelwright complicates his theory of archetypes with a theory of their relation to myth. There is for him a sort of mystery in the way the archetype enters the "living discourse of poetry." Only one thing is certain and that vaguely so: ". . . so far as the poetry is poetically alive, the ingredient universals are somehow concrete, which is to say freshly envisioned and therefore somehow metaphoric, not the static and pre-existent universals which a logical conception involves."[88] This is an effort to keep poetry as archetypal imagining from being swallowed up in metaphysics. Wheelwright turns to myth for aid in this endeavor. He says a number of things that place archetypes previous to myth. Myth is the "archetypal in action." Myth involves "archetypally significant events and situations." But he goes on to declare that "existentially . . . the mythic came first, the archetypal is a later intellectual offshoot."[89] The examples he offers of archetypes are abstract: the good, evil, creative energy. On the other hand, God, Satan, and Mother Earth are concrete and mythic. The distinction seems to turn the archetype into the romantic allegoric, an abstract interpretation of a myth, lacking in the very depth it is supposed to exemplify. It is always "a later intellectual offshoot," it is always this side of the myth, so to speak. But depth meaning has been said to inhere in the myth, which points to the other or far side of itself—the upward threshold.

In short, the concept of archetype, which Wheelwright tries to blend with myth as a "primitive epistemic"[90] is self-contradictory. If it follows upon myth existentially, then it is something projected out from it in the form of interpretation and thus away from depth meaning toward steno symbols. For Wheelwright, archetypes seem sometimes to play only this secondary role, sometimes to have a sort of liminal mystery of their own and become "miraculous" symbols.

I believe that Wheelwright's problem here stems from his effort to keep poetry and religion together, in spite of their apparent desire for amicable separation. Cassirer, we note, recognized their separation, though his distinction between them is not crystal clear. It ought to be clear by now that I regard the "miraculous" symbol as belonging to religion, not to poetry. However, it is best, rather than reasserting the war of religion and poetry that lurks in some medieval theory, to remember Blake's remark that opposition is true friendship.[91]

IO

The Literary Concept of Myth

From this study so far it appears that a philosophy of the literary symbolic requires at its base two fundamental things: first, a concept of language as "creative," abolishing the opposition of language and thought, in which thought is always accorded the primary position and language either copies or signifies it; second, a concept of language as fundamentally poetic, abolishing the opposition of language and poetry deplored by Croce. Language would have to be seen in far broader terms than those which make it a function of the Kantian understanding or assign to it an ideal mathematical form. Certain Blakean principles and Vico's "poetic logic" provide the germ of such a view. Cassirer does not satisfy us here, in part because he does not think consistently of language in the two ways mentioned above, but he helps us by reintroducing Vico's theory of the primordial relation of language to myth in a modern guise. Is it possible to extend this concept (without slipping into "religious" allegory or sentimental archaism) to make an identification of language with poetry by recognizing a connection between poetry and what Cassirer calls "mythical thought," a term reminiscent of Vico's "poetic logic"?

In Wheelwright's concept of "organic-expressive-depth language" and in his enumeration of its "open" traits, we observed an effort to fill a gap left by Cassirer. Yet Wheelwright's analysis leaves us with little if any means to differentiate poetic from religious utterance. It risks the loss of the creative element and a return to "religious" allegory by recourse to the concept of poetry as a "threshold" searching. There seems, therefore, to be a third necessity. It is offered, though undeveloped, in the concept of art as a "universe of discourse"; it must be extended to a concept of the art of language, literature, as itself such a universe. Beyond this, and fourth, we must face the implications of such a view for culture, verging as it does on a broader concept of fictions than Vaihinger expressed and a redefinition of "fiction," emphasizing its connection to the creative act of symbolizing. Vaihinger's positivistic theory of fictions failed effectively to distinguish types of fictions or symbolic forms and to value literary "figments."

In assessing literature as such a form, one would have to see it in parallel and contrast to other forms, perhaps in a dialectical relationship with them. Cassirer hints at this situation at the end of *An Essay on Man*. The dialectical element we can provide, I believe, by recourse to Blake's idea of contraries, sophisticated by the later Yeats.

However, if we could achieve all this we would still have problems, some of which I shall deal with in my last chapter. One, which may be faced here, is the task of rescuing the term "allegory" from the ignominy to which the main lines of romantic criticism condemned it. It would no longer be a term opposed to symbolism and for the most part outside literature but one inside literature conceived of as a symbolic form.[1]

1. *Anatomy of Criticism*

THE MOST comprehensive theoretical effort to gather the strands of romantic and postromantic literary theory together under the guiding terms "symbol," "archetype," "myth," and "allegory" has been Northrop Frye's *Anatomy of Criticism*.[2] Unlike Wheelwright's work, which approached the problem of literary symbolism from a philosophical point of view, Frye avoids making philosophical claims and approaches philosophical questions from the point of view of a specifically *literary* criticism. He claims to create a schema for literary criticism purely out of an inductive study of literature itself. But he does not stop at any known "literary" limits. Rather, he reaches a concept of culture from initially literary concerns, which he develops

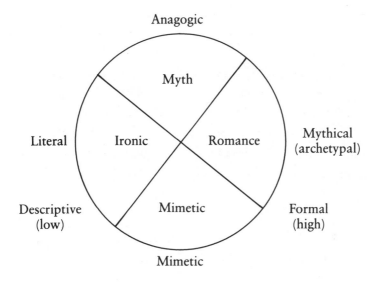

Figure 10.1

later in *The Critical Path*, where he offers his dialectic of the myth of freedom and the myth of concern. In the *Anatomy* Frye begins by claiming that his is a theory of criticism, not of literature, and is thus not a study of literature from its own point of view, which in his view is impossible, but from the point of view of the science appropriate to it. The question before us is how well Frye's theory meets the needs indicated above.

Frye's terminology heavily influenced criticism and need not be discussed at length here. The principal terms representing Frye's well-known phases may be placed on a circle, as in figure 10.1.

If we consider this circle historically (or, in contemporary jargon, diachronically), literary history moves clockwise from the mythic and anagogic to the ironic and literal. Whether it turns back to myth again or our circle ought to be a spiral toward some entirely new historical phase, Frye carefully neglects to tell us. He does not read the stars of his literary universe. In the "Tentative Conclusion" of the *Anatomy*, the veil of the temple only trembles.

When we think of Frye's circle ahistorically (or synchronically), we see it as a charting of fictional and thematic modes, symbols, archetypes, and genres. Frye goes beyond the usual vocabulary of the symbolist tradition, for he seeks to reintroduce terms from theories that have been anathema to symbolists. The principal and most both-

Table 10.1

(1) *Frye's phases*	(2) *Platonic dialogue*	(3) *Mode of imitation*
Anagogic	Phaedrus	of total dream of man
Archetypal	Ion	of other poems
Formal	Symposium	between example & precept
Descriptive	Republic	of externality
Literal	Cratylus	-----

(4) *Medieval scheme*	(5) *Type of metaphor*
Anagogic	universal identity
Moral and Tropological	concrete universal
Allegorical	natural proportion
Literal (historical)	simile
-----	single juxtaposition

ersome reintroduction is Aristotelian "mimesis"; Frye also connects the concerns of certain Platonic dialogues with his five phases. In addition to using the Greeks, he connects his phases to the fourfold scheme of medieval Christian hermeneutics, adding a crucial fifth level that is beyond the scope of any medieval scheme. I organize these relationships in table 10.1.

The addition of a fifth phase I shall examine shortly. First, it is important to consider how Frye introduces the concept of mimesis or imitation into a tradition that has shunned it and opposed the creative to the copying. This is the case as far back as Coleridge's attempt to define poetry in terms of a radically creative, perhaps verbal, imagination. To all of his phases except the literal Frye assigns some mode of imitation, but as we pass up the chart from descriptive to anagogic we discover the term departing from its usual meaning to indicate metamorphosis or liberation of material into a new form.

At the same time, Frye uses "imitation" in other senses as well. Sometimes it means illusion, where the thing produced looks as if it were something else but really is not, as in his remark that there is no direct address in literature, only a mimesis of it.[3] Elsewhere, the ideas of literature are declared not to be real propositions but "verbal formulas which imitate real propositions."[4] Further, all verbal structures with meaning are described as "verbal imitations of that elusive psychological and physiological process known as thought, a process stumbling through emotional entanglements, sudden irrational convictions, involuntary gleams of insight, rationalized prejudices, and blocks of panic and inertia, finally to reach a completely incommunicable intuition."[5] Philosophy itself Frye calls a "verbal imitation" of this process.[6] These remarks imply a conception of imitation as naïve as that of his own "descriptive" phase, and seem to drive a wedge between thought and language. Frye's later remarks, however, qualify his attitude somewhat and insist on a creative, or at least transformative liberating element in imitation itself. In an important statement that applies to all the phases, he states:

> The poet never imitates "life" in the sense that life becomes anything more than the content of his work. In every mode he imposes the same kind of mythical form on his content. . . .[7]

This so-called mythical form, which is for Frye literary or literal form, we would do well to treat not as form in its popular sense of decorative frame, but in Cassirer's sense of an a priori shaping activity. If perhaps Frye does not go quite this far and gives a certain substance to his form, we see him nevertheless trying to keep his phases plastic. This is true even in his treatment of the descriptive phase, which produces at its extremity "documentary naturalism."[8]

Frye thinks of imitation, even in this phase, as fundamentally the means by which literature provides "the vision of something liberated from experience."[9] He believes that is what Aristotle really meant by "mimesis." There are remarks in the *Poetics* to support this claim.

Still it is clear enough that Aristotle had nothing so radical in mind as the literal phase of the symbolic that Frye adds to the medieval scheme. Rather, the literal phase is a requirement dictated by the notion of the symbolic. Ahistorically, Frye sees the literal as lurking implicit in all literature and acknowledged obliquely even in criticism oriented to imitation. For Frye, the remark of Aristotle that it is more important to represent the hind artistically than accurately[10] must be one made from the perspective of the literal phase, "literal" in Frye meaning radically literary and *not* radically descriptive. The literal is purely centripetal or inward with respect to meaning as against the descriptive, which is centrifugal and outwardly referential. The distinction is between what Frye calls symbol as "motif" and symbol as "sign."[11] From the point of view of the literal phase, "a poem's meaning is literally its pattern or integrity as a verbal structure. Its words cannot be separated and attached to sign-values: all possible sign-values of a word are absorbed into a complexity of verbal relationships."[12] The mode of criticism that attaches itself to the literal is the New Criticism or what Frye calls "rhetorical" criticism.

But Frye goes beyond all this to declare that although there are differences between the phases clockwise from literal to descriptive (inward to outward), we shall discover that *literature itself* as a form is centripetal:

> In all literary verbal structures the final direction of meaning is inward. In literature the standards of outward meaning are secondary, for literary works do not pretend to describe or assert, and hence are not true, not false, and yet not tautological either, or at least not in the sense in which such a statement as "the good is better than the bad" is tautological.[13]

By "not true, not false, and yet not tautological either," Frye seems to mean "tautegorical" in Schelling's sense. It is difficult for the reader to keep this idea clearly before him as he passes through Frye's description of the various phases, and its full import is not apparent until the discussion of anagogy, to which I shall turn shortly. It is important to understand at once that though the literal phase is described as the phase of irony, all of literature has to be ironic in this scheme in relation to interpretation. In other words, it is not capturable by commentary, which finds itself in a radically descriptive relation to any literary text. Commentary is not literature itself. It operates by a different form. It must organize what it gazes upon in its own ways, just as poetry operates in its own way: "Poetry organizes the content of the world as it passes before the poet, but the forms in which that content is organized come out of the structure of poetry itself." For Frye this is also imitation, in that a content has been brought in from the world. He does not, however, intend here the old form-content distinction. Rather, the effort is to describe a structure as it makes a unique content which is itself a form. This is similar to what Cassirer was driving at with his claim that art gives us a world of "pure sensuous forms."[14] The aim is not to eliminate content, as in some extreme forms of aestheticism, but to collapse the distinction into the one term "form," and greatly enlarge its scope. The phrase "pure sensuous forms," however, sounds a bit empty in Cassirer, even though it is extended to signify a radically created plentitude. Does "imitation" adequately express this situation, or might Frye have been better off free of the term?

In his "Tentative Conclusion," Frye seems to opt for a theory of symbolic forms similar to Cassirer's and with equal emphasis on the import of cultural creation; but Frye does not diminish the status of the world "out there" as much as some idealists do. There is a Hobbes or perhaps a stone-kicking Dr. Johnson in Frye, and this presence accounts for Frye's maintenance of the term "imitation" no matter how difficult it is for him to square its nuances of meaning with his system.

2. ANAGOGY AND DISPLACEMENT

THE TREATMENT of all literature as ultimately centripetal leads us from the literal phase back to the anagogic. When we come to it we realize that Frye intends his anagogic phase to be not just a phase but a container of all literary phases in an ultimate concept of literature. The anagogic is really literality at a higher or all-inclusive level or total Blakean circumference. (One might remark here that in the anagogic phase existential projection of myth into philosophy takes the form of a coherence theory, while in the descriptive phase the existential projection is a correspondence theory.) This leads us to consider Frye's concept of "displacement," a term he appropriates from Freud, but which has an entirely different and unpsychological meaning in his system. Displacement in Freud is away from the center of meaning of the dream, and interpretation of the dream is an effort to return to that central place—the real dream content. Every manifest dream is a "substitutive" allegory or displaced version of a hidden meaning. In Frye displacement is not the work of a deliberately obfuscating censor. Nor does displacement in Frye proceed from an absolute zero point, as the term might be applied to Mallarmé, or from a "burning fountain," where the deep truth is imageless, as in romantic "religious" allegory. Displacement in Frye is always inward *from* a circumference toward a center which points outward toward a meaning. Thus, "descriptive" works exhibit displaced forms of "anagogy," and the "descriptive" phase is *inside* the "anagogic."

This idea leads us too easily, perhaps, to think of anagogy as a huge substance and literature as an aggregate of all literary works. Sometimes the Hobbes in Frye invites us so to regard it. There is also a Frye who, like Campbell, appears to declare for a world of universal symbols that are abstractable from texts toward a deep truth or monomyth. There is no question that Frye practices this abstracting but only as part of the hypothesizing critical process, which for him must make its own fictive, or as he calls them, "hypothetical" structures in order to escape muteness. Frye's archetypes and myths are best regarded as categories of criticism drawn forth inductively from literary form into the structure of criticism itself. Universal symbols or archetypes are, therefore, strictly speaking, not the components of literature but the components of criticism. This is the burden of the "Polemical Introduction" to the *Anatomy*, where Frye insists on the idea of criticism as a "science" that must get beyond confusing the subject of study with the object of study.

Along with this argument there ought to go, I think, a clearer assertion than Frye makes that literature is to be located not in the aggregate of literary works but *as* a form of symbolic activity. The aggregate is a special fiction necessary to criticism at some stage perhaps but ultimately misleading. If this is so, the center of literature is not in some absolute nothingness, ideal silence, or mystical beyond. It cannot be elsewhere than in the unique form of each creative literary act itself:

> . . . the center of the literary universe is whatever poem we happen to be reading. One step further, and the poem appears as a microcosm of all literature, an individual manifestation of the total order of words.[15]

Frye's "theory" of literature is fundamentally romantic: Literature is expressive. Frye's "science" is an effort to provide a structure of analysis for expressive forms.

As a "scientist" of literature, however, he cannot actually make the act of creation the center of the term "literature." A "scientist" must follow empirical principles. He cannot be privy to the act; he has only the object. The theory and the "science" seem to clash. Frye is well aware of this and goes so far in dealing with it as to call his work an "anatomy,"which is a literary form he discusses in his text. What does this imply? Frye's "scientific" "tentativeness" does not tell us explicitly. But surely it implies that critical theory's "science" is contained in a larger literary form in the same way that allegory is contained in the symbolic. Frye's beginning with science is not a ruse. It is perfectly serious, but Frye's conclusion is the making good of his title, and it looks back into his book ironically. The model of science with which he has begun is transcended and replaced by a notion of fiction-makings, one of which is criticism itself. The literary form known as the anatomy, as Frye describes it, is a curious ironic form of art in which a parade of encyclopaedic learning is given centripetal form. In order for us to understand it we must reject the boundaries between modes of human symbolic expression even as we accept them provisionally. Criticism, or at least Frye's book, would seem to be an ironic form of art which provides a containment and thus a friendly restraint to its own scientific procedures. I have already stated that irony is something that belongs to criticism rather than art, but this is too crude a distinction to sustain longer. What should be said is that criticism differs from art but the line cannot be drawn, that in the case of the *Anatomy* irony pulls us both ways—toward science and away at the same time. In his review of Frye's *Anatomy*, Frank Kermode saw the book as having all the characteristics of a symbolist work, including uselessness. Thus he dismissed it as true criticism.[16] But its subsequent influence on critical practice and the relevance of it to the teaching of romance leads us to revise this estimate and conclude that its own formal structure may disclose something about criticism's ironic middle ground on a continuum of cultural forms.

I have already mentioned that Frye's "literal" has a special relationship to the anagogic. It is clear that if "literal" means something supremely literary, it must in some way become identical with the anagogic concept of literature as a total form. This return of Frye's literal to the anagogic, which renders a simple diagram impossible or, at least, requires it to contain a paradox, is absolutely essential to the whole structure of Frye's book. Frye's anagogic is a descendant of the medieval scheme, but a more recent ancestor is Blake's "Eden." Such a world is "a world of total metaphor, in which everything is potentially identical with [that is, in relation to] everything else, as though it were all inside a single infinite body."[17] Imagistically, this "as though" is the undisplaced core of every work.

At this point in Frye's argument, it seems to me, there is a crisis. It is exemplified by the fact that Frye's anagogic phase is a phase of imitation and his literal phase is not. Is the anagogic, which is a total body, a body of language or a body of human imagination which words try to copy? The question quickly becomes whether Frye makes his identification of literal with anagogic a both-and situation, where we accept the idea of imitation even as we deny it. In such an acceptance we would recognize the anagogic and literal as separate even as we identify them on the model of the mythic identification of macrocosm and microcosm. This would be to look at literature from its own point of view, that is, accepting the principle of identity as the logic of criticism as well as of literature.

But that difficult term "imitation" seems to intervene. In anagogy Frye claims we see literature imitate "the total dream of man, and so imitate the thought of a human mind which is at the circumference of its reality."[18] Imitation of thought in Frye is the emancipation of a previous act into liberating form. But this human mind, as long as it is merely thinking (for Frye describes that act as previous to language), can never be at a circumference. Without language, which is regarded as an imitative form of signification, the mind remains at a center, struggling with a surrounding objectivity. In Frye's description of thought as a "stumbling . . . to reach a completely incommunicable intuition,"[19] thought becomes a movement away from language. Thought is separated from linguistic communication, Frye considering language a form of communication. Thus, though Frye thinks of imitation as the emancipation of experience into literary form, it appears that the experience of the literary thought, let alone the thought itself, can never be emancipated after all, because thought is regarded as an incommunicable form of its own. The idea of the poem as the actual presentation of a linguistic process of thought is impossible, and as a result imitation cannot be emancipation, since intuition is incommunicable.

In the same way, Frye declares philosophy to be the verbal imitation of thought.[20] Obviously by this he means emancipation of thought into communicable form. But the idea of incommunicable intuition clashes with this and forces the more common meaning of imitation on us. It appears at this point that Frye might be better off without the concepts of "imitation" and "thought," at least as he uses them. It may appear later, however, that a submission of them to paradox can save them. This is best seen by returning to the fundamental Blakean paradox of center and circumference.

For Frye, the Blakean center of words—the literal—expands to meet the circumference of words—anagogy. In the literal phase the poem is regarded, as we have seen, as a system of motifs whose meaning, if that is what it can be called, is totally internalized in each motif's relation with all other motifs in the poem. Meaning is *literally* the structural pattern of the work. The literal is ironic because it turns away from external signification and implies the ironic situation of any commentary in relation to it. When we come to the anagogic we see that the same principle applies there, but now we are talking about literature as a total form (not an aggregate) which again contains: "The anagogic view of criticism leads to the conception of literature as existing in its own universe, no longer a commentary on life or reality, but containing life and reality in a system of verbal relationships."[21] It appears, then, that our previous circle or wheel of phases ought now to be represented as a series of concentric circles. Whenever the "descriptive" is passed and the "literal" approached, there is a turning inside out, so that the center becomes a circumference. Frye remarks that in the *Iliad*, Zeus declares that he can pull the whole chain of being up into himself whenever he likes. Even nearer to Frye are Blake's lines from *Jerusalem*:

> I give you the end of a golden string,
> Only wind it into a ball,
> It will lead you in at Heaven's gate
> Built in Jerusalem's wall.[22]

This figure suggests that everything that has been spatialized (stretched out like linear time) and made susceptible to unparadoxical diagram (Wheelwright's "steno language") can be rolled up into a circumferential form. The linear string is a radically "outward" pointing figure. If one takes the outward pointing a little further inward than the descriptive phase, what one has falls completely out of literature into another form with other values such as I have called antimyth. The literary work can seem to verge upon such a center— more radically descriptive than Frye's literarily descriptive—as Zola claimed his work to do. But as Mallarmé and Cassirer both saw in Zola, descriptive literary works in the end admit to, even assert their ultimate literality. As a result there is no center of nothingness, no infinitesimal point inside a literary circumference. Every poem, no matter what its author's pretensions to description may be, springs outward to become a circumferential form itself, like Blake's grain of sand. Thus the appropriate form must be one that violates its own spatial form—a set of concentric circles where in the end every literality expands to become anagogy, as microcosm is macrocosm and imitation is creation, and where the radical center (the black nothingness at the center of figure 10.2) is really "outside" literature.

A more dynamic representation is that of two interlocking, whirling cones, or what Yeats called gyres. Wherever a center seems to be

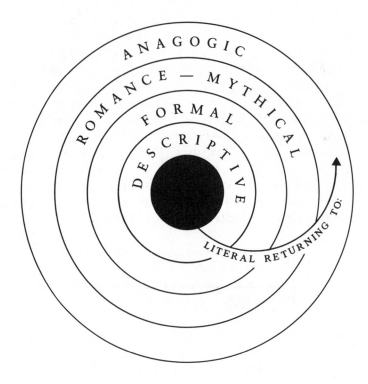

Figure 10.2

reached a circumference is immediately generated (fig. 10.3): Both poem and literature seem to be self-contained universes. The "center" of the order of words, which Frye identifies with the literal and any poem we happen to be reading, is really a circumference. Thus Frye never comes to a zero point or to a nothingness, nor does he come to a situation where a poem is merely a pointer to a Wheelwrightian threshold. When that happens we are outside the two interlocking gyres and have moved to inhabit an entirely different system. Such a system would have to include in its circumference the presumption of an externality—either upward or other—that one is seeking to signify.

In the end this means that we really are, or ought to be, talking about language or languages, claiming that the gigantic body of ana-

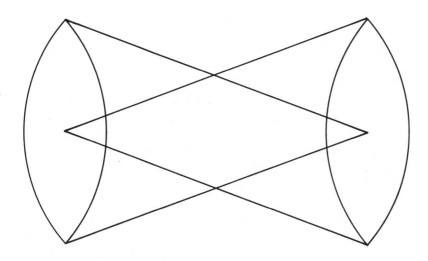

Figure 10.3

gogy is not just an external corporeal object but the human imagination, which is without being except as a linguistic form. Frye's system ought to require the identity of imagination with linguistic form; but, as we have seen, he seems to deny that identity in his various uses of the term "imitation"—unless we find him successful in creating the paradox of the identity of imitation and creation. He does claim that imitation—as the liberation of experience into form—makes more than experience contains. Literature ranges all the way from the "limit of desire" to the "limit of repugnance," the boundaries of imagination.

But what is this raw experience which lies outside literature? Either it must be some sort of manifold of sensation, or it is that which has been constructed inside some other symbolic form. If the former, man as sheer experiencer is in the condition of the passive receptor of sense data. Such a condition can never be known from the inside, there being no inside to know, for such a receptor is at a radical center and everything is outside. Such a condition is an inhuman condition. It is the condition to which behaviorism seeks to reduce man, in which reflection is an impossibility. This suggests that rather than considering literature as the emancipation of raw experience into form, it is better to consider literary form to function dialectically with other symbolic forms to produce from pure potentiality the cultural world.

3. Literature and mathematics

I HAVE SAID that in order to be successful Frye must create the paradox of identity of imitation and creation. But identity is a characteristic of literary works, and criticism as a science cannot achieve it. But what if criticism becomes an art? Then it loses its analytic powers. So it must be both or neither. This returns us to the "Polemical Introduction" and the "Tentative Conclusion" of the *Anatomy*, in which Frye argues for criticism as a science and as an art respectively. The reasons for Frye's beginning with criticism as a science are dictated by his sense of the need to bring some rigor to critical discourse. His ending with criticism as an art has important implications for a general theory of fictions, and I shall come to them in due time. Criticism as science must "objectify," as science must always objectify, but it objectifies. as that word has meaning in its own system. Thus Frye says that physicists study physics, not nature, and critics should realize that they study criticism, not literature.[23] One studies a subject, not objects (that is, constitutes objects within the subject), even if one finds it necessary to claim an empirical connection to objects themselves. The appearance of this fictive construction of the object seems to return us to myth-making and to criticism as an art. Such an art would, however, still verge on antimyth. The presumption of an object external to the subject is a fiction-making that takes the form of antimyth. But such a presumption is a containing circumference which includes that fiction inside itself.

In the conclusion of the *Anatomy* Frye raises questions that verge on a total theory of mythology, a word which in Frye begins to look much like Cassirer's term "symbolic form." If extended from literature the theory would include all forms of human symbolic—the sciences as well as the arts. Frye's movement in this direction in the *Anatomy* is perhaps only a verging, and the rhetoric of it is deliberately tentative, but it is a crucial verging. It occurs most specifically with respect to an analogy Frye develops between literature and mathematics.

The analogy is based on a number of points. First, mathematics, like literature, appears to begin as a "commentary on the outside world," but very soon it becomes clear that the mathematician thinks of his subject as an "autonomous language."[24] The analogy is to the concept of autonomy implicit in Frye's "literal" phase. Second, both literature and mathematics "proceed from postulates, not facts; both can be applied to external reality and yet exist also in a 'pure' or self-contained form."[25] Third, both drive a wedge between the antitheses of being and non-being that is so important for discursive thought. The symbol neither is nor is not the reality which it manifests. The child beginning geometry is presented with a dot and is told, first, that this is a point, and second, that it is not a point. He cannot advance until he accepts both statements at once. It is absurd that that which is no number can also be a number, but the result of accepting the absurdity was the discovery of zero. The same kind of hypothesis exists in literature, where Hamlet and Falstaff neither exist nor do not exist, and where an airy nothing is confidently located and named.[26]

Fourth, there is the analogy of symbolic universes, mathematics and literature for Frye being their own worlds operating according to their own forms. Frye regards mathematics as a "kind of informing or constructive principle" in the sciences: "Mathematics is at first a form of understanding an objective world regarded as its content, but in the end it conceives of the content as being itself mathematical in form, and when a conception of a mathematical universe is reached, form and content become the same thing."[27] This collapse of content into form we have already noted with respect to Frye's theory of imitation.

The analogy leads Frye to consider the possibility that myth may be substantially useful as an "informing or constructive principle" in a variety of human symbolic activities: "psychology, anthropology, theology, history, law, and everything else built out of words."[28] These disciplines or symbolic forms have perhaps been "informed or constructed by the same kind of myths and metaphors that we find, in their original hypothetical form, in literature."[29] Cassirer's view was that myth is a primitive form that gives way to art, science, and other systems as man progresses. Frye's view is not historical but dialectical. Myth endlessly provides the forms of culture, as icons endlessly produce ideas. Myth, then, is artistic process. The whole of symbolic creation is suddenly seen as built upon what we now classify as artistic creation, the most basic of symbolic forms. All of the arts are seen to function in analogous ways as iconic sources for intellectual creation. Frye puts the arts on a wheel and includes mathematics among them (fig. 10.4).[30] This circle with its sets of more intimate and more remote relationships suggests that the shift from *ut pictura poesis* to *ut musica poesis*, which we noted in chapter 5, may be part of an oscillation from emphasizing one to emphasizing the other of the adjoining arts in any discussion of literature. (We

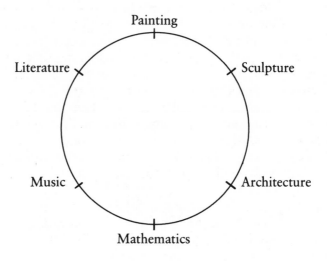

Figure 10.4

might note, incidentally, that mathematics is flanked, like literature, by a principally temporal and principally spatial form.) For Frye, all of these arts provide us with the energy to make a desirable culture. Just as none of the arts is a naïve imitation of nature, so is civilization "not merely an imitation of nature, but the process of making a total human form out of nature."[31]

Frye's discussion of the analogy between literature and mathematics helps us to understand the affinity that poetry and the other arts have traditionally had with mathematics, particularly geometrical form. This matter will be of particular importance when I offer in chapter 11 a concept of the symbolic derived from the later Yeats. It may well be that Frye derived his own interest in the analogy from his study of Yeats.

4. Symbolic universes

Frye's specific treatment of literary symbolism must be taken in terms of his more general interests as I have described them. The symbol is broadly conceived as "any unit of any literary structure that can be isolated for critical attention."[32] This, of course, means literally anything. But, in fact, each of Frye's five phases offers a dif-

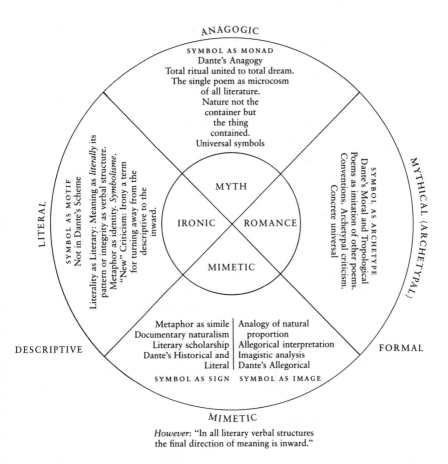

ANAGOGIC

SYMBOL AS MONAD
Dante's Anagogy
Total ritual united to total dream.
The single poem as microcosm
of all literature.
Nature not the
container but
the thing
contained.
Universal symbols

LITERAL

SYMBOL AS MOTIF
Not in Dante's Scheme

Literality as Literary: Meaning as *literally* its
pattern or integrity as verbal structure.
Metaphor as identity. *Symbolisme*.
"New" Criticism: Irony a term
for turning away from the
descriptive to the
inward.

MYTHICAL (ARCHETYPAL)

SYMBOL AS ARCHETYPE
Dante's Moral and Tropological
Poems as imitation of other poems.
Conventions. Archetypal criticism.
Concrete universal

MYTH

IRONIC — ROMANCE

MIMETIC

DESCRIPTIVE

Metaphor as simile
Documentary naturalism
Literary scholarship
Dante's Historical and
Literal

SYMBOL AS SIGN

Analogy of natural
proportion
Allegorical interpretation
Imagistic analysis
Dante's Allegorical

SYMBOL AS IMAGE

FORMAL

MIMETIC

However: "In all literary verbal structures
the final direction of meaning is inward."

Figure 10.5

ferent concept of the symbol. I reduce Frye's discourse on the subject
to a wheel that charts types of symbols by phase (fig. 10.5).

Through the five phases we observe a sliding scale of kinds of
symbols. In the formal phase Frye rescues the term "allegory" from
the by-now venerable negating opposition to symbolism. He treats
what he calls "allegory" as symbolism of the formal phase. The scale
of allegory is as follows:

> naïve allegory (beyond the descriptive and thus
>   out of literature)
> explicit allegory, which is "continuous" in a work
> freestyle allegory

poems with doctrinal emphasis, where internal fictions
   are *exempla*
structure of imagery with implicit relations to events
   and ideas
metaphysical conceits, moving toward increasingly
   ironic modes
heraldic emblems, which arrest narrative and perplex
   meaning
private association, Dada, etc.
and so on outside of literature at this end of the scale.[33]

It is clear enough in Frye's system that allegory is much more than
romantic allegory, which strictly speaking has to be "naïve." As
Angus Fletcher remarks, ". . . allegory often has a literal level that
makes good enough sense all by itself." Fletcher goes on to say, ". . .
this literal surface suggests a peculiar doubleness of intention, and
while it can, as it were, get along without interpretation, it becomes
much richer and more interesting if given interpretation."[34] This
seems to me a little misleading, though with good intentions. If one
misses the allegory, one has simply not *read* the work, much as one
may have enjoyed it. This seems to me true no matter what the so-
called "degree" of allegorical intention,[35] i.e., no matter where on
Frye's scale we are. Literary, apart from naïve allegory or a deliberately secret code, might be seen, equally with Fletcher's view of it,
as commonly moralistic in intent,[36] as forcing morality to face the
world of experience no matter how damaging to the rational consis-
tency of image and idea. The "poetry" of a poem may struggle subversively with and even triumph over the poet's moral intent. If Yeats
had read Spenser's allegorical poetry with a little more sympathy, he
might have discovered just this sort of triumph, with the allegory as
its vehicle. The triumph is a triumph over the ascetic in the larger
sense that all law is ascetic, being abstract and bodiless. The romantics identified only the moral abstraction as allegory, whereas it is
clear enough that allegory is sensuous presentation of abstraction.
Rather than being a "miraculous" incarnation of it, it seems to be
sensuous subversion.

Frye presents a parallel scale of archetypes for the mythical (archetypal) phase. The archetype "connects one poem with another
and thereby helps to unify and integrate our literary experience."[37]
The scale is roughly as follows:

pure convention
translation and paraphrase
deliberate and explicit convention
paradoxical and ironic convention
turning one's back on explicit convention where
    convention becomes implicit
cults of originality, where the conventional patterns
    are deeply submerged.[38]

Reading for Frye involves the inevitable expansion of images into archetypes. The purely unconventional is outside literature entirely. But one assumes that it would belong to some other symbolic form and thus partake of another set of conventions.

Frye rescues allegory from the romantic distinction, and it appears in a different form. He argues that there is "genuine mystery" in art, which he identifies with Carlyle's "intrinsic symbols." There is extrinsic mystery, "which involves art only when art is also made illustrative of something else, as religious art is to the person concerned primarily with worship." This sort of mystery would fall under the class of "religious" or "Platonic" forms of allegory (or perhaps "miraculous" symbolism) as discussed in chapter 1. Frye calls this mystery the "mystery of the unknowable essence." There is also the "mystery which is a puzzle,"[39] a mystery which requires solution and thus annihilation. This corresponds roughly to what I have called the "empirical" mode of allegory and is also outside literature.

Frye tries to formulate the difference between religion and poetry as the difference between the existential and the metaphorical, which in the terms I posited in chapter 1 means that religion posits an "other" beyond itself (though posited by and therefore within its own symbolic form) and insists on differences emanating from a supreme supernatural indifference, while literature tries to preserve identity. Or, as Frye puts it:

In religion the spiritual world is a reality distinct from the physical world. In poetry the physical or actual is opposed not to the spiritually existential, but to the hypothetical.[40]

This remark indicates Frye's critical difference from Wheelwright. Frye's literal, inward, poetic language is not a "threshold" language seeking outward toward a previous independent spiritual reality, but a language embodying a physical world (not a world of physics [that would be a world of mathematical symbolism], but a world of concretion and particularity). Though Wheelwright claims a central formative power for literary language, he puts "religious" limits on it when he makes literature's highest aim the searching for an otherness. Frye does not in the end give a central power to literary symbolism, for there are other symbolic forms, including mathematics and the other arts. Yet here there is some confusion, I think, for (as I have remarked already) Frye calls literature a specialized form of language and language a form of communication.

But now we learn that that is to view language only in one aspect. Language also has a creative aspect and in that aspect language is literature, the maker of myths. With emphasis on the mode of creation rather than communication, it is proper, then, to say,

> For a long time the prestige of discursive reason fostered the notion that logic was the formal cause of language, that universal grammars on logical principles are possible, and that the entire resources of linguistic expression could be categorized. We are now more accustomed to think of reasoning as one of the many things that man does with words, a specialized function of language.[41]

These two views of language as communication and logic on the one hand and language as a form of fictive creation on the other are never resolved by Frye, but it should be clear that as views they are antimythical and mythical respectively.

As in Frye we seem to have more than one definition of language, so do we have in him a plurality of languages, each of which constructs its own fiction:

> The mathematical and the verbal universes are doubtless different ways of conceiving the same universe. The objective world affords a provisional means of unifying experience, and it is natural to infer a higher unity, a sort of beatification of common sense. But it is not easy to find any language capable of expressing the unity of this higher intellectual universe. Metaphysics, theology, history, law, have all been used, but all are verbal constructs, and the further we take them their metaphorical and mythical outlines show through. Whenever we construct a system of thought to unite earth with heaven, the

story of the Tower of Babel recurs: we discover that after all we can't quite make it, and that what we have in the meantime is a plurality of languages.[42]

The term "universe" is employed here in two senses: (1) symbolic universes, and (2) the existential universe (unfortunately, I think, here called "objective," which drags in irrelevant empirical connotations). There is even a third sense implied: the desirable ultimate symbolic universe that man can't quite achieve. This, Frye says, would unite heaven and earth, but it might as well be asked to unite the symbolic and existential that are split in Frye's two uses of the term "universe." The language which accomplished this would have to be an unfictive language. The unity accomplished would be the unity that Kant denied it was possible to know—the unity of the mind's constructs and things-in-themselves.

Another observation to make about the passage above is that Frye describes our situation as one of involvement with a plurality of languages—of symbolic forms. Is there a possibility that the Tower of Babel can be imagined not as a discord but as a prolific contrariety, an order which has conflict as its central form and defines dialectically the role of literature in the building of culture?

5. MYTHS OF CONCERN AND FREEDOM

THIS TAKES US beyond the *Anatomy* to Frye's later work, particularly the dialectic of the myths of concern and freedom that is developed in *The Critical Path*. The main thing about the myth of concern is that it is socially constituted, not "directly connected with reasoning or evidence":

> The typical language of concern tends to become the language of belief. In origin a myth of concern is largely undifferentiated: it has its roots in religion, but religion has also at that stage the function of *religio*, the binding together of the community in common acts and assumptions.[43]

Literature is declared to "represent the *language* of human concern." Literature is not a myth but is always the sustainer of "the total range of verbal fictions and models and images and metaphors out of which all myths of concern are constructed."[44] In this way Frye separates literature from belief. Literature provides "the technical resources for formulating the myths of concern, but does not itself formulate."[45] At the same time it contains more than "any formulation of concern in religious or political myth can express."[46] Literature begins to sound like an aggregate here, rather than a form of expression, but only if we reject Frye's notion that any single literary work (microcosm) has implied in it all of literature (macrocosm).

The other myth is the myth of freedom. For Frye the two myths focus on quite different worlds:

> There is the world [man] is actually in, the world of nature, or his objective environment, a world rooted in the conception of art, as the environment is rooted in the conception of nature. For the objective world he develops a logical language of fact, reason, description, and verification; for the potentially created world he develops a mythical language of hope, desire, belief, anxiety, polemic, fantasy, and construction.[47]

Frye declares that the myth of freedom is part of the myth of concern, by which I assume he means that it emerges from it, though it is never able to replace concern and creates a tension against it.[48] He connects it with "the truths and realities that are studied rather than created, provided by nature rather than by a social vision."[49] The characteristics of this myth are truth of correspondence, objectivity, suspension of judgment, tolerance, and respect for the individual. Just why this should be called a myth by Frye is not clear, since it would appear that what we have here pure and simple is the reception and ordering of sense data according to scientific method and the privileging of object over subject to the extent that the objective is declared to be externally there and human forms expressing it to be copies of it. Since these forms are mathematical abstractions and in the *Anatomy* mathematic form is a constitutor of a reality, perhaps there is reason to call this a myth after all, but *The Critical Path* claims a Hobbesean objectivity free of what I have called antimythical fictive creation.

The problem with this can, I think, be demonstrated by observing what has happened in actual history and practice to Frye's myth of freedom since the eighteenth century and how poets have responded to these events. Frye begins his discussion by identifying concern with society or the mass and freedom with the individual. But these terms shift places historically so that by the twentieth century we have a number of major writers connecting Frye's myth of concern with the individual and Frye's myth of freedom with the tyranny of the mass. The myth of freedom had become the dominant myth of concern. Cassirer's description of the scientist searching for the general law under which differentia can be subsumed shows the triumph of the general over the individual. This movement, glorifying correspondence, objectivity, and suspension of judgment, generated political movements and spread into social science. The romantic poets tried to build myths of concern on the principle of individual freedom. Frye's myth of freedom gradually proved itself, in their eyes, to be a tyrannous destruction of the individual. This occurred not without considerable conflict, of course. In Blake, it is reflected in the relegation of Orcan revolution to cyclical negation. Blake's remarks about Napoleon and Washington reflect skepticism about myths of freedom too easily embraced.[50] In the twentieth century, there are literary attacks on Frye's myth of freedom, or at least on its historical incarnation, as a myth of concern. They are particularly arresting and distressing to many because they happen to be made by some of the greatest writers of the age. Yeats expresses one attitude clearly in a letter to Dorothy Wellesley:

> When there is despair, public or private, when settled order seems lost, people look for strength within or without. Auden, Spender, all that seem the new movement, *look* for strength in Marxian Socialism, or in Major Douglas; they want marching feet. The lasting expression of our time is not this obvious choice but in a sense of something steel-like and cold within the will, something passionate and cold.[51]

These writers' reactionary politics may be seen as responses to a myth of freedom "gone bad." One doesn't have to hold any brief for Yeats's flirtation with Fascism, Eliot's royalism, or Lawrence's mystique of the plumed serpent to recognize negative prophetic power in their attacks on the modernist myth of freedom. Blake's definition of a prophet will serve here: "Every honest man is a Prophet: he utters his opinion both of private and public matters: Thus: If you go on So, the result is so."[52]

Frye does not, of course, intend his myths of concern and freedom to be taken in their historical manifestations. Indeed, he himself remarks of the ". . . interchange of functions that begins with humanism, where the elements of the myth of freedom are seen as perverted into a conspiracy to betray freedom, which only the artist is left to defend,"[53] and he worries about the dogmatism of unliberated concern" and the "skepticism of unconcerned freedom."[54] In a later work, *The Secular Scripture*, he regards the study of literature as helping the student to demythologize, "to become aware of his own mythological conditioning."[55] In history, however, it seems that freedom and concern have the character of cyclical negations and that a contrary to them is necessary. Frye tends to relate literature to religion on the side of concern and science to philosophy on the side of freedom. A true contrary requires something that can stand opposed to this negation. Literature is the contrary of both of Frye's myths. A poet may be very religious, and he may be a scientist, but his poem will rise up against his own religious and scientific themes insofar as they attempt to divest the poem of the body of the world. The poem opposes the struggle of freedom and concern by insisting on having it both ways, or neither way.

This "both-and" or "neither-nor" is "identity," which is the true contrary of "difference/indifference." Frye seems to recognize this in the following remark: "It is identity that makes individuality possible: poems are made out of the *same* images, just as poems in English are all made out of the same language."[56] But Frye's myth of concern is indifference, and his myth of freedom difference, except in history where they change places, so there is no room for identity. This problem is parallel to Frye's occasional privileging of the myth of freedom, even though he has it grow out of concern, and even though he hedges this privileging by indicating that the standards of the myth of freedom are only approximations to objective reality and may be analogous to a model world that doesn't exist. He also raises the question of the "degree to which anything in words can tell the truth at all, in terms of . . . correspondence."[57] This can be read as implying a distinction between two kinds of truth, but the drift has privileged correspondence, now to deny that it can bring truth, leaving us in the state of the romantic "religious" allegorist. Here the contrary must appear. Frye argues that Kierkegaard was in error to think that concern and freedom are the same thing.[58] But Frye's concern and freedom, though they are never the same thing (even when perverted), seem in the end to adopt the same story of an externality always receding from symbolic grasp and end up in history trading places.

II

Stylistic Arrangements of Experience

Astory is told of Yeats in his old age that he startled a professor from India who had asked him if he had any message for the Indian people. Yeats unsheathed Sato's samurai sword, waved it in a circle above his head, and shouted: "Let 100,000 men of one side meet the other. That is my message to India, insistence on the antinomy. Conflict, more conflict."[1] The act was typical of Yeats's tendency to produce farce from his most seriously held ideas—ideas that he certainly at times expressed with solemnity. He created farce early in *The Green Helmet*, where heroism is the subject, in his middle period in *The Player Queen*, subjecting his doctrine of the mask to raillery, and late in life in *The Herne's Egg*, where his concept of historical cycles is the victim. Yeats's tendency toward farce is simply the necessary contrary to the more solemn aspects of his thought— an extreme assertion of the poet's freedom to do what he will with thought. Yeats remarks that Blake had taught him the difference between a contrary and a negation,[2] and the principle of the contrary governs his formulation of the role of the poet in the making of culture as contrary to that of both saint and scientist. We may begin examination of the principle of conflict in Yeats, and its importance to a philosophy of the literary symbolic, by first considering some remarks Yeats made about myth.

1. Myth and Yeatsian conflict

Conflict appears early in Yeats's work, but its being raised to a principle of order was worked out over a period of years as one of the themes of the *Collected Poems*. Writing in the introduction to *The Resurrection*, he remarks of his own antithetical attitude toward the dominant positivistic myth—what I have called antimyth—of his time:

> For years I have been preoccupied with a certain myth that was itself a reply to a myth. I do not mean a fiction, but one of those statements our nature is compelled to make and employ as a truth though there cannot be sufficient evidence. When I was a boy everybody talked about progress, and rebellion against my elders took the form of aversion to that myth. I took satisfaction in certain public disasters, felt a sort of ecstasy at the contemplation of ruin.[3]

In fact, Yeats is really talking about a fiction (as I have come to use the term: something made) here—a fiction or "stylistic arrangement of experience"[4] to be ranged against the dominant, positivistic fiction of his time. Even as a child he made antipositivistic fictions:

> I was unlike others of my generation in one thing only. I am very religious, and deprived by Huxley and Tyndall whom I detested, of the simple-minded religion of my childhood, I had made a new religion, almost an infallible church of poetic tradition, of a fardel of stories and of personages, and of emotions, inseparable from their first expression, passed on from generation to generation by poets and painters with some help from philosophers and theologians.[5]

This antithetical stance impelled the early Yeats to range the poet on the side of mysticism and the "religious." His early effort here only *seems* to emulate Blake's apocalyptic humanism; it is in fact a sort of poetic religiosity—almost the exact opposite of Blake's attempt to raise up art as a "prolific" contrary to "devouring" religion.

This tendency in the early Yeats to confuse art and religion or deliberately to create a new "poetic" religion has strong affinities to the

search for the lost book that became a theme in much modern literature, partly through Mallarmé. Yeats was surely aware of Mallarmé's
oft-quoted statement: "The world is made to end in a beautiful
book."[6] Yeats speaks many times (on occasion comically) of his longing for a sacred book which would give him religious sanction. The
"infallible church of poetic tradition" that he assembled was one
early attempt at a sacred text. His early interests in occultism and
mysticism were part of the search. His attempt with Ellis to turn
Blake into a mystic occultist reflects the same desire.[7] But Yeats's later
career displays a growing realization—and a decisive one—that a sacred book and a poetic book are two different things and that the
sacred book of the arts is in fact a profane book that expresses the
contrary of the "religious."

The later Yeats's remarks about myth are instructive. They reveal
that he had been impressed by Vico, and they declare his sense of the
role of myth in the making of culture. Contrary to some opinions,
Yeats was suspicious of aestheticism and grounded his career at a
crucial moment on the drama:

> during the most creative years of my artistic life, when Synge
> was writing plays, and Lady Gregory translated early Irish
> poetry with an impulse that interpreted my own, I disliked
> the isolation of a work of art. I wished through the drama,
> through a commingling of verse and dance, through singing
> that was also speech, through what I called the applied arts of
> literature, to plunge it back into social life.[8]

Yeats's image of the mask, which arises principally from a consciousness of the dramatic nature of poetry and the contrariety implied
within, is inspired by masks used in the theater. Of myth, Yeats says,
it is not

> as Vico perhaps thought, a rudimentary form superseded by
> reflection. Belief is the spring of all action; we assent to the
> conclusions of reflection but believe what myth presents; be-
> lief is love, and the concrete alone is loved; nor is it true that
> myth has no purpose but to bring round some discovery of a
> principle or a fact.[9]

Yeats sees myth in perpetual, necessary opposition to positivistic
forms of thought, even as he imagines it to be the ultimate source of
those forms. Mythical thinking does not disappear in man's progress

toward the establishment of scientific forms. It is constantly self-renewing, characterized by concretion as against the generalizing tendencies of the reason. Furthermore, philosophy must renew itself in myth: "Giambattista Vico has said that we should reject all philosophy that does not begin in myth."[10] Yeats's "myth" is given the role that art is accorded by Cassirer, but Yeats emphasizes the antithetical nature of myth. The connection of myth with belief is one that Yeats does not, however, always make. Indeed, he attempts to avoid the term "belief" in *A Vision* in favor of the concept of "stylistic arrangements of experience." The abandonment of "belief" makes possible his separation of poet and saint, poem and holy book.

At times, however, his rage against the positivists' capture of philosophy makes him range belief—true belief—on the side of the totally irrational and leads to what Richard Ellmann has aptly called his "affirmative capability,"[11] a state in which one believes everything possible to be believed in contrast to Keats's withdrawal from belief, characterized by his phrase "negative capability."[12] Strangely enough, the two positions have in the end much in common, both being designed to enlarge the scope of the imaginative arts against the power of antimyth. The positivistic way to truth, logic, "is a machine, one can leave it to itself; unhelped it will force those present to exhaust the subject, the fool is as likely as the sage to speak the appropriate answer. . . ."[13] Keats's "negative capability" is paradoxically a form of empathy. Yeats's so-called "affirmative capability" is myth-making—love—also a form of identification with other things. Both are therefore the contrary of the machine of logic, being an involvement of the personality.

But just as Keats's "negative capability" is paradoxically empathy, so is Yeats's myth-making antinomial. His constant recourse to conflict is most succinctly expressed in two passages from *Pages from a Diary Written in Nineteen Hundred and Thirty*. In the first, logic disperses conflict, which is the personal form of all thought:

> I am trying to understand why certain metaphysicians whom I have spent years trying to master repel me, why those invisible beings I have learned to trust would turn me from all that is not conflict, that is not from sword in hand. Is it not like this? I cannot discover truth by logic unless that logic serve passion, and only then if the logic be ready to cut its own throat, tear out its own eyes. . . . Those spiritual beings seem always as if they would turn me from every abstraction. I

must not talk to myself about "the truth" nor call myself "teacher" nor another "pupil"—these things are abstract—but see myself set in a drama where I struggle to exalt and overcome concrete realities perceived not with mind only but as with the roots of my hair.[14]

Here Yeats seeks to valorize a mode of thought transcending logic, for logic is to him a function of the "mind only," and the separation of mind from the rest of man results in what Blake called a "negation," like the ascetic negation of the body when the soul is given its own separate life. Contraries must be maintained in order to achieve the paradoxical order of conflict—the only kind of order that celebrates life. Such celebration is the poet's responsibility. The second passage from the diary asserts this necessity:

I think that two conceptions, that of reality as a congeries of beings, that of reality as a single being, alternate in our emotion and in history, and must always remain something that human reason, because subject always to one or the other, cannot reconcile. I am always, in all I do, driven to a moment which is the realisation of myself as unique and free, or to a moment which is surrender to God of all that I am. I think that there are historical cycles wherein one or the other predominates. . . . Could those two impulses, one as much a part of truth as the other, be reconciled, or if one or the other could prevail, all life would cease.[15]

The two poles described here Yeats elsewhere calls "antithetical" and "primary," characterized by the ideal forms of poet and saint, personality and character, freedom and submission. It is perhaps curious that Yeats should associate the saint with the primary world, which is also the world of the scientist. But it is not curious if we recognize that he is really basing his opposition on the romantic distinction between symbolism and allegory that I set forth in chapter 1. The saint represents the "religious" form of allegory and the scientist the "empirical." How Yeats comes to this requires some scrutiny and takes us back to the beginning of the *Collected Poems*.

2. THE PRINCIPLE OF CONTRARIETY

YEATS's *Collected Poems* is a deliberately constructed book and begins with two lyrics that are paired for contrast. In the first, "The

Song of the Happy Shepherd," the speaker from Arcady (the poem was originally the epilogue to an Arcadian play) advises his listener to forego the world of "grey truth" and "the cracked tune that Chronos sings" and seek

> Some twisted, echo-harbouring shell,
> And to its lips thy story tell,
> And they thy comforters will be.[16]

The world of "grey truth" is the world of the objective, of naïve materialism, of measurable reality, of Locke's primary qualities of experience. That world has been described by A. N. Whitehead in a striking phrase, "a dull affair, soundless, scentless, colourless, merely the hurrying of material, endlessly, meaninglessly."[17]

Yeats's frustration in such a world, or at least in a world where that sort of description of itself was abundantly implied, is expressed not only in this poem, but also in its companion piece, "The Sad Shepherd,"[18] where the escape advocated by the happy shepherd is attempted and found wanting.

If we consider the two poems together, we see that Yeats refuses finally to endorse either the happy shepherd's suggestion or the primary reality from which the shepherd claims we may escape. Yeats became dissatisfied with both subjectivist and objectivist positions as presented in modern philosophy and with the whole principle upon which the division was based. He came to see it as a form of Blakean negation, in which the objective always triumphs. The trouble had all started when Locke created from his mind the distinction between primary and secondary qualities of experience, and, as a result, matter was torn from his side and objectified as nature and its mechanical laws:

> Locke fell into a swoon;
>   The Garden died;
>   God took the spinning-jenny
>   Out of his side.[19]

One can look at Yeats's career as a search to overcome the subject-object split and its inevitable negation of the subject. He had early become disillusioned by Victorian materialism. However, he also became disillusioned by the sort of romantic Platonism that was designed to answer materialism but sent the poetic vision off into abstract essences. Very early he felt that real meaning lay in levels of reality other than those reducible to the laws of matter, but he came to believe that such levels were not the Platonic ideas, and finally he arrived at the antinomial attitude which claimed that we are both in the world and make it too.

Yeats's hatred of Huxley and Tyndall reminds us that in the spirit of Blake he actually created his own triad of villains—"Huxley, Tyndall, and Bastien-Lepage"[20]—on the model of Blake's "Bacon, Newton, Locke." The experimental method that Bacon championed and Newton exploited led to Locke's distinction between primary and secondary qualities and the bifurcation of experience into object and subject. Yeats's contrary, substituted for Locke's objective negation of the subject, is antithetical opposition to the subject-object distinction itself. "Antithetical" is an ironic term implying the embattled position of anyone opposing the dominating cultural force. "Antithetical" is sometimes called "subjective" by Yeats, and this certainly reflects a tendency to slip back into the negative opposition the symbolists struggled with. But Yeats's subjective is a bodily form, and antithetical is sensuous spirit. The second stanza of the poem about Locke and the spinning-jenny asks, "Where got I that truth?" And the answers are:

> Out of a medium's mouth,
> Out of nothing it came,
> Out of the forest loam,
> Out of dark night where lay
> The crowns of Nineveh.[21]

This series of different answers adds up to a refusal to specify a source or meaning behind the poem, so that the poem seems itself to be a bringing of unspecifiable subsidiaries, as Michael Polanyi would call them, to insistence.[22] Truth then would seem to lie in the poem's freedom from a source, in the sense of meaning. This notion of freedom is very important in Yeats, and we shall return to it. Here we can connect it with "antithetical" creativity, which makes the truth in a way baffling even to the maker when he "thinks" upon it.

As the methodology of "Bacon, Newton, Locke" triumphed, so did mythology decline, because an empirical or objectivist method of proof came to be applied to mythic utterances. Thus, the problems we observed among eighteenth-century mythographers who would go to great and fantastic lengths to demonstrate the truths of their theories. The meaning of "belief" not simply narrowed, but changed. In a world of purely measurable truth, myth became publicly acceptable only as poetic decoration. Poetry's thought was not imagined to be independent of scientific categories. There were exceptions, of course. Rather than supporting the rejection of mythology, Blake and Wordsworth rejected its use merely as decoration. Wordsworth attacked the "gaudiness and inane phraseology"[23] of previous poets, and Blake objected to "Bloated Gods, Mercury, Juno, Venus, and the rattletraps of mythology,"[24] in which myth was reduced to the "allegoric." Now, along with the rejection of myth came the misguided subjectivist capitulation to the terms (subject-object) invented by the objectivist enemy that vitiated so much nineteenth-century symbolist thought. One of its forms was a heightened interest in Platonic philosophy, which in the environment of objectivity became a retreat into subjectivity and the "soul." It is reflected in the popularity of Thomas Taylor's translations of Plato and Porphyry and his allegorical readings of myths. Such readings did tend to revive the myths, but, as we have seen, in "Platonic" allegorical form.

Perhaps more pernicious was a romanticized version of the doctrine of the Platonic ideas themselves. With the underpinning of the Platonic ideas poets could relegate science and matter, as Yeats's Happy Shepherd seems to have done, to the imperfect world that vainly imitates the Platonic forms or ideas. According to this view the poet must be a seer, rising to an immediate vision of the forms or ideas themselves, passing from the copies to higher reality. It made no difference that Plato himself held that the poet imperfectly imitated imperfect copies, only rational thought attaining to truth. This romantic, unplatonic, Platonizing view of poetry, of which Shelley is often accused, would tend to dispatch the poet past the threshold to the ephemeral, to what T. E. Hulme called the "circumambient gas."[25] Yeats spoke of Shelley as a "poet of essences" and remarked that such a poet must "seek in the half-lights that glimmer from symbol to symbol as if to the ends of the earth, all that the epic and dramatic poet finds of mystery and shadow in the accidental circumstances of life."[26] That Yeats called Shelley a "poet of essences" and tried to describe such poetry indicates his sense of the special nature of it. But Shelley's poems do not leave this world. They often concretely dramatize a failure to capture the vision of Platonic forms or ideas. One thinks of "Epipsychidion" as the epitome of this drama. But what the poet in the poem fails to perform is what the poem's success requires. Shelley as a poet could not escape the world of the particular even when he spoke of essences. In his terms, Plato was right to the extent that he saw the poet tied to the copies and incapable of rational abstraction toward the Platonic forms or ideas. But unfortunately he saw only danger in the poet's characteristic mode of particularization, for it brought the poet back to the copies. The success of the speaker of "Epipsychidion" would be pure undifferentiation, his failure pure differentiation. The success of the poem is both/ and in the form of its own narrative. It is in defense of the poet's way as a necessary contrary to "Platonic," "religious," and "empirical" modes of abstraction that Yeats broke away from Platonism, and it is because of this that Yeats could rest easy with neither of his shepherds.

Yeats did not deny the efficacy or the value of science. He did not even deny its truth—if we define scientific truth as one side of a dialectical opposition (we shall see this in his attitude toward mathematics). But he denied its truth as soon as it negated the counter-truths represented by the "antithetical" ways to symbolize—including the poetic, which claimed not just to see but to make reality.

At the same time, although he was a student of Platonism, he found romantic Platonism unacceptable as a countertruth to positivistic science because Platonic abstraction was not to his mind really contrary to Lockean abstraction. As a poet he would

> . . . mock Plotinus's thought
> And cry in Plato's teeth.[27]

Yeats came to think of "Platonic" and "empirical" thought as similar in spirit. In the "Platonic," the copies, or the appearances we experience, are really abstractions from eternal forms or ideas. (Experientially, of course, the abstraction goes in the other direction.) In the "empirical," abstraction is achieved by the process of generalization. For Yeats there was a certain half-reality in the results:

> I try always to keep my philosophy within such classifications of thought as will keep it to such experience as seems a natural life. I prefer to keep in my definition of water a little duckweed or a few fish. I have never met that poor creature H_2O.[28]

For him as a poet, the "Platonic" and the "empirical" both abstracted by means of generalization. In both, the particular lost its appropriate status.

In "The Double Vision of Michael Robartes," the speaker Robartes exclaims:

> For what but eye and ear silence the mind
> With the minute particulars of mankind?[29]

"Eye and ear" represent artistic modes of particularization. "Mind" here represents modes of rational abstraction toward the general. "Minute particular" is Blake's term for the form of artistic activity. As we saw in Blake's attack on Reynolds, Blake argues that in art, "To generalize is to be an Idiot. To Particularize is the Alone Distinction of Merit."[30] Blake complains against the adoption in art of modes of abstraction foreign to art, though perhaps proper to science.

In the lines above from "The Double Vision," Yeats uses "mind" much as Keats uses "thought" in "Ode On a Grecian Urn": "Thou, silent form, dost tease us out of thought," where thought refers to the generalizing mode of abstraction that destroys empathy and particularity. Of the romantic poets, Blake and Keats are the least "Platonic" in their assertions about art and most free of the mind/matter, body/ soul, and other such negations that follow upon the "Platonic" view. In their polemics for art they both insist on the "minute particular," as Blake puts it, or the "life of sensations,"[31] in Keats's terms. This makes neither one necessarily a materialist or a sensualist. It means that they do not confuse artistic particularization with "Platonic" or "empirical" abstraction. Artistic thought for Yeats always particularizes from heretofore undifferentiated areas of feeling. Such thought, which for Yeats is "myth," makes possible the subsequent building up of ideas in other symbolic forms. The next step, and the step implied in Yeats, is to consider the "empirical" and the Yeatsian mythic as necessary contraries rather than negations of each other's powers.

In his poetry and, most systematically, in *A Vision,* Yeats saw each individual as belonging to a type in which one form of thought predominates, but never in life wins a clear victory over its contrary (we must remember, of course, that true to his own dialectic, he was skeptical of his own abstract schema). Roughly, man lives between complete, and therefore supernatural, primary being—dominated by what I have called the spirit of "Platonic," "religious," or "empirical" abstraction or romantic allegorization—and complete antithetical being—dominated by the spirit of artistic particularization. Because antithetical artistic particularization is toward the concrete, Yeats associated it with the body; and because the forms of abstraction are toward the general or bodiless idea, he associated them with the soul. Thus Yeats, following Blake, rejected the body's identity with the abstract idea called matter and insisted that the idea of a separable soul is more like the Lockean abstract idea of a substratum of matter than is the body. Neither the soul nor matter can be regarded as particular. Blake held that the body/soul distinction, with its association of primary matter with body, was a false, shapeless negation of that body, created by "Bacon, Newton, Locke." He therefore proposed the existence of a "spiritual body," emanating from man's creative imagination, as a contrary to soul/body.

In the system of *A Vision*, Yeats identified complete abstraction toward the general with phase 1 or the dark of the moon and the full light of the sun. The ideal of artistic particularization he identified with phase 15 or the full moon and the so-called dark of the sun. Each individual belongs by nature to some phase between these extremes on the wheel of life. Neither of the extremes can be attained. Further, should his life be long enough, the individual passes through all the phases. Thus Yeats proposed inevitable conflict in the self. Beyond this he saw historical phases, man being in conflict with his times.

The concept of contrariety at every possible level from microcosm to macrocosm is embodied in Yeats's two famous geometrical fig-

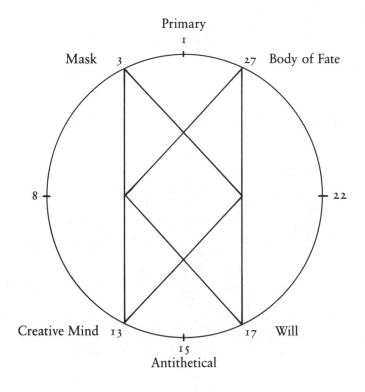

Figure 11.1

ures—the interlocking gyres or cones and the circle. The two figures can be superimposed on each other (though Yeats does not himself provide such a diagram) (see fig. 11.1).

This diagram represents the situation of a man of phase 17 (designated by the position of the will), the phase Yeats assigned himself. Or, it shows man at phase 17 or history at phase 17. Man's four faculties move around the wheel as the gyres expand and contract, Will and Mask move counterclockwise; Creative Mind and Body of Fate move clockwise. Therefore Will and Mask are always opposite, even in the supernatural phases, 1 and 15, where the gyres collapse. Mask and Will in their opposition provide the best example of the poet's creative conflict, but consideration of this point must be delayed somewhat; one illustration must here suffice. Yeats makes much of his own old age in his later poetry and of his movement beyond phase 22 into the phases dominated by "primary," abstract thought. In lines from "The Tower" he complains that at his age,

> It seems that I must bid the Muse go pack,
> Choose Plato and Plotinus for a friend
> Until imagination, ear and eye,
> Can be content with argument and deal
> In abstract things.[32]

But true to his idea that any truly full expression of reality must be antinomial, he insists on continuing to play the role appropriate to him—the poet's role—even against the natural inclination of old age, which is toward sainthood. Yeats creates personae to argue this point. Crazy Jane, an aged poetic type of the tramp, castigates the abstract thinking bishop. The monk Ribh is an "antithetical," heretical monk. All resist becoming saints, who seek to denigrate and escape the body. To turn ascetic is to cease to be a poet; in a primary age, Yeats seems to think, we need all the poets we can get.

Yeats had to insist, therefore, that as a poet Wordsworth was wrong to accept the "enforced peace" of the Immortality Ode. At the beginning of "The Tower," and at the end of "Meditations in Time of Civil War" (poems clearly part of a larger sequence), Yeats rejects the Wordsworthian acceptance, even though he acknowledges that the drift of life is in the direction Wordsworth describes:

> Never had I more
> Excited, passionate, fantastical

> Imagination, nor an ear and eye
> That more expected the impossible—
> No, not in boyhood when with rod and fly,
> Or the humbler worm, I climbed Ben Bulben's back
> And had the livelong summer day to spend.[33]

It is important to remember at this point the quotation from Yeats's *Autobiography* in which he remarked that he had been deprived of the simple-minded religion of his childhood by scientific materialism. Yeats was not speaking here about organized religion as it affected him in childhood, because he had been only superficially exposed to it. He was really lamenting the loss of an imaginative environment friendly to his own tendency toward artistic forms of particularization. He was struggling at this time without yet having developed his theory of the contrariety of poet and saint. But the war was not, as Yeats then thought, between religion and science, for both were primary. The war was between science and religion on the one hand and myth and art on the other.

Yeats's father, John Butler Yeats the painter, had got that much right, though his vehemence negated religion:

> There are two kinds of belief: the poetical and the religious. That of the poet comes when the man within has found some method or manner of thinking or arrangement of fact (such as is only possible in dreams) by which to express and embody an absolute freedom, such that his whole inner and outer self can expand in full satisfaction.
>
> In religious belief there is absent the consciousness of liberty. Religion is the denial of liberty. An enforced peace is set up among the warring feelings. By the help of something quite external, as for instance the fear of hell, some feelings are chained up and thrust into dungeons that some other feelings may hold sway; and all the ethical systems yet invented are a similar denial of liberty, that is why the true poet is neither moral nor religious.[34]

Yeats's own idea of the self is related to his sense of intellectual war as the principle of order in life. Each individual has potentially a personality and a character. The personality, which is "antithetical," he makes from within; the character, which is "primary," is imposed or received from without. The former is identified with poetic thought, the latter with moral and religious thought, as his father defined it. Because character implies subservience to an outer world, it is associated with the "empirical," which creates the antimyth of surrounding materiality. Personality implies the opposite—an imagination which creates, shapes, and contains the world in its own form.

When Yeats has his fictional character Michael Robartes say in *A Vision* that the world is a great egg which is perpetually turning itself inside out without cracking its shell (an image of the gyres),[35] he is making a myth implying the existence of contrary modes of constructing reality. Heraclitus expressed the same attitude gnomically when he said, "Homer was wrong in saying: 'Would that strife might perish from among gods and men!' he did not see that he was praying for the destruction of the universe; for, if his prayer were heard, all things would pass away."[36]

3. ART AND MATHEMATIC FORM

I HAVE suggested that Northrop Frye's classification of mathematics among the arts and the analogy between mathematics and literature he may well have developed principally out of a study of Yeats, whose attitude toward mathematics was an ambivalence that became a prolific contrariety. Yeats's long opposition to science separated from philosophy—"the opium of the suburbs,"[37] as he called it in his 1930 diary—is well known. To the extent that he associated mathematics with the "empirical," which splits experience into subject and object, primary and secondary qualities, he opposed mathematics too. In his last prose work, the argumentative *On the Boiler*, he restated his objection:

> The mathematician Poincaré, according to Henry Adams, described space as the creation of our ancestors, meaning, I conclude, that mind splits itself into mind and space. Space was to antiquity mind's inseparable "other," coincident with objects, the table not the place it occupies. During the seventeenth century it was separated from mind and objects alike, and thought of as a nothing and yet a reality, the place not the table, with material objects separated from taste, smell, sound, from all the mathematician could not measure for its sole inhabitant, and this new matter and space men were told had preceded mind and would live after.[38]

The space of antiquity that Yeats describes here is one of identity— "mind's inseparable 'other'." It is similar to Blake's particular notion of "spaces." This is opposed to the modern Lockean view. It was the fiction constructed by "primary" man: "Nature or reality as known to poets and tramps has no moment, no impression, no perception like another, everything is unique and nothing unique is measurable." He went on to claim that no really educated man today believed in the Lockean world but that nevertheless "deductions made by those who believed in both [objective matter and the space of modern physics] dominate the world."[39] People seemed to want certainty, and mathematics with its undeniable "two and two" provided it. It was the generalizing, measuring authority of science expressed in the image of mathematics which Yeats, as "antithetical" man, opposed. The generalizing tendency, Yeats thought, had led to materialism, which had made possible in its turn the substitution "for the old humanity with its unique irreplaceable individuals something that can be chopped and measured like a piece of cheese."[40] In *Plays and Controversies*, with the same attitude, he wrote: "Somebody has said that every nation begins with poetry and ends with algebra, and passion has always refused to express itself in algebraical terms."[41] Elsewhere he wrote that man had made mathematics, but God reality.[42]

After all that, one might think that mathematics was a red flag to Yeats. In fact, his complaint against mathematics was but one side of a complicated attitude. In his epitaph poem he wrote: "Measurement began our might,"[43] and it is clear that as he became more and more interested in philosophy, he grew to admire mathematics as a self-contained symbolic system. He came to think of it as a "prolific" source for the "devouring" ideas built upon it. It came to have for him a power like that of myth, and even to be a formative source of the western tradition of art. The idea of history by which he assented to the view of nations growing and decaying in some nearly predictable order was inspired by an analogy with mathematics. It is an idea that becomes less and less acceptable to the empirical historian as it develops. Indeed, Yeats comes deliberately to falsify historical and scientific data in order to complete his geometrical history and theory of the great year with the requisite elegance.

It is upon a rather elaborate set of geometrical relations that the system of *A Vision* is based. Ostensibly an occultist explanation of reality, *A Vision* is ultimately a statement about the values and limitations of the poetic form of creation. At the beginning of *A Vision*, Yeats refers to the mathematical or "more than mathematical" structure of the *Cantos*, and *A Vision* keeps returning to geometrical forms at critical points in its treatment of all levels of existence. Yet here it is always a kind of "concrete" mathematical form that interests Yeats—a primitive or mythical form of mathematics, perhaps. Yeats's use of astrology and alchemical symbolism was probably dictated in part by his belief that both were "concrete" or particular sciences developed before mathematics had emancipated itself from its own primitive attachment to things. In primitive language and mythical thought, the idea of number is originally fused with things themselves. "The differentiation of numbers," Cassirer says, "starts like that of spatial relations, from the human body and its members," and proceeds to the designation of objects.[44] These objects are considered by the mythical thinker to be extensions of the human body itself; to the primitive mind the world itself is a human body. Pure mathematics emerges historically as a differentiating form but returns (thought of synchronically) to a fusion of difference/indifference by virtue of its systematic totality.

As long as numbers were identified with objects, there was no mathematics, in our sense of the word. Number was, as Vico might have called it, concrete and poetic. Astrology, for example, though a system of numbers, is also a system of things. It is what Cassirer has called "a kind of hybrid, a semimythical 'science' of nature."[45] It stands between pure myth and mathematics, which is free of reference. But this does not mean it opposes the difference/indifference negation, for its system is an object of belief.

To a certain extent there is an analogy to poetry. It insists on taking such outer world as there may be into its own form. Yeats's great respect for the "mathematic form" of Greek art arose from his sense that art's autonomous power of creation was analogous to that of mathematics, both arising from mythic form, and that indeed art was mythically mathematic. Yeats was fascinated with the relationship of art to mathematic proportion. This implies that though art is concrete and particular, there is something in its own mode of schematizing experience that is like abstraction, though not abstraction toward the general. The formal mathematical abstract seems joined in art with the intuitional concrete. Astrology and alchemy, the "semimythical" sciences, have always attracted poets because of their concrete abstractness, but poets—Yeats included—look foolish when they give belief to these systems. In Yeats's *A Vision* the astrological symbols, combined with his geometrical figures, act as an extended metaphor for the position of his art—formal, but formally particular. Yeats's system leads to what Frye has expressed about the relation of mathematics and literature. The power of mathematics as a self-contained symbolic form, yet one that Yeats clearly saw the limits of, suggests that what reality we can know or form for ourselves is the product of a variety of such "stylistic arrangements of experience," held together by opposition.

Yeats's system or theory or myth—whatever we should decide to call it—is not separable from its expression. It is particular, concrete, "antithetical," yet abstract. *A Vision* constantly evades reduction and forces irony on us. The Yeats whom Yeats presents in *A Vision* is a man struggling with his own reasoning power, continuously skeptical, slow to comprehend the meaning of his instructors' thought. So at times it seems as if he would attribute to mathematics with its abstract purity all the virtues of poetry. "Will some mathematician," he writes, "some day question and understand, as I cannot, and confirm all, or have I also dealt in myth?"[46] The answer in the end is the latter. Mathematics cannot confirm the insights of poetry, nor poetry those of mathematics. Every system at some point closes itself and requires its opposite. Yeats writes that in scientific and other disciplines thinkers have sensed a limit: ". . . some few, meeting the limit in their special study, even doubt if there is any common experience, doubt the possibility of science."[47] The return to sources—to myth— seems inevitable at this point. Frye remarked, as we saw, that no single language has been able to unite heaven and earth. Mathematics' pure form drives it back into itself at the crucial moment when it seems that it may swallow reality whole. In *A Vision*, Yeats comes to see that his own system—and thus poetry—arrives at the same crisis, but that this is not necessarily to be deplored.

The analogy between poetry and mathematics reaches its limit at the point where poetry opts for concreteness. Tobias Dantzig has written in *Number: The Language of Science*: "Only by using a symbolic language not yet usurped by those vague ideas of *space, time, continuity*, which have their origin in intuition and tend to obscure pure reason—only thus may we hope to build mathematics on the sound foundation of logic."[48] Even words which abstractly designate classes "have also the capacity to evoke an image."[49] Mathematics demands complete abstract freedom. Poetry, on the other hand, insists on a "mythical" attachment to the thingness of things. Should it lose this quality it would merge with mathematics or perhaps music. It would cease to have created its own reality. As it is, poetry often claims to attach itself to something called raw experience. Yet it has its own form of autonomy from raw experience, whatever that may be, and its autonomy is the very means by which it presents to us a greater sense of reality than raw experience, always formless and chaotic, can possibly contain in itself.

In his cryptic poem "The Statues," Yeats describes the abstract, even mathematical, yet concretely experiential aspect of art by reference to the convergence of the intuitional concrete and mathematical abstract in Greek sculpture. It will be helpful to follow Yeats through this difficult poem. The roots of the convergence Yeats traces to Pythagoras, the theorist of *qualitative* number (as F. A. C. Wilson has characterized him).[50] A sentence in *On the Boiler* casts light on the poem's first stanza: "There are moments when I am certain that art must once again accept those Greek proportions which carry into plastic art the Pythagorean numbers, those faces which are divine because all there is empty and measured."[51] He refers, of course, to the mathematical proportion to which Greek representations of the human body conformed. This mathematics brought into concreteness, originating in Pythagoras's mythical theory of number, causes the people of Yeats's poem to give the statues startled attention:

> Pythagoras planned it. Why did the people stare?
> His numbers, though they moved or seemed to move
> In marble or in bronze, lacked character.[52]

Number alone is purely abstract, but number embodied in the human forms of art turns into ideal particularity.

> But boys and girls, pale from imagined love
> Of solitary beds, knew what they were,
> That passion could bring character enough,
> And pressed at midnight in some public place
> Live lips upon a plummet-measured face.

The statues bring into particularity the object of desire that remains only abstract in their dreams as well as in pure mathematics.

In an essay called "The Tragic Theatre," written thirty years before "The Statues," Yeats wrote: "And when we love, if it be in the excitement of youth, do we not also, that the flood may find no stone to convulse, no wall to narrow it, exclude character or the signs of it by choosing that beauty which seems unearthly because the individual woman is lost amid the labyrinth of its lines as though life were trembling into stillness and silence, or at last folding itself away?"[53] It is as if Yeats here were trying to describe the ideal form of "antithetical" passion—a paradox, incidentally, since passion is for him always concrete and hardly ideal in the usual "Platonic" sense. Here ideal passion is the ultimate in sensuous human desire. If we examine this essay more closely, we find Yeats holding that in tragic or lyric poetry there is a tendency to destroy the domination of character, which is external and "primary" as opposed to "personality," which is "antithetical" and the form of passion and desire:

> We may not find either mood in its purity, but in mainly tragic art one distinguishes devices to exclude or lessen character, to diminish the power of that daily mood, to cheat or blind its too clear perception. If the real ["primary"] world is not altogether rejected, it is but touched here and there, and into the places we have left empty we summon rhythm, balance, pattern, images.[54]

Here, paradoxically also, those things that are clearly to be associated with mathematic form are brought into the service of heightened "antithetical" life. The "antithetical," then, would seem to be a form which includes opposites under the creative aegis of personality, while character, or the imposition of externality, suppresses or negates its opposite.

Character is "continuously present in comedy alone." The statues, we notice, have "character enough" to provide a form for passion. They have just enough of that which is externally imposed to make for reality. The statues also have "rhythm" and "balance," as well as the image of real life. I am not suggesting that character and personality represent the same opposites as rhythm and image. I am only suggesting that in art all opposites are maintained, that no opposite can be negated, and that the fundamental play of opposites in art is characterized here for Yeats by the mathematic form of the concrete image.

Pythogoras's numbers may not have been works of art, but they had a close relationship to the source of human creativity. They clung to the mythic quality of number that Dantzig says must be purged from true mathematics. However, the artist is greater than Pythagoras—as artist—because he achieves the convergence of abstract and concrete in a way that does not pretend to mathematical truth.

> No! Greater than Pythagoras, for the men
> That with a mallet or chisel modelled these
> Calculations that look but casual flesh, put down
> All Asiatic vague immensities.

The Greek artist's capacity to join number and passion repelled the vague, massive, artistically unformed abstractions of Eastern thought when they threatened Europe,

> And not the banks of oars that swam upon
> The many-headed foam at Salamis.
> Europe put off that foam when Phidias
> Gave women dreams and dreams their looking-glass.

Phidian art represented that balance of opposites which gave to the West its ideal of beauty, which is concrete and sexual, and protected Greece against cultural invasion. In what Yeats calls "Doric vigour" the Eastern extreme was neutralized. In *On the Boiler* he describes the same attempted invasion:

> Europe was not born when Greek galleys defeated the Persian hordes at Salamis, but when the Doric studios sent out those broad-backed marble statues against the multiform, vague, expressive Asiatic sea, they gave to the sexual instinct of Europe its goal, its fixed type. In the warm sea of the French and Italian Riviera I can still see it. I recall a Swedish actress standing upon some boat's edge between Portofino and Rapallo, or riding the foam upon a plank towed behind a speedboat.[55]

This modern Aphrodite is the embodiment of the sexual ideal—which is "antithetical," concrete, particular, and lunar—that Phidias gave to the West. Women became this ideal, as Wildean nature copies art.

History for Yeats is a vacillation between extremes, and in Western art this vacillation may be expressed by contrasting the art of Phidias and that of Callimachus, neither an extreme but tending in opposite directions. In both, there is the convergence with which we are concerned. No art exists without both, but there are subtle shifts of dominance. There is always a historical reaction in art against the extremism of naïve realism. In his essay "Certain Noh Plays of Japan," Yeats views the naturalistic drama of his time and seeks a more "antithetical" form, feeling that naturalism has reached an extreme, its concreteness no longer effective and its forms dying into abstractness under the pretense of concretion.[56] It is similar to a movement that had occurred long ago.

I identify the conquest of Alexander and the breakup of his kingdom, when Greek civilization, formalized and codified, loses itself in Asia, with the beginning and end of the 22nd Phase . . . he is but a part of the impulse that creates Hellenized Rome and Asia. There are everywhere statues where every muscle has been measured, every position debated, and these statues represent man with nothing more to achieve.[57]

This verges on an impossible extreme, where mathematic proportion triumphs over an art that is supposed to contain it. It is a center that cannot hold. Everything is outside, objectified. One notes that in such moments extremes meet. Naturalism can in time become as abstract as the abstract opposite it eschewed in its infancy. Yeats's description of this phase of history is particularly interesting because in phase number it corresponds to the period 1875–1927, during which time the events of stanza 4, Pearse summoning Cuchulain to his side, occurred.

Stanza 3, extremely compressed (excessively so) and gnomic, refers to the Alexandrian movement:

> One image crossed the many-headed, sat
> Under the tropic shade, grew round and slow,
> No Hamlet thin from eating flies, a fat
> Dreamer of the Middle Ages. Empty eyeballs knew
> That knowledge increases unreality, that
> Mirror on mirror mirrored is all the show.
> When gong and conch declare the hour to bless
> Grimalkin crawls to Buddha's emptiness.

Connected with this passage, as several critics have pointed out, is a passage from Yeats's *Autobiography*. Yeats is describing a portrait of William Morris:

> Its grave wide-open eyes, like the eye of some dreaming beast, remind me of the open eyes of Titian's "Ariosto," while the broad vigorous body suggests a mind that has no need of the intellect to remain sane, though it give itself to every phantasy: the dreamer of the middle ages. It is "the fool of fairy . . . wide and wild as a hill," the resolute European image that yet half-remembers Buddha's motionless meditation, and has

no trait in common with the wavering, lean image of hungry speculation, that cannot but because of certain famous Hamlets of our stage fill the mind's eye. Shakespeare himself foreshadowed a symbolic change, that is a change of the whole temperament of the world, for though he called his Hamlet "fat" and even "scant of breath," he thrust between his fingers agile rapier and dagger.[58]

The image of Morris, like that created by the historical movement of Alexandrian Greece into the East, reminds us of the "one image" which crossed the "many-headed" and underwent a change. The result of this convergence is a kind of balance between abstract and concrete, rejecting the domination of purely rational knowledge suggested by the triumph of mathematic proportion over art. The materialistic, "empirical" mind, though it claims to copy an externality, creates an enclosed world of mutually reflecting mirrors. The empty eyeballs—not the pierced eyeballs of naturalistic Roman statuary, but something between "Grecian eyes gazing at nothing,"[59] mentioned in *A Vision* and "those eyelids of China and of India, whose veiled or half-veiled eyes weary of world and vision alike"—indicate the futility of such knowledge as it has come to dominance in a primary age. Empirical or rational form, standing alone, presents such an enclosure, meets the limit, begins to "doubt the possibility of common experience."[60]

When the gong—the midnight gong like that of "All Souls' Night"—sounds, Grimalkin, the witch's cat, crawls into the emptiness of Buddha's eastern gaze. This supernatural cat, which, in his argument with T. Sturge Moore, Yeats claimed scratched John Ruskin,[61] is clearly a concrete particular creature which invades the pure abstract nothingness that Buddha projects, giving it content. If, alas, that content can scratch and hiss at us, nevertheless its imperfection gives our ideals image and body. We are not left in an abstract darkness.

The General Post Office in Dublin was the stronghold of the men who rebelled against English rule in 1916. To commemorate this ill-fated effort, of which Padraic Pearse was the leader, there now stands in the lobby a statue of the Irish mythological hero Cuchulain.

> When Pearse summoned Cuchulain to his side,
> What stalked through the Post Office? What intellect,
> What calculation, number, measurement, replied?

The question of what knowledge, what ideal Pearse summoned up is left unanswered. What appears there now through the sculptor's work is the concrete abstraction of the statue; and whatever the nothingness behind the appearance was, that which Pearse summoned can best be expressed in art, for it preserves passion and desire in the ideal.

In the last lines of "The Statues," Yeats describes the plight of Ireland, whose ancient traditions he believes link it to the golden age of Pythagoras, afloat on the sea of an objective, materialistic, and many-headed civilization. Comparing the dreams of Ireland sadly and ironically to the dreams of the pale youths of stanza 1, Yeats proceeds hopefully to suggest that the dream is worthwhile, to describe the Irish as seeking out the artistic ideal of the spiritual body. Ireland must ascend into the darkness of the decadence of a primary historical era and find the spiritual body of its desires. Cuchulain's appearance to Pearse indicates the continued possibility of such an act, rare as it may be in the present age.

> We Irish, born into that ancient sect
> But thrown upon this filthy modern tide
> And by its formless spawning fury wrecked,
> Climb to our proper dark, that we may trace
> The lineaments of a plummet-measured face.

The Asiatic sea of an earlier historical cycle was "multiform, vague, expressive," paralleling but in contrast to the rubbish of materialism which is today's formless, teeming world. This is like the turn of naturalism from realistic representation to insipid generalization. When the turn is completed, it is time to reintroduce reality and shrink from the "soulless self-reflections of man's skill," medical accuracy, or rhetorical art put to the service of material need. Yeats had rejected rhetoric years before, and he tells us in his *Autobiography* of his dislike for the rhetorical verse much praised in Ireland.[62] On the other hand, it seems to me, Yeats came to see much danger in purely *symboliste* poetry like that of the later Mallarmé, even though he surely sympathized with Mallarmé's antipositivistic attitudes. Frank Kermode, in his *Romantic Image*, has noted Yeats's awareness of the dangers of an autonomous poetic image free of discursive content, a kind of solipsistic poetry.[63] Yeats wanted always the household cat and in his H_2O a few fish.

Looking at the problem from the other side, as early as the volume called *The Rose*, we find an introductory poem calling the mystical cabalistic rose to approach, only to ask it not to approach too close; and the concluding poem of that volume explains to Ireland that the poet has not ceased to write in her behalf despite "the red-rose-bordered hem" which "trails all about the written page."[64] The rose is abstract, spiritual, a symbol of a Platonic sort of beauty. One must keep the rose in sight, but cannot give oneself up to it and still write poetry. In Yeats's later career, other more appropriate (because more mundane) images of autonomy replace the rose. One of these is mathematics.

In his epitaph poem, "Under Ben Bulben," Yeats speaks again of the earthy passion inherent in the mathematic form of Greek art—a humanization of the more strictly geometrical discipline of Egyptian forms. He calls this quality "profane perfection":

> Measurement began our might:
> Forms a stark Egyptian thought,
> Forms that gentler Phidias wrought.
> Michael Angelo left a proof
> On the Sistine Chapel roof,
> Where but half-awakened Adam
> Can disturb globe-trotting Madam
> Till her bowels are in heat,
> Proof that there's a purpose set
> Before the secret working mind:
> Profane perfection of mankind.[65]

We can for our purposes lay aside the sinister racist hints in the poem as a whole to consider the concept of art implicit in the last phrase. From the perspective of what I shall call (even though I claim that it has no perspective) raw experience, the profanity of art lies in its abstract autonomy, its mathematic form, its prideful presumption that it may yet escape from experience. From the perspective of the abstractionist its profanity lies in its attachment to things. The fact that art seems to reach out in both directions is its "profane perfection," and this sort of perfection is that which poetry envisions for man, not the perfection of Buddha's nothingness, but of cultural desire and achievement. This fact leads to Yeats's view of the artist, who by defining his own activity condemns himself to keeping one foot always in what the saint insists is the fallen world.

The saint, who constantly seeks, according to Yeats, the mystical bodily annihilation of complete nothingness (the perfection of the abstract), seeks also to divest himself of the world and thus of the image, which is the poet's life. A creature of phase 27, according to *A Vision*, the saint finds that

> His joy is to be nothing, to do nothing, to think nothing; but to permit the total life, expressed in its humanity, to flow in upon him and to express itself through his acts and thoughts. He is not identical with it, he is not absorbed in it, for if he were he would not know that he is nothing, that he no longer even possesses his own body, that he must renounce even his desire for his own salvation, and that this total life is in love with his nothingness.[66]

The poet, of course, must back away from this ideal, for approach to it gravely threatens the integrity of his symbolic form. In the poem "Vacillation," Yeats expresses the difference between himself and the mystical philosopher Von Hügel:

> Homer is my example and his unchristened heart.
> . . . .
> So get you gone, Von Hügel, though with blessings on
> your head.[67]

He recognizes the necessary contrariety of saint and poet.

Beyond sainthood, between it and the ultimate supernatural in Yeats's system, is phase 28, the phase of the fool, the last human incarnation. Again, this is not the poet's phase:

> At his worst his hands and feet and eyes, his will and his feelings, obey obscure subconscious fantasies, while at his best he would know all wisdom if he could know anything. The physical world suggests to his mind pictures and events that have no relation to his needs, or even to his desires; his thoughts are an aimless reverie; his acts are aimless like his thoughts; and it is in this aimlessness that he finds his joy.[68]

Obviously if the poet cannot be the saint, he cannot be the fool. This idea is stated elsewhere by means of a figure familiar to us:

> If it be true that God is a circle whose centre is everywhere, the saint goes to the centre, the poet and artist to the ring where everything comes round again. The poet must not seek

for what is still and fixed, for that has no life for him; and if he did, his style would become cold and monotonous, and his sense of beauty faint and sickly . . . but be content to find his pleasure in all that is for ever passing away that it may come again . . . in momentary heroic passion, in whatever is most fleeting, most impassioned, as it were, for its own perfection, most eager to return in its own glory.[69]

The figure of circumference and center declares the poet always intent on making and containing life in his forms, while the saint gives himself to the all-powerful deity who surrounds him. But the poet's declaration is also an acceptance of the cyclicity of things, of living it all again, of destruction such as that observed by the sages on Mt. Meru.[70] For Yeats, poetry must seek its profane perfection at neither mathematic nor material extreme, but where the abstracting impulse is always fused with the particularizing imagination. Nor may the poet be the saint, who seeks a freedom from the image ultimately more radical than that of mathematics.

Yeats's distinction between poet and saint separates literature, which is by definition secularly symbolic in the romantic sense I described in chapter 1, from religious utterance and thought. By the analogy between poetry and mathematics, Yeats indicates the creative nature of all symbolic forms—and their variety.

4. A Vision

A Vision is Yeats's most deliberate expression of his concept of the symbolic. From its publication it has been perplexing to readers and commentators. Perhaps the best general statement about it remains Cleanth Brooks's review of it in 1937. Calling it "one of the most remarkable books of the last hundred years," Brooks argues that it is also "the most ambitious attempt made by any poet of our time to set up a 'myth'."[71] The question here is what is meant by a myth. Is it something to which one gives allegiance, the love that is belief, as Yeats remarks? Or has the word "belief" become the property of scientific verification? If belief cannot be given to Yeats's myth, what is its value? Much ink was spilled over this question during the period of the New Criticism. Brooks goes on to claim the usefulness to Yeats of his myth:

The system, to put it concisely, allows Yeats to see the world as a great drama, predictable in its larger aspects (so that the poet is not lost in a welter of confusion), but in a pattern which allows for the complexity of experience and the apparent contradictions of experience (so that the poet is not tempted to oversimplify).[72]

Brooks walks a narrow line between claiming the myth to be an imitation of reality and claiming it to be a purely autonomous creation according to the most extreme art-for-art's-sake tenets. Brooks says, "The system *allows* Yeats to see the world as a great drama" (my italics), as if it may or may not really be one and Yeats, by creating a fiction, can *pretend* that it is. The position verges upon I. A. Richards's famous doctrine of poetry as pseudo-statement[73] and seems to invite a pragmatic or therapeutic view. John Unterecker says, "Yeats's system gave him *what he needed*: a technique,"[74] (my italics) which seems to isolate technique from any formal involvement with truth. R. P. Blackmur says, "Magic . . . for Yeats . . . makes a connection between the poem and its subject matter and provides an *adequate mechanics* of meaning and value,"[75] (my italics) where the idea of adequacy seems to force upon the myth the old split of content and form. These quotations all seem to me not quite right. Their weakness lies in the residue of positivism and behaviorism that early invaded the New Criticism through the psychologistic works of I. A. Richards and from which even in its heyday it never quite recovered.

Perhaps the problem can be said to lie in the word "myth" as Brooks uses it. In spite of himself, I think, he uses the term to denote a sort of verbal structure that is locatable with reference to an external meaning which can be objectified by a text or pointed *to* by it. The language goes back to T. S. Eliot's essays on the metaphysical poets and Blake,[76] where Eliot worries the problem of the purely individual mythology. The concept of myth as a symbolic form or mode of thinking is absent, and myth is hardened into some external religious doctrine or system of verifiable hypotheses—in either case a sort of objectification according to "religious" or "empirical" allegory.

But *A Vision* does not "set up" a myth in this alien objective sense. Instead, it attempts to set up a grammar of the poetic symbolic form of creation. As such it does not describe an externalized object or content. Just as there is no externalized object "mathematics" but instead a subject of study or a circumferential form that makes a mathematical world, so there is no object poetry, only the verbal circumferential form by which man creates a poetic world. Confusion of object and subject in this sense (not the old epistemological sense employed by Coleridge et al.) raises the problem of belief in its most vicious form. One does not believe or disbelieve in a form. One thinks *in* it, according it the category of belief-disbelief, as that category defines itself in that form. Belief in poetry is not belief as projected in the "allegoric" modes. Eliot's essays surely in the end subsume poetic belief under the "religious." Richards's work subsumes it under the "empirical."

There is no question that each symbolic form leads one in a certain direction toward the creation of certain sorts of verbal or other structures. *A Vision* attempts in a poetic way to present a vision of the poetic form. It is a grammar of that form, but a curious grammar, that operates according to the form of its chosen subject.[77] In this sense, it can be said to be reflexive, but it is more explicitly reflexive than so many works said to be metapoetic by contemporary critics. (Indeed, it should be clear from these remarks that *all* poetic works must by definition be metapoetic and that much contemporary critical commentary which pretends to discover metapoetic themes is really only making, over and over again, the assertion that what the critic has before him belongs to the poetic form.)

The extraordinary difficulty of *A Vision*, in addition to its tricky diagrams and curious tone of spoofery, is that what it sets forth so explicitly as a subject is also its own symbolic form. There is, then, no final discursive resting place that is pointed *to*, even though it sometimes seems that there ought to be. It does not adopt the form of the "Platonic," "religious," or "empirical," though its drama makes its fictive author flirt with these forms.

Cecil Salkeld tried to struggle with the critical problem this raised in a review of the book but ended by pointing out how ill-equipped criticism was to deal with it. For Salkeld, *A Vision* was "beyond criticism" because

> a. There is no critical terminology wherewith to treat of a technical work having no border-line between metaphysics, astrology, history, spiritualism, "school" philosophy, poetry, symbolism, geometry (conic sections), and a great deal of humour (an unfortunate man whose Guardian Angel is jealous of his sweetheart is a case in point). b. Symbol and Dogma are both modes that invalidate analysis. This whole section [The Great Wheel] might be termed Dogmatic Symbolism and, as such, either personally valid or invalid *in toto*. In no case can

the original and arbitrary symbol be questioned since we are at no time on common or verifiable ground.[78]

A Vision is not a "technical work," and if "symbol" invalidates analysis then critics will have to close up shop or perform some other act than analysis—at least, the kind of analysis that purports to produce *the meaning*. (I shall have more to say about this matter in the next chapter.) One reason for Salkeld's trouble was the absence at the time of any recognition that works like *A Vision* had been produced before. The genre was brought to our attention by Northrop Frye, who calls such works "anatomies" and cleverly includes his own book in the genre he is describing, thereby inviting the same speculation about his work.

The central quality of the form, says Frye, is "its vision of the world in terms of a single intellectual pattern."[79] This vision takes shape by bringing together a variety of familiar literary mannerisms. There is a "loose-jointed narrative," reliance on humorous observation, and the play of intellectual fancy, the expression of exuberance through intellect by the use of erudition either assertively or ironically, dialogue or colloquy in which the interest is conflict of ideas, and verse interludes. For Frye, the most complete anatomy moves constantly toward the encyclopedic work which contains all genres—novel, confession, romance, etc. Observing Burton's *Anatomy of Melancholy*, Frye notes within it a utopia, a marvelous journey, ironic use of erudition, and satire on the *philosophus gloriosus*, all brought together as a vision of everything in terms of the idea of melancholy.

A Vision certainly takes similar form or similar various forms. It is thus not quite the eccentric document it has frequently been made to appear. Such a work is of the greatest interest to us not only because it stretches toward a containment of all literary genres and conventions but also because its "single intellectual pattern" is that of the symbolic. For that reason, it has distinct affinity with Carlyle's *Sartor Resartus* and Frye's *Anatomy*, both of which deal with the same issue. *A Vision* contains a meditation, a loose-jointed narrative of fantastic events with suggestions of quests, and a satiric narrative in which the characters represent various attitudes; it builds up masses of strange erudition, punctuates them with poems, and perceives human personality, the after-life, and all history in terms of a single pattern. Originally written as a dialogue, the usual shorter form of the Menippean satire according to Frye, it revives some aspects of this form in a letter from the brother of one of the characters of the narrative, criticizing the author, and in the dialogue form of one of the poems. Finally, as might be expected of a twentieth-century anatomy, its intellectual pattern is made immensely complicated by invoking irony. However, the irony it invokes is not just *au courant* but dictated by its subject—poetic symbolism, which, as I have already suggested, always has an ironic relation to discourse and thus to us when we would interpret.

A *Vision* begins with the section called "A Packet for Ezra Pound," which is itself divided into three parts: "Rapallo," "Introduction to *A Vision*," and "To Ezra Pound." "Rapallo" is a piece of meditative prose of five pages written after the five books of *A Vision* proper were completed. Its function is to establish the mood of the main character of *A Vision*—Yeats himself as he looks back over what the reader is yet to move through. Thus the book takes a circular form consistent with one of its major symbols. "Rapallo" is a kind of coda to the dramatic experience which Yeats has just passed through. The tone is one of achieved detachment earned by the experience, which includes (indeed is) the experience of making the book.

Yeats proceeds to discuss Pound's *Cantos* (twenty-seven had been published at that time). He has found the governing principle of the work difficult to grasp. As he describes the poem's "mathematical" structure, it becomes clear that mention of *The Cantos* has something to do with his own endeavors. *The Cantos* seems to him a vast effort to speak in myth. It will contain a descent to Hades and an Ovidean metamorphosis. It will be a poem "in which there is nothing that can be taken out and reasoned over, nothing that is not part of the poem itself."[80] Pound employed a mathematical analogy in describing the poem to Yeats; it will have "mathematic" self-containment. The meditation prepares us for the geometrical gyres and cones, wheels and numbers of *A Vision* itself. Yeats also foreshadows his own role in his own book by casting himself as someone who wishes to understand but has some difficulty capturing and learning to read the language of poetry. The meditation is a fitting introduction to his own grammar of poetic symbolism.

In "Introduction to *A Vision*," one of the most important parts of the book, Yeats reveals what he had kept hidden in the first edition of 1925—the source of the system in his wife's automatic speech and writing. Here he extends and makes more significant the role his own character plays in the book. He makes this character a child of his age—though an antithetical one—skeptical yet desirous of revelation. His capabilities for imaginative thought are constricted by the modern intellectual condition. His first experience with the instructors points this up, for he does not grasp their intent:

> On the afternoon of October 24th, 1917, four days after my marriage, my wife surprised me by attempting automatic writing. What came in disjointed sentences, in almost illegible writing, was so exciting, sometimes so profound, that I persuaded her to give an hour or two day after day to the unknown writer, and after some half-dozen such hours offered to spend what remained of life explaining and piecing together those scattered sentences. "No," was the answer, "we have come to give you metaphors for poetry."[81]

Central to the concept of the poetic form of thought that the instructors had come to communicate was the notion of conflict that we have already examined: "I had made [in *Per Amica Silentia Lunae*] a distinction between the perfection that is from man's combat with himself and that which is from a combat with circumstance, and upon this simple distinction he [the instructor] built up an elaborate classification of men according to their more or less complete expression of one type or the other."[82] True to the notion of inevitable—indeed desirable—conflict, which the poetic ordering always creates, Yeats remarks of the instructors:

> It was part of their purpose to affirm that all the gains of man came from conflict with the opposite of his true being. Was communication itself such a conflict? One said, as though it rested with me to decide what part I should play in their dream, "Remember we will deceive you if we can."[83]

The instructors proceeded to treat human personality, the afterlife, and history in terms of their symbols. Yeats declared the system strange and unknown to both his wife and himself, but in the "expository" books of *A Vision* he gives examples of traditional usage of gyres and wheels or their equivalents. The strangeness asserted at the outset must, therefore, be considered part of the dramatic situation in which Yeats casts himself as typically out of touch with traditional poetic language—"metaphors for poetry"—which the instructors said were their subject. It is important to remember their insistence that they were not conveying a doctrine. That the renewal of poetic

symbolism should come through occult experience is consistent with
the curious nineteenth-century fact that such traditions had died out
in criticism to a great extent and were being preserved in an impure
state by those who appeared to be charlatans.

The introduction is full of an almost slapstick satire on Yeats's
problems with his instructors and, indeed, the instructors' frustration
at having to deal with Yeats:

> A chance word spoken before she fell asleep would sometimes
> start a dream that broke in upon the communications, as if
> from below, to trouble or overwhelm, as when she dreamed
> she was a cat lapping milk or a cat curled up and asleep and
> therefore dumb. The cat returned night after night, and once
> when I tried to drive it away by making the sound one makes
> when playing at being a dog to amuse a child, she awoke
> trembling, and the shock was so violent that I never dared re-
> peat it.[84]

Once the instructors put Mrs. Yeats to sleep sitting down and another time in a restaurant, because they thought from the conversation that the Yeatses were in a garden.

During the instruction, Yeats was constantly criticized for asking
"vague or confused questions,"[85] and one instructor voiced this fear:
"'I am always afraid,' he said in apology, 'that when not at our best
we may accept from you false reasoning.'"[86] And Yeats was aware of
his own limitations: "A Frustrator doubtless played upon my weakness when he described a geometrical model of the soul's state after
death which could be turned upon a lathe."[87] This allusion to Plato is
at the center of the situation. As I read it, Yeats casts himself as by
temperament a Platonist who, affected nevertheless by modern materialism (so that he wishes to see things in solid terms), desires knowledge of things-in-themselves. The instructors, however, deny that this
knowledge is possible, and the frustrators play on his weakness by
delusively closing the gap between mathematic and poetic form and
pretending one can produce a concretion from an abstraction. But
such an object—worked on a lathe—would only be "allegoric."
Yeats's own stance is neither Platonic nor Kantian but Yeatsian and
poetic, though he allies himself in a somewhat curious way with the
Platonists in the following remark: "If Kant is right the antinomy
is in our method of reasoning; but if the Platonists are right may
one not think that the antinomy is itself 'constitutive,' and that the

consciousness by which we know ourselves and exist is itself irrational?"[88] This raising of the irrational to the principle of reality is hardly Platonic, and the claim for antinomies as in fact constitutive is not Kantian. In Kant the antinomies are a product of the merely regulative ideas of the reason, driven to impossible contradiction. For Yeats the contradiction itself is truth, as contrariety is the form of truth.

Concluding this section of *A Vision*, Yeats tentatively identifies his instructors with the muses and argues that his symbols are not outward-pointing designators but "stylistic arrangements of experience"—media for literary creation rather than allegoric representation. This is the reason that Yeats remains, as poets in the end do, Ptolemaic in the face of scientific evidence: The language of poetry is man-centered, humanistic, thus earth-centered:

> . . . because of our modern discovery that the equinox shifts its ground more rapidly than Ptolemy believed, one must, someone says, invent a new symbolic scheme. No, a thousand times no; I insist that the equinox does shift a degree in a hundred years; anything else would lead to confusion.[89]

This passage is laced with a certain ironic humor, but in the end the insistence on independence from scientific verification is a defense of poetic creation and thus even a moral defense against "primary" domination.

The end of such myth-making is the possible achievement in a single thought of both reality and justice, that is, a symbolization that makes an identity of these two things rather than a difference, as, say, reality and law are separated. In a key passage Yeats writes:

> Some will ask whether I believe in the actual existence of my circuits of sun and moon. Those that include, now all recorded time in one circuit, now what Blake called "the pulsaters [*sic*] of an artery,"[90] are plainly symbolical, but what of those that fixed like a butterfly upon a pin, to our central date, the first day of our Era divide actual history into periods of equal length? To such a question I can but answer that if sometimes, overwhelmed by miracle as all men must be when in the midst of it, I have taken such periods literally, my reason has soon recovered; and now that the system stands out clearly in my imagination I regard them as stylistic arrange-

ments of experience comparable to the cubes in the drawing of Wyndham Lewis and to the ovoids in the sculpture of Brancusi. They have helped me to hold in a single thought reality and justice.[91]

This passage separates "empirical" belief from poetry and myth, though it does not denigrate such belief. It separates "religious" belief from poetry and myth, though it does not denigrate such belief. It sees the system as a creation and identifies that with the symbolic. It sees experience cast into the pure forms of that symbolism, resulting in an important holding together.

After the letter to Ezra Pound, there comes the wild satiric episode which provides an alternate, or shall we say contrary, source for the system. The story, narrated by a character named John Duddon, centers upon Michael Robartes's finding the only copy of a book published in 1594 in Cracow by a certain Giraldus. It was being used to prop up a bad bed leg in his mistress's room and was "very dilapidated," the middle pages having been torn out to light the fire.[92] This book is a Yeatsian version of the traditional lost book, but though Yeats tells Pound that he is sending him a book that will "proclaim a new divinity," the book is a profane and not a sacred book, as all poetic books must be. Robartes seeks to recapture the content of the crucial lost middle pages by scholarship but fails. In misery, he considers pilgrimage and prayer, but in the end rejects Jesus as belonging to "order and reason."[93] On the day following, as if the rejection were a sign of Robartes's preparation for poetic knowledge, an old Arab appears at his door and takes up explanation where Robartes's copy of the *Speculum* was defective, connecting the whole system to the doctrines of his tribal sect, the Judwalis or Diagrammatists.

In *A Vision* we learn (through a letter to Yeats from the character John Aherne) that the bulk of *A Vision* itself is Yeats's effort to record in orderly form the words of Robartes taken down by his pupils as Robartes had them from the old Arab. John Aherne remarks to Yeats that he is not surprised that Yeats was able to find "what was lost in the *Speculum* or survives in the inaccessible encampments of the Judwalis." He suggests that Yeats's experience may well have been a "process of remembering,"[94] reminding Yeats that Plato regarded memory as constituting a relation to the timeless. In these remarks hints at both alleged sources of *A Vision* are present.

The whole strange story plays with the ideas of lost truth, a fall, and timeless wisdom. The lost book, which is the grammar of poetic symbolism, is alleged to be (perhaps) timelessly present to the appropriate imagination, who in this case is the archetypal "antithetical" man Michael Robartes. His oracular pronouncements are strangely paradoxical and, in their poetic form, which is their only form, just out of reach of the "primary" Aherne brothers, who will therefore set about *interpreting* them and reduce them to a closed orthodoxy. The conclusion of John Aherne's letter is a parody of scholarly behavior leading in this direction.

We must read the five books of *A Vision* proper in the light of these oblique conflicting introductions, which help to give contrarious form to a text that will claim such form for all experience that is submitted to it. Whatever we want to call it—the literary, the literal, the mythic, the poetic, the symbolic—the form with which Yeats is concerned is in Yeats's mind "antinomial" in the very same way that any metaphor is an identity creatively antithetical to difference/indifference. The poet's resolution of the antinomy is to maintain contrariety as the encompassing design of experience itself.

> Philosophers have tried to deny the antinomy and give a complete account of existence either as a unity (as in the case of Spinoza or Hegel) or as a plurality (as in the case of Leibniz) but the antinomy is there and can be represented only by a myth.[95]

Myth, then, is not a rudimentary form that is surpassed by reflection, but for Yeats the fundamental form of thought, "antithetical" to its "devouring" outgrowths. The frustration of the character Yeats in *A Vision*, rather like the frustration of Carlyle's editor in *Sartor Resartus*, is that of someone who has been imposed on to believe that a final rational solution is possible. The book itself says to us that it is not possible, not even desirable, since such a solution would carry us away from our own being.

A Vision is therefore an infinite regress of contraries from the conflicting versions of its origin to the creation of conflict at all levels of life and history to the opposition of the world of the living and the world of the dead. Whenever resolution appears imminent a new contrary is generated. Yeats comes to learn at the close of *A Vision* that as a poet he no longer desires the closure he has sought and that the poet thrives on antinomies:

> Day after day I have sat in my chair turning a symbol over in my mind, exploring all its details, defining and again defining its elements, testing my convictions and those of others by its

unity, attempting to substitute particulars for an abstraction like that of algebra.[96]

He feels one conviction give way to another at an age when "the mind should be rigid." Then:

> I draw myself up into the symbol and it seems as if I should know all if I could but banish such memories and find everything in the symbol.
>   But nothing comes—though this moment was to reward me for all my toil.[97]

He thinks that something would have to come to him in the days when he meditated under the direction of the Cabalists. But to have sought for that sort of external revelation *through* the symbol is to relax back into the notion of the "miraculous" symbol, thence to the romantic allegoric, and abdicate the poet's role. To have imagined that any form alone can swallow the world whole is an arrogance—the same arrogance as that of "Huxley, Tyndall, Bastien-Lepage":

> Then I understand. I have already said all that can be said. The particulars are the work of the *thirteenth sphere* or cycle, which is in every man and called by every man his freedom. Doubtless, for it can do all things and knows all things, it knows what it will do with its own freedom but it has kept the secret.[98]

When the poet seeks unpoetic resolution nothing comes. The system asserts the power of metaphor, as the instructors promised.

In the epilogue poem "All Souls' Night" the poet is content, even ecstatic in his own meditation, a radical creation, bound, it is true, by its own symbolic form and from the point of view of the "religious," therefore, wound in death like a mummy, but also free:

> Such thought—such thought have I that hold it tight
> Till meditation master all its parts,
> Nothing can stay my glance
> Until that glance run in the world's despite
> To where the damned have howled away their hearts,
> And where the blessed dance;
> Such thought, that in it bound

> I need no other thing,
> Wound in mind's wandering
> As mummies in the mummy-cloth are wound.[99]

The antinomies of death and life here in the image of the poetic as wound in mummy-cloth are deliberately not resolved in indifference but are identified in the poem. To the "religious" this is death. To the "empiricist" it is madness. To the poet it is life and sanity, though the poet is able to recognize and accept the opposite as well and recognizes the nature of the enclosure of his openness. It is he, after all, who has contained in his book two explanations of its genesis—the "empirical" one having to do with Mrs. Yeats and the mythic one having to do with Michael Robartes. This confirms the poet's mythic tendency toward total form including by necessity an opposite.

5. THE MASK

YEATS'S THOUGHT, therefore, glorifies its own radical creativity, but it leads us not to regard that creativity as everything. Indeed, Yeats sees the poet as in certain ways struggling tragically against the encroachments of the powerful primary world. The image of poetic heroism is not in the crossing of a threshold to discover truth but in the power to assert, as Cuchulain does: "I make the truth,"[100] or in Yeats's own constant effort to create anew: "Myself I must remake";[101] or finally the vow to contain the opposite, not to negate it.

The idea of the Mask in Yeats, so important from very early in his career, embodies this emphasis on the poet as creator or Blakean "prolific." The Mask is derived from drama and is intimately associated, as is drama, with conflict.

> If we cannot imagine ourselves as different from what we are
> and assume the second self, we cannot impose a discipline
> upon ourselves, though we may accept one from others. Active virtue as distinguished from the passive acceptance of a
> current code is therefore theatrical, consciously dramatic, the
> wearing of a mask.[102]

"Primary" man should flee his Mask, because it is the external code that he wears. "Antithetical" man should seek to make a mask; it must be a personal one, not externally imposed. The concept expresses the distinction between character and personality, passive and active:

When I wish for some general idea which will describe the
Great Wheel as an individual life I go to the *Commedia dell'*
Arte or improvised drama of Italy. The stage-manager, or
Daimon, offers his actor an inherited scenario, the *Body of*
Fate, and a *Mask* or rôle as unlike as possible to his natural
ego or *Will*, and leaves him to improvise through his *Creative*
Mind the dialogue and details of the plot. He must discover or
reveal a being which only exists with extreme effort, when his
muscles are as it were all taut and all his energies active.[103]

This, Yeats says, is "antithetical" man. The will of "primary" man is
weak and cannot create a role.

For Yeats it follows that in modern life it is the poet who can be
truly heroic—identifying, I think, with the Blakean "reprobate"—by
taking the "antithetical" stance in the face of the massive power of
"primary" or romantically allegoric forms. From the poet's point of
view—in the end—I believe that these allegoric forms must also be
regarded as creative; but they do not recognize their creativity, pre-
ferring to create the antimyth that they *explain* or *describe* or *seek*
out some upper, lower, or outer world. Thus they require "antithetical" redemption from their imprisonment in the externality they
have created. The poetic assertion provides this opposite:

> I mock Plotinus' thought
> And cry in Plato's teeth,
> Death and life were not
> Till man made up the whole,
> Made lock, stock, and barrel
> Out of his bitter soul,
> Aye, sun and moon and stars, all,
> And further add to that
> That, being dead, we rise,
> Dream and so create
> Translunar Paradise.[104]

There is a certain bravado in this, of course, since the forms that
dominate our lives from birth tell us by negation that it is not so. All
the more need for such a voice.

12

Conclusions

In an effort to clarify a role for criticism among the liberal arts and sciences, I now return to the distinction between myth and antimyth and the Blakean principles with which this book began. On the basis of these principles I shall attempt to distinguish a philosophy of the litarary symbolic from a variety of structuralist, phenomenological, and poststructuralist positions. The conclusions reached I identify with the tradition of the symbolic as I have constructed it in a selection of its many transformations—from the romantic distinction between symbolism and allegory through to a true contrary opposing "miraculous" symbol/allegory to "secular" symbolic.

1. DIALECTIC OF FICTIVE CULTURAL FORMS

A SIMILARITY among differences between structuralist and phenomenological positions is the refusal of both to make any sort of fundamental distinction—or sometimes even practical distinction—between kinds of language, as was made by, say, Wheelwright or some theorists of the American New Criticism. Yet on the nature of this one undifferentiated form of language, phenomenologists and structuralists generally disagree. The rejection of such distinctions is also made by certain critics who belong to neither group. For example, E. D. Hirsch, Jr.:

> No literary theorist from Coleridge to the present has succeeded in formulating a viable distinction between the nature of ordinary written speech and the nature of literary written speech. . . . I believe the distinction can never be successfully formulated, and the futility of attempting the distinction will come to be generally recognized.[1]

Not himself a structuralist, and in certain ways harshly critical of them, Hirsch is nevertheless with the structuralists on this point, for his model of discourse is that of symbolic logic. He treats all writing in its terms and thus tends toward a romantically allegoric concept of all verbal structures. Phenomenologists tend to approach the matter from a quite different direction, reasserting variations of the "miraculous" concept of the symbol.

My design is, of course, to argue for the concept of the poem as "secular" symbolic form, identifying language fundamentally with poetry, but recognizing a progression of antimythical emanations from it. In this, I *seem* to be like the phenomenologists, but my conception of language as creative, as I shall try to show, differs from their concept of all language as hermeneutic. At the same time, I am not prepared to claim any absolute fissure between poetic language and any such language as may be set up in opposition to it. In this, I seem to be like Hirsch, the symbolic logicians, and the structuralists. However, my model of language is not the mathematical one, nor is my normative description of it a term such as "logical discourse." As we have seen, Frye has speculated about the relation of poetry to mathematics, and Yeats before him mused on mathematic form as myth. I propose a linguistic continuum that runs from a mythic pole outward through the fictive zones that some philosophers have tried to call "ordinary" language (if it exists) and Wheelwright's "steno language" to mathematical symbolism, which marks the outer limit of symbolic creativity (fig. 12.1). Blake's identification of centers with circumferences applies here. The mythic center is actually a container of all the possibilities implicit in the totality, becoming a circumference, as my diagram (fig. 12.1) attempts to show, the circle turning inside out in the way that Frye's "center" of literality merges with circumferential anagogy in any particular work. There can finally be no lines measuring off these zones, so my diagram is misleading; but unlike Hirsch, I do not believe that because we cannot logically formulate or "measure" where one mode ceases and another begins, we should not make fictive distinctions helpful to our understanding. The principle is a contrary to one requiring a choice between indifference and difference. It states that any verbal structure has *identity*. It will take this chapter to indicate just what I mean by the term.

It should be clear that this notion of identity does not offer the mythic as a necessarily historical origin, as does Vico and as Blake seems to do (though, I think, does not have to do). But it does deny as fundamental the assumptions about language upon which behav-

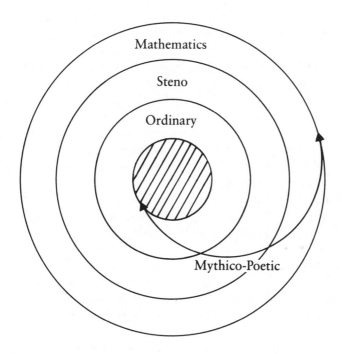

Figure 12.1

ioral social science has based its methodologies. With its quantitative methods, behavioral social science makes mathematics the origin, building abstract behavioral models outward from it. In such a system there is declared to be no containing circumference, all language pointing outward, though one can say, at a higher level, that quantitative social science ends up trying to contain human behavior in a mathematic form. Structuralism, which claims to be a "human" science, or the basis of such a science, is in the end not much different in this matter.

If we are to make the effort as critics to acknowledge (since adoption is finally impossible) the point of view of the poem, we can hardly declare tropes to be deviations from some norm, since they have as much right as anything else to be declared the norm. Metaphor is hardly a transgressive activity, as in some of the headier structuralist flights, unless we are perversely to identify transgression with normality. The idea of discourse that eliminates all tropes from a norm is really an ideal of pure mathematic abstraction.

When the mathematical ideal negates the poetic the result is twofold: (1) All language is regarded as "outward" pointing; it is either transparently mimetic or arbitrarily significatory (allegorical) of a "primary" mathematized universe, that is, it goes to a center and stays there; (2) tropes are regarded as merely devices to lend vividness to discourse or to entertain, or figures to be allegorically interpreted, and poetry becomes decorated outward-pointing language. The idea of such purification toward the bare bones of logic is derived from a positivistic assumption about how the mind works that from the poetic point of view turns things inside out: Rather than computers being regarded as copies of mind, it is implied that the mind is a copy of a computer. Under these conditions "ordinary language" becomes simply a term for how language deviates from a mathematical norm. The argument that there is no ordinary language has been cleverly made by Stanley Fish, who attacks the distinction between ordinary and literary language by declaring the nonexistence of both.[2] Ordinary language seems to me a misleading fiction useless to criticism as long as it is employed to declare poetry as in some way deviant from it. Fish argues that the distinction has forced criticism to claim that poetry is either more than language ("message plus"), which leads to a concept of decorative form, or less than language ("message minus"), which eliminates content and eventuates in theories of "pure poetry." The plus and minus characterizations are simplistic, but in any case Fish's analysis does not

Table 12.1. Dialectic of fictive cultural forms

	Myth	*Antimyth*
Mode:	Sympathy	Analysis
Direction:	Particularity	General or universal law
Movement:	To a circumference	To a center
End:	Individual	Abstract Unity
Paradox:	The particular encompasses the whole	None
Anti-paradox:	None	The particular is inside the aggregate whole
Contrary:	Identity	Difference/Indifference

focus on the issue that is fundamental in this book. That issue is whether we can give to language an expansive, creative character or only an imitative and/or significatory one, whether it is only a dead center, and not a center that is always becoming a circumference.

With that said, I want to locate the arts, history, and criticism as cultural forms of symbolic in their appropriate dialectical positions on a continuum. My dialectic, like Yeats's, does not provide for Hegelian synthesis, but for the constantly renewed conflict of Heraclitus; the notion of identity requires conflict as well as continuum when it is rationally formulated. The dialectic is that of myth and antimyth. Table 12.1 organizes this opposition.

The side of myth is the side of a paradox harbored by the word "identity." Identity is a harbor of individuality *and* relationship. One has an identity, and one can be identical *with* something. A tribe of primitive people can claim that they are crocodiles but do not make the error of jumping in the river that flows by their huts and cavorting with those creatures with which they have established identity. The side of antimyth eschews paradox (as it eschews the identity present in a trope) and abstracts toward general law. In both cases, I shall claim (because I deliberately seek to acknowledge myth's point of view) that what we have are fictions, not untruths, but creations. I say this, even as (indeed, because) I recognize that from antimyth's point of view the antimythic creation is not creation but a correspondence with an external reality. In the end, however, we shall have to say that this too is a fiction—a making.

Let us now imagine these contraries as two extremes or limits. At the antimythical pole we have a vision of the world as external to us, the world of nature and her mathematical laws as object to our subject. Our own bodies are *outside* us, objectified like the world and treatable wholly in terms of behavioristic assumptions. We define ourselves as natural or at least social objects. This is, of course, a myth itself, though what I have chosen, to avoid equivocation, to call a fiction. Antimyth accepts the fiction that the thing to be demythologized is external, in the sense of being an object to a subject. Part of the fiction is that the particular is determined *by* and *in* the world. Extended into religion it is the fiction of man in relation to a sky god, an alien god, or a moral law, external to, usually above, him.

As a limit, antimyth represents the fiction of complete division into primary externality and secondary internality and the consequent privileging of the external. The explicit invention of the division in the history of science, which is usually pushed back to Galileo, is denied by the historian of science Gerald Holton to have been a "wanton act of dehumanization." Rather, he claims it to have been a "strategic decision to reach a worthy human goal, that of understanding nature (including, ultimately, man's nature) in a new way."[3] This is certainly true, but as a pole or limit, it is precisely a dehumanization in that it externalizes man from himself by making man (or at least as much of man as can be gotten hold of in that form) a nature. We might call the notion of antimyth a "category," to use Kantian language, but it would be better to say that it is a pure form (indeed, *the* pure form) of scientific thought. It is not the form of the *process* of scientific thought. It is only a normative concept and as such readily illustrates how normative concepts taken as absolutes can spread over the whole range of a subject and corrupt our understanding of it. The *process* of science is an emergence from myth into antimythical form. Antimyth as a concept contains only "normal science" in Thomas Kuhn's sense or "public science" (S₂) in Holton's.[4]

Both Kuhn and Holton attempt to expand our notions of the process of science by their ideas of paradigms and themata respectively. Holton treats themata as preconceptions in scientific activity that are not verifiable or falsifiable. He treats them as a third (really a primordial) dimension of science in addition to the dimension of the empirical and phenomenal and the dimension of the heuristic-analytic. These latter two alone compose what he calls "public science" or S₂. What is lacking there is part of the process: ". . . the dimension of fundamental presuppositions, notions, terms, methodological judgments, and decisions . . . which are themselves neither directly evolved from, nor resolvable into, objective observation on the one hand, or logical, mathematical, and other formal analytical ratiocination on the other hand."[5] I take it that themata are those fictive acts out of which scientific theories emerge in the process we think of as doing science. "Public science" cannot explain the role of these themata. There is a relation between a public science and the time in which it is practiced that evades scientific explanation. Holton remarks of contemporary science's world: ". . . it is now a profoundly egalitarian rather than hierarchical universe, so much so that a whole theory of relativity (Milne's) has been built around the so-called cosmological principle, the principle that any observer anywhere in the universe interprets data in exactly the same way as any other observer elsewhere."[6] This appears to be an example of the emergence of scientific theory from myth, though not, perhaps, without a doubling back through antimyth to the culture in general. In any case, we can treat it as an emergence into antimyth, because it appears that before a thema can function scientifically in a "public" or "normal" sense it must be shaped into antimythical form.

Holton seems to treat the primary/secondary or subject/object division as a thema, like, say, the thema of fundamental probabilism in physical nature or the notion of the thing-in-itself as a mathematical structure (Heisenberg). His notion of themata as "preconceptions that appear to be unavoidable for scientific thought"[7] would cover the division into primary and secondary qualities. But subject/object is in one sense deeper than a thema and in another sense subsequent to themata. It is deeper in that it is the structure of the pure form to which all themata must accommodate themselves. It is subsequent in that thematic processes of thought that produce science (S_2) go on, or at least can begin, independent of it. Like what Michael Polanyi calls "tacit knowing," the "nature" of such a process is unspecifiable.[8]

Kuhn's notion of paradigms stands in relation to antimyth in the same way that themata do, though in Holton's view themata come more from the individual than from the community. Kuhn's notion of paradigms has been modified considerably since *The Structure of Scientific Revolutions* appeared in 1962. Originally it was very broad, but Margaret Masterman's analysis, in which she showed that Kuhn used the term in at least twenty-one different senses, which she then divided into three basic groups, led Kuhn to redefine down to two fundamental senses.[9] Originally Kuhn offered paradigms of three types: metaphysical (sometimes "quasi-metaphysical," as in Kuhn's description of Descartes' corpuscular theory, which told many scientists "what many of their research problems should be"), sociological, and artificial. Masterman's argument was that though most commentators treated Kuhn's paradigms as metaphysical, their fundamental sense was not that at all; they represented sets of scientific habits prior to theory in their development, sociologically describable and above all concrete and observable. The fundamental form was what she called the "artifact or construct" paradigm that could be a piece of apparatus or anything bringing about puzzle-solving or normal science.[10] Kuhn conspired in this retreat from metaphysics in his postscript of 1969.[11] It is clear, however, that Kuhn's theory must admit paradigms of the metaphysical sort because many of his examples are of that sort. But it is probably true that when they are admitted they are admitted *as* construct paradigms. This is because Kuhn himself has a perfectly natural antimythical bias, as his interest in science might lead us to assume in the first place, though his theory raises all kinds of problems for purely antimythical *beliefs*. Kuhn's abandonment of metaphysics, following Masterman's cue, makes his social science that much harder, a condition which has been devoutly, if on occasion mistakenly, wished for. (In fact, Kuhn eventually drops the term "paradigm" and substitutes for it the term "disciplinary matrix," which he describes as an "entire constellation of beliefs, values, techniques, and so on shared by members of a given community.")[12] For Kuhn, there is always a concrete situation in which a paradigm comes into play. Scientists don't learn concepts, laws, and theories "in the abstract and by themselves." They encounter these tools "in a historically and pedagogically prior unit that displays them with and through their applications."[13] This means that paradigms are relatively silent in the way that the Aristotelian notion of matter can become silent because of its "omnipresence and qualitative neutrality" in Aristotelian physics.[14] But I doubt that because it is omnipresent it can quite be dispensed with. It is, still, paradigmatic. Antimyth is more than paradigmatic, for it is never overthrowable without denying science itself. Except, of course, that we are speaking at this point of public science. It is interesting to see how the notion of necessary externality appears even as Holton, for example, speaks of

> . . . the process of removing the discourse from the personal level . . . to a second level, that of public science, where the discourse is more unambiguously understandable, being pre-

dominantly about phenomena and analytical schemes. . . .
This is a process which every scientist unquestionably accepts,
a process that may be termed externalization or projection.[15]

It is what I call emergence toward antimyth.

What Kuhn calls "normal science" involves acceptance of paradigms and the making of community that this implies. Acceptance of
a paradigm limits as well as liberates, since it tends to select the problems that will be regarded as scientific at any given time. But we can
see, as Holton points out, it is in the nature of science, when limited
to only two rather than his three dimensions, that certain questions
cannot be asked. They are not scientific questions. This is true at a
broader and deeper level than Holton indicates—at the metaphysical
level that Kuhn abandons, the level nearing antimyth, which defines
the limit of scientific projections.

The antimyth of externality is in the end something that the philosophy of science must recognize as the structure of scientific fictions. Once it is assumed that paradigms are fictive, the temptation is
to reinvoke antimythical principle and consider each successive paradigm nearer to an objective (external) truth. That is, the antimyth is
invoked at a higher level than the current paradigm. Kuhn, as a philosopher of science, tries to step out of paradigms, and perhaps even
out of the antimyth (though his retreat from metaphysics is a contrary act), and it is this move that causes him to differ with Karl Popper. Kuhn claims: "We may . . . have to relinquish the notion, explicit or implicit, that changes of paradigm carry scientists and those
who learn from them closer and closer to the truth."[16] From the point
of view of the *philosopher* of science, Kuhn sees the notion of a teleology in science itself as a vacuous concept. His view has outraged
many scientists and philosophers—to the degree that they accept the
absolute dominance of an antimythical world-view and reject so-
called "metaphysical" issues. More precisely, Kuhn refuses to

> compare theories as representations of nature, as statements
> about "what is really out there." Granting that neither theory
> of a historical pair is true, [many thinkers] nevertheless seek
> a sense in which the latter is a better approximation to the
> truth. I believe nothing of that sort can be found.[17]

For Kuhn, to posit an ontological limit, as Popper does, is to imply a
neutral observation language, which he says has never been achieved

(and, in my view, can never be achieved), or implies knowledge of the limit already, which makes the whole search unnecessary. Kuhn goes so far as to consider abandoning the cherished notions that sensory experience is fixed and neutral and that theories are simply man-made interpretations of given data.

The same notion is expressed by Holton in his rejection of ". . . the idea of a perfect entity . . . easily recognizable in scientific thought, from the beginning to this day, as the conception—a haunting and apparently irresistible one despite all evidence to the contrary—of the final, single, perfect object of knowledge to which the current state of scientific knowledge is widely thought to lead us."[18] Holton goes on to speak of it as inexpressible in ordinary language, but the truth must be that it is inexpressible in any language or symbolic form. Yet a positing of such an external limit is so pervasive in science that one must entertain the notion of its necessity as a fiction to the whole enterprise. This means not that the scientist doing Holton's S_1—the unspecifiable imaginative process—need *believe* it, but that normal science adopts it as part of the structure of antimyth. One can argue appropriately that the historian or philosopher of science cannot adopt it, at least not fully. The historian and philosopher perform in the realm of the ironic, and indeed *must* maintain a certain distance from science. Kuhn's quarrel with Popper seems definable in terms of Kuhn's ironic withdrawal. Of course, it ought to be clear enough that for a scientist to adopt the antimythical as a *belief* beyond the activity of S_2 itself is error.

The structures which operate under the aegis of antimyth can be materials for myth and can themselves have fiction-making power. They can create words and images which help to shape the culture, but always from or within an antimythical base. Thus the power is properly called antimythopoeic, but no less therefore fictive. As such it skews things in a certain way. Albert Einstein remarked that experience remains the sole criterion of the utility of a mathematical construct, but he also observed that a creative principle resides in mathematics. In criticizing Mach he wanted to go beyond "phenomenological physics" to achieve a theory, as Holton remarks, "whose basis may be further from direct experience, but which in return has more unity in the foundation."[19] The desire to connect to experience may, indeed, be the scientist's desire to return to a pre-antimythic condition, the place of myth, the origin of making or poesis in the broadest sense, where things are "simple" again. We see this in Einstein's attitude towards his own theories, and his connecting them with classic purity. We see also returns to a sort of image-making. Holton notes a tendency among physicists to evoke visual images of what one would see if it were seeable, which it is not once it becomes assimilated to the form of antimyth.

Michael Polanyi has sought to look beneath what our models of knowing are and invents the idea of tacit knowing. This idea speaks of something deeper than antimyth—something, as Polanyi says, "unspecifiable."[20] This is radically "personal" knowledge not grounded in explicit operations of logic. We can never get antimythically *to* such knowledge because when we try to establish *rules* of tacit knowing we discover that beneath them is always another tacit form and thus an infinite regress. This is perhaps what Yeats offers at the end of *A Vision*, where his ironic language reaches the end of its tether:

> The particulars are the work of the thirteenth sphere or cycle, which is in every man and called by every man his freedom. Doubtless, for it can do all things and knows all things, it knows what it will do with its own freedom but it has kept the secret.[21]

This is a necessarily ironic description of the ground of antimythical fiction-making.

Polanyi goes on to an account of metaphor as an integrative act of tacit knowing or personal knowledge that creates a meaning unspecifiable by recourse to subsidiaries, because it itself is the meaning of the subsidiaries. Meaning here is always located ahead rather than behind the fictive act and thus can never be allegorically recovered. There are some interesting connections here to the Kantian notion of "internal purposiveness" in art and aesthetic experience. If we consider Kuhn's retreat from antimyth and note that it involves refusal to posit an ontological limit, we may come to conclude that Kant's aesthetic theory unintentionally encompasses his critique of pure reason, just as Schiller seems to have tried to make it encompass his ethical theory. Kuhn's retreat is, in these terms, a disestablishment of external purposiveness in science and turns science in the direction of art.

At the mythical pole we have the contrary to the duality of subject/object. The world is part of us, but we are also extended into the world. John Butler Yeats wrote that the poet is involved in a "continual progress in identifying himself with everything that lives, and that does not live, not merely men and women or animals and birds but even trees and plants and rocks and stones."[22] The fundamental quality of mythical thought, as I use the term here, is the drive toward identity, the contrary of difference/indifference. The condition of pure myth would be the successful taking of everything into one's own imagination and the identification of all the elements once inside *with* the whole, yet the maintenance of the individual identity *of* everything so that it is *let be*, to use a phrase of Heidegger. The condition of pure antimyth would be the externalization and objectification of everything except at a central unmoving point, an isolated, purely subjective and totally passive consciousness, alien to everything else. But then there is the turn—the drift back to myth, the yearning for some form of total unification.

Of course, if we try to transcend the opposition I have posed and gain a more spacious view, the antimyth reveals itself as a fiction: The antimyth, the subject surrounded by an alien object, is itself a human creation—something *inside* and emanating from the human imagination. In this light, a shift in my own metaphor is necessary; for my continuum appears to be a sort of fountain whose source is myth and whose jet reaches toward complete analytic or externalizing power but which returns cyclically to its source for replenishment. If this is correct, we can declare that the intellectual life feeds on myth, as Blake's "devourer" feeds on his "prolific," and that the proper organization of the liberal arts and sciences is vertical, the fine arts and literature at the foundation, the pure sciences at the top, with the various humanistic disciplines and social sciences in between. Except, of course, that there is always a flow back, with antimyth at the top returning, often as potentiality for myth.

But full absorption into myth would be impossible to cultural man, as is phase 15 of Yeats's wheel. Yeats calls it a "supernatural incarnation" and thus introduces a "miraculous" though unachievable space. I prefer to call it a fictive limit we never reach. The limit we can reach at this end of the continuum is art. Myth is a term indicating a limit being approached by all symbolic activity that would claim to make, not merely copy or signify. Approaching the limit, language asserts its freedom from antimythical strictures about language. It brings the qualities of myth into action as a contrary to antimythical power. Pure indifference, in the Yeatsian sense of phase 15, impossible in his system, would be unable to grant antimyth its place; and if antimyth is not granted its place, all of the potential vicious social possibilities of myth would be unleashed, and the world would become unlivable, as it threatened to be under Nazism.

By the same token, pure antimyth is reduction to an unlivable center of alienation.

Recently, Northrop Frye, continuing his expansion of the terms "myth" and "mythology" beyond the confines of "literature" to designate larger social verbal structures, has remarked:

> A mythological universe is a vision of reality in terms of human concerns and hopes and anxieties; it is not a primitive form of science. Unfortunately, human nature being what it is, man first acquires a mythological universe and then pretends as long as he can that it is also the actual universe. All mythological universes are by definition centered on man, therefore the actual universe was also assumed to be centered on man.[23]

This passage touches on many of the issues with which I have been concerned. The appearance of science, the creator of Frye's "actual universe," did not destroy or render unnecessary a "mythological universe." Frye makes a very interesting point about this where he suggests that at one time technology seemed to promise a marriage with myth that would produce one dominant structure:

> . . . but poets have dragged their feet in its celebration. Blake, D. H. Lawrence, Morris, Yeats, Pound, are only a few of those who have shown marked hostility to technology and have refused to believe that its peaceful and destructive aspects can be separated. The poets see nothing imaginative in a domination of nature which expresses no love for it, in an activity founded on will, which always overreacts, in a way of life marked by a constant increase in speed, which means also an increase in introversion and the breaking down of genuine personal relationships.[24]

Frye goes on to suggest that for these reasons science fiction began as celebration ("hardware fantasy") of technology but has quickly become "software philosophical romance."[25]

It must always be so. Science is always a movement out of myth and inevitably tends to the contrary end of a continuum. It can never successfully force on society complete victory of what is therefore antimyth without perpetrating its own form of disaster. Frye's remarks point to how a myth that has closed itself and has become a doctrine, demanding subservience, can be the vehicle of terror. Under

Figure 12.2. The Cyclical Fiction of Cultural Forms

Mythic Pole ← Toward Myth		THE IRONIC		Toward Anti-Myth →	Anti-Mythic Pole
Language and Myths	*Art*	*Criticism*	*History*	*Religion*	*Mathematics and Science*
unity of feeling	radical creation	creation/description	past as presence/past as past	upper/lower	object/subject
synthesis	particular	interpretation	ideality of recollection	ethical meaning	numerical determinism
sympathy of relationship (identity)	freedom	art/science	determinism/freedom	God/man	Nature/man
URTHONA (Los)		LUVAH (Orc)		THARMAS (covering cherub)	URIZEN (Satan)

(indifference/difference is opposed by identity.)

Return of anti-myth to myth, of mathematics to art, of religion to myth, of differentiation to poetry in the fictive act.

(indifference and difference are opposed, and indifference is negated.)

such conditions, the contrary is not admitted, as for so long the Copernican theory was rejected because it was not compatible with a man-centered myth that had closed itself into doctrine. Curiously, then, a man-centered myth that closes itself decenters man. Frye points to the opposite terror above, where the antimyth negates the human center and alienates nature.

Figure 12.2 illustrates an attempt to build a dialectical continuum on which can be placed two of the forms that constitute what we call the humanistic disciplines, for the myth/antimyth contrary does not divide up all human activity. Indeed, I have already collapsed it into a more fundamental metaphor of the fountain. The fountain generates a cyclical movement by virtue of a constant return of antimyth to myth. Still the notion of a continuum between contraries is useful for a while longer. There is a ground all along the continuum, to say nothing of a middle ground. All the so-called academic disciplines are somewhere on the continuum, usually described in the more general forms of the fine arts, the humanities, the social sciences, and natural sciences. To read recent philosophy and history of science is to recognize that the ground of scientific activity in its largest sense is unspecifiable and is not a hypothetical-empirical model with an ontological limit, which is the appearance of Holton's S_2. To recognize this offers perhaps some solace to the so-called social scientist, who seems in practice torn between the model of S_2 and various forms of supposedly subjective expression. Talcott Parsons's brief outline of the history of the social sciences describes ideological struggles among competing views of the disciplines. It was not until Weber, he concludes, that a social science balancing contending forces was evolved. Parsons makes a claim for the social sciences as an autonomous disciplinary category, emerging from the contending forces of empiricist-utilitarian monism and idealistic dualism. He defends the tripartite academic division of humanities, social sciences, and natural sciences:

> [the social sciences] are not natural sciences in the sense of excluding the categories of subjective meaning, that is, they must consider knowing subjects as objects. Nor are they humanistic-cultural in the sense that the individuality of particular meanings must take complete precedence over analytical generalities and such categories as causality.[26]

This is almost a fair statement. But one could say a good deal more, since clearly the statement implies that social science always *ex-*

ternalizes the knowing subject. Accepting the notion of internal/ external or subject/object, the statement is grounded in antimyth. Because of the externalization of the knowing subject into an object, the ideal form of social science here is behavioral. (I use this term not in opposition to "instinct" psychology, as it is sometimes used, but to cover both modes as deterministic.) The behavioral form can be thought of as a displacement of the ideal mathematical form of antimyth. Periodically in the social sciences, and most recently with the advent of highly sophisticated computers, there is an ebullient attempt to adopt pure mathematical form in the discipline. But then there is a tendency to pull back. Holton remarks:

> . . . disciplines such as psychology (and certainly history) are so constructed that they are wrong to imitate the habit in the modern physical sciences to depress or project the discussion forcibly to the x/y plane [S_2]. When the thematic component is as strong and as explicitly needed as it is in these fields, the criteria of acceptability should be able to remain explicitly in three-dimensional proposition space.[27]

Social science's relation to mathematics is ironic and not entirely different from natural science's flirtation with an ontological limit. On the other hand, to move toward the mythical passing some point of balance turns a social science into something of recognizably other dimensions. Too often the disciplines of history and literary criticism, placed in the area of the "ironic" on figure 12.2, are battlefields in which opposing sides make efforts to drag the discipline toward the extreme either of myth or of antimyth. If pulled in either direction, these disciplines lose their reason for being. The purely empirical or antimythical historian tends to make no distinction between the writing of history (history as a symbolic discipline) and the flow of events. One simply copies or signifies the other. I have actually known historians who have been unable to distinguish the two or to recognize that there is some sort of problem implicit in this naïvely empiricist notion. This breed ought to be on the decline, given the recent invasion of historical study by analysts of language; but the solution to the problem of the place of history is not to flee to the opposite and identify it as an art, which is only to loosen it from qualities of empiricism that all historical writing must have.

The important thing to recognize at this point is that an empirical act is a constitutive act. Both criticism and history must constitute something as an "object" of study, even as they know that they are "constituting" it, that is, creating a fiction according to certain antimythical categories. *At the same time,* they must reach out toward mythic identification with that object *as if* it were not yet constituted. In a few versions of recent reader-oriented criticism this has been acknowledged, though more often such criticism refuses to constitute the object (even as a fictive object). Blake said that the inexplicit can "rouse the faculties to act," and Keats insisted on art's bringing about a "momentous depth of speculation." Both of these observations insist on an "object" of some sort that is doing these things, but they also require a constitutive act of the reader or viewer before the work can be said to have any value. Neither statement is as sophisticated as we would want it to be today, but with some extension either could be used to show that a text is *there* as potentiality, but that we must always constitute it as there with a certain independence from us, even as we must insist on our involvement with it. It is both/and, as are all activities in relation to whatever they constitute. Recently some critics have seemed to want to become more important than the potentialities from which they constitute their readings; for a while, the style was to claim to be transparent interpreters of superior texts. This is part of the *politics* of critical theory, which appears to be cyclical: either there is a flight from objectification of meaning, even as it seems to be established; or there is a flight from subjectivity, even as it is practiced. Blake describes this sort of cyclicity (on a considerably grander scale than I have here) in the struggle of Orc and Urizen, which goes nowhere; and he has to bring in his character Los as a contrary. It is this cyclical situation that I believe Stanley Fish is attempting to avoid in the last chapters of *Is There a Text in This Class?* There he makes no claim (or almost no claim) that the ways of criticism will change as a result of his arguments, only that one ought to know what kind of game one is playing (and perhaps square one's language with the facts of it: a task that is not easy).[28] It is this cyclicity that I am trying to provide a contrary to.

I am claiming that both criticism and history are creative cultural forms. Their constitutive acts are "ironic" because (from the point of view of a commentary on them) they must maintain both mythical and antimythical stances at the same time. Not to go too far in the direction of either pole as an authority produces the virtue we call scholarly restraint. The growth of literary theory and historiography as separate subjects has recently been accelerated by a greater appreciation of the problems of expression in the two fields that this ironic situation generates.

In figure 12.1 both historical writing and literary criticism would have to be placed somewhere between center and circumference—between where language claims to create and where it claims to "copy" or to describe analytically. I should like to return to the implications of that chart for criticism and for poetry: At the mythico-poetic pole tropes are not tropes in the classical sense, but integrative, creative acts. In the classical rhetorical view there must always be a gap between word and concept; there is always conceivably a better word for the concept. But, if we regard language in action as generating concepts, from a source of unspecifiable subsidiaries, the concept is not an otherness but an emanation (but *not* a lost Blakean one), and the word does not "signify" an externality in the ordinary antimythical sense of the term.

According to this view, language generates out of itself antimyth, and antimyth then demands the verbal fiction of the nonverbal concept or pure idea, or in science the ontological limit. But this fiction, apart from language, has no external substance; it is always created symbolically.

The most radical form of phenomenology would tell us we must get back to things and free ourselves of the tyrannical abstractness of all words and ideas. This, too, would presume the existence of a norm of language distant from the mythic pole. It sets up an idea of signifier and signified and concludes that no poem can connect itself to a signified in the sense of a referent. Therefore, the argument goes, we must abandon language or work through it to the object. This position finds language a prison house from which there is a radical escape through the negation of language.

On the contrary, we must affirm that the imagination and language have a hand in constructing things for culture. From the point of view of the poetic, which is language-centered, therefore imagination-centered, therefore man-centered, a world prior to human culture, which is always proceeding from myth, lacks full reality or is mere potentiality. It is always only subsidiary and unspecifiable because not here yet. The world of culture is something we are *always proceeding to make* rather than *referring back or outward toward*. From the point of view of antimyth, of course, the world is an objective *out there*; it is what Frye has called the "actual universe" to be described by science: But as we think about it, or in any form of our thinking about it, that too is a creation of antimyth. It quickly becomes an abstract idea as fictive as Locke's "primary" qualities were to Blake.

What I have been seeking is a theory of secular creativity in language that gives priority, but not the power that Blake called negation, to the fictive. In this attempt I have chosen to adopt the term "symbolic." Benedetto Croce was quite right to ask what a symbol, used in this sense, symbolizes. I employ symbolization to indicate an act of linguistic creativity. For the symbolic, in my usage, there is no symbolized, only the realm of the potential to be worked up into the symbolic. In Croce's terms, this would involve not the identity of intuition and expression, but the unspecifiability of intuition *outside* of expression. Being is not prior to but *in* the field of language. As such, it is, of course, cultural being and moral being. It does not say there is no world there, but it also does claim that the world there is not the world of the "object." It is a potentiality for the human imagination to work upon, and it throws moral responsibility radically on man. This is why that wise author Joyce Cary said he feared what man would do with imagination and freedom, though he celebrated them in all his books.

Man, then, is not only a devourer of language but is also a constant creator of forms in language in the manner of Blake's "ancient poets," whom Blake declares to have confronted a potentiality and set about making (by naming) the world of culture. Each of us, however, grows up in a language that, like Blake's eternal London, is constantly decaying even as it is being built. True, as continental criticism likes to tell us, we cannot recapture an original undifferentiated innocence. Nor is it important whether it ever existed or not. We have instead the endless task of retrieving language from its own tendency toward ruin or exhaustion. If creation does not go on as decay takes place, the world of human culture becomes Hell. Hell is the diminishment of culture, the result of adoption of the antimyth of human passivity as dogma and the negation of linguistic imagination. But it can also be the result of the negation of antimyth and a seeking for solace in the primitive.

This view directs us radically toward the future, not toward the nothingness and individual death that is the fundamental reality of the existentialists, but toward the continuing act of linguistic creation, toward a passing along of the cultural role. It suggests that the poet's materials are always for him a potentiality to be worked up into form. Every poet begins the day as did Blake's ancients. Each such beginning restores the literal root meaning of "poet." However, as I have suggested, the maker of fictions is not merely the poet as conventionally conceived but everyone who symbolizes, including those opposite makers who seem to be taking apart or "copying" but actually are constructing antimyth. It becomes clear, from this point of view, for example, that history, which seems directed toward copying an outward past, is also the act of creating that past, a symbolic past, which is the only past we have. We are always thus on the threshold of history in an entirely different sense from the common one. We are always making it. Yet, belonging to the "ironic," historians are also hypostatizing a past and "copying" it.

The difference between *signifiant* and *signifié* is itself a fictive creation of language as it operates at a distance from the mythic pole, beyond that unlocatable point where what Vico called "poetic logic" has turned into antimyth. To look back to the poem from a vantage beyond the turning point is to submit it to a mode of thought that is the poem's negation, where the poem is merely its analyzed structure or is only a romantic allegory. But these are all characterizations finally not of the poem but of the limitations of this point of view toward the poem. This allegoric vantage is in the area of antimyth, where language has extended itself to invent the dislocations that we, when we stand *there*, thrust back upon poems.

But one must beware of simply located points of difference on the continuum. That is to be thrust back into an awkward distinction between ordinary and literary, steno and depth language, and overspatializes and quantifies the unmeasurable continuum between center and circumference. The whole continuum is creative. As we pass further and further outward (really, of course, inward, creating more and more externality as we go), what we create is the fiction or antimyth of externality—until we reach mathematics, where something very strange happens—for mathematics proceeds to assert its power to contain, claims that the world is mathematical rather than that mathematics represents the world. Our continuum, by turning inside out, defies measurement, which belongs to antimyth. Heisenberg's notion of the thing-in-itself as a mathematical structure can be read as the assertion of a fictive containment of antimyth.

I have said that the place of criticism on this continuum of language is ironic. Because it must project itself farther out on the radius (or farther inward—therefore pointing outward) than any so-called literary text it treats, it must employ the categories of analysis and reduction, even as it must at some point reject those categories. This is why Frye was compelled in his *Anatomy* to begin by claiming criticism to be a science, but in the end to make his work an anatomy, thus fictively containing his science or antimyth.[29] From this odd perch, irony is one of the things criticism projects back into poetry when critical language cannot hold the poem together in any other way. Certain critics, marveling sweetly over their own condition, imagine that criticism may well be more interesting than poetry today. It should be no surprise that this self-regarding activity should valorize allegory. But this takes us back to a conclusion already reached that criticism is finally, like all symbolic forms, at least partly a *making* of its own. From its ironic area, it produces an antimyth of bifurcations even while it protects the poem's myth. The danger to criticism is to lose the only area where it is distinctly something other than either myth or antimyth, though always in irresolution and always having to be done again.

This theory of "secular" creativity, then, though it refuses to draw a line measuring off poetry from other forms of discourse, and though it argues for the creativity of all language, does not quarrel with our needs as critics to create the dialectical contrariety of myth and antimyth—for the whole system is a creation of criticism—where a continuum is what we apparently have created. The fiction includes the antimyth of difference/indifference and of nature as mathematical law. Blake called antimyth the "starry floor" beneath which, through God's mercy, man could not fall any further than he already had.[30] I do not believe in a fall, but I do believe in a limit.

Criticism, under the ironic condition I have outlined, would seem to be a struggle of radical creation with descriptive analysis, in which neither can be allowed full sway. History would seem to be the product of the historian's mediation between the past regarded as a presence (that is, constructed) and the past regarded as a past (reconstructed or "copied"). We see in both criticism and history an oscillation, at times, between these two poles. A movement to either extreme tends to vitiate the critic's or the historian's ironic strength. At the creative extreme we find par excellence Walter Pater's treatment of the Mona Lisa, which W. B. Yeats quite appropriately turned into verse for his *Oxford Book of Modern Verse*.[31] At the other extreme are a variety of reductive processes, the emphasis on critical "methodologies" and "approaches" and empirical modes.

The diagram of cultural forms (fig. 12.2) converts itself into a circle by virtue of what I call the return of antimyth to myth. This illustrates the point I have made about the creativity of antimyth even as its creation denies creativity. This is a paradox after all, so figure 12.2 must be amended to show that, as a creative force, antimyth in the end (in returning to myth) finally regains possession of its own paradox. The return of antimyth to myth, in this sense, is also the return of mathematics, the language of science, to art, where Frye placed it (see fig. 10.4) as a containing form. It is also a return of religion to myth.

It may seem odd that I have placed religion on the antimythical side, and I admit that it often does not want to stay there. There is little question that religion has its sources in and returns to myth; in the process of emanation it develops two antimythical characteristics. First, it acknowledges a threshold, in Wheelwright's sense—a form of otherness, which it then modifies in some versions with the notion of incarnation or "miraculous" symbol, which in turn implies a Fall. Second, it works toward development of the moral law, an external model of human action that is given supernatural sanction. But though it asserts these differences and posits an ideal realm of indifference, it also returns to myth via its own antimythical form: It tries to create through that form a vision of potential identity—the coexistence of freedom of individual moral choice with the law and the identicality of each individuality with all others. At the level with which we are now concerned, we can find a paradoxical creativity here—a creativity which involves a deliberate discipline of annihilation of the isolated selfhood and the flowing in of the fullness of a vision that is revelation in absence. In the end, such acts are chosen acts from the point of view of the artist. This is, in part, what I think Blake meant when from the point of view of the artist he wrote:

> Prayer is the Study of Art.
> Praise is the Practise of Art.
> Fasting &c., all relate to Art.
> The outward Ceremony is Antichrist.
> The Eternal Body of Man is The Imagination, that is,
> God himself
> The Divine Body[32]

On the other hand, from the point of view of the theologian, art ought to be a form of prayer.

I have somewhat frivolously connected various of the cultural forms with Blake's Zoas and (in parentheses) their "time forms." A fanciful essay could be written on these relationships. I am unable, however, to find a Zoa or other form to represent criticism. Perhaps this is because there ought to be something a little disembodied about the critical act. In Blake's poem it would have to be a ghostly fifth creature never quite anywhere—mediating, educating, and celebrating—somewhat fussy, perhaps, and regarded as rather a noxious vapor by the author.

2. STRUCTURALIST ALLEGORIZING

IF BAUDELAIRE thought of nature itself as a "book" of correspondences, the structuralists (par excellence Claude Lévi-Strauss) consider everything, including nature, to be a "text." A "text" is no longer a book in the conventional sense but anything that can bear structural analysis, and that is everything—poems, clothing, myths, etc. All things are structures of relations, connections, differences composed of signs. For the structuralist, every myth is a text. It is a set of "variants," not from an ideal prototype but embodying a set of laws. In James Boon's *From Symbolism to Structuralism*, for example, the symbolist poem is regarded as a "standard 'hunting ground' for logical structures of fundamental essence":

> But, in another sense it is a set of program notes which reflect on a near-surface level the types of logical processes which maintain any interrelated body of semantic fields. The Symbolists synthesize the sort of orders of experience which Lévi-Strauss assumes as "real" and which lie behind his analyses.[33]

This passage demonstrates how in structuralism the notion of the pure laws of structure or relation become hypostatized into a sort of ur-text which the structuralist reconstructs in the process of deconstructing all the variants he collects.

However, Lévi-Strauss argues that every new variant that is discovered changes the structure, so that on the one hand the structure seems to be a fixed center of a universe of discourse, while on the other it is constantly recreated by the appearance of new variants. Lévi-Strauss sees his own analysis as a variant, and presumably an interpreter of his variant would create a new variant, and so on *ad infinitum*. This notion has some connection with the idea of interpretation developed in the phenomenological tradition, as for example in the work of Hans-Georg Gadamer, where every interpretation involves a new *relation* with a text, though the kind of interpretation is radically different. The structure is the system of relationships, not some ideal substance. One notes here, as in phenomenological hermeneutics, that myth and interpretation are reduced to the same order and that no distinctions are made between them, but the orders discovered in the two systems are opposed.

Still, Lévi-Strauss can himself be evasive on the question of whether the structure is an "empirical" creation or whether it is "Platonic"—a "reality" that analysis recovers from the depths. In the end, it seems to me, he allows the "Platonic" to dominate, and every myth, poem, or other "text" becomes a copy or variant. But it must be remembered that such a "text" does not have the substance of a Platonic idea; in the end it is really the single set of principles or the logic by which all texts operate. It is the law, so to speak, under which everything occurs—a cultural law with the status of external natural law. For Lévi-Strauss, metaphor is fundamental to language, not something that is added on to it or embellishes it, but the act of metaphorical creation is an operation proceeding according to this *a priori* law, which is predicated on the supremacy of logical relations. Metaphor is not, then, a mode of discovery. The law determines how metaphor works, and that is why in the end Lévi-Strauss says that men do not think in myths, but myths think themselves in men.[34] Man is everywhere subject to the laws of structure, which apparently require him to "resolve" logical contradictions in experience by constructing myths. This determinism leads us to what Michel Foucault has called the disappearance of Man.[35] In Jonathan Culler's words, the human sciences have "chipped away at what supposedly belongs to the thinking subject":

> . . . one thinks of speech as the prime instance of individuality; it seems the one area where the conscious self might be master.
>
> But that mastery is easily reduced. A speaker's utterances are understood by others only because they are virtually contained within language. "Die Sprache spricht," claims Heidegger, "nicht der Mensch. Der Mensch spricht nur, indem er geschlicklich der Sprache entspricht." (Language speaks. Man speaks only in so far as he artfully "complies with" language.) A generative grammar goes some way to formalizing this view.[36]

Structuralism, carried far enough, calls the identity of self and consciousness in question.

It would seem that to the structuralist a structure is a human creation of law based upon empirical observation, while on the other hand it is a deconstruction of a "text" in the direction of that ultimate law of relationships which is more real than the objects or events that figure forth its existence. It would seem that in this thought there is a parallel to Joshua Reynolds's eighteenth-century mixture of empiricism and Platonism. It is not surprising that structuralism should find in Freud's similar mixing a modern ally. The structuralists' difference from Reynolds lies, of course, in the treatment of these issues in terms of signification (and therefore language) and the worrying of problems of subjectivity bequeathed by the Cartesian tradition.

For Lévi-Strauss, metaphor and metonym are assumed to be the logical prerequisites for the formation of any system. They signify relationship rather than presence. Metaphor is not something added on to language like a trope in the classical view: "Are not the metonymic and metaphoric functions the very processes by which *rule* is imposed, by which the 'natural order' is disrupted and rearranged into something new, something unnatural, something cultural?"[37] Thus language seems to be a constitutive form, but in fact the real form which gives the rule is the "Platonic" form of law, the system to which language and metaphor conform. This deconstruction is as much a construct as was Locke's deconstruction of all primary qualities of experience to a system of natural law after he had removed the secondary qualities. Blake asked where such a system might exist and answered that it existed in the mind of a fool.[38] That was a harsh verdict, but Blake was a man who thought he was being pressed. It might have been better to utter skeptically the opinion that there is nothing wrong with such antimythical fictions as long as one does not accept them as the single ground of reality, negating all else. In structuralist thought, when man effects a passage from nature to culture it must be that he is obeying the rule of nature which always prescribes the structural law of culture. The creation of culture, however, is seen as a kind of mystification, which in the end must lead to "discontent." (My use of the Freudian term here is not coincidental.) Human creativity is to this extent determined.

The determining structure, as we have seen, is one of logical relations. The function of myth for Lévi-Strauss is to gloss over logical contradictions in a culture. The glossing over is a cultural act. Many years ago Kenneth Burke thought of it as a kind of symbolical problem-solving. A myth displaces the problem (the Freudian term is again not coincidental) to another level. But there is no burking the fact (if you will allow me Burke's pun) that such displacement must always be, from the structuralists' vantage, a mystification. One can call a myth a mediating resolution, but reality is still declared to lie in the logical contradiction, and myth is thus a pyrrhic effort to overcome the real.

Metaphor, of course, is alleged to play an important role in this matter, and though Lévi-Strauss sees it as fundamental to language, its role of displacement and mediation between differences that cannot be logically resolved begins to make it look like a trope in the classical sense after all. It is a covering over, an embellishment. This certainly ought, from this point of view, to be regarded as a "mystification," which itself calls for "deconstruction" back to the logical contradiction, which in turn displays the structure. It would seem, then, that Lévi-Strauss's effort to make aesthetic and logical form one ends in separating a narrowly conceived aesthetic element from logical form in the way that Freud separates the manifest dream from its true meaning. I believe Robert Scholes is correct to remark,

> Lévi-Strauss . . . is concerned not with an aesthetic form but with a logical form: the system of ideas embodied, however obscurely, in primitive mythology. The aesthetic restructuring of a myth, which shapes it into a folk-tale or fairy tale, is for him a form of transformation which obscures the original logic of the myth.[39]

And I would add that Lévi-Strauss negates the aesthetic by referring it always to the logical and considering it *in the latter's terms.*

Boon offers three possible arguments with respect to the function of myth and poetry, the first two being in contrast to the third, which is Lévi-Strauss's structuralist argument (as interpreted by Boon). They are useful for us to consider, for they recall matters with which we have been concerned. First: ". . . a native appreciates myth in the same way that a poetry lover appreciates poetry; both can go to work in their fields (offices), even while they are confronted by irrefutable oppositions (up/down, life/death), thanks to the fact that they know that in the really real realm of myth (poetry) these oppositions are finally resolved." This view, it appears, makes the world of oppositions (and Lévi-Strauss's world of logical relations) dissolve into a higher reality—a sort of religious Platonism, perhaps. The opposition is a dualism of appearance/reality, with appearance negated. Second: ". . . the native actually lives the myth, because for him the

myth *is* the world. . . . Any daily routine would then for the natives
be no more than affirmations of continually reciprocal manifestations of being. 'Real' tilling of the soil is only part of the mythical
story about soil tilling." This, we realize, is the situation proposed by
Eliade, where the religious becomes immanent in nature, so to speak,
and the logical oppositions are negated in the achievement of either a
pure indifference, or if subjected to any notion of a Fall, a "miraculous" incarnation.

Boon declares Lévi-Strauss's third position to be different from
these. For him, myth is a variety of social discourse, myths think
themselves in men, and ritual "surmounts" contradictions by "acting" them: ". . . it translates them out of terms of *ideas* into terms of
act, thereby justifying each in terms of the other, without really 'solving' anything." This goes on by "inversion, assimilation, and transposition of the units . . . what is contradictory on one level is restated
in different terms on another level, and thereby authorized."[40] In all
three of these arguments the real is located on one side of an opposition. In the first, the real is located in a higher reality of total resolution; in the second, it is located in an immanence of the holy; in the
third, which is Lévi-Strauss's position, the level of logical contradiction is privileged, and myth and ritual "surmount" it, "solving" a
problem. The problem is intolerable and made to *appear* to go away.
It is not surprising that this line of reasoning is established at the
same time that a cry goes up among critics and some philosophers
against language itself as the vehicle of "mystification." Since language is rooted in metaphor, and metaphor "surmounts" logical contradiction and the real, then language must be the culprit that separates us from truth. But this cry against language can emerge from
another point of view as well: In this version the logical form of language is still regarded as its fundamental form, and tropes are regarded as deviations from it in a direction (but only in a direction)
that distorts logical form. In this case, the greater the tropological
distortion (the greater the "destruction" of language toward "silence," which is the silencing of logic and reflection) the better. From
my point of view, both of these attitudes adopt the same story and
negate each other. In both of these cases, the desirable but impossible
result—as annihilation of the selfhood is desirable to Yeats's saint—
is the annihilation of language and the attainment of an unmediated
vision. In one case language is too metaphorical and in the other it
can never be metaphorical enough. I am trying to suggest that the
line of thought of structuralism (even as it joins curiously with its

phenomenological opposites in a sort of existentialism) ends in an allegoric concept of language that negates its symbolic contrary. It thus threatens a collapse into the chaos that Heraclitus feared, for it negates in its discontent the idea of culture. In the end structuralism tells us that reality is logical, that language is built on a model of logic, that it reveals logical oppositions that cannot be resolved, that metaphor (a fundamental form of language) tries to resolve them, but when it does so, this resolution is a displacement to another level of discourse (a "surmounting") or the creation of culture, which turns out to be an elaborate mystification, which then must be deconstructed so that truth may come forth.

But of course truth cannot come forth. Deconstruction in these terms must be *construction* (thus mystification) of the primal situation. The construction must go on in language, so that in fact we seem to be gyring back and forth, not between reality and unreality but between two extremes within language itself. The primal situation is as much a human construct as the surmounting. But because the structuralist begins from the externalizing antimythic pole, structuralism has to assume, all along the continuum of language, that language speaks (i.e. controls) man rather than that man can ever speak language. Fundamentally antimythical, the structuralist sees man determined and inside a primary language at all times, in the same way that Locke saw man inside a primary nature. When man seems to be creating, he is always doing so inside a system of rules, drawn forth (i.e. constructed) from his actions and then declared to be a surrounding "Platonic" form. For the structuralist to say that man is unthinkable without language is to say that he is always enclosed in it and spoken by it.

But Lévi-Strauss seems to admit that the rules change whenever a new human creation is added to the system, so it appears that the system is hypostatized after the creative fact. Thus Lévi-Strauss seems to embrace two contrary positions. He does this, I think, with ambivalence. On the other hand, his critic, the philosopher Jacques Derrida, loves the irony.

3. Phenomenology and fallen miracle

Structuralism's predication of language on a single system of rules of logic obliterates the difference between the activities of the poet and of the critic, subjecting the poet to those rules of discourse that the critic has for the most part accepted as his own. Boon identifies Baudelaire as one who "went so far as to deny any fast distinction between the creative function and the critical one."[41] and Peter

Caws argues as a structuralist, "The critic confronted by the book is subject to the same conditions of utterance as the writer confronted by the world."[42] The only difference is that the texts are different—book and world. But both are systems of signification. All fields of experience present the same problem of interpretation, and artistic activity, so-called, is only one level of hermeneutic. But no hermeneutic for a structuralist is ever the pure reading of an object. It is the reading of the system of relations, and this includes the relation of the reader to the "text." One does not as interpreter read the "text" as object but instead the encounter in which one is involved with the "text." And further, in this situation the self has been deconstructed into a set of relations, so that what is being read is the relationship between two sets. This is why it has been said by Lévi-Strauss, who plays with the irony of this situation, that it can't be decided whether the thought of the people he studies is ordered by him or whether their thought forms his.[43] Lévi-Strauss's own work, especially *Mythologiques*, has come to be the story of his growing realization of this situation and "anatomizes" the development of the realization in certain ways similar to the way Yeats's *A Vision* "anatomizes" the growth of Yeats's "contrary" vision. The antimythical theorist becomes a myth-maker.

The claim is that such an orientation deconstructs every text. The term sometimes used is "decenter." Some observations must be made about this. "Center" here is identified with meaning. Such meaning cannot ever be found *in* or behind a "text," since the "text" is always a variant. The meaning is always deferred, that is, there is always a "text" previous to the "text" in question. What any "text" signifies is the difference between a "text" and a previous "text." There is the further twist that such difference can never be located because the hermeneutic act is caught in the encounter between interpreter as "text" and the "text" in question and can only reveal that encounter—the difference. There is therefore a regress backward infinitely unless arrested by the reconciling myth of "center" of an original word with meaning incarnate, as appears at times in Heidegger, or by the myth of a Platonic timeless structure, as sometimes appears, or, if you will, threatens to appear in Lévi-Strauss.

These problems lead out of the area of pure structuralism into concern with the act of reading itself. Jonathan Culler, in an attempt to construct a theory of reader competence, writes:

> . . . it may be misleading to think of texts as "organic wholes."
> This unity is produced not so much by intrinsic features of

their parts as by the intent at totality of the interpretive process: the strength of the expectations which lead readers
to look for certain forms of organization in a text and find
them.[44]

Such competence is clearly determined by the cultural situation. The
center is displaced to the act of reading.

We are also led into that curious marriage of structuralism and
phenomenology that has recently given birth to the critiques of
Jacques Derrida. As I understand Derrida, his concern about structuralism is that its deconstructions are not sufficiently deconstructive,
because the concept of structure itself is a center or "origin." Derrida
begins with a critique of the so-called metaphysics of "presence." Included here would be, in my terms, not only the idea of an "origin"
present in the "miraculous" symbol but also the idea that a word can
be transparent, that is, signify as "present" behind it an object or
thought. For Derrida, we can never proceed from signifier to signified
in the sense of reference or even to a signified in the sense of sense.
We cannot discover a complete meaning or "origin" of a word. This,
for Derrida, is most obvious in poetry, but true of all language, certainly written language, which is freed from its "origin" in a speaker;
and Derrida privileges writing. He connects the metaphysics of
"presence," "origin," or achievable meaning with the traditional concept of *logos*, which in his view has given to the signified primacy
over the signifier. Any view which presumes this primacy is called
"metaphysical."

But for Derrida there is no signified in these senses, only a signified in Saussure's sense of difference, each signifier signifying its difference from other signifiers in a linguistic field. A poem, or any piece
of language, is a play of differences. Interpretation is an endless act of
the production of a new play from this play. In fact, it is merely the
extension of the play. It is the interpreter joining in the play of signification. Only in this sort of creativity can we possibly escape the
nostalgia for a center or an "origin" of meaning, which dominates
objectivist interpretation and imprisons us in an ideology. Derrida
recognizes, however, that the decentering he advocates cannot finally
be achieved, for that would make the principle on which the decentering is based a center. He acknowledges that in this sense we are
trapped, and our task is the endless process of decentering. Thus he
plays, and *would* play, with the irony of this situation, man always
inside language, yet declaring a freedom that he knows he cannot at-

tain except by urging on the dance of language itself, never stopping. The irony is well expressed in a well-known remark in *L'Écriture et la différence*:

> From this language it is necessary for us to try to free ourselves. Not actually to *try* to free ourselves from it, for that is impossible without forgetting our historical condition. But to imagine (rêver) it. Not actually to *free* ourselves from it, which would be senseless and would deprive us of the light of sense. But to resist it as far as possible.[45]

This is, of course, itself a center and has been well named by Culler in a critique of Derridean critical structuralism as the "myth of the innocence of becoming."[46] Murray Krieger has recently remarked that Derrida's critique of language is not a critique of poetry, but Derrida, despite certain flourishes, does not allow a distinction between poetry and other language that Krieger desires to keep.[47] Derrida's view that poetry most obviously exhibits difference is not in any way intended to make poetry different from any other discourse. His model of language is the same antimythical one as that of the structuralists, and it is his dogged clinging to this model that makes his own play possible. Derrida's is a language of *logos* as logical form. The resolutions of myth in such a situation must always be only mystifying false centers or "origins" with regrettable ideological baggage. There are attractive things about this position, not the least of which is its elegant form while at the same time it claims to remain ever open. In the end, though, it assumes a narrow and monolithic view of language, not as a creative power but only as a mode of signification, albeit displaced signification, and allows only for reactionary play within an infinite enclosure.

It is in the concept of imprisonment in language that the structuralist development joins with existential phenomenology in the work of Paul de Man, who perhaps best exemplifies the appearance of this mixture in American critical theory. De Man attacks the concept of the symbol as it was developed out of romanticism. In an essay called "Literary History and Literary Modernity," de Man succinctly reveals his position vis-á-vis language:

> . . . the writer's language is to some degree the product of his own action; he is both the historian and the agent of his own language. The ambivalence of writing is such that it can be

considered both an act and an interpretive process that follows after an act with which it cannot coincide.[48]

However, of these two concepts of writing, it is the latter that dominates his work. In an ingenious and influential essay, "The Rhetoric
of Temporality," he regards the concept of the symbol as a "mystification" that threw the romantics into irresolvable contradictions.[49]
He limits his concept of the symbol to what I have called the "miraculous." He declares that continental criticism "presents a meth-
odologically motivated attack on the notion that a literary or poetic
consciousness is in any way a privileged consciousness, whose use of
language can pretend to escape, to some degree, from the duplicity,
the confusion, the untruth that we take for granted in the everyday
use of language." For de Man, the only language that could escape
this dilemma is "unmediated expression," and that is a "philosophical impossibility."[50]

Both statements proceed *from* the attitude that language is ideally
a copier or a signifier of a preceding reality, but for de Man, language
cannot do what it is supposed to do. It is fallen. It stands between
man and a hidden truth that it can never express. From the point of
view that I am taking, his hidden truth is a creation of language,
which antimythically hypostatizes it as hidden. As language operates
further and further away from the realm of myth, the further beyond
and before itself it appears to thrust its so-called meaning. At the
center-circumference (not in Derrida's sense of center, but Blake's) it
declares its meaning to be generated out of unspecifiable experience.
But for de Man, there is no poetic center-circumference; there is only
an isolated Blakean center that can never discover a Derridean center
even though it hypostatizes the Derridean center as an ontological
ideal; language is a system of signs radically cut off from meaning:

> It is the distinct privilege of language to hide meaning behind
> a misleading sign, as when we hide rage or hatred behind a
> smile. But it is the distinctive curse of all language as soon as
> any kind of interpersonal relation is involved, that it is forced
> to act this way.[51]

Here de Man makes communication of a previous truth or reality definitive, then declares the impossibility of it. I, on the other hand,
take *creation* as definitive. This is a critical difference in perspective
from which all our subsequent differences proceed. De Man holds

that the actual expression always fails to "coincide with what has to be expressed,"[52] while I claim that what we call poems are first of all makings, events in which thought and meaning take place, not copyings or representations or strivings to find an elusive meaning. Indeed, de Man reverses entirely this notion, proclaiming that in the word "fiction" is an admission or self-conscious awareness of the fact that no expression fully reveals meaning. My own view is that the term "fiction" emphasizes that meaning is always being made rather than faultily copied or signified. But de Man argues:

> that sign and meaning can never coincide, is what is precisely taken for granted in the kind of language we call literary. Literature, unlike everyday language, begins on the far side of this knowledge; it is the only form of language free from the fallacy of unmediated expression. All of us know this, although we know it in the misleading way of wishful assertion of the opposite. Yet the truth emerges in the foreknowledge we possess of the true nature of literature when we refer to it as *fiction*.[53]

Several remarks are pertinent here. It is curious for de Man to insist that we seem only to declare this to be true by stating the opposite. It is interesting that the word "fiction" has spread its influence into areas other than literature—physics, for example, where it clearly is identified with creation or making of thought. But the fundamental observation I want to make here is that the passage says that language vainly attempts to communicate a fully pre-existent meaning, that language and thought do not create, and that a "fiction" is a deviation from an established reality or meaning (though how we can think this if we cannot ever arrive at the meaning from which deviation occurs is unclear). De Man's and my emphases may appear logically independent, but there is a fundamental disagreement between us about the role of language in thought, the nature of the imagination, and the human condition.

The difference of orientation is well displayed, as I have implied, by contrasting the valorization of "secular" symbolism in my position and that of allegory in de Man's. In approaching this matter, de Man points out, "Hans-Georg Gadamer makes the valorization of symbol at the expense of allegory coincide with the growth of an aesthetic that refuses to distinguish between experience and the representation of this experience."[54] This is the common distinction, but it does not do justice to the development in the tradition from which I have tried to select, where the distinction that is obliterated or at least softened is one between experience and the verbal *formation* of it, not between experience and the *representation* of it. With Gadamer, de Man goes on to treat the symbol as something with indefiniteness of meaning. Priority in his analysis is given to a clear meaning. By the very way he puts the issue, the symbol is made to be a representation of a previously existent meaning, rather than the other way around, where the symbol is a forming. Indefiniteness of meaning is for de Man always to be deplored. It is mystification, weak thought. It is, in fact, a debasement of allegory, which properly expresses the relation of sign to meaning. A symbol can only be, to use Fish's terms, "message minus." But what if this apprehension of an indefiniteness of meaning is really a sign in itself of the inevitable failure of a naïve theory of interpretation to reach an assumed preexistent meaning that has never really existed? Does not the unexamined use of the term "meaning" itself here require de Man to separate sign and meaning? Is "meaning" then an appropriate term? The huge commentary in modern criticism about the impossibility of translation and the "heresy" of paraphrase can be taken as an effort to say that it is not. Put another way, the question before us is whether man is only an *animal significans*, in Culler's terms, or also the *animal symbolicum* that Cassirer hoped to establish.

The symbol in de Man, as in most of the continental *nouvelle critique*, is treated as a trope (despite Lévi-Strauss's connection of language with metaphor), and a very inadequate trope at that, for it can never deliver on its promises of the "miraculous." In much romantic practice the irony of the trope *as such a trope* is often the poetic theme, but I believe romantic theory and practice of the symbol has been a searching in the direction of a description of the poem as a whole, where the characteristics of the so-called trope "symbol" are ultimately seen as pertaining not to a device or element in the poem but to the poem as a whole. De Man's treatment of irony as a trope is, of course, completely different from that of the American New Critics, who came to use the term "irony" as descriptive of whole poems rather than of parts of poems. By the same process the romantics made allegory a term that means "nonpoem." What de Man must see as supremely important—the *meaning* of the poem—is what the romantics called allegorical and what to them and later critics became the hated paraphrase. A twofold confusion resulted from this: First, the poems containing allegory as it was traditionally understood were routinely denigrated when disliked, even though it is difficult to find a major poem that does not contain allegory in this sense. Second, the term "symbol," on its way to becoming a "secular" term for a poem, kept slipping back to its usage as designating a special sort of trope with "miraculous" powers. This led to much flying off into what T. E. Hulme called the "circumambient gas."[55] Insofar as de Man is complaining about this sort of miraculism in the so-called trope called the symbol, I am with him. It is another language in which to complain about romantic sentimentality and the tendency of romantic symbolism to turn into allegory of the "religious" type. But ironically this is exactly what de Man's view of poetry is.

It is also regrettable that in making the term "allegory" mean nonpoem there was no term left available to criticism to describe, let alone do justice to, traditional allegorical usage, or what I call the hypostatization of meaning. But this is not the immediate issue of concern. When de Man attacks romantic theorists, he attacks them for valorizing the symbol as "miraculous" *trope*, while I see them as struggling with the classical terminology of tropes against its fundamental assumptions about poetic wholes and toward a new theory of poetic wholes. As so often occurs in the history of language, romantic critics appropriated, or in Kenneth Burke's terms stole,[56] the terms of the old rhetorical criticism, wrenching them for their own uses. Ultimately their struggle allows us to move from their declaration that a poem contains symbols (and for that reason is valuable) to claims that the whole of a poem is a symbolic form.

In de Man and much structurally influenced continental criticism there exists a continuation of that profound disillusionment with language that is one dominant mood of romanticism and perhaps comes to its logical conclusion in Derrida's *reductio ad absurdum*. Derrida seems to play the role with respect to structuralism that Berkeley did in the empiricist movement. There comes a time in each case, however, when someone must kick a stone or recast the terms of argument. Therefore, I look at another romantic mood that continually seeks to formulate the full range of the possibilities of language. Certainly romanticism was incomplete and in many respects abortive. E. E. Bostetter was correct in so viewing it:

What seems at first glance triumphant affirmation is revealed on close observation as a desperate struggle for affirmation against increasingly powerful obstacles. The ultimate impression left by the poetry is of gradual loss of vitality and confidence too easily won and precariously held; of diminishing faith in the power of man; of a growing gap between the material and the spiritual and a deepening doubt; of affirmation hardening into an incendiary rhetoric sharply at odds with the perceptions and experience it conveys. Romantic poetry becomes in part the testing of a syntax that proved inadequate to the demands placed upon it.[57]

De Man connects this failure—though for him all language ultimately fails—with the romantic concept of the symbol, which would be a vehicle supposedly to achieve the ultimate—a form of language transcending language. He sees Wordsworth renouncing the "seductiveness and the poetical resources of a symbolical diction" and turning to allegory. This retreat he thinks inevitable to any right-thinking poet, the union of signified and signifier, subject and object, and so on being impossible. Further, for de Man, an allegorical sign refers always to a temporally "previous sign with which it can never coincide" in the enclosure which is language. "It is the essence of this previous sign," he says, "to be pure anteriority."[58] Here de Man mixes structural and existential traditions, from which all he has to say follows: In a temporal system of allegorical signs there is, from the point of view of any given moment or word, only a regress back through an infinite series of escaping meanings. The present can never capture the ultimate meaning. In any case, de Man's claim against the symbol is a claim against the "miraculous" form of the symbol as I have described it—against the symbol as incarnation. He does not admit as an outgrowth of romanticism the "secular" form of the symbolic.

All of this means that in de Man's view, for any kind of discourse there can only be misreadings in an infinite chain, though de Man's notion of misreading is different from Harold Bloom's well-known and ingenious psychologically oriented idea of misprision.[59] One might normally conclude that if there are *mis*readings there must be their Hegelian negation, a *reading*, but de Man's answer here, no doubt, would be that the notion of a *reading* is merely an example of language's hiding "behind a misleading sign." This misleading sign turns out to be the trope or figure. Figurality provides the deceit, and for de Man it is clearly a deceit, even perhaps the original sin, since the notion or model of language upon which his discourses are based is that of symbolic logic. Then, when he finds no discourse that measures up to this model, which he accepts absolutely with no reservations and without subjecting it to query, he can claim that figures are the culprit, particularly metaphor, because metaphor not only frustrates the hope of pure philosophical discourse but also glosses over difference with its illicit form of indifference. Thus figurality, which for him is the defining term of rhetoric, is responsible for what he calls "epistemological damage."[60]

De Man's argument turns on the Blakean kind of negation I have called difference/indifference: There is an ideal form of language, a pure and undifferentiated form of symbolic logic; there is our fallen linguistic state, which is one purely of difference in a semiotic field. Metaphor would delude us into its illicit form of indifference, but falsely: "It appears that philosophy either has to give up its own constitutive claim to rigor in order to come to terms with the figurality of its language or that it has to free itself from figuration altogether."[61] But de Man must know that he has already made the latter impossible and the former deceitful. Thus philosophy can only be rhetoric, subject to deconstruction in terms of the deceit it is continually performing with respect to a positivistic notion of truth, which requires a pure "unfigurality." I shall not say here "literality," because I agree with Northrop Frye that if literality means anything it ought to have to do with the literary.[62]

So, in order to play his language game, de Man posits the ideal of the logical positivists as a norm which he then comes to claim no discourse can reach. But rather than calling in question the norm, he exploits the predicament this positing creates. This ideal is *not* for de Man a fictive ontological limit, such as I mentioned in connection with Kuhn's disagreement with Popper. De Man's critique is radically antimythical, locating truth at that limit, then never finding it. As a result every discourse becomes a candidate for a deconstructive essay, a fact that ought to keep young academicians busy much longer than the methodology that grew out of the New Criticism did. For there is really no end to the sophistic discourse this can generate. Or rather, the only end is a myth of the fallen condition of figurality itself. For de Man, this fall is either an unredeemable sin or it is a fixed condition into which Adam was born: Man is in language; language is not in man. There is no contrary: Man is in a fallen state where in practice difference negates indifference, the unattainable ideal by which everything must be judged. The one notion of language triumphs over and remains aloof from its fallen deceitfulness, as aloof as the Gnostic deity, signifiable, but only ironically so, by a "religious" form of romantic allegory.

Martin Heidegger, whose work has influenced de Man, but whose views de Man revises in the direction of poststructuralist enclosure, seems to offer a fictive beginning for de Man's otherwise infinite regress. But for de Man it is a beginning we can never recapture and make our condition, because of its involvement in a chain of infinite deferral. In Heidegger's *Introduction to Metaphysics* there is perhaps the best example of his characteristic etymologizing. It is not merely a quirk of the professor; it is quite central to his fundamentally theological approach. He presses words back to "origins," where it can be imagined that word and concept were one. With the modern word "being," he reaches back past Aquinas, Aristotle, and Plato all the way to Parmenides and Heraclitus, where he restores a unity of meaning to the original word, before it was, Osiris-like, torn apart. This modern Isis reconstructs its meaning by deconstructing its history. The myth behind all this is that of the single original word given by God to man, which broke up in the Babel of tongues. Language as *we* know it thus represents the condition of the Fall. Heidegger finds the primordial word to have been radically creative in a special sense I shall later discuss, but the fallen word is a mere sign.[63] For de Man, allegory faces up to the fact of the Fall and "designates primarily a distance in relation to its own origin, and, renouncing the nostalgia and the desire to coincide, it establishes its language in the void of this temporal difference."[64] According to this view, the authentic voice of romantic literature is indeed a romantic irony, emphasizing failure to reach ultimate meaning, acknowledgment of the victory of nature over man, and suspicion of the presumptuousness of the "miraculously" symbolizing imagination. The myth of past origin halting the infinite regress of meaning is balanced in the future, in the existentialist view, not by a myth of achievement but by the fact of death. This word, incidentally, is never uttered in de Man's essay, but it lurks unspoken.[65] Indeed, this fact obliterates all other meaning. Every fallen word looms toward it—the one authenticity. De Man demystifies the symbol only to provide a new mystification in the supreme symbol of the Fall.

Is it possible to find in romanticism an alternative to the disillusionment attendant upon the fixation on death and the desire to transcend language and earth? Such an effort will, of course, be called "mystification" in its turn. But de Man's version of romantic agony seems to me excessively centered upon what Blake called the "selfhood" and its attendant egoism. If the symbol could be purged of its connections with, on the one hand, the Pyrrhic effort at transcendence, which turn it into a form of the allegoric—in this case the "religious" allegoric—and, on the other hand, its connections with "miraculous" incarnation, if we could find in it a reasonably mundane creative principle—one that concerns itself concretely with human culture—perhaps what begins in romanticism could be declared to have outgrown the crisis Bostetter saw in it.

I agree that as long as we hold that (A) language is a system of signs, of differences, of perpetual deferral of meaning, we find ourselves locked inside language and have only romantic irony to assuage our *angst*. I agree that given this highly abstracted notion of language, man is *in* language and thus always in some way determined by it. But I also see (B) history as *in* man and determined by man. Language in the sense of *langue* may be merely a system of differences, but *langue* is an abstraction from concrete human linguistic acts which are each radical, formative expressions of experience that are the ground of *langue*'s fictive existence. Thus I also hold that language can emerge from man anew every day as a creative form. De Man, it seems to me, claims that A is our condition, either from eternity or by virtue of a Fall, and that B doesn't solve the problem of our yearning for a hidden truth: We would best be rid of the illusion that we can make miracles, as modern poets have rid themselves of the illusion and realistically embraced the discontinuities of allegory. This view is a "religious" form of antimyth. Derrida chooses to declare A all we can know and any positing of how A came about a fiction, which illicitly assumes an "origin." This does not prevent us from creative activity in the form of the play of signifiers, but history is never *in* us, nor is language contained by us. His view is deliberately "secular" but not symbolic. My view is that both A and B are fictions in the sense not of pretenses but of creations. A is an antimythical creation; B is mythical.

Obviously, rather than deconstruct Derrida, I would like to turn him inside out so that one could see him as representative of antimyth, with the poetic as his contrary. However, the situation is not that simple. For a long time the dominant modes of philosophy have been antimythical, modeled on the antimythical "certainties" of symbolic logic. As a philosophical ironist Derrida won't stay at the antimythical end, even though his model of language seems to be antimythical. But it is inadequate to him, and he adopts something of the poetic stance himself. There has always been this curiosity in philosophy—a curiosity that impelled Hans Meyerhoff to divide philosophers into two groups, the literary and the scientific.[66] However, it might be better to view Meyerhoff's literary philosophers as ironists who, having met the limit of antimyth, seek the balance afforded by the poetic contrary, still never actually becoming poets. Such philosophy would inhabit the area of the "ironic," though it sometimes struggles to devour the whole continuum—without success. The importance of Derrida may be his awareness, renewed for our time, of the need to restore irony to philosophy in the face of modern philosophy's almost total commitment to an antimythical stance. Derrida's irony comes from his acceptance of antimyth at the outset and then his exploration of the void into which this takes us. The ultimate book of Derrida ought to be what Northrop Frye calls a Menippean satire. This might better explain Plato's recourse to myth without declaring him to be a poet, which the Platonic antimyth, offered by Plato himself, denies him to be.

The contrary which I want to hold to as the fundamental fictive opposition might be treated as that of nature containing culture (and man) and culture containing nature. Unlike Derrida, I say that we need not *try* to escape language (culture) even though we know we cannot (not actually *try*). Instead we have to learn to hold both sides of the opposition in our minds as equal forms of human *creativity*. As Empedocles said of concord and discord, "Never will boundless time be emptied of that pair."[67] In the end, of course, I claim that in experience myth contains antimyth, but only as the seed contains the tree, and that what we have is Yeatsian conflict and Blakean creation. This we must accept with a gaiety balanced against our dread, lest Homer's prayer be answered. Clearly, in Derrida's terms I have established a "center." It is a fictive center, which even Derrida in the end thinks we must have, though continually abandon. I claim mine to be the necessary one, because I think it insists on the moral necessity of projecting a vision of culture and attempting to achieve it. Such a vision would avoid the tyranny of mythical and antimythical extremes and is directed toward a future in which humankind recognizes responsibility for the world. Both critical structuralist and existential visions seem to me to end in forms of reaction.

My brief discussion of de Man's views ends by claiming that for him poetry and finally, of course, all discourse, falls under the category of "religious" allegory. But phenomenological literary theory has not often resulted in de Man's own mixture of it with structuralism and existentialism. If we look at the most influential precursors of contemporary phenomenological thought—for example, Heidegger himself or Karl Jaspers—I think we shall see that de Man has sacrificed Heidegger's hermeneutic phenomenology and Jaspers' existential phenomenology, both of which represent theories of "miraculous" symbolism, to structuralist allegorizing. In a recent book, Robert Magliola draws a distinction between a phenomenological view and a Neo-Kantian one. Phenomenology, he claims, is an epistemological theory of mutual implication of subject and object. Knowledge is a mutual grasping between subject and object.[68] It is in this concrete experience that the essence of being is disclosed.[69] The Neo-Kantian view is that knowledge is not a grasping but the construction of an object. It is a mistake to think of Heidegger, or Jaspers, as beginning with a prior subject/object situation. Heidegger's point is that the subject/object distinction is already fallen, like the word. It is fallen as the result of subjectism (*Subjektität*), which, as Richard Palmer has put it, "is a broader term than subjectivity, for it means that the world is regarded as basically measured by man."[70] This leads to the idea of mastery of the world (seen as object) and results in the domination of technology, the extremity of antimyth. In such a frame of mind we are unable to let the world be. In Heidegger's view the Neo-Kantian cannot let be; all construction or creativity in the Neo-Kantian sense leads to the dangers of mastery. In his typical way, Heidegger examines the ancient word *techne* and declares that in connection with poetry it originally meant "making manifest" rather than simply "making." Modern *techne* has fallen and lost this sense; it has become making for use, or technology. As Harold Alderman has observed in an excellent treatment of Heidegger's critique of science and technology, the old poetic *techne* was responsible and contemplative, and modern technology is domineering and challenging. The result is the loss of the mutuality of man and world. Similarly, the word *physis* meant originally emergence or coming to being. Alderman notes that Heidegger's distinction between science and technology is based on his view that science maintains a pretense of letting be and treats beings as objects, while technology treats beings as resources.[71]

It is difficult to escape subjectism because it is so difficult to probe beneath its foundation—as difficult as it was for Vico and Cassirer to rid themselves of certain preconceptions in their studies of myth. As Karsten Harries has pointed out,

> Traditional ontology must lack a foundation as long as it seeks to exhibit the structures constitutive of the things man encounters, while taking for granted a particular interpreta-

tion of the encounter, which gives priority to detached observation, without questioning the adequacy of that interpretation. Heidegger's fundamental ontology attempts to meet this deficiency by giving more careful attention to the many different modes in which man exists and encounters things.[72]

Heidegger insists on the fundamental ontological field of poetic grasping, which is at the same time a letting be. The subjectism of science is a special mode of thought with a special purpose. Letting be is actually an unconcealment or disclosure. But the term "unconcealment" is not quite right. Rather, what occurs is a bringing into being. Such an act is what hermeneutic properly is, rather than interpretation as it was practiced through the time of Wilhelm Dilthey. Meaning is never, Heidegger claims, "a property attaching to entities, lying 'behind' them, or floating somewhere in an intermediate domain."[73] Meaning is not, in other words, romantically allegorical.

Heidegger's hermeneutic phenomenology is an effort to allow for the poetic act as itself a bringer into being and for language itself as the vehicle. It is in this spirit that Heidegger offers the remark that Culler quotes (page 348) to the effect that language speaks man, rather than man speaking language. By this he does not, as the structuralists would, argue that man is enclosed in the prison house of language. On the contrary, he sees language as a condition of liberation. Not an enclosure, neither is it a tool that man masters. It is a power. So he says elsewhere,

> . . . we cannot say, "Language speaks." For this would be to say: "It is language that first brings man about, brings him into existence." Understood in this way, man would be bespoken by language.[74]

He is trying to say that man dwells poetically with the power of language. Language is prior to being but is not a thing:

> There is some evidence that the essential nature of language flatly refuses to express itself in words—in the language, that is, in which we make statements about language. If language everywhere withholds its nature in this sense, then such withholding is in the very nature of language. Thus language not only holds back when we speak it in the accustomed ways, but this its holding back is determined by the fact that lan-

guage holds back its own origin and so denies its being to our usual notions.[75]

Language is the place where being is spoken. Questions about the invention of language by man are absurd because it is human power: "How could man ever have invented the power which pervades him, which alone enables him to be as a man?"[76] Poetic naming is the filling of the place with being. It does not involve something already known being given a name: ". . . it is rather that when the poet speaks the essential word, the existent is by this naming nominated as what it is. . . . Poetry is the establishing of being by means of the word."[77] This linguistic space of language is fundamentally poetic. Indeed, poetry as a term means for Heidegger something prior to language, but only insofar as the poetic is the essence of language. Poetic naming would seem to nominate beings *to* their Being.

Heidegger sometimes treats this poetic naming as creation. It not only opens up but also seems to set up a world; yet in the end the hermeneutic act, which Heidegger identifies with the poetic, is always more disclosure than creation. That which is is never of our making. When Heidegger speaks of creation he means bringing forth, and the model of this is "miraculous" incarnation. Behind the idea is specifically the "miraculous" incarnation of the word in the Gospel of St. John. *Logos* is for Heidegger not the language of reason but *poesis* as *techne*. In these terms Heidegger seeks to balance disclosure and creation. The same balancing occurs in the doctrine of incarnation and rituals containing it, where there is claimed to be the perfect identity of symbol and referent. Gadamer's remark that a symbol is a "coincidence of sensible appearance and suprasensible meaning . . . the union of two things that belong to each other,"[78] leads to the necessity of claiming that the gods need men as much as men need the gods. But an equality of mutuality, which is the basis of phenomenology, can never quite be sustained. The gods must be superior. Thus there emerges from the idea of the "miraculous" the idea of fallen analogy, where the symbol becomes imperfect and allegorical in the "religious" sense. Gadamer notes that in religion there is always the need to maintain tension between image and referent. For Gadamer, the religious symbol involves always the "dividing of what is one and reuniting it again."[79] There is a constant movement from "miraculous" symbol to "religious" allegory and back.

In Heidegger, too, the word falls, and his own work becomes as it develops a ritual act of restoration to symbol. In such a system, such acts must be regarded as supreme. Hermeneutic philosophizing takes precedence over other forms as the true vehicle of knowledge. All other forms are alienated from being and must be reduced to special ways of making use of the world. Science becomes inevitably technology and its discontents.

Characteristically, Heidegger would return the term "hermeneutics" to its original meaning. He does not claim to invent a new hermeneutics, nor for that matter to invent anything new, only to discover the truth implicit in pre-Socratic thought, and in language itself:

> The expression "hermeneutic" derives from the Greek verb *hermeneuein*. That verb is related to the noun *hermeneus*, which is referable to the name of the god Hermes by a playful thinking that is more compelling than the rigor of science. Hermes is the divine messenger. He brings the message of destiny; *hermeneuein* is that exposition which brings tidings because it can listen to a message.[80]

This last remark leads to Heidegger's conception of the hermeneutic enterprise as a conversation with a "text." The interpreter brings a "fore-sight" to the text: "An interpretation is never a presuppositionless apprehending of something presented to us." An interpretation presupposes an understanding:

> In interpreting, we do not, so to speak, throw a "signification" over some naked thing which is present-at-hand, we do not stick a value on it; but when something within-the-world is encountered as such, the thing in question already has an involvement which is disclosed in our understanding of the world, and this involvement is one which gets laid out by the interpretation.[81]

This view, which leads the way to the phenomenological hermeneutics of Hans-Georg Gadamer, accounts for Heidegger's own hermeneutical essays in which texts become disclosed by Heidegger's own poetic contemplation upon them. Thus every text must in any historical moment be brought into being by a new text, and so on. Each text would then seem for that moment of conversation to recede behind its newly formed being in the hermeneutic act. The critic and poet would seem to be one, the poem incarnate in the critic's words. The role of incarnate symbol is transferred into the critic's conversation with the poem itself. But is the poem not now a husk? Or is it not lost behind its fallen form—the critic's discourse?

The philosophy of *existenz* of Karl Jaspers presents a powerful concept of "miraculous" symbolism through the idea of the "cypher-script of being." The cypher, which is really a symbol in the "miraculous" sense, harbors both sensuousness and transparence out of which it makes a new whole. If one finds transparency alone, one has "disassociation from sensuousness" and the loss of the real encounter with being, which can come with "the defection from the cypher to the pure concept." At the same time, "absolute adherence to the sensuous draws one into the darkness of transparentlessness" or the "slipping into groundlessness."[82] Jaspers rejects the flight to absolute concept which was the dialectical end for Hegel, in which art and religion are surpassed. Instead, Jaspers valorizes a state similar to the condition of Hegel's romantic art—a halfway state that becomes religious:

> This religious corporeality—if one compares it with being bound to transparentless realities—causes an upswing into the suprasensuous. . . . Not the transparency of sensuousness but the concreteness of Transcendence in a particular empirical reality of the world is the result.[83]

The new whole is signified by "transcendence," where Being is grasped in a going-beyond, but a going-beyond not in the direction of a pure concept or Hegelian absolute.[84] This idea can be nothing other than a restoration of the idea of incarnation, to which Jaspers frequently refers. Jesus himself is a cypher or symbol in which we read being, but it is incarnation with a difference, for the Christ myth is "a cypher for the justification of the cypher as mediation between God and man":

> . . . there is in the Christ myth the indication that everything human has in it the possibility of relatedness to God, God-nearness, and that the way to God goes through the world and through the reality of our historically to be determined human nature, and not by-passing the world.[85]

The space of transcendence which is the way through the world is the cypher or symbol itself. We can never grasp the One directly. To do so leaves us with an empty concept. Theology itself falls short by trying to go too far. To try to image God except in the "vanishing mediation of cyphers falls short of the mark."[86]

The cypher or symbol, then, does not signify a beyond. Its signification lies in its presentness. And signification is "only a metaphor for being-a-cypher."[87] When one seeks to provide a cypher's signification, the cypher becomes "fixed and definite and turns into an object in the world," thereby losing its essential reality.[88] This is not to say that we do not question the cypher's meaning, but we do not do so, or should not do so, in the usual sense of interpretation:

> Genuine symbols cannot be interpreted; what can be interpreted through an "other" ceases to be a symbol. On the other hand, the interpretation of symbols through their self-presentation penetrates into them but does not explain them. Such interpretation encircles and circumscribes, penetrates and illuminates. It becomes itself at once a part of the symbol. By interpreting it, it participates in symbol-status.[89]

Thus Jaspers sees proper interpretation as an "endless movement" set in motion by the symbol. Every hermeneutic act is part of a chain of being, of questioning, of conversing:

> Interpreting is not a form of cognition of the meaning of the cypher, but is itself a metaphorical act, a game. To interpret is impossible; Being itself, Transcendence, is present. It is nameless. If we speak of it, then we use an infinite number of names and cancel them all again.[90]

Here the difference between symbol and interpretation, poem and criticism, is obliterated and all is hermeneutic. The ultimate form of philosophizing would be "the penetration of objectivity in such a way that everything is a metaphor (cypher), nothing is without language, nothing is left to mere existence. . . ."[91]

But there are all sorts of ways to slip from transcendence in the symbol: superstition, allegory, aesthetic detachment, dogmatic metaphysics, and magic.[92] These are all ways by which we erroneously seek for "truth itself." We cannot find "truth itself" by giving precedence to one mode or another.[93] The idea of a "universally valid truth" is always being subverted by existence itself, which is radically historical and thus makes every hermeneutic event tied to the conditions of that moment and a conversation rather than an objectivization. A past can only be present as cypher through the "mode of its sensuous presentness."[94]

This view, which has much to recommend it, is, as I have said, a theory of the "miraculous" symbol, where though all is declared to be present in the cypher, yet the cypher also draws being into itself from elsewhere. As such it stands in contrast to a "secular" view, though clearly it secularizes its own miraculism to a considerable extent. Still, it seems to me that in the end it puts all human activity at the behest of a fundamentally religious view that allows no other forms of human truth to emerge as a contrary. In *The Philosophy of Existence*, Jaspers remarks:

> The fact that all modes of the meaning of truth *come together* in actual human life, and that man thus exists within all the sources of all the modes, urges us on to the *one* truth in which no mode of the encompassing is lost. And only clarity about the multiplicity of meanings of truth brings the question of the one truth to that point where breadth of view becomes possible, and an easy answer—in the presence of an intense urgency of the One—becomes impossible.[95]

But in the end his own miraculism seems to do just what he warns against. This is inevitable in a view that places discovery before creation and flirts with what Wheelwright called threshold experience. The dominant form is the "religious" and the seeking out of the hidden god. The result must ultimately be a reactionary turning away from the possibilities of culture and human concern.

The phenomenological hermeneutics of Hans-Georg Gadamer follows Heidegger and Jaspers in accepting man's radical historicity. Gadamer is thus distinguishable from the historicist interpreters of history in the nineteenth century who attempted to eliminate the interpreter's "horizon." This inevitable horizon or perspective is always involved in an interpretation. It must not, however, be regarded as an imprisoning subjectivity but an opening out into conversation with the past, a fusion of a present horizon with a past one. Language is the medium of the conversation, of course. Experience is linguistic:

> . . . the illusion that things precede their manifestation in language conceals the fundamentally linguistic character of our experience of the world.[96]

Language cannot be regarded as fundamentally instrumental; instrumental uses of language are special and narrow. Gadamer's views provide an apparent contrast to those of Hirsch, who argues for a methodology of "objective interpretation" by which one reading of a text is preferable to another by virtue of its being more probable.[97] While Gadamer's position requires a view of language as originally poetic in Heidegger's sense, Hirsch's model of language is "fallen," that is, it assumes that the proper model is that of symbolic logic. Gadamer would swallow Hirsch by claiming that Hirsch's positivistic horizon is exceedingly limited (though he has no criterion for determining horizontal scope). Hirsch can claim that Gadamer's view is purely relativistic and gives us nowhere to stand. It seems to me, without discussing these two views at length, that this is an impasse that might be resolved by taking an independent position such as I have already suggested. Perhaps Heidegger's model of language *was* originally the right one, but it seems almost quixotic today to insist on it as still language's only authentic being. It is a look backwards nostalgically to an impossible purity and to return to a theology of the Fall. Still, Heidegger's criticism of technology is powerful, though not powerful enough to demand that we require science to abandon its claims to truth or to disclosure of being in its own mode. I believe that we must instead abandon nostalgia for the merely poetic on the one hand and a desire for an overarching positivism on the other, adopting a theory of "secular" creativity in a variety of interlocking or contrary symbolic forms, where poetry and science play reprobate to one another. Symbolic forms are not prisons but means by which we can liberate ourselves. In them we establish our visions, or, in my terms, fictions of a possible culture, accomplished by intellectual strife.

4. METAPHOR AND SECULAR SYMBOLIC

THE NOTION of the symbol has usually been closely related to that of metaphor, either in its technically rhetorical tropological sense or in the broader sense which makes it virtually the defining idea of language itself. The latter sense has appeared frequently in our investigation to this point. Paul Ricoeur has recently studied metaphor in the former sense. His *Rule of Metaphor* (published in France in 1975) nearly eliminates the term "symbol" from a discourse that in his previous books was dominated by it and by an approach to the symbol heavily in the debt of the tradition of phenomenological hermeneutics.[98] However, Ricoeur seems not to have abandoned the symbol, because it plays a role in relation to metaphor in a series of lectures given at Texas Christian University in 1973 and published in 1976 under the title *Interpretation Theory: Discourse and the Surplus of Meaning.*[99] The turn from discussion of the symbol in *The Rule of Metaphor* I regard as a shift from emphasis on a "miraculous" form of symbolism to seeking establishment of a "secular" form, but the "miraculous" is nevertheless present in *Interpretation Theory.* This flow and ebb of the "miraculous" symbol in Ricoeur's thought is worth study, because to follow it demonstrates, in my opinion, the necessity of identifying the poetic with the "secular"—an identification which during the period 1973–76 Ricoeur is apparently not willing entirely to concede, though there are moments when the reader may think he has.

In his earlier work, *The Symbolism of Evil*, Ricoeur offers a notion of myth and symbol that is subsequently elaborated in his work on Freud and elsewhere.[100] Myth, which may once have been explanatory, Ricoeur says, actually reveals its "exploratory significance," that is, its "symbolic function." This exploration involves discovery of "the bond between man and what he considers sacred."[101] Myth must be seen "as myth,"[102] but at the same time it is awareness of myth *as* myth that is to revive philosophy. It appears that philosophy is an end toward which man uses myths and symbols. (I shall come back to this point to query the privileging of philosophy.) Myth is a "species of symbols,"[103] and symbols are the lowest constituent level of consciousness.[104] The obligation placed upon man by the symbol is to think. In the symbol, everything has in a sense been said enigmatically, and the symbol thus makes it necessary to begin everything again "in the dimension of thinking."[105] This idea is repeated in the statement that symbols are gifts of language; but here beginning is limited to symbols:

> . . . this gift creates for me the duty to think, to inaugurate philosophic discourse, starting from what is always prior to and the foundation of that discourse . . . philosophy does not begin anything, since the fullness of language precedes it.[106]

Ricoeur never abandons this position, even when the symbol disappears for a time from his discourse. But there is a paradox here, because philosophy also "begins from itself, since it is philosophy which inaugurates the question of meaning and of the foundation of meaning."[107] For Ricoeur, meaning comes into play only with philosophy and is not something allegorically extracted from symbols, even though Ricoeur also says:

> . . . in their mythical form symbols themselves push toward speculative expression; symbols themselves are the dawn of reflection. The hermeneutic problem is not imposed upon reflection from without, but proposed from within. . . .[108]

There are reasons Ricoeur would have it both ways: The symbol stands *on* or, better, *as* a threshold between *bios* and *logos*. Rather than making "symbol" his all-inclusive term, as Cassirer does, Ricoeur chooses the term "sign."[109] The symbol is a kind of sign that "conceals in its aim a double intentionality."[110] The primary intentionality gives the second meaning analogically.[111] A technical sign is perfectly "transparent," but symbolic signs are "opaque"; the obvious meaning points analogically to the second meaning, and the second meaning is given only in the first: "This opacity constitutes the depth of the symbol, which . . . is inexhaustible."[112] Thus a symbol requires interpretation of a meaning "attainable only in and through the first intentionality."[113] This interpretation involves a living in the first meaning, so as to be drawn by it beyond itself to the symbolic meaning, but in the process one can never "intellectually . . . dominate the similarity,"[114] that is, "objectify the analogical relation that connects the second meaning to the first."[115] Initially, this seems to suggest a hopeless enigma, but Ricoeur claims that it is the kind of enigma that actually provokes understanding, for there is something to "unfold" or "disimplicate" in symbols.[116] Thus the meaning of "symbol" cannot be discovered in the analogical model (*A* is to *B* as *C* is to *D*).[117] Ricoeur's symbol is not formalized, as in symbolic logic, for the symbol is "bound to its content."[118] Therefore, it contains the paradox of showing and hiding.[119]

At this point, I want to look ahead to Ricoeur's later work, which comes under the influence of structuralism and Anglo-American language analysis—especially the analysis of metaphor. In this later work, the symbol and the metaphor are described as having an "excess of signification," but this excess, strictly speaking, belongs to the interpretation:

> As in metaphor theory, this excess of signification in a symbol can be opposed to the literal signification, but only on the

condition that we also oppose two interpretations at the same
time. Only for an interpretation are there two levels of signification since it is the recognition of the literal meaning that
allows us to see that a symbol still contains more meaning.
This surplus of meaning is the residue of the literal interpretation. Yet for the one who participates in the symbolic signification, there are really not two significations, one literal
and the other symbolic, but rather a single movement, which
transfers him from one level to the other and which assimilates him to the second signification by means of, or through,
the literal one.[120]

At this point in his later work, Ricoeur invokes his version of the
symbol/allegory distinction, which has been with him since *The Symbolism of Evil*. In an allegory, he said there, the "literal" meaning is
contingent, and the secondary meaning is independently accessible.[121]
This is a way of saying, as he does, that symbols precede hermeneutics, while allegory *is* hermeneutic. Symbols are "spontaneously
formed and immediately significant," not another dimension of hermeneutic.[122] In the later work, even with the assimilation of new terminologies, he holds to this definition:

Allegory is a rhetorical procedure that can be eliminated once
it has done its job. Having ascended the ladder, we can then
descend it. Allegory is a didactic procedure. It facilitates
learning, but can be ignored in any directly conceptual approach. In contrast, there is no symbolic knowledge except
when it is impossible to directly grasp the concept and when
the direction towards the concept is indirectly indicated by
the secondary signification of a primary signification.[123]

The question raised by these more recent statements is the exact status of interpretation with respect to the symbol. Is "participation" in
the process of getting from one signification to the other part of hermeneutic? In *The Symbolism of Evil*, Ricoeur says no: Symbol and
allegory are not two directions of hermeneutic brought to bear on the
same content.[124] Participation must then be prehermeneutic, and
Ricoeur's theory requires a hermeneutic of the symbol that is not allegorical. The notion of philosophy as playing this role, as finishing
off the symbol in thought, seems to devalue the state of participation

itself in favor of a higher state reminiscent of Hegel's surpassing of art and apotheosis of reason, even though (as we shall see) Ricoeur criticizes Hegel's concept of absolute knowledge.

There is, indeed, for Ricoeur an allegorical or allegorizing form of hermeneutic—the hermeneutic of "suspicion" limited by its recognition of only a single dimension of the symbol, as in Freud's work.[125] Ricoeur raises the question of whether Freud was right to restrict the idea of the symbol to that of the stenographic sign,[126] and he goes on to distinguish dreams from art on the basis of the *expressive* nature of dreams and the *progressive* nature of art, which promotes "new meanings by mobilizing old energies initially invested in archaic figures."[127] Rather than quarrel with Freud, he thinks of symbols as of three types—religious, oneiric (dream), and poetic, each of which presumably requires a different hermeneutic, thus allowing Freud his method, so long as it is worked upon dreams. However, all three modes of symbolic activity stand on a threshold and cannot be "completely inscribed within the categories of logos."[128] This is hard to square with Freud's assumptions or with a hermeneutic of "suspicion," which appears to be allegorical and based on a principle of the substitution of a symbol for a word the dream desires to hide.

In his remarks about thresholds we begin to see that Ricoeur's symbol—despite his attitudes toward dream symbols—is modeled on the idea of a "miraculous" incarnation, which is treated in terms of a secondary meaning coming to inhabit the primary or so-called literal. This is what Ricoeur intends when he says that the symbol is "bound" or "rooted," in contrast to the metaphor, which is a free invention of discourse:[129]

> Metaphor occurs in the already purified universe of the *logos*, while the symbol hesitates on the dividing line between *bios* and *logos*. It testifies to the primordial rootedness of Discourse in Life. It is born when force and form coincide.[130]

Ricoeur's distinction between metaphor and symbol is crucial for him, but it is a very slippery one as he describes it. I believe it can be clarified by showing that Ricoeur's symbol is in the end "miraculous" and belongs ultimately to religion, while his metaphor is "secular" and ought properly to belong to poetry. Of the two, the symbol, for Ricoeur, remains the deeper, and it is privileged. Metaphor is "just the linguistic procedure—that bizarre form of predication—within which the symbolic power is deposited."[131]

In quoting these remarks, I have leapt, as I warned I would, from Ricoeur's earlier work to the 1973 lectures. In the same period Ricoeur was working on *The Rule of Metaphor*, a book which never mentions the symbol, in his own sense of it, but which paves the way for the distinction between metaphor and symbol later on. I have said that *The Rule of Metaphor* comes at the question through rhetoric and not symbolic theory. It begins with a commentary on Aristotle and post-Aristotelian rhetorical theory, and it argues convincingly that Aristotle's notion of metaphor as deviation from *common* usage became changed in later classical rhetoric to deviation from *proper* usage and/or *original* usage. This led to an erroneous distinction between figurative and proper and paved the way for a model of discourse that in its nonfigurative purity represents a "zero degree of rhetoric."[132] This is clearly what I have already called an antimythical fiction. It has the characteristics of Blakean "negation" by virtue of the accusatory morality it seems to practice in its use of the terms "deviation" and "transgression." In classical rhetoric, the metaphor was a figure that either filled a lacuna in the language or made an ornamental substitution in a discourse. The metaphor thus offered no new information. After reviewing this history, Ricoeur would shift the idea of metaphor from that of denomination to that of predication; this means that the metaphor *is* the predication and is not lodged merely in the noun. It is lodged in the tension of the copula itself. Further, metaphor as deviation (as destroyer of order through what Gilbert Ryle calls "category mistake") is also the inventor of a new order on the ruins of the old.[133] It is the complement of the logic of discovery, as it is regarded in Max Black's integration of the epistemological concept of the model and the poetic concept of the metaphor.[134] Finally, metaphor as radically predicative requires (to use Emile Benveniste's distinction) not a semiotics of the word, but a semantics of the sentence.[135] The sentence must be recognized as the "primary unit of meaning."[136] Discourse cannot be reduced to the "semiotics of lexical entities."[137] This leads to metaphor's own special kind of "rootedness" in the concrete act of discourse rather than in merely a semiotic code and revives, for that reason, the concept of reference, which drops out of the purely semiotic treatment of language with its binary opposition only of signifier and signified. The contrast is between the synthetic character of predication and the "mere interplay of differences and oppositions among signifiers."[138] Reviving the third element—reference in the sense employed in Gottlob Frege's famous essay[139]—Ricoeur limits the authority of Saussure's semiotics and Derrida's deconstruction. However, for Ricouer the relation of sense to reference in literature is not "suspended" in the way Frege claimed. Indeed, his aim is to do away with the restriction of reference to scientific discourse and such subsequent distinctions as relegated literature to the connotative and emotive.[140] Reference will have to appear, however, in a "more fundamental mode . . . whose explication is the task of interpretation."[141] Thus we have a semiotics of the word, a semantics of the sentence, and a hermeneutics of the work, the last of which will reveal the referential aspect that is suspended only in the sense that it awaits interpretation or disclosure. Of these three activities, the semiotic is for Ricoeur the narrowest, the least challenging, and the least fruitful. Ricoeur's view is that any other route than the semantic-hermeneutic lands us in what Blake would have called a "negating" distinction between descriptive and emotive:

> Critiques shaped by the school of logical positivism state that all language that is not *descriptive*, in the sense of giving information about *facts*, must be emotional. Furthermore, the suggestion is that what is "emotional" is sensed purely "within" the subject and is not related in any way whatsoever to anything outside the subject. . . . this postulate . . . says that there is no truth beyond the pale of verification.[142]

What Ricoeur attacks here is a negating acceptance of the subject/object antimyth in which literature is negated by relegation to the subjective—a phenomenon we have seen occur even among those who oppose the positivistic but end up embracing its antimythical postulates. Ricoeur explicitly mentions this and adds cogently: "The new rhetoric in France confronts us with the same scene: Literary theory and positivist epistemology support each other."[143] In his view, Northrop Frye's term "mood" and Tzvetan Todorov's "opaque discourse" embrace the positivistic while opposing it, though one might wish to question whether Frye's conclusions do not so enlarge the centripetally organized enclosure of "mood" as finally to swallow even the centrifugal and force the very notion of reference back upon us indirectly, just as Ricoeur desires.[144] What Ricoeur desires is a new notion of literary reference or of getting to reference that is released by interpretation. There is still in my mind, however, and perhaps still in Ricoeur's, the question of how complete the release from the symbol or metaphor into interpretation can be.

What I want to follow out here is Ricoeur's idea of the metaphor as creative of the possibility of "new meaning, which truly has the status of event."[145] The metaphorical event is repeatable. The event's adoption in the linguistic community indicates that it has created common meaning. But at this point, for Ricoeur, the event ceases to be metaphor as such and dies. It is no longer "authentic," no longer at once meaning and event. Ricoeur's distinction between authentic and dead metaphor is necessary to his attack on Derrida's refusal to differentiate between the two and his making all discourse carry the "trace" of dead metaphor in an endless semiotic chain down which one chases an always elusive original meaning. It also allows Ricoeur to make a distinction between metaphorical utterance and speculative or philosophical discourse.

Ricoeur's metaphor *is* the tension between the literal and the figurative in the relational function of the copula. This means that he demands a sense of "to be" that includes in itself an "is not." This "is not" insists (in Vivas's sense) *in* the tension, and evidence of it is the impossibility of the literal interpretation; it presents itself as a part of "filigree" in the metaphorical "is."[146] The result is a relation of "identity and difference in the interplay of resemblance."[147] (Ricoeur's use of "identity" is not mine; it is what I have called "indifference," as I shall later show.) This interplay is absolutely critical for Ricoeur (and for me), but there is a question between us as to how it ought to be characterized.

Ricoeur characterizes it in ways I shall attempt to illustrate, partly through quotation. He cheerfully acknowledges the argument that "anything resembles anything else . . . except for a certain difference!"[148] And he goes on to say that the conceptual structure of resemblance opposes and unites identity and difference. I think it is important to say not quite this, but that metaphor operates *in spite of* the categories of the same and different, that is, contrary to them. In interpreting a metaphor either the "is" or "is not" is likely to suffer negation, but Ricoeur wants to preserve both. Indeed, Ricoeur goes to some lengths to attack the theorists of the same as indulging in "ontological vehemence" or "naïveté," Philip Wheelwright being for him an example of this. On the other side, Ricoeur attacks theorists of "difference," as examples of the influence of logical positivism. Colin Turbayne's *Myth of Metaphor* succumbs to this influence, in Ricoeur's opinion.[149]

Ricoeur tries to mediate here by arguing, according to his theory of tension, that the "metaphor is that place in discourse where . . .

the identity and the difference do not meet together but confront each other."[150] However, this runs a danger of privileging one or the other. Another approach renders the following:

> Now, in saying that this is (like) that—whether the *like* is "marked" or not—the assimilation does not reach the level of the identity of meaning. The "similar" is not the "same." To see the similar, in Aristotle's words, is to apprehend the "same" within and in spite of "difference." This is why we were able to refer this schematization of a new sense back to the productive imagination.[151]

But is it not true that to see the similar is to apprehend the difference within the same? Can we not offer a word that allows us to oppose the opposition while yet allowing the opposition its contrary role? The opposition is clearly antimythical: Ricoeur's "identity" is my "indifference."

I would like to reserve the term "identity" for the mythic pole of a contrariety. Does it suffice? Not quite, if we engage in the effort to say what it means. I would propose the following "ironic" effort, nevertheless: I offer two examples. The first requires us to imagine again the primitive river bank people who call themselves crocodiles, yet do not rush into the river to frolic with their "sames." The second requires us to transpose over into a notion of "secular" metaphor the substance of some annotations Blake made to Swedenborg's *Wisdom of Angels Concerning Divine Love and Divine Wisdom*:

> Essence is not Identity, but from Essence proceeds Identity & from one Essence may proceed many Identities, as from one Affection may proceed many thoughts.
>
> That there is but one Omnipotent, Uncreate & God I agree, but that there is but one Infinite I do not; for if all but God is not Infinite, they shall come to an End, which God forbid.
>
> If the Essence was the same as the Identity, there could be but one Identity, which is false. Heaven would upon this plan be but a Clock; but one and the same Essence is therefore Essence & not Identity.[152]

Blake's notion of the infinite variety of identity has been remarked on by Northrop Frye in the process of making a distinction between things identical with everything else (as in metaphor) and things merely like everything else. The latter would be, Frye points out, a world of "monotonous uniformity."[153] But identity preserves the unique. In this effort to get between myth and antimyth there is indeed the tension of our own irony generated by our realization that we are breaking down a notion of what is proper according to the same/different negation. But we must keep proceeding with this. Ricoeur's description of the copula as tensive is itself from the antimythical point of view. Mythically the tension is not so tense; it is a situation in which is included all difference/indifference in the form of what Blake called emanations. They go out from myth in the form of concepts, of meanings, of interpretations, and they must also constantly return: ". . . all human forms identified, living, going forth and returning wearied. . . ."[154]

Ricoeur's idea of interpretation in *The Rule of Metaphor* is that of a going-beyond—a "horizon of speculative logos"—that frees conceptual thought from the play of double meaning and hence from the semantic dynamism characteristic of the metaphorical order.[155] The effort here is again to guard against entrapment in the Derridean labyrinth of metaphor, from which there is no escape once we bring to notice all the submerged or dead metaphor in any discourse. Ricoeur mounts this effort even though he has already declared that metaphoric discourse in the sentence is referential and *about something*.

The question, on the other hand, is whether this conceptual order in its freedom can ever fully devour the metaphorical. Ricoeur's "inclination" is to hold that "the universe of discourse [is] a universe kept in motion by an interplay of attractions and repulsions that ceaselessly promote the interaction and intersection of domains whose organizing nuclei are off-centered in relation to one another; and still this interplay never comes to rest in an absolute knowledge that would subsume the tensions."[156] The language is reminiscent of Blake's "Attraction and Repulsion, Reason and Energy, Love and Hate are necessary to human existence." Blake goes on to imply that some serious problems can arise from this situation. "From these contraries spring what the religious call Good & Evil," in other words, negations.[157] So there is the necessity of return to metaphor for regeneration of the language. Ricoeur, in a criticism of Hegel, calls for an endless quest that does not posit absolute knowledge.

We are now at the point where we notice the symbol reappearing in Ricoeur's work, and in the light of what I would call a "secular" theory, which is what Ricoeur's theory of metaphor is. In the new treatment of the symbol, its metaphorical dimension is granted, but the metaphor is limited to the arena of the semantic. There is something nonsemantic in the symbol, something deeper than any semantic appearance.[158] The symbol functions metaphorically, and its semantic nature can be fully apprehended by a study of metaphor. It is inexhaustible to conceptual language. But this does not invalidate conceptual thought; it means only that "no given categorization can embrace all the semantic possibilities of the symbol." On the other hand, only the concept can "testify to this surplus of meaning."[159] The metaphor is free, though located in the linguistic act of the sentence. The symbol is "rooted" and "bound" by its threshold situation—in and out of language at the same time. It is not merely a phenomenon of the linguistic surface. Consequently some of its inexhaustibility comes from its nonsemantic side. It is this very rootedness that caused Walter Benjamin to regard the symbol as fixed, as against the dynamism he assigned to allegory.[160]

Poetic symbols are "privileged" images in a poem or the images that dominate an author's work or a school of literature or, presumably, literature itself, as in Frye's theory of archetypes.[161] The nonsemantic traits of symbols—opacity and rootedness—indicate that the symbol lacks autonomy, and it becomes the task of various disciplines to "reveal the lines that attach the symbolic function to this or that nonsymbolic or pre-linguistic activity."[162] When Ricoeur comes to declare that poetic language (one of the three forms of symbolism Ricoeur mentions) is itself "bound," he is hard pressed to show exactly how without subsuming it under the religious form of symbolism. It is free of the intended references of scientific and ordinary language. It is "hypothetical" in Frye's sense. It "destroys" the world, but is "bound" by what it creates. It brings to language modes of being that ordinary vision obscures or even represses.[163] This "boundedness" seems, however, quite different from the "boundedness" of the symbol in a previous nonsemantic order. It is a whole new creation. At this point Ricoeur seems to have been compelled to distinguish levels of symbols, some more deeply rooted than others.[164] But something is either irreducible or it is not. To resolve this problem we must separate the symbolic from the poetic and identify the poetic with the creative metaphor.

Indeed, Ricoeur's identification of the symbol with the venerable notion of correspondences tends to turn his symbol toward the "religious" form of allegory, as is characteristic of the drift in most theories of the "miraculous" symbol. In any case, it would appear that the following quotation implies that any poem must be a failure in the same way that de Man's notion of the poem condemns it to a failure to achieve truth: "What asks to be brought to language in symbols, but which never passes over completely into language, is always something powerful, efficacious, forceful."[165] So Ricoeur holds for that *other* and thinks of hermeneutic as disclosure, as its being brought into being from a threshold, except that it never can quite be! Poetry is an incomplete medium. Yet his description of the symbolic act varies: It is sometimes an "augmentation of reality," it is sometimes a revelation of a more real reality, it is sometimes a metamorphosis. These all seem to imply success, and in the first and last cases a success unrelated to correspondence, though in every case the activity implies knowledge of the reality previously there in order to gauge the act. In his insistence on reference that breaks out of *langue*, Ricoeur has held for the uniqueness of every speech act *as art*, but he has also found it difficult to declare for creativity and yet hold on to the "rooted" symbol.

This important emphasis on the act raises new problems when that act is one of writing or "inscription." Ricoeur remarks that when we write, "what we inscribe is the noema of the act of speaking, the meaning of the speech event, not the event as event."[166] In any interpretation of writing it is clear that some things are more available than others. The locutionary act may be transcribed and preserved; the illocutionary act can be inscribed to some extent; and the prelocutionary act to an even lesser extent. But Ricoeur also recognizes that there can be human thought directly brought to writing without the intermediary of spoken language. The poetic would have to belong to this class, for all the rest would have to be hermeneutic in itself, according to Ricoeur's idea of where meaning resides. In any case, inscription always involves for the interpreter the "semantic autonomy of the text," which escapes from the horizon of the author.[167] Inscription involves what Ricoeur calls a world and not merely a situation, as the term is used in speech-act theory. It is not a closed-in semiotic world but a world referred to.[168]

There is some question as to what this breaking out of the prison house of *langue* via the sentence and the overall signification of the metaphor is *in to*. The earlier Ricoeur's search is, like Cassirer's, into man:

I am, I think; to exist, for me is to think; I exist *insofar as* I think. But this truth is a vain truth; it is like a first step which cannot be followed by any other, so long as the *ego* or *ego cogito* has not been recaptured in the mirror of its objects, of its works, and, finally, of its acts.[169]

That recovery is achieved only by the decipherment of the documents of the life of the *ego*.[170] This tends to return us to the mirrored enclosure of human symbolic activity in which man must discover an outside that is really the emanation of his expressive power. Yet Ricoeur seems to hold for an outside that is not such a projection but is that *bios* constituting what the nonsemantic opacity of the symbol "miraculously" calls up.

In Ricoeur there is some question as to whether this miracle that is both speech and silence, revelation and opacity, as Carlyle said, is anything more than part of a process or teleology that ends in the triumph of philosophy over the symbol, despite claims for the symbol's inexhaustibility. The notion of the inexhaustible was expressed as follows in *The Symbolism of Evil* and is repeated in a number of places later on: "What we need is an interpretation that respects the original enigma of the symbols, that lets itself be taught by them, but that, beginning from there, promotes the meaning, forms the meaning in the full responsibility of autonomous thought."[171] The latent *logos*, later *bios*, which demands to be exhibited, seems more amenable to Freud's mode of "suspicious" interpretation than promotion. It seems to suggest allegorization, but we know that Ricoeur protests against this, trying to preserve his version of the symbol/allegory negation: ". . . no longer an allegorizing interpretation that pretends to find a disguised philosophy under the imaginative garments of the myth, but a philosophy that starts from the symbols and endeavors to promote the meaning, to form it, by a creative interpretation."[172] Creative interpretation provides for the phenomenological "horizon" of the interpreter and his particular understanding: ". . . to understand is not merely to repeat the speech event in a similar event, it is to generate a new event beginning from the text in which the initial event has been objectified."[173] But sometimes "promotion" of a meaning is called "manifestation and restoration" of a meaning,[174] which seems "suspicious" again. Nevertheless, we are told that this sort of interpretation is opposed to "demystification, as a reduction of an illusion," which characterizes the various "hermeneutics of suspicion" in Freud, Marx, and Nietzsche.[175] Ricoeur holds that the two types of interpretation—promotion and suspicion—can work on the same symbols. He connects promotion with the emergence of figures that are always ahead of us, while suspicion treats of figures that are behind us.[176] This suggests that both modes are somehow equal, but Ricoeur implicitly privileges promotion at this time, explicitly later on; even though there is ambiguity in the way he presents the matter: "The sense of a text is not behind the text, but in front of it. It is not something hidden but something disclosed."[177] But disclosure has to be of something hidden behind or in the text, and it implies completeness, so that we have the illusion here that the text is exhausted.

But Ricoeur is concerned about the triumph of promotion, which constructs the meaning in front of the text, because it may give rise to Gnostic modes of interpretation, "dogmatic mythology," or the fixing of symbols.[178] The escape from this, which lies in a truly creative interpretation that allows thought to manifest itself alternately as reflection (demythologization? suspicion?) and speculation (promotion?), is having it both ways, while yet arranging interpretations in a hierarchy of value, promotion above suspicion. In any case, the distinction seems to be symbol/allegory all over again. Symbol would become connected with teleology, allegory with archeology.

At this point Hegel looms up again behind Ricoeur's hermeneutic theory. The Hegelian teleology leaves the symbol behind in the apotheosis of absolute reason, and this Ricoeur rejects. The symbol is opaque by virtue of its relation to *bios*. Also, it is never completed in reason because of the temporality of the hermeneutic event, which involves a constantly changing horizon and thus a continuing renewal of the act of interpreting. Ricoeur has rejected the notion of interpretation by recourse to the intention of the author, the genius-to-genius idea of romanticism, the recreation of the understanding of the text's contemporaries, and the placing of interpretation under the *final* control of any one reader. Every interpretation is a making of a text "one's own," but obviously it cannot be final.[179] The only choice is interpretation and interpretation again. Ricoeur sees this situation as having teleological possibilities, though not as Hegel would have. Whether the difference is great enough from Hegel to save poetry from being devoured by Hegel's reason is one question. Whether or not poetry is devoured by Ricoeur's religion is another.

Ricoeur's reading of Hegel finds spirit to be

> . . . a progressive and synthetic movement through various figures or stages, in which the truth of one moment resides in

the truth of the following moment. For this reason . . . consciousness is a task and is never complete and fulfilled until it comes to an end. . . . Thus, the meaning of consciousness is not in itself but in Spirit, that is, in the succession of figures that draw consciousness forward away from itself.[180]

The relation between this and a progression of hermeneutic acts in which meaning is always coming to reside is clear enough. But for Ricoeur, Hegel failed by giving absolute knowledge as an end to this process. Ricoeur instead invokes a religious view that implies an eschatology:

> Would it not be possible to say . . . that the end is not absolute knowledge, that is, the completion of all reflections in a whole, in an all-inclusive totality, but rather that the end is only a *promise*, promised through the symbols of the sacred?[181]

Though symbols give rise to thought there is always something more in symbols than in philosophy (and, indeed, in language). Therefore a philosophical interpretation of symbols cannot become absolute knowledge. The symbol remains inscrutable in the Goethean sense, but by virtue of this, holds out an eschatological promise. For Ricoeur, interpretation seems to be always on the move to embrace a religious mystery, even as philosophy must "comprehend everything, even religion."[182] Completion cannot occur, however, without a false allegorizing. There is no triumphant ontology, and interpretation is a risk that must be taken. There is always the conflict of a multiplicity of interpretations—both from behind and ahead,[183] though, as we have seen, the "ahead" is privileged.

The opposition appears, then, to be a negation. Both, despite his protests to the contrary, depart from the symbol, one into a chain of interpretations which chase the promise of an end, albeit an end beyond the Hegelian end; the other into allegorical demystification via the route of "suspicion." The privileged former seems to me not a return to the symbol but a probing generated by the promise of a nonsymbolic truth behind appearance. Here search triumphs over creation, religion swallows the poetic. Both sides of Ricoeur's opposition adopt the same story.

Ricoeur's theory of the symbol was first an attempt to mediate between "religious" allegory and the "miraculous" symbol. His later theory of metaphor seems to develop a "secular" notion of the symbolic, where a new vision of reality springs forth from the semantic tension.[184] But Ricoeur also fears this freedom, since it leads into the enclosure of language and the Derridean free play of the signifier. So the "miraculous" rooted symbol is privileged over the merely metaphorical. We find here the typical romantic reversal of the direction of the Fall, a fall upward into the semiotic chain from a depth of *bios*.

But Ricoeur has already said that the metaphorical utterance is a phenomenon of predication, not denomination, and that the sentence is a semantic, not a semiotic, phenomenon. This roots metaphor in the semantic act, in the moment, in experience and grounds it in *reference*, but a reference which is a creation. From an antimythical point of view, this rootedness is describable in terms of signification and imitation and appears to lose the very rootedness posited. A mythical perception of such reference would have to be repetition of the predication. Somewhere in the ironic middle lies an appropriate hermeneutic which would be neither of these, nor a free play upon an alleged free play of signifiers, as Derrida's work has tended to become. The rootedness of the metaphoric lies in the concreteness of its predications. This rootedness is indeed, as Ricoeur says of his symbols a rootedness in *bios*, but Ricoeur insists finally on going beneath or past *bios* to the sacred. The rootedness of the poem is in the *bios* of the experience of the act. Language draws its nourishment in *bios* but grows from it, making as it does. Poetry may be a free play, but it is a free play bringing a nowness into language, or rather, making a nowness in language. A theory of literature does not need Ricoeur's symbol. It needs only his metaphor. The "miraculous" symbol belongs to the antimythical realm of the theological.

The ironic realm of critical interpretation certainly has a creative element; phenomenological hermeneutics tells us that all hermeneutic acts have their own horizons. But to inhabit the area of interpretation is not merely to bring a text into that horizon, for a text is always properly *over there* in its being, even though it has in a very real sense brought its moment *here*. If the over thereness is not preserved by criticism, there is only devouring for use or creative "misprision," to use Harold Bloom's well-known term.[185] Of course, the text is not *merely* over there. It is a Blakean prolific and is available for use. But not for the use of criticism, which must limit itself to the cultural role of celebration, mediation, and education. This is often a process of reviving the poetic from what has appeared to be a complete and final devouring. It is an activity that never ends because of the movement of time, the change of language. It always has to be done again, yet it is not the work of Sisyphus, since the dialectic of meaning and significance in time makes every moment a new critical challenge, requiring the reestablishment of the historical relation between work and reader. I am not talking about making a work, in the recent jargon, "relevant," nor am I taking sides in the argument E. D. Hirsch has made against H-G. Gadamer over objective interpretation.[186]

I discover a contrary to this negation in the notion that accepting Gadamer's horizontal interpretation, which requires constant renewal—but not accepting the hopelessness implied in de Man's version of this activity or the necessity of psychological swerving in Bloom's theory—does *not* require that we cease to strive methodically within our horizon for the "naïve" objectivity that Hirsch demands, though Hirsch recognizes that it is not reached. I shall call it a fictive ontological limit, harmless (indeed valuable) as long as recognized as a fiction in the same way that Karl Popper's ontological limit is so recognized by theorists of science like Kuhn and Holton. Gadamer without Hirsch threatens to turn criticism into the sort of devouring that alienates man from his own home in history, albeit a constructed history, and results in poems on poems on poems. Hirsch without Gadamer is an antimythical literalization of the past that alienates man from the text.

Many works cannot stand up to the repeated making available of criticism. Cultures come to agreement that some texts are exhausted, though sometimes these texts merely sleep for a while; however, I think it must be held that interpretation never fully releases what Ricoeur, following Frege, calls the reference of the text. Thus the continued necessity of interpretation is not caused entirely by the change in horizon. It is also true that at any given time something is genuinely left over. It is also not merely what has been lost from an earlier reading that we fail to grasp. It is what lies there in the form of reference as potentiality for our discourse that discourse can never grasp *as such*. Every critical tradition of any value has made a term for this. When Ricoeur says that speculative discourse has its condition of possibility in the semantic dynamism of metaphorical utterance but has its *necessity* in itself—putting the resources of conceptual articulation to work, and when he says that the speculative does this only by breaking with the metaphorical, he is correct enough to sustain his criticism of a Derridean deconstruction which chases down the trace of dead metaphor; but the statement is fraught with danger, even so. In the end, speculative discourse cannot long be without metaphor, cannot progress ever on its own. If we look again at the remarks of Kuhn and Holton, we must conclude that the dialectic is constant, that the speculative is constantly impoverishing itself and moves by constant infusions of metaphoric power. The contraries—to employ a phrase Yeats liked—live each other's death, die each other's life.

Ricoeur comes close to my own formulation of the ironic role of criticism in the following remarks:

> . . . destruction of the metaphorical by the conceptual in rationalizing interpretations is not the only outcome of the interaction between different modalities of discourse. One can imagine a hermeneutic style where interpretation would conform both to the notion of concept and to that of the constitutive intention of the experience seeking to be expressed in the metaphorical mode.
>
> Interpretation is then a mode of discourse that functions at the intersection of two domains, metaphorical and speculative. It is a composite discourse, therefore, and as such cannot but feel the opposite pull of two rival demands. On one side, interpretation seeks the clarity of the concept; on the other, it hopes to preserve the dynamism of meaning that the concept holds and pins down.[187]

Such a hermeneutic style would for me be "ironic." At this point, Ricoeur invokes the Kant of Section 49 of *The Critique of Judgment* and his notion of the "aesthetical idea," but we saw early on that Kant falls into a romantic allegorical notion at the very moment that he seems to be establishing a "secular" symbol. This amounts to privileging speculative discourse, as Ricoeur finally must: ". . . the ultimate meaning of the reference of poetic discourse is articulated in speculative discourse: indeed, actuality has meaning only in the discourse on being."[188] The war between poetry and philosophy has extended from before Plato's time into our own.

5. SECULAR SYMBOLIC AS THE CONTRARY

IT IS time to summarize: The phenomenological can claim to be anti-"Platonic" because it holds that language is not a system of signs that is applied to a prior set of objects or ideas. Some versions of it—though not, I think, Ricoeur's—can claim to be anti-"religious" because they hold that being is not *there* but *here*. Nothing is *there*. It can claim to be anti-"empirical" because it refuses to accept the subject/object distinction (fundamental to antimyth) by rejecting any idea of an object, which is for the phenomenologist nothing except when brought to being by consciousness. It is not "secularly" symbolist because it emphasizes terms like "drawing forth" and "unconcealment" rather than cultural creation.

In phenomenological hermeneutics nothing is brought into being or "arrives" at "presence" in language. The only pure example of this must be (have been) the primal act of the original word. Facing nature, the poet attempts to speak again an original word. The poem which participates in this bringing into being is a hermeneutic act, but not in the structuralist sense. The structuralist model of all language is symbolic logic. Poems are regarded as deconstructible back to it. The phenomenological model of all language is a verbal act of drawing forth, of sheer naming. In both systems, criticism and poetry are identical, but in structuralism all is consumed by antimyth, while in phenomenology all is consumed by myth. Each interpretation of a poem is itself the same drawing forth into presence from a text that the text was. The character of the drawing forth is variously described. In Gadamer, as we have seen, the hermeneutic act is one of dialogue and mutual questioning.

The phenomenological concept of the symbol is "miraculous" and makes the poetic act active. However, there are significant differences between this miraculist activism, albeit a secularized miraculism, and the purely "secular" view:

1. The rhetoric of phenomenology plays with a paradox in the concept of nothingness: how nothing can be a something. Thus the phenomenologist seems to have his being and nonbeing simultaneously, claiming poetic creativity at the same time that he claims transformation. The "secular" symbolic theorist claims that artistic creativity works with the verbal materials of the culture melted back down, so to speak, to their potentiality to be made into new forms.

2. Phenomenology is a criticism built upon and supposing poetry to be fundamentally a poetry of nature. It is a postromantic development. The poem hermeneutically draws forth an *other* (albeit "nothing") into being. Symbolic theory is a criticism that supposes poetry to be always a poetry of culture, even when it claims to be a poetry of nature. It assumes that nature itself is a cultural creation, formed by antimyth as an abstract other and by myth as particular presence.

3. Phenomenology is a criticism that supposes all utterance, including criticism, to be poetry. Thus we observe certain claims today that the critic is no different from the poet. It is here that structural-

ism and phenomenology seem to meet, with both sides recently having representatives who claim that criticism is more interesting than poetry in its conventional sense. The structuralist achieves this superiority by deconstruction to a zero-degree. The phenomenologist achieves this by his hermeneutic dialogue with the previous text. The symbolic theorist holds to fictive differences along a continuum of language. This requires always a distance by ironic contrariety of poem and criticism of it.

4. Phenomenology regrets (regarding it as a Fall) the conflict that this book identifies as the fundamental cultural necessity. Behind the phenomenological disclosure of being there gapes forth an existential nothingness that takes precedence over culture. Nature's blankness triumphs. One suspects that Heidegger speaks of "deconcealment" rather than "opening up" because he believes in the end that there is nothing *there*; thus the emphasis is necessarily entirely on clearing away that which conceals, and the direction of its gaze is to the past. Poetry as hermeneutic has to be both a making and a clearing away of the rubbish that conceals; but the rubbish can easily be regarded as that very same language of the poem that was designed to perform the deconcealment. The paradoxical aim of the poem becomes therefore in later existential phenomenology its own silence. But silence is a word equivocated upon. It can be a silence insofar as from the antimythical point of view anything without logical form is not language and is therefore silent. But in more radical phenomenological forms it can mean that language by any definition is rubbish and must be cleared away, indeed as a poem clears itself away. But in this case, a poem can hardly be declared to bring anything into being unless its hatred of itself can be regarded as a deconcealing of nothing. But the very act of doing this—using language—must obfuscate. Why not then silence from the beginning? No matter which choice, it is the choice of the Yeatsian saint, and the poem moves toward a form of "religious" allegory. This is far from Heidegger, but it is also an emergence from Heidegger. From the point of view of secular symbolic theory, this nothingness is an antimythical fiction like Locke's primary qualities of experience.

It seems to me that in most phenomenological views it is ultimately supposed that two cultures are possible. One is an artificial culture of technology, in which man loses contact with being. The other is a free culture of *hermeneuein* which establishes mutuality with the world, a nature that is rife with meaning, but a meaning that can be produced only in the hermeneutic process itself. In the struc-

turalist view the second possibility ceases to exist. Man cannot surpass the conditions of the first possibility, because man is entrapped
in the play of signs, the prison of language. Language is not a space
of disclosure but a system of signification of difference in an infinite
field. Structuralism comes to deconstructive skepticism, assuming
that language is supposed, in man's eyes, to perform disclosure, but
in fact cannot, and thus provides a field for mystifications. What is
necessary is constant deconstruction back to an absolute nothing.
This is not the nothing of Heidegger, which produces being in the
hermeneutic act and is therefore present always as *something*. It is
instead a nothing of blankness produced by rationalistic deconstruction, resulting not in being but in the contemporary parallel to that
void which Blake's Urizen contemplates from his decentered center.
This seems to me a profoundly reactionary view. But phenomenology ends in mysticism and Fall. Its miracles slip back to "religious"
allegory.

The theorist of the "secular" symbol offers a concept of artful
creativity which regards language as a liberation (as do the phenomenologists) and yet presumes not the task of disclosure of being but
the task of conservation of value and improvement of culture. The
task for art is not the mystical one of knowing an other, of seeking
before making. Rather, it is the constant development of a cultural
reality from the potentiality of experience through particular linguistic acts and what is built from them. Blake wrote:

> The Angel that presided o'er my birth
> Said, "Little creature form'd of Joy and Mirth,
> Go love without the help of any Thing on Earth." [189]

Here he locates all responsibility in man. This seems to me the basis
of a purely "secular" concept of poetic creativity, which provides the
contraries to the three Blakean negations mentioned at the beginning
of this book. Difference/indifference and subject/object are opposed
by "identity"; symbol/allegory is opposed by the "secular" symbolic.
This presumes the idea of the mythic as both a source and a counter-
fiction to science and to religion, which in its insistence on fallen
analogy as inevitable to the concept of incarnation, holds artistic behavior back from an unbearable egoism by providing *its* own countertruth. The battle between negations, as I have tried to show, is cyclical, endless, and without progression, both sides adopting the
same story. The mythic contrary to a negation can include the nega-

tion *as* its opposite. The negation can never include its contrary. This is another way of arguing that the mythic side of the contrary—"identity" and "secular" symbolic—can be called the *source* of anti-mythical negations, while in our experience of the world it acts as counterforce to the negations emanating from it. This is why we cannot say it is privileged over the negations. In our experience, in time, in history, in culture, it is appropriately contrary.

A theory of the "secular" symbolic declares that creation need not be what Heidegger laments as "mastery," that we have via return to the contrary the means to control technology. In this mode of thought language is fundamentally poetic, out of which culture is built. Man projects his gods vertically into the sky and his nature horizontally into an other; but both the gods and nature are his, and to abuse them is to abuse himself. If man abandons contrariety and declares the absolute domination of any single form, he condemns himself to a Hell he has made. By the same token, he corrupts truth by claiming to discover the one truth that he declares transcends them all. The "secular" symbolic theorist constructs an image of culture, knowing it is a construction which will generate its antimythical contraries. They will wear it out so that it must be returned to myth for refurbishment:

> All Human Forms identified, even Tree, Metal,
>   Earth & Stone; all
> Human Forms identified, living, going forth & returning
>   wearied.[190]

Appendix
"On the Subjects of the Plastic Arts"
by Johann Wolfgang von Goethe

Of the plastic arts one requires clear and definite representations. Whether they can be achieved to the highest degree of accomplishment depends on the subjects, and it is therefore most important what subjects the artist chooses and which he is inclined to treat.

The most advantageous subjects are those which determine themselves by their own being.

The first kind of these is the natural. It represents well known, common things as they are, although certainly raised to an artistic whole. They are mostly physiological, sometimes commonly pathetic and in this sense possess nothing ideal, although as works of art they must in another sense participate in the idealistic.

The second kind is the idealistic itself. One grasps not the subject as it appears in nature; rather one captures it on a level where, divested of all commonality and individuality it does not become a work of art through treatment, but rather meets this treatment as an already completely formed subject. Nature produces the former, the human spirit in the most intimate association with nature the latter; the artist raises the former through mechanical treatment to a certain worth, but all mechanical handling is hardly able to express the worth of the latter. Representation of the former has been brought to the highest perfection by the Dutch, that of the latter by the Greeks. These latter are also either physiological or highly pathetic.

It is a requirement of this whole class that it be self-explanatory at first sight as a whole as well as in its parts; of the former the aforesaid school provides endless examples, of the latter a Jupiter, a Laocoön may be mentioned.

Now it is possible that a certain cycle of subjects together will form, as it were, a mystical subject, such as the nine muses with Apollo, Niobe with her daughters. Here the various modifications of a character or of a state appear, and after a happy concatenation together close the circle.

The subjects of which we have just spoken are the most perfect of all, since those of the second sort coincide in their perfection with those of the first. Now there are also subjects which by themselves would be neither intelligible nor interesting, unless they were interconnected and interpretable in a sequence; this may be a sequence of actions, as for example the feats of Hercules, or of parts of an action, as for example a bacchanal. In this way Julio Romano carried out a march of troops accompanying Emperor Siegmund in the form of a frieze. The whole art of the bas-relief rests on the correct insight in this kind of treatment.

Exactly, then, as a single action out of such a sequence, when it is well enough known, can be represented, as for example, one of the feats of Hercules on a gemstone, so too is it not incorrect to select such subjects as are generally known through fable or history; certainly they will never reach the highest worth, yet one cannot reprimand the artist who proceeds to work with the requisite care.

Although in all works of art the subject can never be considered by itself, except as it is treated, it must be said of the three kinds so far described that they have been considered chiefly with reference to the object. In the following we shall consider more the treatment and the spirit of the treater, and so then are subjects determined:

Through deep feeling, which if it is pure and natural will coincide with the best and highest subjects and possibly make them into symbols. Subjects represented in this way only seem to stand naked by themselves but are freshly and deeply significant on account of the ideal, which always carries universality with it. When the symbolic attests to anything beyond the representation it does so always in an indirect manner.

However, deep feeling may border on fanaticism and seek out mystical subjects; of this type are most of the representations of the Catholic religion, which too have to some extent their own common large cycle; among them are, however, occasional pictures, such as when several patrons of a city or of a family are brought together; but one can consider this kind as occasional works, although they may be raised to a high level by their execution, as the St. Cecilia of Raphael shows.

But even shallow feelings make claim to art; thence arise the sentimental pictures of which our time produces such great numbers through a false combination of the ethical-beautiful and the medium of the representational arts; one might say that the artist and the lover of this kind of art are really quite economical.

Now there also exist works of art that scintillate through intellect, wit, gallantry, among which we also include all allegory: of these one can expect the least good, because they too destroy the interest in the representation itself and drive the spirit back into itself, so to speak, and remove from its eyes what is actually represented. The allegorical distinguishes itself from the symbolic in that the former signifies directly, the latter indirectly.

Now there also exists a false application of poetry to the plastic arts. The plastic artist must be a poet, but not a poetaster, that is, unlike the poet, who by his work must properly incite the imagination, the plastic artist should not, when working at sensible representation, also work for the imagination. Most of the works of Henry Fuseli sin in this respect.

However, the three aforementioned kinds are hardly so blameworthy as the last, which we owe to the most recent times: that is, of course, the attempt to embody the highest abstractions in sensible representations.

Stafa, Friday, 13 October 1797

Notes

ONE: INTRODUCTION (*text pages* 3–28)

1. Northrop Frye, *Anatomy of Criticism* (Princeton: Princeton University Press, 1957), p. 90. The notion is seconded by Angus Fletcher in his *Allegory: The Theory of a Symbolic Mode* (Ithaca: Cornell University. Press, 1964), p. 14, a book influenced by Frye's work: "The word 'symbol' in particular has become a banner for confusion, since it lends itself to a falsely evaluative function whenever it is used to mean 'good' ('symbolic') poetry as opposed to 'bad' ('allegorical') poetry, and in this way it clouds distinctions that are already difficult enough to make." Fletcher goes on to observe that in more recent criticism the term "myth" seems to have taken over the role of the rather worn term "symbol." Several recent critics have enlisted on the side of allegory in this matter, and thus the moraine grows. Fletcher, who sees allegory as a type—a ubiquitous type—of symbolic, reveals why the romantics used the term pejoratively when he remarks, "Allegory belongs ultimately in the area of epeidictic rhetoric, the rhetoric of praise and ceremony" (p. 121).

2. Walter Benjamin, *The Origin of Germanic Tragic Drama*, trans. John Osborn (London: Nottingham, Loughridge, and Billingsgate, 1977), esp. pp. 159–85 [*Ursprung des deutschen Trauerspiels* (1928), Frankfurt am Main: Suhrkamp, 1963]; Paul de Man, "The Rhetoric of Temporality," in *Inter-*

pretation: Theory and Practice, ed. Charles S. Singleton (Baltimore: Johns Hopkins University Press, 1969), pp. 173–209.

3. There is no full historical study of the theory of the literary symbol, though there are several important works on some aspect of the problem and some histories of certain periods. Among the most valuable of the latter are B. A. Sørensen, *Symbol und Symbolismus in der ästhetischen Theorien des 18. Jahrhunderts und der deutschen Romantik* (Copenhagen: Munksgaard, 1963); A. G. Lehmann, *The Symbolist Aesthetic in France 1885–1895* (1950) (Oxford: Basil Blackwell, 1968). My *Philosophy of the Literary Symbolic* was nearly completed when Tzvetan Todorov's *Théories du symbole* (Paris: Seuil, 1977) was published, but his book has been helpful to me, though its position differs from mine by virtue of its emphasis on semiotics. With respect to allegorical and other modes of interpretation of myths in the eighteenth century, the indispensable study is Frank Manuel's *The Eighteenth Century Confronts the Gods* (Cambridge: Harvard University Press, 1959).

4. Ernst Cassirer, *The Philosophy of Symbolic Forms*, trans. Ralph Manheim, 3 vols. (New Haven: Yale University Press, 1953, 1955, 1957) [*Philosophie der symbolischen Formen* (1923–1929) (Darmstadt: Wissenschaftliche Buchgesellschaft, 1964)]; *An Essay on Man* (New Haven: Yale University Press, 1944). Paul Ricoeur, *Freud and Philosophy* (New Haven and London: Yale University Press, 1970), pp. 10–22 [*De l'interprétation: essai sur Freud* (Paris: Seuil, 1965)]; *The Conflict of Interpretations: Essays in Hermeneutics* (Evanston: Northwestern, 1974), p. 11 [*Le Conflit des interprétations: essais d'herméneutique* (Paris: Seuil, 1969)].

5. In "Dialectic of *The Marriage of Heaven and Hell*," in *The Ringers in the Tower* (Chicago and London: University of Chicago Press, 1971), p. 58, Harold Bloom distinguishes Blake's dialectic from Plato's and Hegel's: Blake is neither a rational mystic nor a mystic rationalist. It is fair, I think, to say that Blake's dialectic is historical but refuses the notion of synthesis at any point. Synthesis always involves a negation.

6. *The Complete Writings of William Blake*, ed. Geoffrey Keynes (London: Nonesuch; New York: Random House, 1957), p. 153 (plate 11).

7. Ibid., p. 153.

8. Letter to Butts, January 10, 1802, ibid., p. 812.

9. Ibid., p. 155.

10. Blake's imagery is full of instances of expansions and contractions, circumferences and centers. See, for example, *Jerusalem*, plate 71, ibid., p. 709.

11. For example, see *Jerusalem*, plate 10, ibid., p. 629.

12. René Girard, *Violence and the Sacred*, trans. Patrick Gregory (Baltimore: Johns Hopkins University Press, 1977), p. 159 [*La Violence et le sacré* (Paris: Bernard Grasset, 1972)] argues that inside a cultural system only differences are perceived. Outside, all the antagonists seem alike. Further, "wherever differences are lacking, violence threatens" (p. 57). I seek a stance beyond Girard's inside/outside, beyond his difference/indifference, which can be the contrary to that negation. Girard also remarks, "The rite

selects a form of violence as 'good,' as necessary to the unity of the community." (p. 115). This differentiating form of violence is perhaps preferable to the undifferentiating form that Girard sees the culture terrified of
and managing in this way. But clearly both are Blakean "negations," corresponding to the opposition of Orc/Urizen in Blake's poetry. A contrary is
needed, which would imply the possibility of a higher form of culture, not
a return to a primitive state. Blake offers his figure Los as a contrary form.
I offer the as-yet-undeveloped notion of "identity." Where identity is lacking, alienation reigns.

Fletcher remarks with pertinence: "Moral fables assert, symbolically,
that some objects are sacred and some are sinful, and the true believer
should avoid the one and embrace the other. . . . But when we seek the
true meaning of 'sacred' [that is, the 'contrary' meaning] in religious usage,
we meet a paradox, for it turns out that 'sacred' means both good and
evil" (*Allegory*, p. 225).

13. Ibid., p. 1.
14. Isaiah Berlin, *Vico and Herder: Two Studies in the History of Ideas* (London: Hogarth, 1976), particularly pp. 42–55. The standard Italian commentary is that of Fausto Nicolini, *Commento storico alla seconda scienza
nouva*, 2 vols. (Rome: 1949–50).
15. *The New Science of Giambattista Vico*, rev. trans. of the 3d ed., 1774,
trans. Thomas Goddard Bergin and Max Harold Fisch (Ithaca: Cornell
University Press, 1968), pp. 71, 33 [*La scienza nouva*, ed. Fausto Nicolini,
2 vols. (Bari: Gius. Laterza & Figli, 1928), 1:87, 42]. For this, a study of
the Hebraic biblical tradition will not do because of the miraculous incur-
sion of the deity into the history of the Hebrews, which makes them a special case. (Thus Vico avoids religious disputation.) They received their law
direct from God and never went through the long historical process that
the gentile tribes—dispersed descendants of Noah—experienced. The gentiles, therefore, had to discover and make laws for themselves by a long
process of development which everywhere began in religion. The similarities among myths arose not because of a common historical and geo-
graphical origin but because of a common human nature.
16. Ibid., p. 116 [1:145–46].
17. See, for example, Antoine Court de Gebelin, *Monde primitif analysé et
comparé avec le monde moderne* (Paris, 1773). Gebelin is under the domineering influence of Cartesianism with its supreme confidence in the mathematical structure of reality. A good rationalist, he makes no distinction
between allegory and symbolism.
18. Vico, *The New Science*, p. 314 [2:21].
19. Ibid., p. 105 [1:130].
20. Berlin, *Vico and Herder*, points out that Joseph de Maistre's remark "la
pensée et la parole sont un magnifique synonyme" one hundred years later
probably comes from Vico (p. 42).
21. See Berlin, ibid., who quotes from *De nostre temporis studiorum ratione*
(1708).

22. Vico, *The New Science*, p. 131 [Vico, 1:167].
23. Ibid., p. 128 [1:162].
24. Ibid., p. 118 [1:148].
25. Ibid., p. 74 [1:91].
26. Ibid., p. 312 [2:18].
27. Ibid., p. 129 [1:164].
28. Ibid., p. 130 [1:165].
29. Ibid., p. 297 [1:380].
30. Ibid., p. 167 [1:213].
31. Ibid., p. 120 [1:151].
32. Benedetto Croce, *The Philosophy of Giambattista Vico*, trans. R. G. Collingwood (New York: Russell and Russell, 1964), p. 50.
33. The terms "poetic" and "nonpoetic" are themselves problematic in this context, first, because the romantics did not identify the poetic with a poem in the modernist sense of a particular sort of verbal structure, and, second, because in contemporary theory the notion of literature or the literary as a particular sort of verbal structure has been called in doubt by many. See, for example, Alan Bass, "'Literature'/Literature," in *Velocities of Change: Critical Essays from MLN*, ed. Richard Macksey (Baltimore: Johns Hopkins, 1974), pp. 341–53, and Jacques Derrida's remark, quoted by Bass, that "literature annihilates itself through its own illimitability" (*La Dissémination* [Paris: Seuil, 1971], p. 253). On this point, also note Tzvetan Todorov, "The Notion of Literature," *NLH* 5, no. 1 (Autumn 1973): 5–16. Both structuralist and phenomenological critics tend to annihilate literature by enlarging its boundaries. I would try to find the contrary to the negation literature/nonliterature.
34. When I use these terms in my special sense of them as denoting three types of romantic allegory, I shall put them in quotation marks.
35. At this point I use "expressive" in the sense developed by M. H. Abrams in *The Mirror and the Lamp* (New York: Oxford, 1958), and widely adopted since. For example, see Charles Taylor, *Hegel* (Cambridge: Cambridge University Press, pp. 13 ff.).
36. On Reynolds, see my "Revisiting Reynolds' *Discourses* and Blake's Annotations," *Blake and His Time*, ed. Robert N. Essick and Donald Pearce (Bloomington: Indiana University Press, 1978), pp. 128–44.
37. A. N. Whitehead, *Science and the Modern World* (New York: Macmillan, 1941), p. 80.
38. John Crowe Ransom, "Poetry: A Note in Ontology," in *The World's Body* (New York and London: Charles Scribner's Sons, 1938), pp. 120–28.
39. *Aristotle's Theory of Poetry and Fine Art*, trans. S. H. Butcher (New York: Dover, 1951), p. 35.
40. Walter Benjamin argues in *The Origin of German Tragic Drama* that the "genuine" notion of the symbol was "theological"—that is, a figure in which is embodied the paradox of the "unity of the material and transcendental" (p. 159). If "genuine" means historically prior here, this is incorrect, since the Greek term antedates the theological notion and meant

nothing more than what we now call a sign. Benjamin's main point in any case is that the romantics substituted the paradoxical joining of appearance and essence or "manifestation of an idea" for the theological joining of material and transcendence (p. 160). This may be so, though I do not see what makes one more genuine than the other. Benjamin, who valorizes allegory and regards the romantic valorization of symbol as "worthless" (p. 161), stops probing it with his conclusion that the distinction is between expressing a concept (allegory) and expressing an idea (symbol) (p. 161). He does not see the romantic distinction as possibly part of a prolific *process* on the way to a secularization. This process will stake out a cultural role for the poetic that will not suffer negation by religion; it will involve a joining of neither of the opposites he mentions.

41. Ibid., p. 201.
42. This is an important point. On the basis of it I distinguish my views of the literary symbolic from those of Paul Ricoeur or theologians of the symbol like Edwyn Bevan, *Symbolism and Belief* (1938) (Boston: Beacon Press, 1957), and finally even Hegel. All in their different ways make theology negate art, while I see the two as contraries.
43. It is, of course, possible to read Locke, Hume, Kant, etc., through our present preoccupation with language and construct a linguistic Locke, etc. See, for example, Paul de Man, "The Epistemology of Metaphor," *Critical Inquiry* 5, no. 1 (Autumn 1978): 13–30. This hindsight demonstrates the difficulties created by an orientation paying inadequate attention to language. It does not make these people into language philosophers, or perhaps it makes them into not very good ones.
44. Vico, *The New Science*, p. 100 [1:123–24].
45. Cassirer, *An Essay on Man*, p. 76.
46. In this regard note the penetrating analysis of the struggle of the human sciences to throw off positivistic and historicist tendencies in the nineteenth century and after made by Hans-Georg Gadamer, *Truth and Method* (New York: Seabury, 1975), esp. pt 2, pp. 153–234 [*Wahrheit and Methode* (Tübingen, 1960)].
47. *Humanist without Portfolio: An Anthology of the Writings of Wilhelm von Humboldt*, trans. Marianne Cowan (Detroit: Wayne State, 1963), p. 246 [*Gesammelte Schriften*, 17 vols. (Berlin: Königlich Preussischen Akademie der Wissenschaften, 1903), 4:27].
48. Ibid., p. 293 [7:59].
49. Ibid., p. 249 [3:167].
50. Herder begins to use "myth" as a term referring not merely to a primitive and bygone mode of thought or to ancient stories, but with respect to the possibility of the creation of a new mythology out of contemporary experience. Though there is a theory of "constitutive" language in Herder and a connection among language, myth, and poetry, Herder's concentration on origins, created partly by an anxiety about present, leads him away from developing a full theory of poetry out of his notion of the original poetic nature of language.

51. Von Humboldt, *Humanist without Portfolio*, p. 298 [4:432].
52. Ibid., p. 223 [7:197].
53. Ibid., p. 245 [7:621].
54. Ibid., p. 248 [3:170].
55. Ibid., p. 248 [3:169].
56. Ibid.
57. Ibid., p. 246 [4:27].
58. Ibid., p. 218 [5:343].

Two: The Kantian Symbolic (*text pages 29–45*)

1. *Critique of Judgment*, trans. J. H. Bernard (New York: Hafner, 1951), p. 197 [*Kritik der Urteilskraft* (Hamburg: Felix Meiner, 1963), p. 211].
2. Ibid.
3. Ibid., p. 197 [pp. 211–12].
4. Ibid., p. 198 [p. 212].
5. Ibid.
6. Ibid.
7. Ibid., p. 198 [p. 213].
8. Ibid., p. 199 [p. 213].
9. Ibid., p. 192 [pp. 205–6].
10. Ibid., p. 20 [p. 21].
11. Ibid., p. 23 [p. 24].
12. Ibid., p. 157.
13. Ibid., p. 15.
14. Ibid., p. 16 [pp. 16–17].
15. Ibid., p. 22 [p. 22].
16. Ibid., p. 17 [p. 17].
17. Ibid., p. 20 [pp. 20–21].
18. Ibid., p. 26 [p. 26].
19. Ibid., p. 26 [pp. 26–27].
20. Ibid., p. 45 [p. 48].
21. Ibid., p. 54 [p. 58].
22. Ibid., p. 73 [p. 77].
23. Ibid., p. 77 [p. 82].
24. Ibid., p. 39 [p. 41].
25. Tzvetan Todorov points out (*Théories du symbole*, [Paris: Seuil, 1977], p. 190) that the idea of internal as against external end is enunciated by Karl Philipp Moritz in 1785, five years before the publication of Kant's *Critique*. Moritz's distinction between the beautiful and the useful is like Kant's. See Moritz's "Versuch einer Vereinigung aller schönen Künste und Wissenschaften unter dem Begriff des in sich selbst Vollendeten," *Schriften zur Ästhetic und Poetik*, ed. H. S. Schrimpf (Tübingen: Max Niemeier, 1962), pp. 3–9. In connection with this, see Moritz's short essay on allegory: ". . . one does not contemplate Guido's *Aurora* in order to awaken in oneself thoughts of dawn—thoughts of dawn are rather added only in order to explain the painting which is here predominant and which by itself arrests the attention. The idea is subordinated by the power of the

brush—the idea serves the work of art, the work of art does not serve the idea" (*Schriften*, p. 115). Further, Moritz connects the concept of myth with the aesthetic, all of the tropological elements of myth constituting also the world of poetry. The mythological is joined to the Kantian aesthetical by an assertion of the purposefulness without purpose of the poem. See his *Götterlehre oder mythologische Dichtungen der Alten* (Berlin: Verlag von F. V. Herbig, 1843).

26. *Critique of Judgment*, pp. 146–47.
27. Ibid., p. 148 [p. 158].
28. Ibid., p. 150 [p. 160].
29. Ibid., p. 157 [pp. 167–68].
30. Ibid., p. 157 [p. 168].
31. Ibid., pp. 157–58 [pp. 168–69].
32. Ibid., pp. 170–71 [p. 183].
33. Ibid., p. 171 [p. 183].
34. Ibid.
35. Paul de Man, "The Epistemology of Metaphor," *Critical Inquiry* 5, no. 1 (Autumn 1978):26–27.
36. *Critique of Judgment*, pp. 158–59.
37. Ibid., p. 85. In *Allegory: The Theory of a Symbolic Mode*, (Ithaca: Cornell University Press, 1964), p. 307, Angus Fletcher denies that allegory can ever be judged according to a standard of beauty, since it is a "sublime modality": "That is, applying the Kantian requirement of disinterestedness to allegory and then finding it wanting would be in error, in that the sublime is by definition never disinterested." This is not strictly true. Kant argues for a certain kind of disinterest in the sublime in the *Critique*, pp. 99–104; also, "The sublime is what pleases immediately through its opposition to the interest of sense" (p. 107).
38. *Critique of Judgment*, p. 96.
39. Ibid., p. 101.
40. Ibid., p. 89; see also p. 88.
41. Ibid., p. 107.
42. Ibid., p. 166 [p. 177].
43. Charles Taylor (*Hegel* [Cambridge: Cambridge University Press, 1975]) notes a shift in Kant's view, "from a view of beauty as founded on the sheer play of our faculties of intuition and understanding, to a view which sees the beautiful object as a shadowy and necessarily fragmentary representative of a higher reality which cannot be fully presented in experience" (p. 34). Thus Taylor locates this shift as toward a position somewhere between romantic allegory and "miraculous" symbol. I do not believe this was a shift so much as a struggle inside Kant's language, and that Taylor is really talking not about the Kantian beautiful but the Kantian sublime.
44. According to my understanding, Paul Ricoeur (*Symbolism of Evil*, trans. Emerson Buchanan [Boston: Beacon Press, 1969] [*Le Symbolique du mal* (Paris: Aubier-Montaigne, 1963)], esp. p. 355) wants to free the symbol from its subsumption under the Kantian reason by a philosophy of interpretation that develops meaning from symbols: ". . . no longer an alle-

gorizing interpretation that pretends to find a disguised philosophy under the imaginative garments of myth, but a philosophy that starts from the symbols and endeavors to promote the meaning, to form it, by a creative interpretation. I shall venture to call that endeavor, at least provisionally, a 'transcendental deduction' of symbols. Transcendental deduction, in the Kantian sense, consists in justifying a concept by showing that it makes possible the construction of a domain of objectivity." Ricoeur's view seems to be that interpretation of the symbol is a process by which meaning does finally replace the symbol, but by a drawing out, so to speak, rather than discovering a hidden meaning on the other side of the symbol. This position privileges the process of interpretation.

45. *Critique of Judgment*, p. 97.

46. Fletcher, *Allegory*, passim.

47. In his provocative work *The Romantic Sublime* (Baltimore: Johns Hopkins University Press, 1976), Thomas Weiskel remarks: ". . . the judgment of the sublime experience is a direct function of the impossibility of realizing (in any way) the idea of humanity (or any supersensible idea)" (p. 45). I am not speaking of discovery of an idea when I speak of a Blakean prolific. Weiskel's examination of Blake's attack on transcendence and the sublime raises important questions which suggest to me, though not necessarily to Weiskel, that the effort of transcendence by the artist is inevitably foiled by the secularly symbolic nature of art. See Weiskel: "In both Kant and Wordsworth the sublime conducts us, as it were, to the frontier of the 'invisible world' but leaves us as soon as that world is consciously represented, or given any positive content" (p. 43) and: ". . . if the fact or existence of the invisible world—as opposed to its content—is called into question, the possibility of a sublime moment evaporates. And if the sensible world is too strongly negated, the usurpation loses its 'strength,' and the sublime is reified into a permanent attitude of alienation from nature" (ibid.).

48. *Critique of Judgment*, p. 199 [p. 213].

49. Ibid., p. 111 [p. 118].

50. This merging of the beautiful with the moral ("the unlimited immanence of the moral world in the world of beauty") is lamented as decadent by Walter Benjamin, *The Origin of German Tragic Drama*, trans. John Osborn (London: NLB, 1977), p. 160 [*Ursprung des deutschen Trauerspiels* (1928), (Frankfurt am Main: Suhrkamp, 1963)]. But he connects the beautiful with the "miraculous" or, in his terms, the "theological" symbol, rather than with the "secular" symbol, which would produce a secular morality. Benjamin does not historically analyze in any detail the merger he laments.

THREE: ROMANTIC DISTINCTIONS BETWEEN SYMBOL AND ALLEGORY (*text pages 46–98*)

1. The distinction between symbol and allegory is a matter that has been much studied, and I can add little to the historical treatment of it or even to the close analysis of the terms in the romantic period. This work has

been done with great care by B. A. Sørensen, *Symbol und Symbolismus in der ästhetischen Theorien des 18. Jahrhunderts und der deutschen Romantik* (Copenhagen: Munksgaard, 1963). A discussion of Goethe and Schelling in these terms, in addition to treatment of others, is accomplished also by Tzvetan Todorov, *Théories du symbole* (Paris: Seuil, 1977), pp. 235–59. Of special usefulness is B. A. Sørensen's anthology of texts on allegory and symbol, *Allegorie und Symbol: Texte zur Theorie des dichterischen Bildes im 18. und frühen 19. Jahrhundert* (Frankfurt am Main: Athenaum, 1972).

2. To William Godwin, 22 September 1800, *Collected Letters of Samuel Taylor Coleridge*, ed. E. L. Griggs, 4 vols. (Oxford: Clarendon Press, 1956), 1:352.

3. Shelley, "A Defense of Poetry," in Hazard Adams, ed., *Critical Theory since Plato* (New York: Harcourt Brace Jovanovich, 1972), p. 500.

4. René Wellek, *A History of Modern Criticism*, 4 vols. (New Haven: Yale University Press, 1955), 1:4.

   On A. W. Schlegel's definition of the symbol, see Wellek, 2:41–42. On Friedrich Schlegel's see Liselotte Dieckmann, "Friedrich Schlegel and Romantic Concepts of the Symbol," *Germanic Review* 34 (1951):276–83.

5. Winckelmann, for example, did not distinguish between the terms "allegory" and "symbolism."

6. Heinrich Meyer, "Über die Gegenstande der bildenden Kunst" (1798). Meyer used the same title as Goethe did for his essay, written in 1797.

7. The translation is based on the German text in Johann Wolfgang Goethe, *Schriften zur Kunst* (*Gedenkausgabe der Werke, Briefe und Gespräche*, ed. Ernst Beutler [Zurich und Stuttgart: Artemis, 1949]), pp. 122–25. Translations are mine unless otherwise stated.

8. This essay and Goethe's theory of the symbol have been discussed at length by many, particularly Sørensen, *Symbol und Symbolismus*, pp. 86–132; Werner Keller, *Goethe's dichterische Bildlichkeit* (Munich: Wilhelm Fink, 1972), esp. p. 210ff.; and Maurice Marache, *Le Symbole dans la pensée et l'œuvre de Goethe* (Paris: Nizet, 1960), esp. pp. 94–129, 206–19; Curt Müller, *Die geschlichtlichen Voraussetzungen des Symbolbegriffs in Goethes Kunstanschauung* (Leipzig: Mayer & Müller, 1937), discusses Goethe and the symbol in connection with his forerunners (pp. 213–41).

9. Goethe, "Über die Gegenstande der bildenden Künst," p. 122.

10. Ibid., p. 123.

11. Ibid.

12. Ibid.

13. Ibid.

14. Ibid.

15. Ibid., p. 124.

16. Ibid., p. 125.

17. Quoted by Ernst Cassirer in "Goethe and the Kantian Philosophy," *Rousseau, Kant, Goethe*, trans. J. Guttman, P. A. Kristeller, and J. H. Randall, Jr. (Princeton: Princeton University Press, 1945), p. 73.

18. Ibid., p. 81.

19. Ibid., pp. 73–77.
20. *Conversations of Goethe with Eckermann*, trans. John Oxenford (New York: E. P. Dutton, 1930), p. 205 [Johann Peter Eckermann, *Gespräche mit Goethe* (*Gedenkausgabe der Werke, Briefe und Gespräche*), ed. Ernst Beutler (Zurich und Stuttgart: Artemis, 1949), p. 635].
21. Ibid., pp. 205–6 [p. 636].
22. Ibid., p. 206 [p. 636]. Angelo Bertocci in his *From Symbolism to Baudelaire* (Carbondale: Southern Illinois University Press, 1964), points out that Goethe "seems to illustrate unintentionally his own definition of allegory, as when he praises the Greek sculptor Myron's group" as representing an abstract idea (p. 18). Bertocci also notes that Goethe tended to distrust metaphor as not direct and clouded (p. 207).
23. Ibid., p. 205 [p. 636].
24. Ibid., p. 206 [p. 636].
25. Ibid., p. 8 [p. 48].
26. "Es ist ein großer Unterschied, ob der Dichter zum Allgemeinen das Besondere sucht oder im Besondern das Allgemeine schaut. Aus jener Art entsteht Allegorie, wo das Besondere nur als Beispiel, als Exempel des Allgemeinen gilt; die letztere aber ist eigentlich die Natur der Poesie, sie spricht ein Besonderes aus, ohne ans Allgemeine zu denken oder darauf hinzuweisen" (*Maximen*, no. 279; *Gedenkausgabe der Werke, Briefe und Gespräche*, ed. Ernst Beutler [Zurich und Stuttgart: Artemis, 1949], p. 529).
27. René Wellek, *A History of Modern Criticism*, 1:211.
28. "Das ist die wahre Symbolik, wo das Besondere das Allgemeinere repräsentiert, nicht als Traum und Schatten, sondern als lebendig-augenblickliche Offenbarung des Unerforschlichen" (*Maximen* no. 314; *Gedenkausgabe der Werke*, p. 532).
29. Bertocci, *From Symbolism to Baudelaire*, p. 17.
30. Karl Viëtor, *Goethe the Thinker* (Cambridge, Mass.: Harvard University Press, 1950), p. 63.
31. Ibid., p. 62.
32. Ibid., p. 56.
33. Cassirer, *Rousseau, Kant, Goethe*, p. 82.
34. "Die Allegorie verwandelt die Erscheinung in einen Begriff, den Begriff in ein Bild, doch so, daß der Begriff im Bilde immer noch begrenzt und vollständig zu halten und zu haben und an demselben auszusprechen sei" (*Maximen*, no. 1112, p. 693). "Die Symbolik verwandelt die Erscheinung in Idee, die Idee in ein Bild, und so, daß die Idee im Bild immer unendlich wirksam und unerreichbar bleibt und, selbst in allen Sprachen ausgesprochen, doch unaussprechlich bliebe" (*Maximen*, no. 1113, *Gedenkausgabe der Werke*, p. 693).
35. T. E. Hulme, "Romanticism and Classicism," *Speculations* (1924) (New York: Harcourt, Brace, n.d.), p. 120.
36. Moritz, *Götterlehre oder mythologische Dichtungen der Alten* (Berlin: Verlag von F. Herbig, 1843). Moritz's "symbolic" view of myth may be contrasted to that of the influential and controversial theorist Friedrich

Creuzer (*Symbolik und Mythologie der alten Volker* [1820–1812], 4 vols. [Leipzig: Darmstadt, 1819]). Creuzer claimed that the symbol contains *at once* what allegory or other expression must lay out consecutively. In spite of statements giving the symbol the power to contain its referent, the idea of the synthesis of discrete representations in a single instant is basically allegorical. On the other hand, Creuzer's symbol is "inscrutable," though not always "miraculous," at least in a theological sense. Creuzer also draws a distinction between symbol and myth. The original symbols are interpreted by the myths which follow upon them. Thus myths, too seem to be allegorical, as Schelling remarked of Creuzer's theory. Note C. Otfried Müller's criticism of Creuzer's view in his *Introduction to a Scientific System of Mythology* (London: Longman's, 1844) [*Prolegomena zu einer wissenschaftlichen Mythologie* (Göttingen: Vandenhook und Ruprecht, 1825)]: ". . . even the religious mythus by no means sprang *always* from the symbol as explanatory and interpretive, but was often quite an immediate expression of the idea" (p. 272). See also Walter Benjamin, *The Origin of German Tragic Drama*, trans. John Osborn (London: NLB, 1977), pp. 163–169, also 186–197 [*Ursprung des deutschen Trauerspiels* (1928) (Frankfurt am Main: Suhrkamp, 1963)], in which he quotes Gorres to Creuzer on the distinction between "mystic" and "formal" symbols on the one hand and the "real" symbol on the other, where the "bodily form absorbs the spiritual." In this whole argument, it seems to me, the terms are Blakean negations.

37. Moritz, *Götterlehre*, p. 5.
38. Of the vast scholarship on Schelling, perhaps the most helpful works with respect to these matters are Jean Gibelin, *L'Esthétique de Schelling d'après la philosophie de l'art* (Paris, 1934); Sørensen, *Symbol und Symbolismus*, pp. 248–60; T. Todorov, *Théories du Symbole*, pp. 243–49.
39. Schelling, "On the Relation of the Plastic Arts to Nature," trans. J. E. Cabot, *in* Hazard Adams, ed., *Critical Theory since Plato*, (New York: Harcourt Brace Jovanovich, 1971), p. 446 [*Schellings Werke*, ed. Manfred Schroter, 13 vols. (Munich: C. H. Beck und R. Oldenbourg, 1927–59), suppl. vol. 3, p. 392]. All subsequent quotations are from this text.
40. Frederick Copleston, *A History of Philosophy*, vol. 7, *Modern Philosophy*, pt. 1, "Fichte to Hegel" (Garden City, N. Y.: Image, 1965), p. 137.
41. Schelling, *System of Transcendental Idealism*, trans. Peter Heath (Charlottesville: University Press of Virginia, 1978), p. 232 [*System des transcendentalen Idealismus, Sämtliche Werke*, ed. K. F. A. Schelling, 14 vols. (1856–1861), 3:629], which is the text used by Heath.
42. Ibid., p. 232 [p. 629].
43. Adams, p. 447 [Schelling, "On the Relation of the Plastic Arts to Nature," p. 392].
44. Ibid., p. 447 [p. 396].
45. Ibid., p. 447 [p. 399].
46. Ibid., p. 449 [p. 399].
47. Ibid., pp. 448–49 [p. 403].

48. *Schellings Werke*, vol. 5, *Darstellung des Naturprozesses*, p. 395.
49. Schelling, "On the Relation of the Plastic Arts to Nature," p. 409 [p. 404].
50. Ibid., p. 449 [p. 402].
51. Ibid.
52. *Schellings Werke*, vol. 6, *Philosophie der Mythologie*, p. 95.
53. In Shelley's *A Defense of Poetry* (written 1821, published 1840): "A man cannot say 'I will compose poetry'. The greatest poet even cannot say it; for the mind in creation is as a fading coal, which some invisible influence, like an inconstant wind, awakens to transitory brightness . . . Could this influence be durable in its original purity and force, it is impossible to predict the greatness of the results; but when composition begins, inspiration is already on the decline, and the most glorious poetry that has ever been communicated to the world is probably a feeble shadow of the original conceptions of the poet."
54. Schelling, "On the Relation of the Plastic Arts to Nature," p. 448 [p. 401].
55. Ibid., p. 449 [p. 403].
56. Ibid., p. 453 [pp. 411–12].
57. *Schellings Werke*, vol. 3, *Philosophie der Kunst* (1802), p. 427.
58. Todorov, *Théories du symbole*, pp. 244–45.
59. "On the Origin of Language" (from *Über die Sprache und Weisheit der Indier* [1808]), *On the Language and Philosophy of the Indians, The Aesthetic and Miscellaneous Works of Friedrich Schlegel*, trans. E. J. Millington (London: E. Bohn, 1849), p. 457.
60. Schlegel, "Talk on Mythology," *Dialogue on Poetry and Literary Aphorisms*, trans. Ernst Behler and Roman Struc (University Park and London: Pennsylvania State University Press, p. 82 ["Rede über die Mythologie," *Gespräch über die Poesie* (Stuttgart: J. B. Metzlersche, 1968), p. 313].
61. Ibid., p. 81 [p. 312].
62. Ibid., pp. 81–82 [p. 312].
63. Ibid., p. 86 [p. 319].
64. "Introduction," ibid., p. 28.
65. *Schelling: Of Human Freedom*, trans. James Gutman (Chicago: Open Court, 1937), p. 22 [*Philosophische Untersuchungen über das Wesen der menschlichen Freiheit* (1809), *Schellings Werke*, 4:241].
66. Paul Ricoeur, *Symbolism of Evil*, trans. Emerson Buchanan (Boston: Beacon, 1969), p. 350 [*Le Symbolique du mal* (Paris: Aubier-Montaigne, 1963)]. Ricoeur regards myths as a "species of symbols" (p. 18). For a discussion of Ricoeur's views see my chap. 12, pp. 372–89.
67. The point is basic to Schelling's *Philosophie der Mythologie* (Stuttgart, 1856).
68. Quoted by Emil L. Fackenheim, "Schelling's Philosophy of the Literary Arts," *Philosophical Quarterly* 4 (1945):322, from "Über Dante in philosophischer Beziehung," *Werke* (Stuttgart und Augsburg, 1856–61), 1:686.
69. Coleridge, *The Statesmen's Manual; or, The Bible the Best Guide to Political Skill and Foresight: A Lay Sermon addressed to the Higher Classes of Society* (London: S. Curtis, 1916), p. 34. This work has necessarily been

at the center of any discussion of Coleridge's notion of the symbol, of which there have been many, but not many of any particular length and concentration. The most recent, that of M. Jadwiga Swiatecka, O. P., *The Idea of the Symbol: Some Nineteenth-Century Comparisons with Coleridge* (Cambridge: Cambridge University Press, 1980), is interested exclusively in the theological, or what I call the "miraculous" symbol; but it does address the problem that Coleridge has drawing the line between the Bible as symbol and such purely secular works as Shakespeare's. The book also contains a chapter on Carlyle.

70. Ibid., p. 35.
71. Ibid., pp. 36–37.
72. *Miscellaneous Criticism*, ed. T. M. Raysor (London: Oxford, 1936), p. 30.
73. *The Statesman's Manual*, p. 36.
74. Ibid., pp. 36–37.
75. René Wellek, *Immanuel Kant in England, 1793–1838* (Princeton: Princeton University Press, 1931), p. 115.
76. *The Friend*, ed. Barbara E. Rooke (Princeton: Princeton University Press, 1975), 1:155–56.
77. A term Kenneth Burke introduced in his *Attitudes toward History*, 2 vols. (New York: The New Republic, 1937). See especially 2:229–30.
78. *The Statesman's Manual*, Appendix C, p. xiv.
79. Ibid., pp. 44–45.
80. *Poems*, ed. E. H. Coleridge (London: Oxford University Press, 1912), p. 132. Swiatecka (p. 63) argues that there is no inconsistency between the "shadow" here and the "translucence" Coleridge attributes to the symbol elsewhere. But surely the Platonic image he employs indicates at the least the shakiness of the idea of translucence.
81. *The Statesman's Manual*, Appendix B, p. xiii.
82. Ibid., Appendix C., p. xv.
83. *Biographia Literaria*, ed. J. Shawcross, 2 vols. (London: Oxford University Press, 1962), 1:202.
84. *The Statesman's Manual*, Appendix C, p. xv.
85. Ibid., p. 42.
86. *Biographia Literaria*, 1:3.
87. Ibid., 1:13, 25.
88. To William Godwin, 22 September 1800, *Collected Letters of Samuel Taylor Coleridge*, 1:352.
89. *The Notebooks of Samuel Taylor Coleridge*, vol. 3 (text), ed. Kathleen Coburn (Princeton: Princeton University Press, 1973), p. 4237.
90. *Biographia Literaria*, 1:13.
91. Ibid., 2:115–16.
92. Ibid., 2:16.
93. Coleridge, "Shakespeare's Judgment Equal to his Genius," *in* Hazard Adams, ed., *Critical Theory since Plato*, p. 462.
94. Ibid.
95. *Biographia Literaria*, 2:202.

96. "On the Principles of Genial Criticism," ibid., 2:243.
97. Ibid., p. 239.
98. Ibid., p. 288.
99. Northrop Frye, *Anatomy of Criticism* (Princeton: Princeton University Press, 1957), esp. pp. 308–14.
100. Thomas Carlyle, *Sartor Resartus* (New York, Chicago, and Boston: Charles Scribner, 1921), p. 180.
101. Ibid., p. 195.
102. Ibid.
103. Ibid.
104. Ibid., p. 46.
105. Ibid., p. 49.
106. Ibid., p. 195.
107. Ibid., p. 197.
108. Ibid., p. 198.
109. Ibid.
110. Ibid., p. 44.
111. Ibid., p. 199.
112. Ibid., p. 200.
113. Ibid., p. 63.
114. Hegel, *The Philosophy of Fine Art*, trans. F. P. B. Osmaston, 4 vols. (London: G. Ball and Sons, 1920), 1:9 [*Ästhetik*, 2 vols. (Frankfurt am Main: Europäische Verlagsanstalt GmbH, 1966), 1:19].
115. Hegel, *The Phenomenology of Mind*, trans. J. B. Baille (New York and Evanston: Harper & Row, 1967), p. 69 [*Phänomenologie des Geistes*, 2 vols. (*Werke*, [Berlin: Duncker & Humblot, 1841]), 2:9].
116. Ibid., p. 90 [p. 23].
117. Ibid., p. 81 [p. 15].
118. Ibid., p. 83 [p. 16].
119. W. T. Stace, *The Philosophy of Hegel: A Systematic Exposition* (New York: Dover Press, 1924), p. 300.
120. Copleston, *A History of Philosophy*, 7:206.
121. Hegel, *The Philosophy of Fine Art*, 1:8 [*Ästhetik*, 1:19].
122. Ibid., p. 51 [p. 48].
123. Ibid., pp. 51–52 [p. 48].
124. Ibid., p. 53 [p. 48].
125. Ibid., p. 139 [p. 109].
126. Benedetto Croce, *What Is Living and What Is Dead in the Philosophy of Hegel*, trans. Douglas Ainslie (London: Macmillan, 1915), p. 122.
127. Hegel, *The Philosophy of Fine Art*, 2:8 [*Ästhetik*, 1:299].
128. Ibid., 2:50 [p. 300].
129. Ibid., 1:106 [p. 85].
130. Ibid.
131. Byron, *Manfred* II, iv, 57.
132. Hegel, *The Philosophy of Fine Art*, 1:107 [*Ästhetik* 1:85–86].
133. Ibid., p. 107 [p. 86].
134. Ibid., p. 108 [pp. 86–87].

135. Ibid., p. 109 [p. 87].
136. Ibid., p. 119 [p. 94].
137. Ibid., 4:22 [2:339].
138. Ibid., 4:23 [2:340–41].
139. Werner Marx, *Hegel's Phenomenology of Spirit: A Commentary on the Preface and Introduction*, trans. Peter Heath (New York: Harper and Row, 1975), p. xxii.
140. Hegel, *The Phenomenology of Mind*, p. 73 [*Phänomenologie des Geistes*, 2:8].
141. Hegel, *The Philosophy of Fine Art*, 1:141 [*Ästhetik*, 1:110].
142. Ibid., 1:12 [1:21–22].
143. Croce, *What Is Living and What Is Dead*, p. 122.
144. Ibid., p. 125.
145. Charles Taylor, *Hegel* (Cambridge: Cambridge University Press, 1975), p. 477.

FOUR: THE BLAKEAN SYMBOLIC (*text pages 99–116*)

1. *The Complete Writings of William Blake*, ed. Geoffrey Keynes (London: Nonesuch; New York: Random House, 1957), p. 825. All quotations from Blake are taken from this edition, hereafter referred to as *K*.
2. *K*, p. 578.
3. *K*, p. 240.
4. *K*, p. 605.
5. *Jerusalem* 50:2, *K*, p. 681.
6. *K*, p. 789.
7. *K*, pp. 333, 345.
8. *K*, pp. 656, 730, 733, 734, 735.
9. *K*, p. 758.
10. *K*, p. 77. Lavater: "Whatever is visible is the vessel or veil of the invisible past, present, future—as man penetrates to this more, or perceives it less, he raises or depresses his dignity of being." Blake: "A vision of the Eternal Now."
11. Quoted by Blake in a letter to George Cumberland, 26 August 1799, *K*, p. 795.
12. To Trusler, 23 August 1799, *K*, p. 793.
13. Ibid.
14. Edward B. Hungerford, *Shores of Darkness* (Cleveland and New York: World Publishing Co., 1963), p. 44. Hungerford also errs in assuming that the confused thinking in Blake's sources carried over into Blake when he used those sources, described as "undignified" and "ridiculous" (p. 5).
15. *A Vision of the Last Judgment*, *K*, p. 605.
16. Letter to Butts, 10 January 1802, *K*, p. 812.
17. See Northrop Frye, *Fearful Symmetry* (Princeton: Princeton University Press, 1947), for "The Case Against Locke," pp. 3–29. See also my *Blake and Yeats: The Contrary Vision* (Ithaca: Cornell University Press, 1955), pp. 22–44, on Blake's epistemology and theory of artistic vision.
18. Letter to Trusler, 16 August 1799, *K*, p. 792.

19. Remarks on Malkin's *A Father's Memoir of His Child, K,* p. 439.
20. *Milton,* 24:38, *K,* p. 509.
21. *Milton* 29:20, *K,* p. 516.
22. *A Descriptive Catalogue, K,* p. 576.
23. *K,* p. 446.
24. *A Public Address, K,* p. 596.
25. *K,* p. 473.
26. *Discourses on Art* (New York: Collier, 1961), pp. 46–48.
27. Ibid., p. 48.
28. *K,* p. 460.
29. *K,* p. 459.
30. *K,* p. 460.
31. See in *K, A Descriptive Catalogue,* p. 567: "Of Chaucer's characters, as described in his Canterbury Tales, some of the names or titles are altered by time, but the characters themselves remain unaltered and consequently they are the physiognomies or lineaments of universal human life, beyond which Nature never steps."
32. *K,* p. 774.
33. Charles Taylor, *Hegel* (Cambridge: Cambridge University Press, 1975), p. 195.
34. *A Vision of the Last Judgment* in *K,* p. 605: "The Nature of my Work is Visionary or Imaginative; it is an Endeavour to Restore what the Ancients call'd the Golden Age."
35. Plate 11, *K,* p. 153.
36. Note Northrop Frye's remark in *The Critical Path* (Bloomington: Indiana University Press, 1971): "Poetry is continually bringing us back to the starting point, not necessarily of time, but of social attitude" (p. 89).
37. Plate 15, *K,* p. 153.
38. See "There is no Natural Religion," *K,* p. 97, and "Auguries of Innocence," *K,* p. 433, for examples of Blake's idea that the mind is what he sees.
39. *The Laocoön, K,* p. 776.
40. *Jerusalem, K,* p. 668.
41. 53, *K,* p. 684.
42. *K,* p. 631.
43. 11, *K,* p. 630.
44. 10, *K,* p. 629.
45. Ibid.
46. *Milton* 28, *K,* pp. 514–15.
47. 28, *K,* p. 515.
48. Ibid.
49. *Europe* 13, *K,* p. 243.
50. 98, *K,* p. 746.
51. Ibid.
52. Letter to Butts, 22 November 1802, *K,* p. 818.
53. 77, *K,* p. 717. This whole book was written before the appearance of Leopold Damrosch's *Symbol and Truth in Blake's Myth* (Princeton: Prince-

ton University Press, 1980). His argument is that Blake was a dualist who would have liked to be a monist. Damrosch's notion of the symbol is that of what I call the "miraculous," and he believes Blake needs that notion because he needs the incarnate Jesus as a transcendent principle. My view is that Blake's Jesus, even in the late prophecies, is human before miraculous and that Blake did not want to be either a monist or a dualist but to find the contrary in myth to that antimythical negation.

FIVE: SYMBOLIST SYMBOLISM (*text pages* 117–53)

1. Of the many books on the *symboliste* movement, the one most pertinent to my concerns is A. G. Lehmann's penetrating analysis of symbolist theory, *The Symbolist Aesthetic in France 1885–1895* (Oxford: Basil Blackwell, 1968; first published, 1950). This book is heavily influenced by Croce and Cassirer and seeks to treat symbolist theory as potentially a theory of constitutive language. The most exhaustive analysis of the symbolist movement from Baudelaire to Valéry, Claudel, and others is Guy Michaud's *Message poétique du symbolisme*, 3 vols. (Paris: Nizet, 1947). Of use for a brief overview are the introductory sections of Lloyd James Austin, *L'univers poétique de Baudelaire* (Paris: Mercure de France, 1956). The connection between the French *symboliste* theory and Cassirer's secularization and broadening of the concept of the symbol has not always been seen. Austin mentions Cassirer's work in his general overview (pp. 19n, 27n) but remarks that Cassirer's notion of the symbol is "so vast" that it is of no use in pursuing the distinctions he wishes to make between direct and indirect presentations of value.

2. For example, Albert Mockel, Jean Moréas, or Charles Morice. See Paul Delsemme, *Un theorician de symbolisme: Charles Morice* (Paris: Nizet, 1958), pp. 208–9.

3. I realize that there has been much debate over whether to call Baudelaire a *symboliste* or not. Such debate I intend to ignore as not pertinent to my concerns. I am interested in what Baudelaire says or implies about symbols, not in whether or not he belongs to a movement.

4. "The Salon of 1846," *The Mirror of Art: Critical Studies by Charles Baudelaire*, trans. Jonathan Mayne (Garden City: Doubleday, 1956), p. 58 [*Œuvres complètes* (Paris: Gallimard [Bibliothèque de la Pléiade], 1968), p. 891].

5. "The Salon of 1859," ibid., p. 239 [p. 1041].

6. Ibid., p. 239 [p. 1041].

7. "Since It Is a Question of Realism," *Baudelaire as a Literary Critic*, trans. Lois Boe Hyslop and Francis E. Hyslop, Jr. (University Park: Pennsylvania State University Press, 1964), p. 88 [*Œuvres complètes*, p. 637].

8. "The Salon of 1859," *The Mirror of Art*, p. 241 [ibid., p. 1044].

9. Mallarmé, "Sur l'évolution littéraire," in *Œuvres complètes* (Paris: Gallimard [Bibliothèque de la Pleiade, 1945], p. 872.

10. Mallarmé, "Le livre, instrument spirituel," ibid., pp. 378–82.

11. Guy Michaud, in *Mallarmé*, trans. M. Collins and B. Humez (New York:

New York University Press, 1965), pp. 4, 164–68, argues that Mallarmé's ultimate "book" was not a mere myth but was actually planned out in the manuscript notebook published by Jacques Scherer, *Le "Livre" de Mallarmé* (Paris: Gallimard, 1957).

12. Lehmann, *The Symbolist Aesthetic*, p. 162.

13. Mallarmé, "Crise de vers," *Œuvres complètes*, p. 367.

14. Ibid.

15. Lehmann, *The Symbolist Aesthetic*, p. 159.

16. See Anna Balakian, *The Symbolist Movement: A Critical Appraisal* (New York: Random House, 1967): "The Symbolists and their international coterie agreed on accepting a common origin in the philosophy of Swedenborg, which had already succeeded in infiltrating the art forms through such literary illuminists as Gerard de Nerval, Novalis, Blake, and Emerson" (p. 11).

17. Angelo Bertocci, *From Symbolism to Baudelaire* (Carbondale: Southern Illinois University Press, 1964), takes symbolism beyond the movement proper back to Plotinus, remarking: "The ancient occultist view of the world seems to crop up wherever there is symbolism" (p. 18).

18. The work was originally done by George Nicholson (1800). It was abridged and published in 1841, with a second edition in 1847. The thirteenth edition appeared in 1931 and was reprinted in 1955: *A Dictionary of Correspondences, Representatives, and Significatives, derived from the Word of the Lord. Extracted from the Writings of Emanuel Swedenborg* (New York: Swedenborg Foundation, 1955). However, Swedenborg's own most influential texts were *Angelic Wisdom concerning the Divine Providence* and *Heaven and Hell: Things Seen and Heard*.

19. Arthur Symons, *The Symbolist Movement in Literature*, 1899; rev. eds. 1908, 1919, (New York: E. P. Dutton, 1958).

20. Maurice Bowra, *The Creative Experiment* (London: Macmillan, 1949), p. 5.

21. Austin, *L'Univers poétique*, pp. 54–56.

22. Charles Chadwick, *Symbolism* (London: Methuen, 1971), pp. 2–3, 8, 14, 60.

23. Austin, *L'Univers poétique*, p. 40.

24. Ibid., p. 17.

25. Ibid., p. 49.

26. See my *William Blake: A Reading of the Shorter Poems* (Seattle: University of Washington Press, 1963), esp. p. 38. Austin warns against choosing one over the other in Baudelaire, since both play a role (p. 54).

27. Joseph Chiari, *Symbolisme from Poe to Mallarmé: The Growth of a Myth* (Folcroft, Pa.: Folcroft Library, 1956), p. 53.

28. Baudelaire, *The Mirror of Art*, p. 49 [*Œuvres complètes*, p. 884].

29. Baudelaire, "The Exposition Universelle, 1855," ibid., p. 218 [p. 947]. Austin (pp. 179–80) warns us that this is not quite what Poe said. Poe refers merely to an intensity of interest, not a supernatural intensity.

30. Balakian, *The Symbolist Movement*, p. 35.

31. Baudelaire, "Richard Wagner and Tannhäuser in Paris," *Baudelaire as a Literary Critic*, p. 199 [*Œuvres complètes*, p. 1213].
32. This distinction is succinctly reviewed in A. D. Woozley, *Theory of Knowledge* (London: Hutchinson, 1949), esp. pp. 129–75.
33. Lehmann, *The Symbolist Aesthetic*, p. 261.
34. Quoted by Margaret Gilman, *Baudelaire the Critic* (New York: Octagon, 1971; first published, 1943), p. 162.
35. Lehmann, *The Symbolist Aesthetic*: "For Baudelaire the term 'symbol' is almost entirely—but not quite—bound up with a theosophical view of the universe" (p. 260).
36. It is perhaps unnecessary to say that this is not the classical mathematically conceived principle of harmony but an idea emphasizing the *identity* of all things.
37. Lehmann, *The Symbolist Aesthetic*, p. 270.
38. Bertocci, *From Symbolism to Baudelaire*, p. 4.
39. Austin, *L'Univers poétique de Baudelaire*, p. 145, connects Baudelaire's symbolism—not necessarily by direct influence—with Goethe's concept of universal in particular and the romantic concept of infinite in finite. In his view, Baudelaire's symbol leads to nostalgia, romantic agony, and guilt. In my view, these are the results of a "miraculous" concept of the symbol slipping back to "religious" allegory and acknowledgement of a fallen state. For speculation on the intellectual sources of Baudelaire's symbolism, see ibid., pp. 139–61.
40. Walter Pater, *The Renaissance* (New York: Boni and Liveright, 1919), p. 196.
41. Poe, "The Poetic Principle" (1848, 1850) and "The Philosophy of Composition" (1848). For a critique of Poe's aesthetics along these lines, see Chairi, *Symbolisme*, pp. 97–99.
42. Baudelaire, "Madame Bovary," *Baudelaire as a Literary Critic*, p. 147 [*Œuvres complètes*, p. 655].
43. "Exposition Universelle, 1855," ibid., pp. 81–82 [ibid., p. 956].
44. Baudelaire, "Philosophic Art," ibid., p. 187 [ibid., p. 1099].
45. Mallarmé, "Sur l'évolution littéraire," *Œuvres complètes*, p. 869.
46. Ibid.
47. Mallarmé, "L'art pour tous," ibid., p. 257.
48. Letter to Trusler, 23 August 1799, *The Complete Writings of William Blake*, ed. Geoffrey Keynes (London: Nonesuch; New York: Random House, 1957), p. 793. This work will hereafter be referred to as K.
49. Mallarmé, "Sur l'évolution littéraire," p. 869; also the following: "Les monments, la mer, la face humaine, dans leur plénitude, natifs, conservant une vertu autrement attrayante que ne les voilera une description, évocation dites, allusion je sais, suggestion," "La musique et les lettres," ibid., p. 645. Showing, like description, Mallarmé seems to regard as a term implying the analytical processes of positivistic science.
50. Mallarmé, Letter to Henri Casalis, October 1864, *Correspondance, 1862–1871*, ed. Henri Mondor (Paris: Gallimard, 1959), p. 137.

51. Mallarmé, "Sur l'èvolution littéraire," *Œuvres complètes*, p. 869.
52. Ibid.
53. Mallarmé, "L'art pour tous," ibid., p. 258.
54. Baudelaire, "Richard Wagner and Tannhäuser in Paris," *Baudelaire as a Literary Critic*, p. 201 [ibid., p. 1215].
55. *K*, p. 459.
56. T. E. Hulme, "Romanticism and Classicism," *Speculations* (1924) (New York: Harcourt, Brace, n.d.), p. 120.
57. T. S. Eliot, "Hamlet and His Problems," *Selected Essays 1917–1932* (New York: Harcourt, Brace, 1932), p. 124.
58. Baudelaire, "New Notes on Edgar Poe," *Baudelaire as a Literary Critic*, p. 132 [*Œuvres complètes*, ed. S. de Sacy avec C. Pichois, 2 vols. (Paris: Club de Meilleur Livre, 1955), 1:645]. The "Notes" are not available in the Gallimard edition.
59. Mallarmé, "Richard Wagner," *Œuvres complètes*, p. 542.
60. Mallarmè, "La musique et les lettres," ibid., p. 649.
61. Gilman, *Baudelaire the Critic*, p. 225.
62. "New Notes on Edgar Poe," *Baudelaire as a Literary Critic*, p. 127 [*Œuvres complètes* (1955), 1:639].
63. "The Salon of 1859," *The Mirror of Art*, pp. 234–35 [*Œuvres complètes* (1968), pp. 1037–38].
64. On Mrs. Crowe see G. T. Clapton, "Baudelaire and Catherine Crowe," *Modern Language Review* 25 (1930):286–305.
65. "The Salon of 1859," *The Mirror of Art*, p. 230 [*Œuvres complètes* (1968), pp. 1033–34].
66. Ibid., p. 242 [p. 1044].
67. Ibid., p. 233 [pp. 1036–37].
68. Ibid., p. 234 [p. 1037].
69. "Since It Is a Question of Realism," *Baudelaire as a Literary Critic*, p. 88 [ibid., p. 636].
70. Baudelaire, "New Notes on Edgar Poe," ibid., p. 132 [*Œuvres complètes* (1955), p. 644].
71. Lehmann, *The Symbolist Aesthetic*, p. 85.
72. Ibid., p. 279.
73. Balakian, *The Symbolist Movement*, p. 12.
74. Mallarmè, "Sur l'évolution littéraire," *Œuvres complètes*, p. 870.
75. Mallarmé, "La musique et les lettres," ibid., p. 647.
76. "The Salon of 1845," *The Mirror of Art*, p. 17 [*Œuvres complètes* (1968), p. 830].
77. Baudelaire, "On the Essence of Laughter," ibid., p. 146 [ibid., p. 987].
78. Baudelaire, "Richard Wagner and Tannhäuser in Paris," *Baudelaire as a Literary Critic*, p. 218 [ibid., p. 1231].
79. Michaud, *Message poétique du symbolisme*, 1:74. Michaud argues that allegory appeals to Baudelaire because he was able to restore its "authentic and primitive reality." This is consistent with Michaud's own tendency to emphasize the mystical side of symbolist poetry, but always with reserva-

tion. In the conclusion to volume 2, Michaud argues that poetry is a "veritable religion," a sort of priesthood (p. 416). Poets are the "ordainers of sacred festivals of truth and joy." Poetry's way is that of the mystic. But Michaud goes on to say that finally poetry is not mystical. There is an analogy, but the ways of poetry and mysticism are different: "Poetry is creation, and the poet is a sort of demiurge. . . . The mystic tends toward silence, the poet toward the word." The priestly element tends to express itself in allegory. Michaud clearly here expresses the two sides of *symboliste* thought that are, I think, never really finally resolved with each other, and indeed cannot be.

80. Baudelaire, "The Salon of 1846," *The Mirror of Art*, p. 127 [*Œuvres complètes* (1968), p. 950].
81. Ibid., p. 127 [p. 950].
82. Ibid., p. 85 [p. 915].
83. Ibid., p. 83 [pp. 912–13].
84. Bertocci, *From Symbolism to Baudelaire*, p. 126.
85. Baudelaire, "New Notes on Edgar Poe," *Baudelaire as a Literary Critic*, p. 131 [*Œuvres complètes* (1955), p. 644].
86. See note 106 below. The phrase is Arthur Symons's.
87. Michaud, *Mallarmé*, p. 53. In his earlier book (*Message poétique*, pp. 177–78), Michaud is not so quick to connect Mallarmé with Hegel but insists on some differences.
88. I distinguish this from a source of archetypes, as in Jung.
89. Michaud, *Mallarmé*, pp. 53–54. See also Chadwick, *Symbolism*, p. 35. Thus, for Chadwick "Ses purs ongles . . ." is the archetypical Mallarmé poem. But Chadwick is wrong, I think, in claiming that the "ideal form of the infinite world" contained within "le Néant" flows into the poet.
90. Mallarmé, "Crise de vers," *Œuvres complètes*, p. 368.
91. Mallarmé, "Le Livre, instrument spirituel," ibid., p. 378.
92. Mallarmé, Letter to Francis Coppée, December 5, 1866.
93. Mallarmé, "Crise de vers," *Œuvres complètes*, p. 367.
94. Ibid., p. 368.
95. Ibid., p. 367.
96. Mallarmé, "La musique et les lettres," ibid., p. 653.
97. Lehmann, *The Symbolist Aesthetic*, p. 256. Lehmann's own position is one derived from Croce, Cassirer, and perhaps Langer, and he claims a distinction between imaginative and discursive knowledge similar to Langer's presentational and discursive. Of the symbolists he says: "Instead of realizing that we find in art imaginative, not discursive knowledge, they mostly took it for granted that anything entitled to the name must deal with material abstracted from and distinct from the knowing subject" (p. 108). But the weakness of Lehmann's excellent book is his failure to discuss in any detail the nature of "imaginative knowledge," to explain what it is knowledge of, or, if it is not knowledge of anything, how the term "knowledge" can be so used.
98. Ibid.

99. Ruth Z. Temple, *The Critic's Alchemy: A Study of the Introduction of French Symbolism into England* (New York: Twayne, 1953).
100. Edward Engelberg, *The Vast Design: Patterns in W. B. Yeats's Aesthetic* (Toronto: University of Toronto Press, 1964), pp. 107–8. This is the only book devoted to the whole of Yeats's aesthetic theorization.
101. See Ellmann's introduction to Arthur Symons, *The Symbolist Movement in Literature*, p. xi.
102. Symons, "To W. B. Yeats," ibid., p. xx.
103. Temple, *The Critic's Alchemy*, p. 155.
104. Symons, *The Symbolist Movement*, p. 2.
105. Ibid., p. 5.
106. The phrase is from *The Symbolist Movement*, p. 3, and refers to Zola in particular: ". . . he is quite sure that the soul is a nervous fluid, which he is quite sure some man of science is about to catch for us." Symons's statement is a recasting of an idea of Mallarmé.
107. Yeats, "The Symbolism of Poetry" (1900), in *Essays and Introductions* (London: MacMillan, 1961), p. 155.
108. Symons, *The Symbolist Movement*, p. 2.
109. Yeats, "The Autumn of the Body" (1898), *Essays and Introductions*, p. 189.
110. Yeats, "The Symbolism of Poetry," ibid., p. 163.
111. The intelligence of Symons's work on Blake is vitiated almost as much as that of Yeats's work on Blake by this attitude. Symons does not, however, clutter his discourse with a Swedenborgian terminology. See his *William Blake* (New York: E. P. Dutton, 1907).
112. Symons, *The Symbolist Movement*, p. 1.
113. Ibid.
114. Yeats, "The Autumn of the Body," *Essays and Introductions*, pp. 192–93. The idea of modern writers as "but critics" persists in Yeats, turning up in the poem "Ego Dominus Tuus" (*Collected Poems* [New York: Macmillan Co., 1965], p. 158) in the same sense as it is used here. The idea of a lost book or store of poetic wisdom is also persistent, appearing in *A Vision* and elsewhere. In connection with this, see my "The 'Book' of Yeats's Poems," *Cornell Review* 1 (1) (Spring 1977):119–28.
115. *The Works of William Blake: Poetic, Symbolic, and Critical*, ed. Edwin J. Ellis and William Butler Yeats, 3 vols. (London: Bernard Quaritch, 1893), 1:235–45.
116. Ibid., p. 245.
117. Two points: (1) The secondary qualities of Locke are qualities, but the primary qualities are really *quantities*, being all that is subject to or defined in terms of measurement. (2) "Creation" for what Urizen does may seem odd, but Blake's view is that Urizen does create the error that he believes to exist. From his own point of view, of course, the creation is just there, and he is in it.
118. Letter to Thomas Butts, January 10, 1802, *K*, p. 812.
119. Yeats, *Memoirs: Autobiography—First Draft Journal*, ed. Denis Donoghue (New York: Macmillan Co., 1973), p. 23.

120. *The Works of William Blake*, 1:236.
121. Ibid., p. 239.
122. This is not to say that Blake denies that there is a body or husk left behind after death, but death and resurrection result in the rising of a spiritual body that is still sensual. The best discussion of the body in Blake's work is Thomas R. Frosch, *The Awakening of Albion: The Renovation of the Body in the Poetry of William Blake* (Ithaca: Cornell University Press, 1974).
123. The spectacle of Yeats and Ellis trying to apply a dualistic vocabulary to Blake is equaled in its futility by I. A. Richards's effort to convert Coleridge's thought into a materialist vocabulary in his *Coleridge on Imagination* (New York: W. W. Norton, 1950).
124. Yeats, "The Moods," *Essays and Introductions*, p. 195.
125. *The Works of William Blake*, 1:241.
126. Yeats, "William Blake and his Illustrations to the *Divine Comedy*," *Essays and Introductions*, p. 116.
127. Ibid.
128. Yeats, "Symbolism in Painting," ibid., p. 146.
129. Ibid.
130. Yeats, "William Blake and the Imagination," ibid., p. 114.
131. Ibid.
132. Eliot, "William Blake" (1920), *Selected Essays 1917–1932*, pp. 275–80.
133. Yeats, "William Blake and his Illustrations," *Essays and Introductions*, pp. 119–20.
134. Yeats, "Edmund Spenser" (1902), ibid., p. 368.
135. Ibid., p. 382.
136. Ibid., p. 383.
137. Yeats, "Symbolism in Painting," ibid., pp. 146–47.
138. Yeats, "Discoveries" (1906), ibid., p. 293.
139. Yeats, "Magic," ibid., p. 46.
140. Yeats, "The Philosophy of Shelley's Poetry," ibid., p. 79.
141. Ibid., pp. 78–79.
142. Yeats, "Magic," ibid., p. 49.
143. Yeats, "The Symbolism of Poetry," ibid., pp. 156–57.
144. Yeats, "Magic," ibid., p. 49.
145. Yeats, "The Symbolism of Poetry," ibid., p. 160.
146. Yeats, "The Body of Father Christian Rosencrux" (1895), ibid., p. 197. "I cannot get it out of my mind that this age of criticism is about to pass, and an age of imagination, of emotion, of moods, of revelation, about to come in its place: for certainly belief in a supersensual world is at hand again."
147. Yeats, *Memoirs*, p. 24.
148. *The Autobiography of William Butler Yeats* (New York: Macmillan Co., 1953), p. 115.
149. Yeats, "Discoveries," *Essays and Introductions*, p. 271.
150. Ibid., p. 292.
151. Even in "Symbolism in Painting" there are hints or even direct assertions of this more mundane, but not materalistic, celebration of the poet as a

man of sense: "The systematic mystic is not the greatest of artists, because his imagination is too great to be bounded by a picture or a song . . ." (*Essays and Introductions*, p. 150).

152. Ibid., p. 145.
153. *The Writings of Oscar Wilde*, 12 vols. (New York: Gabriel Wells, 1925), 5:113–14.
154. Wilde, "The Decay of Lying," ibid., p. 26.
155. Ibid., p. 7.
156. Wilde, "The Critic as Artist," ibid., p. 137.
157. Wilde, "The Decay of Lying," ibid., pp. 47–48.
158. Ibid., p. 49.
159. Wilde, "The Critic as Artist," ibid., pp. 141–42.
160. Wilde, "The Decay of Lying," ibid., p. 50.
161. Wilde, "The Critic as Artist," ibid., p. 175.
162. Ibid., pp. 201–3.
163. Ibid., p. 203. This idea is exploited by the later Yeats in his own doctrine of the mask.

SIX: THE MODERN DREAM (*text pages* 154–76)

1. See chap. 5, pp. 134 and 136.
2. See chap. 5, p. 123.
3. K. A. Schermer, *Das Leben des Traumes* (Berlin, 1861).
4. Walter Pater, *The Renaissance* (New York: Boni and Liveright, 1919), p. 196.
5. Sigmund Freud, *The Interpretation of Dreams* (first version, 1900), trans. James Strachey (New York: Avon, 1965), p. 39 [*Die Traumdeutung, Gesammelte Werke* II–III (Frankfurt am Main: S. Fischer, 1942), p. 5]. There were eight editions of *The Interpretation of Dreams* from 1900 to 1930, each with some changes.
6. "The Scientific Literature dealing with the Problems of Dreams," ibid., pp. 35–127 [pp. 2–99].
7. Ibid., p. 135 [pp. 107–8].
8. Ibid., p. 96 [p. 66].
9. It was still possible in 1916 to write a whole book on dreams and visions in poetry without mention of Freud. For example, Marjorie N. How, *Dreams and Visions in English Poetry* (1916) (Folcroft, Pa.: Folcroft Library, 1969), but a Freudian criticism soon developed. See Claudia C. Morrison, *Freud and the Critic: The Early Use of Depth Psychology in Literary Criticism* (Chapel Hill: University of North Carolina Press, 1968). One of the earliest Freudian works is F. C. Prescott's *Poetry and Dreams* (Boston: Four Seas, 1921). To separate art and dream became also a trend, for example, Roger Fry, *The Artist and Psychoanalysis* (London: Hogarth, 1924).
10. See, for example, Prescott, *Poetry and Dreams*, pp. 28–32, on John Keble's theory of poetry.
11. Many writers have noted the conflicting views of the artist in Freud. See

particularly Lionel Trilling, "Freud and Literature" (1940), *The Liberal Imagination* (Garden City, N.Y.: Doubleday Anchor, 1953), pp. 44–64, esp. p. 51.

12. *The Interpretation of Dreams*, p. 129 [p. 101].
13. Ibid., p. 130 [p. 102].
14. Ibid., p. 136 [p. 108].
15. .The major figure here is Jacques Lacan. See "The Function of Language in Psychoanalysis," in *The Language of the Self*, trans. Anthony Wilden (Baltimore: Johns Hopkins University Press, 1968). I say "had to have meant" because Lacan is clearly "completing" Freud according to principles derived from structuralism.
16. Freud, *On Dreams* (1901), trans. James Strachey (New York: W. W. Norton, 1952), p. 74 [*Über den Traum, Gesammelte Werke* II–III, p. 679]. *On Dreams* is a short version of the theory of dreams expressed in *The Interpretation of Dreams*.
17. Ibid., p. 26 [p. 653].
18. Ibid., p. 53 [p. 667].
19. Jack J. Spector, *The Aesthetics of Freud* (New York: McGraw-Hill, 1974): "Freud often allied himself to the artists and writers whose remarks on dreams he found so much more rewarding than the dry scholarship of academic investigators. But Freud never regarded the artist's insights as really comparable to the rational understanding of the psychoanalyst" (p. 78). Hyman's remark occurs in his *The Tangled Bank: Darwin, Marx, Frazer and Freud as Imaginative Writers* (New York: Atheneum, 1962), p. 351.
20. *On Dreams*, p. 110 [*Über den Traum*, p. 698].
21. In connection with this, see Paul Ricoeur, *Freud and Philosophy* (New Haven: Yale University Press, 1970) [*De l'interprétation: essai sur Freud* (Paris: Seuil, 1965)], p. 27, whose book is a "dialogue" with Freud: "According to one pole, hermeneutics is understood as the manifestation and restoration of a meaning addressed to me in the manner of a message, a proclamation, or as sometimes said, a kerygma; according to the other pole, it is understood as a demystification, as a reduction of illusion. Psychoanalysis, at least on a first reading, aligns itself with the second understanding of hermeneutics." Ricoeur's treatment of Freud has much in common with mine here on this point. The alternative he offers above is that of phenomenological hermeneutics, the coming into meaning of the hermeneutic act. Ricoeur sometimes seems to take a position near to the one I shall take in chap. 12: "Dreams look backward, toward infancy, the past; the work of art goes ahead of the artist; it is a prospective symbol of his personal synthesis and of man's future, rather than a regressive symbol of his unresolved conflicts" (p. 175). But for Ricoeur, art is ultimately swallowed by religion. For Ricoeur on Freud's use of "symbol," see p. 98.
22. *On Dreams*, p. 101 [*Über den Traum*, p. 696].
23. Ibid., p. 108 [p. 697].
24. Ibid., p. 107 [p. 696].
25. Ibid., p. 75 [p. 680].

26. Ibid., p. 76 [pp. 680–81].

27. Spector, *The Aesthetics of Freud*, pp. 117–18, criticizes E. H. Gombrich's attempt ("Freud's Aesthetics," *Encounter*, January 1966, pp. 30–40) to find an acceptable sense of aesthetic form in Freud as follows: "'Far from looking in the world of art only for its unconscious content of biological drives and childhood memories,' he [Gombrich] maintains, Freud insisted that the dream had to adjust to reality before becoming a work of art. According to Gombrich, Freud's view is that the 'wrapping' determines the content so that 'only those unconscious ideas that can be adjusted to the reality of the formal structure become communicable, and their value to others rests at least as much in their formal structure as in the idea.'" Spector is quite right to remark that Gombrich's case rests on isolated remarks and is inaccurate when the drift of Freud's analysis is perceived.

28. "The Relation of the Poet to Day-Dreaming" (1908), *On Creativity and the Unconscious: Papers on the Psychology of Art, Literature, Love, Religion*, ed. Benjamin Nelson (New York: Harper & Row, 1958), p. 54 ["Der Dichter und das Phantasieren," *Gesammelte Werke* 7:223].

29. Freud, "The Moses of Michelangelo," ibid., p. 11 ["Der Moses des Michelangelo," *Gesammelte Werke* 10:172].

30. It is not surprising, then, that, as Spector points out (*The Aesthetics of Freud*, pp. 23–25), Freud was inclined in his tastes toward naturalists like Zola, whose content at least *seems* to be more than their form, and showed little interest in Fauvism, Cubism, and German Expressionism, those movements where formal matters seemed to be a fundamental concern.

31. Ibid., p. 79.

32. Freud, "The Relation of the Poet to Day-Dreaming," p. 46 ["Der Dichter und das Phantasieren," p. 215].

33. Ibid., p. 47 [p. 216].

34. Ibid., p. 50 [p. 219].

35. Prescott, *Poetry and Dreams*, p. 17.

36. See Jung's "Psychology and Literature," *The Spirit in Man, Art, and Literature*, trans. R. F. C. Hull (New York: Pantheon, 1966), pp. 84–108.

37. An excellent analysis of this phenomenon is provided by Frederick J. Hoffman, *Freudianism and the Literary Mind* (1945) (New York: Grove, 1959), pp. 40–42. See also Spector, *The Aesthetics of Freud*, p. 90.

38. Freud, "The Relation of the Poet to Day-Dreaming," p. 53 ["Der Dichter und das Phantasieren," p. 222].

39. Freud, *On Dreams*, pp. 60–61 [*Über den Traum*, pp. 671–72].

40. Jung, "Freud and Jung—Contrasts," *Modern Man in Search of a Soul* (1933), trans. W. S. Dell and Cary F. Baynes (New York: Harcourt, Brace, n.d.), p. 124 ["Der Gegensatz Freud und Jung," *Gesammelte Werke*, vol. 3, *Freud und die Psychoanalyse* (Zurich und Stuttgart: Rascher, 1969), p. 393].

41. Jung, "Dream-Analysis and its Practical Application," ibid., p. 11 ["Die Praktische Verwendbarkeit der Traumanalyse," *Gesammelte Werke*, vol. 16, *Praxis der Psychotherapie* (Zurich und Stuttgart: Rascher, 1958), p. 157].

42. Ibid., p. 21, [p. 166].
43. Jung, "Psychology and Literature," ibid., p. 160 ["Psychologie und Dichtung," *Gesammelte Werke*, vol. 15, *Über das Phänomen des Geistes in Kunst und Wissenschaft* (Olten und Freiburg im Breisgau: Walter, 1971), p. 107].
44. Jung, "On the Relation of Analytical Psychology to Poetry," *The Spirit in Man, and Literature*, p. 66 ["Über die Beziehungen der Analytischen Psychologie zum dichterischen Kunstwerk," ibid., p. 76].
45. Jung, "Dream-Analysis," p. 13 ["Die Praktische Verder Traumanalyse," pp. 158–59].
46. Ibid., p. 21 [p. 166].
47. See, for example, "On the Relation of Analytical Psychology to Poetry," p. 70 [pp. 80–81].
48. Jung, "Dream-Analysis," p. 21 [p. 166].
49. Ibid., p. 22 [p. 167].
50. Jung, "On The Relation of Analytical Psychology to Poetry," p. 76 [p. 87].
51. Jung, "Dream-Analysis" p. 21 [p. 166].
52. Jung, "On the Relation of Analytical Psychology to Poetry," p. 70 [p. 81].
53. Ibid., p. 70 [p. 81].
54. Ibid., p. 70 [p. 81].
55. Jung, "Psychology and Literature," p. 171 ["Psychologie und Dichtung," ibid., p. 118].
56. Yeats, "Magic" (1901), *Essays and Introductions* (New York: Macmillan Co., 1961), pp. 28–52.
57. Jung, "Psychology and Literature," p. 164 ["Psychologie und Dichtung," p. 110].
58. Jung, "On the Relation of Analytical Psychology to Poetry," *The Spirit in Man, and Literature*, p. 80 ["Über die Beziehungen der Analytischen Psychologie zum dichterischen Kunstwerk," ibid., p. 92].
59. Ibid., p. 81 [p. 93].
60. Ibid., p. 73 [p. 85].
61. Jung, "Psychology and Literature," p. 155 ["Psychologie und Dichtung," p. 102].
62. Ibid., pp. 156–157 [p. 103].
63. Ibid., p. 162 [p. 108].
64. Jung, "Two Kinds of Thinking," *Symbols of Transformation*, trans. R. F. C. Hull (Princeton: Princeton University Press, 1970), pp. 7–33 ["Über die zwei Arten des Denkens," *Symbole der Wandlung* (Olten und Freiburg im Breisgau: Walter, 1973), pp. 25–54].
65. *The Philosophy of Giambattista Vico*, trans. R. G. Collingwood (New York: Russell and Russell, 1964), p. 50.
66. Jung, "On the Relation of Analytical Psychology to Poetry," *The Spirit in Man, and Literature*, p. 77 ["Über die Beziehungen der Analytischen Psychologie zum dichterischen Kunstwerk," ibid., p. 89].
67. Ibid., p. 82 [p. 95].
68. Ibid.
69. Ibid., p. 83 [p. 95]. One wonders whether or not Jung would be willing

to imagine a poetic society like Vico's in which the scientific impulse becomes compensatory and therefore that society's true art: This would presumably be a profoundly antiarchetypal art, but not the psychological art
he describes.

70. Jung, *Symbols of Transformation*, p. 11 [*Symbole der Wandlung*, p. 29].
71. For Herder, language is not merely the expression of thought but the form
of it, without which thought could not exist: "A nation has no idea, for
which it's [*sic*] language has no word: the liveliest imagination remains an
obscure feeling, till the mind finds a character for it, and by means of a
word incorporates it with the memory, the recollection, the understanding,
and lastly the understanding of mankind, tradition: A pure understanding,
without language, upon Earth, is an utopian land." *Outline of a Philosophy of the History of Mankind*, trans. L. Churchill (London: L. Johnson
1800), p. 233 [*Ideen sur Philosophie der Geschichte der Menscheit* (Berlin
und Weimar: Aufbau, 1965) 1:346].
72. Jung, *Symbols of Transformation*, p. 17 [*Symbole der Wandlung*, p. 36].
73. Ibid., p. 11 [pp. 29–30].
74. "Archaic Man," *Modern Man in Search of a Soul*, p. 144 ["Der archäische
Mensche," *Zivilisation im Übergang* (*Gesammelte Werke* 10) (Olten und
Freiburg im Breisgau: Walter, 1974), pp. 82–83].
75. Ibid., p. 126 [p. 68].
76. Ibid., p. 140 [p. 80].
77. "The Symbolism of Poetry," *Essays and Introductions* (London: Macmillan, 1961), p. 155.
78. "Psychology and Literature," p. 172 [p. 120].
79. "Archaic Man," pp. 141–42 ["Der archäische Mensch," pp. 81–82].
80. "The Basic Postulates of Analytical Psychology," *Modern Man in Search of
a Soul*," p. 174 ["Das Grund problem der Gegenwärtigen Psychologie,"
Die Dynamik des Unbewußten (*Gesammelte Werke* 8) (Zurich und Stuttgart: Rascher, 1967)].
81. Jung, "On the Relation of Analytic Psychology to Poetry," p. 73 [p. 85].
82. Ibid. This situation accounts for Jung's version of the impersonality of the
poem: "A work of art is not a human being, but is something supra-
personal" (ibid., p. 71).
83. Ibid., p. 77 [p. 90].
84. Ibid., p. 77 [p. 89].
85. Ibid., p. 78 [p. 90].
86. Charles Lamb, "On the Sanity of True Genius," *New Monthly Magazine*,
May 1826.
87. Jung, "On the Relation of Analytic Psychology to Poetry," p. 78 [p. 90].
88. Bachelard's phenomenology is of a special sort, and one must not draw
general conclusions about phenomenological criticism from it.
89. Bachelard, *La psychoanalyse du feu* (1938) (Paris: Gallimard, 1949); English translation, *The Psychoanalysis of Fire*, by Alan C. M. Ross (Boston:
Beacon Press, 1968).
90. Bachelard, *The Poetics of Space*, trans. Maria Jolas (Boston: Beacon Press,
1969), p. xi [*La poétique de l'espace* (Paris: Presses Universitaires, 1964),
p. 1].

91. Bachelard, *The Poetics of Reverie*, trans. Daniel Russell (Boston: Beacon Press, 1969), p. 149 [*La poétique de la rêverie* (Paris: Presses Universitaires, 1965), p. 128].
92. Ibid., p. 22 [p. 20]. Bachelard's book circles around this idea. See repetitions on pp. 145, 147.
93. Ibid., p. 147 [p. 126]. See also p. 145, where the night dream is an "abductor, the most disconcerting of abductors: it abducts our being from us."
94. Ibid., p. 150 [p. 129].
95. Ibid.
96. Ibid., p. 158 [p. 136].
97. Ibid., p. 166 [p. 143].
98. Ibid., p. 162 [p. 140].
99. Ibid., p. 167 [p. 144].
100. Bachelard, *The Poetics of Space*, p. xvii [p. 5].
101. Ibid., p. xxv [p. 12].
102. Bachelard, *The Poetics of Reverie*, p. 3 [p. 3].
103. Bachelard, *The Poetics of Space*, p. xiv [p. 2].
104. Ibid., p. xx [p. 7].
105. Bachelard, *The Poetics of Reverie*, p. 7 [p. 7].
106. Bachelard, *The Poetics of Space*, p. xix [p. 7].
107. Bachelard, *The Poetics of Reverie*, p. 57 [p. 49].
108. Ibid., p. 159 [p. 137].
109. Ibid., p. 154 [p. 132].
110. Bachelard, *The Poetics of Space*, p. xx [p. 8].
111. Bachelard, *The Poetics of Reverie*, pp. 157–59 [pp. 135–37].
112. Ibid., p. 157 [p. 135].
113. Bachelard, *The Poetics of Space*, p. xxiii [p. 10].
114. Ibid., p. xxiii [p. 10].
115. Bachelard, *The Poetics of Reverie*, pp. 158–59 [p. 136].
116. Bachelard, *The Poetics of Space*, p. xxiii [p. 10].
117. Ibid., p. xxviii [p. 14].
118. Bachelard, *The Poetics of Reverie*, p. 1 [p. 1].

SEVEN: SYMBOL, FICTION, FIGMENT (*text pages 177–99*)

1. *Estetica come scienza dell'espressione e linguistica generale* was first published in 1902 and was revised through the fourth edition of 1911. The English translation used here is *Aesthetic as a Science of Expression and General Linguistic*, trans. Douglas Ainslee, rev. ed. (1922) (New York: Noonday Press, 1963).
2. *Die Philosophie des Als Ob* was first published in 1911. The English translation used here—a condensation—is *The Philosophy of "As If,"* trans. C. K. Ogden (New York: Harcourt, Brace, 1925). "Part I: Basic Principles" was Vaihinger's inaugural dissertation at Strassburg in 1876. The work was taken up again in 1906.
3. Croce, *Aesthetic*, p. 231 [*Estetica come scienza dell'espressione e linguistica generale* (Bari: G. Laterza & Figli, 1965), pp. 254–55].
4. Ibid., p. 225 [p. 247].

5. Ibid., p. 142 [pp. 155–56]. But he is not thinking of linguistics in all the contemporary senses of the term.
6. Croce, *Terze pagine sparse*, 3 vols. (Bari: G. Laterza, 1955), 2:164.
7. See chap. 1, pp. 7–12.
8. Croce, *Aesthetic*, p. 69 [*Estetica*, p. 77]. An excellent account of Croce's criticism of tropes occurs in Gian N. G. Orsini's *Benedetto Croce, Philosopher of Art and Literary Critic* (Carbondale: Southern Illinois University Press, 1961), pp. 78–84.
9. H. Wildon Carr, *The Philosophy of Benedetto Croce: The Problem of Art and History* (London: Macmillan, 1917), p. 39. On the contrast to scientific hypothesis: "The sciences increase our control of nature, they widen the range of our knowledge and therewith enlarge the sphere of our activity, they give us a deeper and more penetrating insight into reality; but they are turned from and not towards reality itself, they take us further and further from the individual, indivisible, concrete whole which alone is actual" (p. 6).
10. Croce, *Aesthetic*, p. 256 [*Estetica*, p. 283].
11. Ibid., p. 42 [p. 49].
12. Orsini, *Benedetto Croce*, p. 67.
13. Croce, *Aesthetic*, p. 147 [*Estetica*, p. 160].
14. Orsini, *Benedetto Croce*, p. 69.
15. Croce, *Aesthetic*, p. 4 [*Estetica*, p. 6].
16. Ibid., p. 15 [p. 18].
17. Croce, *Guide to Aesthetics*, trans. Patrick Romanell (Indianapolis: Bobbs-Merrill, 1965), p. 44 [*Breviario de Estetica* (1913) (Bari: Gius. Laterza & Figli, 1938), pp. 58–60].
18. Croce, *Aesthetic*, p. 8 [*Estetica*, p. 11].
19. Croce, *Guide*, p. 40 [*Breviario*, pp. 54–55].
20. Croce, *Aesthetic*, p. 16 [*Estetica*, p. 19].
21. Ibid., p. 16 [p. 18]. This verbal manipulation only serves to show how stubborn the form-content terminology is, even for someone who wishes to eliminate it.
22. Ibid., p. 17 [p. 21].
23. Ibid., pp. 23 ff. [pp. 26 ff.]. Croce deals with objections to this idea here. Principally, they are (1) that one can think in other sorts of symbols than language (but Croce means to include all symbols in the expanded term "speech"); (2) that animals reason without speech (but Croce argues that if they do reason, there is no doubt in his mind that in some way or other they express); (3) that some books are well thought but ill expressed (but Croce argues that this really means that some parts of the book are well thought and well expressed and the rest ill thought and ill expressed).
24. Ibid., p. 44 [p. 51].
25. Ibid., p. 42 [p. 48].
26. Croce, *Guide*, p. 23 [*Breviario*, p. 34].
27. Croce, *Aesthetic*, p. 34 [*Estetica*, p. 39].
28. Ibid., [p. 40]. See also Croce's essay: "On the Use and Abuse of the Term 'Symbol'," *Letture*, pp. 216–26, quoted by Orsini, *Benedetto Croce*: It is

impossible to define "the symbol in itself, as if it were an independent mental activity possessed of its own theoretical rights, whereas, if it is so defined, it becomes immediately identified with the undesired [deprecata] allegory. If this identification is rejected, one cannot define it for the good reason that it is not a new and original act additional to that of poetic creation, but is a synonym of poetry itself, which is always 'symbolic,' i.e., always (the tautology is here inevitable) *poetic*" (pp. 328–30).

29. Croce, *Guide*, p. 22 [*Breviario*, p. 33].
30. Croce, *Aesthetic*, pp. 34–35 [*Estetica*, p. 40].
31. Ibid., p. 34 [ibid., p. 39].
32. Ibid., p. 116 [ibid., p. 128].
33. Ibid., p. 111 [ibid., p. 122]. The concept of will in Croce has traditional and Kantian limits. The will is that spiritual activity which is not merely theoretical contemplation but is productive of actions. Externalization is a fact of will, a practical as against an aesthetic act (pp. 47, 50). The distinction between intuition and the purposive will preserves a Kantian purposiveness without purpose for intuition but gives to will the purpose of communication, though it is not always clear, I am afraid, that externalization has such purpose.
34. For a critique of Croce on this point see Joyce Cary's *Art and Reality: Ways of the Creative Process* (New York: Harper, 1958). Cary insists on the distinction between intuition and expression from the artist's point of view. The present study was to have included a chapter on Cary's views, but it has been necessary to delay that discussion for a book on Cary, recently completed but not yet in print.
35. Croce, *Aesthetic*, p. 103 [*Estetica*, p. 113].
36. Carr, *The Philosophy of Benedetto Croce*, p. 53.
37. Orsini, *Benedetto Croce*, p. 73. Orsini notes that Saussure's distinction between *parole* and *langage*, speech as individual utterance and speech as a collective product might be invoked to claim that individual speech must conform to *langage* and that the artist therefore always faces an "external obstacle," but Croce denies concrete reality to *langage*, which is a sort of "fiction."
38. Croce, *Guide*, p. 16 [*Breviario*, p. 25].
39. Ibid. [ibid., pp. 25–26].
40. Ibid., p. 17 [ibid., p. 26].
41. Vaihinger, "Autobiographical," *The Philosophy of "As If,"* p. xxvii.
42. Vaihinger, *The Philosophy of "As If,"* p. 107 [*Die Philosophie des Als Ob* (Berlin: Reuther & Richard, 1913), p. 191].
43. Ibid., p. 77 [pp. 114–15].
44. Ibid., p. 168 [p. 304], a statement that anticipates Cassirer.
45. Vaihinger, "Autobiographical," p. xxx.
46. Ibid., p. xliii.
47. Ibid., p. xlvii.
48. Vaihinger, *The Philosophy of "As If,"* p. 65 [*Die Philosophie des Als Ob*, p. 93].
49. Ibid., p. 123 [p. 215].

50. Ibid., p. 137 [p. 232].
51. Vaihinger, "Autobiographical," ibid., p. xlii.
52. Vaihinger, *The Philosophy of "As If,"* p. 86 [*Die Philosophie des Als Ob,* p. 145].
53. Ibid., pp. 18–19 [p. 27].
54. Ibid., p. 88 [p. 148].
55. Ibid., p. 79 [p. 124].
56. Ibid., p. 63 [p. 88].
57. Ibid., p. 171 [p. 311].
58. Ibid., p. 67 [p. 97].
59. Ibid., p. 81 [p. 130].
60. Ibid., p. 81n [p. 129].
61. Ibid., p. 138 [p. 236].
62. Ibid., p. 98 [p. 172].
63. Ibid., p. 82 [p. 131].
64. Ibid., p. 83 [p. 132].
65. Ibid., p. 84 [p. 142].
66. Ibid., p. 208 [p. 404].
67. Frank Kermode, *The Sense of an Ending: Studies in the Theory of Fiction* (1966) (New York: Oxford University Press, 1970), pp. 39–42; Harold Toliver, *Animate Illusions: Explorations of Narrative Structure* (Lincoln: University of Nebraska Press, 1974), pp. 37–49. Standard histories of criticism rarely mention Vaihinger.
68. Donald A. Stauffer, *The Golden Nightingale: Essays on Some Principles of Poetry in the Lyrics of William Butler Yeats* (New York: Macmillan, 1949), pp. 6–7.
69. Ibid., p. 4.
70. Ibid., p. 6.
71. Ibid.
72. Ibid., p. 17.
73. Ibid., pp. 22–23.
74. Ibid., p. 17.
75. Kermode, *The Sense of an Ending*, p. 34.
76. Stevens, *Opus Posthumous* (New York: Alfred Knopf, 1957), p. 163. Kermode quotes part of this (p. 36).
77. Kermode, *The Sense of an Ending*, p. 39.
78. Ibid., p. 40.

EIGHT: THE PHILOSOPHY OF SYMBOLIC FORMS
(*text pages* 200–242)

1. Ernst Cassirer, *The Philosophy of Symbolic Forms*, trans. Ralph Manheim, 3 vols. (New Haven: Yale University Press, 1953, 1955, 1957) [*Philosophie der symbolischen Formen*, 3 vols. (Darmstadt: Wissenschaftliche Buchgesellschaft, 1964)].
2. Northrop Frye, "Myth as Information," *Hudson Review* (Summer 1954): 228–35.

3. Ernst Cassirer, *An Essay on Man* (New Haven: Yale University Press, 1944). After he had come to America, Cassirer had been asked to provide an English translation of *Philosophie der symbolischen Formen*, which had appeared in Germany from 1923 to 1929. He declined and wrote the much shorter *Essay* instead, warning readers that his ideas had developed and changed and that he would not merely return to the former work. At the same time, he directed readers to *Philosophie der symbolischen Formen* for more extended demonstrations of many points.

4. *The Philosophy of Symbolic Forms*, vol. 1: *Language*, p. 75 [*Philosophie*, 1:5].

5. Ibid., p. 78 [p. 9].

6. Ibid., p. 76 [p. 7].

7. Ibid., p. 77 [p. 7].

8. Ibid., p. 85 [p. 17].

9. Ibid., p. 111 [p. 48].

10. Ibid., p. 147 [p. 90].

11. Ibid., pp. 147–48 [p. 90].

12. Ibid., p. 149 [p. 91].

13. Ibid., p. 153 [p. 96].

14. Ibid., p. 153 [p. 97].

15. Ibid., p. 158 [pp. 102–3].

16. Ibid., p. 159 [p. 103].

17. Ibid., p. 159 [p. 104].

18. Ibid.

19. Ibid., p. 215 [p. 170].

20. Ibid., p. 218 [p. 173].

21. Ibid., p. 226 [p. 183].

22. Ibid., p. 228 [p. 185].

23. It sometimes seems as if Cassirer sees mathematics as the Aristotelian final cause of language, but in *An Essay on Man* he rejects the Aristotelian natural teleology.

24. Cassirer, *The Philosophy of Symbolic Forms*, 1:280 [*Philosophie*, 1:251].

25. Ibid., p. 281 [p. 253].

26. *The Philosophy of Symbolic Forms*, vol. 2: *Mythical Thought*, pp. 2–3 [*Philosophie*, 2:5].

27. Ibid., p. 3 [p. 5].

28. Ibid., p. 3 [p. 6].

29. Ibid., p. 4 [p. 7].

30. Ibid., p. 14 [p. 19].

31. Ibid., p. 16 [p. 21].

32. Ibid., p. 37 [p. 50].

33. Ibid., p. 47 [p. 62].

34. Ibid., p. 62 [p. 81].

35. Ibid., p. 63 [p. 81].

36. Ibid., p. 64 [p. 82].

37. Ibid., p. 99 [p. 123].

38. Ibid., p. 105 [p. 130].
39. Ibid., p. 187 [p. 224].
40. Ibid., p. 239 [p. 286].
41. Ibid., p. 249 [p. 298].
42. Ibid., p. 256 [pp. 305–6].
43. Ibid., p. 257 [pp. 306–7].
44. Ibid., pp. 260–61 [p. 311].
45. Paul Ricoeur, *Freud and Philosophy* (New Haven: Yale University Press, 1975), p. 20 [*De l'interprétation: essai sur Freud*, (Paris: Seuil, 1965)]. Also: "If we use the term symbolic for the signifying function in its entirety, we no longer have a word to designate the group of signs whose intentional texture calls for a reading of another meaning in the first, literal, and immediate meaning" (p. 11). Thus Ricoeur sees symbol as a kind of sign, while Cassirer sees sign as a function of symbolic. For Cassirer, Ricoeur's symbol is allegorical. For me it is either "miraculous" or allegorical. See chap. 12, pp. 372–93.
46. Cassirer, *An Essay on Man*, p. 24.
47. Ibid., p. 25.
48. Ibid., p. 218.
49. Ibid., p. 49.
50. Ibid., p. 143.
51. Ibid.
52. Ibid.
53. Ibid., p. 144.
54. Ibid., pp. 156–57.
55. Ibid., p. 157.
56. Ibid., p. 168.
57. Ibid., p. 169.
58. Ibid., pp. 169–70.
59. Susanne K. Langer, *Feeling and Form* (New York: Charles Scribner's Sons, 1953).
60. Langer, *Philosophy in a New Key: A Study in the Symbolism of Reason, Rite, and Art* (1942) (New York: Mentor, 1951).
61. Langer, *Feeling and Form*, p. 376.
62. Ibid.
63. Ibid., p. 26.
64. Langer, *Philosophy in a New Key*, pp. 83–84.
65. Langer, *Feeling and Form*, p. 10.
66. Langer, *Philosophy in a New Key*, p. 85.
67. Ibid., p. 129.
68. Ibid., p. 91.
69. Ibid., p. 186.
70. Langer, *Feeling and Form*, p. 377.
71. Ibid., p. 376.
72. Ibid., p. 120.
73. Ibid., p. 384.

74. Ibid., p. 240.
75. Langer, *Philosophy in a New Key*, pp. 126–27.
76. Ibid., p. 127.
77. Ibid., p. 83.
78. Ibid., p. 88.
79. Langer, *Feeling and Form*, p. 369.
80. Langer, *Philosophy in a New Key*, p. 225.
81. Ibid., p. 220.
82. Ibid., p. 237.
83. Ibid.
84. Langer, *Feeling and Form*, p. 120.
85. Langer, *Philosophy in a New Key*, p. 93.
86. Langer, *Feeling and Form*, p. 31.
87. Langer, *Philosophy in a New Key*, p. 204.
88. Ibid., p. 92.
89. Ibid., p. 89.
90. Ibid., p. 173.
91. Ibid.
92. Ibid., p. 113.
93. Ibid., pp. 106–7.
94. Ibid., p. 128.
95. Susanne K. Langer, *Problems of Art* (New York: Charles Scribner's Sons, 1957).
96. Langer, *Philosophy in a New Key*, p. 130.
97. Ibid., p. 125.
98. Langer, *Feeling and Form*, p. 81.
99. Langer, *Philosophy in a New Key*, p. 172.
100. Ibid., p. 173.
101. Ibid., p. 174.
102. Ibid., p. 223.
103. Ibid., pp. 173–74.
104. Ibid., p. 217.
105. Langer, *Feeling and Form*, p. 28.
106. Ibid., p. 40.
107. Ibid., p. 28.
108. Ibid., p. 32.
109. Ibid.
110. Ibid., p. 82.
111. Ibid., p. 211.
112. Ibid., p. 252.
113. Ibid., pp. 242, 253.
114. Ibid., p. 242.
115. Ibid., p. 227.
116. One of the exceptions is Charles Feidelson's *Symbolism and American Literature* (Chicago: University of Chicago Press, 1953), one of the first critical books to come consciously under the influence of Cassirer. To this may

be added Walter Brylowski's *Faulkner's Olympian Laugh: Myth in the Novels* (Detroit: Wayne State University Press, 1968).

117. Eliseo Vivas, *D. H. Lawrence: The Failure and the Triumph of Art* (Bloomington: Indiana University Press, 1960), p. 283.

118. Vivas, "What Is a Poem?" *Creation and Discovery* (1955) (Chicago: Henry Regnery, 1965), pp. 134–35.

119. Ibid., p. 112.

120. Vivas, "Animadversions on Imitation and Expression," *The Artistic Transaction* (Columbus: Ohio State University Press, 1963), p. 161.

121. Vivas, "Preface," *Creation and Discovery*, p. xix.

122. Vivas, *The Artistic Transaction*, p. 10.

123. Ibid., p. 13.

124. Vivas, "What Is a Poem?" *Creation and Discovery*, p. 127.

125. Vivas, *The Artistic Transaction*, p. 14.

126. Ibid., p. 4.

127. Vivas, "Literature and Knowledge," *Creation and Discovery*, p. 181.

128. Vivas, "What Is a Poem?" ibid., p. 125.

129. Ibid., p. 126.

130. Ibid.

131. Vivas, "Preface to the Gateway Edition," ibid., p. xiii.

132. Vivas, "Literature and Knowledge," ibid., p. 191.

133. Vivas, "What Is a Poem?" ibid., p. 115.

134. Vivas, "Preface to the Gateway Edition," ibid., p. x.

135. Vivas, "What Is a Poem?" ibid., p. 115.

136. Vivas, "Literature and Knowledge," ibid., pp. 163–64.

137. Vivas, "What Is a Poem?" ibid., p. 116.

138. Vivas, *The Artistic Transaction*, p. 19.

139. Vivas, "A Definition of the Aesthetic Experience," *Creation and Discovery*, p. 146.

140. Vivas, "What Is a Poem?" ibid., p. 133.

141. Ibid., pp. 132–33.

142. Ibid., p. 127.

143. Vivas, "The Object of the Poem," ibid., p. 206.

144. Ibid., p. 207.

145. Ibid., p. 213.

146. Vivas, *D. H. Lawrence*, p. 276.

147. Ibid., p. 280.

148. Ibid., p. 279.

149. Ibid.

150. Ibid., p. 281.

151. Vivas, *The Artistic Transaction*, p. 7.

152. Vivas, "What Is a Poem?" *Creation and Discovery*, p. 123.

NINE: SENTIMENTAL ARCHAISM (*text pages* 243–62)

1. "The Metaphysical Poets," *Selected Essays 1917–1932* (New York: Harcourt, Brace, 1932), p. 247.

2. Frank Kermode, *Romantic Image* (New York: Macmillan, 1957), pp. 138–66.
3. Joseph Campbell, *The Hero with a Thousand Faces* (1949) (New York: Meridian, 1956).
4. Ibid., p. 3.
5. Ibid., p. 387.
6. Ibid., p. 4.
7. Ibid., p. 388.
8. Ibid., p. 255.
9. Joseph Campbell and Henry Morton Robinson, *A Skeleton Key to Finnegans Wake* (1944) (New York: Viking Press, 1961).
10. *The Hero with a Thousand Faces*, p. 256.
11. Ibid., p. 4.
12. Ibid., pp. 251, 258.
13. Ibid., p. 236.
14. Ibid., p. 258.
15. Ibid., p. 267.
16. Ibid., p. 258.
17. Ibid., p. 34n.
18. Ibid., p. 259.
19. Ibid., p. 266.
20. Ibid., p. 382.
21. Ibid., p. 37.
22. Ibid., p. 381.
23. Ibid., p. 382.
24. Ibid., p. 257.
25. Mircea Eliade, *Myth and Reality*, trans. Willard R. Trask (New York and Evanston: Harper and Row, 1963), p. 163 [*Aspects du mythe* (Paris: Gallimard, 1963), p. 199].
26. Eliade, *Myths, Dreams, and Mysteries: The Encounter between Contemporary Faiths and Archaic Realities* (1957), trans. Philip Mairet (New York and Evanston: Harper and Row, 1960), p. 16 [*Mythes, rêves et mystères* (Paris: Gallimard, 1957), p. 10].
27. Ibid., p. 24 [p. 19].
28. Ibid., p. 15 [p. 10].
29. Eliade, *Cosmos and History: The Myth of the Eternal Return* (1949), trans. Willard R. Trask (New York: Harper & Brothers, 1959), p. 85 [*Le mythe de l'éternel retour* (Paris: Gallimard, 1949), p. 127].
30. Ibid., p. 34 [p. 63].
31. Ibid., p. 34, [p. 64].
32. Ibid., p. 123 [pp. 184–85].
33. See, for example, *Myths, Dreams, and Mysteries*: "archaic man, the man who has been called (though wrongly) the 'primitive'" (p. 236) [*Mythes, rêves et mystères*, p. 67].
34. Eliade, *Cosmos and History*, p. 147 [*Le mythe de l'éternel retour*, p. 218].
35. Eliade, *Myths, Dreams, and Mysteries*, p. 36 [*Mythes, rêves et mystères*, p. 34].

36. Eliade, *Myth and Reality*, p. 192 [*Aspects du mythe*, p. 232].
37. See p. 105.
38. Eliade, *Myths, Dreams, and Mysteries*, p. 36 [*Mythes, rêves et mystères*, pp. 33–34].
39. Ibid., p. 35 [p. 33].
40. Ibid., p. 36 [p. 34].
41. Blake, see p. 102.
42. Eliade, *Myths, Dreams, and Mysteries*, p. 36 [*Mythes, rêves et mystères*, p. 34].
43. Ibid., p. 27 [p. 23].
44. Ibid., p. 31 [p. 28].
45. Eliade, *Myth and Reality*, p. 141 [*Aspectes du mythe*, p. 174].
46. Blake, "Milton" 25:72, *Complete Writings*, ed. Geoffrey Keynes (New York: Random House, 1957), p. 510.
47. Philip Wheelwright, *The Burning Fountain: A Study in the Language of Symbolism* (Bloomington: Indiana University Press, 1954; new and rev. ed., 1968).
48. Ibid. (1954 version), p. 4.
49. Ibid. (1968 version), p. 4.
50. Ibid., p. 37.
51. Ibid. (1954 version), p. 8.
52. Ibid. (1968 version), pp. 18–19.
53. Ibid., p. 272.
54. Ibid.
55. Ibid., p. 7.
56. Ibid., p. 9.
57. Ibid., p. 10.
58. Ibid., pp. 12–13.
59. Ibid., p. 13.
60. Ibid., p. 12.
61. Ibid., p. 17.
62. Ibid., p. 74; see also p. 17.
63. All discussed ibid., pp. 73–101.
64. Ibid., p. 76 (1954 version, p. 55).
65. Ibid. (1968 version), pp. 76–101 (1954 version, pp. 55–60). The discussion in the 1968 edition is considerably revised.
66. Ibid. (1968 version), p. 74.
67. Ibid., p. 147.
68. Ibid., p. 100.
69. Ibid., p. 21.
70. Ibid.
71. Ibid., p. 22.
72. Ibid., p. 24.
73. Ibid.
74. Ibid.
75. Ibid.

76. Ibid., p. 35.
77. Ibid., p. 37.
78. Ibid., p. 38.
79. Ibid., p. 79.
80. Ibid.
81. Ibid., p. 80.
82. As enunciated in Bullough's "'Psychical Distance' as a Factor in Art and an Aesthetic Principle," *British Journal of Psychology* 5, no. 2 (1912).
83. Wheelwright, *The Burning Fountain* (1968 version), pp. 46–47.
84. Ibid., p. 52. See also: ". . . Goethe holds that the world is intrinsically symbolic: by which he means that every quality, character, happening, is at once concrete event (Phänomenon) and archetype (Urphänomenon). The Goethean archetype, however, is not like the Platonic *eidos* something separate in existence or even in thought from the particular" (p. 53).
85. Ibid., p. 54.
86. Ibid., p. 67.
87. Ibid., p. 70.
88. Ibid., p. 142.
89. Ibid., p. 149.
90. Ibid., p. 150.
91. Blake, "The Marriage of Heaven and Hell," *Complete Writings*, p. 157.

TEN: THE LITERARY CONCEPT OF MYTH (*text pages 263–86*)

1. As I implied in chapter 1, my way here is not to leave the issue, as Walter Benjamin does, in a situation where allegory is privileged over (negates) "miraculous" symbolism, but to find allegory as a form of symbolic.
2. Northrop Frye, *Anatomy of Criticism* (Princeton: Princeton University Press, 1957).
3. Ibid., p. 250.
4. Ibid., p. 85.
5. Ibid., p. 83.
6. Ibid.
7. Ibid., p. 63.
8. Ibid., p. 79.
9. Ibid., p. 93.
10. Aristotle, *Poetics* 25, 5.
11. Frye, *Anatomy of Criticism*, pp. 73–82.
12. Ibid., p. 78.
13. Ibid., p. 74.
14. Ernst Cassirer, *An Essay on Man* (New Haven: Yale University Press, 1944), p. 144.
15. Frye, *Anatomy of Criticism*, p. 121.
16. Frank Kermode, "Northrop Frye," *Puzzles and Epiphanies* (New York: Chilmark, 1962), pp. 64–73.
17. Ibid., p. 136.
18. Ibid., p. 119.

19. Ibid., p. 82.
20. Ibid.
21. Ibid., p. 122.
22. Blake, "Jerusalem," *The Complete Writings of William Blake,* ed. Geoffrey Keynes (London: Nonesuch; New York: Random House, 1957), p. 716.
23. Frye, *Anatomy of Criticism,* p. 11.
24. Ibid., p. 350.
25. Ibid., p. 352.
26. Ibid., p. 351.
27. Ibid., p. 352.
28. Ibid.
29. Ibid.
30. Ibid., p. 364.
31. Ibid., p. 105.
32. Ibid., p. 71.
33. Ibid., pp. 89–92.
34. Angus Fletcher, *Allegory: The Theory of a Symbolic Mode* (Ithaca: Cornell University Press, 1964), p. 7. The argument continues along the same lines on p. 8.
35. Ibid., p. 314. Fletcher (p. 220) contrasts allegory (thought, *dianoia*) and mimesis (action, *praxis*), but his book eventually turns everything into allegory or at least into writing that will bear an allegorical reading. As we proceed through the book the distinction between allegory and *praxis* weakens, though the distinction is still invoked. At the end we do not know quite how to take Fletcher's discussion of the limits of allegory, since allegory has spread so far.
36. Ibid., p. 8.
37. Frye, *Anatomy of Criticism,* p. 99.
38. Ibid., pp. 103–4.
39. Ibid., p. 88.
40. Ibid., p. 148.
41. Ibid., p. 331.
42. Ibid., p. 354.
43. Northrop Frye, *The Critical Path: An Essay on the Social Context of Literary Criticism* (Bloomington: Indiana University Press, 1971), p. 36.
44. Ibid., p. 98.
45. Ibid., p. 101.
46. Ibid., p. 103.
47. Ibid., pp. 56–57.
48. Ibid., p. 131.
49. Ibid., p. 44.
50. Blake, Letter to Hayley, 28 May 1804.
51. W. B. Yeats, letter to Dorothy Wellesley, July 6, 1935, *The Letters of W. B. Yeats,* ed. Allan Wade (New York: Macmillan, 1955), p. 836.
52. Blake, "Annotations to Watson's *Apology* for the Bible," *Complete Writings,* 1957, p. 392.
53. Frye, *Critical Path,* p. 93.

54. Ibid., p. 157.
55. Northrop Frye, *The Secular Scripture: A Study of the Structure of Romance* (Cambridge, Mass.: Harvard University Press, 1976), p. 167.
56. Ibid., p. 23. Frye's notion of identity goes back at least as far in his writings to an essay on Blake's *Milton*. More about this in chapter 12.
57. Ibid., pp. 117–19.
58. Ibid., p. 130.

Eleven: Stylistic Arrangements of Experience
(*text pages 287–324*)

1. Quoted by Joseph Hone, *W. B. Yeats, 1865–1939* (New York: Macmillan, 1943), p. 491.
2. William Butler Yeats, *A Vision* (New York: Macmillan, 1938), p. 72.
3. Yeats, *Explorations* (London: Macmillan, 1962), p. 392.
4. Yeats, *A Vision*, p. 25.
5. Yeats, *Autobiography* (New York: Macmillan, 1953), pp. 70–71.
6. ". . . le monde est fait pour aboutir à un beau livre": Mallarmé, "Sur l'evolution littéraire," *Œuvres complètes* (Paris: Gallimard [Bibliothèque de la Pléiade], 1945), p. 872.
7. *The Works of William Blake*, ed. Edwin J. Ellis and William Butler Yeats, 3 vols. (London: Bernard Quaritch, 1893).
8. Yeats, "Pages from a Diary Written in Nineteen Hundred and Thirty," *Explorations*, p. 300.
9. Yeats, Introduction to "The Cat and The Moon," ibid., p. 400.
10. Yeats, "Bishop Berkeley," *Essays and Introductions* (London: Macmillan, 1961), p. 409.
11. Richard Ellmann, *The Identity of Yeats* (New York: Oxford University Press, 1954), p. 238.
12. Keats, Letter to George and Thomas Keats, December 21, 1817, *Complete Poems and Selected Letters*, ed. C. D. Thorpe, (New York: Odyssey Press, 1935), p. 528.
13. Yeats, "Estrangement," *Autogiography*, p. 279.
14. W. B. Yeats, *Explorations*, pp. 301–2.
15. Ibid., p. 305.
16. W. B. Yeats, *Collected Poems* (New York: Macmillan, 1956), p. 8. In earlier volumes and in the two-volume signed edition, "The Wanderings of Oisin" is the first poem. It was originally intended as the first poem but was relegated to the back of *Collected Poems* on advice of the publisher. See my "The 'Book' of Yeats's Poems," *Cornell Review* 1, no. 1 (Spring 1977): 122–23.
17. A. N. Whitehead, *Science and the Modern World* (New York: Macmillan, 1941), p. 80.
18. Yeats, *Collected Poems*, pp. 8–9.
19. Yeats, "Fragments," ibid., p. 211.
20. Yeats, *Autobiography*, p. 76.
21. Yeats, "Fragments," *Collected Poems*, p. 211.

22. Michael Polanyi and Harry Prosch, *Meaning* (Chicago and London: University of Chicago Press, 1975), p. 39.
23. Wordsworth, in the preface to the second edition of *Lyrical Ballads.*
24. Blake, "A Public Address," *Complete Writings*, ed. Geoffrey Keynes (London: Nonesuch; New York: Random House, 1957), p. 599.
25. T. E. Hulme, *Speculations* (1924) (New York: Harcourt, Brace, n.d.), p. 120.
26. Yeats, "The Philosophy of Shelley's Poetry," *Essays and Introductions*, p. 87.
27. Yeats, "The Tower," *Collected Poems*, p. 196.,
28. *W. B. Yeats and T. Sturge Moore: Their Correspondence, 1901–1937*, ed. Ursula Bridge (London: Routledge and Kegan Paul, 1953), p. 69.
29. Yeats, *Collected Poems*, p. 168.
30. Blake, *Complete Writings*, p. 451.
31. Keats, Letter to Benjamin Bailey, November 22, 1817, *Complete Poems and Selected Letters*, p. 524.
32. Yeats, *Collected Poems*, p. 192.
33. Ibid., p. 192.
34. *Further Letters of John Butler Yeats*, ed. Lennox Robinson (Dundrum: The Cuala Press, 1920), pp. 22–23.
35. W. B. Yeats, *A Vision*, p. 33.
36. John Burnet, *Early Greek Philosophy* (New York: Meridian, 1957), p. 36.
37. W. B. Yeats, *Explorations*, p. 340.
38. W. B. Yeats, *On the Boiler* (Dublin: The Cuala Press, n.d.), p. 25.
39. Ibid., p. 26.
40. Ibid., p. 26.
41. Yeats, "The Irish Dramatic Movement," *Plays and Controversies* (New York: Macmillan, 1924), p. 121.
42. Yeats, *On the Boiler*, p. 26.
43. Yeats, "Under Ben Bulben," *Collected Poems*, p. 342.
44. Cassirer, *The Philosophy of Symbolic Forms*, 3 vols. (New Haven: Yale University Press, 1953), 1:229 [*Philosophie der symbolischen Formen*, 3 vols. (Darmstadt: Wissenschaftliche Buchgesellschaft, 1964), 1:187].
45. Ibid., 2:66 [2:85].
46. Yeats, *A Vision*, p. 213.
47. Ibid., p. 300.
48. Tobias Dantzig, *Number: The Language of Science* (Garden City: Anchor, 1954), pp. 98–99.
49. Ibid., p. 100.
50. F. A. C. Wilson, *Yeats's Iconography* (London: Gollancz, 1960), p. 296.
51. Yeats, *On the Boiler*, p. 37.
52. Yeats, *Collected Poems*, p. 322.
53. Yeats, *Essays and Introductions*, pp. 243–44.
54. Ibid., p. 243.
55. Yeats, *On the Boiler*, p. 37.
56. Yeats, *Essays and Introductions*, pp. 221–37.

57. Yeats, *A Vision*, p. 271.
58. Yeats, *Autobiography*, p. 87.
59. Yeats, *A Vision*, p. 277.
60. Ibid., p. 277.
61. *W. B. Yeats and T. Sturge Moore: Their Correspondence 1901–1937*, pp. 63–108.
62. Yeats, *Autobiography*, pp. 58–61.
63. Frank Kermode, *Romantic Image* (New York: Macmillan, 1957).
64. Yeats, "To Ireland in the Coming Time," *Collected Poems*, p. 49.
65. Yeats, "Under Ben Bulben," ibid., p. 342.
66. Yeats, *A Vision*, pp. 180–81.
67. Yeats, *Collected Poems*, p. 247.
68. Yeats, *A Vision*, p. 182.
69. Yeats, "Discoveries," *Essays and Introductions*, pp. 287–88.
70. Yeats, "Meru," *Collected Poems*, p. 287.
71. Cleanth Brooks, "W. B. Yeats: The Poet as Myth-maker," reprinted in *The Permanence of Yeats*, ed. J. Hall and M. Steinmann (New York: Macmillan, 1950), p. 67.
72. Ibid., p. 92.
73. I. A. Richards, in his *Science and Poetry* (New York: W. W. Norton, 1926).
74. John Unterecker, *A Reader's Guide to William Butler Yeats* (New York: Noonday, 1959), pp. 28–29.
75. R. P. Blackmur, in *The Permanence of Yeats*, ed. J. Hall and M. Steinmann, p. 42.
76. T. S. Eliot, *Selected Essays, 1917–1932* (New York: Harcourt, Brace, 1932), pp. 241–50, 275–80.
77. The concept of such a grammar was presented by Northrop Frye in "Yeats and the Language of Symbolism," *Fables of Identity* (New York: Harcourt, Brace and World, 1963), pp. 218–37.
78. Quoted by Joseph Hone, *W. B. Yeats, 1865–1939*, p. 495.
79. Northrop Frye, *Anatomy of Criticism* (Princeton: Princeton University Press, 1957), p. 310.
80. Yeats, *A Vision*, p. 4.
81. Ibid., p. 8.
82. Ibid., pp. 8–9.
83. Ibid., p. 13.
84. Ibid., p. 10.
85. Ibid., p. 11.
86. Ibid., p. 21.
87. Ibid., p. 13.
88. *W. B. Yeats and T. Sturge Moore*, p. 131.
89. Yeats, Introduction to "The Resurrection," *Explorations*, p. 396.
90. Blake wrote "pulsations," not "pulsaters."
91. *A Vision*, pp. 24–25.
92. Ibid., p. 38.
93. Ibid., p. 41.

94. Ibid., p. 54.
95. Quoted by A. N. Jeffares, *W. B. Yeats: Man and Poet* (New Haven: Yale University Press, 1949), p. 267.
96. Yeats, *A Vision*, p. 301.
97. Ibid., p. 301.
98. Ibid., p. 302.
99. Yeats, *Collected Poems*, p. 226; *A Vision*, p. 305.
100. W. B. Yeats, "The Death of Cuchulain," *Collected Plays* (New York: Macmillan, 1953), p. 441. Ironically, this remark of Cuchulain is made on the verge of his death, when he no longer makes the truth; but he has made it in his life.
101. Yeats, "An Acre of Grass," *Collected Poems*, p. 299.
102. Yeats, "Estrangement," *Autobiography*, p. 285.
103. Yeats, *A Vision*, pp. 83–84.
104. Yeats, "The Tower," *Collected Poems*, p. 196.

TWELVE: CONCLUSIONS (*text pages 325–93*)

1. E. D. Hirsch, Jr., *The Aims of Interpretation* (Chicago: University of Chicago Press, 1976), pp. 90–91.
2. Stanley Fish, "How Ordinary Is Ordinary Language?" *New Literary History* 5, no. 1 (Autumn 1973):41–54.
3. Gerald Holton, *Thematic Origins of Scientific Thought: Kepler to Einstein* (Cambridge, Mass.: Harvard University Press, 1973), p. 440.
4. Thomas Kuhn, *The Structure of Scientific Revolutions*, 2d ed. (Chicago: University of Chicago Press, 1970), pp. 10–42; Holton, *Thematic Origins*, pp. 19 ff.
5. Holton, *Thematic Origins*, p. 57.
6. Ibid., p. 103.
7. Ibid., p. 23.
8. See Polanyi, *Personal Knowledge* (1958) (Chicago: University of Chicago Press, 1962), and Polanyi and Harry Prosch, *Meaning* (Chicago: University of Chicago Press, 1975).
9. Margaret Masterman, "The Nature of a Paradigm," *Criticism and the Growth of Knowledge* (1970), ed. Imri Lakatos and Alan Musgrave (Cambridge: Cambridge University Press, 1972), pp. 59–89. Kuhn's response, "Reflections on My Critics," occupies pp. 231–78.
10. Masterman, "The Nature of a Paradigm," p. 65.
11. Kuhn, *The Structure of Scientific Revolutions*, pp. 174–210.
12. Ibid., pp. 182, 175.
13. Ibid., p. 46.
14. Kuhn, "Reflections on My Critics,",p. 269.
15. Holton, *Thematic Origins*, p. 101.
16. Kuhn, *The Structure of Scientific Revolutions*, p. 170; Karl Popper, *The Logic of Scientific Discovery* (London: Hutchinson, 1935).
17. Kuhn, "Reflections on My Critics," p. 265.
18. Holton, *Thematic Origins*, p. 104.

19. Gerald Holton, *The Scientific Imagination* (Cambridge: Cambridge University Press, 1978), p. 145.
20. Polanyi, *Meaning*, p. 39.
21. W. B. Yeats, *A Vision*, p. 183.
22. *Further Letters of John Butler Yeats*, ed. Lennox Robinson (Dundrum: The Cuala Press, 1920), p. 22.
23. Northrop Frye, *The Secular Scripture: A Study of the Structure of Romance* (Cambridge, Mass.: Harvard University Press, 1976), p. 14.
24. Ibid., p. 180.
25. Ibid.
26. Talcott Parsons, "Unity and Diversity in the Modern Intellectual Disciplines: The Role of the Social Sciences," *Daedalus* 94, no. 1 (Winter 1965): 63.
27. Holton, *Thematic Origins*, p. 65.
28. Stanley Fish, *Is There a Text in This Class?* (Cambridge, Mass., and London: Harvard University Press, 1981), pp. 303–71.
29. Frye's naming of his book as he did calls for some thought. The anatomy as a literary genre might well be regarded as an evoker of irony in my sense of the term. I claim irony to be the product of the relation of or difference between the poem and its commentary. Frye's work is "literary" but at the same time it stands outward from the poetic center (though not so far outward as to be "science" after all) because it hypostatizes an object, "literature," and is a commentary on that object. Yeats's *A Vision* has similar qualities, but I place it closer in to the poetic center because it doesn't really have an object. It ends up commenting on itself. Of course, when I say center above, I really mean circumference.
30. In Blake's "Introduction to *Songs of Experience*," *Complete Writings of William Blake*, ed. Geoffrey Keynes (London: Nonesuch; New York: Random House, 1957), p. 210.
31. *Oxford Book of Modern Verse*, ed. W. B. Yeats, (New York: Oxford University Press, 1936), p. 1.
32. Blake, "The Laocoön," *Complete Writings*, p. 776.
33. James Boon, *From Symbolism to Structuralism* (New York: Harper & Row, 1972), p. 59.
34. Claude Lévi-Strauss, *Mythologiques*, 4 vols. (Paris: Plon, 1964), 1:20.
35. Michel Foucault, *The Order of Things* [Les mots et les choses] (New York: Random House, 1973).
36. Jonathan Culler, *Sturcturalist Poetics* (Ithaca, N.Y.: Cornell University Press, 1975), p. 29.
37. Boon, *From Symbolism to Structuralism*, p. 77.
38. Blake, "Annotations to Reynolds' Discourses," *Complete Writings*, p. 459.
39. Robert Scholes, *Structuralism in Literature* (New Haven: Yale University Press, 1974), p. 68.
40. Boon, *From Symbolism to Structuralism*, pp. 99–100.
41. Ibid., p. 27.
42. Peter Caws, "What Is Structuralism?" *Partisan Review* 35, no. 1 (Fall 1968): 89.

43. Lévi-Strauss, *Mythologiques* 1:21.
44. Culler, *Structuralist Poetics*, p. 91.
45. Jacques Derrida, *L'Écriture et la différence* (Paris: Seuil, 1967), p. 46.
46. Culler, *Structuralist Poetics*, p. 251.
47. Murray Krieger, *Theory of Criticism* (Baltimore: Johns Hopkins University Press, 1976), p. 226.
48. Paul de Man, "Literary History and Literary Modernity," in *In Search of Literary Theory*, ed. Morton W. Bloomfield (Ithaca: Cornell University Press, 1972), p. 250.
49. Paul de Man, "The Rhetoric of Temporality," in *Interpretation: Theory and Practice*, ed. Charles S. Singleton (Baltimore: Johns Hopkins University Press, 1969), pp. 173–209.
50. Paul de Man, *Blindness and Insight* (New York: Oxford University Press), p. 9.
51. Ibid., p. 11.
52. Ibid.
53. Ibid., p. 17.
54. De Man, "The Rhetoric of Temporality," p. 174.
55. T. E. Hulme, *Speculations* (1924), ed. Herbert Read (New York: Harcourt, Brace [Harvest], n.d.), p. 120.
56. The concept of linguistic theft is nicely expressed in Burke's *Attitudes Toward History*, 2 vols. (New York: New Republic, 1937), 2:229.
57. E. E. Bostetter, *The Romantic Ventriloquists* (Seattle: University of Washington Press, 1963), p. 5.
58. De Man, "The Rhetoric of Temporality," p. 190.
59. For example, see de Man's "Nietzsche's Theory of Rhetoric," *Symposium* (1974), p. 50; Harold Bloom, *The Anxiety of Influence* (New York: Oxford University Press, 1973).
60. This argument is presented and the phrase used in de Man, "The Epistemology of Metaphor," *Critical Inquiry* 5, no. 1 (Autumn 1978): 13–30.
61. Ibid., p. 13.
62. Northrop Frye, *Anatomy of Criticism* (Princeton: Princeton University Press, 1957), pp. 76–77.
63. See quotation, 5, p. 000.
64. "The Rhetoric of Temporality," p. 191. One might compare de Man's "religious" interest in allegory to Walter Benjamin's socialistic interest, the latter valorizing allegory because he regards it as dynamic and worldly.
65. It *is* uttered in a related essay by de Man, "Intentional Structure of the Romantic Image," *Romanticism and Consciousness*, ed. Harold Bloom (New York: W. W. Norton, 1970), pp. 65–77.
66. Hans Meyerhoff, *Time in Literature* (Berkeley: University of California Press, 1955), esp. pp. 136–47.
67. Yeats quotes this line in *A Vision*, p. 67, in connection with his gyres and wheel.
68. Robert Magliola, *Phenomenology and Literature: An Introduction* (West Lafayette, Ind.: Purdue University Press, 1977), p. 17.

69. Ibid., p. 63.
70. Richard Palmer, *Hermeneutics* (Evanston, Ill.: Northwestern University Press, 1969), p. 144.
71. Harold Alderman, "Heidegger's Critique of Science and Technology," *Heidegger and Modern Philosophy*, ed. Michael Murray (New Haven and London: Yale University Press, 1978), pp. 44–47.
72. Karsten Harries, "Fundamental Ontology and the Search for Man's Place," ibid., p. 67.
73. Heidegger, *Being and Time*, trans. John Macquarrie and Edward Robinson (Oxford: Basil Blackwell, 1967), p. 193.
74. Heidegger, "Language," *Poetry, Language, Thought*, trans. Albert Hofstadter (New York: Harper, 1975), p. 192.
75. Heidegger, "The Nature of Language," *On the Way to Language*, trans. Peter D. Hertz (New York: Harper and Row), p. 81.
76. Quoted by Palmer, *Hermeneutics*, pp. 153–54.
77. Heidegger, "Hölderlin and the Essence of Poetry," *European Literary Theory and Practice*, ed. Vernon Gras (New York: Delta, 1973), p. 34.
78. Hans-Georg Gadamer, *Truth and Method* (New York: Seabury, 1975), p. 69.
79. Ibid., p. 70.
80. Heidegger, "A Dialogue on Language," *On the Way to Language*, p. 29.
81. Heidegger, *Being and Time*, pp. 190–92.
82. Karl Jaspers, *Truth and Symbol* (New Haven: College and University Press, 1959), pp. 52, 44.
83. Ibid., p. 46.
84. Ibid., p. 44.
85. Ibid., pp. 76–77.
86. Ibid., p. 75.
87. Ibid., p. 42.
88. Ibid., p. 49.
89. Ibid., p. 53.
90. Ibid., p. 42.
91. Ibid., p. 66.
92. Ibid., pp. 58–60.
93. Karl Jaspers, *Philosophy of Existence*, trans. R. F. Graban (Philadelphia: University of Pennsylvania Press, 1972), p. 42.
94. Jaspers, *Truth and Symbol*, p. 42.
95. Jaspers, *Philosophy of Existence*, p. 42.
96. Hans-Georg Gadamer, *Philosophical Hermeneutics*, trans. David E. Linge (Berkeley: University of California Press, 1976), pp. 77–78.
97. See Hirsch, *Validity in Interpretation* (New Haven: Yale University Press, 1967), esp. pp. 209–64.
98. Paul Ricoeur, *The Rule of Metaphor*, trans. Robert Czerny with Kathleen McLaughlin and John Costello, S.J. (Toronto: University of Toronto Press, 1977) [*La Métaphore vive*, Paris: Seuil, 1975].
99. Paul Ricoeur, *Interpretation Theory: Discourse and the Surplus of Mean-

ing (Fort Worth: Texas Christian University Press, 1976). (Chapter 3, "Metaphor and Symbol" is translated by David Pellauer.)

100. Paul Ricoeur, *The Symbolism of Evil*, trans. Emerson Buchanan (Boston: Beacon Press, 1967) [*Symbolique du mal*, (Paris: Aubier-Montaigne, 1963)]; *Freud and Philosophy*, trans. Denis Savage (New Haven: Yale University Press, 1970) [*De L'interprétation: essai sur Freud*, (Paris: Seuil, 1965)]; *The Conflict of Interpretations*, ed. Don Ihde (Evanston: Northwestern University Press, 1974) [*Le Conflit des interprétations*, (Paris: Seuil, 1969)].

101. Ricoeur, *The Symbolism of Evil*, p. 5.

102. Ibid., p. 350.

103. Ibid., p. 18.

104. Ibid., p. 9.

105. Ibid., p. 349.

106. Ricoeur, *Freud and Philosophy*, p. 38.

107. Ibid.

108. Ibid., p. 39.

109. Ibid., pp. 11–12.

110. Ricoeur, *The Symbolism of Evil*, p. 15.

111. Ibid., p. 16.

112. Ibid., p. 116.

113. Ricoeur, *Freud and Philosophy*, p. 16.

114. Ricoeur, *The Conflict of Interpretations*, p. 290.

115. Ricoeur, *The Symbolism of Evil*, p. 15.

116. Ricoeur, *Freud and Philosophy*, p. 18.

117. Ibid., p. 17.

118. Ricoeur, *The Symbolism of Evil*, p. 17.

119. Ricoeur, *Freud and Philosophy*, p. 7.

120. Ricoeur, *Interpretation Theory*, p. 85.

121. Ricoeur, *The Symbolism of Evil*, p. 16.

122. Ibid., p. 18.

123. Ricoeur, *Interpretation Theory*, p. 56.

124. Ricoeur, *The Symbolism of Evil*, p. 18.

125. Ricoeur, *The Conflict of Interpretations*, p. 14.

126. Ricoeur, *Freud and Philosophy*, p. 102.

127. Ibid., p. 175.

128. Ricoeur, *Interpretation Theory*, p. 60.

129. Ibid., p. 61.

130. Ibid., p. 59.

131. Ibid., p. 69.

132. Ricoeur, *The Rule of Metaphor*, p. 137.

133. Gilbert Ryle, *The Concept of Mind* (London: Hutchinson, 1949); Ricoeur, *The Rule of Metaphor*, p. 197.

134. Max Black, *Models and Metaphors* (Ithaca: Cornell University Press, 1962); Ricoeur, *The Rule of Metaphor*, p. 21.

135. Emile Benveniste, *Problems in General Linguistics*, trans. M. E. Meek

(Coral Gables: University of Miami Press, 1971) [*Problèmes de linguistique générale* (Paris: Gallimard, 1966)].

136. Ricoeur, *The Rule of Metaphor*, p. 44.
137. Ibid., p. 66.
138. Ibid., p. 216.
139. Gottlob Frege, "On Sense and Reference," *Philosophical Writings*, ed. Max Black and Peter Geach (Oxford: Basil Blackwell, 1970), pp. 56–78 ["Über Sinn und Bedeutung" (1892)].
140. Ricoeur, *The Rule of Metaphor*, p. 221.
141. Ibid., p. 229.
142. Ibid., p. 227.
143. Ibid.
144. Ibid.; Frye, *Anatomy of Criticism*, p. 80; Tzvetan Todorov, *Littérature et Signification* (Paris: Larousse, 1967).
145. Ricoeur, *The Rule of Metaphor*, p. 99.
146. Ibid., p. 248.
147. Ibid., p. 247.
148. Ibid., p. 196.
149. Ibid., pp. 249–54.
150. Ibid., p. 199.
151. Ibid., pp. 296–97.
152. Blake, *Complete Writings*, p. 91.
153. Northrop Frye, "Notes for a Commentary on *Milton*," *The Divine Vision*, ed. V. Pinto (London: Gollancz, 1957), p. 107.
154. Blake, "Jerusalem," *Complete Writings*, p. 747.
155. Ricoeur, *The Rule of Metaphor*, p. 302.
156. Ibid.
157. Blake, "The Marriage of Heaven and Hell," *Complete Writings*, p. 149.
158. Ricoeur, *Interpretation Theory*, p. 45.
159. Ibid., p. 57.
160. Walter Benjamin, *The Origin of German Tragic Drama*, trans. John Osborne (London: NLB, 1977), pp. 159–85 [*Ursprung des deutschen Trauerspiels* (1928) Frankfurt].
161. Ricoeur, *Interpretation Theory*, p. 65.
162. Ibid., p. 58.
163. Ibid., p. 59.
164. Ibid., pp. 61–62.
165. Ibid., p. 63.
166. Ibid., p. 27.
167. Ibid., p. 29.
168. This is an important issue for Ricoeur because by insisting on this point he separates himself, as I have already indicated, from the structuralists and Derridean deconstruction: "A linguistic analysis which would treat these significations as a whole closed in on itself would ineluctably set up language as an absolute. This hypostasis of language, however, repudiates the basic intention of a sign, which is to hold 'for,' thus transcending itself and

suppressing itself in what it intends. Language itself, as a signifying milieu, must be referred to existence" (*The Conflict of Interpretations*, p. 16).
169. Ibid., p. 17.
170. Ibid., p. 18.
171. Ricoeur, *The Symbolism of Evil*, pp. 349–50.
172. Ibid., p. 355.
173. Ricoeur, *Interpretation Theory*, p. 75.
174. Ricoeur, *Freud and Philosophy*, p. 27.
175. Ibid., pp. 27 and 32ff.
176. Ricoeur, *The Conflict of Interpretations*, p. 326.
177. Ricoeur, *Interpretation Theory*, p. 87.
178. Ricoeur, *The Conflict of Interpretations*, p. 299.
179. Ricoeur, *Interpretation Theory*, p. 91.
180. Ricoeur, *The Conflict of Interpretations*, p. 331.
181. Ibid., p. 332.
182. Ricoeur, *The Symbolism of Evil*, pp. 347–48.
183. Ricoeur, *The Conflict of Interpretations*, pp. 330–34.
184. Ricoeur, *Interpretation Theory*, p. 61.
185. Bloom, *The Anxiety of Influence*, pp. 19ff.
186. Hirsch, *Validity in Interpretation*, pp. 245–64.
187. Ricoeur, *The Rule of Metaphor*, p. 303.
188. Ibid., p. 307.
189. Blake, "Notebook," *Complete Writings*, p. 541.
190. Blake, "Jerusalem," ibid., p. 447.

Bibliography

A selection of texts consulted during the writing of this book. Where translations are available I have cited the translation rather than the original.—H. A.

Auerbach, Erich. "Figura." In *Scenes from the Drama of European Literature.* New York: Meridian Books, 1959.

Austin, Lloyd James. *L'Univers poétique de Baudelaire.* Paris: Mercure de France, 1956.

Bachelard, Gaston. *The Poetics of Reverie.* Translated by Daniel Russell. Boston: Beacon Press, 1969.

———. *The Poetics of Space.* Translated by Maria Jolas. Boston: Beacon Press, 1969.

———. *The Psychoanalysis of Fire.* Translated by Alan C. M. Ross. Boston: Beacon Press, 1968.

Balakian, Anna. *The Symbolist Movement.* New York: Random House, 1967.

Baudelaire, Charles. *Baudelaire as a Literary Critic.* Translated by Lois Boe Hyslop and Francis E. Hyslop, Jr. University Park: Pennsylvania State University Press, 1964.

———. *The Mirror of Art: Critical Studies by Charles Baudelaire.* Translated by Jonathan Mayne. Garden City, N. Y.: Doubleday, 1956.

Benjamin, Walter. *The Origin of German Tragic Drama.* Translated by John Osborn. London: NLB, 1977.

Benveniste, Emile. *Problems in General Linguistics*. Translated by M. E. Meek. Coral Gables, Fl.: University of Miami Press, 1971.

Berlin, Isaiah. *Vico and Herder*. London: Hogarth Press, 1976.

Bertocci, Angelo. *From Symbolism to Baudelaire*. Carbondale: Southern Illinois University Press, 1964.

Bevan, Edwyn. *Symbolism and Belief*. Boston: Beacon Press, 1957.

Bigg, Charles. *The Christian Platonists of Alexandria*. Oxford: Clarendon Press, 1968.

Black, Max. *Models and Metaphors*. Ithaca: Cornell University Press, 1962.

Blake, William. *Complete Writings*. Edited by Geoffrey Keynes. London: Nonesuch Press; New York: Random House, 1957.

Bloom, Harold. "Dialectic of *The Marriage of Heaven and Hell*." In *The Ringers in the Tower: Studies in Romantic Tradition*. Edited by Harold Bloom. Chicago and London: University of Chicago Press, 1971.

———. *Kabbalah and Criticism*. New York: Seabury, 1975.

Boon, James. *From Symbolism to Structuralism*. New York: Harper and Row, 1972.

Bowra, Maurice. *The Creative Experiment*. London: Macmillan, 1949.

Bryant, Jacob. *A New System, or An Analysis of Ancient Mythology*. London, 1774.

Burke, Kenneth. *Language as Symbolic Action*. Berkeley and Los Angeles: University of California Press, 1968.

Campbell, Joseph. *The Hero with a Thousand Faces*. New York: Meridian Books, 1956.

Carlyle, Thomas. *Sartor Resartus*. New York, Chicago, and Boston: Charles Scribner, 1921.

Cassirer, Ernst. *An Essay on Man*. New Haven: Yale University Press, 1944.

———. *Language and Myth*. Translated by Susanne K. Langer. New York: Harper and Brothers, 1946.

———. *The Philosophy of Symbolic Forms*. Translated by Ralph Manheim. 3 vols. New Haven: Yale University Press, 1953, 1955, 1957.

———. *Rousseau, Kant, Goethe*. Translated by J. Guttman, P. A. Kristeller, and J. H. Randall. Princeton: Princeton University Press, 1945.

Chadwick, Charles. *Symbolism*. London: Methuen, 1971.

Chadwick, Henry. *Early Christian Thought and the Classic Tradition: Studies in Justin, Clement, and Origen*. New York: Oxford University Press, 1966.

Chase, Richard. *Quest for Myth*. Baton Rouge: Louisiana State University Press, 1949.

Chiari, Joseph. *Symbolisme from Poe to Mallarmé*. Folcroft, Pa.: Folcroft Library, 1956.

Coleridge, Samuel Taylor. *Biographia Literaria*. 2 vols. Edited by J. Shawcross. London: Oxford University Press, 1962.

———. *The Friend*. Edited by Barbara E. Rooke. Princeton: Princeton University Press, 1975.

———. *Miscellaneous Criticism*. Edited by T. M. Raysor. London: Oxford University Press, 1936.

———. *The Statesman's Manual; or, The Bible the Best Guide to Political Skill and Foresight: A Lay Sermon Addressed to the Higher Classes of Society.* London: S. Curtis, 1916.

Creuzer, Friedrich. *Symbolik und Mythologie der alten Völker.* 4 vols. Leipzig: Darmstadt, 1819.

Croce, Benedetto. *Aesthetic as a Science of Expression and General Linguistic.* Translated by Douglas Ainslie. New York: Noonday, 1963.

———. *Guide to Aesthetics.* Indianapolis: Bobbs-Merrill, 1965.

———. *The Philosophy of Giambattista Vico.* Translated by R. G. Collingwood. New York: Russell & Russell, 1964.

———. *What Is Living and What Is Dead in the Philosophy of Hegel.* Translated by Douglas Ainslie. London: Macmillan, 1915.

Culler, Jonathan. *Structuralist Poetics.* Ithaca, N.Y.: Cornell University Press, 1975.

Danielou, Jean. *From Shadows to Reality: Studies in the Biblical Typology of the Fathers.* Translated by Wulstan Hibbard. Westminster: Newman, 1960.

Davies, Edward. *Celtic Researches.* London, 1804.

De Man, Paul. *Blindness and Insight.* New York: Oxford University Press, 1971.

———. "The Epistemology of Metaphor." *Critical Inquiry* 5 (Autumn 1978): 13–30.

———. "The Rhetoric of Temporality." In *Interpretation: Theory and Practice.* Edited by Charles S. Singleton. Baltimore: Johns Hopkins University Press, 1969.

Derrida, Jacques. *Writing and Difference.* Translated by Alan Bass. Chicago: University of Chicago Press, 1978.

Dieckmann, Liselotte. "Friedrich Schlegel and Romantic Concepts of the Symbol." *Germanic Review* 34 (1951): 276–83.

Eckermann, Johann Peter. *Conversations of Goethe with Eckermann.* Translated by John Oxenford. New York: E. P. Dutton, 1930.

Eliade, Mircea. *Cosmos and History: The Myth of the Eternal Return.* Translated by Willard R. Trask. New York: Harper and Brothers, 1959.

———. *Myth and Reality.* Translated by Willard R. Trask. New York and Evanston: Harper and Row, 1963.

———. *Myths, Dreams, and Mysteries.* Translated by Philip Mairet. New York and Evanston: Harper and Row, 1957.

Ellis, Edwin J., and Yeats, William Butler, eds. *The Works of William Blake: Poetic, Symbolic, and Critical.* 3 vols. London: Quaritch, 1893.

Engelberg, Edward. *The Vast Design: Patterns in W. B. Yeats's Aesthetic.* Toronto: University of Toronto Press, 1964.

Feidelson, Charles. *Symbolism and American Literature.* Chicago: University of Chicago Press, 1953.

Feldman, Burton, and Richardson, Robert, eds. *The Rise of Modern Mythology, 1680–1860.* Bloomington: Indiana University Press, 1972.

Festugière, A. J. *La Révélation d'Hermès Trismégiste.* 4 vols. Paris: J. Gabalda, 1944–54.

Fletcher, Angus. *Allegory: The Theory of a Symbolic Mode.* Ithaca, N.Y.: Cornell University Press, 1964.

Foerster, Werner, ed. *Gnosis: A Selection of Gnostic Texts.* 2 vols. Oxford: Clarendon Press, 1972.

Frege, Gottlob. *Philosophical Writings.* Edited by Max Black and Peter Geach. Oxford: Blackwell, 1970.

Freud, Sigmund. *The Interpretation of Dreams.* Translated by James Strachey. New York: Avon, 1965.

———. *On Creativity and the Unconscious.* Edited by Benjamin Nelson. New York: Harper and Row, 1958.

———. *On Dreams.* Translated by James Strachey. New York: W. W. Norton, 1952.

Frosch, Thomas R. *The Awakening of Albion: The Renovation of the Body in the Poetry of William Blake.* Ithaca, N.Y.: Cornell University Press, 1974.

Frye, Northrop. *Anatomy of Criticism.* Princeton: Princeton University Press, 1957.

———. *The Critical Path.* Bloomington: Indiana University Press, 1971.

———. *Fearful Symmetry: A Study of William Blake.* Princeton: Princeton University Press, 1947.

———. *The Secular Scripture: A Study of the Structure of Romance.* Cambridge, Mass.: Harvard University Press, 1976.

Gadamer, Hans-Georg. *Philosophical Hermeneutics.* Translated by David E. Linge. Berkeley and Los Angeles: University of California Press, 1976.

———. *Truth and Method.* New York: Seabury, 1975.

Geertz, Clifford, ed. *Myth, Symbol, and Culture.* New York: W. W. Norton, 1971.

Gibilen, Jean. *L'Esthétique de Schelling d'après la philosophie de l'art.* Paris, 1934.

Gilman, Margaret. *Baudelaire the Critic.* New York: Octagon Press, 1971.

Girard, René. *Violence and the Sacred.* Translated by Patrick Gregory. Baltimore: Johns Hopkins University Press, 1977.

Goethe, Johann Wolfgang von. "Maximen." In *Gedenkausgabe der Werke, Briefe, und Gesprache.* Edited by Ernst Beutler. Zurich und Stuttgart: Artemis, 1949.

———. *Schriften zur Kunst.* Edited by Ernst Beutler. Zurich und Stuttgart: Artemis, 1949.

Goodenough, E. R. *By Light, Light: The Mystic Gospel of Hellenistic Judaism.* Amsterdam: Philo, 1969.

———. *An Introduction to Philo Judaeus.* New York: Barnes and Noble, 1962.

Grant, R. M. *Gnosticism and Early Christianity.* New York: Columbia University Press, 1959.

Hawkes, Terence. *Metaphor.* London: Methuen, 1972.

Hegel, Georg Wilhelm Friedrich. *The Phenomenology of Mind.* Translated by J. B. Baillie. New York and Evanston: Harper and Row, 1967.

———. *The Philosophy of Fine Art.* Translated by F. P. B. Osmaston. 4 vols. London: G. Ball and Sons, 1920.

Heidegger, Martin. *Being and Time*. Translated by John Macquerrie and Edward Robinson. Oxford: Blackwell, 1967.

———. "Hölderlin and the Essence of Poetry." In *European Literary Theory and Practice*. Edited by Vernon Gras. New York: Delta Books, 1973.

———. *An Introduction to Metaphysics*. Translated by Ralph Manheim. New Haven: Yale University Press, 1959.

———. *On the Way to Language*. Translated by Peter D. Hertz. New York: Harper and Row, 1971.

———. *Poetry, Language, Thought*. Translated by Albert Hofstadter. New York: Harper and Row, 1975.

Herder, J. G. *Outline of a Philosophy of the History of Mankind*. Translated by L. Churchill. London: L. Johnson, 1800.

———. *The Spirit of Hebrew Poetry*. Translated by James Marsh. Burlington, Vt.: Edward Smith, 1833.

Holton, Gerald. *The Scientific Imagination*. Cambridge: Cambridge University Press, 1978.

———. *Thematic Origins of Scientific Thought: Kepler to Einstein*. Cambridge, Mass.: Harvard University Press, 1973.

Humboldt, Wilhelm von. *Humanist Without Portfolio: An Anthology of the Writings of Wilhelm von Humboldt*. Translated by Marianne Gowan. Detroit: Wayne State University Press, 1963.

Hungerford, Edward. *Shores of Darkness*. Cleveland and New York: World, 1963.

Jaspers, Karl. *Philosophy of Existence*. Translated by R. F. Graban. Philadelphia: University of Pennsylvania Press, 1972.

———. *Truth and Symbol*. Translated by Jean T. Wilde, William Kluback, and William Kimmel. New Haven: College and University Press, 1959.

Jonas, Hans. *The Gnostic Religion*. Boston: Beacon Press, 1958.

Jung, Carl G. *Modern Man in Search of a Soul*. Translated by W. S. Dell and Cary F. Baynes. New York: Harcourt Brace, n.d.

———. *Psychology and Alchemy*. Translated by R. F. C. Hull. New York: Pantheon Books, 1953.

———. *The Spirit in Man, Art, and Literature*. Translated by R. F. C. Hull. New York: Pantheon, 1966.

Kant, Immanuel. *Critique of Judgment*. Translated by J. H. Bernard. New York: Hafner, 1951.

Keller, Werner. *Goethe's dichterische Bildlichkeit*. Munich: Wilhelm Fink, 1972.

Kermode, Frank. *Romantic Image*. New York: Macmillan, 1957.

———. *The Sense of an Ending: Studies in the Theory of Fiction*. New York: Oxford University Press, 1970.

Krieger, Murray. *Theory of Criticism*. Baltimore: Johns Hopkins, 1976.

Kuhn, Albert J. "English Deism and the Development of Romantic Mythological Syncretism." *PMLA* 71 (5): 1094–1116.

Kuhn, Thomas. *The Structure of Scientific Revolutions*. 2d ed. Chicago: University of Chicago Press, 1970.

Lakatos, Imri, and Musgrave, Alan, eds. *Criticism and the Growth of Knowledge*. Cambridge: Cambridge University Press, 1970.

Langer, Susanne K. *Feeling and Form*. New York: Charles Scribner's Sons, 1953.

———. *Philosophy in a New Key: A Study in the Symbolism of Reason, Rite, and Art*. New York: Mentor Books, 1951.

Lehmann, A. G. *The Symbolist Aesthetic in France, 1885–1895*. Oxford: Basil Blackwell, 1968.

Lévi-Strauss, Claude. *The Savage Mind*. Translated by George Weidenfeld, and Nicolson Ltd. Chicago: University of Chicago Press, 1966.

———. *Structural Anthropology*. Translated by Claire Jacobson and Brooke Grundfest Schoepf. Garden City: Doubleday Anchor Books, 1967.

MacQueen, John. *Allegory*. London: Methuen, 1970.

Mallarmé, Stéphane. *Œuvres complètes*. Paris: Gallimard, 1945.

Manuel, Frank. *The Eighteenth Century Confronts the Gods*. Cambridge, Mass.: Harvard University Press, 1959.

Marache, Maurice. *Le Symbole dans la pensée de Goethe*. Paris: Nizet, 1960.

Meyerhoff, Hans. *Time in Literature*. Berkeley: University of California Press, 1955.

Michaud, Guy. *Mallarmé*. Translated by M. Collins and B. Humez. New York: New York University Press, 1965.

———. *Message poétique du symbolisme*. 3 vols. Paris: Nizet, 1947.

Moritz, Karl Philipp. *Götterlehre oder mythologische Dichtungen der Alten*. Berlin: von F. V. Herbig, 1843.

———. *Schriften zur Ästhetic und Poetik*. Edited by H. S. Shrimpf. Tübingen: Max Niemeier, 1962.

Muller, C. Otfried. *Introduction to a Scientific System of Mythology*. Translated by John Weitch. London: Longman's, 1844.

Müller, Curt. *Die geschlichtlichen Veraussetzungen des Symbolbegriffs in Goethes Kunstanschauung*. Leipzig: Mayer & Müller, 1937.

Murray, Gilbert. *Five Stages of Greek Religion*. Garden City, N.Y.: Doubleday, 1955.

Murray, Michael, ed. *Heidegger and Modern Philosophy*. New Haven and London: Yale University Press, 1978.

Orsini, Gian N. G. *Benedetto Croce, Philosopher of Art and Literary Critic*. Carbondale: Southern Illinois University Press, 1961.

Owen, A. L. *The Famous Druids: A Survey of Three Centuries of English Literature on the Druids*. Oxford: The Clarendon Press, 1962.

Palmer, Richard. *Hermeneutics*. Evanston, Il.: Northwestern University Press, 1969.

Philo Judaeus. *The Essential Philo*. Edited by Nahum N. Glatzer. New York: Schocken Books, 1971.

Polanyi, Michael. *Personal Knowledge*. Chicago: University of Chicago Press, 1962.

Polanyi, Michael, and Prosch, Harry. *Meaning*. Chicago and London: University of Chicago Press, 1975.

Read, Herbert. *Icon and Idea*. Cambridge, Mass.: Harvard University Press, 1955.

Ricoeur, Paul. *The Conflict of Interpretations*. Evanston: Northwestern University Press, 1974.
———. *Freud and Philosophy*. New Haven and London: Yale University Press, 1970.
———. *Interpretation Theory: Discourse and the Surplus of Meaning*. Fort Worth: Texas Christian University Press. 1976.
———. *The Rule of Metaphor*. Translated by Robert Czerny, with Kathleen McLaughlin and John Costello, S. J. Toronto: University of Toronto Press, 1977.
———. *The Symbolism of Evil*. Translated by Emerson Buchanan. Boston: Beacon Press, 1969.
Saurat, Denis. *Blake and Modern Thought*. Glasgow: Dial, 1929.
———. *Literature and Occult Tradition*. London: G. Bell and Sons, 1930.
Schelling, Friedrich Wolfgang von. "On the Relation of the Plastic Arts to Nature." In *Critical Theory since Plato*, edited by Hazard Adams, pp. 444–58. New York: Harcourt Brace Jovanovich, 1972.
———. *Werke*. Vol. 6, *Philosophie der Mythologie*. Munich: C. H. Beck und R. Oldenbourg, 1927–1959.
———. *System of Transcendental Idealism*. Translated by Peter Heath. Charlottesville: University Press of Virginia, 1978.
Schlegel, Friedrich. *Aesthetic and Miscellaneous Works*. Translated by E. J. Millington. London: E. Bohm, 1849.
———. *Dialogue on Poetry and Literary Aphorisms*. Translated by Ernst Behler and Roman Struc. University Park and London: Pennsylvania State University Press, 1968.
Schneider, Daniel J. *Symbolism: The Manichean Vision*. Lincoln: University of Nebraska Press, 1975.
Seligmann, Kurt. *The Mirror of Magic*. New York: Pantheon Books, 1948.
Senior, John. *The Way Down and Out: The Occult in Symbolist Literature*. Ithaca, N.Y.: Cornell University Press, 1959.
Seznec, Jean. *The Survival of the Pagan Gods*. Princeton: Princeton University Press, 1953.
Shumaker, Wayne. *Literature and the Irrational: A Study in Anthropological Backgrounds*. Englewood Cliffs, N.J.: Prentice-Hall, 1960.
Sørensen, B. A., ed. *Allegorie und Symbol: Texte zur Theorie des dichterischen Bildes im 18. und frühen 19. Jahrhundert*. Frankfurt am Main: Atheneum, 1972.
———. *Symbol und Symbolismus in der ästhetischen Theorien des 18. Jahrhunderts und der deutschen Romantik*. Copenhagen: Munksgaard, 1963.
Sowers, Sidney G. *The Hermeneutics of Philo and Hebrews*. Zurich: EV X, 1965.
Spector, Jack J. *The Aesthetics of Freud*. New York: McGraw-Hill, 1974.
Stevens, Wallace. *Opus Posthumous*. Edited by S. F. Morse. New York: Alfred A. Knopf, 1957.
Strelka, Joseph, ed. *Perspectives in Literary Symbolism*. University Park and London: Pennsylvania State University Press, 1968.

Stukeley, William. *Abury, A Temple of the British Druids*. London, 1743.
———. *Stonehenge, A Temple Restor'd to the British Druids*, London, 1740.
Swiatecka, M. Jadwiga, O. P. *The Idea of the Symbol: Some Nineteenth Century Comparisons with Coleridge*. Cambridge: Cambridge University Press, 1980.
Symons, Arthur. *The Symbolist Movement in Literature* (1899). New York: E. P. Dutton, 1958.
Tagliacozzo, Georgio, and White, Hayden V., eds. *Giambattista Vico, An International Symposium*. Baltimore: Johns Hopkins University Press, 1969.
Taylor, Charles. *Hegel*. Cambridge: Cambridge University Press, 1975.
Taylor, Thomas. *Thomas Taylor the Platonist: Selected Writings*. Edited by Kathleen Raine and George Mills Harper. Princeton: Princeton University Press, 1969.
Temple, Ruth Z. *The Critic's Alchemy: A Study of the Introduction of French Symbolism into England*. New York: Twayne, 1953.
Tindall, William York. *The Literary Symbol*. New York: Columbia University Press, 1955.
Todd, Ruthven. *Tracks in the Snow*. London: Grey Walls Press, 1943.
Todorov, Tzvetan. *Théories du symbole*. Paris: Seuil, 1977.
Vaihinger, Hans. *The Philosophy of "As If."* Translated by C. K. Ogden. New York: Harcourt Brace, 1925.
Vickery, John B., ed. *Myth and Literature: Contemporary Theory and Practice*. Lincoln: University of Nebraska Press, 1966.
Vico, Giovanni Battista. *The New Science of Giambattista Vico*. Translated by Thomas Goddard Bergin and Max Harold Fisch. Ithaca, N.Y.: Cornell University Press, 1968.
Vivas, Eliseo. *The Artistic Transaction*. Columbus: Ohio State University Press, 1963.
———. *Creation and Discovery*. Chicago: Henry Regnery, 1965.
———. *D. H. Lawrence: The Failure and the Triumph of Art*. Bloomington: Indiana University Press, 1960.
Vygotsky, Lev Semenovich. *Thought and Language*. Translated by Eugenia Hanfmann and Gertrude Vakar. Cambridge, Mass.: Massachusetts Institute of Technology Press, 1965.
Wallis, R. T. *Neoplatonism*. London: Duckworth, 1972.
Weiskel, Thomas. *The Romantic Sublime*. Baltimore: Johns Hopkins University Press, 1976.
Wellek, René. *A History of Modern Criticism, 1750–1950*. 4 vols. New Haven: Yale University Press, 1955–65.
Wheelwright, Philip. *The Burning Fountain: A Study in the Language of Symbolism*. Bloomington: Indiana University Press, 1954; new and revised edition, 1968.
White, Hayden. *Metahistory*. Baltimore: Johns Hopkins University Press, 1973.
Wilde, Oscar. *The Writings of Oscar Wilde*. New York: Gabriel Wells, 1925.
Wilson, R. McL. *The Gnostic Problem*. London: Allenson, 1958.
Yates, Frances A. *Giordano Bruno and the Hermetic Tradition*. Chicago: University of Chicago Press, 1964.

Yeats, W. B. *Autobiography*. New York: Macmillan, 1953.
———. *Collected Plays*. New York: Macmillan, 1953.
———. *Collected Poems*. New York: Macmillan, 1956.
———. *Essays and Introductions*. London: Macmillan, 1961.
———. *Explorations*. New York: Macmillan, 1962.
———. *A Vision*. New York: Macmillan, 1938.

Index

459

UTSA